*Mask of Treachery*

*Also by John Costello*

THE BATTLE FOR CONCORDE (with Terry Hughes, 1971)
D-DAY (with Warren Tute and Terry Hughes, 1974)
THE CONCORDE CONSPIRACY (with Terry Hughes, 1976)
JUTLAND 1916 (with Terry Hughes, 1976)
THE BATTLE OF THE ATLANTIC (with Terry Hughes, 1977)
THE PACIFIC WAR (1981)
VIRTUE UNDER FIRE (1985)
"AND I WAS THERE" (with Rear Admiral Edwin T. Layton and
Captain Roger Pineau, 1985)

# Mask of Treachery

## JOHN COSTELLO

COLLINS
8 Grafton Street, London W1
1988

William Collins Sons & Co Ltd
London · Glasgow · Sydney · Auckland
Toronto · Johannesburg

BRITISH LIBRARY CATALOGUING IN PUBLICATION DATA

Costello, John, 1943
Mask of treachery : the first documented
dossier on Blunt, M15, and Soviet subversion.
1. Anti-British espionage. Blunt, Anthony.
Biographies
I. Title
327.1′2′0924

ISBN 0-00-217536-3

Works of Louis MacNeice quoted by permission of the Louis MacNeice Estate:
Letters copyright © by John Stallworthy, 1988.
Poems by permission of Faber & Faber.

Letters of Virginia Woolf and Vanessa and Julian Bell in the King's College Archives quoted by permission.

Photographs from King's College Archives reproduced by permission of the Provost and Fellows of King's College, Cambridge.

Photographs from Trinity College Archives reproduced by permission of the Master and Fellows of Trinity College, Cambridge.

Crown copyright material in the Public Record Office reproduced by permission of the Controller of Her Majesty's Stationery Office.

Letters from the Davidson papers reproduced by permission of the Clerk of the Records, House of Lords.

Originated and first published in the United States by
William Morrow and Company, Inc.
First published in Great Britain 1988

Coypright © 1988 by Atlantic Communications, Inc.

Typeset in Linotron Janson by
Rowland Phototypesetting Ltd, Bury St Edmunds
Printed and bound in Great Britain by
Butler and Tanner Ltd, Frome and London

*For Robin and Julia*

# *Preface*

Shortly after I started my investigation of the Cambridge spies, two bizarre encounters provided a foretaste of just how tortuous the trail of Blunt would become.

First, an extremely reticent former member of the thirties' Communist cell in Trinity College quickly agreed to see me. It was only after he had talked frankly about the cell's activities that he found out that I was not the son of a former comrade of the same name. With that the interview quickly came to an end. On the second occasion my name proved a drawback when I tried to contact a reclusive senior figure in the American counterintelligence community. He, too, believed mistakenly that I was the son of Desmond Patrick Costello.

The little-known case of this New Zealander of Irish extraction illustrates the problems confronting a historian.

The facts of Desmond Patrick Costello's academic history and subsequent career in World War II military intelligence conform to the classic pattern of the Cambridge moles. After graduating in classics from the University of Auckland in 1932, Costello arrived at Trinity that same year on a traveling fellowship. He became active in the Trinity Communist cell before becoming an assistant lecturer in classics at Exeter University in 1936. After joining the army he quickly made a name for himself as an intelligence analyst when the Germans drove the British forces out of Greece and Crete in 1941. General Freyberg, the New Zealand forces commander, appointed Costello to be his divisional intelligence officer during the subsequent campaigns in North Africa and Italy. His importance to the Soviets was his direct access to Ultra. That Costello was a "bit left-wing" did not deter the New Zealand prime minister from appointing him in 1944 as second secretary to their legation in Moscow with the cheery assurance: "It won't hurt to have one or two Communists in Moscow."

After six years in the Soviet Union, during which he taught himself Russian and made many Russian friends — including the writer Boris Pasternak — Costello served in the New Zealand diplomatic service at the Paris embassy until 1955. He then accepted an appointment as professor of Russian at Manchester University.

Professor Costello first came under MI5 suspicion as a result of information given by Anatoli Golitsyn, the senior KGB officer who defected in 1961. His debriefing revealed that it was "Paddy" Costello who had provided New Zealand passports for Peter and Helen Kroger (the former New York Communists Morris and Lena Cohen), who were convicted as members of the so-called Portland Spy Ring for stealing anti-submarine-warfare secrets.

The Manchester University academic was put under surveillance by the watchers of MI5. He was observed meeting suspected Soviet agents. But this was not enough to charge a professor of Russian literature with espionage. Not until *after* Anthony Blunt confessed to his own treason in April 1964 did Blunt provide Peter Wright with the confirmation that Costello had indeed been another Cambridge recruit. But it was too late to confront Professor Costello with his treachery. According to his *Times* obituary, Costello had "died unexpectedly at the age of 52" on February 24, 1964. It does not seem a coincidence that Blunt "burned" Costello only after he was dead.

What justification is there to conclude that Costello was a Soviet spy? There is no confession, no primary source evidence, and no declassified MI5 investigation or other official documentation that proves he was yet another Soviet mole recruited at Cambridge. The case against Costello rests on information given in defiance of the Official Secrets Act by the former MI5 investigating officer Peter Wright to Harry Chapman Pincher, the veteran British journalist with a reputation for accurately relaying intelligence information. Although his book *Spycatcher* makes no mention of Costello, Pincher confirmed that he made notes about Costello during his 1981 interviews with Wright in Tasmania.

Further confirmation that Paddy Costello was a long-term Soviet agent was provided to me on a nonattributable basis by a senior American intelligence source who cited his own debriefing of Golitsyn. This still begs the question of absolute proof, but it does provide credible corroboration that Costello was another Soviet spy whose career appears to have begun in the peculiar circumstances of Cambridge in the thirties.

For the historian, the problem of charting the progress of an espionage network is the lack of documentary proof. Intelligence officers who have devoted a lifetime to counterespionage operations repeatedly stress that without a confession, or the arrest of a spy in the act of passing secret information to a hostile power, the lack of evidence is what makes espionage such a difficult crime to prove.

Yet counterintelligence case officers also emphasize that espionage networks do not grow spontaneously: They must be directed and managed. This basic truth is supported by the reports and investigations that intelligence services — especially the British — are loath to declassify. This is because documentary records that span a long time frame establish a paper trail — the essential spoor of counterintelligence methodology that the case officer talks about, but for which he has no hard proof. Nonetheless, if one studies the paper trail of Soviet intelligence efforts, one finds that they betray themselves by their remarkable consistency of purpose and operational technique — especially when supplemented by the minutiae provided by defectors from Moscow's intelligence apparatus.

At an early stage in the course of my work on this book, I was fortunate to locate part of that historic paper trail: a large volume of British MI5 reports in the confidential archives of the U.S. Department of State. Supplemented by FBI reports that I obtained under the Freedom of Information Act and buttressed by files that had escaped the official "weeders" of the British Foreign Office and Home Office, this significant new documentation leaves no doubt about the scope of the secret Anglo-American "special relationship" that began during World War I. It also reconstructs the elusive spoor of Soviet operations — especially in the context of the Cambridge spies.

Working from the clues presented by these documentary records, it is now possible to examine — for the first time from a case officer's viewpoint — an accurate picture of the pattern of Soviet subversive operations against Britain and then the United States from the mid-1920s onward. By using the documents to cross-check the testimony of British and American participants in this secret war, fresh interpretations of events emerge. We can now understand for the myths that they are the self-serving accounts promoted both by the British government and by those, such as Kim Philby, who betrayed it.

Like all skillful disinformation, the corrosive fabrications promoted by Anthony Blunt himself, echoing those orchestrated from Moscow by Burgess and Philby in their books, and Philby's final interviews just before he died in 1988, all were constructed around a connective tissue of truth. Where I have chosen to rely on statements by Blunt, Philby, or Burgess, or others in the conspiracy, it is because these particular statements can be corroborated by documents or other reliable intelligence sources. Where suspect sources conflict with events as they can now be documented, I have endeavored to make that fact clear with supporting analysis in the source notes.

The Official Secrets Act has necessarily restricted the attribution of certain information contributed by former MI5 and MI6 officers. But such conclusions as I reached have been drawn only after considerable documentary analysis and many hundreds of hours of discussion of my findings with informed opinion on both sides of the Atlantic.

Just as the case officer is responsible for his judgment calls, I take full responsibility for the conclusions arrived at in this work. They cannot be complete and unequivocal, but they were reached after the careful weighing of new documentary evidence and in the spirit of historical objectivity. Some of my distinguished fellow countrymen, who have made it clear that they regard the freedom of speech enshrined in the American Constitution as a dangerous threat to the profession of intelligence, may find some of my conclusions contentious, and possibly offensive.

I would, however, remind those who challenge my thesis and my conclusions with special pleading of their access to "informed sources" that the faintest ink is usually a more reliable foundation for historical analysis than the strongest memory. I acknowledge that I have not seen every MI5 report, but I cannot apologize for the message conveyed by the documents I studied, nor for the assessments given me by informed sources. So if that portion of the MI5 record that provides the core of this book speaks falsely, then would it not be appropriate for the British government to declassify the remainder of these secret-service records that are half a century old?

The *Spycatcher* debacle, and the mass of secret data from Britain now openly available to historians in the United States, argues that the time has now come for Parliament to pass a Freedom of Information Act appropriate to a democratic nation. Yet in a policy decision that challenges one of the most basic of Western freedoms, the right to know, the British government proceeds with legislation intended to revise the Official Secrets Act in a way that will make it impossible for historians ever to have access to secret archives. Under the proposed new law, interviewing MI5 or MI6 officers, even off the record as I have had to do, would attract criminal prosecution.

When it comes to the verdict of history, it is ironic how official secrecy continues to hold Britain's leaders in thrall. It was an obsession that Blunt and his associates so effectively turned to the Soviet advantage, and it flies in the face of Shakespeare's time-tested axiom:

> Time's glory is to calm contending kings,
> To unmask falsehood, and bring truth to light.

# Acknowledgments

This project would not have come to fruition but for the very considerable individual contributions made by three people behind the scenes, contributors who deserve equal billing with the author:

Bruce Lee, my editor at William Morrow, whose expertise as a former newsman not only inspired, sustained, and drove this project, but whose singular editorial skills, wisdom, and patience have fashioned the final result.

Robert T. Crowley, whose encyclopedic study of the KGB and knowledge drawn from firsthand experience have made sense of the many multiple images as he guided me through the "wilderness of mirrors."

Andrew Lownie, whose Cambridge historian's training and intellectual stamina have been tested and vindicated by four years of persistent spare-time interviewing and rigorous archival research.

My reasons for gratitude to these three unsung contributors may not be immediately apparent to the reader, but the text and source notes also reveal that this book would not have been possible without the personal testimony and insights that flesh out the book's documentation. To some of those I cannot name I owe my deepest debt of gratitude.

To Lord Noël Annan, Andrew Boyle, Robert Cecil, Robert J. Lamphere, Verne Newton, Harry Chapman Pincher, Michael Straight, and Nigel West (Rupert Allason, M.P.) I owe a special word of thanks. Not only have they afforded both Andrew Lownie and me many hours of interviews, but in long transatlantic telephone discussions and correspondence over many years, each has unhesitatingly permitted me to tap his fund of personal knowledge, reminiscence, and perceptive analysis. They may not agree with all my conclusions, but their advice was indispensable and most carefully considered.

More than a hundred others contributed directly or indirectly to my research, either by letter or interview, or by supplying photographs or information. I should like to single out for special thanks:

In the United Kingdom: Dr. Christopher Andrew, Alan Berends, Simon Blunt, the late Professor John Bowle, Professor R. Braithwaite, Dr. Anita Brookner, Dr. Christine Carpenter, Mrs. Robert Cecil, the late Sir John Colville, John E. C. Costello, Mr. and Mrs. F. Cowgill, Professor Dan Devin, Lady Mary Dunn, Sydney Elwood, Rachel Gould, Peter Fairbarn, Professor Henry Ferns, Bruce Fireman, Sir Charles Fletcher-Cooke, Sir Dudley Forwood, Dr. Martin Gilbert, Jean and

Peter Gimpel, Dr. Anthony Glees, Sir Ernst Gombrich, Hugh Gordon, Paul Greengrass, Robert Harbinson, Duff Hart-Davis, Margot Heinemann, Jack Hewit, Charles Higham, Mr. and Mrs. John Hilton, Professor Sir Harry Hinsley, David Irving, Timothy and Mrs. Kemball Johnston, Tyler G. Kent, Dr. George Knuppfer, Rosamond Lehmann, David Leigh, Peter J. Liddell, Alan Liddell-Hart, Mr. and Mrs. Alastair MacDonald, Sir Dennis Mahon, Patricia Meehan, Mr. and Mrs. Arthur Martin, Dr. Janet Morgan, Mr. and Mrs. Donald McCormack, Leonard Miall, the late Joan Miller, Malcolm and Kitty Muggeridge, Alexis Racine, Guy Rais, John Richardson, Michael Robertson, Dr. A. L. Rowse, Kenneth Rose, Andrew Roth, Andrew Rothenstein, James Rushbridger, Brian Sewell, Andrew Sinclair, Professor Jon Stallworthy, Professor George Steiner and Dr. Zara Steiner, Malcolm Turnbull, Lord Thurlow, W. J. West, Jasper Wight, Christopher Wright, Philip Ziegler; and a cordial acknowledgment to Mrs. Cherry Hughes.

Harold J. Ketzer of Frankfurt and Hansruedi Zellweger of Zurich provided hospitality and valued assistance with research in Germany.

In the United States, I should like to thank: Professor James Barros and his son Andrew, Emily Crowley, Laughlin Campbell, Dr. George Carver, Dr. Ray Cline, George Constanedes, Dr. Robert Conquest, Dr. John Dziak, Professor Sydney Hook, Stephen Koch, Robert Haslach, John Hawkins, Hayden Peake, the late Rear Admiral Edwin T. Layton and Mrs. Layton, Janetta Lee, Nicholas Lawford, John Loftus, Judge Robert Morris, Desmond MacCrae, Captain and Mrs. Roger Pineau, Walter Pforzheimer, Professor Ronald Radosh, William Rusher, Dr. Arnold Kramish, Dr. Wilfred Basil Mann, Stephen J. Koch, Timothy Naftali, Daniel J. Mulvenna, the late Dr. Karl Wittfogel, John Saxon, Professor Robert Chadwell Williams, Professor Simon Schama, Thomas S. Troy, Professor Robin W. Winks, Natalie Grant Wraga.

I must also acknowledge the supportive mosaic of indirect contributions made by the other writers whose works have provided valuable background detail and anecdote. Their books are identified in the appropriate source notes, which also serve as the bibliography.

The documentation that provided the telephone underpinning of this book would not have come to light without the patient help provided by the archivists and staff of the National Archives in Washington. John Taylor has, for over a decade now, been both counsellor and guide in the excavation of new data to fuel and inspire my historical writing. I would like to take this opportunity to add my own endorsement to numerous accolades paid to this unique historical resource at a model national institution. Among its informed, ever-willing and helpful staff who have been of particular assistance to this book are John Butler, Terri Hammett, Dane Hartgrove, William H. Lewis, Wilbur Mahoney, Timothy Nennigan, Richard von Doenhof, William Harris, Sally Marks, Katherine Nicastro, Edward R. Reese, and Ronald Swerczek.

Special thanks are also extended to Dr. Michael J. Halls, the archivist of King's College, Cambridge, for considered and insightful guidance to the affairs of the Bloomsberries. Also to the librarian of Trinity College; Marion Stuart and the staff of the Churchill College Archives; the Manuscripts Division of the Cambridge University Library and the Bodleian Library, Oxford; the archivist of Christ Church, Oxford; the staff of the Cambridge County Library; the chief clerk of the Cambridge Union Society; and the archivists of Eton College, Marlborough College, and Westminster School.

Thanks are due to the staff of the Public Record Office, Kew; the Foreign Office Library; the Courtauld Institute; the Beinecke Rare Book and Manuscript Library, Yale University; the Hoover Institute, Stanford, California; the London Library; the New York Public Library; and the Library of Congress, Washington, D.C.

Robin and Julia Wight have made many major contributions to the project through their sustaining friendship, generous hospitality, and logistical support. I thank my parents and many friends on both sides of the Atlantic, especially John Alston, Patricia Greenwood, John and Kari Hegarty, Gerald P. Jantzi, David Kagan, Kenneth Nicolls, Laurence Pratt, Chauncey Smith, and Milo O'Sullivan and all the others on both sides of the Atlantic who by hospitality, chauffeuring, or sympathetic attention have shared in some of the trials and triumphs of a four-year research project — and to Sharon and Stak Aivaliotis and Peter Jones, for improving my image.

Gary Lazarus, Frederic M. Schulman, and Fred Biehl in New York, with the diligent assistance of Anthony Rubinstein, Julia Palca and Simon Olswang in London, have helped shepherd this complex project through some very tangled legal thickets. But this book would not have been possible at all without my publishers, who nurtured this project with all the patience and skill of a parent raising a temperamental and sometimes rather wayward child. My gratitude is extended to the house that first signed up this book, William Morrow, and all its staff, but especially to Abigail Stackpole, John Harrison, Andy Ambraziejus, Cheryl Asherman, Joan Amico, Bernard Schleifer, Mark Stein, and John Wahler, my heartfelt thanks. Roger Schlesinger brought William Collins into the project in midstream and to him and Ariane Goodman, Simon King, and Juliet Annan, who have acted as parents for the English edition — and to Teresa Sacco of Pan Books — again my grateful thanks.

AT&T provided the telephone communications facilities that bridged the Atlantic and had it not been for the Microsoft's "Word," the narrative would never have flowed. A final mention for "Slap and Tickle," whose contribution as companionable, kitten-sized furry paper-weights is marred only by their ability to shred chapters and chew floppy discs.

*New York*
*London*
*August 1988*

# Contents

# List of Illustrations

# List of Documents

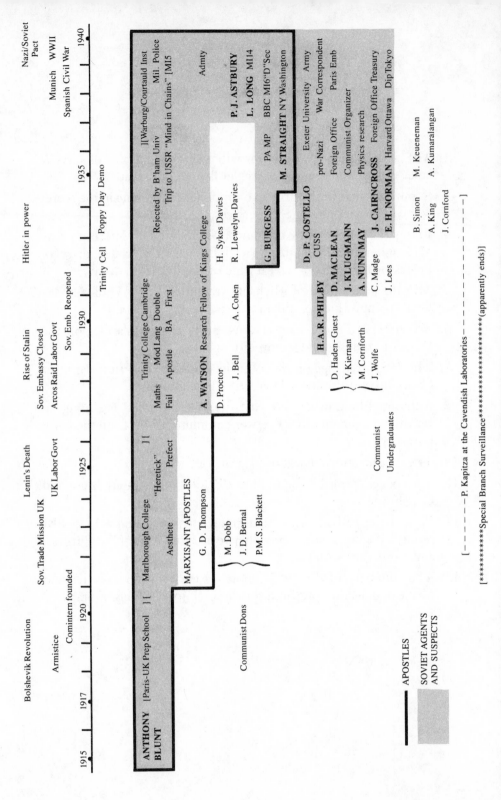

Dunkirk  Hitler's Attack on Russia  Hiroshima  Defeat of Nazis  USSR A Bomb  Korean War  Burgess & Maclean  Stalin's death  Suez Debacle  Cuban Crisis  Philby Defects  Blunt Confesses

1940    1945    1950    1955    1960    1965    1969

"C" MI5 "B"    SHAEF    Surveyor Royal Art & Courtauld Director    Contacted by Modin    Queens Gallery    Immunity Deal    BLUNT
    Royal Missions    Defection Cover    Knighted    WATSON
Admiralty Research    Sonar and NATO anti-sub warfare research    Interrogated no confession    ASTBURY
Radar research with Blackett    London University    Physicist CERN Nuclear Accelerator Geneva    Refused interrogation    LONG
Military Intel    Germany    Columbia Pictures UK    Named and confesses    BURGESS
USA    BBC    USAAF    USA    Defects    STRAIGHT
State Dept    "New Republic"    Moscow/Driberg book    dies    COSTELLO
    Contacts Burgess    PHILBY
Army Intelligence ULTRA    NZ Embassy Moscow    NZ Embassy Paris    Professor Russian Manchester    Dies and named by Blunt    MACLEAN
SOE    MI6 Sec "V"    "IX"    Turkey    USA MI6    Interrogated    Exonerated    MI6 rehires Beirut    Defects    KLUGMANN
Foreign Office    Washington    Cairo    Moscow Press Conf. Soviet Foreign Ministry    NUNN MAY
SOE    Balkans Ops    London Defects    CAIRNCROSS
Atomic Bomb project    Communist Party    Physics professor in Ghana    NORMAN
    Exposed and convicted    Retires under suspicion to live in Rome
GCHQ ULTRA    MI6    Treasury
Tokyo    Ottawa    Assistant to MacArthur in Japan    Ambassador Egypt    Suicide after Communist accusations in Congress

# CHAPTER 1

# "How Can You Ever Forgive Me?"

At 10:30 every weekday morning, a dapper man in his mid-fifties emerges from London's Chancery Lane underground station and hurries through traffic-clogged Fleet Street on his way to work. His neat gray moustache, stylish suit, and black briefcase give the impression that he belongs to the legal profession. Well it might be, for Guy Rais's journalistic beat is the High Court of Justice, which deals with the most important civil cases in England. But his real "office," as he prefers to call it, is the bustling newsroom of *The Daily Telegraph*.

On Tuesday morning, February 12, 1980, Rais arrived at his desk expecting an assignment to cover a major libel case that would be bread-and-butter reading for the British public. But before he could check the assignment roster, his telephone rang. It was a tipster who calmly said: "A man has jumped from the top floor of Portsea Hall."[1]

The deep male voice on the other end of the line told Rais the address of the incident: a block of luxury flats just north of Marble Arch. The man politely declined to identify himself and hung up. At first Rais believed it was just a crank call. "People ring up with the most ridiculous tip-offs," he told me, "and half of them don't lead to stories." But after some seconds of reflection, this call aroused his interest.

Portsea Hall was the address of some newsworthy names. Among them was the flamboyant former foreign secretary, Lord George Brown. It was also the home of Anthony Blunt, a self-confessed spy, notorious homosexual, and recently-forced-to-retire surveyor of the queen's pictures.

Three months earlier, Prime Minister Margaret Thatcher had made a sensational statement in the House of Commons and confirmed for the first time that Blunt had been a Soviet agent. Rais had covered the story. The prime minister's disclosures scandalized England. Blunt had been made a knight of the realm for his service to the royal collections and was a courtier at Buckingham Palace for nearly forty years. He was a third cousin of the queen mother. He had extensive connections and influence. He was a former Slade professor at London University, a long-serving director of the world-famous Courtauld Institute of Art, and an honorary fellow of Trinity College, Cambridge. But he was also linked to three college contemporaries who had defected to Moscow.

23

They were the so-called Cambridge traitors: one the former senior British intelligence official Kim Philby, and two renegade diplomats named Guy Burgess and Donald Maclean.

Immediately after Thatcher's disclosure, the queen had stripped Blunt of his knighthood. The spy had gone into seclusion at his flat at Portsea Hall. But by using a journalistic trick, Rais had managed to telephone Blunt and interview him.

"Are you still a Communist, Sir Anthony?" Rais had asked.

"No, of course I'm not," Blunt replied in a plummy voice. "In the thirties, you know, it was not unusual to be strongly anti-Fascist." It was the self-serving statement that Rais had expected. But he used it anyway in his article.

Now he told the assignment editor of the suicide tip and ran for a taxi and the twenty-minute cab ride to the six-story, brick-and-concrete building that was the scene of the incident. As his taxi swung past Connaught Square into Portsea Place, Rais saw there were two police cars parked at the Art Deco front entrance of Portsea Hall.

He asked the police what had happened but did not get anything helpful except confirmation that an elderly man had fallen from the sixth floor early that morning. Rais was gratified that his telephone informant had his facts straight. But once he stepped inside the door he realized that the story was not his exclusively. Other Fleet Street reporters were gathered at the doorman's semicircular desk underneath the chandelier in the lobby.

The doorman, William Druce, was adamant. Only a tenant could enter the building and use the elevators. So Rais decided to pull an end run. He located the doorman's flat and approached his wife.

Gladys Druce was a stoutish woman in her fifties, and proved eager to describe the early-morning drama. The Druces lived in the back, in a basement flat at the foot of the fire escape. She had been woken "just before five o'clock by a terrific thump. At first we thought some masonry had fallen from the roof. My husband went out in his nightclothes and found this man outside our daughter's bedroom window."

Her husband identified the victim as a Mr. Gaskin, who had lived with Anthony Blunt ever since the two men had moved into Flat 45 five years earlier. "It was a miracle that Mr. Gaskin was still alive," she said. Indeed, it was miraculous that anyone could survive a sixty-foot fall from the tiny iron balcony above. Mrs. Druce also told Rais she had heard the injured man gasp: "I came out for a breath of fresh air."

Gaskin proved to be doubly lucky. St. Mary's Hospital was only a half-mile away, and the ambulance crew, along with a fire engine, arrived just a few minutes after Mrs. Druce called the 999 emergency number. After that the police arrived in force, including plainclothes detectives.

"Where is Blunt?" Rais asked.

Mrs. Druce said that he had left around half past seven, "very upset and very concerned."

Rais had been a reporter too long to accept this at face value. "It was their duty to protect the residents," he told me. "At first I thought he was still there." So he went off to find the nearest telephone and dialed Blunt's number. When the familiar voice did not answer, he set off up the Edgware Road toward Paddington Station.

At the grimy Praed Street entrance of St. Mary's Hospital, Rais joined the other reporters milling around the entrance. A hospital spokesman appeared and read a short statement. He confirmed that a patient identified only as William John Gaskin was making "satisfactory progress," recovering from an emergency operation for "internal bleeding and treatment for a number of fractures." The only concession to the press was the doctor's admission that it was "amazing" that the fall had not killed the sixty-five-year-old man.

"Hospitals never do give out much useful information because they protect the privacy of patients," Rais observed. In such circumstances, he explained, reporters suspend their normal cutthroat competition. "We leaned on each other," Rais said, recalling how the reporters spread out to question every doctor and nurse in sight. "Persistence is what counts. Someone let slip, 'I was in the operating theater,' another that 'Dr. So-and-so was in charge,' and so we pieced the story together."

The reporters learned that the injured man was originally from Belfast, was a former Irish guardsman, and for thirty years had been Blunt's live-in lover. They joked that the two men had probably had "a rough night of it." One man from the *Daily Express* provided a more dramatic slant to the story. He said that a woman living in the fifth-floor flat below Blunt had claimed that she had been woken around five by loud noises and people shouting. Then, it had "stopped, all of a sudden."

"When anyone falls from a balcony in such curious circumstances there is a great deal of speculation," Rais said. The question was whether it was a simple suicide or if Blunt had pushed Gaskin over the balcony in the heat of a blazing row.

"Speculation is all very well," Rais continued, "but it seemed to me that to hang around at the hospital was just banging our heads against a wall." So he returned to Portsea Hall to take another look at the site. From the far side of the Edgware Road he could see that the fire-escape railings were well above waist height. Another puzzle was why an elderly man should go outside during the chill midwinter dawn. And if Gaskin needed a breath of fresh air, why had he picked the cramped iron fire escape when he could have used the large sheltered balcony opening off the flat's front room with its view over tree-lined Connaught Square?

Rais then checked Metropolitan Police Headquarters for an official comment. The Scotland Yard press office would say only that detectives had taken fingerprints from the balcony and had found nothing suspicious. There was no evidence of a struggle. Blunt had made a sworn statement that he was "sound asleep" at the time of the incident. And when Gaskin regained consciousness he insisted he had missed his footing and fallen. The matter was to be logged as an accident. No further investigation would be made. Criminal charges were not contemplated.

Rais went back to his office and typed up the hard facts. No responsible newspaper would publish unsubstantiated rumors and risk a libel suit. Still Rais was not satisfied. After filing his story with the copydesk he went back to Portsea Hall.

No lights were visible in Flat 45 when he came by at seven. So Rais headed on to St. Mary's Hospital. Reporters and several cameramen were still staking out the main entrance. They believed that Blunt would make a bedside visit to his injured friend. There were bantering comments about "how to spot an old queen," but the joke was wearing thin.

"I took the view that with all the trouble Blunt was in, a public appearance at the hospital was the last thing he would do," Rais said. "After all, what could a visit achieve that a phone call could not, especially if his friend was so badly hurt?"

Rais then departed for home, leaving his colleagues to keep the vigil. He later heard some Fleet Street gossip that Blunt had disguised himself as an old woman and given the press the slip while visiting his lover. The idea was not quite so outlandish as it seemed. There is a Cambridge photograph that shows a girlish-looking, young Anthony Blunt languidly posing in ringlets and gown in imitation of the romantic Victorian poet Elizabeth Barrett Browning.

The truth of the matter is that the former surveyor of the queen's pictures did *not* get up a 'drag act' to visit Gaskin. I have been assured of this by one of Blunt's close friends, who told me exactly what Blunt *did* to elude the reporters that night.

"Nobody, but nobody spotted him going into the hospital," my source insists. He is a respected international art consultant. On condition that his name would not be mentioned, Blunt's friend agreed to see me in his New York City townhouse on the Upper East Side. Amid an impressive collection of art, he offered cocktails and proceeded to tell me what he knew.

A short time after Gaskin's mysterious fall, he lunched with Blunt at Portsea Hall. He recalled: "It was an unusually hot day for early March, but every window in the apartment stayed tightly closed. Finally I had to say, 'God! Anthony, the heat is unbearable!'"[2]

"I haven't been able to go near a window since John's accident," Blunt replied. "Would you mind opening it for me?"

The art consultant said that Blunt swore that he had been fast asleep when Gaskin fell. He was awakened by a door banging in the wind. "I left the bedroom," Blunt explained, "but couldn't find John anywhere."

According to the New York art consultant, the strain of living with Blunt had proved too much for the former Irish guardsman. Another of Blunt's confidants, Brian Sewell, a former pupil from the Courtauld Institute, agreed. Alluding to the incident, which some of Blunt's circle still darkly referred to as the "Defenestration of Portsea Hall," Sewell said that the couple's domestic affair had been falling apart for some time.[3]

"While in no way camp," he told me, "Gaskin was both wife and manservant. He cooked for Anthony and put out a clean shirt for him every morning." But Sewell said that Gaskin also "greatly distressed Anthony" with his early-morning domestic chores and fetish for spending hours slicing carrots paper thin. "Food meant nothing beyond eating to Anthony," said Sewell, and Blunt was never generous with his praise for Gaskin's cooking. "Lady John would often launch into his 'I slave-my-guts-out-for-you' routine like a regular harridan, and a dreadful row would simmer on for days like a bad soap opera."

The publicity that followed Blunt's exposure proved to be the final straw. Gaskin became increasingly paranoid and was drinking too much. "John was fanatically loyal and protective," the art consultant said. "He felt terribly destroyed when all the espionage business came out because he realized that for all those years Anthony had excluded him from his confidence. Gaskin, he believes, was suicidal.

"John was from lower-class Belfast," Blunt's art consultant friend observed, sniffing disdainfully. "He was not unattractive physically, but was of limited intelligence." He said that Blunt had fallen for the former Irish guardsman when he was a handsome, muscular thirty-year-old.[4]

"Anthony chased soldiers and 'rough trade' out of sheer naughtiness," said Blunt's New York friend. He revealed that Anthony preferred sexual adventures with lower-class men. Even after he had been knighted by the queen, he continued to pick up soldiers by night in the bars and public lavatories frequented by the men who guarded Buckingham

Palace by day. The suave expatriate Englishman explained that paid liaisons with soldiers in the Guards and Household Cavalry regiments were a common practice in London's upper-crust homosexual scene.[5]

"The key to understanding Anthony," the New York consultant told me, "is to know the tremendous charge he got out of living his life on many different levels." Blunt, he said, obtained an immense satisfaction from escorting the president of France around the queen's pictures at Buckingham Palace, knowing that at six o'clock he had a rendezvous with his Russian controller and could then go on to a homosexual encounter with a guardsman. "Anthony skipped nimbly from one role to the other. All the time I knew him he was drinking heavily to keep his hideously complicated life together." Blunt was cold and emotionless, but could be surprisingly loyal to his friends. That was why he appeared filled with remorse when he discussed the incident over lunch. Blunt had been determined to get into the hospital to see his injured friend and had managed to slip in through a side entrance to spend an hour at Gaskin's bedside.

Blunt regarded his coup against the press as a personal triumph. So did his inner circle of friends. As the New York art consultant polished off his tumbler of whiskey, he assured me with a nod of approval: "Now it takes an old spy to get away with that!"[6]

What precisely had the "old spy" got away with? How did he do it? What type of man was he? What was the significance of the roles he lived and played? These questions have been the focus of a three-year search involving hundreds of interviews and the sifting of thousands of documents in archives on both sides of the Atlantic. Many attempts have been made to piece together the Blunt story from inadequately sourced interviews that cannot be cross-checked. The accounts obtained for this book — even when given by "confidential sources" — have been checked for consistency by intelligence experts with firsthand experience of Soviet cases on both sides of the Atlantic.

More important, many of the facts that emerged in these interviews have been checked against contemporary MI5 reports, which the British government never intended should become available to researchers. For example, in this account are published, for the first time, organizational charts and personnel lists of Britain's wartime intelligence services. Contemporary "Most Secret" reports shared with the American government in the twenties are reproduced here which show that early warnings about Soviet efforts to penetrate the university system had been picked up long before Anthony Blunt reached Cambridge.

Despite all that had been written about Blunt, it was difficult to distinguish fact from fiction, gossip from truth. "Anthony himself remains a shadowy figure" was the considered opinion of Robert Cecil, a former British diplomat who interviewed Blunt extensively before his death. I had approached Cecil in the early stages of my research and he was convinced that the old spy remained a figure of shadows and speculation — precisely because he was so successful at compartmentalizing and concealing his life. To find the real Blunt, I would have to open each compartment of his secret lives.[7]

Blunt's impassive masklike countenance was his primary asset. It was a throwback to his Norman ancestors, and his face camouflaged a ruthless intellect. Its glacial self-assurance enabled Blunt to pursue a fifty-year career of high scholarship and low treachery. Of all the people I interviewed who believed they knew Blunt well, there was only one who could recall seeing more than one side of his multifaceted personality. This was Rosamond Lehmann, one of Britain's most distinguished novelists. She was able to penetrate Blunt's mask to catch glimpses of the intensely vulnerable and guilt-ridden rebel who hid his real face from everyone else. Now in her mid-eighties, Miss Lehmann nonetheless looked no older than a comfortable sixty on the autumn afternoon when she opened the door of her pink-stucco London townhouse in a quiet backwater of Kensington.

Soft-spoken and hesitant at first, Miss Lehmann apologized for not being able to see properly after her recent eye operation. But when she had settled down in her cozy front room surrounded by the mementos of a lifetime of literary success, she quickly relaxed. Unprompted, she seemed to anticipate my questions and began to pour out her vivid memories of that lost hothouse world of Cambridge intellectuals of which she and Blunt had once been a part.

"It doesn't seem possible that we're living in the same country as the one I knew before the war," Rosamond Lehmann sighed. Her first novel, *Dusty Answer*, was published to enormous critical success in 1927. Set in post-World War I Cambridge, it is a personally revealing account of a young woman's struggle to come to terms with the emotional complexities of her adult love for childhood boyfriends, and her yearning to understand the realities of homosexual attachments. The heroine of *Dusty Answer* sets out to "dissect him and make notes, learn him by heart and marvel at" the mysteriously attractive boy in her life. But she never does, and finally she leaves Cambridge, which "had disliked and distrusted her and all other females."[8]

Talking with Rosamond Lehmann about the Cambridge she knew

and wrote about so brightly, it becomes clear that time has not dimmed the psychological insight that made her an international literary celebrity before she was twenty. Blunt, she recalled, had been introduced to her by her brother, John, in 1928 or 1929, when she was an undergraduate at Trinity College. The two often encountered one another in later years as they both shared friends in intellectual circles of the so-called Bloomsbury group. Miss Lehmann explained that most of the brilliant Cambridge graduates of her generation gravitated toward this loose but influential group of writers, artists, and thinkers who were challenging the conventional English cultural, political, and artistic values.

The center around which this celebrated circle of friends and lovers revolved was novelist Virginia Woolf and her husband, Leonard, an active socialist and publisher who ran the Hogarth Press. The stellar throng included novelist E. M. Forster, economist John Maynard Keynes, biographer Lytton Strachey, artist Roger Fry, art critic Clive Bell, and Vanessa, his artist wife, who was Virginia Woolf's younger sister. On the periphery hovered the philosopher-mathematician Bertrand Russell and the expatriate American poet T. S. Eliot.

"Bloomsbury" was synonymous with a style that was outspoken, iconoclastic, and well to the left of the political center. But Miss Lehmann could not recall any occasion when Blunt ever mentioned politics. "In fact, I never thought of him as anything other than a rather aloof and erudite academic," she said. She was aware that he was fond of her because he always singled her out. "But I never really liked him," she added firmly. "I always found Anthony too aloof and too coldly intellectual."

Miss Lehmann struck up close relationships with many of Blunt's Cambridge friends. The outrageous and sharp-witted Guy Burgess was her particular favorite. "In contrast to Anthony, Guy was not only brilliant, but very affectionate and warm-hearted," she explained. "I was very fond of him." He was a welcome weekend guest at her country home near Oxford. "He'd bathe in the river," she recalled, "then sit up very late talking politics to anybody who would listen."

Blunt, Burgess, and many other friends of Rosamond Lehmann were intellectual Marxists. She explained that many of them sympathized with the Communists because they were violently opposed to appeasement of Hitler. In 1928 she had married Wogan Philipps, an Oxford graduate and an old Etonian who went off to Spain in 1936 to drive an ambulance for the Republicans. After her husband was wounded, he made a Pauline conversion to communism. They were divorced before Philipps succeeded to the title of Lord Milford in 1962. As Britain's first publicly declared Communist baron, he took his seat in the House of Lords only to demand the abolition of that hereditary chamber. The writer and critic Cyril Connolly, who was also a friend and admirer of Rosamond Lehmann, compared her, with her own moderate political views, to "the Alcazar of Toledo, an irreducible bastion of the bourgeoisie entirely surrounded by Communists."[9]

"I was probably the first person outside those immediately involved to know that Anthony was involved in some way with spying or treason," Miss Lehmann told me. The first inkling of his treachery came from Goronwy Rees, a promising young fellow of All Souls, Oxford's elite graduate college. Rees was also a close associate of both Blunt and Burgess. Miss Lehmann revealed that Rees arrived "awfully flustered and stressed" one afternoon toward the end of 1936. He insisted on a confidential talk.

"Goronwy said that he had just had the shock of his life," Miss Lehmann recalled. "His staggering news was that Guy Burgess had told him that he was a Comintern agent and had tried to recruit him to the Communist cause.

"Goronwy was very fond of me. He said he needed to tell somebody and he thought that I was discreet. But if I ever mentioned it to anybody, he said he'd strangle me." Miss Lehmann quickly added: "He said it in such an alarming way that I knew that he meant it."

"Have they recruited you too, Goronwy?" Miss Lehmann said she asked him. "Are you going to work with Guy Burgess?"

"Goronwy gave me an ambiguous answer," she said. Looking back she was sure that he had not told her the truth.

"Goronwy was a thumping liar," Miss Lehmann added quite forcefully. "But at the time I buried it deep inside me." She admits that she wanted to believe Rees. She explained that his deviousness and fascination for women were well portrayed by novelist Elizabeth Bowen. Rees appears in thin disguise in her *Death of the Heart*, a novel published in 1938, which describes the fatal love affair between a teenage girl and an "arriviste" philanderer named Eddie. "It is not an entirely accurate portrait of Goronwy because no novelist makes a portrait as a journalist would," Miss Lehmann cautioned. "But Eddie's manners, his emotion, and his treachery capture Goronwy very well."[10]

So by the mid-1930s, Miss Lehmann knew that Burgess was a Communist agent. She suspected Rees, and wondered about the involvement of their friend Blunt. But it was not until Burgess defected to Moscow in 1952 that an incident convinced her that it was Blunt, not Burgess, who had been at the center of the web of treachery that had ensnared her friends.

Miss Lehmann explained Blunt was always solicitous whenever he encountered her after 1938. He finally blew his cover in 1956, after Guy Burgess and another diplomat, Donald Maclean, had appeared at a press conference in Moscow. Blunt immediately sought her out at a small cocktail party at a mutual friend's flat in Eaton Square.

"Can I give you a lift home?" Blunt asked after a few moments of polite conversation. Miss Lehmann thought his offer strange. He knew that she lived only two hundred yards away at the other corner of London's grandest residential area. But he pressed her to accept, explaining that he had arranged a car to take him on to a dinner engagement.

"The moment I got into the cab, Anthony burst into tears," she said. "He covered his face with his hands and muttered in a choked voice, 'Can you forgive me? Can you ever forgive me?'

"'Forgive you for what?' I asked. 'Whatever's the matter, Anthony?'" He kept shaking his head until the cab drew up to her front door.

"Anthony sort of waved me away, so I got out." She remembers watching him with his face over his hands, shaking with sobs, as she shut the door and the cab drove away. "It was an extraordinary scene."

At the time, Miss Lehmann thought Blunt was very drunk. But twenty years later, after Blunt's public exposure as a spy, she learned two important facts that caused her to revise her opinion: The British government revealed that Blunt had been repeatedly subjected to rigorous interrogation throughout the fifties, and Blunt's eldest brother, Wilfred, told her that around the time of his brother's tearful breakdown in the cab, their mother had also become worried about his strained and gaunt appearance. Miss Lehmann is now convinced that in 1956 Blunt was on the verge of cracking under the strain and had tried to appeal to her in a moment of intoxicated weakness in the cab.

"Anthony wanted me to forgive him for something for which he was deeply, deeply guilty. But it was something that he just could not bring himself to reveal." Miss Lehmann believes she caught sight of a tortured man that evening in Eaton Square, a man who had lived so long behind the mask of treachery that he was permanently trapped by his own deceit.

"After that I did not see Anthony again for over twenty years," Miss Lehmann mused. Then, a few weeks after his exposure, he telephoned her out of the blue and asked whether he could come over. "As he was an old friend, I thought it would be kind, but I could not think why he should want to come and see me."

After Blunt arrived, they chatted inconsequentially while she poured him drink after drink. Not until he had consumed what Miss Lehmann described as "an immense quantity of gin," did he explain the real reason for his visit.

"I came to tell you that there was not a word of truth in anything Goronwy Rees said," Blunt blurted out. Miss Lehmann told me that she thought at first he was referring to Rees's deathbed confession to author Andrew Boyle, whose book *The Fourth Man* had blown Blunt's cover once and for all. But on reflection she believes Blunt may have suspected all along that Goronwy had told her about Burgess's attempt to recruit him. "I confessed as soon as I knew all my friends were safe," Blunt assured her. But he was also careful to assert that he was of far more use to the British than he ever was to the Russians.

"Anthony then got up, gave me a kiss, and said, 'I must go now.'" Miss Lehman asked him to visit her again. "He said he would, but he never even telephoned me. I think Anthony was anxious to discover how much I knew about him from Guy and Goronwy. He was really only checking up on me. He wanted to know how much I knew about him and whether, in any sense, I could still be dangerous to him."

The silences between my questions and Rosamond Lehmann's answers grew longer. "This is going to be a very difficult book for you to write, because you will have to tell the story of an enigma." She paused, then offered a final bit of advice: "The only way you will be able to make sense of Anthony Blunt's story is to treat it like a psychological thriller."

Our discussions had evidently stirred many memories. When I left that evening I worried that I might have raised too many ghosts. My concern was allayed when I heard a few days later that she had told her grandson that our afternoon had brought her closer to a new understanding of a man she believed to be "a very alarming personality."

It is one thing to unravel a psychological thriller of fiction. But it is an entirely different matter when it comes to real life. It had taken a long, long time to reach the point where my research could prompt someone so knowing as Rosamond Lehmann to tell a confidant that I was on the right track. I had been dealing with the results of hundreds of interviews, and over a period of years, I had found discrepancies in people's stories that complicated the story of Blunt in unexpected ways, which raised the problem, of course, of what twist or turn was the proper lead for me to follow.

I had discussed these problems with my editor, a heartless man in terms of his response to these complexities, because he insisted that I locate *documents* on Blunt. "There is always a paper trail" was how he put it.

"You have to take the paper trail and build a chronology of Blunt's life. Lawyers would call this charting. It's what a good case officer would do in intelligence. It takes time. It's hard work." Once this chronology was done, then I could return to my interviewing. The paper trail would give me the necessary checks and balances to help evaluate the leads of what people were telling me about Blunt. And in some cases, seemingly innocuous pieces of paper would force truly telling new information from people who had never spoken for the record.

I believed at first that documents would be nearly impossible — if not totally impossible — to find. To the best of my knowledge, other authors writing on British intelligence had always told me that their work was always hampered by an almost total lack of documents in the British archives. But I had been given my marching orders, and I began to dig into the U.S. archives in Washington. To my surprise a large body of British material surfaced. I began cross-checking the sources. In one instance there amounted to thousands of pages of documents and reports on Communist agents and associated countersubversion. In England my researcher Andrew Lownie, a Cambridge history graduate, found more documents, including letters, official records, and writings that had never been analyzed by other historians. This documentation enabled me to go back to sources to ask for confirmation or denial of what existed on paper.

Here, I faced a new problem. The more I worked with this new documentation, the more I cross-checked it with interviews, the more I became impressed with the mask of treachery that Blunt had built as a shield for his operations.

I came to the conclusion that Blunt had lived his whole life as a lie. Unfortunately, as time passed, the lies of Blunt's life had come to be accepted as truth by the public. For the real story of Anthony Blunt's life shows how a superbly sophisticated Soviet intelligence operation exploited the failures of British society for Soviet purposes. The Blunt story would not have been possible but for the problems of the British educational system, the ambiguities of its political system, and the weakness of its intelligence operations. It is also possible to conclude that these flaws in the British system, which were so skillfully manipulated by the Soviets, were so great that they explain why for so many years the British government has never allowed the story of Anthony Blunt to be told. Unraveling of the psychological-thriller aspects of Blunt's life therefore has great significance for the governments on both sides of the Atlantic.

Today, it is common knowledge that the British security services suspected Blunt's treason in the 1950s. As far as the public was concerned, however, the first break in the case occurred in 1979 when British journalist Andrew Boyle concluded a series of remarkable investigative interviews and published his shocking book, *The Climate of Treason*. (It caused an immediate sensation in London and was published a short while later in America under a new title: *The Fourth Man*.) Boyle made the case that there had to have been a Fourth Man in a ring of upper-class English spies that the Russians had recruited from Cambridge University. That spy ring had come to light when Guy Burgess and Donald Maclean had defected to Moscow in 1952. The "missing diplomats," as they became known, were assumed to have been the First Man and Second Man in the ring. Their Cambridge contemporary, Kim Philby, had also come under suspicion of being their accomplice. Many years after official exoneration, the former high-ranking British intelligence officer confounded his investigators by identifying himself as the so-called Third Man when he fled to Moscow in 1963.

That same year Blunt's secret career was uncovered, and in return for immunity from prosecution, he confessed to MI5 and became the Fourth Man. It had taken Boyle years to overcome what he described as "Britain's highly restrictive Official Secrets Act and the natural deceitfulness of spies" to build his case. Britain's stringent libel laws prevented him from naming Sir Anthony Blunt as the Fourth Man in the first edition of his book. But Boyle's work provided sufficient pointers to the real identity of the person he code-named "Maurice" for the press and members of Parliament to force the government's hand. Prime Minister Margaret Thatcher surprised everyone, including Boyle, by not attempting to sweep the whole matter under the carpet of official secrecy. On November 15, 1979, in a statement to the House of Commons, she named Blunt as a former Soviet spy.[11]

The prime minister's revelation that, for sixteen years, Blunt had been kept safe from exposure under a secret immunity deal shocked the nation almost as much as her confirmation that the queen's art adviser was a self-confessed Russian spy. But Boyle's success in piercing the cocoon of official silence to expose Blunt did not bring the full disclosures he had hoped for. The government quickly reimposed its traditional bureaucratic secrecy. It refused a parliamentary commission of inquiry and did not make any comment beyond the prime minister's brief statement. A week later, the veil of official secrecy became a veil of official hypocrisy. Blunt, without so much as a blush, invoked the Official Secrets Act to avoid answering questions at his one and only press conference.[12]

Outraged newspaper editors condemned Blunt's brief appearance as a "cynically stage-managed Establishment set piece." It was not insignificant that Blunt had said that the British system was "better than the American." His preference was not simply an admission of his antipathy toward the United States. Blunt knew that he could rely on British law to protect him from the full consequences of his treacherous secrets. Whereas, if he were an American citizen, congressional inquiries and the Freedom of Information Act would have enabled journalists and elected officials to root out the real extent of his treachery and the conspiracy behind the subsequent official cover-up.

Criminal prosecution and imprisonment threaten anyone in Britain who publicly discloses or passes to an unauthorized person any bureaucratic document or fact that the government deems officially secret. Ever since 1911, when the fear of German subversion and Irish nationalism panicked Parliament into passing the all-embracing Official Secrets Act, this draconian law has muzzled debate and screened from public access information on many sensitive issues. Newspapers and book publishers can be prohibited from printing facts obtained by anyone from government documents or officials. In other words, there *are* limits on the free press in England. The government has the absolute right to withhold any fact or document it does not choose to release or declassify under the so-called thirty-year rule.[13]

British official secrecy also goes to extreme lengths to protect the two principal intelligence and security organizations: MI5, the Home Office's internal-security network, and MI6, the Foreign Office's overseas Secret Intelligence Service (SIS). So secret is MI6 supposed to be that no government official knowingly admits to its existence. The London headquarters of both organizations, though well known to journalists, are an official secret not to be printed in newspapers. Although both MI5 and MI6 have been in existence since before World War I, no records of either organization have ever been formally declassified. Furthermore, current or former members of MI5 and MI6 who communicate intelligence information to outsiders do so at the risk of criminal prosecution. So do those who "incite" them to give information, or anyone who publishes it.

Despite all these deterrents, the skeletons in closets have continued to rattle; disturbing information about Blunt and his associates has continued to leak out. Many former British intelligence officers, who played a key role in Blunt's case, are more concerned about the continuing governmental cover-up than possible prosecution. They have continued to leak information that suggests Soviet penetration of Britain's intelligence services has been — and perhaps still is — far more serious than officially admitted.

In response to these and other charges, the government has been forced to acknowledge that Britain's security services conducted a series of intensive secret internal investigations. These officially unproductive inquiries were intended to root out long-term Russian penetration agents like Blunt, Burgess, Maclean, and Philby, who because of their deep cover were dubbed "moles." "Mole hunting" has become a lucrative field for British journalists, writers, and even academics.[14]

Circumstantial evidence has surfaced to suggest that the most important Soviet mole of all was the late Sir Roger Hollis, the head of MI5 from 1956 to 1965. The charges were made by Peter Wright, MI5's former "mole-hunter-in-chief," who wrote his memoir *Spycatcher* from retirement in Australia, where he is safe from imprisonment under the Official Secrets Act.[15]

The British government, perhaps fearing that Wright's disclosures would set a dangerous precedent and encourage other intelligence officers to spill even more politically damaging revelations, took the issue of confidentiality of its former intelligence agents to the courts in Australia, England, Scotland, New Zealand, and Hong Kong. In the furor the legal battle provoked, writers and journalists who had consulted with former intelligence officers were threatened with prosecution, and stern official letters of warning were sent to all surviving MI5 and MI6 officers reminding them of their lifetime oath of secrecy. As a result, the posthumous memoir of one MI5 officer has been banned in Britain, and the publication of another has been ruled illegal.

The government in Britain may be able to muzzle its own citizens, but it cannot silence former American intelligence officers. These professionals have long shared the belief of their British colleagues that it is time for the full truth to be told. In the United States, former CIA and FBI agents can speak more freely on the record than their British counterparts.

Among the readily accessible and hospitable network of retired intelligence officers centered on Washington there exists a group with strong British connections and interests. This group was led, until his death in 1986, by James Murphy, the London chief of the OSS (Office of Strategic Services) counterintelligence section known as X-2, which had access to the most sensitive British wartime secrets. Murphy was the mentor of the CIA's legendary spycatcher, the late James Angleton, who liaised with Kim Philby in London and later in Washington. Angleton shared a Ryder Street office at MI6 headquarters in London with Norman Holmes Pearson, a Yale professor of English, the unofficial American representative on Sir John Masterman's XX Committee (Double-Cross Committee), running German double agents. Also in this group is Robert J. Lamphere, a former FBI counterintelligence agent who provided the British security services with the information that led to the exposure of the atomic physicist Klaus Fuchs and Donald Maclean.

The constraints of the Official Secrets Act make such frank disclosures about the real nature of Soviet operations impossible in Britain. Former MI5 and MI6 agents cannot go on the record. But the information they have provided me has helped their American colleagues construct a professional reinterpretation of the Blunt case. Thanks to their help it has been possible to make sense of the clues that lie at the heart of the case.

This analysis shows that Blunt must have been a much more dangerous Russian agent than the British government has revealed.

"Blunt's true importance to his Russian masters," said Robert Crowley, a former senior member of the CIA, in a wide-ranging interview, "can be determined from the fact that he was the only identified, native-born Briton known to have achieved a supervisory level in directing and controlling his fellow countrymen. By that I mean people who were supporting and servicing Soviet intelligence."[16]

Crowley bases his assertion on his solid professional knowledge of Soviet undercover operations. He can dissect the arcane minutiae of KGB operations with the incisiveness and detail of a Harvard Law professor. His mental card index of Russian agents is phenomenal. His years at the CIA studying Soviet operations have given him an encyclopedic knowledge of the KGB.

Tall and contemplative, Crowley projects a courtliness that belies his many years in the tough world of military intelligence. His patient courtesy and ability to detect the vital connections in an enormous volume of data made him a formidable counterintelligence officer and debriefer of Soviet defectors. Crowley's authority is highly respected by the former MI5 agents who know him. So while they may be legally constrained from speaking on-the-record for themselves, they have concurred with much of Crowley's thoughtful reconstruction of the Blunt case.

The first point that Crowley made to me — and he made it very strongly — was that he does not believe that convincing answers have yet been given to three central questions:

1. Why did Blunt and his contemporaries from the privileged English class turn traitor?
2. How did the Russians recruit and expand their Cambridge network so rapidly?
3. What was the full extent and nature of Soviet penetration?

"It is difficult to find a Soviet anywhere in the Blunt story as it has been told so far," says Crowley. "They are the missing players in the drama." The reason, he speculates, is the nonavailability of MI5 surveillance records from the twenties and thirties. Without an accurate picture of the Russian presence in Britain at the time, it has been impossible to identify how the Soviets might have recruited, trained, directed, disciplined, sustained, and rewarded their British spies.

"It's a simple fact of life that major Soviet espionage networks are not spawned in a laboratory dish. Their spies are initiated, organized, and run by Soviet case officers." Therefore, Crowley suggested, any self-respecting counterintelligence officer taking on the case would start by trying to establish the How? When? and By Whom? of Blunt's recruitment.

"No one has yet come up with an explanation of Blunt's recruitment that fits what we know about Soviet operational practice," Crowley declares. "Everyone has accepted Blunt's version and, at best, that is highly suspect." He points out that Blunt and Philby were the only two members of the spy ring to have gone on the public record and that both have been taken at their word. That, suggests Crowley, was astonishing; spies invariably try to conceal the roots of their treachery with false justifications.

"Focus on *how* the Russians carried out their recruiting of the Cambridge ring," Crowley advised, "and then you will discover how the seemingly disconnected pieces of the Blunt case come together."

Thanks to the guidance of Crowley and others, I turned up a remarkable number of new pieces of the puzzle in still secret British documents that have been uncovered in the United States. The Official Secrets Act does not extend offshore and these discoveries contradict assertions made in other books whose writers had to rely on unsupported interviews.

For example, new information on Burgess, Maclean, Philby — and Blunt — has been culled from FBI files obtained under the U.S. Freedom of Information Act. A hoard of "Most Secret" British MI5 reports in the files of the U.S. Embassy in London was gathering dust for years on the shelves of the National Archives in Washington. These reveal the secret counterintelligence data that was provided to the United States on a regular basis by the British between the wars. It shows, for the first time, that the extent of the Soviet penetration effort was indeed recognized by the British authorities at an early stage in the 1920s. Then there are the papers of Professor Norman Holmes Pearson at Yale. They include not only the diaries he kept while an intelligence officer during World War II, but also many confidential reports on the inner workings of the British counterintelligence services. Taken all together, the material reveals the weakness that enabled Russian moles like Philby to take control of a whole section of MI6 in 1945.

Assembly of these intelligence snapshots in chronological order illuminates both the details *and* the broad picture of the clandestine Soviet assault on Britain and the United States. The documents reveal that the nature if not the objective of the Russian subversion *was* known to the British authorities — and *was* communicated to the United States — even before Blunt and his associates went up to Cambridge. This must raise serious questions of either negligence or criminal high-level conspiracy within the British security services years before MI5 opened its doors to Blunt, Philby, and Burgess.

A more alarming overall picture of Soviet penetration emerges from the new evidence. Many of its aspects confirm the dire warnings issued by MI5's former mole-hunter Peter Wright: "The British establishment has never accepted that it was, en masse, penetrated by the Russians." But now that it has been documented that this penetration began earlier, went deeper, and was more extensive than previously recognized, it supports Wright's conclusion that "it was simply not correct to say that the extent of the penetration was thoroughly investigated."[17]

With documents to work from, with interviews that cross-check the documents, it is now possible to view the recruitment of Anthony Blunt in the same way a professional counterintelligence officer would do it. (One of the questions I will discuss later is the failure of MI5 and MI6 to create a Research and Analysis Department [R&A] prior to the 1970s, and the effects of this failure.) Using as a starting point the close examination of Blunt's background and character, it becomes obvious why he was such a potentially valuable agent for the Russians. In turn, this gives new insight into how the Russians recruited him, why he was trusted by Moscow with a supervisory role, whom else Blunt recruited and their importance, and what information Blunt betrayed.

Building the case step by step, certain patterns and hitherto unappreciated facts emphasize the critical importance of the Blunt case. They include:

- One of Lenin's first acts after coming to power in Russia in 1917 was to order two émigrés in London, Maxim Litvinov and Theodore Rothenstein, to set up a network of subversion. They were funded by diamonds smuggled into England.

- By 1920, the Soviet Union had a trade delegation in London. It was led by Leonid Krassin, who imported all the tools and talents necessary to establish a far-reaching intelligence underground in Britain.

- From the outset, the Soviet Union has been sophisticated and successful in penetrating the British ruling establishment and government on many levels. The case of Anthony Blunt is a perfect example of the cleverness with which the Soviets have manipulated the idiosyncrasies of the British system.

- There were two waves of Soviet penetration in England before Blunt was recruited in the third wave. This wave was the agents recruited in the late 1920s not only at Cambridge and Oxford but also, and possibly even more importantly, at Birmingham and other universities that specialized in electronics, mathematics, and engineering.

- Contrary to popular belief, there were Marxists in the secret society of the Apostles of Cambridge before Anthony Blunt joined their ranks. In terms of treason, however, Blunt was not the Fourth Man. He was the First Man, the primary agent.

- Also contrary to popular belief, Guy Burgess did *not* recruit Anthony Blunt.

- A major key to Blunt's success was sexual blackmail and his network of homosexual contacts within the British establishment.

- With the outbreak of World War II, Soviet agents were slipped into positions of power in MI5 and MI6 with special attention being paid to the infiltration of the counterespionage divisions. This was deemed vital to Moscow, because such penetrations were the best way to keep tabs on the success of Soviet operations. They also allowed Moscow to monitor the intentions of the principal enemies of the Soviet state, Great Britain and the United States.

- Blunt personally recruited agents who penetrated British intelligence according to the guidelines established by Moscow.

- Blunt also recruited agents at Cambridge who penetrated the administration of President Franklin D. Roosevelt.

- The Cambridge moles associated with Blunt helped insert Communist agents into the State Department and the wartime Office of Strategic Services (OSS), the predecessor of the CIA.

- Blunt's personal handling of diplomatic pouches belonging to Allied embassies during World War II helped facilitate the Soviet takeover of Eastern Europe at the conclusion of the war.

- Scientists associated with the Cambridge network played a critical role in stealing the secrets of the atomic bomb and passing them to Moscow.

- The Blunt network in MI5 falsified legends so that after World War II the CIA hired, for covert operations, agents who were allegedly anti-Communist but who were, in reality, working for the Soviet cause.

- Instead of protecting documents that compromised the pro-Hitler activities of the Duke of Windsor and the Duke of Kent, Blunt passed this damaging information to the Russians.

- Blunt was always one step ahead of MI5 because of help he received from one of the most senior officers within MI5, who has so far escaped investigation for being a Soviet mole.

- Blunt remained "an agent of influence" for the Russians long after he was suspected by the British of being a Soviet spy.

- In 1951, Blunt orchestrated the escape of Burgess and Maclean to Moscow.

- In 1957, Blunt was reactivated to contact Philby and six years later was the principal beneficiary of Philby's defection to Moscow.

- Blunt left two deadly legacies: The first involved the fact that the Blunt case embarrassed both American and British intelligence agencies so that both governments had a vested interest in preventing the Blunt story from being told. More important, the Blunt case soured the relations between the American intelligence-operations people and their British counterparts. This distrust continues today.

# CHAPTER 2

# *"French Leanings"*

"You must admit," Anthony Blunt bragged to his elder brother Wilfrid, after his treason had been made public, "I'm a very good actor."[1]

Published six months before his death in December 1986, Wilfrid Blunt's memoir reveals just how good an actor Anthony was. Despite Wilfrid's close, lifelong relationship with Anthony, he never suspected that his brother was a Soviet agent. Anthony, he insisted, withheld the "whole ghastly truth" until after the prime minister exposed him in the House of Commons.

"I searched my memory," Wilfrid wrote, "trying in vain to see whether, in the light of the disclosures, I could identify anything (other than his close friendship with Guy [Burgess]) that should have forewarned me." That Anthony had so successfully concealed his double life from his brother is only a small measure of his remarkable powers of deceit. Long after he was unmasked and underwent interrogation, Anthony also lied successfully to the British intelligence services about when and how he became a Soviet agent.[2]

Wilfrid Blunt's account shows that he, like other writers, accepted Anthony's explanation as to how he became a Marxist and "was ensnared by the machinations of Guy Burgess." (Anthony had read and by implication approved the draft of Wilfrid's memoir before his own death.) We also know now that Anthony went to considerable lengths, both privately and publicly, to portray Burgess as his recruiter and to implicate his friend as being the First Man in the Cambridge spy ring.[3]

In his only post-exposure press statement, Blunt insisted: "I was persuaded by Guy Burgess that I could best serve the cause of anti-Fascism by joining him in his work for the Russians." Like all the best alibis, this one seemed to fit the facts. It seemed so watertight that when Blunt first promoted it at his 1979 press conference, *The Daily Telegraph* headlined its report by Guy Rais: BLUNT BLAMES BURGESS.[4]

Close scrutiny, however, shows that Blunt had carefully worded his only public pronouncement so as to minimize his role in the Cambridge spy ring. He declared that he had become a Marxist "in the mid-1930's," when the Western governments were appeasing Hitler, and it had seemed to him "that the Communist Party constituted the only bulwark against Fascism." Guy Burgess was "one of the most remarkable, brilliant people I had ever known," Blunt said. Burgess also had persuaded him "that the Marxist interpretation was right."[5]

Blunt portrayed Burgess as the mastermind of the Cambridge Communists. And by inflating his friend's influence, Blunt successfully diminished the public's idea of his own role in the conspiracy, describing it merely as being an impulsive response to his friend's "brilliant" appeal to "assist" him to defeat the forces of Fascism.

When questioned by reporters, Blunt said that it had been Burgess's idea that he should become the resident Soviet talent spotter in Cambridge. Blunt then said that after the war he realized what he called "the true facts about Russia" and that helping the Soviets had been "a huge mistake." But, Blunt declared, he had put his conscience before his country. For this reason he had not warned the authorities about Burgess because he "could not denounce my friends."[6]

To believe Blunt's story — and to date too many have taken him at his word — is to accept that Guy Burgess was his Marxist mentor. But on closer examination it appears that Burgess was Blunt's scapegoat. Moreover, we now know that Blunt had given this same version of events to his MI5 interrogators fifteen years earlier. After his exposure by Prime Minister Thatcher, Blunt carefully embellished his story. He suggested to at least one writer that anyone with whom Burgess was friendly should be regarded as a possible suspect. Wilfrid, as one of his brother's executors, read Anthony's uncompleted 35,000-word hand-written memoir. Since it evidently contained "nothing of significant interest" for his own memoir, we have to assume that Anthony enshrined his version of his recruitment by Burgess for posterity.[7]

Blunt went to great lengths to ensure general acceptance of his account. And one reason why no one has yet challenged it is that Blunt — and the British government — have shared a continuing interest in creating a smokescreen that hid the real story. As we shall see, Blunt and British intelligence combined forces to keep the truth from the public and England's allies.

So far, no published accounts have challenged this official cover story. Every British writer who has followed Andrew Boyle's ground-breaking analysis of the Cambridge Comintern appears to have accepted Blunt's version of events.

The endorsements began with the veteran Fleet Street espionage specialist Harry Chapman Pincher's book *Their Trade Is Treachery*, which became a sensational British best seller in 1981. "Burgess," Pincher stated, "was among the earliest to be actively recruited to the cause of what is now called the KGB." That same year, Rupert Allason, writing under the pen name of Nigel West, said in the first installment of his two-part history of MI5 that "it was Guy Burgess who remained the key organizer of the Cambridge-orientated ring." West, whose unsourced books are remarkable for the detail he obtains from his confidential contacts with former British intelligence officials, also revealed that he had interviewed and corresponded with Blunt. The following year, his second volume on MI5 unequivocally stated that Blunt "had confirmed that he had been recruited as a Russian spy by Guy Burgess in 1936."[8]

Chapman Pincher's *Too Secret Too Long* (1984) went further. His "confidential sources," one of whom later turned out to be Peter Wright, said that Blunt had told MI5 that Burgess "tried to recruit anybody he admired." And Blunt is reported to have admitted that, "in late 1934 or early 1935," Burgess had confided that he was "already committed to work secretly for peace" when he demanded of Blunt: "Are you prepared to help me?"[9]

The following year Dr. Christopher Andrew, a Cambridge historian specializing in intelligence affairs, endorsed Blunt's version in a volume of scholarly essays gathered under the title *Diplomacy and Intelligence in the Second World War*. According to Andrew: "The first step in the making of the Cambridge moles was probably Guy Burgess's decision in 1933 to join the Comintern's secret war against the growth of Fascism and form a ring of five." Dealing with the Cambridge moles more briefly in his comprehensive account of *Her Majesty's Secret Service*, published some years later, Andrew asserts that the prime burrowers were "Kim Philby and Guy Burgess, the two earliest recruits (probably during the 1933–4 academic year)."[10]

Wilfrid Blunt, in his memoir, stirred this same pot by stating that Burgess did not recruit his brother Anthony until the winter of 1936, *after* he and Anthony had both returned from a summer trip to the Soviet Union. Wilfrid notes that when Anthony saw the complete draft of the manuscript, he requested the deletion of his reference to "the vile Burgess." Then London *Sunday Times* reporters Simon Freeman and Barrie Penrose, in their *Conspiracy of Silence*, disputed Blunt's public assertion that he "became a communist, or more particularly a Marxist, in 1935–36." They said Blunt was "attempting to disguise the fact that, by the beginning of 1934 at the latest, he was, like his friend Guy Burgess, a communist."[11]

Apart from the wide variety of dates for Blunt's actual recruitment, there has been a truly remarkable agreement that Burgess's recruitment preceded and was instrumental in determining Blunt's own decision to become a Soviet agent. It has been echoed with surprising unanimity by such disparate authorities as Peter Wright in *Spycatcher* and Kim Philby himself. But Philby was speaking from Moscow under the KGB's nose and was out again to deceive. Philby therefore refused to be drawn on "operational details." However, he encouraged British journalist Phillip Knightley to infer that Burgess was indeed the "mastermind," with a Delphic assertion that Burgess was the one "who maintained all the links with all of us."[12]

The real facts, according to the documented record that has now been uncovered, are very different. Taking these into account a counter-intelligence officer would point out that:

1. Blunt was a self-confessed Russian agent who liked to boast about his ability to deceive.
2. None of the dates given for Blunt's conversion are consistent.
3. The Russians would not have employed a newly graduated Burgess with his mercurial temper to recruit Blunt, an aloof research fellow who was six years his senior.

Blunt's apparent inability to recall the pivotal date of his supposed "Damascus Road" conversion to Marxism is a glaring flaw in his alibi. Did it take place in 1935, as he insisted after his exposure – or was it two years earlier, as he suggested in a farewell lecture in 1972 to the Courtauld Institute? More significant still is how such a meticulous mind as Anthony Blunt's could have forgotten so momentous a milepost in his career. The logical conclusion is that Blunt went to his grave an unrepentant spy.

Robert Crowley and other American authorities on Soviet undercover operations have always been skeptical about the role ascribed to Guy Burgess. They point out that he was an undergraduate until the summer of 1933 and then failed to obtain even a junior fellowship at Cambridge. Blunt implied that he was homosexually infatuated with the younger Burgess. But the presumption that the Russians would have trusted Burgess to sign up an agent so many years his senior does not match with what they know about Soviet operations. Moreover, Home Office files have come to light that show that by the mid-twenties Moscow was operating a highly sophisticated network of Soviet nationals and sympathizers in Britain and at various universities. Under these circumstances, they would not have been likely to use Burgess as a recruiter. More importantly, they never recruited any of their important agents overnight, as Blunt's own account asks us to believe.

The only writer to date to have touched on the deceptive nature of the stories about the date of Blunt's recruitment has been Professor George Steiner of Cambridge. His essay was published in 1980 by *The New Yorker*, as a result of which Steiner found himself being snubbed by some of his fellow professors at the university.[13]

It is also clear that Blunt's version of events was not swallowed hook, line, and sinker by those MI5 officers who were assigned to handle his case. Arthur Martin wrote to *The Times* of London and complained that he had been hampered by higher authority in his investigations of Soviet moles. Peter Wright, who in 1965 took over the task of hunting them down, testified in 1986, "It is simply not correct to say that the extent of penetration was thoroughly investigated."[14]

The British authorities dismissed Wright's assertions and in 1986 still refused to release for an Australian judge the results of their top-secret investigations. But the Most Secret British contemporary documents that have come to light while researching this book reveal that MI5 knew about Russian subversion in British universities in the early 1920s — long before Blunt came along. This new documentation undermines the credibility of the convenient cover story that it was not until a decade later that Guy Burgess became the prime recruiter of the so-called Cambridge moles.

Blunt, in the supposedly full and frank confession that he made in 1964 in return for a secret immunity deal, was careful to overplay Burgess's importance. According to Arthur Martin, however, who obtained Blunt's first confession, Blunt never told him the whole truth. Martin remains skeptical about how truthful Blunt was with him. Although Martin did not himself investigate all the Cambridge connections, he considered it significant that not until the year after Burgess's death in the Soviet Union was he able to persuade Blunt to confess.[15]

Dead men tell no lies. They cannot contradict the living. Given the extent to which it has become clear that Blunt lied and obfuscated about his career as a Russian spy, it would be more plausible to assume that his excuse that he "could not confess until all my friends were safe" was self-serving.[16]

Blaming a friend for leading you astray is the oldest ploy in the book. But it worked for Blunt because everyone believed his eldest brother's account that Anthony's recruitment by Burgess occurred in "late 1935 or early 1936." Research has, however, revealed that the British government wanted the public to believe Blunt's story about the late date of his recruitment almost more than the old spy himself did. So no one bothered to check the available records inside and outside the

United Kingdom. These put quite a different interpretation on the sequence of events — and how the Russians *really* went about recruiting spies at Cambridge.[17]

The question now becomes this: If Guy Burgess was *not* the so-called First Man, as has been believed for so long, who was? The clues emerge from Blunt's attempts to deflect attention from the real culprit.

Cambridge University was, and still is, an intensely hierarchical society. The same holds true for Russia's secret service, the KGB. Therefore, when it was desired to recruit a senior member of the university such as Blunt, no one would have known better than the Russians that this was not a task for an undergraduate. Nor would they have picked as their number-one recruiter in Cambridge a drifting postgraduate student like Burgess. If he was as brilliant as Blunt claimed, surely Moscow would have asked why he could not secure tenure at any college. Counterintelligence experts repeatedly stress that the Soviets ran a highly disciplined and centrally controlled network. They believe that Moscow would not have given any authority to someone with Burgess's disreputable character and notorious lack of self-discipline because he would have been difficult, if not impossible, to control.

"On the basis of extensive research of Soviet operational practice," Crowley told me, "Blunt, rather than Burgess, emerges as a more probable First Man." Crowley contends that with Blunt at the center instead of the periphery of the Cambridge net, the inconsistencies with Soviet practice which he sees in the "official" account, disappear. The most important of these inconsistencies, he stresses, is the supposedly central role of Guy Burgess.[18]

"From what is known about Burgess," Crowley says, "he appears an increasingly unlikely candidate for the Cambridge recruiter." Moscow could not have failed to note all of Burgess's failures and personality weaknesses. "All these add up," Crowley concludes, "to a negative argument against the recruitment of Burgess as prospective 'principal agent.'

"Blunt on the other hand," Crowley explained, "would have impressed the Russians as very sound agent material." Moreover, he points out that it was very significant that Michael Straight's account showed that it was Blunt, not Burgess, who was the chosen channel to inform the young American that Moscow had given him the "assignment" of returning to New York and making a career of banking on Wall Street. Straight protested. He wanted to stay in England. Again, it was Blunt who warned him that this would be difficult. Blunt then promised Straight's appeal "would be considered in the highest circles in the Kremlin." Straight made not one but two pleas to stay in Britain. And in each case it was

Blunt who rejected them. He reminded Straight that "our friends" in the Communist International had decided his mission was very important.[19]

Straight's account demonstrates that by 1936, only a few months after Blunt claimed Burgess had recruited him, it was Blunt who was acting as a Soviet recruiter with apparently direct lines to Moscow. According to Crowley, "Blunt just could not have achieved the sort of supervisory status implied by his directions to Straight in so short a time." Crowley also points out that it was a matter of regret among his former colleagues that neither the FBI nor the CIA was given the opportunity to participate in any of the debriefings of Blunt. Nonetheless, both agencies devoted considerable effort to follow up Straight's revelations and to investigate the American end of the Oxford and Cambridge network. Crowley leaves no doubt that both the FBI and the CIA concluded Blunt must be considered the most talented, and therefore the most dangerous, of all the Cambridge group.[20]

"The Soviets are thorough and cautious in the process of agent selection," Crowley explains. "They would have spent much time and considerable effort on a prospect as potentially important as Blunt." He stresses the endless patience that the Russians take in vetting foreign recruits. It is a long, disciplined procedure. It could not have taken place in the brief period allowed by Blunt's chronology.

Crowley believes that the Soviet officers who identified Blunt as a potential recruit would have given him high marks for his icy self-control and his obvious intelligence. As a rising young academic, he had promising access to potentially valuable information and people in authority. Blunt's well-connected family would also have been of interest to Moscow because it held the promise of even greater access.

"Access leads to information, and information was what Moscow wanted," Crowley says. "But make no mistake about it — they would also have taken endless trouble to satisfy themselves that the brilliant young Blunt was driven by a commitment: a commitment that they could divine and one that made him susceptible to discipline and control."

To establish whether Blunt's commitment was controllable, the Russians would have examined the minutiae of his family background and school career. They would have been looking for clues to "his personality, his prejudices and motivations."

To conduct an analysis of Blunt as Crowley believes the Soviets would have done, the details of his early life and parental influence provided by his eldest brother Wilfrid must be more carefully examined than has been done to date.

\*     \*     \*

The real story of Anthony Blunt's extraordinary life begins during an unseasonal heat wave on September 26, 1907, in the vicarage of Holy Trinity Church, Bournemouth. Anthony was born on this date into an upper-middle-class family that already consisted of two brothers: Christopher, a chubby two-year-old, and Wilfrid, who was six.[21]

The Reverend Arthur Vere Stanley Blunt was a solid, hearty man, well attuned to the conventional propriety of his parishioners. Bournemouth was a south-coast town that was the very model of Edwardian respectability; it was a favorite with retired Indian Army officers and convalescents.

The Reverend Blunt, who preferred to be called Stanley, was the son of the suffragan bishop of Hull. Like his father, Stanley considered himself a "broad evangelical" in the mainstream of the Church of England. He had a deep suspicion of Roman Catholics and distrusted anything "popish" such as Baroque architecture. He pronounced God as "Guard" in accordance with established Church of England practice. A good social mixer, he was just as much at home on the tennis courts as in the pulpit.

According to Wilfrid, his father was a "good man" but regarded by his sons as "hearty" and "distant." There is a suspicion that there was a resentment of the cold showers and daily family prayers that their father considered part of the regimen necessary to build a Christian character. Wilfrid also noted that their parents both "tacitly assumed we would all eventually want to be ordained."[22]

Mrs. Blunt was a puritanical teetotaler who forbade the consumption of strong drink under her roof and fussed about her husband's pipe-smoking. Wilfrid describes his mother as a "woman of infinite goodness and almost puritanical simplicity, incapable of telling the whitest of lies." A reserved woman, her natural shyness was exaggerated by her deafness in one ear.

Hilda Violet Masters was ten years younger than her bridegroom when Stanley Blunt married her at the turn of the century. As the youngest daughter of an iron-willed matriarch, she had been well trained on how to rule over a household that eventually consisted of maids and governesses in addition to her husband and three sons. She had also brought some needed money and aristocratic connections to the Blunt family. Both were essential to maintaining an upper-class social status on a vicar's modest stipend.

*Burke's Landed Gentry*, the indispensable guide to England's leading families, listed the Reverend Blunt and his heirs until 1922. But then they were dropped because their closest aristocratic relative was judged "politically and morally unsound." He was the Victorian poet, diplomat, and adventurer Wilfrid Scawen Blunt. A kind of latter-day Lord Byron, Scawen Blunt had devoted his life to writing passionate verse and martyring his popularity to a campaign for Irish, Indian, and Egyptian independence. But it was his seductions of titled ladies that really scandalized Victorian society. According to Wilfrid, his parents never once mentioned the family's second cousin whose name he bore.

If cousin Scawen Blunt's immorality so offended Hilda's high-minded piety, what would she have thought if she had lived long enough to see her favorite son denounced as a traitor? She doted on her intelligent sons, who soon learned the importance of concealing from their overbearingly strict mother their secret childhood transgressions. Anthony became her "Benjamin," and Hilda cosseted him because she was convinced that he was a "delicate" infant who needed frequent doses of proprietary nursery tonics.

Anthony returned his mother's affection; they remained devoted to each other until the end of her life. This strong maternal bond may well have contributed to Anthony's ability — and determination — to conceal that for most of his life he had systematically betrayed the most cherished ideals and standards of his patriotic, puritanical mother.

The Masters family claimed an aristocratic lineage superior to that of the Blunts. Hilda Masters was a second cousin of the Earl of Strathmore, whose daughter, Lady Elizabeth Bowes-Lyon, became the consort of King George VI and mother of Queen Elizabeth II. According to Wilfrid's recollections, royal connections were also important to the family because of their maternal grandmother's close friendship with the Duchess of Teck.

Grandma Gertrude Emma Masters was the personification of a Victorian matriarch. Although a semi-invalid with a bad leg, she ruled over her family from her pramlike invalid carriage, waving her smelling salts and thumping her silver-topped ebony cane. A formidable campaigner on behalf of temperance and a supporter of Christian charities, she was an "alarming" figure to her grandsons. By contrast, they held their white-bearded grandfather in special affection. A mild-mannered man, he had served as colonial magistrate in Madras, and retired early from India to a genteel if unostentatious house near the River Thames at Richmond.

Finding herself conveniently close to the Duke and Duchess of Teck's residence at White Lodge in Richmond Park, the redoubtable Grandmama Masters toadied with enthusiasm her aristocratic neighbor's heavy round of Christian charity and temperance work. A punctilious correspondent, she once dispatched a servant with paper and pen to White Lodge when the Duchess failed to respond to one of her letters. But the two remained on warm terms. Their daughters learned to skate together on the park's ponds, and the Blunt boys' Aunt Mabel became a close friend of the Tecks' daughter Princess Mary. Mary later married George, Duke of York, the oldest surviving son and heir of Edward VII.

When King George V succeeded to the throne in 1910, the Blunts proudly counted the new queen of England as a family patron and friend. According to Wilfrid, his Aunt Mabel and his mother had become confirmed "royalty snobs." The whole family went en masse to cheer the coronation procession. Aunt Mabel bound the family's royal correspondence in leather, and for many years his mother and aunt were the honored recipients of hand-me-down dresses, hats, and parasols from the royal wardrobe. This was a great family confidence — and one of the "state" secrets that Anthony never divulged.

The Blunts' royal connections may have been responsible for a dramatic transformation in their lives that took place in 1911. The Reverend Blunt applied to become chaplain of the British embassy church in Paris, and Wilfrid recalls his father announcing matter-of-factly at breakfast one April morning that the family was moving to France. And so the stage was set for the pivotal educational experience that led the Reverend Blunt's youngest son into a career of treachery.

In Anthony's own words, Paris "coloured the whole of my future development." The city's effect on Anthony was far-reaching and dramatic. It aroused and shaped his precocious interest in art and architecture. During the formative childhood decade when his home was in the cosmopolitan French capital, he became more and more alienated from what he perceived as the stuffy conventionalities and philistinism of Britain and the British way of life.[23]

Anthony's father had become a person of some importance in the embassy in Paris. The splendor of being part of the most glittering outpost of the British Empire in Europe would have been apparent to Anthony when the king and queen made a state visit to Paris in 1912.

Even the Reverend Blunt's hearty sermons seemed more bearable. Obliged to attend two services each Sunday, Anthony and his brothers now had more to hold their attention than the damp hymnbooks and dull congregation of Holy Trinity Church, Bournemouth. The worshipers at St. Michael's were colorful and intriguingly cosmopolitan. The handsomely appointed Gothic church had been built in 1833 with donations, including a hundred pounds from Queen Victoria, to "set in order those things which are wanting among such natives of Great Britain who choose to be resident in Europe."[24]

A short walk from the chaplain's residence past the mouth-watering *pâtisseries* was the domed Greek temple guarding the entrance to the Parc Monceau. This grandest of all Parisian gardens has the cultivated rusticity of the classical vistas so beloved of the French sixteenth-century painters. It is easy to imagine you are stepping out of the traffic of the Rue de Courcelles into a painting by Claude Lorrain or Poussin. The greensward leads to gravel paths that meander through the middle distance like the roads of the Roman *campagna* into groves of trees shading a dark lake where a waterfall, framed by fragmentary Doric columns, tumbles past the stony stare of carved nymphs. This must have been a magical world for the six-year-old Anthony Blunt and his brothers accustomed to the municipal geranium borders and geometric rose beds of Bournemouth.

"Paris was gloriously and endlessly exciting," Wilfrid wrote. He must have communicated his own sense of adventure to his youngest brother, for whom he became role model, confidant, and guide. Keeping up spurred Anthony's physical and intellectual development. At the age of six he was too tall for the mark painted on Parisian trams that showed who had to pay full fare. The switch in 1912 from age to height caused much anguish to the self-righteous Hilda Blunt. She carried a copy of Anthony's birth certificate in French to persuade the skeptical Paris tramcar conductors that her son rode at half fare.[25]

"My earliest recollection connected with works of art is that I can just remember going to the Louvre before the 1914–18 war," Anthony recalled a half century later. He could not remember which pictures had impressed him, but we have Wilfrid's word that he was soon collecting picture postcards of religious paintings. The eldest brother's detailed account of their childhood trips of exploration to Versailles, Malmaison, and Saint-Cloud reveal how close he and Anthony became as a result of their shared interest in art.[26]

Christopher, their middle brother, was the odd-boy-out. According to Wilfrid, he showed no interest in painting or architecture and appears to have rather deliberately distanced himself from them with his single-minded pursuit of coin collecting. Childhood photographs of the three invariably show Christopher scowling. Wilfrid's pointed references to his middle brother's reputation for "naughtiness" suggest that, as often occurs in sibling trios, the eldest and youngest Blunts may have ganged up on him and seen to it that Christopher was unfairly blamed for their mischievousness. Wilfrid also recounts how they played elaborate practical jokes such as dangling coins attached to virtually invisible black threads out of their windows, and rigging up their father's Pianola to startle visitors with ghostly music.[27]

World War I left its own imprint on Anthony's intellectual and artistic development. When the guns roared out of the crystalline summer skies in 1914, the Blunt brothers were on vacation with relatives in England. Wilfrid, much to his regret, was packed off to his preparatory school. Not until October, after the German advance on Paris had ground to a halt along the banks of the River Marne, was it considered safe for Anthony and Christopher to rejoin their parents in Paris.

Anthony's formal education began when he left his nursery governess and joined Christopher at the L'École Villiers, a nearby Parisian day school. He quickly became fluent in French, and although the war had closed the city's museums, he continued his exploration of Paris architecture when Wilfrid came home for vacations. Anthony recalled how he had been "compelled to look at architecture" and so began a lifelong fascination with the structure, form, and decoration of buildings.

Summer holidays in wartime were spent on economical bicycling holidays with the whole family pedaling through Normandy, the Auvergne, and Fontainebleau. Wilfrid provides a revealing insight of Mrs. Blunt's "materfamilias" role in his account of how they lodged at the simplest — and presumably cheapest — hotels. But the accommodation was never settled until their mother had been upstairs to "vet the lavatories."[28]

Wilfrid also related how they had already begun to compare the frugality of their own home with the generous hospitality of their adopted aunt, an American named Vandervoort. "Vandy," as she liked to be known, lived in a smart residence in the Boulevard Malesherbes. She was an expatriate with a fortune to match her ample figure. Expensive presents, trips to the circus, and drives in the Bois de Boulogne were usually followed by sumptuous teas at Pré-Catelan. It was at Vandy's insistence that the Blunt brothers took their first deliciously sweet sips of Château d'Yquem. When Hilda Blunt found out that her sons had tasted the forbidden liquor, she fretted about Vandy's harmful influence on her sons.

"The chaplain's house," as Wilfrid wryly observed, "was not a good jumping-off point for Bohemia." But thanks to Vandy the Blunt boys began to develop a taste for the pleasures of the world and, perhaps, secretly to question the puritanical values imposed on them at home.[29]

Wilfrid admits that from an early age he fostered Anthony's developing artistic consciousness as a shared reaction against the worthy dullness of their home. Their parents' principal cultural artifacts were wishy-washy Victorian watercolors and shelves of blue-bound devotional works such as *The Psalms in Human Life.*

The Blunts took it for granted that their children were embracing the family's Christian beliefs. But Wilfrid's memoir and the recollections of Anthony's schoolfriend Louis MacNeice reveal that both brothers had begun to question their parents' religiosity at an early age. But neither dared give any voice to their advancing skepticism. They appear to have unconsciously redirected their nascent rebellion against purita-nical Christian values into a more acceptable form: a personal crusade against the cultural values of their parents. Yet a strong emotional bond tied Anthony to his mother. Throughout his life, according to Wilfrid, his youngest brother appears to have gone to considerable lengths to avoid hurting his mother's feelings. Rosamond Lehmann had also noted Anthony's deep concern. But the need to preserve that tie also demanded a degree of deviousness and self-concealment on Anthony's part that can only have intensified and deepened his rebellion.

There are clues in Wilfrid's account of their boyhood suggesting that there existed other reasons for Anthony's lifelong rebellion against conventional English life. In 1916, the three brothers, who by that time were all at school in England, spent the Christmas season at the Lancashire estate of their uncle Sir Ralph Assheton. He was a member of Parliament and managed to maintain the life of an Edwardian country gentleman throughout the war.

The liveried footmen, shooting parties, English country-house life alternately fascinated and offended Anthony and his brothers. The snob-bish Asshetons, with their obsession with their ancient pedigree and the rows of ancestral portraits lining Downham Hall, made their visiting cousins feel unwelcome. The Eton-educated Asshetons constantly re-minded the Blunts of their "poor-relation" status. Wilfrid noted how they had been made to "feel inferior, ungrateful and even rebellious."[30]

The Assheton snubs, both real and imagined, made a deep impact on Anthony. Although he never regarded himself as anything other than a member of the English privileged class, the Asshetons' unbearable snootiness appears to have reinforced his growing conviction that every-thing in France was more sophisticated and vastly superior to what he knew of in England. "I developed a very strong French leaning," Anthony would write, "which has coloured my whole attitude toward things ever since."[31]

The first recorded manifestation of Anthony's rebellion was against his father's preference for Gothic architecture. "At that time my taste was extremely conventional," Anthony later conceded, noting that this was because his father "did not encourage him to look at anything later than medieval architecture." The Reverend Blunt considered seventeenth-century Baroque churches "vulgar and decadent" expressions of "popishness" and "idolatry." Wilfrid recalled that he was "rapped over the knuckles for enticing Anthony away from the Gothic which alone it was respectable to admire."[32]

The values Anthony increasingly rejected were those of his parents. He owed a bigger debt to brother Wilfrid, "who was six years older and was becoming a painter by the time I was growing up, and had far closer contacts, naturally, with the artistic world."

Wilfrid set Anthony an example of how to be a cultural and social rebel. Confounding the Reverend Blunt's expectations, his eldest son showed no inclination for the Church. Then he abandoned Oxford for a brief spell to become apprentice painter in a Paris atelier. Wilfrid was a gifted artist, whereas Anthony, by the evidence of the one picture of his that has survived, was not. The irony is that while Wilfrid, through unconventionality and talent, eventually found himself a niche teaching art, Anthony managed to climb to the pinnacle of the art world by dint of conventional scholarship.

In 1916, Anthony's parents considered him mature enough to join Christopher at a preparatory school in Sussex, one of the more successful of a number of smallish private schools at Seaford. The two brothers traveled to and from England by train and the Channel steamers that braved drifting mines and prowling U-boats. Wartime travel set the brothers apart from their classmates, whose only experience of the great conflict was sticking pins marked with flags into schoolroom maps.

The war also brought Anthony's baptism by fire. There had been sporadic air raids on Paris by Zeppelin airships and later, in the spring of 1918, by Gotha bombers. But it was during the final German effort to advance that August that a German shell from the legendary Big Bertha railway gun exploded in the Rue Jouffroy near the chaplain's house. Windows shattered and glasses broke. Anthony's account would later enthrall his classmates at St. Peter's. The Blunts were to be virtually on the lines of the Western front compared with the other boys.

# CHAPTER 3

# *"Sexual Politics"*

"Anthony Blunt had that special ability to enter any role and play it marvelously well," Robert Cecil said. "He was a languid man, certainly, but he had a very cute brain."[1]

Interviews with Blunt at his London flat shortly before his death reinforced Robert Cecil's impression of Blunt as a calculating and ruthless man. As he poured out a sherry before the lunch that punctuated our daylong conversation, Cecil observed how he invited Blunt down to his home. He had offered to drive Blunt over to his brother Wilfrid's nearby home afterward. But Blunt always politely declined.

"I got the impression Anthony would have been most uncomfortable accepting my hospitality," Cecil observed. "It would have put him under an obligation to me."

The setting, we speculated, would have discomfited Blunt. The Cecils' house is on the outskirts of a Hampshire village where cricket matches have been played on the local green since the seventeenth century. Its windows look out past Mrs. Cecil's lush flower beds, to cows grazing on the gentle downland slopes beyond the rosebushes. It was the home of a diplomat who retired after a career devoted to preserving the very English values that Blunt set out to destroy. The careers of the two men may have been very different, but they sprang from similar social backgrounds and shared a common heritage and education.

Like Blunt, Cecil's courteous yet authoritative manner is deeply rooted in the traditions of Britain's privileged class. His family connections are woven more tightly than Blunt's into the fabric of British history. Lean and bespectacled, Cecil still maintains in his mid-seventies the upright bearing of the urbane and confident young diplomat who in 1945 joined his friend Donald Maclean as a first secretary at His Britannic Majesty's Embassy in Washington. He had known Maclean at Cambridge and is preparing his own book on him.

Recalling Maclean and his own experience in Washington, Cecil explained that Blunt shared, along with Philby and Burgess, a peculiarly British hauteur toward the United States. Cecil speculated that this traditional upper-class British attitude may have played a part in prompting his Cambridge contemporaries to look toward the east rather than west. In the thirties a few intellectuals had begun to sense that the British Empire was on the decline. The United States, by contrast, was a power on the rise. So was the Soviet Union. This was a source of inspiration to young people with leftist sympathies. Cecil's generation had expected to grow up to inherit and rule an empire on which the sun never set. But the cataclysmic upheaval of the First World War had upset that comfortable notion. It had also provided — for those who cared to read it — the writing on the wall that Britain's imperial power was envied by America and hated by the Soviet Union.

"The mistake that Maclean and the others made was to pin their colors to the Russian mast because of the latent anti-Americanism that infected so many of my generation," Cecil said. "Englishmen went to the United States not to a foreign land, but to a country they regarded as populated and run by a race of socially inferior Englishmen."

It was while traveling by train from New York to Washington in 1945, Cecil told me, that he had been brought face to face with the reality of Anglo-American relations. He had a pleasant conversation with a U.S. marine sergeant, and as they were about to part, the marine had the last word.

"You're not a bad guy, but you can't be English," Cecil recalls the marine telling him as he got off the train at the Baltimore railroad station.

"'Yes,' I said, 'I'm English, actually.'"

"'You're new here. Let me give you a piece of advice,' the marine said. 'In this country you can be an Irishman, a Welshman, or a Scot — but don't be a goddamn limey.'"

"It was," said Cecil, who went on to become head of the Foreign Office American department, "the best piece of advice that anyone ever gave me."

After postwar service in embassies in Europe, Cecil headed the British information services in New York and the Cultural Relations Department. Then he retired to make a second career as a university lecturer and writer of books and articles on contemporary history. When Blunt was publicly unmasked as a Soviet agent, Cecil's intimate knowledge of Blunt's wartime operations caused him to wonder what kind of man could have betrayed so much.

Blunt's calculated and cold-blooded inhumanity puzzles and still concerns Cecil. He was as interested as I was in discovering what motivated the man's treachery. He did not believe that there had been sufficient attention paid to why Blunt's Cambridge contemporaries, Maclean, Burgess, and Philby, all highly intelligent members of Britain's privileged class, so readily betrayed their country. Their university experience and the seeming impasse of contemporary British politics played their part, of course. But Cecil believed there might have been a more sinister Soviet involvement in which Blunt had an important role.

Cecil pointed out that Cambridge played a part in Maclean's conversion to Marxism, and he admitted that he, too, had once been almost hooked. He recalled that after a long political discussion with Marxist friends, he had returned one evening to his rooms almost convinced that the future hope of mankind was the great Soviet experiment.

"Fortunately," Cecil said with a wry smile, "when I woke up the next morning, I realized that my commitment to communism had not survived the night."

Maclean, Cecil believes, became a Marxist because he was genuinely committed to change society. He at one point wanted to abandon Cambridge for the Soviet Union and drive a tractor on a collective farm. "Donald became involved in the student rights movement," Cecil recalled, "because he genuinely believed in the struggle of the masses."

Consideration for the proletariat was not, Cecil believes, Blunt's motivation for becoming a Communist. He was driven by a different set of values than Maclean. The only aspect of Marxism that appealed to Blunt, Cecil believes, was his determination to obtain access to the power that came with being on the side of the future.

"The welfare of the masses did not interest Anthony. His objective was to effect some major change in British society which would leave him on top." Whatever that change was to be, Blunt would not work for it by selling copies of *The Daily Worker*, or passing resolutions at a meeting. Anyone could do that. Politics on this level was boring: beneath the dignity of a member of the intellectual elite such as himself.

"Secret power, I am sure, was the real appeal to Anthony for becoming an undercover Communist agent," Cecil said. He reached this conclusion during his interviews with Blunt. Cecil believes Blunt's desire for social change was also rooted in the nature of his peculiarly personal vendetta against British society.

"As Blunt rose higher in public and academic esteem, all the time Anthony was privately laughing at everyone," Cecil observed. He also agrees that Blunt's dislike of British society must have been triggered by a reaction to his family's puritanical Christianity and his boyhood experience in France. He said that Blunt's school career was instrumental in giving direction to reinforcing that rebellion.

"You have to grasp that Anthony was a very exceptional character, not merely another traitor," Cecil advised me. It is impossible to make sense of Blunt, he believes, unless you can show that he was an exceptionally talented manipulator. Furthermore, the intricacies of his quite astonishing character reveal that he had a unique ability to gain power over people and make them trust him.

Blunt made no specific admissions during his three interviews with Cecil, who theorized from his own educational experiences that Blunt must have learned the lesson at his public school that if you want to have power over people you first have to gain control over someone else.

The British public schools were not "public" — except in the sense that they were open to any boy whose parent could afford the fees and who could pass the entrance examination. Rugby school under its reforming headmaster Dr. Thomas Arnold (immortalized in *Tom Brown's School Days*) became the model for the British public school. In keeping with the good doctor's Victorian perception of Great Britain's global destiny, Rugby and its imitators provided a spartan education aimed at turning out Christian gentlemen worthy of becoming British leaders. The curriculum relied heavily on the Bible and Greek classics, leavened with organized team sports to instill "manly spirit." A hierarchical prefect system reinforced the "muscular Christianity" that imposed discipline and beat out what Dr. Arnold had characterized as the "surprising wickedness of young boys."[2]

Cecil explained that his public school, Wellington College, had the same reputation for toughness as Marlborough, where the three Blunt brothers were educated. The pupils at Marlborough and Wellington, like those at the more famous Eton and Harrow, represented a cross-section of British middle- and upper-class society. The prefects and athletes were the privileged class. They lorded their juvenile authority over the other boys with brutal thrashings administered by thin bamboo canes.

"Anthony discovered the secret of obtaining power over people at an early age," said Cecil, "when he found out that the way to beat the system was to gain control over a prefect or a senior boy." What Cecil alluded to was sexual blackmail.

Today, when one walks through the school quadrangle by a girl and boy chatting eagerly about classwork as they hurry with their rackets on the way to the tennis courts, it is difficult to visualize just how rugged an establishment Marlborough College was in the 1920s. (The admission of female students is a relatively recent innovation.) The red-brick Georgian buildings have a warmth that belies the school's earlier reputation for toughness. Even the institutional Victorian buildings and the austere Gothic-revival chapel are softened by the clinging red creeper and framed by the spreading branches of beech and lime trees.

When Marlborough College was founded in 1843, the school moved into a mansion that had originally been built by Lady Hertford. For many years her once-elegant property had been functioning as a Bath

Road hostelry, but the advent of the nearby Great Western Railway had killed the London to Bath coaching traffic. The transformation of the Castle Inn into a public school often caused mirth among the boys of an educational establishment that prided itself on spartan discipline and strong ecclesiastical ties.

What Marlborough lacked in prestige and ancient heritage it quickly compensated for with its glowing record of academic success — thanks to the many intelligent and industrious vicars' sons it attracted. Church of England clergymen received a discount on the tuition, and that is why it became the Blunt brothers' school. Their father could not afford to send three boys to Eton.

In the five years he was there, Anthony Blunt grew to know and love the picturesque setting, if not the school itself. Situated at the north end of the one-street Berkshire market town of Marlborough, the college is within easy bicycling distance of some of the most beautiful countryside in England. To the north rears Martinsell Hill and the wild Wiltshire downs with their beech coppices and prehistoric burial mounds. South up the hill from the small town were the mysteries of the ancient oak forest of Savernake with its herd of deer. It was not the idyllic location of Marlborough College or its surrounding countryside that impressed arriving new boys as they walked warily down Granham hill from the railway station. It was the school's harsh reputation. Their fears were soon realized when they found themselves assigned to a dormitory in an ugly Victorian building. New boys were told Junior House was the work of the same architect who had designed London's notorious Wormwood Scrubs prison. This was a bit of local folklore, but for those boys who worked, ate, and slept in this great square building, the similarity of their life to prison was painfully real.

The spacious open stairwell at the center of the Junior House was the scene of the sadistic initiation rituals. At one time, new boys had been tossed from the top of the well into a blanket; a practice that was banned after one of these unfortunate initiates was killed. Anthony had to endure nothing more dangerous than being made to crawl the length of a long, hot cast-iron radiator while singing a popular song. Yelling boys jammed the landings above and then rushed down to join in a face-slapping ceremony that completed the initiation.

According to Wilfrid Blunt, "any modern gaol would seem a paradise" compared with Junior House, where new boys lived "in constant fear of infringing petty regulations laid down by our oligarchy of tyrants." His contemporary T. C. Worsley also noted that "Marlborough prided itself on its toughness." He wrote that "life was lived on the barest of bare boards, at the smallest and hardest of desks, in the coldest of cold classrooms, in the total absence of any possible privacy. One was always cold, usually hungry."[3]

Recalled the poet Louis MacNeice, Anthony's contemporary, "physical discomfort and futile ritual — those were the first things I noticed." For up to a year they stayed in Junior House, supposedly being hardened before transfer to Upper School. "Boys of that age being especially sadistic," MacNeice noted ruefully, "life in the Junior House was more uncomfortable than the supposedly more frightening life we moved on to."[4]

New boys often went hungry in the bleak dining hall until they had learned the knack of fighting five hundred others for food. Marlborough had a particularly nasty ritual called "Rushing." This required junior boys to plant a spoon or fork in a dish of food, such as "College Bolly" before it could be "Condescended" and snatched away by more senior boys. The burly MacNeice remembered how the mealtime ritual filled him with such confusion and terror that for three days he avoided using the lavatory. He was too embarrassed to ask for the location of the large covered shed with its two long doorless rows of back-to-back cubicles.

The shock of incongruous tribal rituals did not hold nearly so much terror for the fourteen-year-old Anthony Blunt when he arrived at Marlborough in January 1921. He had learned about the school's peculiar customs from his older brothers. But no amount of foreknowledge could have spared him from the humiliating duty of "fagging" for senior boys. Bullying was also institutionalized and tolerated by the masters as a necessary part of the hardening-up process in the Junior House, where the length of stay depended on sexual development rather than educational accomplishment. Junior housemasters made periodic bathroom inspections to watch for the sprouting pubic hair, the signal for a boy's promotion to Upper School.

Most boys faced the prospect of their promotion with considerable apprehension. It meant that in the two years before they became members of the sixth form, they ran the constant risk of beatings and sadistic rituals. Recollections of Upper School still chill the memories of those who endured it. Wilfrid Blunt remembered the hall that contained nearly two hundred desks where the boys of fourteen to sixteen worked day and evening as a "brutal, junior hell." Worsley described it as "a cold and barbarous barn."[5]

A single master aided by six junior prefects selected primarily for their athletic prowess — and their ability to wield a cane — maintained strict discipline. "The only law was a jungle law of force; and the special sufferers were the individualists and non-conformers," recalled Worsley. He avoided the worst of the bullying because his ability at sports earned him rapid promotion to junior-prefect status. Seniority and physical strength established the bullying order among the members of Little Fire and Big Fire, the two large grates on either side of the hall. Every evening the prefects came marching up and down the rows of desks lashing out with their canes. The most junior boys cleaned up the day's litter and deposited it into an enormous wastepaper basket.

This receptacle also served to imprison the unfortunate boy whom the prefects every once in a while singled out for Marlborough's supreme disciplinary penalty — the much-feared "basketing."

"They would seize him," MacNeice wrote, "tear off most of his clothes and cover him with house paint, then put him in the basket and push him round and round the hall." As a finale a rope would be produced and the basketed victim hauled thirty feet into the air.

"Government of the mob, by the mob, and for the mob" was how MacNeice described the scene. He roundly condemned what the deliberately absent masters considered "a fine old tradition" as "a perfect exhibition of mass sadism."[6]

Sadism was also encouraged in the thrashings administered by older boys on their juniors for the most minor transgressions. Cuthbert Worsley recalled that even when he was a junior prefect, senior boys still contrived to find excuses to beat him: "It was all done in the spirit of semi-ragging," he wrote, "rough but good natured, ending usually in the cane being shoved up me, a crude form of sexual play." There was also an unhealthy sexual element in the ritual dormitory beatings which were known at Marlborough as "bum shaving." Victims were made to stand back to back, their naked buttocks remaining in contact until cut apart by the slicing cane. Too soon a move by either one brought more lashes. The alternative to beatings was "hot potting." This involved cupping each cheek of the boy's naked buttocks with mugs containing a flaming paper scrap. The vacuum created left the two mugs clinging to the boy, who paraded up and down between the row of beds with the cups on his bottom swinging like a pair of pendulous breasts. The victim could then be beaten again for "obscenity."[7]

Those who were beaten, and most of those doing the beating, were prudishly ignorant of the sexual undertow of such escapades. One critic coined the term "sexual concentration camps" to describe Britain's public schools. Recent research has shown that sexual activities, from widespread masturbation to actual cases of rape of junior boys, were not uncommon in Britain's public schools. But it was not until after

World War II that serious medical and psychological investigations into human sexual behavior revealed the contradictions inherent in segregating boys in boarding schools.[8]

Instead of lessening the pent-up sexual energies of the boys, the standard public-school regime of physical exercise actually fanned the flames of the healthy young libidos. In these segregated environments, boys who were sent away from home from the age of eight inevitably transferred their affection to members of their peer group. In English public schools, romance was, by physical necessity and educational inspiration, homosexual.

Much of the Greek literature used as set texts in schools emphasized that the love of man for man was on a higher plane than the carnal love of a man for a woman. This came as no surprise to generations of English boys raised on *Tom Brown's School Days, Eric, or Little by Little, The Hill,* and other such books that celebrated the virtues of male comradeship. But the worthy Victorian clerics who wrote homoerotic titles such as *A Garland of Ladslove, The Romance of a Choirboy,* and *Passing the Love of Women* may have been inspired by more than comradeship. The latter volume moved a reviewer to praise the vicar who authored it for being "as alive to the beauty of unsullied youth as Plato."[9]

Platonic admiration of male youth was socially and legally acceptable only as long as it remained "unsullied." As the homoerotic cult blossomed in public-school boys, the British Parliament voted in 1885 to make homosexual acts a criminal offense. The conflicting currents of law and morality generated a unique state of confusion and anxiety. "Beautiful sins," quipped Oscar Wilde, "are the privilege of the ruling class." The furor that erupted with Wilde's trial for sodomy in 1895 was symptomatic of this collective fear and guilt about "the love that dare not speak its name," a term coined appropriately by Wilde's one-time lover, Lord Alfred Douglas.[10]

On the basis of many confidential interviews, the author of a recent British study, *The Public School Phenomenon,* believes that an average of a quarter of the boys attending Britain's public-school system during the first decades of this century engaged in regular sexual contact. More than 90 percent owned up to "fact or fantasy" love affairs with other boys. The majority were purely romantic affairs like the distant passion for another Marlborough boy recalled by John Betjeman. A year ahead of Anthony Blunt, the future poet laureate of Britain "never dared touch anyone," because of his fear that he "would have gone to gaol — and hell."

Betjeman, like many public-school boys, found his intense amorous feelings for a fellow Marlburian both frustrating and confusing. And Wilfrid Blunt recalled that the headmaster's advice on sex to his confirmation class was that "if we treated all women as we would our mothers and sisters we would never go far wrong."[11]

Some public-school boys learned to fear and even despise the opposite sex; many more grew up confused and hostile toward women. Their dilemma became the butt of a smutty Eton joke, about a laundress who raised her skirt to expose her passion for a young student.

"There! What do you think of that?"

"Gosh, ma'am," said the astonished boy. "If you wait a minute I'll run to my room, get my cricket bat and come back and kill it."[12]

Marlborough housemasters treated the onset of puberty as "a sort of disease like measles." Wilfrid Blunt, like most homosexuals who became teachers, considered any physical contact with a pupil to be a violation of trust. Some did not. The Reverend Blunt's godfather, Dean C. J. Vaughan, resigned the headmastership of Harrow under the threat of public exposure by one of his former pupils.

While Britain's public-school system may not have increased significantly the incidence of homosexuality in the national population, it instilled subconscious homoerotic attitudes in successive generations of middle- and upper-class males. And their shared proclivities in public school resulted in the development of extensive underground "old boy networks" of practicing homosexuals. In turn, because the law made practicing homosexuality a criminal offense punishable with a harsh jail sentence, the homosexual networks among the British elite offered great opportunities to any blackmailer — or spy — who gained admission.

Not every homosexually inclined boy managed to gain admission into the magic ruling circle. Wilfrid claims to have been so sexually immature that he was ignorant of "the pleasures of masturbation" and therefore "did not really understand those whispered, sniggering references to certain arcane practices alleged to take place in the denser thickets of Manton Coppice."[13]

The more precocious boys at Marlborough rendezvoused for illicit sexual practices in the woodlands half a mile from the school, but they did not always have enough regard for the secrecy that was essential for their protection. Indiscretion was the downfall of one group. Their conversation offended the prudish Cuthbert Worsley and he reported them. Much to his surprise, he wrote, an investigation resulted in the expulsion of three senior boys.

Rumors about "The Cult of Priapus," as MacNeice termed it, spread quickly in a closed institution. What Anthony Blunt made of the gossip about Manton Coppice is not recorded. But we do know from his close friend MacNeice that "nearly all the elder boys had their mild homosexual romances — an occasion for 'billets' and giggling and elaborately engineered rendezvous." He admitted writing a poem to "a dark-haired boy of sixteen who had large grey feminine eyes." Blunt criticized the verse as too heavily influenced by Tennyson.[14]

MacNeice insisted that this was his only flirtation with another boy, but Blunt's liaisons were more serious, according to their mutual friend John Hilton. He told me of an incident during their final year when, on a pouring wet day, he had been waiting under the arcade across from the dining hall, waiting for it to open.

"Anthony, who as a prefect had an umbrella, suddenly darted forward and I darted with him," Hilton recalled. "It turned out that he had seen a 'love object' and intended offering 'it' a share of the umbrella — he was very, very angry." The boy could well have been "the Beautiful Basil" whom MacNeice refers to frequently in letters to Blunt that date from their last year at school. Their homoerotic tone suggests that Anthony was involved in a series of such liaisons. Other Marlborough boys referred to only by their first names are cryptically described as members of the "Elect."[15]

In one letter to Blunt, MacNeice signed off, "I wish you dreams of Edward's eyes. I am afraid they are not pure." Another contained a reference to a boy called John: "I should say the satisfactory end for violent affection is a break."[16]

On the evidence of this correspondence, Blunt appears, at the very least, to have formed a number of romantic attachments to other boys during his senior year. Other members of his circle were certainly doing so; their contemporaries remember at least one boy was expelled from Marlborough after being caught indulging in homosexual practices.

It is impossible to do more than speculate about the origins of Anthony Blunt's homosexuality, but a parallel can be drawn to the experience of another of his contemporaries, Thomas Driberg. He also was the son of a distant older father and dominant middle-class mother. Driberg graphically described in his memoir *Ruling Passions* how he became homosexually active before going to public school. Like Blunt, Driberg became a Communist. For many years he was a member of Parliament and a Russian agent who also fed information to MI5.[17]

Also like Blunt, Driberg was an aggressive homosexual who relished the danger involved in searching for sexual partners in public lavatories. They shared a preference for lower-class men, a common trait of Britain's privileged classes in search of illicit sex partners. The services of a whore or lower-class male pickup could be paid for, and this made the relationship less inhibiting because the unequal social status of the participants did not induce feelings of guilt.

So if Blunt's initial homosexual experience was with a soldier in a public lavatory, it would explain why the scenario always had a powerful erotic fascination for him. There would have been plenty of opportunity for such an encounter during his trips back and forth to Paris. (His family did not move back to England until the end of 1921, when his father became rector of St. John's Paddington, a dowdy middle-class parish north of Hyde Park, near the Great Western Railway's London terminal.)

Anthony Blunt was then in his first term at Marlborough College and he considered himself vastly superior to his contemporaries. His foundation scholarship attested to his intellectual ability. He read French better than any master and had amassed a precocious knowledge of art. But he was also intensely cynical toward the hearty Christianity and orthodox Britishness that Marlborough considered its duty to instill in all its boys.

So although Blunt had acquired from his brothers a useful insider's survival guide to the school's rules and tribal rituals, he would have become an obvious target for bullying and cutting down to size by more senior boys. Forty-five years later, when Sir Anthony Blunt — as he then proudly was — recalled for the benefit of two Marlborough boys how "perfectly beastly" were his first terms, he said he "lived in perpetual fear" that he might be "basketed."[18]

"My life," Blunt declared, "was made a misery for me for two terms by the bullying of one boy." He did not elaborate, nor did he explain how or why the bullying ceased. But his admission that it did not continue beyond the second term of the school year suggests that something might have made the bully desist.

How did Blunt manage to neutralize the bully? Robert Cecil wonders. Why had such an obviously offensive junior boy managed to escape a ritual basketing?

Drawing on his own background knowledge of the similarities between Wellington and Marlborough, Cecil believes that Blunt obtained some hold over the prefects and senior boys to relieve him of the bully's wrath.

"Sexual politics," Cecil said. "That is the only way I can describe it." He believes Blunt discovered that sex was the key to survival in a society where adolescent boys were alternately beating or competing with each other for favors and privileges. Cecil speculates that Marlborough, like Wellington, would have had its share of homosexual witch hunts to root out what the headmasters euphemistically described as "vice." Invariably the senior boy faced expulsion but not the younger boy. The presumption was always that the junior partner in a sexual crime would have been bullied or corrupted against his will. A junior boy could therefore entice an older one to his advantage in the game of "sexual politics."[19]

"You see," Cecil said, "Anthony would have been attractive to the older boys because he could turn on considerable charm." When bullied he would, after a term or so, have learned how to get his own back in a peculiarly feminine way.

"At Wellington," Cecil explained, "the athletes, despite the rules against fraternizing with the juniors, would have their friendships with smaller boys." Although protective of their favorites, they were terribly exposed because of the other seniors. According to Cecil, although prefects may also have been protecting a young chap on the side, they were not going to let anyone who was caught breaking the rules off the hook.

"Anthony was clever enough," Cecil believes, "to exploit this complex web of sexual entanglement to escape sadistic bullying." Blunt might have found himself a protector, Cecil theorizes, or even provoked an overtly homosexual encounter to entrap the bully who might have been trying to force his attentions on him. "Now I'm going to the housemaster, or else!" would, Cecil believes, have been a powerful threat. If the blackmail worked — and it seems it did — it would explain why Blunt was no longer threatened by senior boys. Other would-be bullies, forewarned that the youngest Blunt boy was dangerous, would not molest him. Cecil also points out that Blunt would thereby have acquired an enormous contempt for the system as a result of his own ability to bend its weakness to his advantage.

"In later life," Cecil emphasized, "Anthony knew that much of Britain was run by former prefects vulnerable to the same kind of blackmail." Cecil's theory explains why Blunt was so important to the Soviets. He knew how to manipulate the semisecret homosexual networks that were extensions of the public-school system.

# CHAPTER 4

# *"Image Breaking"*

"Anthony Blunt became a spy because he wanted to get back at the establishment," said Oxford historian John Bowle. "There is no doubt in my mind about that."[1]

A year senior to Blunt at Marlborough College, Bowle ended his career as a fellow of Wadham College. The wispy white-haired professor was the very image of a crusty old don who made little effort to conceal his personal animosity toward Blunt. Yet, during our interview, Bowle provided a revealing insight into Blunt's character. Personal experience of Blunt and his recollections of similarly precocious boys during his own career as a history master at Westminster School and Eton had convinced him he was right.

"Intense conceit," Bowle declared firmly. "That was the secret of Blunt's personality." He explained that Blunt was a brilliant scholar who easily won academic honors. This, however, was not enough for him. He wanted to prove his superiority by excelling at everything. He yearned to be a leader at school. But he faced a major hurdle. Blunt did not excel at team sports. At Marlborough, as at the other British public schools, the real test of leadership potential came on the playing fields.

"Blunt felt ostracized and slighted because he was bad at games," explained Bowle. "He was not the brilliant all-rounder that he thought he was." The resulting wound to his self-esteem was deep and permanent. According to Bowle, Blunt tended to harbor grudges. This, Bowle believed, fired Blunt's personal insurrection against the public-school system, a rebellion that underpinned his secret antiestablishment work for the Soviets.

Bowle's firsthand view of Blunt as a precocious adolescent rebel who translated his personal insurrection against his school into a betrayal of his country in later life coincides almost exactly with the independent assessment of his motivational impulse made by Robert Cecil.

That Blunt was immensely conceited about his intellectual abilities squares with the Marlborough records, which reveal him as a scholastic high-flier. He excelled in mathematics and steadily climbed up the academic ladder, winning a great many prizes and scholarships until he became the undisputed top of his class in his final year. He was so fluent in French that one master let him take over the class. But Blunt's arrogance often grated on his contemporaries. John Hilton recorded in his diary how "that terrible boy Blunt came to ask for the key of classroom and of course had to stay to tea and monopolized the conversation."[2]

Blunt's unshakable self-assurance was apparent even at fourteen. "Old for his years in the knowledge of the world and knowledge of where he was going," according to his closest friend at Marlborough, Louis MacNeice, who described him as "a dominating figure both in his assurance and incandescent spirit and with his imposing height and large handsome, long-haired head." Blunt became "the dominant intellectual" of his generation while making a reputation for a "precocious knowledge of art and an habitual contempt for conservative authorities."[3]

"Socially and in power terms, these boys carried no weight at all," Cuthbert Worsley wrote in his memoir of Marlborough. "Public approval among the masters as well as boys was reserved for the athlete." The Marlborough motto, "Virtu, Studio, Ludo," might more appropriately have reversed the order of "Study" and "Play" to acknowledge the preeminence of games. The tyrannical games master, T. G. C. Sandford, was a middle-aged Oxford triple-blue who made all the boys turn out in shorts and shirts to cheer their rugby teams at every game.[4]

Games were compulsory for all. On afternoons when it was too wet to play, the whole school was sent on cross-country runs. The hated "Sweats" sent straggling lines of miserable boys toiling over the windswept downs with prefects clocking them along. Dawdlers and those who took shortcuts were beaten. Games worship reached its peak in the summer term when Sandford made cricket "a kind of pagan religious rite," according to Worsley, who spoke with the authority of a member of the Marlborough First XI, the school's top team.

Blunt himself admitted that he "hated compulsory games." Certainly it was not because of any physical incapacity, because at Cambridge he played hockey and he is also on record as saying how he enjoyed running "rather slowly over long distances" across the downs.[5]

Blunt, it seems, was psychologically ill-equipped to be a team player. Those who would not accept him on his own terms, he despised. He grew his hair long, causing the local barber to remark to MacNeice that he "didn't think THAT gentleman would be any good at games because his hair would get in the way." Shortly afterward the bursar issued instructions to the hairdresser to cut all boys' hair shorter. "He couldn't have people going about like a lot of poets," MacNeice reported home. "The Bursar doesn't like poets."[6]

Blunt was delighted to be regarded as an aesthete. He liked to recall how he showed contempt for the athletes by playing catch with a large, brightly colored ball right across their game.

"We went out of the way to be irritatingly provocative," Blunt admitted in a 1967 interview with the two schoolboy editors of *The Marlburian*, the college's magazine. He recalled how he and his friends delighted in ostentatiously taunting the prefects by flouting nonexistent rules as they flaunted blue silk handkerchiefs from their wristwatches in chapel. He also told the Marlborough boys how he helped organize a more adult and focused "revolt against the absolute dominance of games."[7]

In these published recollections, Blunt portrayed himself as one of the leaders, along with John Bowle and John Betjeman, of a group of more senior boys who systematically mocked Marlborough's sacred code of athleticism. By calling themselves aesthetes and associating themselves with the "art for art's sake" sentiments of Oscar Wilde, they deliberately set out to shock. Betjeman was the leading spirit of this cult of aesthetic dilettantism. His hoarse laughter and childish behavior included rolling a hoop around the school while wearing a green feather behind his ear. It infuriated the hearties. The future poet laureate's eccentric passion for Gothic-revival architecture, Victorian trams, and Methodist chapels Blunt regarded as contrived, because he dismissed them as a "wilful passion" and a "joke."[8]

Blunt had more respect, it seems, for John Bowle, whom he claimed to have rescued from marauding hearties. "He used to come into my study, absolutely terrified, and say: 'Can you give me shelter, they're trying to throw me in the swimming pool.'"[9]

Bowle thereby put himself under an obligation to the younger boy, who thereby gained an entrée to the circle of older Marlborough aesthetes. Blunt said he became a member of the group who founded "a paper called *The Heretick*, which was intended to express our disapproval of the Establishment generally."[10]

John Bowle said this was a typical Blunt fabrication. Blunt had nothing to do with founding the magazine. *"The Heretick,"* he said, was his brainchild. Betjeman had thought up the magazine's name. Blunt had not even helped with the magazine; he had merely contributed two articles. Bowle angrily recalled how the tactlessness of Blunt's second piece had been instrumental in closing down *The Heretick*.[11]

*The Heretick*, according to Bowle, was not nearly as anti-establishment as Blunt claimed. Bowle and Betjeman edited a more literary alternative to the school magazine, which was dull and devoted too much space to games reports and obituaries of old Marlburians. The first issue of *The Heretick* in March 1924 proclaimed "Upon Philistia Will I Triumph" above Bowle's cover drawing of a scowling hockey player taunted by a mischievous faun.

Far from declaring open war on the school establishment, Bowle revealed that the headmaster himself had encouraged and supported the publication. Dr. Cyril Norwood was a reformer who tried to strike a balance between the classroom and the games field by reforming the curriculum and giving more emphasis to science. Norwood sympathized with Bowle and his group of "aesthetes" because of the jeering that had greeted his own first appearance in the school hall. The athletes had vociferously expressed their snobbish resentment that the new Marlborough head was a former grammar-school headmaster. They had sarcastically nicknamed him "Boots" because he had weak arches and could not wear shoes. But Bowle respected the "Great Grim Man," as he said he was later popularly known. Norwood — whose abilities led to his appointment to the headmastership of Harrow in Blunt's final year — was nevertheless considered dangerously liberal by some parents because he spoke out in favor of the League of Nations.

Norwood's support for *The Heretick* collapsed when the second issue appeared in June 1925. The games master violently objected to the opening article, which attacked the "ludicrous pomposity" of the belief that "the foundations of our mighty Empire are laid on the playing fields of our schools." But it was Blunt's provocative piece on the Wildean theme of art and morality that caused an uproar. "To call a work of art immoral is like calling an ink spot sympathetic," he wrote, adding that: "To say that a painting is immoral merely shews a lamentable incapacity for appreciation." Blunt later claimed that his housemaster had provoked him to write the piece because he "thought that the Matisse and Rouault which I had in my study were indecent." This was confirmed by Hilton, who remembers that Blunt was "at loggerheads with his housemaster over books picturing unclothed and amorous persons."[12]

"A typical Blunt piece of work," Bowle snorted. "Priggish, boring and conceited." Considering his later espousal of Marxism, it is surprising that at the age of nineteen he insisted that "great artists could not be moral reformers." Nevertheless, one Marlborough parent found this whiff of the scandalous Oscar Wilde so offensive that he wrote to the headmaster threatening to remove his son from the school. Norwood thereupon banned *The Heretick*.[13]

Bowle blamed his magazine's demise on Blunt's "intense conceit." But Blunt, predictably, told a different story to the *Marlburian* editors in 1967. He made no mention of the furor provoked by his article, merely stating that the second issue went into debt because it was "duller than the first" and did not sell. "A fitting end for such an ephemeral production" was Blunt's haughty comment.[14]

Blunt's conceit was so great that it seems he found it difficult ever to accept responsibility for his own mistakes. Whether it was the folding of the school magazine, the attribution of a painting, or his conversion to communism, Blunt always had to pass the blame to someone else. The trait is particularly evident in his repeated insistence that he was never interested in politics. The Marlborough record is very revealing when weighed against the picture Blunt contrived to present of himself as having been always the naïve, detached, apolitical academic.

"Politics was simply a subject never discussed at all at Marlborough," Blunt is on record as telling his Courtauld students in a farewell lecture. Since it was later published under the title of "From Bloomsbury to Marxism," Blunt presumably approved and corrected it before he retired in 1973. In his rambling and self-serving monologue he said that "the most striking feature about this whole period at Marlborough was its complete unreality, and the fact that we lived in this little self-contained world of art and literature with no awareness of what was taking place in the outside world."[15]

But neither Marlborough nor the boys were as politically detached or unaware of what was going on outside the school walls as Blunt found it convenient to "remember" fifty years later. The records of the school debating society, of which he was a one-time secretary, reveal that politics was a frequent subject for discussion. Socialism, the Labour government, the Victorians, Fascism, and the general strike were all eagerly debated. Blunt's close friends MacNeice and Basil Barr regularly spoke as the advocates of a left-wing viewpoint. But the reactionary attitudes of the majority usually won the day, until a single vote defeated them when the Debating Society voted to deplore the British Fascist party in February 1925.

When Blunt gave his talk about the influences of Marx and Bloomsbury, he had already given MI5 his secret confession blaming Guy Burgess for recruiting him to the Communist cause. He therefore found it convenient to stress his youthful political naïveté to reinforce assurances that his espousal of Marxism was an aberration of his Cambridge years.

Yet Blunt's own rebellion against the athleticism of Marlborough was a consciously political act. He and the other literary aesthetes may well have been aware that they were taking up the gauntlet thrown down by Alec Waugh, the author of *The Loom of Youth*, which created a sensation in 1920. The autobiographical novel of this twenty-year-old survivor of Sherborne school and the Western Front assailed the hypocrisy of games worship and the homosexual undercurrents of the public school.

His biting novel was as penetrating a work of social satire as anything his younger brother Evelyn would later pen about Britain's other cherished institutions. But the outraged denials of rampant homosexuality in the public schools left his central theme that "athleticism is ruining the country" largely ignored.

Furious headmasters banned the book and the Establishment condemned *The Loom of Youth*. After watching so many Marlborough boys march off to die in the mud of Flanders, Dr. Norwood had been deeply affected by the bravery of those "old boys" whose sacrifice was seen as a vindication of the importance of the team spirit of the games field. "The ideas of chivalry which inspired the knighthood of medieval days have been combined in the tradition of English education which holds the field today," Norwood wrote in 1927 after he became head of Harrow School.[16]

Although Norwood was not nearly as reactionary as some public-school headmasters, this defense of the system fostered the idea that the flower of England's manhood had perished in the war. The postwar economic crises also helped promote the popular belief that Great Britain was left adrift because of the loss of its strongest, bravest, and most intelligent men in World War I. The searing war memoirs, such as Siegfried Sassoon's *Memoirs of a Fox-Hunting Man* and Robert Graves's *Goodbye to All That*, intensified the belief among the war's survivors that their generation had been victims of a ruthless historical trick perpetrated by the old guard of political leaders. Many battle-scarred young men came home only to be bitterly disillusioned at not finding the promised "land fit for heroes."

Britain's "lost generation" myth, like all rationalizations for national failure, was inflated by the retelling. The German and French armed forces had suffered twice the casualty rates, but Britain's peculiarly class-bound elite accentuated the significance of their high mortality rates. One in five former public-school boys became war casualties, with the rate approaching one in four for Oxford and Cambridge recruits. But even so, machine-gun bullets and high-explosive mortar shell did not selectively cut down the "brightest and the best." Ninety percent of the British officer corps survived. But they had to come to terms with the new social and political realities that had swept away the comfortable Edwardian values and undermined the shaky economics of Britain's imperial legacy.[17]

In Europe the old order was under siege. Socialism, with its emphasis on the rights of the masses rather than the privileges of the few, had become a major political force in Germany and France. The Russian

Revolution of 1917 had given birth to a Communist state dedicated to the worldwide subversion of capitalism. Even in Britain the whiff of revolution was in the air. The enfranchisement of women in 1918 and the expansion of organized labor unions, together with the growth of bureaucracy and business during wartime, presented an increasing challenge to the traditional ruling class. In the wake of a succession of postwar economic crises and deepening industrial unemployment, the rise of socialism among the working class threatened the traditional division of parliamentary rule between the Liberal and Conservative parties.

The Labour party preached class war by way of industrial strikes and the ballot box. When Liberal wartime Prime Minister David Lloyd George's coalition government broke up in 1922, the Conservatives returned to power. Labour emerged from the election for the first time as the radical opposition in a Parliament that included two Communist members. Labour's leader, Ramsay MacDonald, became Britain's first socialist prime minister when he formed a minority government at the beginning of 1924.

"Today 23 years ago dear Grandmama dies," King George V noted in his diary on January 22, 1924. "I wonder what she would have thought of a Labour government." Queen Victoria might not have been amused to find that for the first time in two centuries there was not a single old Etonian in the Cabinet. But this was not the dawn of the socialist revolution so many conservatives feared. Overwhelmed by economic problems and their decision to give official recognition to the Soviet Union, the Labour government collapsed after only eight months.[18]

The Conservatives swept back to power in the fall elections of 1924. With their avuncular pipe-smoking champion Stanley Baldwin as prime minister, the former public-school prefects were once again firmly in charge of the British government. The politics of nostalgia, however, did nothing to arrest Britain's economic decline.

Despite Baldwin's soothing reassurances, the bitterness released by a rising unemployment rate deepened the sense of collective class-guilt in a growing number of British intellectuals. There was increasing disenchantment with the "headmasterly" prime minister and the "prefect" mentality of Britain's ruling class. The public schools themselves had responded to the postwar political and economic upheavals with reaction and retrenchment. But while zealous headmasters banned from school libraries subversive works like *The Loom of Youth* and the *Daily Herald*, Britain's young socialist newspaper, they could not prevent boys from reading them during their vacations.

The changing British political landscape and increasing disenchantment among the educated elite were also reflected in the cultural shock of Bloomsbury. New forms of literature, poetry, and art, fomented in the drawing rooms of the quiet London square, were soon reaching from the universities down to the public schools like Marlborough, where the embryo intellectuals like Blunt were smoldering with unfocused discontent. Impressionable young minds, already in reaction against starchy parental values, devoured Lytton Strachey's anti-establishment assault on *The Eminent Victorians*. Another catalyst for young minds groping for a new definition of cultural values was the powerful fragmented imagery of T. S. Eliot's *The Waste Land*.

Like many of his contemporaries, even the precociously bright Anthony Blunt may not have fully grasped the scope of one of the twentieth century's seminal works of poetry that Eliot himself described as the portrayal of "the immense panorama of futility and anarchy that is contemporary history."[19]

*The Waste Land* nonetheless had a powerful impact on a generation of rebellious young intellectuals intent on toppling the towers of the old cultural order in their quest for the elusive "city over the mountains."

"We were very much aware of the Eliot movement," Blunt recalled, "and we all knew *The Waste Land* off by heart." Strachey's histories "justified," he said, his schoolboy "hatred of the Establishment." This antipathy found its chief expression through his ardent championship of modern art. He explained that his "great desire to proselytize" was because of a "genuine admiration of the new" and his determination to preach the decadence of the old order. But art for the young Blunt was also a political cause and a vehicle for self-promotion. He himself admitted as much in a rare moment of self-revelation, saying that his intention was to "exasperate the other boys and masters at school."[20]

Blunt had been laying the foundations of his crusade ever since the autumn term of 1923, when he finally escaped from the brutality of Upper School. Emerging with distinctions in the school-certificate examinations, he entered the sixth form and shared a study. He stocked it with his growing collection of art books and decorated the walls with modern prints. He set himself up as Marlborough's revolutionary prophet of modernism and began lending out books and prints of French paintings that many masters and boys considered shocking and subversive.

The first Postimpressionist exhibition had outraged London in 1910. Roger Fry, the painter and Bloomsbury art critic, had organized the first showing of Cézanne, Matisse, Gauguin, and van Gogh. As director of painting at the Metropolitan Museum of Art in New York from 1905 to 1910, Fry had introduced Americans to the brightly colored paintings. But the staid British cultural establishment had violently rejected the art, which was already popular in the United States. Ironically, it was Blunt's second cousin Wilfrid Scawen Blunt, who had taken the lead in denouncing the canvases of the Postimpressionists as "a pornographic display." *The Times* warned that paintings such as van Gogh's *Sunflowers* were a "bad influence on the younger generation," and the conservative *Morning Post* compared the show to a plague and demanded that "the source of infection ought to be destroyed."

A decade later Blunt appreciated that after the outcry over Fry's prewar London exhibition, French Impressionist paintings were still considered shocking and that Picasso's Cubist canvases represented a frontal assault on staid British taste. Paintings, rather than political slogans, therefore became the banners of Blunt's schoolboy rebellion.

Louis MacNeice, who became the principal lieutenant of Blunt's attack on the bastions of Marlborough's aesthetic conventionality, provides an arresting image of the sixteen-year-old rebel. He described Blunt as "very tall and very thin and drooping, with deadly sharp elbows and the ribs of a famished saint." He particularly noted his friend's "cold blue eyes, a cutaway mouth and a wave of soft brown hair falling over his forehead." According to MacNeice, Blunt had not yet learned the knack of concealing his emotions. Whenever he became angry, MacNeice observed how it affected Blunt's "pre-Raphaelite beauty." He would pout and stick out his lip and "his good looks vanished and the sulkiness was all."[21]

"Anthony was an austere hedonist," wrote John Hilton, another contemporary, who described Blunt as "living for gratification of the senses, with an eye for social esteem and seeking anchorage in a system of scholarly detail." A fellow member of the mathematical sixth form, Hilton was keenly aware of the sharp difference between his two friends. MacNeice he described as "a ribald seer, an anarchic and mocking seeker after the deep springs of action and faith."[22]

MacNeice, who was in the classical sixth, was a husky, untidy youth, who was remembered as Blunt's sidekick and proselytizer among the hearties, to whom he had an entrée because he played a useful game of rugby. MacNeice had a ferocious Celtic talent for words that made him a gifted poet and orator. He shared with Blunt the common revolt against their clergyman fathers, whose moral values "were a delusion, and politics and religion a waste of time." The boys concluded that "the only values were aesthetic," which appears to have been the way they both disguised from their parents their rejection of Christian values as they immersed themselves in what MacNeice described as "the bacchanalian chorus of adolescence."[23]

MacNeice and Blunt both separately insisted that their mutual attraction was not physical. "It is important that you understand that Louis was always totally, irredeemably heterosexual," Blunt assured Oxford Professor Jon Stallworthy, MacNeice's biographer, shortly before his death. But Stallworthy agrees that MacNeice's letters to Blunt suggest that Louis was aware of his friend's preferences because of many overt homosexual references in their decade-long correspondence.[24]

Blunt seems to have found in MacNeice's creative brilliance the necessary grist for his more analytical intelligence. Blunt was "infinitely more intelligent than MacNeice" but "not nearly such a genius," observed their mutual friend Hilton. But there can be no doubt that it was Blunt's dominant personality that drew the trio together at Marlborough. He drilled them in the need to display their intellectual superiority over other boys who were merely clever.[25]

"Anthony was usually the nucleus of a cloud of circling electrons," Hilton said. According to Blunt, his circle proved their intelligence "avidly and extremely widely but in a very eccentric manner." Their cultural philosophy reflected their chorus master's deep-seated anti-establishment prejudice. They rejected Shakespeare as "part of the establishment" in favor of Marlowe; Shelley and Keats were romantic and passé. They devoured Voltaire's philosophical novel *Candide* because it attacked established institutions. They despised Tennyson but approved Victorian Gothic horror stories. Grimms' fairy tales together with the prose and limericks of Edward Lear became props for a child-cult. They admired the contemporary verse of T. S. Eliot and the Sitwells. They read Gertrude Stein aloud "up and down the dormitories to exasperate our neighbors."[26]

"Anthony and I went in for eclectic reading," MacNeice wrote in later life. "It was either stark and realistic or precious and remote and two dimensional." Blunt, he noted, had "a flair for bigotry" and "every day he blackballed another musician." They liked Bach, Handel, and Mozart, but despised Wagner. According to Blunt he was "establishment, romantic, all the things that we thought were most wicked."[27]

Blunt's presumptuous confidence in his aesthetic sense came from his familiarity with the Postimpressionist pictures he had seen in the Paris galleries. His brother Wilfrid, then an art master at Haileybury school, kept him informed about the latest trends, eventually introducing Anthony to Roger Fry. Blunt reinforced his juvenile preconceptions about modern art with technical expositions that he had gleaned from his growing collection of books. His aesthetic bible in his formative years was a slim volume by the Bloomsbury critic Clive Bell.

*Art*, as it was simply titled, was the first English book to attempt a modern definition of the essential aesthetic values of painting. "Significant Form" was the label Bell coined to define the combination of lines, colors, and spatial relationships that "stir our aesthetic emotions." What he had read in these art books may well have influenced Blunt's decision to specialize in mathematics at Marlborough. "Art transports us from the world of man's activity to a world of aesthetic adulation," Bell had written, suggesting that the "pure mathematician rapt in his studies knows a state of mind which I take to be similar, if not identical."[28]

Bloomsbury's principal artistic theorist may have been responsible for Blunt's pursuit of mathematics, but there can be no doubt that Anthony embraced Bell's belief in significant form. Blunt personalized the doctrine as "pure form" and employed it to discount the representational elements in painting. Pure form became a dogmatic obsession. Even MacNeice recorded how reluctant he had been to challenge Blunt's fixed opinions by liking the "jugness of the jug and bowlness of the bowl" in the colored print of a Picasso still life on the wall of the study they shared. For Blunt, "anything else but Pure Form was out," MacNeice wrote, "literary content was wrong or irrelevant, and naturalism was an insult."[29]

Form, rather than representation, was an article of faith for Blunt. So was everything French. Paris was the standard by which he judged everything else. He admitted he was "extremely snooty about all English art" because he considered it "either literary or derivative." The only exception was William Blake and his passion for the mystical artist-poet was a lifelong enthusiasm. But Blunt accommodated his prejudices if it suited his proselytizing purposes, as it did in 1925 when there was a public outcry at sculptor Jacob Epstein's primitive *Rima*. Despite his belief that Epstein "was not a good sculptor" he boldly defended the statuesque relief "because it was Modern Art."[30]

Blunt's youthful bigotry revealed a great deal. He justified his single-mindedness as the result of "a great desire to proselytize." But his use of religious terms to describe his challenge to the old aesthetic gods and identification with the new was surely significant. It shows that he realized that he was aligning himself with a revolution in the visual arts as sweeping as any since the Renaissance. Recognition that the French Cubist and Postimpressionist painters "were still regarded as dangerous revolutionaries" reinforced Blunt's sense of mission. He knew that their preoccupation with abstraction and nonrepresentational form challenged the most basic assumptions of Western art and was no less "revolutionary" than Marx's political doctrine that challenged the fundamental human need for material possessions.[31]

Pride of place on Blunt's study wall at Marlborough was given to Cézanne's *Montagne Sainte-Victoire*. This was his homage to the precursor of the modernist movements, who had overturned the precepts of representational art by breaking down three-dimensional forms into a series of two-dimensional planes. Blunt was well versed in explaining to his disciples how Cézanne's followers had diverged into two main schools. Matisse became the leader of the "Fauves" — literally, the "Wild Beasts" — who broke their images into bold areas of bright colors. Picasso was the leading light of the "Cubists," who dissected figures and objects into a myriad of shifting geometric planes.[32]

Cubism, and particularly Picasso's pre-World War I still lifes, had special appeal for Blunt. Their bold planes and sharply defined, colorful forms lent themselves to a mathematical rationalization about art that appeared "scientific." This appealed to his keenly analytical mind just as he later found his sympathies drawn to the "scientific" approach of Marxist political dialectic.

"Blunt does not like Cubism very much except the theory," MacNeice noted perceptively. An impromptu exposition had left the school's Astronomical Society "quite lost." The irony for Blunt was that even as he was championing Picasso's bold geometric forms at Marlborough, the century's most prolific artistic genius was advancing beyond the simple Cubist approach into a more emotive style that did not afford such simple analysis. Blunt never forgave his youthful godhead for abandoning the Cubist faith. His vindictive disappointment was given expression a decade later when he roundly condemned Picasso's masterpiece *Guernica*.[33]

Blunt himself admitted that his youthful approach to art was too formularized and dogmatic. He accepted many of his juvenile attitudes as misconceptions, especially his dismissal of the High Renaissance art that became central to his professional career. In his later years he excused his blinkered views as the enthusiasm of youth for clearcut definitions. But such was Blunt's conceit that he blamed his teenage errors of judgment on the "wrong ideas" perpetrated by the artists themselves.[34]

Yet at Marlborough Blunt was uncritically accepted as the leader of the circle of rebellious aesthetes. "We traipsed along eagerly with him," John Hilton wrote, acknowledging that Blunt was "far ahead of us in sophistication." Blunt also showed his political skill by contriving to get himself elected secretary of the school debating society. This coup especially impressed Hilton because Blunt had "hardly ever attended a debate before."[35]

The debating society, however, was an inadequate launching pad for Blunt's grandiose plan for demolishing Marlborough's bastions of philistinism. He was scheming to set up a more influential cultural forum, one that would involve sympathetic masters and senior boys. But Blunt's proposal for a full-fledged Art Society ran into opposition from the art master, Christopher Hughes.

"I did not get on well with Hughes," Blunt recalled in his Courtauld lecture fifty years later. He said this was because Hughes "believed all art stopped at the pre-Raphaelites."[36]

His contempt for Hughes became a vendetta after the master tried to block his plans. He first tried to outflank the art master by inviting Clifford Canning, a boyish-looking master who had been a friend to all the Blunt boys, to become president of the Art Society. Canning had taken holy orders in 1924, but this did not faze MacNeice and Blunt. They regarded him, in contrast to their clerical fathers, as an "intelligent Christian." Many of the disciplinarians in the staff common room thought Canning was too close to his boys. In particular they criticized the way he had turned his rooms into a salon and a refuge for budding aesthetes.[37]

Blunt's society quickly became a staff-room issue. His housemaster, Dr. Gullebaud, who evidently had little sympathy for the one boy in C3 House who caused him more problems than any other, supported Hughes. The art master insisted that if there was going to be an Art Society at Marlborough, then he was going to be president. That did not please Blunt. But with Canning's help he outmaneuvered the opposition by calling his forum the "Anonymous Society" and enlisting George C. Turner, a sympathetic senior master, as its nominal president.

"I've been bullied by Blunt into joining his society," John Hilton wrote to his parents. It was not, he took care to reassure them, "really eccentric" because masters as well as members of the school teams were members.[38]

Blunt's objective for his new society was anything but the promotion of eccentricity. He wanted to project his influence and authority with the aid of members of the Marlborough establishment. Besides Canning and G. C. Turner (who the following year succeeded Dr. Norwood as headmaster), the senior classics and science masters were regular participants. Thanks to MacNeice's contacts among the athletes, three leading school-team players were also persuaded to join up.

The prestige of Blunt's Anonymous Society as a forum in which boys joined with masters for stimulating discussion rapidly eclipsed the school's established Literary Society, which was "rather dull" by comparison. Within a year it had become a kind of juvenile Bloomsbury. Marlborough's brightest intellects plied each other with philosophical debate while they munched on the egg sandwiches provided by the hospitable Canning at his house, the Priory, off Marlborough High Street. Formal presentations ranged from the lighthearted paper given by MacNeice on "The Mailed Fist of Common Sense and How to Avoid It" to avant-garde piano recitals of Debussy by Dr. Goad, the science master, to a succession of Blunt's precocious dissertations on modern art.[39]

Blunt was relentless in his campaign against Hughes. In debating such topics as the rival merits of Picasso and Michelangelo, he wore his opponents down with long perorations supported by prints and quotations from his many art books. His sheer persistence and mastery of detail usually demolished his opponents.

"I remember reading a paper proving that art went underground at the end of the Renaissance," Blunt recalled, "reemerged at El Greco, and then submerged again until Cézanne and the Impressionists." Hughes was "so roused" at Blunt's polemics that he insisted on giving an answering paper. He was invited to give his paper the following term. The feud between them was worsened the following month when Hughes refused to allow Wllfrid Blunt to exhibit a still life in the annual exhibition of paintings by Old Marlburians.

"It was unworthy of a pavement artist," fumed the art master. To which Blunt remarked that the art master's paintings "seemed to have been scrubbed with soft soap."[40]

The January meeting of the Anonymous Society, when Hughes set out to get his own back on the scornful Blunt, was, according to MacNeice, "very tense." But Hughes's blustering defense of Pre-Raphaelite painting became so confused that Blunt collapsed into sarcastic laughter. The art master could stand the humiliation no longer.

"You've hurt me many times, and now I'm hurting you," Hughes blurted out. According to Blunt's recollection, this "delightful" confrontation reduced the art master to tears of frustrated rage.[41]

Such triumphs greatly enhanced Blunt's self-esteem. The importance and respectability of "Blunt's Society" was never higher. It even included the senior prefect and rugger XV team player Michael Robertson. Most of the school's other leading lights participated, including James Mason, the future film star. Younger boys who admired Blunt grew their hair long and called themselves aesthetes. He established himself as a prominent figure and did his best to live up to his reputation. He and his circle strove to appear avant-garde as they strolled around the school, posturing as though to admire the details of an imaginary Baroque church.

"Sometimes I was conscious that Anthony and I were spending too much time being 'enfants terribles,'" MacNeice admitted. But Blunt's career received its final accolade in 1926 when he won a scholarship to study mathematics at Trinity College, Cambridge. Blunt self-effacingly said that he topped the candidates' list in *The Times* only because of alphabetical order. But the scholarship fixed his star securely in the school firmament. The highly competitive Trinity College scholarship had marked him out as one of the brightest young men of his age in Britain, and a recruit for the ruling elite. The aesthete rebel became, overnight, a respectable school hero, helped by a newspaper article on the examination results that noted, "Marlborough is not a public school, it is a miracle."[42]

"I think it is less cruel to people with minds than any other public school," MacNeice assured his mother in a letter in January 1926 announcing that his friend Blunt had been made a senior school prefect. "There are so few prefects with any intelligence," MacNeice observed.[43]

To impress his circle with his newfound prefectorial authority, Blunt proposed adding an art magazine, *The Apollo*, to the sixth-form papers. This infuriated his fellow prefects who objected to the "horrible" art journal. But it was impossible to keep the new school hero down. Marlborough boys paid tribute to the rebel's success by adapting verses of the school song: "Yes, We Are Collegiate" became "Yes, We Are Aesthetic," with Blunt's name linked to MacNeice's and Hilton's in the refrains. Even *The Marlburian* satirized his success as a cultural revolutionary. But it is doubtful whether Blunt liked the reference to his "inane though slightly malicious smile" or "the wave of hair of which I am not a little proud."[44]

For his final two terms Blunt basked in the esteem of his schoolfellows and lorded it over them as prefect. According to MacNeice, who had himself won a classical scholarship to Oxford, they had little to do in their final two terms at school except "amuse ourselves and infuriate everyone else." They made long bicycle rides to sleepy Wiltshire hamlets, where they rang the East Kennet church bells in anticipation of the coming freedom. "Anthony says this really is the best country in the world," MacNeice wrote after a trek gathering wild-apple blooms and bluebells.[45]

During the late-spring days, when Britain teetered on the brink of civil disorder during the general strike, Blunt and MacNeice lazed naked in the buttercups beside the chalky banks of the meandering Kennet. According to Blunt, the strike was treated very largely "as a sort of joke, when one's elder brothers and one's parents went and did curious things."[46]

Anticipation of their coming triumph at Cambridge and Oxford was celebrated with tea parties for their friends. At the very last one they stuffed themselves on walnut cake and solemnly dispatched the tea service, piece by piece, out of the window to smash against the wall opposite. "We kept the best till last," MacNeice recorded. "The sugar bowl, still full of lumps, burst on the wall like a round of machine-gun fire and the large teapot sailed to its doom trailing tea from the spout. 'Ruins of Carthage,' we said and washed our hands of Marlborough."[47]

On the afternoon of June 28, 1926, seven hundred boys filed past the tall Doric columns and into the newly completed Marlborough College Memorial Chapel. Fidgety in their high collars and formal black flannel jackets, they waited for the Prize Day speeches to begin.

The annual ritual did not get off to a smooth start. Despite an earlier practice, the school rebelliously left it to the choir to intone the Latin school song, "Carmen Marlburiensis." The disapproval was evident on the headmaster's face when he rose to begin his address. George C. Turner was "cultured, attractive and tactful," according to MacNeice. In his short speech Turner paid tribute to his predecessor, Dr. Norwood, whose transformation of the curriculum had produced record numbers of Oxford and Cambridge scholarships.[48]

It was Anthony Frederick Blunt whom the headmaster singled out as Marlborough's top scholar. The crowning moment of Blunt's school career came when Turner put him at the top of the list to be congratulated for the scholarship he had won to Trinity College. But this was only by way of an introduction to his remarks about "Blunt's propaganda of Modern Art."

"I cannot refrain from congratulating him also," said the headmaster, "on his persistent efforts to interest an incurably sentimental society in modern aims in art and literature."

A discernible snicker snaked around the huddled ranks of boys as the headmaster confessed, with a smile, that he found Blunt's "world of angles, dissonance and mis-shaped objects" a "very odd one." Some disapproving throat clearing from some of the more stiffly seated fathers greeted Turner's assertion that "it is a world in which many people are trying to find, if not beauty, at least truth."[49]

Anthony Blunt sat proud and detached. Junior boys, accustomed to hearing praise lavished on cricketers and rugby players, looked around to glimpse this unusual school hero. Their housemaster, Dr. Guillebaud, "was enraged," according to MacNeice.

Any nineteen-year-old would have found his head swelling with pride. But before the rush of self-satisfaction must have reached Blunt's toes, he was stung by a sharp rebuke. "Blunt and some others may go image breaking, but" — the headmaster paused — "that is no bad thing so long as the hammer is swung fair and square at the image and not the heads of rival worshipers."[50]

Laughter erupted throughout the hall. Blunt had been cut down to size in his moment of glory. The headmaster had touched a raw nerve by publicly exposing Blunt's willingness to turn his high-minded championship of the cause of modern art into personal vendettas.

The moment brought some satisfaction to Christopher Hughes. The art master had already turned down "nearly all" the paintings Blunt and MacNeice had submitted for the Prize Day exhibition. Blunt had fired off a final scornful salvo entitled "De Cubismo," which appeared in *The Marlburian*. "Modern art," Blunt declared, should be judged by the same standards as Persian rugs," which, he said, were the "formal qualities of pattern and color." He attacked the "evil tradition" of "purely imitative" pictures and storytelling painting, singling out the art master's cherished Pre-Raphaelites as exemplifying a "peculiarly English failing." The French, Blunt claimed, had "revolutionized the art of all European countries, except England."[51]

Hughes had the last word. "Unless the critic grasps something of that feeling for nature," Hughes wrote in the next issue of the school magazine, "it is easy to understand how he missed the finer points of Art." This parting shot struck Blunt's exposed flank. For all his pedestrian aesthetic values, Hughes was a creative artist who had instinctively put his finger on Blunt's great failing: He had little artistic ability himself, and this lack of understanding of the creative impulse flawed his critical judgments.[52]

Did Blunt harbor a resentment against art and artists because of an inferiority complex? Blunt's lack of ability on the games field appears to have been a contributory factor in spurring his rebellion against the Marlborough athletes. Could the recognition of his lack of artistic ability have prompted him to take a similar revenge on art?

MacNeice's recollections reveal that he and Blunt had experimented with painting in the style of the artists they admired. Together they daubed watercolors of Matisse-like goldfish and painted Picasso-style still lifes. On one occasion an angry bathing master confronted Blunt when he set up his easel at the school swimming moat. Anthony managed to get permission to continue his canvas by assuring the master it was not the naked boys he wished to record for posterity but the corrugated-iron bathing shed.

Unfortunately, neither this nor any other Blunt picture survives. But research for this book turned up an example of his work. It suggests that Blunt's inability to draw may have prompted his passion for objects rather than people, and also his fanaticism for Cubist art. The only known genuine Blunt is preserved for posterity in a photograph of his Marlborough study. It is propped up against the wall over his desk. An enlargement reveals a still-life watercolor of a small urn atop a pyramid of books. The painting probably dates from September 1925, when a MacNeice letter mentions that Anthony had brought "a superb piece of lustre ware" from his summer trp to Belgium. But Blunt's effort clearly did not do justice to the urn. The painting's clumsy composition and lack of form confirms that the young critic was a poor artist whose dogmatic, intensely analytical approach to art ignored the emotional value of a painting. It also suggests why Blunt was so determined to set himself up as the arbiter of cultural values: to compensate for his own lack of talent.

On the eve of his departure for university life, Anthony Blunt was already a deadly combination in terms of his psychological profile. He was prepared to rebel and strike out against the society in which he lived. He was blessed with a superb intelligence that allowed him to spot the weak points in people and organizations. He had learned the secrets of sexual blackmail. He was capable of manipulating his peers and his teachers. And, as Robert Cecil has pointed out, he was cold-blooded enough, calculating enough, that he could achieve his goal of secret power over other people's lives. And since Blunt's "cute brain" ensured his success at an early age, the only questions were: How would he achieve his adult goals, and who would help him achieve them?

# CHAPTER 5

# *"Exporting the Revolution"*

Two years before Anthony Blunt went to Marlborough College and discovered his talents for manipulating people, momentous events were being played out on the world's stage that would have a dramatic impact on his adult life. In March 1919, Vladimir Ilyich Lenin, chairman of the people's commissars and virtual dictator of the emerging Soviet Union, summoned foreign sympathizers to the motherland of communism to discuss the future of the Revolution.

It would take another two years for the Bolsheviks to win the bloody civil war and secure total control of all Russia, but Lenin was planning with deadly precision. With Leon Trotsky standing at his side, Lenin gave his overseas battalions their marching orders: He announced the Third Communist International, or Comintern as it came to be known. Lenin thereby proclaimed that the Bolsheviks were the leaders of the world socialist movement, and the Comintern would be the agent by which the dreaded enemy known as capitalism would be destroyed. What Lenin and Trotsky intended was a global revolution that was to be coordinated and directed by Moscow.[1]

Trotsky drew up the plan of battle: It called for applying every means — legal and illegal — to undermine and abolish all other forms of government, including democracy. When it came to establishing the so-called dictatorship of the proletariat, the end justified the means. In a ringing recasting of Marx's famous phrase, Trotsky called on the workers of the world to unite in the name of the Comintern, telling them they had "nothing to lose but your chains."

A principal target for the Comintern was Great Britain. Over the years, the pattern of the onslaught can be seen as three successive waves of subversion, each one more dangerous than the last. Simply put, the first wave would call for spontaneous combustion, the explosion of hatred created by the British class system. The second wave would involve trade; by opening these lines of communication, Moscow hoped to infiltrate and suborn the labor movement. The third would be the most dangerous of all to the British government because Moscow had learned from its previous failures. It would take a new tack and spend years infiltrating the system from within to gain control of the British government's counterintelligence system. This was the sophisticated plan that activated Blunt and the Cambridge spies.

To understand the story of Blunt, one has to go back to the abdication of Tsar Nicholas II in March 1917, an event that was warmly welcomed by British radicals. The subsequent overthrow of Kerensky's socialist provisional government by the Bolshevik Revolution in November of that year cooled their ardor somewhat and the Parliamentary Labour party declared itself opposed to Lenin's dictatorship of the proletariat.

British socialists nevertheless protested the launching of military expeditions by Allied forces (British, American, and Japanese) to Archangel and Siberia in March 1918. The declared objectives of these operations were to protect Allied war matériel against capture by the Germans, with whom the Bolshevik government had just signed a peace treaty. Then the Labour party joined its voice to Moscow's furious protests at the invasions by capitalist powers in support of the White Russian armies who were fighting to overthrow the six-month-old Revolution. Britain was also suspected of complicity in the August assassination attempt on Lenin. (The shots that wounded the architect of the Bolshevik Revolution were actually fired by a disaffected Russian socialist named Dora Kaplan.) In a retaliatory move, Moscow arrested Robert Bruce Lockhart, a Foreign Office envoy, along with two of his officers. The British government responded in kind by detaining Maxim Litvinov and several other Russians who were serving as the Bolsheviks' unofficial emissaries in London. This practical demonstration of the realpolitik of Anglo-Soviet relations may have lacked the traditional niceties of diplomatic protocol, but it produced a speedy exchange of prisoners.

As a trusted member of the Bolshevik old guard, Litvinov had been living in exile in London since the 1905 abortive uprising against the tsar. He had fled after taking part in "expropriation raids" — a Soviet euphemism for robbing Russian banks of millions of rubles. Litvinov had married an English girl, Ivy Low, and had become an accomplished socializer and an astute exploiter of class conflict. His polished manners and many connections in British left-wing circles had earned him Lenin's respect and a key role in organizing the Soviets' subversion and intelligence apparatus in Britain.[2]

Litvinov's abrupt repatriation to Moscow — where he eventually became Stalin's commissar for foreign affairs in 1930 — obliged Lenin to make some significant changes in his scheme for exporting the Revolution to Britain. Litvinov's mission was taken over by Theodore Rothenstein, another resident Russian émigré with extensive contacts with the left wing. His mission was to unite the fractious and splintered British Marxist groups into a coherent revolutionary movement. It proved to be an uphill struggle and in the 1919 "Referendum on Socialist Unity," the British Marxists rejected the call to form a single Communist party.

Historically, the writings of Marx had made little impact on either the workers or the intellectuals of the capitalist nation. Dialectical materialism aroused little enthusiasm in British socialists who regarded themselves as heirs to the older radical tradition of the seventeenth-century Leveller sects and the nonconformist Christian Methodism of the eighteenth century. Violent revolution was also alien to the moderate views of the genteel socialists in the Fabian Society, which, since its foundation in 1884 by middle-class intellectuals, had been guided by economists Sidney and Beatrice Webb and critic and writer George Bernard Shaw.

British socialists believed in achieving social reform by "permeation" of existing political institutions. The Fabian moderates greatly outnumbered the hard-core Marxist organizations such as the Social Democratic Federation, founded in 1881 by the eccentric financier Henry Hyndman. Ramsay MacDonald, who became Britain's first socialist prime minister thirty years later, had abandoned the SDF in 1894, to join his fellow Scot Keir Hardie in the Independent Labour party. Six years later the Labour Representation Committee of the Trades Union Congress formally disavowed the extreme Marxism of the SDF in favor of moderate Fabianism. The querulous alliance between the trade-union movement and socialist intellectuals gave birth to Britain's parliamentary Labour party, which won twenty-nine seats in the 1906 general election.[3]

The Marxist hardliners refused to give up. Among the workers, a Plebs League took root with the coal miners in South Wales. The Socialist party, an offshoot of the SDF, drew its strength from the workers in the Scottish shipyards along the River Clyde, while Guild Socialism, as it was called, emerged as a force among the left-wing intellectuals in the Fabian movement on the eve of World War I. The war was seen by true Marxist believers as ushering in the final crisis of capitalism as predicted by the Second International which had resolved in 1889 "to accelerate the fall of the bourgeoisies." But the Labour party, which had rashly affiliated itself with the International in 1908, broke its pledge to oppose "an imperialist war." It declared in support of the British government, as did the Trades Union Congress, which called for an "industrial truce."[4]

The socialist leaders on Clydeside defied the truce and fomented a series of strikes. By 1917, the government was obliged to intervene to halt the spread of industrial anarchy that threatened to disrupt the war effort. The enormous expansion in Britain's counterintelligence organizations during World War I enabled the government to move surely against the homegrown Marxist revolutionaries to contain the

Communist menace. By 1918 this activity overshadowed their original mission to round up German sympathizers and spies.

The Secret Service Bureau, formed in 1909, was divided into two departments: one responsible for domestic counterintelligence and the other for overseas operations. In 1916, as a direct reflection of their particular wartime responsibilities to the Military Intelligence department in the War Office, they were renamed MI5 and MI6 (pronounced M-eye-five and M-eye-six). They were headed by two powerful personalities who possessed a uniquely British talent for combining eccentricity with ruthlessness: Captain Vernon Kell and Commander Mansfield Smith-Cumming.

Kell, a mustachioed army officer and veteran of the Boxer Rebellion in China, was every bit as talented a bureaucratic empire builder as Cumming, a naval officer with a passion for fast cars. Cumming was known simply as "C," a title inherited by succeeding directors of MI6. His spies — who included the much romanticized Sidney Reilly — attracted considerable fictionalized attention as spy literature became a fashionable genre. But it fell to the less glamorous MI5 to maintain the mundane filing cards in the Central Registry. These, as we shall see, made by far the greater contribution to the empire's security. By 1917, Kell's department had grown from 19 people to 844, and its register of suspicious characters had increased to a quarter of a million cards. These were constantly updated by 130 trusted female clerks.[5]

By the end of the war, the Central Registry had become the heart of MI5's operations; its alphabetized "Special Intelligence Black List" index was coded by nationality, credentials, and a suspect's subversive activities. The data on these cards were collected from the chief constables of the British police services, and the Special Branch — the elite undercover force of London's Metropolitan Police, founded in 1887 to counter Irish Fenian terrorism — carried out investigations and arrests on behalf of MI5. Dominion and Indian police, informants, port disembarkation records, and government censors — who monitored all telegraphic and postal communications — also contributed their reports to MI5; additional intelligence was obtained from wartime allies. Almost from the beginning, the "Precautionary Index," as the "Black List" was euphemistically renamed once the war was over, was shared with MI6, the police, the Foreign Office, and — as newly uncovered British MI5 documentation shows — with the United States.[6]

The rapid expansion of MI5's Registry was eyed enviously by Sir Basil Thomson, assistant commissioner of the Metropolitan Police and head of Scotland Yard's Criminal Investigation Division. The Bolshevik takeover of Russia's provisional socialist government convinced Thomson that undercover Marxist revolutionaries would soon replace German spies as the new enemy. He regarded Bolshevism as a "sort of infectious disease, spreading rapidly but insidiously, until like a cancer it eats away the fabric of society and the patient ceases to wish for his own recovery."[7]

Thomson cast himself in the role of the surgeon summoned by destiny to rid Britain of the Communist cancer. In 1919, the specter of a "Triple Industrial Alliance" among miners, railwaymen, and transport workers was threatening a general strike that could paralyze the country. As head of the Home Office's newly formed Directorate of Intelligence, Thomson had authority rivaling that of MI5, which had suffered a peacetime staff cut and loss of the Passport Control Service to the Foreign Office. But the assistant commissioner of the Metropolitan Police still had to rely on Kell's MI5 Registry for the intelligence on which he based his weekly report for the Cabinet. Thomson always led off his report, appropriately titled "Revolutionary Organizations in the United Kingdom," with the latest summaries of the rising unemployment figures. These, he was fond of pointing out, represented "the best recruiting agent for revolutionaries."[8]

Stamped SECRET, the early copies of these reports in the declassified British Cabinet records, as supplemented by the later reports in the U.S. State Department files, reveal the extent and depth of the surveillance operation run by MI5, Special Branch, and the local police forces in Britain during the twenties and thirties. From Communist activities on "Red Clydeside," to the Irish Sinn Feiners, to information on Moscow's devious efforts to fund the financially strapped socialist *Daily Herald* newspaper, and the plans for a Youth International to infiltrate schools and universities, Thomson's weekly reports suggest that Scotland Yard was anything but complacent when it came to monitoring Comintern subversion in Britain.

"There is no worse way of meeting danger than to enter the fight trembling in one's shoes," Thomson advised the home secretary in his February 1920 report on "Revolutionaries and the Need for Legislation." This memorandum, despite its alarmist "Red Menace" tone, was an accurate summary of Comintern strategy for exporting the Bolshevik Revolution "not by force of arms, but by the far cheaper and more effective method of underground propaganda." It was based on MI5 evidence that Soviet agents were "training emissaries for India." They were "in correspondence with the Sinn Feiners in Ireland." Furthermore, a secret report received from the Hungarian commander in chief in Budapest revealed that Lenin had ordered 50 million rubles deposited in Berlin banks in November 1919 to fund Comintern subversion overseas. As a result, Thomson called for tough new antirevolutionary legislation, modeled on that already introduced in the United States and Canada, to make it a criminal offense to advocate the overthrow of the government by force, and to accept financial support or propaganda from the Soviets.[9]

Prime Minister Lloyd George's coalition government of Liberals and Conservatives balked at introducing these measures. Thomson was fettered by having to work within the existing sedition and conspiracy laws to monitor the Comintern operations against Britain. In contrast to Commander Cumming and Admiral Sir Hugh Sinclair, who succeeded him as "C" in 1923, neither MI5 nor Special Branch underestimated the skill and ruthlessness of the opposition they faced.

Feliks Edmundovich Dzerzhinski, C's principal adversary in Moscow, was a spymaster of very different mettle from "Quex" Sinclair, who continued the tradition of recruiting Britain's spies from the upper-class members of London gentlemen's clubs. Handpicked by Lenin in December 1917 to head the All-Russian Extraordinary Commission to Combat Counterrevolution and Sabotage (Vserossiyskaya Chrezvychaynaya Komissiya or VChK), better known as the feared Cheka secret police, Dzerzhinski was a veteran Bolshevik. His goatee and beady blue eyes gave him a gnomelike appearance There was nothing benign, however, about the Polish revolutionary who had already spent over eleven of his forty years in the tsar's jails or Siberian exile.

An instinctive master at predicting human behavior, Dzerzhinski was an awesome interrogator. According to one of his victims, his "eyes made you feel that he could see into your very soul." He proudly bore on his wrists the scars of handcuffs as evidence of the apprenticeship that uniquely qualified him to carry out Lenin's orders "to Combat Counterrevolution, Speculation and Sabotage" with a ruthless secret-police system whose mission was both offensive and defensive: the "Sword and Shield" of the Revolution.[10]

The Cheka became the weapon by which Lenin and his Bolshevik minority swiftly imposed their authority on the Russian civilian populace and the Red Army. At the same time the Cheka branched out into overseas espionage to counter the threat posed to the Revolution by White Russian émigrés. The organization that Dzerzhinski built discharged its functions so thoroughly that it grew in numbers and authority. Soon it was an indispensable part of the Soviet *apparat* that, after a succession of name changes, became the State Security Committee (Komitet Gosudarstvennoy Bezopasnosti), the all-pervasive KGB.[11]

Dzerzhinski's first major foreign success was the infiltration of the White Russian émigré networks by means of a brilliantly executed deception known as "The Trust." The British security services, which secretly supported the anti-Bolshevik émigrés, never appreciated how Soviet penetration had undermined the 1918 "Envoys Plot" and later exploits of Sidney Reilly on behalf of MI6.[12]

During the final year of World War I, the British and Americans entered into a secret treaty for sharing counterintelligence information. The treaty is still in force, although this particular "special relationship" has never been officially acknowledged on either side of the Atlantic. While the British Empire was Moscow's principal target in the interwar years, English-speaking Soviet agents were often switched between the two countries and subversion on both sides of the Atlantic was, as we shall see, linked and coordinated by the same directorate in the Comintern's Moscow bureau.

The secret MI5 and Special Branch reports in the National Archives in Washington reveal how wartime exchanges on German spies quickly gave way to peacetime swapping of information about Bolshevik revolutionaries and subversion. The United States was better equipped to meet the Communist subversion when J. Edgar Hoover became director in 1924 of what became the FBI and assistance was provided by British reports passed via the U.S. embassy in London. They were circulated by the State Department to the Justice Department and thence to military and naval intelligence organizations which, when the situation required, called on the services of the local police forces to arrest spies and subversives.

Commencing in February 1920, the Special Branch reports listing "prominent revolutionaries in the United Kingdom," along with digests of Thomson's weekly reports on subversive activities, were hand-carried to the first secretary of the U.S. embassy in London by senior Special Branch officers. The State Department's initial lack of security and facilities for handling such sensitive information very nearly ended this unique secret collaboration only a month after it began. In March, information from one of Thomson's reports appeared in *The New York Times*, which printed details of Britain's secret emergency plans to meet a Communist-inspired national strike. Investigation by the Justice Department confirmed the leak had occurred despite a Strictly Confidential classification. It was only after Washington tightened up security in May that Thomson proposed setting up with the Americans "a Clearing House in London for all undesirable Bolsheviks."[13]

While the Clearing House operation was never made official, it is obvious that it went into effect because of the volumes of documentation under 800 B "Bolshevik" in the State Department records in Washington. These reveal that American requests for data from the Central Registry were being met on a regular basis. In turn, the Americans supplied information for the MI5 files on the Comintern. As mutual confidence and trust developed between MI5 officers and their contacts in the U.S. embassy, cooperation extended way beyond exchanging visa applications from known and suspect Communists. The details of Comintern personnel, organization, and operations that appear in the U.S. records are documentary testimony — where none is available in Britain — of the remarkable early success of MI5 in intercepting Moscow's secret communications and penetrating the evolving Communist organizations.

A sobering realization confronts any researcher delving into the indigo leather-bound confidential London Embassy files. They contain actual MI5 and Special Branch reports that represent only the tip of the iceberg of data that remains locked away by the British Official Secrets Act. How this intelligence (still top secret in Britain) was used remains a mystery. But from the scope and detail of the files that were passed to the Americans, it is difficult to see how MI5's expertise and early success could have been squandered in such appalling later failures.

The British security services were, as the new documentary evidence shows, more than a match for the primitive Soviet efforts to subvert Britain from within and without. After Litvinov's abrupt repatriation in 1918, it is clear that both Kell of MI5 and Thomson of Special Branch quickly discovered that his mission and his authority had passed to Theodore Rothenstein, on whom they had already an extensive dossier.

A long-standing member of the British Socialist party, Rothenstein had funneled Soviet funds to and sought to impose Moscow's direction upon the British revolutionary organizations. The breakthrough came in June 1919 with the arrest of Jacob Novosivitsky, an American Bolshevik, at Liverpool. After interrogation he was "turned" into a double agent and his confession to working for Rothenstein as a trusted courier enabled Special Branch to monitor Comintern orders to and contacts with Ludwig C. A. K. Martens, the self-proclaimed Soviet representative in New York. The secret Anglo-American exchanges led to Martens's deportation from the United States in January 1921, along with forty members of his staff, for advocating the overthrow of Congress.

The Special Branch report on Rothenstein provides a detailed picture of how he ran the Soviet underground network in Britain from his mother's house in Highgate. His summer home was a converted railway Pullman car near Lake Windermere, situated conveniently near the shipyards, mines, and factory areas of the industrial north of England. His son Andrew, who, according to the secret report, "assists him," was a Brackenbury Scholar at Balliol College, Oxford. Andrew Rothenstein was later to become the first English-born member of the Soviets' London-based Communist cell while managing Moscow's news agency in Fleet Street.[14]

Theodore Rothenstein, MI5 established by 1921, communicated with Moscow mainly by courier. The British had learned — through infiltrators and by censoring his mail — that he used a secret password with trusted contacts in the British Socialist party. He also employed a code for his secret cables to the Comintern, of which, Thomson reassured the Cabinet, "the Authorities possess a copy." MI5 monitored how the Comintern's principal agent in Britain received the substantial funding to pay subsidiary agents, contribute to the former suffragette leader Sylvia Pankhurst's organization, and even dole out funds to Italian Bolsheviks.[15]

"Among the remittances received by Rothenstein from Russia," the Special Branch report noted, "was a packet of diamonds." These were not industrial diamonds, but gems looted from tsarist nobles. Mrs. Rothenstein, according to the British report, enjoyed adorning herself and her daughter with diamond necklaces, earclips, and brooches. The most surprising revelation was that Rothenstein had worked until 1919 for MI7, a branch of Britain's military intelligence. This made him one of the first Soviet moles because he had used his position of trust to feed reports from Russian newspapers to George Lansbury, editor of the *Daily Herald*, and to supply Sylvia Pankhurst with information for her People's Russian Information Bureau.[16]

Rothenstein's "contempt for Sylvia Pankhurst's intelligence and discretion" was also revealed to MI5. In January 1920 Pankhurst appealed directly to Lenin to recognize her Workers Socialist Federation as the "Communist Party (British Section of the Third International)" after attending a secret convocation in Holland of European Comintern leaders. Unfortunately, the militant suffragette's opposition to Communists' standing as parliamentary candidates conflicted with Lenin's ruling that "Soviet propaganda can and ought to be carried on from within the bourgeois parliaments."[17]

Without a united British Communist party to take the lead, the threat of imminent revolution was remote. The British revolutionary groups indulged in "too much theatrical cloak and dagger" for Thomson to believe that their secret meetings constituted "a real menace." But Thomson did not hesitate to caution the Cabinet against under-estimating Lenin's capacity for "composing quarrels" and "dictating policy." Thomson's real concern was with the next wave of Comintern activity. This he believed would automatically follow the diplomatic recognition of the Bolshevik regime by the Liberals because Lloyd George had a naïve belief that opening commercial activity with the Soviet Union was the best way to blunt Moscow's subversion.[18]

"The moment trade was established Communism would go," declared Prime Minister Lloyd George with a myopic miscalculation that belied his reputation as a *realpolitiker*. An invitation was issued to the Soviets to send a delegation to London in the spring of 1920 to begin talks about a trade treaty.[19]

The fear of MI5 and Special Branch that the Soviets would exploit this diplomatic overture proved justified that May when the British trades unions rallied to the "Hands Off Russia" campaign instigated by London dockworkers. They refused to load ships with munitions destined for the Polish army in the final phase of the Russian civil war.

When the official trade delegation from Moscow arrived in London, Winston Churchill, the secretary of state for war and air in Lloyd George's coalition government, absented himself from the formal reception for the Soviets rather than "shake the hands with a hairy baboon." But Leonid Krassin, the tall and elegantly spoken Soviet commissar for foreign trade, was the exact opposite of a primatelike Bolshevik revolutionary. As head of the delegation he promised that members of his staff would not "interfere in any way in the politics or internal affairs of the country."[20]

It gave Thomson, however, a certain grim satisfaction to report that Krassin's assistant, N. K. Klisko, had wasted no time in contacting "Communist elements" immediately after the delegation's arrival. When Rothenstein "attached himself" to the delegation despite written Soviet assurances not to interfere in Britain's domestic politics, MI5 was confirmed in its belief that such promises were not worth the paper they were written on. Thomson's predictions about Lenin's determination to impose his authority on the fractious British Communists was also borne out. After their leaders attended the Second Congress of the Third International in Petrograd and Moscow that June, Mrs. Rothenstein was observed to be wearing fewer diamonds. The congress, chaired by Grigori Zinoviev, adopted Lenin's "twenty-one points," a plan to bring about the overthrow of capitalism by splitting the European socialist parties into warring factions and then bringing the radical elements under Soviet control.

The British delegates to the Second Congress continued to feud among themselves until Rothenstein arrived in Moscow to exert his authority on the dozen delegates who finally agreed to unite into the Communist party of Great Britain (CPGB). At a conference in London at the end of August, some 154 delegates of the CPGB adopted the Soviet leadership, the dictatorship of the proletariat, and adherence to the Comintern's revolutionary objectives. Communications intercepted by MI5 revealed that Rothenstein was secretly designated CPGB "chairman appointed by Moscow Executive." He was promptly barred from reentering Britain after Thomson dryly acknowledged he should be credited "for such unity as was achieved" because "he supplied the funds."[21]

That money played midwife to the birth of the CPGB, an irony additionally compounded because, contrary to Marx's prediction that the workers would be led by the intellectuals, only three of the intelligentsia played any significant part in the formation of Britain's Communist party. They were Sylvia Pankhurst, Colonel Cecil L'Estrange Malone, and William Mellor, a former Oxford divinity student who openly derided the notion that the only good Communist was one "whose arse stuck out of his pants." Malone, a former wartime aviator and sitting Liberal M.P., switched his affiliation to become the only sitting Communist member of Parliament. But the failure of the British party to attract intellectual supporters ensured that it was a worker-led organization, a factor that played its part in leading the Soviets to attempt an alternative penetration of Britain's ruling elite.

So while the CPGB played an important part in the first wave of the Soviet assault on Britain, it was doomed to a minority appeal after the four million strong Labour party — the largest socialist body in Europe — rejected affiliation with the "intellectual slaves of Moscow." Party membership in Britain remained at the bottom of the Comintern league, reaching a peak of ten thousand only during the 1926 general strike. It is also now clear that the CPGB was undermined from within by MI5 informants who relayed the details of Zinoviev's plan for infiltrating the armed forces and the trade unions with Communist cells "to fan the already existing flames of discontent, to foment revolt, and finally to bring about revolutionary action."[22]

It was a scheme that, had it not been "mere verbiage," Thomson warned, "would have plunged the country into revolution within a month." MI5 and Special Branch therefore concentrated their efforts on monitoring the "incessant intrigues of the Russian Trade Delegation," whose members communicated "daily" with the Councils of Action of the CPGB. The distinctive cut of Russian diamonds smuggled into Britain in Soviet diplomatic bags helped derail the delegation's efforts to fund their subversive plans. Scotland Yard arranged for one dealer to purchase a packet of these Soviet gems with £75,000 of marked banknotes. These were then traced to Francis Meynell, a director of the *Daily Herald*, who later boasted how he had smuggled diamonds in chocolates and jars of cold cream.

Britain's only socialist daily had self-righteously proclaimed that it received "not a bond, not a sou, not a rouble" of foreign subsidy. But Scotland Yard's irrefutable evidence of the paper's financing by the Russian Trade Delegation cost Meynell the editorship in 1921. At the same time, it confirmed the Intelligence Directorate's warnings that the enemy had been let in by the gate.[23]

Comintern agents were multiplying in Britain, but MI5 and Special Branch possessed the secret weapon needed to contain and counter Communist subversion. Since 1917 British code breakers had been able to read the Soviet cipher traffic. The Bolsheviks' disdain for all things tsarist had prompted them to reject the sophisticated codes of the imperial government, replacing them with a simple transposition system in plain Russian. With the assistance of F. C. Fetterlein, one of the leading cryptanalysts of the ousted regime, and his team of émigré women translators, British intelligence was kept abreast of the Kremlin's most secret exchanges as its envoys fanned out to export the Revolution.

"We were able to attack their systems step by step with success from the days of Litvinov's first visit to Copenhagen, of Kamenev as their first representative in London, followed by Krassin, until the famous Arcos raid in 1927." This authoritative insight comes from the private papers of Commander Alexander Denniston, the head of Britain's top-secret Government Code and Cipher School" (GC&CS) which operated in a ten-story Westminster office block known as the Broadway Buildings. A wiry Scot with a quizzical expression, Denniston had been a member of the Royal Navy's famous World War I code-breaking team in Room 40 of the Admiralty.[24]

Led by the legendary code breaker Captain (later Rear Admiral) William Reginald "Blinker" Hall, the GC&CS staff had broken the German foreign minister's cable to the German ambassadors in Washington and Mexico City that signaled Berlin's imminent intention to begin unrestricted U-boat warfare. After the contents of the notorious "Zimmermann" telegram was leaked to the press, public opinion in America hardened in favor of entering the war against Germany in 1917. This demonstration of the value of "signal intelligence" in twentieth-century diplomacy convinced the British government of the necessity for continuing and expanding its eavesdropping operations after the war. Accordingly GC&CS was set up under Foreign Office control.[25]

The discovery in the archives of Churchill College, Cambridge, of Denniston's detailed and uncensored history of the GC&CS code-breaking establishment blows a large hole in the British government's refusal to acknowledge the extent of its peacetime code-breaking effort. Denniston headed the secret organization for over two decades. Its most spectacular triumph was the breaking of the German Enigma machine codes in World War II, to provide the Allies their so-called Ultra secret. Denniston's paper, moreover, reveals that while he was put in charge of GC&CS to "advise on the security of codes and ciphers," its real objective was "to study the methods of cipher communications by foreign powers." In his 1944 memoir, Denniston concedes Britain made a priority of eavesdropping on its allies: French ciphers were read with ease, and "good progress" had been made in penetrating the American diplomatic ciphers.[26]

Denniston reported that the "only real operational intelligence" GC&CS provided in the twenties came from the Soviet traffic. It was his code-breakers who kept the British government abreast of the Russian Trade Delegation's clandestine mission of subversion and spying during Britain's lengthy negotiations with Krassin in 1920–21. The intercepted telegrams reveal how the Soviets began the talks with a typically hard line. "That swine Lloyd George has no scruples of shame in the way he deceives," Lenin warned Krassin. "Don't believe a word he says and gull him three times as much."[27]

The British government, with the advantage of knowing its opponent's hand, held firm with their demands for Moscow to repay the Russian loans repudiated by the Bolsheviks and for an end to subversive activities against the British Empire. The ability to monitor the instructions sent to Krassin after he returned in July with Lev Kamenev (chairman of the Moscow Soviet and the new head of the delegation) kept MI5 and Special Branch aware of the developing threat. They warned the prime minister of the trade delegation's central role in the "plot to create red revolution and ruin in this country."[28]

Lloyd George decided, nevertheless, that despite the "flagrant breach of the conditions" by the trade delegation, there was an "undoubted advantage" in "our being able to tap these messages as it gives us real insight into Bolshevist interests and policy." He wanted to keep the Soviet trade deal alive because he hoped it would stimulate the faltering British postwar economy and bring votes for his ailing Liberal party.[29]

The prime minister adopted a stick and carrot approach. He confronted the Russian delegation on September 10, 1920, and accused Kamenev, who was due to depart for Moscow next day, of a "gross breach of faith." He made it clear that the head of the Moscow Soviet would not be readmitted to Britain. But his deputy Krassin would be permitted to remain, provided he adhered strictly to the agreement not to engage in subversion. The government then began a crackdown after an October miners' strike persuaded the Cabinet to pass an Emergency Powers Act authorizing MI5 to step up action against civilian Communist subversives.[30]

Scotland Yard, acting on information received from MI5, arrested Sylvia Pankhurst. She was sentenced to six months' imprisonment for publishing seditious articles. Cecil Malone, the Communist M.P., was also taken into custody and charged with "incitement to revolution" after telling a meeting held at the Albert Hall to mark the third anniversary of the Bolshevik Revolution: "What are a few Churchills or Curzons on lampposts compared to the massacre of thousands of human beings?" Special Branch suspected Malone's contact, Erik Veltheim, was a Comintern courier. A search of his lodgings turned up coded messages for Moscow and a manual — "The Red Officers' Course" — for training recruits to an underground Communist army. The police found more copies in the London Underground's left-luggage offices. Claim checks led them back to Malone. On this evidence the Communist M.P. and his courier were jailed for six months.[31]

The British government's public crackdown against Communist subversion was not lost on Lenin. His regime was struggling to stave off a collapse of the Soviet economy. Trade was seen as a vital road to economic rejuvenation after the debilitating period of "war communism," so talks with the British resumed in November. By January 1921 Leonid Krassin took a draft agreement back to Moscow. With Lenin's New Economic Policy putting a high priority on exporting products for badly needed foreign capital, the Soviets "capitulated" to the British terms, and the Anglo-American Trade Agreement was signed on March 16, 1921. Three months later the Russians, despite their devastated economy, invested a third of a million pounds in one of the City of London's most expensive office buildings at 49 Moorgate.

Renamed Soviet House, it served as Russia's London headquarters for three years until Moscow was granted the right to maintain an embassy in Britain. Meanwhile, its trade delegation enjoyed limited diplomatic immunity, which the Comintern turned to its advantage by launching into a new course of subversion, propagandizing the British trade unions to affiliate with the Profintern, the so-called Red International of Labor Unions.

Ironically, shortly after the Foreign Office opened a file headed "Violations of the Russian Trade Agreements," the activist Sir Basil Thomson was sacked and his Intelligence Directorate disbanded. This came after Lloyd George's shaky coalition government was faced with charges by the Labour party that Special Branch had become a "system of domestic espionage" aimed at the working class. General Kell welcomed the demise of the powerful assistant commissioner of the Metropolitan Police because it removed a rival whose authority had been forcing MI5 into a subsidiary role.

If the Intelligence Directorate had survived, it could have provided Britain's security services with the coordination necessary to deal with the increasing sophistication of the second Soviet assault. The new beachhead was the All Russian Co-Operative Society — better known as Arcos Limited — a £1 million limited liability company formed in London. With an Anglo-Soviet board of directors and a staff that grew in five years to more than two hundred Russians, Arcos was ostensibly engaged in conducting commercial operations. But behind the commercial front, Arcos was a cover for the operations of the Soviet intelligence service and representatives of the control commission who supervised the CPGB.

The majority of Arcos managers were handpicked officers of Soviet Military Intelligence — the GRU (Glavnoye Razvedyvatelnoye Upravleniye). Their mission was to be industrial espionage agents, and their role was indicative of the importance that Lenin gave to rehabilitating and modernizing the Soviet economy. Obsolete Russian factories needed technology and know-how that could only be bought at inflated prices for hard currency from greedy capitalist businessmen. The trade delegation quickly became the cover for the systematic GRU-masterminded theft of Western technology with only a minimum investment in legal trade. This developed into an industrial-espionage operation on a global scale. It was managed under the auspices of the Commissariat for Foreign Trade, Narkomvneshtorg, the NKVT, whose Torgpredstva or trading delegations, nominally offshoots of Arcos in Britain, sprang up in every European capital by the end of 1921.[32]

The Soviets had to wait three years before the United States — Russia's biggest potential market — permitted any direct trading because Congress had passed a law prohibiting any trade with the Soviets after they had repudiated their war debts. But Ludwig Martens — with the help of sympathetic American bankers, businessmen, Marxists, and smuggled diamonds — functioned as the "unofficial" Soviet ambassador and trade representative in New York until his deportation in 1921.

One of the Martens's closest associates was a doctor of medicine, a Jewish émigré from Odessa named Julius Hammer. According to State Department records, Hammer was a generous contributor to the U.S. Socialist party and "believed to be at present part of the Bolshevik regime." That explained why he was "one of the first to establish one of the 'fronts,' corporations and purchasing agencies" that were in reality controlled by "Soviet Jewish elements under the direction of the Soviet Government of Russia." Hammer, with Abraham Heller — "a notorious Bolshevik" and associate of Martens — was the founding partner in the Allied Drug and Chemical Company. A State Department investigation revealed that this company, incorporated in 1917 with Martens holding half the stock, was "utilized by the Soviet Government in starting trade with the United States."[33]

Dr. Armand Hammer, the youngest son of Julius, and a graduate of Columbia University Medical School, began his business career as company secretary for Allied Drug. The international philanthropist and octogenarian head of the Occidental Petroleum conglomerate has actively championed trade with the Soviet Union throughout his long and remarkably successful career. Armand Hammer has counted among his personal acquaintances every Soviet leader. He met Lenin in Moscow in 1921. This was after his father's business career had been curtailed by his father's arrest and conviction for manslaughter after the death of a woman for whom he had performed an illegal abortion. Lenin was evidently impressed that Julius Hammer's letter introducing his son Armand was written from Sing Sing prison. The Soviet revolutionary leader seems to have felt that the capitalist system had harshly punished the good doctor not for medical malpractice but for his socialist convictions. As a gesture of goodwill to Julius for his commitment, Lenin awarded his son one of the first foreign concessions and put private railroad cars at Armand's disposal. Feliks Dzerzhinski, the head of the Cheka, was appointed to head the commission administering the concessions. This suggests that industrial contracts were not regarded by the Soviets as mere business transactions, but as an integral part of the subversive strategy.[34]

It appears significant, moreover, that Armand Hammer's trip to Russia, which included a stopover in London, also aroused the interest of MI5. On July 8, 1921, the U.S. embassy in London was alerted that his father, Dr. Julius Hammer, was "noted on our files as having been a close associate of Trotsky and later of Martens." There is, however, no concrete evidence that the youngest Hammer son shared his father's commitment to the Bolshevik cause.

The Hammers' concession to mine asbestos in the Urals was signed by Maxim Litvinov, the Soviet trade commissar. The original contract was made with Allied Drug and Chemical, but this corporation had "disappeared as an active institution." On Armand's return to the United States in December 1921, his brother Harry J. Hammer and three business associates had formed the Ural-American Refining and Trading Company, which changed its name to the impressive-sounding Allied American Corporation in 1922. Nor does it appear insignificant that Allied American became the first Soviet-American trading agency or that one of its subsidiaries, Allied American Fur Sales Company, maintained what State Department officials called its "real" bank account at the Midland Bank in London, "where it receives the supervision of certain individuals connected with the Russian government."[35]

The "individuals" in question were officials of Soviet House. Documents discovered by Special Branch in the possession of an Arcos employee named Anton Miller linked payments of $5,000 made by Harry Hammer in 1925 to Joseph Moness and Julius Heiman. The pair were Comintern agents known to be involved in channeling funds to the American Communist party. But the demands of espionage and subversion in the United States outstripped the resources of a single trading corporation. In 1921 orders came from Moscow to expand the American operation. Allied American was then obediently merged with two smaller Soviet-controlled trading fronts: Products Exchange Corporation (Prodexco) and the All-Russian Textile Corporation (Derutra).[36]

The amalgamation gave birth to Amtorg — American Trading Organization — with its "home offices" at 14 Kuznetsky Most, Moscow. The attorney who engineered the deal, Charles Recht, had acted as legal adviser to Ludwig Martens. He contrived to set up Amtorg as a "licensee" of Russian goods with a charter of incorporation that artfully circumvented the congressional ban on direct trade with the Soviet Union. But once in operation, Amtorg sponsored an influx of Soviet managers and "inspectors" to conduct its licensing operations. As with Arcos, its key personnel were GRU officers trained in espionage, who worked alongside officials of the GPU and control commission posing as commercial agents. Amtorg's secret mission was to fund a network of Communist groups using the cover of legitimate business. Its officials practiced some highly creative accounting, drawing its funds from Arcos in London and then shunting the transfers around its numerous accounts in Canada and the United States. In this way Amtorg disguised the huge sums it fed to the Soviets' North American espionage and subversion network.[37]

The establishment of Amtorg in 1924 coincided with the controversial decision by Britain's first Labour government to grant full diplomatic recognition to the Soviet Union.

This Red Letter year for the Communist Revolution opened with Lenin's death in January and a struggle for power among Joseph Stalin, Leon Trotsky, and Grigori Zinoviev. The triumvirate that Lenin designated as his titular successor and guardian of the Revolution was quickly dominated by Stalin, who gained the upper hand by allying himself with the chief of the secret police.

Feliks Dzerzhinski had consolidated the real behind-the-scenes power in the Kremlin two years earlier, when Lenin authorized the transformation of the Cheka into the State Political Administration, the GPU (Gosudarstvennoye Politicheskoye Upravleniye). Through his able lieutenant, Mikhail Abramovich Trilisser, who became the chief of the GPU Foreign Department, Dzerzhinski gained the power to veto Comintern activities when they affected security, and to coopt the services of foreign Communist parties for intelligence gathering.

Stalin, who believed in "building socialism in one country," was a pragmatist. Evidently he did not share the messianic belief of Trotsky or Zinoviev in the immediacy of the global Communist revolution. The Comintern's disastrous failure to precipitate a workers' uprising in Germany in 1923 cost Zinoviev a further loss of authority. His prestige was already on the line when the British, citing wholesale violations, threatened to cancel the trade agreement. The rapidity with which the Kremlin agreed to renew promises "not to support with funds" or "spread discontent or to foment rebellion in any part of the British Empire" indicated the value, both covert and commercial, that the Soviets put on the trade agreement.[38]

Yet neither Lenin nor his successors had any intention of sticking to their agreements. They believed that to achieve the goals of communism, the end justified any expedient, especially when it came to taking advantage of the fact that Britain's first Labour administration was all for granting Moscow full diplomatic recognition.

This was one of the first acts of Ramsay MacDonald's shortlived government. After some initial concern about his trustworthiness, Britain's security-service chiefs concluded that MacDonald was "loyal and straightforward" — but not enough, it seems, to have access to his own Special Branch file! After a wave of strikes, MI5 chief Kell set up a Committee on Industrial Unrest to ascertain "whether any appreciable percentage of the unfortunate aspects of these strikes was due to Communist activity."[39]

MI5 was able to inform the Cabinet it had "irrefutable evidence" that the Communist party received weekly financial payments from the Russian Trade Delegation. The CPGB had been brought firmly under Comintern direction in 1922 when it adopted a report on organization, prepared by two members of its executive: Harry Pollitt and Rajani Palme Dutt. Pollitt, a Lancashire boilermaker of rare oratorical skill, and Dutt, an austere Anglo-Indian theoretician who had graduated from Balliol College, Oxford, formed a partnership that led the party on an unswerving course dictated by Moscow for more than two decades.

The Labour government's apprehension about taking firm action against Communist subversion for fear of prejudicing the signing of commercial treaties with the newly established Soviet embassy helped bring down MacDonald's government. MONEY FOR MURDERS was the outcry of the Tory press that greeted Moscow's agreement to acknowledge prerevolutionary debts in return for loans guaranteed by the British government. But the prime minister's decision not to release John Campbell, a Communist journalist arrested under the Incitement to Mutiny Act for writing seditious articles aimed at the military, cost the Labour party its Liberal support in Parliament. After losing a vote of confidence on October 8, 1924, MacDonald's minority government resigned.

The Red Menace issue dominated the general election, whose outcome was never in any doubt after the *Daily Mail* of October 25 printed a letter leaked from MI5 purporting to have been sent by Comintern chief Zinoviev on September 15. It ordered the British Communist party to "strain every nerve" to ensure that the government accept the Anglo-Soviet trade treaties. The instructions to the CPGB to step up "agitation-propaganda work in the armed forces" made it appear that Moscow was preparing to unleash the Red Revolution in Britain.[40]

Genuine or not, the Zinoviev letter gave Stanley Baldwin's conservatives a landslide victory. Ironically, Trotsky and Zinoviev welcomed the downfall of Britain's first socialist government. To them it was an article of faith that true socialism could be achieved only by bullets, not by ballots. But the affair brought more discredit to the Comintern, as Stalin and his ally Dzerzhinski called for concentrating the GPU's efforts on internal control rather than dissipating resources on fomenting world revolution. The split in the Soviet leadership widened the following year, allowing Stalin to engineer Trotsky's dismissal as war commissar. This enabled Dzerzhinski to extend the authority of the GPU over the foreign operations of the Comintern.

Baldwin's second administration also consolidated the authority of Britain's counterintelligence services by halting general circulation of Soviet intercepts and Special Branch reports to the Cabinet. But despite continuing evidence of subversive activities from Soviet House in Moorgate and the new Soviet embassy in Belgravia, the prime minister accepted the Foreign Office view that continuing peaceful relations with Moscow were preferable to "a definitely outlawed Russia" that would increase its efforts at secret subversion.[41]

It was not simply a matter of clandestine subversion. "The Bolshevisation of the British Trade Union Movement has begun," announced *The Times* of London in April 1925 after the Profintern announced a Joint Anglo-Soviet Advisory Committee. The hardline anti-Bolshevik home secretary, Sir William Joynson-Hicks and Sir Wyndham Childs, who had succeeded Thompson as chief of Special Branch, believed it was only a matter of time before the Soviets would have to be sent packing. Rising unemployment and industrial unrest were the background to intercepted Comintern communications to the CPGB and the Profintern-sponsored National Minority Movement. These claimed ten thousand trade-union members should be "prepared to fight" in a civil war for "the seizure of power by the working class." Communist agitators were told to educate Britain's sailors and soldiers to "turn their guns on the masters as the workers of Russia had done."[42]

In response to the growing economic crisis Prime Minister Baldwin declared: "All the workers of this country have got to take a reduction in wages." The trade-union movement rallied behind the militant miners, who refused to accept the savage wage cuts threatened by the private colliery owners in order to make their coal prices competitive on the international market. The Cabinet postponed the inevitable confrontation by offering the miners a nine-month pay subsidy until the Royal Commission reported on the crisis the following May. The Conservative press accused Baldwin of a sellout.

To demonstrate the government's resolve, the prime minister called on the home secretary to make preparations for combating subversion and beating a general strike. Sir William Joynson-Hicks, "Jix," as he was known in the popular press, was an iron-jawed reactionary who had stepped up police raids on London's fashionably notorious nightclubs. But it was not cocaine-snorting flappers or brothel madams whom Scotland Yard's Special Branch was looking for on October 13, 1925, when they raided the headquarters of the Communist party of Great Britain. They arrested the leading party officers and carted off a large haul of documents and propaganda leaflets. Sedition charges resurrected from the 1797 Mutiny Act enabled the government to try Pollitt and eleven other executive members of the CPGB. They were found guilty and sentenced to prison terms of six months to a year. This was a precedent-setting punishment since it signaled that political opinions rather than demonstrable subversive acts would be used to secure convictions in the courts.

As the showdown with Britain's labor unions edged closer in the spring of 1926, the Comintern communications intercepted by MI5 disclosed that Moscow expected the confrontation with the miners to spark the "gigantic struggles" of the British working class. "Only a well-organized strike movement can prepare the way for active revolutionary struggle," Zinoviev advised the CPGB in February.

Well in advance of the impending showdown, the British took care to keep the Americans fully briefed on Arcos and its connections with Amtorg via Captain Guy Maynard Liddell of Special Branch, who proposed visiting Washington in April. When Liddell delivered his March 27 report to the U.S. embassy in Grosvenor Square, he suggested that his forthcoming marriage to Calypso Baring, the sister of Lord Revelstoke, a distinguished banker, offered the perfect cover for him "to meet some of the men in the [State] Department who are interested in the same sort of work," while on his honeymoon trip. Liddell was a Special Branch officer who had liaised with U.S. embassy officials. The State Department was advised that he was "one of the cleverest and most intelligent of 'our friends.'"[43]

Liddell's photographic memory and ruminative brain had taken him to the top of Scotland Yard's section responsible for tracking Communist subversion. The thirty-four-year-old son of an army captain and a professional violinist, Liddell was a gifted cellist whose promising musical career was cut short by World War I when he joined the field artillery. After winning the Military Cross for bravery under fire on the Western front, he had been selected for Special Branch by Metropolitan Police Commissioner Thomson in 1919. For thirty-three years, Liddell was at the heart of Britain's counterintelligence operations, working with MI5, the armed forces, MI6, and the code breakers of GC&CS. It is now clear that his visit to Washington resulted in closer Anglo-American cooperation to secretly combat Soviet subversion.[44]

The Americans were kept posted, through their London embassy, of Moscow's efforts to exploit the industrial unrest and create all-out class warfare on the streets. When the general strike erupted in Britain on May 3, 1926, after the miners refused to accept the pay cuts recommended by the Royal Commission, the government proved better prepared than the Comintern and its CPGB agitators. The Conservative Cabinet did not send in troops, as Zinoviev predicted it would, when the transport and dock workers joined the striking miners in an all-out bid to bring the country to a halt. Instead, with calm headmasterly authority, Baldwin rallied his Tory supporters in the middle class to keep essential transport services running. This tactic took the Comintern and its British agents by surprise. With no barricades for the proletariat to man, there was no class warfare in the streets. No workers were shot and within a week the general strike collapsed.

Even Moscow's attempts to fuel the British strike with funds was met by rejection. The Trades Union Congress was so apprehensive of charges of bribery by "Red Gold" that it returned the strike donations sent by the Profintern and the Soviet Union. Not even the rabidly anti-Bolshevik home secretary could substantiate his initial claim that Moscow was "providing money on the first day of the general strike for financing." Joynson-Hicks buttressed his convictions, however, by publishing a so-called Blue Book of selected documents seized from Communist party headquarters. These included a message to Comintern headquarters referring to "transmitting money by the secret channel." Only after the general strike collapsed did the locked-out miners openly accept a £1.25 million supposedly donated by their Soviet counterparts.[45]

When the striking miners began drifting back to work in September 1926, the Red Menace appeared defeated. But far from giving up, the Soviets renewed their subversive assault by extending their efforts to India, where a rejuvenated Communist party with funds from Moscow began fomenting political and industrial unrest. In Britain, despite a stiff warning delivered to the Soviet ambassador in February 1927, Foreign Secretary Austen Chamberlain informed the Cabinet a month later of "highly secret information" he had received about "the activities of the Soviet Union in this country."

What exercised the Cabinet's concern was the growing threat of espionage and subversion networks operating out of Arcos. The arrest in March of Soviet spy Ethel Chiles had alerted MI5 to this danger. The twenty-five-year-old German Comintern agent, whose real name was Kate Grüssfeld, had used a forged British passport for her work for International Workers' Relief. This was a Comintern front organization that MI5 described as "a flagrant case of fraudulent perversion."[46]

The secret reports supplied to the U.S. State Department reveal that Chiles was part of the ring run by Jacob Kirchstein, an elusive Comintern agent whom British and American authorities had spent two years trying to track down. Grüssfeld remained tight-lipped under interrogation and refused to name any American associates. The extent of Kirchstein's espionage ring was only revealed after addresses found by Special Branch at Arcos headquarters led New York police to raid the headquarters of the Moness Chemical Company at 426 Broome Street in Manhattan. There, papers stuffed in a stove confirmed that Moness had received substantial loans over the signature of Harry J. Hammer.[47]

MI5 reports in the U.S. Archives show that the Grüssfeld/Kirchstein case played an important part in persuading the British government to curb such blatant violations of the Anglo-Soviet trade treaty. But before the home secretary could authorize any direct move against Arcos headquarters, MI5 had to find a pretext that would allay Moscow's suspicions that the raid was a result of breaking their codes or penetrating their British operations.

In a curious twist of fate, it was an old boy of Marlborough College named George Monckland who provided the evidence that Special Branch needed to justify a raid on Soviet House. A Lloyd's underwriter, Monckland told Special Branch how in March 1927, a man by the name of Wilfred McCartney had approached him in an illegal Mayfair gambling club and offered a retainer of £50 a month to supply the Soviets with information on arms shipments obtained in the course of his work at Lloyd's. On March 22 McCartney produced a letter from a man named K. J. Johnson. He claimed that Johnson was "the superior Russian spy agent in the country," telling Monckland that in an emergency he could call on the Soviet military attaché and say that he was "one of the firm."[48]

Monckland evidently was not cut out for spying. A week later he informed the authorities about McCartney. An MI5 officer identified only as "Peter Hamilton" persuaded him to become a double agent with the code name of "M2." His role was to provide Special Branch with the justification for mounting a surprise raid on Soviet House when, at the end of April, MI5 supplied Monckland with a manual titled "Regulations for Training Flying Personnel of the Royal Air Force." Monckland's instructions were to pass this manual to McCartney. It was prominently marked SECRET even though sources in the RAF knew it was out of date. McCartney returned the manual to Monckland a few days later, saying it was "no good because it was obsolete." MI5 therefore knew that a Soviet agent familiar with RAF operating procedures must have read the manual and that it would certainly have been copied in the Arcos headquarters.

A foolproof trap had been set by MI5. But the carefully planned "sting" operation went awry on May 11, 1927, after the home secretary advised the Cabinet that the secret report was in the trade delegation. The RAF manual supplied to McCartney was obviously intended to provide the cast-iron evidence of espionage that could be "discovered" to send the whole Soviet delegation packing.

It is now clear that Jix was able to persuade the prime minister to authorize the raid only because the British secret service had an informant *inside* Soviet House who *tipped off* MI5 that a copy of that secret RAF report had been made. That much is obvious from an original draft of Baldwin's announcement stating that the Soviets had been caught redhanded. It has come to light in declassified British Cabinet records and specifically refers to a "missing" document of "an official and highly confidential nature, so marked" that the government knew "from information voluntarily furnished by a person lately in the employment of Arcos" has been "conveyed to 49 Moorgate and there reproduced by means of photographic apparatus."[49]

On the strength of this assurance from the home secretary, the Cabinet agreed on the afternoon of May 11 to authorize a police search of the Arcos premises.

The meticulously planned raid began at 4:30 the following afternoon. A squad of blue-uniformed policemen converged on 49 Moorgate, just north of the Bank of England. Within minutes, fifty plainclothes detectives of Special Branch emerged from the nearby underground station, having traveled from Scotland Yard on the Circle Line so as not to attract suspicion. They raced up the steps into the main entrance of 49 Moorgate, the office building that served as headquarters for the four hundred staff members of Arcos and the thirty-five diplomatically accredited members of the Soviet Trade Delegation.[50]

Brushing aside the angry protests of Soviet officials, the detectives fanned out according to a rehearsed plan. One detachment headed downstairs to the basement, which they found barred by a massive locked steel door. Upstairs, panic broke out. Secretaries shrieked hysterically at the sight of detectives' pistols as the plainclothes police officers hustled them into corridors and demanded keys to locked filing cabinets and safes. In one office the manager barred the door in an effort to gain time to contact the Soviet chargé d'affaires at Chesham House. But the telephone lines had been cut off.

Acrid smoke began curling up from a ground-floor office window and the clanging bells of fire engines added to the chaos and confusion in the narrow city streets. The stench of burning paper drifted into the corridor outside the office of the head of the trade delegation, who happened to be away in Geneva. When Special Branch officers burst into the locked code room, after threatening to shoot the door down, they saw through the choking smoke two men and a middle-aged woman feeding a small bonfire with the contents of a large dispatch box on the table. The detectives stamped out the flames, rescuing charred documents. From the pocket of one of the men fell a roll of papers that confirmed he was Anton Miller, the trade delegation's cipher clerk. In his possession he had lists of names and addresses of Comintern agents across the world.

When the police broke into the underground room with its battery of photographic apparatus they did not find the copy of the secret RAF manual they had been told was there. They did arrest an illegal immigrant, Robert Kolling, who acted as a courier between Soviet House and the Russian legation on Chesham Place. Under interrogation, Kolling later confessed to using a whole string of aliases in his assignments as an official of the Russian Seamen's Union and a full-time Red agitator.[51]

While the raid was under way at Soviet House, there was also turmoil at Chesham House. Alerted to the arrival of the police by a phone call from Moorgate just before the lines were cut off, Rosengolz, the chargé d'affaires, wired a warning cable to Moscow. Then this heavyset Russian set off by embassy car to deliver a personal protest to the foreign secretary. But it was after six o'clock by the time he puffed up the marble steps of the Foreign Office. An undersecretary greeted him with the news that Sir Austen Chamberlain had left for the day.

Displaying a hard-nosed Bolshevik's disregard for the niceties of diplomatic protocol, Rosengolz hurried across Parliament Square for a hastily convened meeting with the Labour party's front bench. Opposition Leader Ramsay MacDonald was in the United States, but the angry Soviet envoy was given a sympathetic hearing from Labour's chief whip. He promptly put down a parliamentary question protesting a shameful violation of Soviet diplomatic immunity. This brought counteraccusations from Conservatives about Rosengolz's behavior, and accusations that the names of prominent Labour M.P.'s had been found in the compromising documents discovered in Soviet House files.

Despite protests from the Soviet embassy, the intensive police search of Arcos headquarters continued late into the night and all through the next day. The enormous steel doors in the basement of 49 Moorgate had to be cut down with pneumatic drills and the oxyacetylene torches that had been brought in to open the many safes to which keys had mysteriously vanished. When the police broke into the vault they found stacks of files, propaganda films, and crates of guns that the Soviets disingenuously claimed were hunting rifle "samples." The floor-to-ceiling search went on through the weekend, yielding two truckloads of material, which were driven off to Scotland Yard.

Not a single page of the planted RAF manual was found among the quarter-million documents that took more than a week of round-the-clock sifting by a team of translators from the Foreign Office supervised by MI5 officers. While the search for the incontrovertible evidence of espionage continued, a major diplomatic and parliamentary row erupted. Maxim Litvinov, the assistant commissar for foreign affairs, protested that diplomatic relations with Britain and millions of pounds in trade had been put at risk "in the grossest and most insulting manner" by the police raid, which he called "a most serious hostile act."[52]

The failure to come up with the proof of redhanded espionage gave the British government fits. The Cabinet had resolved to break diplomatic ties with the Soviet Union and send the trade delegation packing. But without blowing the secret interception of the Soviet cable traffic, they lacked the hard evidence to justify such a radical course of action. More than a week passed while the parliamentary row grew worse. Labour members sympathetic to Moscow's propaganda accused the British government of engineering the Arcos raid as a diplomatic insult, timed to discredit the opposition to the government's pending trade-union legislation.

All the home secretary would tell the House to quell the storm of criticism was that he was "satisfied that a certain official document was or had been improperly in the possession of a person employed in the premises occupied by Arcos." His subsequent admission that the document could not be found prompted another noisy outburst from the opposition benches. Weakly, Joynson-Hicks assured the House that "the police have taken possession of certain papers which might bear upon the case."[53]

The U.S. military attaché reported to Washington that a War Office source had said that the postponement of a full statement by the prime minister on the raid was because the "situation demanded the most careful handling." Lacking the military manual to prove a Soviet espionage ring operated from Arcos, the British government took twelve days to decide there was no choice but to reveal some of the intercepted secret Comintern messages.[54]

When the prime minister rose to address the House of Commons on May 24, his carefully worded statement justified the raid because of "information secured, and supported by documentary evidence" that led the government to believe that a missing War Office document "had been conveyed to Soviet House and there reproduced by means of a photo-static apparatus, the exact character and location of which were described." What Baldwin did not describe was the RAF manual, or how it reached the Soviets, or the existence of a British mole on the Arcos staff. In his most imperturbable manner he merely referred to "secret staff records" and "other documents" that it was "unnecessary to describe."[55]

To bolster the government's contention that the Soviets had violated the terms of their trade agreement, the prime minister read verbatim the text of three secret Soviet telegrams, two to Moscow from the Soviet chargé d'affaires in London. These official communications left no doubt about the degree to which the Soviets had been abusing the terms of their trade agreement by using their officials in London to conduct subversive and propagandizing activities. Nevertheless Baldwin did not identify the source of the cipher cables that had "come into the possession of HM government."[56]

The Labour opposition spokesman protested that none of the documents seized in the Arcos raid nor the Soviet telegrams provided conclusive proof of the government's charges of "both military espionage and subversive activities." With a cavalier disregard for security that horrified the British code breakers, the home secretary wound up the six-hour debate by reading four more incriminating communications that Rosengolz had recently sent to Moscow.[57]

The House of Commons voted overwhelmingly in favor of the expulsion of the Russians and the abrogaton of the Anglo-Soviet Trade Agreement. But the GC&CS code breakers were left wringing their hands in frustration since Moscow would know beyond any doubt that their ciphers had been broken.

The Arcos raid, which the Conservative government regarded as a major victory in its undeclared war against socialism and communism, in fact proved to be a strategic disaster in the long run. The Soviets, as Denniston and the GC&CS code breakers predicted, promptly changed their code system to one-time pads that were theoretically unbreakable. The failure to find the RAF manual in Soviet House cost MI5 and Special Branch the one sure weapon with which to fight the second wave of Moscow's penetration and subversion of Britain.

An explanation of why the planted evidence was not at Arcos headquarters did not emerge until the trial of McCartney in December 1927, a month after his arrest along with a German named Georg Hansen, who had arrived in London as an undercover Comintern agent after the Soviet diplomats had returned to Moscow. Monckland testified that McCartney had telephoned and warned him to "get rid of any incriminating documents" *at the very hour* the raid on Soviet House was actually in progress. McCartney had also boasted that "he had been warned that the raid would take place and that he had been able to warn the people at Arcos."[58]

Under cross-examination, McCartney denied that he had alerted the Soviets. It is possible that Monckland, as the Crown's witness, was primed to provide an "official" and plausible explanation of why the copy of the RAF manual that triggered the raid was never found. But only five people outside the Cabinet knew the day before that the operation against Arcos had been set for the following afternoon. This suggests that a ranking MI5 or Special Branch officer tipped off the Soviets. A joint MI5–Foreign Office investigation into the leak never produced a culprit; and their official report on the affair is still an Official Secret.

So, too, are the contents of the two truckloads of Soviet paperwork seized by the British in the Arcos raid. Only six examples were given in a special government White Paper titled "Documents Illustrating Hostile Activities of the Soviet Government and the Third International Against Great Britain." But the counterintelligence value of the largest haul of Soviet documents ever taken in the West has now become evident from one report on the Arcos files that found its way into State Department archives via the U.S. embassy in London. We now know that the raid provided the British with extremely valuable information about Soviet methodology and operations. Seized documentation ranged from the code system "used between the Soviet authorities and the Workers (Communist) Party of America" to MI5's assessment of an interlocking network of Moscow-directed Communist cells radiating out from Arcos.[59]

"The Constitution and Duties of Russian Communist Party (V.K.P.(b)) Cells Abroad" — a post-Arcos report still an Official Secret in Britain — illustrates the insights MI5 obtained in 1927 on Soviet objectives and the interrelation between the GRU's foreign industrial espionage, the GPU's undercover operations, and the Comintern-directed CPGB. The heart of this network of spying, propaganda, and subversion was the (Vsesoyuznaya Kommunisticheskaya Partiya (Bolshevikev) — All Union Communist Party (Bolshevik) — or V.K.P. (b) "cell."[60]

The secret British report on the V.K.P. prepared for the Americans explained the key role played by the primary cell based in Soviet House, which had been "confirmed from documents obtained during the raid on 49, Moorgate." Documents showed that it "consisted of members of the staff of Chesham House, The Russian Trade Delegation and of

Arcos, and its subsidiary companies." The cell's function was "to increase its circle through conversion of others to Communist ideas and to carry out any special instructions that may be received from its own Central Committee through its Party Executive."[61]

This report is pivotal. It conclusively shows that, contrary to later official British assertions, MI5 had unraveled the "genetic code" of the Soviet virus by 1927. The mechanism by which the "disease" of communism was transmitted was known even as the repercussions of the Arcos raid were felt in Moscow. One of the most important outcomes was to hasten the takeover of the Comintern by the GPU for the second wave of Soviet clandestine war against Britain. American counterintelligence experts confirm that the thirty-page V.K.P. memorandum reveals that the British authorities must have compiled a very detailed dossier on the direction and depth of this second assault on the political system, trade unions, armaments factories, and intellectual elite.

MI5, for example, must by 1927 have been fully aware that the Comintern had set up and used the Society for Cultural Relations as a front organization for recruiting Communist and left-wing sympathizers in the universities as part of a coordinated scientific and technological espionage. The evidence contained in this section of the report suggests that Special Branch had not only penetrated the SCR, but appreciated how the scientific research at Cambridge made it a special target for the Soviets.

For example, six years earlier, when MI5's prime concern was sedition in the armed forces and subversion of the trade unions, a brilliant young Russian electrical engineer from the Petrograd Polytechnic Institute had obtained a visa for Britain even though Germany and France had refused him entry visas on suspicion that he was a Bolshevik agitator. By 1927, Peter Kapitza was associated with the leading members of the brilliant band of pioneering nuclear physicists at Cambridge's renowned Cavendish Laboratory.[62]

In 1920, Kapitza was called on by Abram Joffe, the Soviet Union's leading physicist, under whom he had studied at Petrograd, to join a delegation of scientists. The Soviet Scientific Mission was set up with the ostensible objective of establishing links between Russia and the scientific community in the West and as a purchasing agent for laboratory instruments, supplies, and machine-shop equipment. But, as with the trade delegation, its members were also expected to spy out useful research and act as Communist proselytizers for the Soviet Union as the world's first "scientific" political system.

Kapitza himself would later deny that the efforts he made to join

Lord Rutherford's team at the Cavendish were motivated by anything other than the purest scientific ambitions. But the historical record shows that Soviet scientists, whose skills Lenin ranked as important state assets, were never permitted to leave unless they could be trusted to continue serving the Revolution abroad. Nor can there be any denial that Kapitza was singularly persistent and successful in establishing himself as one of Cambridge's most prominent scientific figures.

Kapitza's arrival in England shortly after the setting up of Arcos is also significant. It was under its auspices that he first contacted Rutherford as a purchaser of scientific equipment. Moreover, by 1927, when the Soviet Trade Delegation was sent packing, the undercover GRU officers engaged on scientific intelligence would have assembled a clear picture of the advanced work being done at Cambridge into radioactivity, X-ray crystallography, and nuclear physics. What Kapitza learned from his participation with the team working at the Cavendish Laboratory, which within seven years would split the atom, gave Russian nuclear physics a major boost.

Even if Kapitza was as reluctant a Soviet repatriate as he protested from Leningrad in 1934 when his exit visa was withdrawn, he nonetheless served as part of the first and most successful of the Soviet Union's scientific penetration operations. American intelligence sources are aware that the GRU considered Cambridge such an important scientific target that it maintained a resident control officer there. This confidential disclosure to the author confirms the documentary evidence that the Soviet intelligence apparatus was already in place at Cambridge when Anthony Blunt entered Trinity College as a freshman scholar in October 1926.

# CHAPTER 6

# *"Mathematical Gloom"*

While Moscow was doing its best to spread socialist revolution through-out Great Britain – and the world – Anthony Blunt arrived at Cambridge University. He signed the Trinity Admissions Book on September 26, 1926, after his tutor, Reginald Vere Lawrence, a historian fellow who was then the junior bursar.

To Blunt, as to most freshmen who came up from the politically cloistered public schools, socialism – if it was of any concern at all – seemed doomed after the Conservative government's defeat of the general strike only six months earlier. The general strike had pricked the social conscience of the student body. But as one undergraduate wryly commented: "Even the most hardened socialist was apt to break down before the lure of realizing at last a latent but long cherished desire to drive a real train."[1]

However, the current of left-wing sympathy among senior members of the university – known as dons from the Latin *dominus*, "master" – was more consistent. A hundred of the more radical, led by Trinity College fellows, had publicly urged the government to negotiate with TUC. Among them was a young fellow from Pembroke College named Maurice Dobb, who, after a visit to Moscow in 1925, made no bones about his Communist sympathies. A frequent speaker in the Union Society, the undergraduate debating forum modeled on the House of Commons, Dobb tirelessly reminded those who would listen how science and art were flourishing under the new "aristocracy of intellect" in the Soviet Union.

Six years earlier, the secretary of the Heretics Club, a radical discussion forum founded in 1904, had told the president: "I wish we could all be Bolsheviks quick and have done with it." This enthusiastic supporter of the Soviet Union was Dora Black, a don from Girton – one of only two women's colleges – who was to marry Bertrand Russell, the left-wing philosopher-mathematician whose wartime imprisonment for pacifist pamphleteering had cost him his fellowship at Trinity College. Nor was the future Mrs. Russell the only member of the Heretics infatuated with the bold new socialist experiment in Russia. Preoccupied with such diverse issues as psychology, art, science, and economics, the Heretics, during Blunt's time at Cambridge, became one of the principal centers in the university for intellectual socialist debate and the promotion of the "social relations of science move-ment."[2]

"The Russian experiment has aroused very great interest inside the university," observed Claude W. Guillebaud of St. John's College, who noted how undergraduates seemed less conservative than previous generations. The intellectual fascination with Marxism was spreading beyond the more progressive members of the Economics Faculty such as Dobb. The supposedly "scientific" rationale of dialectical materialism held an immediate appeal to the Cambridge physicists, biologists, and chemists who were responsible for the university's illustrious reputation as one of the world's foremost centers of scientific research.[3]

Cambridge's obsession with scientific rationalism after World War I was the product of a long analytical tradition and a unique brand of intellectual Puritanism. Ever since thirteenth-century clerics like those of Chaucer's "Reeve's Tale" taught grammar, logic, and rhetoric in "Canterbrigge's" ramshackle wooden halls, Cantabrigians had prided themselves on a more rigorous academic attitude than that of their Oxonian rivals. The Dutch humanist Desiderius Erasmus arrived in Cambridge in 1511, to be followed by many adherents of Martin Luther's rebellion against the Church of Rome, who helped make the younger university the intellectual center of the Reformation in England. In fact, its professor of divinity, Thomas Cranmer, became Henry VIII's Archbishop of Canterbury and the architect of the Church of England.

The "new learning" offered by the rapidly expanding colleges lining the banks of the River Cam produced some of the most illustrious Elizabethan poets, philosopher-scientists, and dramatists. Edmund Spenser, John Fletcher, and Francis Bacon were all Cambridge graduates. So too was Christopher Marlowe, the playwright and diplomat who was one of the founder members of Her Majesty's Secret Service.

The self-analytical Puritanism of Cambridge, which manifested itself in John Milton and Oliver Cromwell during the Puritan revolution of the sixteenth century, was also a dominant force in the Restoration. Samuel Pepys and the "metaphysical" poets John Dryden and Andrew Marvell gave a new direction to literature as the genius of Christopher Wren put a bold new face on English architecture. At the same time, the mathematics of Isaac Newton charted a new conception of the universe, establishing Cambridge's reputation as a center of scientific learning.[4]

The Newtonian influence was so pervasive a century later that young William Wordsworth complained that he was driven away from the university before graduation by the university's "mathematical gloom." Nonetheless, Cambridge was the cradle of the English Romantics, producing not only Wordsworth, but also Thomas Gray, Samuel Taylor Coleridge, and Lord George Byron. Nor did the university's scientific tradition hold back Thomas Babington Macaulay, William Makepeace Thackeray, or Alfred Tennyson from reaching the pinnacle of Victorian literary achievement.

The natural-sciences tripos (examination) was established in 1848 while Charles Darwin was producing his seminal work on the origin of species. After 1882, when it no longer became compulsory for dons to take holy orders and vows of chastity, the study of science and philosophy accelerated as fellows married and put down roots beside the Cam and raised families. Their sons, and by the turn of the century their daughters also, were graduating, intermarrying, and forming the "intellectual aristocracies" whose Victorian parlors became the meeting grounds between fellows and up-and-coming undergraduates.

Cambridge's preeminence in science was confirmed in 1874 with the founding of the Cavendish Laboratory under the first professor of experimental physics, J. Clerk Maxwell, the pioneer of electromagnetic theory. His successor, Professor J. J. Thompson, was the discoverer of the electron, and his experiments set the course for modern physics before World War I demonstrated the potential destructiveness of twentieth-century technology.[5]

"We are living in the heroic age of physics," Sir Ernest Rutherford declared in 1923, four years after taking over from Thompson. The New Zealand-born Nobel laureate, who discovered the atomic nucleus, presided over the Cavendish's golden age. In the laboratory complex built on the site of the friary where England's Protestant reformers had assembled more than two and a half centuries before, Rutherford was gathering the most talented concentration of physicists the world had yet seen. Cambridge's professor of astronomy, Arthur Eddington, and P. A. M. Dirac had forged the theoretical link between Einstein's theory of relativity and quantum mechanics. But it was at the Cavendish that Rutherford's team conducted the experiments that led to the splitting of the atom and ushered mankind into the nuclear age.[6]

Intellectual electricity was crackling through the Cambridge lectures when the nineteen-year-old Blunt arrived in 1926 (a year that saw women become eligible to serve as university teachers, and the individual colleges lost their control over lecturing and examinations). The scientific rationalism generated by the Cavendish powerhouse had even invaded lectures in English literature. Ivor A. Richards, the iconoclastic literary critic from Magdalene College, was given to drawing electrical circuits on the blackboard to illustrate his lecture on Shelley's "Ode to the West Wind." Richards's razor-sharp intellect and his "scientific" approach presented a stark contrast to the Victorianism of Sir Arthur

Quiller-Couch, professor of English literature, a celebrated novelist whose lectures were notable for his wearing full morning dress and refusal to acknowledge the presence of female undergraduates.[7]

Meanwhile, Professor George Edward Moore, a pioneer of the linguistic approach to philosophy, was emphasizing the importance of asking the right question in order to elicit the right answer. His assertion of the moral value of the "pleasures of human intercourse and the enjoyment of beautiful objects" had exercised a profound influence on the turn-of-the-century generation of graduates. Neoplatonism, and Moore's teachings that common sense was a valid criterion for weighing moral certainties, had provided the philosophic underpinning for such eminent Cambridge disciples as Bertrand Russell, Leonard Woolf, John Maynard Keynes, Roger Fry, Lytton Strachey, and E. M. Forster. They had forged the intellectual, moral, and social reaction to Victorian liberal Christianity that became known as Bloomsbury.[8]

Bloomsbury embodied the essence of Cambridge's questioning, liberal-humanist tradition. The skepticism of its prominent intellectuals produced the debunking histories of Lytton Strachey, the revolt against literary realism in Virginia Woolf's novels, and the rationalistic view of modern art of Clive Bell and Roger Fry. The upsurge of scientific rationalism persuaded many of the group that moral imperatives could be reduced to simple equations and that theology would eventually become a branch of anthropology. This notion prompted Bertrand Russell's aphorism that the Ten Commandments, like a Cambridge examination paper, required that "only six need be attempted."[9]

Yet it was not to Bloomsbury that Blunt was first committed. Mathematics was his chosen field of study. It was also the choice of two of the brightest intellects in the undergraduate firmament when Blunt arrived at Trinity: Jacob Bronowski and William Empson. Bronowski composed poems alongside algebraic theorems in his notebooks. At the end of his life, his *Ascent of Man* television series popularized his belief that art and science represented the same expression of human imagination. He later told how he and his Cambridge ally, Empson, had "wanted, almost without thinking, to carry the language of science into literature."[10]

Bronowski's enthusiasm cannot have been too dissimilar to Blunt's schoolboy campaign to apply his mathematical talents to the rationalization of modern art. Blunt also shared Bronowski's and Empson's enthusiasm for William Blake's prophetic vision. But as a freshman mathematician, Blunt was very much in their shadow. Empson, whose attendance at Richards's controversial English lectures had not prevented him from getting a first-class grade in Part I Math, was already a popular speaker in the Union and an innovative poet and playwright.

"Life at Cambridge," Blunt once boldly declared, "was to an extraordinary extent for me an extension of life at Marlborough." But the actual record — and the recollections of his undergraduate friends — suggest otherwise. Like other freshmen who had glittered brightly in their public-school environment, Blunt did not measure up immediately to the brilliance of the intellectual competition of Cambridge. Although he had been a dominant figure at Marlborough, his self-esteem suffered a severe shock at finding he was outshone by such contemporaries as Bronowski and Empson, who were more brilliant and creative.[11]

At Marlborough, modern art had been the vehicle for Blunt's remarkably successful protest against the system. At the university, he found that French Postimpressionist painting had long ago lost its novelty value. His fellow undergraduates hung prints of van Gogh's sunflowers in their rooms. The dons were followers of Bloomsbury and just as familiar as Blunt with the finer points of Cubism. The tutorial system, which supplemented lectures with "supervisions" where teachers and undergraduates exchanged ideas and criticism on a one-to-one basis, made it more difficult to find a target for extending his schoolboy rebellion.

When it came to flamboyance, Blunt also discovered that he would need more elaborate props than the toy balls and hoops he had used at Marlborough to make an impression. Cecil Beaton, for example, had arrived in Cambridge wearing an evening jacket, red shoes, black-and-white trousers, and a huge blue cravat, and had already been sent down. The elegant Steven Runciman, however, remained as Trinity College's resident aesthete, cutting elegant poses with a parakeet perched on his heavily ringed fingers and his hair cropped in an Italianate fringe.[12]

Competing with Runciman's parakeet and "aesthetic" banquets featuring costly delicacies like plover's eggs was far beyond Blunt's financial resources. To be an aesthete at Cambridge or Oxford required wealthy parents. Neither the Reverend Blunt's stipend nor Hilda Blunt's small independent income permitted Anthony to live luxuriously. His £100-a-year scholarship covered less than half the cost of his university admission, tuition and examination fees, books and lodging. Because he was a scholar, Blunt enjoyed a large set of rooms in Bishop's Hostel, known as "The Ritz." But his small allowance would not stretch to scarlet walls and vodka parties like those of the Etonian aesthete in Jesus College who ventured out only in a hired Daimler, which he referred to as "my barouche."[13]

To be an aesthete, social status was as important as scholastic attainment. Learning "was what the grammar school boys did" according to

Blunt's bosom friend MacNeice, who wrote from Oxford scornfully of "those distorted little creatures with black teeth who held their forks by the middle and were set on making a career." Public-school boys went to university "either for sport and beer drinking," or, according to MacNeice, "for the aesthetic life and cocktails."[14]

Public-school boys and the attitudes of the privileged class dominated Cambridge. Instead of schoolboy "fags," there were regiments of college servants called "gyps," and "bedders," who deferred to the whims of young gentlemen by drawing an undergraduate's washing water, making his bed, fetching coal, and waiting on him at mealtimes. Young gentlemen were made to feel in every way that they were the future prefects and proconsuls of the British Empire. Most public-school undergraduates regarded their nine-term degree course as a glorified selection process. A "good" second-class "Oxbridge" degree, respectable family connections, and an "old school tie," were the standard passport for future success in Britain's legal, financial, political, and academic institutions. And since the undergraduate population turned around every three years, the ambitious freshman with an eye to making lifelong friends and connections was under pressure to establish himself in the Oxbridge pecking order during his first year.[15]

What is surprising about Blunt is that his first year was such a disaster. He had no platform to speak from or attack. Nor did he join any of the undergraduate societies such as the Union — as Empson and Bronowski had done — from which he might have dazzled his contemporaries with his theories about art.

Unlike MacNeice, who threw himself into Oxford life with gusto, playing rugger for his college, writing poetry for *Cherwell*, the university newspaper, and beagling with the Christ Church pack, Blunt lost out in the undergraduate status race. He sought only the company of a select few of his school friends; one of the closest of these was Michael Robertson, who had been one of Marlborough's senior prefects and a star rugger player.

A measure of their attachment was that Blunt was best man at Robertson's wedding in 1931 and godfather to his eldest son — a fact that Robertson proudly pointed out when he received me at his timbered country cottage deep in the heart of East Anglia's "Constable country." A tall, diffident man wearing a tweed jacket and plus-four breeches, Robertson insisted he "wasn't frightfully bright like Anthony," when recalling how he had come up to read law and history. He still held an intense loyalty toward Blunt, admitting that he continued seeing him even after his exposure as a spy. This feeling may have accounted for his difficulty in recalling details of his Cambridge friendship with Blunt, but he vividly remembered how their Marlborough circle was dismayed at the overbearing attitude of the old Etonians who dominated Trinity.[16]

"Our tutor was a frightful snob," Robertson said. "But he was a great entertainer and through him I got to know a lot of people." He and Blunt saw one another frequently, even though Robertson lived out of college during his first year. Each evening Blunt and his Marlborough cronies would gather together for the first dinner sitting in Trinity's great Elizabethan hall.

Alastair MacDonald, who had been in the Anonymous Society and was now in Caius College reading history, remembers being flattered that during their first term, he and Blunt regularly received invitations to dinner at Mrs. Granville Gordon's. A large, somewhat overbearing lady whose grating voice was accentuated by loose false teeth that flapped as she talked, Mrs. Granville Gordon's passions were music and claret, which she was careful to serve a degree or two above room temperature to accompany a lavish spread. She ran a society called the Echo Club, to which Blunt managed to get himself invited through his friendship with MacDonald, who considered himself a budding composer, along with their Trinity contemporary, L. G. D. Wraith, who was a fine pianist.[17]

"Mrs. Granville Gordon used to refer to us as the Three Marlborough Musketeers, although we never discovered which one of us she thought of as her D'Artagnan," MacDonald told me with some amusement. "We were all three of us rather poor so none of us dressed up in dinner jackets. We simply turned up in the gray flannel bags and jackets that we wore all the time."

MacDonald's recollections of how much they prized these regular invitations to dinner from a prominent Cambridge hostess at whose table they could talk knowledgeably with dons — suggest that Blunt had not yet found a mentor to replace Clifford Canning of Marlborough. Three years before, a history scholar at Corpus Christi named Christopher Isherwood (who had enjoyed a similar close relationship with his history master at Repton School) found himself likewise adrift and in conflict with his tutor. His obligations as a scholar weighed heavily. When he found Cambridge lectures "grave, magnificent, remote" and "began to feel with alarm that I was badly out of my depth." After "feverish attempts" to pull himself together, he abandoned academic work in favor of the distractions of Cambridge. He spent most of his time in bookshops, or at the cinema, where the films "even in those days were not silent, because the audience supplied the popping of champagne corks, the puffing of trains, the sounds of horses' hooves and the kisses." Isherwood finally flunked by writing defiant limericks as answers to his first-year examinations papers.[18]

Blunt's defiance was not nearly as dramatic. But his failure to obtain the first-class math examination results suggests that, like Isherwood, he found himself at odds with his subject and his mathematics supervisor. This would not be surprising. Blunt's principal lecturer and examiner was Ralph H. Fowler, a large, hearty golfing Trinity don who was Cambridge's first professor of physical mathematics. A survivor of the beaches of Gallipoli during World War I, Fowler had done his most original theoretical work, a paper on improving the flight of spinning projectiles, while recovering in the hospital from serious shrapnel wounds.

Blunt's dislike of heartiness, his distaste for all things mechanical, could not have endeared him to Fowler. According to John Hilton, "Anthony was the best pure mathematician at Marlborough." But this penchant was not for analyzing the dynamics of artillery shells, or for the physics or optics problems that accounted for fully half the Cambridge first-year math syllabus. Blunt was attuned to the symmetry and order of pure mathematics, which he identified with the aesthetic principles of modern art. But he also knew that his academic standing, his status as a Trinity scholar, *and* his financial security depended on getting high marks.

"Mathematics enjoys the advantages, and suffers the penalties of being a secret doctrine," cautioned one of Blunt's lecturers in a contemporary student handbook. Mathematics as it was taught at Cambridge in the twenties was a stern and uncompromising discipline. It required intellectual toughness for staying the three-year course. More than half of every first-year class dropped out, or switched to other subjects, rather than face two more years of an intellectual obstacle course in which "pure math" — algebra, trigonometry, calculus, and analytical geometry — required additional study for the "applied math" of dynamics, elementary electricity, and optics. Even so, Part I of the Cambridge Math Tripos was not much more taxing than the examinations in which Blunt had excelled at school. As one of a dozen undergraduate scholars in his first-year class of 132, Blunt might have been expected to sail through the first-year exam with distinction.[19]

On June 14, Blunt's failure to do justice to his scholarship became public when the tripos examination results were ceremonially posted on the west wall of the Cambridge Senate House.

"Blunt, A. F." was not among the candidates who were on the first-class list. He was among the also-rans, who received an undivided second. It was the first time he had failed to acquit himself with distinction in a mathematics examination. To make his fall from academic grace even harder to live down, the relative easiness of the Part I papers permitted more than 40 percent of the examinees to get firsts.

What went wrong?

Why had Marlborough's star pupil failed to live up to his schoolboy reputation as one of his generation's ablest mathematicians?

The most obvious explanation for his second-class performance was the result of mediocre grades in the applied-math subjects: dynamics, optics, and elementary electricity.[20]

That Blunt's poor grades caused a deep personal sense of failure was evident from his refusal ever to acknowledge that his Cambridge degree was anything other than a double first in modern languages. This was in keeping with his desire to portray his career through school and university as an uninterrupted success story. Alastair MacDonald believes, however, that "Anthony was very much disturbed during his first year and was unable to concentrate."[21]

I finally discovered, in the archives of King's College, Cambridge, evidence that confirms just how unsettled and unhappy Blunt was during his freshman year.

Halfway up a worn stone staircase marked PRIVATE, MEMBERS OF THE COLLEGE ONLY, a landing leads off to a Gothic portal. An iron-bound, wooden door opens on to a long library where tall stacks of books flank tables polished by the sleeves of generations of students. Through the mullioned windows, a placid green lawn washes up from the River Cam and laps the pale stones of King's College chapel, one of the architectural masterpieces of the Tudor age.

In the library, as nowhere else in the university, there exists the interplay of concentrated scholarship and glorious environment that is the very essence of the Cambridge mystique that inspired E. M. Forster to observe: "Body and spirit, reason and emotion, work and play, architecture and scenery, laughter and seriousness, life and art, these pairs which are elsewhere contrasted were fused together into one."[22]

This distillation of the Cambridge spirit in the handwriting of the Bloomsbury novelist, one of the most celebrated of King's College's literary sons, can be read, "by appointment only," in a small air-conditioned annex at the end of the library. Here too are kept the original manuscripts of *A Passage to India*, *A Room with a View*, and *Maurice*, books that have made one of the twentieth century's most reclusive novelists into a posthumous Hollywood box-office success.

Royalties from the Forster films help maintain the Modern Literary

Archives. Knowledgeably managed by Dr. Michael Halls, a surprisingly youthful archivist, his vault contains many of the letters, papers, diaries, and manuscripts of other Bloomsbury members for whom King's is a spiritual home. But sharing shelf space in a vault lined with boxes of the voluminous correspondence of Virginia Woolf, Forster, and John Maynard Keynes are four cartons of letters deposited in 1969 by Anthony Blunt. His scrawled notes on the brown-paper envelopes state that he wanted them sealed until after his death. The collection consists of postcards and letters sent to Blunt over the course of ten years by his friend Louis MacNeice, the Oxford poet. These letters provide a revealing, intimate, and sustained insight into a close friendship that did not break up until 1936, the eve of the Spanish Civil War.

The MacNeice letters are tantalizingly incomplete. Like so much else about Blunt, they provide fresh insights and clues to his elusive character, but they also raise as many questions as they answer. The evidence of the postmarks suggests that Blunt withheld, or destroyed, some of the letters. Nor did a search of the MacNeice Papers at the Bodleian Library at Oxford turn up a single one of Blunt's replies. Nevertheless, MacNeice's letters provide far more information than Blunt ever did about his early aspirations and frustrations and his circle of intimate friends and lovers during the first decade of his enigmatic career.

The picture the letters give contrasts sharply with Blunt's own autobiographical accounts, on which other investigators have had to rely. The MacNeice correspondence reveals how the harsh reality of competition shattered the daydreams of two teenage rebels who had set out from their public school full of confidence that their scholarship and wit would bring them the glittering prizes of Oxbridge. The many references to their schoolmaster mentor, Clifford Canning, and to Blunt's homosexual attachments, suggest they both had great difficulty cutting their emotional ties to Marlborough.

"You are really rather sublime, I can imagine you preaching to a spellbound Cambridge Anonymous Society," MacNeice wrote encouragingly in the summer of 1926 before Blunt arrived at Cambridge. Blunt was then in Italy, where his father had taken a temporary summer chaplaincy that provided his family with an economical vacation at Stresa, on the northern shores of Lake Maggiore.

"My dear child," MacNeice wrote affectionately two weeks later, assuring his friend that he looked like Apollo and admitting he was "still averse to women." A Poussin painting MacNeice had seen in the Dublin Art Gallery left him "rather taken with that paint like golden tea with milk." Blunt later borrowed this simile when writing about the painter, who was his first and greatest love.

At the age of fifteen, Blunt, according to Ellis Waterhouse, had become convinced that Poussin was a figure of immense stature waiting to be rediscovered. As a schoolboy, Blunt may have calculated — like other art historians before him — that by dedicating his own lifetime to the patient rediscovery of Poussin, he could achieve a lasting and posthumous glory from the greatness of his chosen artist.[23]

From a reference to *Crime and Punishment*, Dostoevski's novel about a student's psychological struggle to overcome social and academic rejection, these early MacNeice letters make it clear that Blunt was suffering from some underlying insecurity. "Are you sure you'll bear Cambridge all right?" MacNeice wondered, suggesting a concern that rolling hoops and trailing blue handkerchiefs were not sufficiently "adult" manifestations for an undergraduate aesthete. "And how is your toy?" he quipped. "I am thinking of getting a wooden dog on wheels to draw after me at Oxford."[24]

Once at Oxford, MacNeice found that the undergraduate decadence satirized by Evelyn Waugh in *Brideshead Revisited* was fading fast. Two years had passed since Harold Acton, the old-Etonian model for Waugh's effete Anthony Blanche, had taunted the Christ Church boat club by reading them Eliot's "Waste Land" from a megaphone. Acton's rooms had been smashed in retaliation, and his friends Cyril Connolly and Brian Howard ceremonially "debagged." Howard was another old Etonian who regarded himself as a cross between Marcel Proust and Beau Brummel, and whose loud silk ties MacNeice affected. He was therefore neither surprised, nor "altogether displeased," when the Merton College hearties attacked him and tore his trousers off.[25]

An aesthete's duty was to be "tastefully insane, inanely obscene and obscenely tasteful," MacNeice proudly told Blunt, insisting that "the banner of Intelligence had to be kept flying." But his Cambridge friend had already abandoned any pretense of being a flamboyant aesthete. "But my dear Anthony, you must not become a hypochondriac," MacNeice pleaded. "University is really rather amusing."[26]

Evidently Blunt did not find Cambridge that amusing. After little more than a month, his disillusion reached a critical point, and he drove across England to Marlborough with two school friends to see Clifford Canning. On the way back they stopped at Oxford unannounced. While his friends changed a flat tire, Blunt sought out MacNeice. Anthony was in a "black mood" when they encountered one another outside Merton College hall. The hurried meeting did little to resolve Blunt's personal crisis. From the explicit nature of the letter MacNeice sent after their talk, it is evident that Blunt's tangled homosexual relationships contributed to his insecurity at Cambridge.

"I hope you did not go away enraged," MacNeice wrote. "Your appearance was so meteoric." He advised Blunt that the "continuing of this affection" for a mutual school friend then at Oxford was "quite hopeless," except for "a little emotion which might be called platonic." Blunt's passion for another boy at Marlborough, called Edward, was "far superior in every way." But concern that Basil, his other Marlborough favorite, was too involved with another boy called Colin, MacNeice said was altogether unfounded, because that relationship was "platonic from Basil's standpoint."[27]

"I still believe in the ideal of mutual affection," MacNeice reassured Blunt, "but I have never yet seen two people capable of it." Anticipating that his advice would upset his friend, he apologized for "a brutal letter" and for being a "didactic and moralizing pig." But the correspondence suggests that Blunt was in the midst of a serious emotional crisis by the end of his first term when MacNeice wrote on December 6 that "Canning is very worried about your hatred of Cambridge and wouldn't believe me when I told him it was probably exaggerated."

MacNeice's early success in getting his own poems published in the Oxford undergraduate magazines and newspapers must have been a painful reminder to Blunt that his former acolyte was outshining the high priest. But MacNeice was not entirely free of his own sense of insecurity either. Citing Dostoevski's *The Brothers Karamazov*, he compared himself to the "precious little boy in there who is just like us, picks up fag ends of a dozen latest ideas and says 'Look at me smoking!'" Blunt shared a preoccupation with the mordant Russian's novels and it may well have drawn a parallel between his predicament and that of the hero of *Crime and Punishment*. Raskolnikov's belief in his own superior intellect alienates him from his fellows and leads him to murder a defenseless old woman to prove his defiance of, and power over, a society he believes has rejected him. Blunt's "hatred" of Cambridge appears to reflect the insecurity that haunted him throughout his first year — a symptom of the frustration that he felt. He believed himself to be a superior person, but had as yet received no such recognition from his peers.[28]

The MacNeice letters suggest that Michael Robertson must have seen more of Blunt during his freshman year than Robertson was willing to recall during our conversation. MacNeice's letters always end with a salutation to Robertson and one of the envelopes bears a note from Robertson informing Blunt that a book on the painter Blake was in the

Union Library. Furthermore, Blunt's inability to break away from his immediate circle of Marlborough contemporaries may also have encouraged his growing disillusionment with Cambridge. His friend at Oxford also found that the hoped-for intellectual stimulation had fallen short of expectations. MacNeice complained of the "jargon and false profundity" of dons who "caught little facts like flies in a web of generalization." They were so detached that they "might just as well have been at Cambridge."[29]

The two friends had an opportunity to commiserate when MacNeice came to stay with the Blunts in London during the Christmas vacation. They both attended the annual Varsity Rugby match at Twickenham; a measure of Blunt's frustration was that he apparently considered taking up athletics. Running "would be good for you, but don't [let it] turn your looks," MacNeice advised in a letter expressing surprise that Blunt had decided to abandon being an aesthete.[30]

"Just because you yourself are affecting to be unaffected," MacNeice riposted, "why on earth shouldn't I wear a red tie?" He wrote of the "tangerines and ginger beer" John Betjeman had offered him at his candlelit lodgings in north Oxford, and of a visit to Marlborough "to inspire people there." To raise Blunt's spirits he planned a midsummer canoe trip up the Kennet to the scene of earlier triumphs.[31]

"The Prince of Wales will declare open the first Phallic procession to the accompaniment of Marine bands," MacNeice enthused. "We shall skip through the hoops of the seven spheres and sway by our toes upon the balls of heaven." He assured his friend: "Out of you will come a great Boreas searing the earth to a perfect nudity." These flights of language with their allusions to Blake's poems were, it seems, calculated to bolster Blunt's flagging self-confidence.[32]

"In the new Jerusalem, what will happen when the sea suddenly vanishes?" MacNeice wondered in an April letter. It was mailed to Downham Hall in Lincolnshire, where Blunt was spending the Easter vacation with his snobbish Assheton cousins. Blunt's earlier "hatreds" seem to have been mellowing at the prospects of lazy summer afternoons punting down the willow-hung Cam, to be followed by a summer job as a paid tutor in Italy. His good fortune impressed MacNeice, who wrote home explaining that his friend's tutoring might be "a menagerie" but at four pounds a week it was "highly lucrative."[33]

Blunt's dreams came crashing down at the end of May, after he had labored through three-hour exam papers on such taxing subjects as orthogonal geometry and the behavior of magnetic fields. Even before he had handed in his final math paper, he must have known that he had failed to get a first. He would, therefore, have anticipated the summons from his tutor to explain why his performance fell below the standards expected of a Trinity Foundation scholar. He would be warned that he had to improve or he would lose his scholarship status and the hundred pounds a year grant.

To limit the damage to his reputation and career, Blunt moved with a swiftness that suggests he had expected his poor examination results.

"Anthony got a second in his schools, he is going to drop Math and do Modern Languages," MacNeice informed his parents matter-of-factly. Blunt's decision to switch to French came as a surprise to his parents, who believed that a degree in math was a more secure passport to the academic career their youngest son was contemplating. Was it possible for an immensely conceited twenty-year-old like Blunt to swallow his pride and concede that his mental equipment was not, after all, up to the rigorous demands of the Cambridge Math Tripos? Or did he see his stumble as another failure of the "system" to accord him the distinction he believed was his due?[34]

Blunt now had to live with the public verdict of Professor Fowler and his four examiners. They had judged him not to be a first-class intellect. To someone as convinced of his own superiority as Blunt, this was the unkindest cut of all. He had set his sights on an academic career and had stumbled at the first hurdle. His self-esteem had suffered a double blow: Having to live down a second-class examination result when the majority of his class had firsts was galling enough. Blunt's friend Hilton, who himself "felt the lack of a pilot in Oxford's mathematical seas," says that Blunt blamed the Marlborough math master, who "spoon-fed us."[35]

Whatever the reason for his failure, to an aspiring academic accustomed to top-dog status, the public announcement of his lackluster performance added further injury to his pride. He could imagine the Marlborough masters he despised gloating, as they read the tripos listings in *The Times*, which showed how the examiners had finally cut Blunt down to size.

Blunt, as his contemporaries attested, harbored grudges. He would not easily forgive the Cambridge mathematicians for what he believed to be a vicious snub. And it contributed to Blunt's decision to take a unique revenge against the British system as a whole.

Blunt's egotism ruled out any attempt to salvage his reputation as a mathematician. Nor was his decision to switch subjects simply because he "thought that languages would be more relevant than the mental gymnastics of pure mathematics." If that were the case, he could have read for Part II of the Modern Languages Tripos. His fluency in French and his general facility with languages made this a "soft" option. But his belief that he was a first-class intellect did not permit half-measures. He had to wipe his academic slate clean by starting afresh and devoting his second year to another Part I. This meant writing off his entire first year and joining a new freshman class the following October. It would not only set him back from his peer group, but it would cost him an additional year of study. That was the price Blunt decided to pay for a crack at the coveted "double first." (Only by the award of first-class results in *both* Part I and Part II could a Cambridge undergraduate aspire to the universty's highest academic accolade that guaranteed to open the door to a fellowship.)[36]

Blunt put the best possible construction on his academic setback. But he did not fool MacNeice, who now characterized their Marlborough trip as "a Wake up the river." The exam results were evidently still grating on Blunt when he journeyed to Oxford a week after the public announcement because John Hilton noted in his diary how Blunt's arrival "further upset the universe." Supper at the Trout Inn at Godstow in the company of the Marlborough clique restored his humor for the trip to the old school the next day. After punting up the Kennet for a picnic amid the moonlit downs, Blunt stayed on with the Canning household. That he conducted a serious review of his future is evident from MacNeice's letter to his mother, in which he said that it was agreed that he should become a writer. "Anthony is wavering in his decision to be a schoolmaster," MacNeice observed. "I expect his tutoring in Italy will finish that off."[37]

The three boys whom Blunt had agreed to tutor were the sons of Réné Gimpel, who was a friend of one of the Reverend Blunt's more well-to-do parishioners. The Gimpel galleries were among the most famous in London. Gimpel had married the daughter of Edward Duveen, the wealthy British collector who had built up an art empire selling old masters to American millionaires. Blunt set off for Menaggio with high hopes that he would make influential friends who could help him establish himself in the art world.

At the Hotel Victoria, a grand-luxe establishment on the picturesque shores of Lake Como, Blunt first met his charges. The three Gimpel brothers — Jean, nine; Peter, twelve; Charles, fourteen — proved more of a menagerie than he had anticipated.

"We must have been quite difficult," Jean Gimpel recalled to me with a smile. There was no actual academic tutoring, he explained, but Blunt supervised them during the day: swimming, walking, or sailing on the lake. Jean told me that their mother was most upset when Blunt did not carry out his duties properly by swimming with his charges. Since there is no evidence that Blunt actively disliked the water, his refusal may have had more to do with retaliating for the affront delivered to his pride by the Gimpel parents.[38]

"My father was a 'grand bourgeois,'" Jean explained. "He did not believe it was proper for servants — which is how he regarded Anthony — to be seen eating with us in the evenings when everyone dressed up for dinner." Looking back, Jean reflected that their young Cambridge tutor would have taken his father's action as a personal slight.

Blunt wasted no time in paying back the snub. When the Gimpels returned to London, they discovered that he had put it about that the boys had behaved badly. "We took a long time to forgive him for that," Jean Gimpel said. The experience taught him to be suspicious of men like Blunt, who he said "cultivate art as a compensation for their lack of creativity." Many years afterward, Jean recalled, during an interview with his son at the Courtauld Institute, Professor Blunt had tartly remarked: "My goodness, how *you* have changed."

Jean Gimpel also pointed out that Blunt later went to great lengths to cast doubt on the authenticity of a self-portrait of Poussin the family owned. Jean and his brother Peter believe this was another retaliation for their father's refusal to admit the young tutor to the dinner table. This gave Blunt a grudge against the family. "It may even have helped make him a Marxist," he said, only half seriously.

There may be more truth than Jean Gimpel realized in his statement. Having had his ego badly wounded by his first year at Cambridge, Blunt would have magnified out of all proportion any personal slight by the Gimpels. The snub Blunt felt he suffered by his exclusion from the dining room of the Hotel Victoria — and his subsequent spreading of vindictive rumors about the three brothers — dashed his hope for a friendship with an influential figure in the art world. And it could only have added another smoldering ember to his determination to get even with the Establishment.

# CHAPTER 7

# *"Boys of Rough Trade and Laddies of Leisure"*

Anthony Blunt liked to convey the impression that the Bloomsbury group welcomed him with open arms. "Their ideas were very firmly planted in all of us," he once said, "so that going to Cambridge and coming into direct contact with these people was only a direct extension." Apparently content to take their cue from Blunt, those who have written about him have portrayed his Cambridge career as a meteoric rise to academic and aesthetic distinction. But the record shows this to be another myth.[1]

Blunt failed to take Cambridge by storm in his first year, and so began his second year a long way short of being the freshman most likely to succeed. He also knew that it would be more difficult to win admission into the Apostles, the elite intellectual fraternity with close associations with the charmed Bloomsbury circle. He had already discovered that members of this society played a dominant role in the intellectual life of Cambridge because most of Bloomsbury's founding members had sprung from the patrician worldliness of Trinity and King's College, where John Maynard Keynes was now the bursar. While Keynes formulated the theories that were to transform the global economy, he acted as a father-figure for the Apostles and made the college the spiritual home of what was known as Bloomsbury-on-Cam.

When Blunt returned to Cambridge at the beginning of October 1927, to join that Michaelmas term's intake of freshmen reading modern languages, he worked doubly hard to make his mark, spurred on by the failure of his summer tutoring in Italy.

MacNeice tactfully referred to this setback in a letter. "I want to hear more about your Italian Purgatory and your Bavarian Paradise," he wrote, referring to his friend's bitter experiences with the Gimpels and subsequent recovery amid the baroque architecture of Munich, which he visited with Wilfrid Blunt on the way back to England. MacNeice strove loyally to bolster Blunt's self-esteem. "I am writing a novel featuring you," he informed Blunt in December. "I hope you don't mind, but I am giving you dark hair and some athletic prowess." Blunt must have been flattered and amused to hear about his appearance as the white-flanneled hero of a public-school cricket team. The opening line was: "Downs dozing in the distance was all he could remember and the light beneath them."[2]

Regrettably, the manuscript of MacNeice's first novel has not surfaced among his papers in the Bodleian Library. His letters indicate that he sent the finished draft to Blunt the following year with an appeal to help find a publisher. John Hilton, his Oxford and Marlborough compatriot, read the manuscript and pronounced it memorable chiefly for its "very brilliant portrait of Anthony."[3]

Tantalizing glimpses of the youthful Blunt emerge in the letters MacNeice sent him. "You might have been a cardinal, but I fear you missed your epoch," MacNeice wrote teasingly to his friend. "However, you lighten up this one a good deal, like a water-snake of bright colours come by mistake out of the bathroom tap." At a New Year's party in January 1929, thrown by their Oxford contemporary Richard Moore Crosthwaite, a lifelong friend who became a British ambassador, Blunt and the celebrated authoress of *The Constant Nymph* played charades. "Anthony and Margaret Kennedy," according to MacNeice, "both very tall and thin, were Hyde Park orators, one with a placard saying THE EARTH IS ROUND and one THE EARTH IS FLAT and gesticulating appropriately."[4]

"Lots of luck in your schools," MacNeice wrote to Blunt before his 1928 examinations. "I feel it would be superfluous to wish you mental agility." It was. Already fluent in French, Blunt had made an Easter vacation trip to Vienna "to improve his German." This time Blunt easily managed a French first class and a respectable 2:1 in Part I of the Modern Languages Tripos. His translations and essays in both received A's from the examiners, who praised his understanding of the "literature, history or institutions of the country concerned."[5]

Blunt had redeemed his academic reputation and saved his Trinity scholarship. He was back on course for a double first as he began studying for Part II of the tripos, which was concerned not so much with languages as with European "literature, history and thought." Lectures ranged from Rabelais to Dante to Goethe, covering French, Italian, or German culture up to the end of the nineteenth century. Later in life, Professor Blunt pointed out to his own students that he did not "wholly neglect" his academic work to pursue his artistic interests. But this was another distortion, because his Cambridge studies meshed well with his extracurricular passion for Poussin. He specialized in French and wrote essays on the discourses of philosopher-scientist Réné Descartes and the plays of Jean Baptiste Racine and Molière. The restrained aesthetic intellect that set the seal on French classicism harmonized with Blunt's coolly analytical temperament. His enthusiasm for French culture was reinforced by studying the rationalist philosophy of Jean Jacques Rousseau and Voltaire, whose philosophic writings underpinned the Age of Reason.

The 1930 Cambridge Register records that Blunt took a first class in the Part II Modern Languages examinations with a distinction for his special papers. After a false start, he could now proudly claim to have achieved his goal of a double first, a success that Trinity recognized by awarding him a research scholarship and an Allhusen Scholarship.

The following year the university awarded him the coveted Allen Scholarship; a Trinity fellowship was now a foregone conclusion. He was elected the next year for his dissertation on "The History of Theories of Painting with Special Reference to Poussin" — essentially the same thesis on which he was to be awarded his doctorate degree in 1935.

The university register also discloses, however, that Blunt had actually graduated a year earlier. Regulations permitted his Part I in the Mathematics Tripos to count with his Part I Modern Languages to qualify for the degree of bachelor of arts. A clue to the reason for Blunt's decision to take his degree at the end of the third year appears in the MacNeice correspondence. In 1929 Blunt was considering applying for a graduate vacancy as a curator at Cambridge's art museum. "Is it a good job at the Fitzwilliam?" MacNeice enquired that May. "I am going to be a colonial professor I expect," he declared flippantly, adding: "My life hangs on getting a first at the moment."[6]

A more serious family crisis seems to have prompted Blunt's decision to equip himself without delay for a junior curatorial post in the Fitzwilliam Museum art department. His father's health was failing. If Trinity did not renew his scholarship for a fourth year of undergraduate studies, he might have to get a university job in order to complete his studies.

Fortunately, the college awarded Blunt a senior scholarship. But that summer the fifty-nine-year-old Stanley Blunt was stricken by his worsening stomach complaint. An exploratory operation in September 1929 revealed cancer. Surgery followed, but the doctors found the disease had spread too far to be operable. That November Hilda Blunt was left a widow. "What a loss he will be," Queen Mary wrote condolingly to Blunt's mother. "Why should he have been taken, who was doing such good work on earth, when such useless, evil people are allowed to live?"[7]

It has been speculated that Reverend Blunt's death was a pivotal event in turning his youngest son into a Soviet agent. No evidence has yet been uncovered suggesting his father's death provided the psychological release that sent Blunt down the slippery path to treachery. Neither

Anthony nor his brothers had been especially close to their father, and as Wilfrid has made clear, his father's death intensified the bond between his mother and her favorite son. The most important point that has emerged from an investigation of the facts behind the Blunt myth is that very little about his career allows for such a superficial explanation. This is especially true of published accounts of his homosexual affairs. According to one recent story, Blunt's "first love affair" was with a college contemporary called Peter Montgomery, a second cousin of British World War II hero Field Marshal Bernard Montgomery.

The Trinity Register, however, reveals that Peter Montgomery, who became a music director with the BBC after serving as a wartime army-intelligence staff officer, did not come up to Cambridge until Blunt was in his second year. Friends confirm Montgomery did become one of Blunt's longtime homosexual lovers, but the MacNeice letters make it clear that Montgomery cannot have been the first.

Analysis of the published record shows that reminiscences provided by Cambridge contemporaries *after* Blunt's exposure as a spy in 1979 are also suspect. This is especially true in the case of some distinguished figures whose memories of Blunt have been blurred so as to deliberately distance themselves from the self-confessed traitor. For example, the late Sir Michael Redgrave, who actually came up to Magdalene in 1927, described himself in his autobiography as a "University aesthete" who "thought of himself as a socialist." Redgrave would have us believe that he arrived in Cambridge in 1928, the year he teamed up with Blunt — a "young postgraduate student [sic] at Trinity" — to edit a literary magazine called *The Venture*.[8]

According to Redgrave it was his friend the undergraduate poet Robin Fedden "who suggested we should have a third editor." But Redgrave must already have known Blunt for a year because he was a classmate of Blunt's in the 1927 Part I Modern Languages lectures. Yet Redgrave, perhaps anxious to allay suspicions about his own left-wing leanings (which had led to his wartime ban from the BBC for signing a 1941 antiwar pro-Soviet manifesto), insisted: "I never got to know Anthony well, and he did not, as I recall, take a very active part in editorship."[9]

Alastair MacDonald distinctly remembers being introduced to both Redgrave and Fedden by Blunt. The yellowing copies of *The Venture* in the New York Public Library belie Redgrave. Blunt's name disappeared from the masthead after the third issue, articles by him and his friends appear in every one of the six issues of the magazine. The late John Lehmann, a Trinity friend of Blunt's and a fellow contributor to *The Venture*, stated, moreover, that Redgrave and Blunt were "very close."

The first issue of *The Venture* appeared in Bowes & Bowes and the other Cambridge bookstalls in September 1928, at the start of Blunt's third undergraduate year. To beat the competition — *The Experiment*, a more avant-garde literary magazine edited by Empson and Bronowski — Redgrave hired a man with a sandwich board to parade advertisements around Cambridge. Despite *The Venture*'s "arty crafty" floral woodcuts by Lehmann, and a cover by Blunt's artist friend Guy Barton that depicted a heavy mermaid and two nudes in fashionably primitive Bloomsbury style, the established journal *Granta* panned *The Venture* as "scarcely the more venturesome" of the two magazines.[10]

*The Experiment*, however, even without any illustrative material, was iconoclastic and startlingly original. "Anti-poetical" was how one critic described Empson's celebrated poem "Camping Out," which began with the arresting line: "And now she cleans her teeth into the lake." Even the loyal MacNeice, who edited an Oxford literary magazine called *The Galahad*, admitted that the *Venture* issues that carried his poems were "dangerously safe." In later life Blunt poured scorn on the magazine he helped found and edit. He called it "short-lived" and "jejune," hinting perhaps that editorial differences had caused Redgrave to remove his name from the masthead. Nevertheless, Blunt continued to contribute articles to *The Venture* until it folded in 1930, when Redgrave succeeded John Lehmann as editor of the semi-official *Cambridge Review*.[11]

Anthony Blunt's articles did, however, stake out his claim to fame as Cambridge's premier undergraduate art critic. With topics ranging from Flemish art to Cubism, from Gothic architecture to the baroque, his writings are as impressive for their diversity as for their forcefully expressed opinions. The pieces also have more in common with his spirited schoolboy dogmatism than with the frosty rationality and dry dissection of minutiae that became the hallmark of his later writings as an art historian.

The article that made the biggest impression on the Cambridge mind was based on a trip to Bavaria and Austria during the 1928 Easter vacation with Michael Robertson and John Hilton. Robertson recalled that Blunt was already "hooked" on the baroque. "I was very much the pupil," Robertson said. "Anthony just told me what to think about all that fascinating baroque stuff in those churches."

Hilton recalls the trip, which, he says, was made before Blunt's "aesthetics were overlain by politics." They had been so awed by the "dazzling white and ochre without; explosive gold and colour in the church" of St. Florian in Vienna that they packed their rucksacks and set off on an aesthetic pilgrimage to the baroque monasteries on the

Lower Danube. Blunt took care of all the details, according to Hilton, who said he knew exactly what they ought to see and how to get to it, and took care of details such as train times. "The fitting climax was fabulous Melk, whose photographs we had pored over in the close confines of our studies at Marlborough. From the hotel window Anthony preached a sermon to the empty moonlit street."[12]

Robertson told me that Blunt's enthusiasm for the opulent decoration and the "sacred theater" of the churches of southern Germany had first been aroused by his father's strong disapproval during a family tour seven years earlier. To an English Protestant minister, the marble, stucco, and gilt religious stages, crowded with emotive statuary and cherubs soaring aloft to garish depictions of heaven, were gaudy popish tabernacles. But what intrigued the young Blunt was the religiosity of the architectural rhetoric of the Counterreformation of seventeenth-century Rome. He remained captivated throughout his life by the sheer technical virtuosity of the baroque architects and painters who "aimed at arousing astonishment, at creating strongly emotional effects and imposing them instantaneouly, even abruptly, on their audience."[13]

Interest in the baroque in England had only recently revived following the publication of Osbert Sitwell's book *German Baroque Art*. This was a high-minded tourist guide, which compared the ice-cream-sundae confection of rococo decoration in the Munich palaces of the Wittels-bachs to "the ease and swiftness of some divertimento or serenade by Mozart." Blunt's approach was altogether more analytical. He was concerned with understanding how baroque art achieved its impact on the eye rather than describing its emotional impact on the heart.[14]

"The first impressions which a visitor receives are of immense size and of a riot of ornament and unexpected colour," Blunt wrote of the spectacular interior of the abbey church at Ottobeuren. "Gradually, however, the different parts sort themselves out; colour and ornament become more coherent, and the size not overpowering but impressive." For Blunt the symmetry and synthesis achieved by the architects of these churches was not so much Mozartian as it was a reaffirmation in stone, paint, and stucco of the spiritual grandeur and geometric musical logic of Johann Sebastian Bach. Blunt's analytical eye discerned that the coup de theatre succeeded because of the skillful arrangements of large window areas. The masterful Johann Michel Fischer and his fellow architects had learned how to use light to fuse structure, space, ornament, and painting into a single spiritual drama — the "fantastic atmosphere" of baroque churches, which became Blunt's lifelong passion.[15]

Blunt's love of the baroque suggests that he was essentially a Stoic who was fascinated by the discovery that he too was not immune to the powerful emotional appeal of this unique flowering of art and architecture. The austerity of his writing reveals a deep-rooted belief that only by putting aside passion and indulgence can an individual reach true wisdom and insight. Yet while one side of his scholarly temperament pulled him toward becoming the supreme historian of the rationality of Poussin and French classicism, his other half wrestled with coming to terms with the emotionalism of the baroque period.

Again and again throughout his career we find Blunt, like an addict in search of a fix, making pilgrimages to southern Europe in his quest for the architecture that, he conceded, "to a northerner, often influenced, though perhaps unconsciously, by the traditions of Puritanism, may seem vulgar, even irreligious." Blunt justified his addiction for baroque by insisting that it was "entirely wrong to suppose that, because this rhetorical art made a direct appeal to the emotions and even to the senses, the artists who produced it were not intellectual."[16]

Blunt delighted in analyzing every detail of these churches. His decidedly mathematical approach emerges clearly in his article on the French Postimpressionist painter Georges Seurat in the June 1929 *Cambridge Review*. It was part of Blunt's technique — a carryover from his Marlborough days — to attract attention for his articles by picking a topical theme. On this occasion it was the Tate Gallery's controversial purchase of *Une Baignade* (*The Bathing Place*), which Seurat had created by meticulously applying dots of pure color. Blunt was full of praise for the artist's ability to combine "the advantages of impressionism with a classical sense of form." His pictures were "calculated with almost geometrical accuracy," which appealed to Blunt's mathematical sensibility because Seurat's "figures, like Poussin's, restricted in a perfectly rigid contour, seem to have been turned to stone in a moment of energy." He concluded that "as an artist pure and simple" Seurat was "at least the equal" of the more emotional Monet.[17]

In his praise for Seurat, it is interesting to note, Blunt was echoing the opinion of Roger Fry, Bloomsbury's leading art theorist. Fry had also studied science as a Cambridge undergraduate, and he too sought to dissociate aesthetics from ethics. John Maynard Keynes was also an avid Seurat collector. So Blunt may have been writing his appreciation with an eye to currying favor with two of the most influential Cambridge figures in the Bloomsbury movement at the very time when his father's illness might have required him to pursue a curatorial job at the Fitzwilliam.

It is significant that even at university, Blunt's articles appear carefully timed to further his career. They certainly succeeded in capturing the satiric attention of his contemporaries. "Is Anthony Blunt?" asked *The Trinity Review*. It quipped: "We wish we could have seen Mr. Anthony Blunt wheeling Daan Hubrecht round the Italian pictures in a bath chair." Hubrecht, a former Marlburian who was also at Trinity, accompanied Anthony to the exhibition at Burlington House during the 1929 Easter vacation. Blunt's critique appeared in the summer issue of *The Venture*, where he asserted that "Michelangelo marks the summit of Renaissance painting."[18]

Blunt, it seems, had now come full circle from his adolescent rejection of the High Renaissance. He also appears to have changed his mind about Victorian Gothic revival architecture. Although he had dismissed Betjeman at Marlborough for his faddish neo-Gothic cult, Blunt now gushed with praise for the "dazzling architectural ensemble" of Fonthill Abbey, which had been built by the early-Victorian eccentric William Beckford. He now regarded it as "artistically the best production of the Gothic revival" — even though it had collapsed under the weight of its lofty but ill-constructed spire.[19]

Despite Blunt's later suggestions to the contrary, it is clear that *The Venture* made his Cambridge reputation by promoting his utterances on art. But more important, during his second undergraduate year, Blunt became a member of the exclusive literary and artistic circle orbiting around the stars of the older Bloomsbury generation. He gained access to this charmed circle of dons and intellectually minded undergraduates partly by cultivating a friendship with John Lehmann.

Lehmann was a Trinity contemporary who had also aimed high only to swoop dangerously low academically during his first year. An Eton College classics exhibitioner, Lehmann switched subjects after failing to get a first. Again like Blunt, Lehmann had discovered his homosexuality at school. He later claimed "no bitter regret at having turned out to be a lover of my own sex." Yet both young men faced "the guilty feeling of being a misfit" and "the danger of being pursued by the law and being branded as a criminal." And both became Marxists. Lehmann's conversion came after a 1934 trip to Russia. Interrupting his career as a writer and left-wing editor with the Woolfs' Hogarth Press, Lehmann went to Vienna where he cooperated with the Communist underground as a courier at the same time as Kim Philby.[20]

It is a matter for speculation whether an intrinsic homosexuality contributed to Blunt's or Lehmann's decision to become a Communist. But finely chiseled features and a yearning to be taken seriously as a poet were certainly no drawbacks when Lehmann aspired to join the salons of Bloomsbury-on-Cam. His sister Rosamond, whose celebrated novel had made her an instant literary celebrity in 1927, facilitated his entrée. She had dedicated her best-selling book to her friend George Rylands, a golden-haired young fellow of King's, who was known to his friends as "Dadie." Out of friendship for Rosamond Lehmann, he became her brother John's literary mentor.

John Lehmann was one of those who introduced Blunt to Dadie. He in turn brought him into his circle of influential friends. Rylands's friendship was an endorsement for any aspiring Cambridge aesthete. Cast in the same mold of romantic male beauty and intelligence as Rupert Brooke, he combined charismatic charm and scintillating intelligence. Like Brooke, Rylands had made his reputation as an undergraduate poet and actor. He was a popular lecturer in English literature and a member of Keynes's Arts Theater Trust. Alastair MacDonald, who had an elder brother at King's, confirms that Blunt knew Rylands "very well." He believes the friendship may well have been assisted at Mrs. Granville Gordon's soirées, where the organist of King's, Bernard "Boris" Ord, a Cambridge contemporary and friend of Rylands's, was a frequent performer.

Networking — or the technique of making friends and influencing people — was the key to Blunt's success during this year. The most influential and elitist network at Cambridge was that of the Society of the Apostles — and Rylands was one of the prominent senior members. The "Cambridge Conversazione Society" was a century-old intellectual brotherhood founded in 1820 by twelve evangelical-Christian undergraduates who had taken to referring to themselves as Apostles. Kingsmen dominated the society throughout the 1920s, so Rylands's support counted during the vetting of the "embryos," as potential Apostles were known to other members.

Blunt's friendship with Rylands was certainly a factor that helped him find a "father" to sponsor his election to Cambridge's most elite secret society. The membership lists compiled by a distinguished senior member of the society from the secretary's records, known as the Ark, show that Blunt was elected on May 5, 1928. This was rather late in his second year. Since embryos were usually invited to join after proving themselves first-class material in their freshman tripos papers, it suggests that Blunt received his invitation after some considerable lobbying by his supporters. If he did, his eventual election was a tribute to his subtlety. Embryos who reached above themselves were quickly disposed of as "unapostolic." Anthony, however, had already proved that he had a sixth sense when it came to ingratiating himself with the right sponsors.

That Blunt was an Apostle, and so was Guy Burgess, together with at least three other Cambridge graduates suspected of spying for Moscow, has led to the popular belief that the society was the only forum for Soviet recruiting at Cambridge. This myth has been encouraged by the traditional apostolic fetish for secrecy. Understandably this has brought embarrassment for a super-elitist fraternity that traditionally restricted new elections to an average of one or two of the best and brightest of each undergraduate year. Among the society's select membership of over a century and a half are many eminent intellects. The best known of the Apostles of the nineteenth century are Poet Laureate Alfred Lord Tennyson, physicist James Clerk Maxwell, historian Thomas Babington Macaulay, and philosopher Bertrand Russell. Twentieth-century luminaries include economist John Maynard Keynes, writer E. M. Forster, poet Rupert Brooke, philosopher Ludwig Wittgenstein, Nobel Laureate Sir Alan Hodgkin, and the contemporary author, theater director, TV personality, and polymath Jonathan Miller.

Blunt openly declared in 1973 that he was a member of the Apostles, insisting that it was "no longer indecent" to refer to the society in public. But most of his surviving contemporaries are still too outraged at his betrayal to discuss him. George Rylands (elected in 1922) has repeatedly declined invitations to comment, although he could have shed some light on Blunt's election over academically better qualified embryos. Richard Bevan Braithwaite, the outstanding mathematician and moral scientist of his generation at Cambridge (elected in 1921), did agree to discuss his contemporaries. But the then eighty-four-year-old professor abruptly terminated the interview when asked about the Apostles, whose affairs, he reminded me, were strictly confidential.[21]

Fortunately for history, some of the more junior members of the society have adopted a more liberal interpretation of the fearsome oath of apostolic confidentiality. According to a recent paper on the history of the society, secrecy was considered necessary by the Victorian Apostles who played a leading role in opposing the doctrinaire authority of the Church of England. Members adopted a quasi-religious ritual, referring to themselves as "brethren" and outsiders as "phenomena." Graduate Apostles who had "taken wings" and become "angels" were released from the obligation to attend every meeting. Ritual secrecy continued even when the aggressive logical humanism of the 1890s replaced liberal Christianity.[22]

The philosophers James MacTaggart, George Edward Moore, and Bertrand Russell ensured that the Apostles became the intellectual nursery for the Bloomsbury generation. "It was to be a principle in discussion that there were to be no taboos, no limitations, nothing considered shocking, no barriers to absolute freedom of speculation,"

Russell recorded in his autobiography. At the Saturday evening meetings the chosen member took to the "hearthrug" to deliver a discourse while the assembled brethren feasted on "whales," as the Apostles referred to their quasi-sacramental sardines-on-toast, which were served in lieu of the original anchovies.[23]

Topics of discussion ranged from parapsychology to Fabian socialism. Cleverness and wit counted in addressing such philosophically profound issues as "Why we like nature," "Is this an awkward age?," "Must a picture be intelligible?," and "Shall we elect God a member?" By this time the society, according to a paper on its history read to the members in 1985, was "agnostic in religion and liberal in politics.[24]

The society had already become something of a sanctuary for homosexual discussion after Oscar Wilde's trial and conviction for sodomy in 1895. That was the year in which Goldsworthy Lowes Dickinson, a leading exponent of "romantic friendship" between older and younger men, became an Apostle. Goldie, as he was known to E. M. Forster and other admirers, was an inspiring Hellenist who subscribed to Socrates's teaching "that the love for men is of a higher kind than that for women." This contrasted oddly with his desire for humiliation by young men wearing boots. Not surprisingly his romantic affairs with a succession of undergraduates invariably ended in anguish.[25]

Platonic affairs between members of the society were regarded by homosexuals such as Dickinson as one path to the "good states of mind" preached by the Apostles' philosopher George Moore. But a distinct change had overtaken the society by the turn of the century; the members no longer discussed politics but became "obsessed by homosexuality," which was "discussed in terms of Moore's criterion that good states of mind involved the contemplation of art or of the beloved object." It was Lytton Strachey who persuaded the brethren that it was silly and affected to talk of a love that dared not speak its name. Breaking with Dickinson's idea of romantic love, Strachey and his homosexual confrere Keynes pursued what they called "the higher sodomy."

Keynes, who would later dismay homosexual brethren by marrying the Russian ballerina Lydia Lopokova, conceded that his generation of Apostles had repudiated "customary conventions and traditional wisdom" to become "in the strict sense of the term immoralists." He and Strachey regarded the Apostles as their special preserve for the pursuit of that "true combination of passion and intellect." According to the records, "birth" became difficult, with only seven members elected between 1903 and 1911. Male beauty and homosexual inclination became a qualification for embryos, as Strachey and Keynes competed for the election — and seduction — of their "adorables." One such case was that of the poet Rupert Brooke, reputedly the "handsomest man in England." He resisted their physical advances but, as new evidence has shown, was not as homosexually innocent as he maintained.[26]

Squabbles over apostolic boyfriends inevitably led to friction. Keynes's philandering led Strachey to describe his friend spitefully as a "safety-bicycle with genitals." Ludwig Wittgenstein, the ascetic Viennese philosopher who was Russell's protégé, was elected in 1912, then walked out. He rejected the prevailing atmosphere of sexual indulgence, protesting that the Apostles "had not yet learned their toilets, a process which though necessary, was indecent to observe."[27]

Virginia Woolf took such amorous apostolic love spats in her stride. "They were men who tended to be devoid of female company," she noted, subscribing to the Bloomsbury view that homosexual relationships were a necessary demonstration of individual freedom. She tartly referred to them as "the society of equals enjoying each other's foibles."[28]

World War I saw a decline in the society's preoccupation with homosexuality as an essential qualification for election, although the influence of such older members as John Tresidder Sheppard, a scandalously affected fellow of King's, continued to be felt. His habit of suggestively greeting handsome undergraduates reputedly once brought the stinging rebuff "I'm not your dear boy, I'm in Selwyn." Sheppard's behavior led to "mutterings among the old Kingsmen about the college's reputation."[29]

Many at Cambridge were taken aback by the abandon with which homosexual dons and undergraduates treated what was at that time criminal conduct. Another overtly homosexual Apostle was Dennis Robertson, who later received a knighthood as one of Britain's leading economists. He was elected to the society in 1926 and, as a Trinity don, would have encouraged the election of Blunt, whose own homosexuality and lean boyish good looks were certainly no drawback to ensuring his own election two years later.

By the late twenties, when Blunt entered the society, the idealism and pacifism engendered by World War I had begun to fade. Evidence of the lack of apostolic political interest came when the society concluded that sociology was more important than socialism. This was no surprise to Arthur Benson, the master of Magdalene, who, when he heard of the decision on the high-table grapevine, acidly remarked: "Most Apostles seem to come from King's and for more than twenty years King's has regarded sociology as more important than the Ark of the Covenant."[30]

The predominance of King's and the society's preoccupation with sociology make it all the more surprising that Blunt, a Trinity College aesthete and failed mathematician, was ever elected member 273. In his university generation he was preceded by his first-year mathematical classmate Alister Watson and classicist Philip Dennis Proctor, both of whom obtained firsts as freshmen and were King's College scholars. They were elected in January and October 1927. Since it was tradition-ally the role of the junior Apostles to vet the embryos, there is some significance that Blunt's immediate predecessors — Watson and Proctor — were both in later years suspected of and investigated for spying for the Soviets.[31]

No matter who engineered it, Blunt's apostolic elevation was reassur-ing recognition of his intellectual superiority, and it wiped out the stigma of his first-year academic stumble. "I really felt I had reached the pinnacles of Cambridge intellectualism" was how Julian Bell felt when he became the next member six months after Blunt. There could never have been doubt that Virginia Woolf's nephew, then in his second year at King's, would be elected. But it is ironic that it fell to Blunt, as the most junior Apostle and the sixty-seventh secretary of the society, to arrange for the election of the son of Clive Bell, the art critic who had been a major formative influence over him at Marlborough.[32]

"Bloomsbury un peu passé," was how Julian Bell described the Apostles' philosophical anarchism "in the mode of Blake and Dostoievsky." According to Bell, "Practical politics were beneath discussion." He observed that the aesthetic discussions in which Blunt, who delivered no fewer than eleven papers, played a leading part assumed "a classic post-impressionist view of the arts." Rather surprisingly, in view of the eleven occasions he took to the hearthrug, Blunt later insisted that "on the whole my own activities lay very largely outside" the society. The record suggests otherwise. During his first two years as an Apostle Blunt devoted considerable effort to trying to raise the artistic consciousness of the members. According to Bell, the discussion of aesthetics figured prominently in their weekly evening meetings. In a letter dated March 14, 1929, to his mother, Vanessa, he expressed the hope that Roger Fry "may come up this Saturday to listen to a paper of Anthony's to be read to the apostles."[33]

Blunt was particularly anxious for Fry to attend because he had deliber-ately chosen his subject — the Elder Breughel — to take issue with the keeper of Bloomsbury's artistic conscience. The previous year Fry had dismissed the Flemish painter as "essentially an illustrator," the sixteenth-century equivalent of "a great cartoonist." Blunt, who had also visited the Flemish exhibition at Burlington House, disagreed with Fry's "misconception" that Breughel's paintings of bucolic peasants were the work of a "mere illustrator and not an artist." Blunt, with customary attention to detail, argued that Breughel's carefully balanced compositions deserved better than Fry's dismissal that he was "a sort of fungus which had grown mysteriously" onto the main tree of European art.[34]

MacNeice's letters show that Blunt devoted almost a full year to honing his case. He even gave an early version of his paper, eventually published in *The Venture*, to his brother Wilfrid's art class at Haileybury College. Blunt, it seems, invested considerable time preparing his artistic studies, which explains why he recycled his work in several guises. Perhaps because he failed to persuade Fry to change his mind over Breughel, Blunt sourly insisted that the Apostles "were never primarily interested in art."[35]

Despite Blunt's disparaging attitude, these were heady times to be a young Apostle. Fry and his friends Keynes and Forster were then at the height of their fame. Membership in the society opened the doors to one of the inner sanctums of Bloomsbury, the rambling country home of Lytton Strachey at Ham Spray. The red-bearded sage held court for junior Apostles as he strolled the downland familiar to Blunt from his schooldays at nearby Marlborough. A tall stooped figure in baggy pants and "wopsical" sun hat, Strachey peered out at his coterie through round tortoiseshell eyeglasses, fluttering his long delicate hands as he delivered dismissive witticisms in a high-pitched voice.

Blunt had finally realized his schoolboy dream. Bloomsbury would also open the door to future connections, which he would exploit in both his public and secret careers. The society played an especially important role by introducing ambitious undergraduates to the twin clans of the Trinity and King's dons who constituted a dominant force in Cambridge. Dadie Rylands, for example, was close friends with Andrew Gow, a Trinity don and a member of "The Family," a dining club of Jacobite origin, whose members included the master of Trinity, J. J. Thompson, and A. E. Housman, the celebrated poet and university professor of Latin. As an undergraduate twenty years earlier, Gow had co-founded with Rupert Brooke The Marlowe Society, the university acting club, whose leading man was Rylands — and Rylands also shared Gow's enthusiasm for bridge.

Blunt, who played a polished hand of cards, quickly became Rylands's regular partner at Gow's bridge sessions. But it was art and not cards that was Blunt's principal reason for cultivating Gow.[36]

Aloofly austere, this Trinity classics don nursed a deep feeling for art, especially Renaissance painting. A fine connoisseur, Gow inherited his eye from his father, a clergyman headmaster who was a member of the Royal Society of British Artists. His mother was also the daughter of a noted Victorian painter. Gow's keen interest was fostered by an uncle, who was keeper of the Royal Academy.[37]

A lifelong friendship between Blunt and Gow arose, not from a Marxist conspiracy as it has been misinterpreted but from a shared intellectual passion for the arts. After graduating in 1908, Gow had embarked on a systematic study of early French, Italian, Dutch, and Flemish painting, visiting the museums and picture galleries of Europe during Cambridge vacations. Unlike Blunt, he never made art his career, but he appears to have put his knowledge and connections in the art world at Blunt's disposal. Gow spent liberally from a substantial inheritance to acquire a fine collection of nineteenth-century drawings, which he bequeathed to the Fitzwilliam Museum. His contribution to British art led to his appointment, with support from Blunt, as a trustee of the National Gallery and a member of the National Art Collections Fund.

In a rare public statement in 1978, Blunt persuaded *The Times* to print his personal embellishment to Gow's formal obituary. He declared that even though Gow's influence "only spread to a small circle of undergraduates, it had a vitally important effect on them and through them on others in Cambridge and eventually elsewhere." This unusual tribute prompted Brian Sewell, Blunt's friend in later life, to conclude that Gow — who once spoke of his influence over Blunt — was the *éminence grise* and original recruiter of the Soviets' Cambridge espionage network. But interviews with Sewell and those who knew Gow, along with investigation of his papers, have failed to reveal anything more sinister than his dominant influence over Blunt's aesthetic development.[38]

Gow's political views — in so far as he held any — appear to have been those of a "rock-ribbed conservative" according to those who knew him. This is borne out in the decidedly anti-Communist tone of his public statement decrying the "bellow from the biochemical department" that greeted the wartime government's suppression of the Communist *Daily Worker* in 1941. "I have never understood," Gow waspishly noted, "the link between biochemistry and communism, but in Cambridge it is close."[39]

Blunt's obituary makes it clear that his esteem for Gow was because "he did more than anyone to foster a real understanding of the arts in a Cambridge that had very little feeling for them." He went on to describe him as "almost the only don to take a positive interest in the art of the past and his rooms were one of the few places where one could find good library books about the Italian Renaissance, a fine collection of photographs of paintings and above all stimulating conversation about the arts in general." Gow assumed the role of Blunt's artistic guide at a critical juncture in the young man's development. Blunt's reference to his mentor's enthusiasm for the Renaissance is most significant in light of his own rejection at Marlborough of Italian painters of the sixteenth and seventeenth centuries. It was Gow who opened his eyes to the importance of the Renaissance and "was willing to discuss the ideas of even the most heterodox student, *and often helped him clarify his thought*" — apparently a direct reference to his own artistic education.[40]

"Granny Gow," as he was known for his bespectacled gaze and legendary fastidiousness, could be scornful to the point of derision with those he considered slipshod or pretentious. Because Blunt was conscious that his intellectual relationship with his natural father had been lacking, his devotion to his Cambridge mentor was strong and enduring. Hilton says that Blunt always spoke of Gow "in tones of reverence, as though he was the embodiment of all wisdom." Until Gow's death at ninety-one, Blunt made a point of regular visits to Neville's Court, where the installation of a special lift enabled the progressively crippled arthritic to get to his suite of rooms overloking the Cam and the glorious reach of lime trees across the Trinity Backs.[41]

Some of Blunt's friends suspected that there was a homosexual element to Gow's special fondness for Blunt. Gow was widely regarded as one of Cambridge's "bachelor dons," who made no secret of his enjoyment of the company of intelligent and attractive undergraduates. "He spent most of his time in his room in Neville's Court and was very hospitable, if you happened to be a member of a certain sort of circle," Michael Robertson told me archly. He reluctantly added that aesthetes, such as his friend Blunt, received a warmer welcome at Gow's Saturday evening sherry parties than rugby players like himself.[42]

Gow's homosexuality appears to have been more sublimated than predatory. He was the typical product of an Edwardian generation of Cambridge graduates raised on the precious Victorian homoerotic poetry of Gerard Manley Hopkins and the so-called Uranian writers who spoke largely in code. His friend Housman's love for an Oxford undergraduate named Moses Jackson inspired "A Shropshire Lad." The surprising popularity of this poem, which gave acceptable expression to the yearnings of upper-class intellectual homosexuals for blond English youth, inspired Forster to write *Maurice*. It also promoted a national cult of homoerotic patriotism. By the outbreak of World War I this peculiarly British obsession extended far beyond the Bloomsbury group's worship of Rupert Brooke to reach the corridors of power in Whitehall, and even into the Cabinet.[43]

The all-male Oxford and Cambridge colleges have been described as a "homosocial" environment because of the high proportion of bachelor dons ministering to a majority of undergraduates fresh from the homo-erotic subculture of their public schools. The educational system of the British elite was steeped in the Socratic Greek tradition of an older teacher sharing his cultural heritage with budding male intellects. Discussing the so-called romantic friendships of Hellenist dons such as Gow, the former provost of King's College and noted Cambridge historian Lord Noël Annan states in his unpublished essay "The Cult of Homosexuality" that "it can safely be said of these bachelors that they were never guilty of any homosexual act that went further than the chaste kiss or caress."[44]

Annan concedes, however, that dons like A. E. Housman who would never have attempted to seduce an undergraduate of their own social class "probably made love with soldiers or working class boys." He also cites the Victorian poet John Leslie Barford who wrote under the "Platonic pseudonym of Philebus": "Boys of rough trade and the laddies of leisure/All give me equal and infinite pleasure."[45]

Most of the homosexual dons, Annan says, sublimated their passion. Some, like the left-wing economist from King's, Arthur Pigou, enjoyed taking handsome undergraduates mountaineering. Others haunted the bathing sheds on the Cam where male members of the university swam in the buff. According to Annan, Gow favored the university library as "a convenient place to cultivate new friendships."[46]

There were, Annan also acknowledges, some notorious exceptions to the unwritten Cambridge rule forbidding amorous homosexual adventures between dons and undergraduates. He asserts that by the twenties the gossip circuit at Cambridge distinguished between "good Trinity," who were "susceptible dons who formed romantic attachments — and didn't," and "bad Trinity," who were "a few of the younger fellows such as Dennis Robertson — who did." Annan believes that the overt homosexuality of such dons as the Trinity economist fed on the social reaction to World War I.[47]

"The homosexuals of the nineties treasured their secret passwords," he observes, "but the homosexuals of the twenties came out of the closet into the drawing room." While a minority wrote manifestos, or boasted publicly of their criminal conduct, many made no attempt to conceal their differences. "One no longer had to admire chi-chi or pose lily in hand or court choirboys. Homosexuality became a way of jolting respectable opinion and mocking the Establishment that had 'made' the war." In support of his contention, Annan points out that for Blunt's generation homosexuality "had all the thrill of being illicit (as taking drugs has today) and all the pleasure of being certain to outrage the older generation."[48]

Annan's view is confirmed by John Lehmann, who wrote, "It was definitely considered bad form, in fact ridiculous to show embarrassment or guilt." He observed that "this was to some extent due to the liberating influence of Bloomsbury with which King's was permeated at the time." Lehmann's friends "made no bones about preferring their own sex." They talked "openly of their romantic attachments to choristers, telegraph boys, and young beauties of our own generation." Another Cambridge fellow, the international literary critic George Steiner, pointed out in a *New Yorker* essay on Blunt that proper account has yet to be taken by historians, sociologists, and psychologists of "the vast theme of homosexuality in western culture since the late nineteenth century."[49]

Investigation for this book has shown that historians have yet to explore the importance of homosexual networking. The existence of extensive lines of personal influence and favors goes a long way toward explaining the power that Blunt attained — power he was to manipulate for the Soviets, as well as for his own ends. The homosexual network reached out like a cobweb across the pinnacles of the British Establishment, with connections in Whitehall ministries, the universities, the foreign service, the church, and the armed services. Its communicating filaments were powerful strings of hidden influence, so fine that they were not easily detectable.

What does become obvious, however, is that several of the lines of this web of homosexual influence were spun by Apostles who, by the twenties, had anchored themselves firmly in the upper reaches of Whitehall. Although Keynes was without doubt the society's most prominent influence, the leading behind-the-scenes string-puller in the interwar years was Edward Marsh. Elected to the society in 1894, "Eddie," as he was known, ascended the senior ranks of the civil service while pursuing his avocation as one of London's leading literary impresarios. A prominent apostolic "angel," he regularly journeyed up to Cambridge from London for society meetings. His London bachelor flat and his extensive address book of government and social contacts were always open to Apostles seeking to advance their careers.

Marsh was always ready to pull strings and arrange favors for eligible Cambridge men of intellect, talent, and good looks. Successive generations of Apostles, including Blunt and later Guy Burgess, discovered this to their advantage. The Marsh network included bureaucrats, publishers, parliamentarians, and prominent members of London society. Marsh was longtime personal secretary to Winston Churchill, to whom "dear Eddie" would attach himself like a faithful hound whenever Churchill had a ministry. When his master was out of office — an increasingly frequent occurrence in the thirties — Marsh was always at hand to polish the statesman's prose, happily performing the unsung role of editor and literary critic.

Given the importance of the apostolic connection that Blunt certainly was aware of, it is surprising to find that he spoke so dismissively of the society. Declaring that "the Saturday evening meeting of the Apostles was the centre of their life" for the senior members, he claimed that "in my generation the importance had become less great." This remark, made in 1977, was like so much of Blunt's autobiographical statements: part of his effort to conceal the true importance of the secret society in which he was an active member for six years.[50]

Julian Bell, by contrast, wrote that the society "played a more important part in my life than any other institution." Since Bell's frank correspondence with his mother documents his homosexual affair with Blunt, it appears that the Apostles must also have played a central part in Blunt's undergraduate career.[51]

Julian Bell's letter to his mother, dated March 14, 1929, announces that his "great news is about Anthony." Couched in the matter-of-fact terms that might be expected of the eldest son of Virginia Woolf's sister, he informed Vanessa: "I feel certain you won't be upset or shocked at my telling you that we sleep together — to use the Cambridge euphemism." There is good reason to believe that this affair was Bell's first full-blown sexual encounter with either man or woman. Blunt, on the other hand, did not seem exhilarated by the relationship. The two men shared little in common but their membership in the Apostles and a passion for France. Julian Bell — described by Strachey as "fat and rather plain — socialistic I fancy" — was hardly the ideal partner for the handsome Adonis of MacNeice's letters. Perhaps pedigree and Bloomsbury connections compensated for Bell's lack of physical attraction?[52]

Julian Bell's infectious enthusiasm and his fondness for debating were more than a match for Blunt's intellect. But it is a significant reflection on the nature of Blunt's long-standing relationship with MacNeice that his letters betray no hint of the friendship, let alone an affair.

Blunt may have felt slighted by MacNeice's courting of Mary Ezra, the daughter of a Jewish intellectual, of whom he disapproved. "Mary doesn't like you," MacNeice wrote on March 18, 1929. "I gather you don't like her, which is very bad taste on both sides." The feelings of animosity for MacNeice's future wife did not prevent him from inscribing *Blind Fireworks*, his first published poetry volume: "To Anthony (I'm not going to put anything magnaminous here, or anything witty or soulful or even improper) with love ever, Louis."[53]

Blunt, it appears, had already learned how to compartmentalize his life. "It's a great mercy thinking that you aren't a moral and disapproving parent," Julian wrote to his mother. "Still, don't let it go any further, or it might get round to Virginia [Woolf] and then one might as well put a notice in *The Times*." Bell made his plea for confidentiality to protect Blunt! He explained to Vanessa that since Anthony's "parents were strict and proper clergymen of the Church of England, and a number of his friends highly shockable athletes, we have to take our precautions."[54]

Certainly Blunt always took the greatest care to hide his homosexuality from his mother. One example of Blunt's preoccupation with his public image was his captaincy that spring of a scratch Cambridge hockey team, for which he recruited a member of the university rugger team. In the event, Blunt's team easily beat a side of Oxford aesthetes captained by a young poet, Stephen Spender, who managed to score a goal against his own side. At the celebratory tea party the guest of honor was E. M. Forster, who disappointed the Oxford visitors because he "talked solely to the rugger blue."[55]

The out-of-character excursion onto the games field succeeded in camouflaging Blunt's homosexual affair with Bell from most of their friends. But it did not fool the knowing Forster — or Keynes, who delighted in incestuous apostolic dalliances. Keynes appears, however, to have taken a dislike to Anthony. He wrote to Vanessa Bell in May 1929, wondering "whether Anthony Blunt (with whom he's completely and helplessly infatuated) is quite all that Julian thinks him." Vanessa, to whom Julian was deeply attached, wanted to believe her confidant. Writing in 1937 after her son's death in Spain, where he was driving an ambulance for the Loyalists in the Civil War, she consoled herself that her son's "first love affair with A.B. [Anthony Blunt] was not a very real one."[56]

Real or not, the affair continued for six months. Blunt was a guest of the Bell family at their home in Charleston in Sussex. "Please God I say these delightful & divine people don't come and make me concentrate again all in my face & brain," neighbor Virginia Woolf confided to her diary on September 21, 1929. She was spared that visit — and a month later Julian admitted to Vanessa that, "Anthony and I being about equally bored with each other," he intended to "make the acquaintance of more young women." That summer he had begun his first serious relationship with an undergraduate at Girton, the first of a series of affairs with women that, as Lehmann noted, led to a "succession of mistresses."[57]

Blunt's six-month homosexual affair with Bell must have exposed him to Julian's left-wing political enthusiasms. Under the influence of his uncle Leonard Woolf, Bell had become a socialist at the age of fifteen. At Cambridge he distinguished himself with his passionate antigovernment speeches in the Union, culminating in a condemnation of the Conservative government's budget of April 1929. Bell never espoused the Communist cause either openly or secretly, as Blunt was to do. But he was a Marxist in all but name by the time he went off to Spain "to throw overboard all weak charity-mongering idealism and get down to guts and brawn." Blunt, however, would never have agreed with Bell's conviction that "what is sauce for the proletarian goose is surely sauce for the intellectual gander." He preferred covert plotting and manipulation to "guts and brawn."[58]

In light of Blunt's intimate relationship with a fiery and persuasive socialist whose "interests and feelings were almost equally divided between politics and poetry," his repeated pretensions to political naïveté are incredible. Yet he always insisted that his Cambridge years were spent in a "sheltered existence" and a "kind of dreamworld" where he and his friends occupied themselves with "spinning our own intellectual webs."[59]

New information emerging from Blunt's association with Bell give the lie to his claim to political celibacy. Julian's letter to his mother telling her that they intended to travel together to France in the autumn of 1929 contains one clue. They planned to attend "the session of Pontigny in September." The prevailing scientific-humanist tone of these annual gatherings of European intellectuals in this picturesque former abbey in Burgundy attracted Marxist intellectuals. The novelist philosopher André Gide, a member of the Pontigny Directorate, was a Communist convert in the early thirties. So was the Russian émigré intellectual Dimitri S. Mirsky, a London University lecturer and a Pontigny regular like his Bloomsbury friends.[60]

Whether Blunt attended Pontigny in 1929 as planned is not clear. But his association with Bell had politicized him, as is made clear from a divisive apostolic dispute in which he sided with Bell. Politics, rather than aesthetics, contributed to their distaste for the Viennese logician Ludwig Wittgenstein. The birdlike appearance of the author of *Tractatus Logico-Philosophicus* belied his numbing preoccupation with the precision of language implicit in his assertion: "What can be said at all can be said clearly; and whereof one cannot speak, thereof one must remain silent."[61]

Wittgenstein had arrived back at Cambridge in 1929 as an un-apologetic "old time conservative of the late Austro-Hungarian Empire." At the reunion dinner of the Apostles in Wittgenstein's honor, he appears to have offended Bell's fiercely socialist morality. Blunt sprang to his friend's defense. A fierce verbal dispute erupted. Keynes sent a sharp "My dear Blunt" note to Anthony on March 19, taking him to task for being "upset by what you think happened when Wittgenstein returned to the Society." Keynes curtly told Blunt, "The facts are not at all as you suppose." Both he and Julian were to be summoned to lunch "early next term to talk about it."[62]

Despite Keynes's talking to, neither Bell nor Blunt reconciled themselves to Wittgenstein. According to John Hilton, Blunt made Cambridge's adopted philosophical genius "one of his not rare, 'bêtes noires.'" The assignment of Wittgenstein to a suite on Blunt's staircase in Bishop's Hostel further increased the young man's discomfort.[63]

Never one to abandon a vendetta, Blunt encouraged Bell to write four pages of barbed couplets for *The Venture*, attacking Wittgenstein's self-righteousness. The most poisonous sting came in its reference to Wittgenstein's "ascetic life," which supposedly made him "intent to shun/The common pleasure known to everyone."[64]

The running feud with Wittgenstein contributed to the souring of Blunt's relations with Keynes. When it came to infighting, Blunt applied the calculated cunning he had learned at school. The overtones of the feud do not jibe with Anthony's protestations of political innocence — nor does his pretense at detachment measure up to the radicalism of his intimate friends.[65]

John Lehmann recorded that the "atmosphere of intellectual Cambridge at the time was strongly pacifist since there were many younger dons who had been through the war or who had some of their dearest friends killed." The ghost of Rupert Brooke haunted Cambridge in the twenties, stirring conflicting currents of pacifism, cynicism, and guilt. "It was always there in the background," Lehmann recalled, "conditioning the prevalent sensibility, with its preference for tragedy and bitter wit."[66]

This mood had fueled the fires of Bell's socialism and Lehmann's own disillusion led to his dalliance with Marx. George Steiner, who has written about Blunt's intellectual psyche, believes that he was not immune to the political forces that deeply affected his friends and contemporaries.

"It is thought likely," Steiner asserts in his provocative essay "The Cleric of Treason," "that Blunt became actively interested in and sympathetic to Communism as an undergraduate at Trinity College, Cambridge between 1926 and 1929." When I put it to Steiner that Blunt had stressed, "the sense of detachment" at Cambridge in the twenties, he smiled knowingly. This he did not believe to be so. Steiner advised me to examine the primary sources.[67]

Subsequent research exposed the dimension of another of Blunt's myths. The Cambridge Union minute books, college magazines, letters of dons, and records of undergraduate societies show that university life was anything but "detached" during Blunt's undergraduate years.

Still more intriguing are British records uncovered in Washington that show MI5 knew that the Soviets had targeted Cambridge for penetration long before Blunt was recruited as one of Stalin's Englishmen.

# CHAPTER 8

# "A World Doomed to Destruction"

Cambridge was becoming increasingly politicized leftward by the end of the twenties. The Labour Club membership had risen to over two hundred, and there was even a vocal Communist society of thirty. While this does not prove that Blunt was a Marxist during his undergraduate years, it does indicate a far more powerful left-wing political undercurrent among his contemporaries than he ever admitted.[1]

This was especially true for scientists like Alister Watson, who later joined the Cambridge Communist party. Only after Blunt's secret confession in 1963 was Watson interrogated by MI5 on suspicion that he too had been recruited by the Soviets. No confession was extracted, but this did not lay to rest the strong suspicion that Watson, a scientist who later worked on top-secret submarine-detection systems, had become another of the Soviet network during his Cambridge years.

In disentangling the intellectual clues that may have led both Watson and Blunt to Marx, a common factor is their undergraduate interest in the prophetic philosophy of William Blake. Watson, it turns out, wrote the *lead* article of the first issue of *The Venture* on "The Wisdom of Blake." England's eighteenth-century iconoclast painter/poet was praised for being "the passionate enemy of the traditional ideas of the judgment of human actions and affairs by ethical and moral philosophies." According to Watson's interpretation, which Blunt later reflected in his own published study, Blake put the study of Science "beside the exercise of Art as one of the greatest objects of human life."[2]

In the *Venture* article, which presumably Blunt endorsed by giving it such prominence, Watson pointed out that Blake had been pilloried "by the skeptical and leisured gentlemen of his time," whose definition of reason "did not apply to scientific investigation but to moral thought — and it is still there." This statement clearly expresses the author's strong personal conviction that even in the twentieth century the reactionary British Establishment was still prejudiced against men of science and vision.[3]

Mutual identification with Blake as a symbol of the predicament of budding intellectuals in Britain appears to be the first expression of a shared resentment. It led the two apostolic confreres to conclude that the future belonged to the more "scientific" organization of society reflected in Marx's vision. They were not alone. Such views were common enough among Watson's fellow scientists, who resented the traditional lack of political recognition and respect the British accorded to those who were dedicated to pushing back the frontiers of human knowledge.

This atmosphere in the world's most advanced research center made Cambridge rather than Oxford the focus for Soviet intelligence and propaganda efforts, and Cambridge was to pay the price. In time Britain's second-oldest university gained an unenviable reputation as the alma mater of spies and traitors. Yet research shows that British authorities for some reason chose to ignore the mounting evidence that Cambridge's scientific reputation had made the university a special target for Moscow's intelligence and subversion. Declassified papers in Cambridge scientific archives, as well as MI5 and Special Branch police files, indicate that although the threat was perceived, neither its magnitude nor its danger was appreciated.

After the lessons learned from fighting Germany in World War I, the British government had no excuse for ignoring the role of science in contributing to the advancement of the peacetime economy. Although much of the Cambridge effort was concentrated in the area of "pure science," bequests from industrial foundations such as that set up by Lord Alfred Melchett, founder of the giant Imperial Chemical Industries, provided much of the special funding for nuclear research at the Cavendish Laboratory. Under Rutherford's direction, the team led by John Cockcroft and E. T. S. Walton was making steady progress toward the first actual splitting of the atom. A crucial contribution to Cavendish research was made by the Russian physicist Peter Kapitza.

Just how important his efforts were is evident in the recently released Cockcroft papers. His enthusiastic report to Rutherford, dated April 16, 1930, discloses that in less than four years after Kapitza's appointment as assistant director of the Magnetic Laboratory, funded by the Department of Scientific and Industrial Research, it had developed the equipment to produce enormously powerful magnetic fields "of over 300,000 gauss" which "proved that a wide field of research was open which take several men's lifetime to cover." In less than a year Kapitza's experimental genius had perfected "a very efficient liquid hydrogen plant which we made ourselves," enabling them to extend their work "to the region of 14 degrees absolute. I think that, without exaggeration," Cockcroft wrote to Rutherford, "our magnetic laboratory possesses unique facilities for further investigation of a new region in modern physics."[4]

The significance of Kapitza's low-temperature and magnetic work was recognized by the British scientific establishment within six months. Although he had only become a fellow of Britain's prestigious Royal Society a year before, in November 1930 he was made its Messel Professor and awarded a £15,000 grant to establish a permanent magnetic and cryogenic laboratory.

British recognition of Kapitza's achievements came less than a month after his return from a trip to Leningrad. He had begun making these annual trips in 1926, when his appointment as assistant director of the Cavendish brought an invitation and promise of a safe return to England from Leon Trotsky. But in 1929, Lev Kamenev, Trotsky's successor as president of the Collegium of the High Council of the People's Economy Board of Science and Technology, put Kapitza on a retainer as a consultant for the establishment of a new Technical Institute at Kharkov. According to Kapitza's wife, Anna, Kamenev had warned Kapitza that he would be expected to return to complete his important work in the Soviet Union as soon as suitable laboratories were built.[5]

Two other leading Russian scientists, physicist Lev D. Landau and mathematician George Gamow, also appear to have been part of the same long-term Soviet technical espionage operation. Both graduated from the University of Leningrad before working in the Institute of Theoretical Physics at Copenhagen University, where Nobel Laureate Niels Bohr developed the relation between the quantum theory and nuclear structure that paved the way to the splitting of the uranium atom. Both Landau and Gamow worked for a time alongside Kapitza at Cambridge. Landau returned to play a leading role in the Soviet atomic-bomb project and was elected in 1946 to the Academy of Sciences. Gamow went back to Leningrad in 1931 and was denied an exit visa for two years. Kapitza's retainer as an adviser for the Kharkov project was a clear indication that the Soviets regarded him as essential to their scientific effort. Another indication was the visit to Cambridge in 1931 by Nikolai Bukharin, then president of the Soviet Academy of Sciences. Following Stalin's personal instructions, his mission was to persuade Kapitza to return permanently to the Soviet Union. Kapitza demurred and continued to return to Cambridge after his annual visits to Leningrad until the summer of 1934, when his exit visa was denied.[6]

Significantly, this was a year *after* his new Mond Laboratory, lavishly equipped for low-temperature and magnetic research, had been completed. Despite Rutherford's lobbying of the British government and protests by the international scientific establishment, Moscow refused to relent, claiming that Kapitza was "a citizen of the U.S.S.R., educated and trained as a scientist at the expense of his country" who "was sent to England to continue his studies and research work" and had "stayed in England rather longer than he should have done."[7]

Kapitza at first protested his forced detention and refused to continue his research. Or that was the story that was believed by his former colleagues in Cambridge. Whether he was a witting or unwitting tool of Soviet scientific espionage can never be known for sure. The Stalin regime certainly made their prodigal son comfortable with a spacious new home, cars, and a dacha. Most important of all, Moscow succeeded in persuading the British government to sell them at knockdown prices the entire contents of the Mond Laboratory. These were carefully packed up under the supervision of Kapitza's erstwhile colleague John Cockcroft and shipped to the Moscow Physics Problems laboratory in 1935.

The scheme to purloin Western technology was hatched a decade earlier by Mikhail Abramovich Trilisser of the OGPU Foreign Department and later the Comintern in collaboration with Russian Military Intelligence. The plan, ironically, appears to have been inspired by the Grand Tours young eighteenth-century English gentlemen of substance made to acquire aesthetic knowledge, and European paintings and sculpture to bedeck their country houses. The Soviet Union sent its most brilliant young physicists abroad in the twenties and recalled them in the early thirties with a priceless haul of technical data and equipment.[8]

The Soviet scientific espionage plan succeeded in part because after World War I it had become a matter of faith to many researchers that science had transcended political creeds and national boundaries. This was especially true in the field of theoretical physics, where investigations into the structure of matter depended on the free interchange of technical information. The Soviet Collegium assiduously fostered this belief.

The importance of Cambridge to the Soviet technical espionage operation in the early thirties has been confirmed by a former senior U.S. counterintelligence official, who was told by the British that MI5 had uncovered evidence that the GRU had actually stationed one of their undercover officers there to manage the operation. The real payoff came twenty years later, when the scientific foundation provided by physicists like Kapitza, Landau, and Gamow played its part in the Soviets' crash program to develop their own atomic bomb. Kapitza always denied playing any personal role in this work, but his work made an important contribution to the Soviet scientific effort.

On evidence currently available it is impossible to give credence to the claim, recently revived, that Kapitza fathered the Soviet hydrogen bomb with secrets stolen from Cambridge. His research at the Cavendish was not directly connected to atomic fission. But it is interesting to note that Kapitza's annual trips back to Leningrad began only in 1926, *after* his own magnetic-research program started to produce significant results. Obviously his masters in the Kremlin wanted him to keep his former colleagues in the Leningrad Institute abreast of the groundbreaking work at the Cavendish Laboratory. However long a leash Kapitza had been given, he could not have been unaware of his obligations to Moscow. Soviet intelligence agencies would have known that Kapitza moved in a remarkable circle at Cambridge. He counted as his associates and friends some of the most brilliant physicists and mathematicians in Europe.

"The inexhaustible resources and the diversity of matter are becoming clearer every day," noted an intriguingly explicit *Pravda* report less than a year after Kapitza's return. Commenting on the work being done at Cambridge, a Soviet scientist named Lapirov-Skobolo noted: "Research into the nature of the atom is in its turn calling into existence new methods of producing a vacuum, new methods of super-high voltage techniques." The article, noting the "leftward" tendencies among the new generation of Cambridge scientists, called on them to "break with a world doomed to destruction."[9]

Was it therefore beyond the flight of fancy of a scientific commissar in the Kremlin to divine the ultimate significance of the work being done at the Cavendish Laboratory? A simple equation of basic physics revealed that by splitting the atom energy could be released. Whether this was practical in the laboratory was still a matter of theoretical debate in the mid-twenties, even among Cambridge scientists. But Russian researchers took it as an article of political faith that Lenin had decreed that "Communism equals electrification plus Soviet Power." Kapitza's experiments with harnessing electricity to generate powerful magnetic fields encouraged some scientists in Leningrad to discuss the feasibility — as early as 1932 — of experiments to produce "controlled thermonuclear reaction."[10]

This astonishing fact is recorded by Gamow, who had returned to the Soviet Union to lecture at Leningrad that year. Nikolai Bukharin, as president of a Kremlin committee supervising the development of science and engineering, attended a lecture Gamow gave on thermonuclear reactions in stellar energy production. "After the talk he made the proposal to head a project for the development of controlled thermonuclear reactions," Gamow recorded, emphasizing "and that in 1932!" To persuade him to take on the project, Bukharin promised to put at his disposal "for a few minutes one night a week the entire electric power output of the Moscow industrial district." Bukharin's scientific committee believed that nuclear fusion could be induced by pumping huge amounts of power through very thick copper wire impregnated with small bubbles of lithium-hydrogen mixture. "I decided to decline the proposal," Gamow wrote. "I am glad I did because it would not have worked." Ironically, Bukharin provided Gamow and his wife with exit visas to attend the 1933 Solvay Convention of international physicists, from which they never returned.[11]

Achieving nuclear *fusion* — the basis of the hydrogen bomb — was not achieved for more than twenty-five years, and then only by nuclear explosion. What is surely significant is that some Russian scientists and their Kremlin masters were seriously contemplating fusion at a time when the team at Cambridge was still two years away from the first step toward nuclear *fission* — the splitting of the atom.

Dr. Arnold Kramish, a distinguished nuclear physicist who was a member of the American Manhattan Project and historian of the Soviet Union's nuclear research effort, believes Bukharin's remarks to be significant. "The Russians, through Kapitza and Gamow, had opened the window into the technical advances being made in the Cavendish Laboratories," Kramish said. "It is not impossible that an exceptional scientific mind like Bukharin's could guess that the work being done by Cambridge physicists would eventually turn the key to releasing the energy of the atom."[12]

Kapitza's notebooks reveal that Gamow was a member of his close circle in 1929. The members of the so-called Kapitza Club were a score of the university's most talented physicists, mathematicians, and experimental scientists. This exclusive group met in Trinity on Tuesdays to discuss subjects that ranged from "Investigation of the Upper Atmosphere by Means of Wireless Waves" to "Shape of Orbits of Core Electrons." The schoolboy-style notebooks, which record the subjects debated by the scientists who were at the cutting edge of atomic physics, reflect the catalytic influence of a unique personality. Charming, bullying, and flattering by turns, Kapitza drove his colleagues with a force every bit as powerful as the magnetic fields produced by the generators he had cajoled from the Manchester Tram Corporation. One club member, whose mathematics were evidently more polished than his verse, penned an anonymous limerick after a stormy session in January 1925:

> In discussion our chief P. Kapitza
> Goes off suddenly like a Howitzer.
>   He's been known to say: "No!
>   It is not at all so.
> It is True, as you're bound to admit, sir!"[13]

Cockcroft, one of the Kapitza Club's founding members, later acknowledged the role these lively intellectual brainstorming sessions played in helping fuse together the theoretical and experimental scientific effort that resulted in his success, along with Walton, another club member, in splitting the atom in 1932.

Alister Watson was a junior member of Kapitza's famous club. Here the political views of Blunt's fellow Apostle and devotee of Blake were subject to the influence of more mature Cambridge scientists who had already openly embraced the Marxist philosophy. Chemist J. D. Bernal, a pioneer of X-ray crystallography, was a beetle-browed Irishman who followed an extreme socialist ideology fired by his Jesuitical education. His enthusiasm for dialectical materialism was inspired by his belief — later dubbed "Bernalism" by an Oxford scientist — that the duty of science was to improve the welfare of society and that pursuit of knowledge for its own sake was as irrelevant to social progress as the solution of crossword puzzles. Bernal did not hesitate to apply the torch of Marxism to scorch the political nonbelievers and fire the left-wing enthusiasm of P. M. S. Blackett, another physicist in Kapitza's influential Club.[14]

The "scientific" rationale of dialectical materialism also found a ready audience at the Heretics Club. Founded in 1909 as another intellectual talking shop, the club had a radical tradition. As its name implied, it was founded to promote scientific-rationalism as an alternative to the Christian view promulgated in college chapel. The Heretics became an important platform for the dissemination of the "social relations of science movement," which influenced many members of Britain's scientific establishment between the wars. This club had none of the exclusivity of the Apostles — although many of the society's leading lights participated. Heretics meetings were open and advertised in the local press. But the Heretics, like the Kapitza Club and later the Apostles, were an obvious target for Comintern infiltration.

Nowhere outside the Soviet Union itself was there such a vigorous and influential Communist movement as in Britain, according to Neil Wood, author of a ground-breaking study, *Communism and the British Intellectuals*. The Cambridge intellectual establishment held the essentially Marxist view that science was an ideology like religion, philosophy, law, literature, and art. Under capitalism, science was made to serve the interests of the ruling classes. Only in the supposedly classless Soviet Union, where the abolition of capitalism had also abolished the distinction between "pure" and "applied" research, could science truly serve the needs of the community.[15]

The Cambridge physicists and biochemists who were thrusting back the frontiers of science were those most influenced by proto-Marxist philosophy. Brilliance combined with powerful egocentric personalities led men such as Bernal to adopt radical philosophies and nonconformist life-styles. This was certainly true of J.B.S. Haldane, the idiosyncratic biochemistry professor whose extramarital relations offended the staid Trinity dons as much as his habit of bringing bottles of urine to the college's high table. The radicalism of J.B.S. Haldane and Joseph Needham, who succeeded him as professor, was stimulated by Sir Frederick Gowland Hopkins, the director of the Institute of Biochemistry, whose greatest interest after biochemistry was socialism.

In 1928 Haldane followed Maurice Dobb in making the Cambridge left-wing intellectual's obligatory pilgrimage to Moscow to observe the new scientific state at first hand. But unlike Keynes and Russell, whose innate liberal humanism had been affronted by their encounters with Stalin's emerging police state, Haldane and his second wife, Charlotte, an American journalist, returned as ardent champions of the supposedly scientific foundations of the Soviet Union. While Charlotte joined the Communist party and became an underground agent for the Comintern until her break with the Soviets in World War II, Haldane did not officially become a card-carrying Communist until 1942 — after his divorce from Charlotte. Although Haldane believed firmly that the scientific mind was best employed outside politics, until he left for University College, London, he was Cambridge's most outspoken proselytizer for the cause of scientific materialism.[16]

No less egocentric, and dedicated to the same brand of scientific left-wing idealism — although he never joined the Communist party — was Dr. Joseph Needham, a biologist who believed in the unique blend of socialism and Social Gospel of the Reverend Conrad Noel. A prewar Cambridge graduate and friend of composer Gustav Holst, the so-called Red Vicar of Thaxted was an Anglo-Catholic who preached that Christ was a "militant revolutionist" and placed the Red Flag and a Sinn Fein banner alongside the Cross of St. George in his church.[17]

Needham and his left-wing Cambridge colleagues were among the influential voices who called throughout the thirties on the need for scientists to be given a more responsible role in the British social and political process. One of the leaders in this movement was Julian Huxley, the radical Oxford biologist and president of the Union of Scientific Workers — an organization that already had an influential cell of Communists in its Cambridge branch, including Maurice Dobb.[18]

Needham, Huxley, Bernal, and many others echoed the theme of the Soviet scientific delegation who had made a dramatic arrival in London by air at the end of June 1931. An outraged *Daily Mail* protested that Stalin himself had elevated Bukharin, his "notorious propaganda agent," into a professor just so that he could obtain a visa to lead the Soviet delegation to the International Congress on the History of Science. Professor or not, the short balding figure whose goatee and bulbous cranium gave him a striking resemblance to Lenin, managed to electrify the strong left-wing contingent at the conference. Bukharin contrasted the economic crisis of the capitalist world with the "entirely new phenomenon" of scientific Marxism and the collective organization of scientific research on a vast scale in the Soviet Union. According to Bukharin, this "new type of intellectual culture which dominates the mental activity of millions of workers is becoming the greatest force of the present day."[19]

"Shall science enslave the masses or serve them?" This was the central theme of eleven papers prepared by the eight-man Soviet scientific delegation. In a brilliantly orchestrated public-relations coup, the solution appeared self-evident when *Science at the Crossroads*, which contained their arguments, was printed, bound, and on sale in the London bookstores within the week.

"I can say that the inspiration for my own work and that of many others in science," Bernal later wrote, "can be definitely traced to the visit of Marxist scientists to the History of Science Congress in 1931." Even those less ideologically committed than Bernal felt the impact of their first exposure to dialectical materialism. They were impressed with the status and importance the Soviets apparently accorded to their scientists. Here was an example to be emulated.[20]

The Congress and its potential impact did not go unnoticed by Special Branch, which obtained copies of Bukharin's papers and intercepted a Tass telegram to Moscow reporting on the proceedings. The Soviets had been "impressed" by the younger delegates. Singled out for special mention was the Cambridge group, led by Needham, who "called themselves mechanists," not because they opposed dialectical materialism but because they had as yet "unheeded it."[21]

Special Branch reports on the revolutionary leader's visit indicate how by 1931 the MI5 Registry contained some bulky files on Cambridge scientists who were potential targets of, and sympathizers with, the Soviet Union. The records that have come to light show that elaborate measures were in place to monitor the activities of Needham and his cohorts, especially Maurice Dobb, who had been identified as a longtime member of the Communist faction of the Union of Scientific Workers. Dobb was already the university's leading spokesman for the new vision of the classless, scientifically run society that was to hypnotize the third wave of Cambridge undergraduate recruits to Marxism in the years to come.

Until the end of his life, Maurice Dobb steadfastly played communism's John the Baptist, preaching the Decline of Capitalism to successive generations of undergraduates. In 1965, when I attended his classes, he was white-haired and weary after nearly half a century in his self-appointed role. But he still mustered the persuasive enthusiasm of the true convert who was also an inspiring teacher. Unlike some of his younger colleagues in the Economics Faculty, whose ferociously statistical arguments were virtually impossible to follow, let alone take notes on, Dobb's twice-weekly classes were a breath of common sense to a confused newcomer to the Economics Tripos. His plausible rendering of the serpentine twists of Soviet economic policy were models of clarity and memorability. Dobb earned this former student's gratitude because attendance at his biweekly Soviet Economic History class enabled me to confound my college tutor's predictions of a "third" because I had skipped most of the other economics lectures!

Dobb was a patient teacher and this made him a highly effective spokesman for Marxism. He was a patient academic; he could make abstruse economic theory convincing. Although he was often suspected of being a Soviet agent, he was always able to defend himself by pointing to the openness of his communism. After reading one of the 1925 Home Office reports on Communist subversion, King George V wrote to the chancellor of Cambridge demanding to know why such a well-known Marxist was permitted to indoctrinate undergraduates.[22]

Dobb was not a simple ideologue, propagandist, or undercover agent. He studiously avoided activities that could have led to his prosecution or being turned out of his Cambridge teaching position. Dobb's skill lay in appearing to keep his teaching separate from his politics, although in reality they were one and the same. His was a unique ability to portray the inconsistencies of communism as consistent and to make the unfathomable Marxist mysteries appear logical. As an economics lecturer and later a Trinity fellow, Dobb was in a unique position to be adviser and father confessor to radical undergraduates. Given the intellectual environment in which he operated, his unswerving loyalty to Moscow, and the scores of committee positions he held in such front organizations as the Union of Scientific Workers and the Society for Cultural Relations, Maurice Dobb was one of the Comintern's most influential assets in Britain.

Dobb's activities had not escaped the notice of MI5 and the Special Branch officers responsible for monitoring Soviet subversive activities. In one of the files reporting on the Society for Cultural Relations, which has turned up in the U.S. Archives, Dobb is noted as "the Cambridge economist, a well known Communist and a prominent member of the S.C.R." The file contains a 1929 letter from a Comintern official to a London subordinate, in which Dobb is characterized as "one of the staunchest friends of Soviet Russia in England, and in view of his position at Cambridge, he can do much for cultural rapprochement."[23]

Cultural rapprochement was, as this report makes plain, only a euphemism. The Society for Cultural Relations was one of a number of front organizations that mushroomed in the late twenties as a cover for Moscow's increasingly sophisticated subversion. The SCR had been formed in 1924 with the support of many leading members of Britain's progressive intelligentsia, while the Friends of Soviet Russia was set up to appeal to the masses. Both organizations were identified as "component parts of the vast machinery of propaganda directed from Moscow." Most of the early meetings were devoted to "enthusiastic accounts of conditions in Russia" by returning travelers, almost all of whom were "of strong Left Wing or Communist sympathies."[24]

Reflecting Soviet interests, the SCR's "cultural" orientations became increasingly "scientific." In 1925, at a London meeting to mark the bicentenary of the Soviet Academy of Sciences, a resolution, supported by many Oxford and Cambridge dons including Dobb and Lowes Dickinson, had favored closer relations. In 1929 the SCR sent a circular letter to British businessmen stating that "one of the objects of the Society is to facilitate a knowledge of scientific and technical developments."[25]

The Soviets made special efforts to develop the Cambridge branch of the SCR. The strictly "cultural" side of activity consisted of an exhibition of Russian drawings, although the SCR planned to support the Workers' Educational Association (WEA), which held a world conference in Cambridge in 1929. The WEA was set up to provide a channel for bringing the benefits of higher education to the less privileged members of society. Although not itself a front organization, its lecture programs were used by Marxist academics like Dobb to proselytize among the working class and trade unions. Dobb was not only a keen champion of the WEA but himself a trade unionist. While researching at the London School of Economics after graduating from Cambridge in 1922, Dobb became a founding participant in the "nucleus membership," of the original Communist cell of the National Union of Scientific Workers.

Counterintelligence officers were keeping a close watch on Dobb and his Cambridge associates. Monitoring by MI5 and Special Branch revealed a more sinister "cultural rapprochement," according to the evidence in the Home Office records. One area of particular concern, as we can now see, was Soviet film propaganda.

The Special Branch file titled "The Cambridge Film Society" provides a tantalizing glimpse of the extent of surveillance mounted on one specific area of the Cambridge Communist network's activities. The Scotland Yard files reveal that neither Special Branch nor MI5 had dropped its guard after the expulsion of the Arcos mission and the Soviet delegation to Britain. In fact, surveillance and monitoring of mail to organizations like SCR and individuals such as Dobb had uncovered a new area of Comintern propaganda activity.

Just six months after the Arcos raid, Special Branch intercepted a "Yours fraternally" letter from Willi Münzenberg inviting the Honorable Ivor Montagu to a November conference in Berlin to organize the production and distribution of "proletarian films and letting them out of bourgeois film-theaters."[26]

Lenin himself had decided that "of all the arts, for us the cinema is the most important." In 1919 D. W. Griffith's silent masterpiece *Intolerance* had made such a deep impression on the Soviet leader that Russian filmmakers Vsevolod Pudovkin and Sergei Eisenstein were soon turning out powerful cinematographic revolutionary films such as *The Mother* and *Strike*. Münzenberg, the Comintern's mastermind of front organizations, saw the potential of using these movies to appeal to both intellectuals and the masses. Western governments also appreciated the propaganda power of the Soviet cinema, and Britain attempted to ban the import and public showing of these movies. But Münzenberg devised a scheme to use the front organizations he was operating from Berlin, under the banner of the International Workers Relief, to arrange for the clandestine distribution of films.[27]

Ivor Montagu, a member of the immediate postwar generation of Cambridge Communists, was already running Comintern front organizations. Montagu was a younger son of a Liberal peer and banker, Lord Swaythling. Educated at Westminster School, where he claimed to have become a socialist before attending the Royal College of Science, he went on to King's College, Cambridge. After graduating in 1925 he turned his hand to left-wing journalism and became interested in filmmaking. Special Branch identified his participation in a number of Communist causes, including his directorship of the Film Society in 1924.

A Special Branch report, obviously based on intercepted mail, indicated that Montagu had invoked the aid of the Russian Trade Delegation and a number of leading British Communists such as Page Arnot "in

pressing the claims of his Society on Sovkino, the Central Cinemato-
graph Section in Moscow." Montagu's proposal was that the Russian
films which had been "refused on the score of politics" would be
imported privately to avoid censorship, "titled in English at their own
expense," and then "passed on to other people, Society of Cultural
Relations, etc." to "make them generally known." The list of Soviet
films on the Home Secretary's proscribed list included Eisenstein's *The
Armoured Cruiser Potemkin*, which the British Board of Film Censors
refused to certificate in 1926 on the ground that "it dealt with mutiny
against properly constituted authority" and "depicted scenes showing
the armed forces firing on the civil population."[28]

Customs officers had been alerted to look out for the banned Soviet
films, and police warrants for the seizure of fourteen titles had been
issued. Captain Guy Liddell, acting on information MI5 passed on of
a Soviet scheme to flood Britain with Soviet films smuggled into the
country from the Irish Free State, asked the police to extend "existing
arrangements" to west-coast ports. The list included pure propaganda
titles, such as *Communist International and Young Communist International
Congress*, along with *Potemkin* and Pudovkin's *The Mother*, which are now
accepted as masterpieces of cinematographic art. But the revolutionary
imagery of Pudovkin's screen version of Maxim Gorki's harrowing saga
of a mother's violent conflict with tsarist oppression had resulted in its
exhibition being banned in New York. The incandescent passion in *The
Mother* reaches a climax when the peasant woman, having witnessed her
son's murder by the police, raised the Red Flag before the thundering
hooves of an imperial cavalry charge in the 1905 St. Petersburg
uprising.[29]

"That they are of high technical merit is undoubted. Pudovkin, the
producer of many of them, is in a class apart," noted a critically attuned
British Home Office official, "but that is not the only criterion. The films
are *clearly propagandist* in character and if publicly exhibited are *quite likely
to lead to disorder*." The secret Special Branch reports, however, reveal that
the concern was not so much with the supposedly inflammatory nature of
the films, as with the widening Soviet infiltration and subversion of which
these two films were only the most prominent examples.[30]

Intercepted mail to the London office of the Friends of Soviet Russia
exposed the extent of the scheme cooked up by Münzenberg (who was
described in the report as "the notorious Communist, who presides in
Berlin on behalf of Moscow over the doings of the League against
Imperialism and the Friends of Soviet Russia"). Pudovkin came to
Britain at Montagu's invitation to speak at a private viewing at the Film

Society of *The End of St. Petersburg*. This screening of a film whose public showing was banned had prompted angry questions from Conservatives in the House of Commons.

Another report concerned Emil Burns, a 1922 Cambridge graduate, who was the London branch secretary of the Friends of Soviet Russia. Münzenberg's February 18, 1929, letter to Burns evidently caused the British authorities some concern. The secretary of the Friends of Soviet Russia was requested to report to Berlin the following week for a meeting on "a whole lot of political and personal questions . . . which must however be taken up between us personally and verbally." Münzenberg's caution in not committing the agenda to paper suggests that he was probably aware — either by suspicion or information — that the British authorities were intercepting his letters. Not until November did MI5 issue a report on the latest move in the Comintern's cinema offensive: the setting up of the Federation of Workers Film Society British branch. As with all Moscow's front organizations, its ample council included eight "professed communists." Among the party stalwarts were Maurice Dobb, Emil Burns, Harry Pollitt, and Willi Gallacher. The report noted "the great majority of the remainder being active in almost the same sense."[31]

Some idea of the extent of MI5 interest and Special Branch surveillance of leading British academic Communists in the late twenties — particularly of those at Cambridge — emerges in the Special Branch reports on the showing of Russian films in the university that same year. Letters intercepted before delivery to Montagu alerted MI5 and Special Branch that an undergraduate named G. Moxon and a left-wing fellow of St. John's College, Dennis Arundell, had set up a Film Society based in King's in November 1928 to "show film privately in a local cinema on Sundays." The local Cambridge police were "discreetly" instructed to investigate.[32]

A letter to Montagu two months later revealed that Dobb, who had met Pudovkin in London, was making arrangements with a local supporter named Poynter to hire a projector to show *The Mother* at Malting House School. On investigation, Special Branch detectives learned that a final-year undergraduate at Clare, a left-wing socialist named P. A. Sloan, had been present at Pudovkin's London Film Society lecture and was helping Dobb make arrangements to have Pudovkin's masterpiece screened at Cambridge.[33]

"There is a great deal of interest being shown in the prospects of the film," Dobb wrote to Montagu on February 16, inviting him to give the introductory lecture at the March 9 showing. He suggested hiring a local musician, as "some form of musical accompaniment would be preferable to the rather irksome ticking of the projector." Dobb had easily raised the twenty pounds necessary to cover the costs, thereby making it a private "invitation only" affair to forestall action by the police. Calculating that the home secretary would be reluctant to obtain a warrant to stop a genuinely private viewing, Special Branch efforts to thwart Dobb and his friends came to naught. They waited until March 23 before alerting the chief constable of Cambridge, advising of the need to "be careful to hide the source of our information."[34]

The Special Branch reluctance to prejudice its sources of information, even in this relatively minor operation, is a pointer to the extent of the efforts then under way against the Comintern and its agents. The file on the Cambridge Film Society is the only such group of MI5 records so far released. Only one of the three sets of files indicated on the docket has been declassified — a decision that probably reflects the lack of bureaucratic concern for "Disturbance of Entertainments," as the entry is headed, as a possible source of disclosure of Home Office secret information to future historians.

This Special Branch file, which must be representative of other more weighty operations, is an important indicator of the true extent of British counterintelligence operations. It reveals not only that the mail of known British Communists was being regularly intercepted but also that particular attention was being paid to the Cambridge circuit of Comintern sympathizers.

The myth has been perpetrated by Blunt and others that Soviet recruitment at Cambridge did not start in earnest until the mid-thirties. It has even been asserted that MI5 and Special Branch were slow in following up the evidence of a growing network of friends and supporters of the Comintern among university dons.[35]

Yet those MI5 reports and Special Branch memoranda that have come to light in the course of research for this book do not justify this view. For example, a Cambridge graduate named Philip Spratt had been arrested at Meerut in 1929 and charged with leading a conspiracy of Communists in India. As a result, throughout the thirties MI5 sent the Indian police the Special Branch dossiers on Oxford and Cambridge graduates with Communist associations who went out to the Far East.[36]

The records of secret liaison meetings between Special Branch officers and their contacts at the U.S. embassy in London just do not support the promoted view that the British intelligence services turned a blind eye to Comintern agents operating in Cambridge — or elsewhere in Britain — during Anthony Blunt's undergraduate years.

CHAPTER 9

# "You Can Hang Them
# or Burn Them Alive —
# If You Can Catch Them!"

Reports from MI5 still bearing their old secret classification show that, following the raid on Arcos, the security service, far from ignoring Soviet subversion in England, increased its nationwide surveillance. The expulsion of Soviet diplomats in 1927 had been a setback for the Comintern's British operations, but the British authorities did not drop their guard.

Countering Russian subversion had certainly become more difficult after MI5 and Special Branch lost the advantage of eavesdropping on Moscow's communications with the Soviet embassy. But the Russian Trade Delegation, much reduced in numbers, continued to maintain a small presence in London. Within months the diplomats who had been expelled from London began to reappear in various Western European capitals. The Soviet embassy in Berlin, for example, was much expanded. Strong Soviet influences were at work in the Weimar Republic, as the German government's former antipathy toward the Soviets faded and the secret codicils of the Rapallo Treaty of 1922 cleared the way for German soldiers to train with the Red Army.

Berlin became the site of a growing number of Soviet facilities. These included centers for the fabrication of documents and altering of passports. Large printing establishments were set up, as well as safe houses for agent training and commercial companies used as fronts. To control the Berlin center and coordinate its extensive non-German activities, Moscow gave increased decision-making authority to its local representatives. Berlin was soon the communications center not only for OGPU but also for Comintern-front activity.

Propaganda and subversion after 1927 were directed through a system of sympathizers and couriers recruited by mushrooming front organizations. The League Against Imperialism and International Workers Relief were based in Berlin. So were the Russian Red Cross, the Friends of the Soviet Union, and the Society for Cultural Relations.

Wrapping political subversion and propaganda in the trappings of cultural or humanitarian objectives proved a favorite strategy of the Kremlin. Many British public figures, not just established left-wing intellectuals, became unwitting allies of the Comintern. By agreeing to lend their names as members of worthy committees, they endowed an organization like the Society for Cultural Relations with a cloak of respectability and authenticity. It is now clear that it was a nine-page Secret British report of 1929 that alerted the Americans to the central subversive role of VOKS, the Russian acronym for the Society for the Promotion of Cultural Relations abroad, that is, SCR. The nominal head of the British SCR was Margaret Llewelyn Davies, a radical matriarch of one of Cambridge's leading academic families. Through her efforts distinguished visitors such as John Maynard Keynes, H. G. Wells, and Bernard Shaw were persuaded to make the trip to the Soviet Union, the "bait" of VIP reception with free travel and accommodation.[1]

Just as in Britain, when Arcos had been the nerve center for much of Moscow's clandestine activity, so the Berlin trade mission called Westorg assumed a new importance in 1927. The trade representatives launched an aggressive recruitment program among the foreign embassies, telephoning low-paid clerks and messengers and asking them out to dinner. Those from the U.S. embassy who accepted the invitation usually were met by a "Mr. Poull," who proceeded to offer the clerk a monthly salary of $300 with an extra $100 for expenses. In exchange for these payments — a princely sum in Germany at the time — the clerk provided access to the contents of the U.S. embassy's diplomatic pouch for a brief time prior to its dispatch. Germany was also the field headquarters for the massive Soviet maritime operation, which had infiltrated crews of all nationalities. Thus Moscow's center in Berlin had an extensive network of couriers and agents who were able to move easily from port to port and country to country under cover of their seamen's papers.

To meet the increased threat from the Soviets, the British made more and more requests for confidential American assistance in tracking down suspected Comintern and OGPU operatives. The British complained that English-speaking agents acting under cover of Amtorg, the Soviet-American trading company, entered the United States with "false passports prepared and issued in Moscow." The U.S. State Department rejected this charge. Amtorg visas were subjected to special scrutiny; but State did concede "the possibility of Soviet agents (not posing as Amtorg representatives) fraudulently securing quota visas." The extent of the Soviet illegal operation was uncovered the following year when a naturalized U.S. citizen, Jacob Kreitz, was arrested, ostensibly on a watch-smuggling charge. Customs officials found he was carrying a leather-bound book containing the names of sixty-five Soviet agents operating in the United States, China, and Japan. He also had a supply of signed American baptismal certificates, birth certificates, passport applications, and other documents.[2]

The records reveal that the U.S. embassy in London was being provided, on a regular basis, with copies of telegrams in both plaintext and cipher, which MI5 had intercepted between Comintern headquarters in Moscow and the New York secretariat. In one instance, the British, by mistake, actually passed on a photostat of the front page of a telegraph company's file copy of a February 12, 1929, message from "LCO Wolfe" in New York to "LUX" in Moscow. "You will notice that this cable was sent on the northern route," the U.S. embassy pointed out in a cover memo to Washington, drawing attention to the implication that U.S. traffic was also being similarly intercepted. The memorandum pointed out that "no doubt Washington would be interested to know that there is a [British] Government peace-time censorship on certain cable lines from America to Europe."[3]

Interception of telegrams and mail was still MI5's most reliable source of information on the Comintern. The northern route, which relayed transatlantic cable traffic through Britain to Europe, was especially useful in monitoring communications to and from the Netherlands. The Hague had become another center of Soviet efforts to infiltrate Soviet intelligence agents into Britain. These were principally "illegals" who used forged passports and identities to pose as residents. Confirmation of The Hague's strategic importance was later provided by Walter Krivitsky, a high-level Soviet intelligence official who defected through France in 1937. In the late twenties and early thirties Krivitsky was a rising young officer with the Third Setion of Soviet Military Intelligence, which worked alongside the OGPU with the European "illegals and with the Communist international."

Krivitsky may not have been the chief of Soviet Military Intelligence for Western Europe, but he was one of the most highly placed Soviets ever to defect. Too highly placed, it seems, for the comfort of Stalin. On February 10, 1941, he was found by the chambermaid in the bedroom of a seedy Washington hotel. Three apparent suicide notes on the bedside table, plus a lack of suspects, led the D.C. police department to conclude that Krivitsky had taken his own life. It is now suspected that Stalin's emissaries were responsible for eliminating Krivitsky.[4]

In 1939, when Krivitsky was interviewed by British intelligence, he charged that Moscow had managed to infiltrate the Foreign Office. Unfortunately, most of his information was intriguingly imprecise, gathered from documents he remembered seeing in Moscow many years earlier. These referred to a Soviet agent "from a good family" in the

British diplomatic service: It was eleven years before this Soviet spy was identified as Donald Maclean. So much has been made of this *ex post facto* discovery that the significance of other concrete evidence Krivitsky provided has been overlooked. The former Soviet spymaster also identified two low-level Foreign Office spies who had been recruited long before Donald Maclean. They were both cipher clerks. John Herbert King was quickly identified, and in 1939 secretly tried and convicted. The other spy could not be brought to justice. He had been dead for six years. The official verdict at the time was suicide, but now it appears he, too, was a victim of the sinister skills of the OGPU's Operations Division. The British have *never* officially identified this second Soviet spy, but the evidence shows he was Ernest Holloway Oldham. Disgruntled over his failure to obtain a pay raise in 1929, Oldham had gone to the Soviet embassy in Paris to offer information on British codes. Oldham provided a double bonus for Moscow when he persuaded his colleague Captain King to join his treachery.[5]

King, as we now know, proved to be the more damaging long-term agent. The pressure of spying soon weighed too heavily on Oldham. He broke off his communications with the Russians after resigning from his Foreign Office post in September 1932. Twelve months later, he was found unconscious in the gas-filled kitchen of his Pembroke Gardens flat and pronounced dead on arrival at nearby St. Mary Abbot's hospital. Oldham's convenient death bought Soviet intelligence seven additional years of King's tapping of Foreign Office code and traffic.[6]

The coroner's verdict was that Oldham had taken his life by "coal gas suffocation" while of "unsound mind." But a favorite OGPU saying in the thirties was: "Anyone can commit murder but it takes an artist to commit a suicide." This seems especially appropriate in the Oldham case, a fact that had never been officially admitted by the British government. Not until 1945 did the British learn, from the Dutch intelligence service, that Oldham had been run by Hans Gallieni, an OGPU illegal, who operated from Holland. The information came from an associate on the same underground circuit, Hans Pieck, who defected after World War II. Pieck had been introduced to the Oldhams in the thirties by Gallieni and MI5 arranged in October 1945 that he should come over to London to help Mrs. Oldham identify Gallieni. The day before the meeting was due to take place, she was suddenly taken ill and died before identification could be made.[7]

Oldham and the other Soviet spies in the Foreign Office code room were run by an OGPU illegal operating from Europe and not by the British Comintern chief. After Arcos, the Soviet intelligence services were having to be far more careful of the threat posed by MI5 and Special Branch. The resident Comintern agent in Britain until 1929 was a bulbous-nosed Ukrainian with protruding ears. His name was A. D. Pestrovsky, but he used the English alias A. J. Bennet. He had married Rose Cohen, an English Communist, and his mission was not to recruit agents but bring the Communist party of Great Britain under Moscow's full control. This required "cleansing the party of all right wing and conciliating tendencies" and engineering the removal of the independent-minded Andrew Rothenstein from the party's central committee. Pestrovsky then secured the authority of Moscow loyalists Clemens Palme Dutt and Harry Pollitt over the CPGB. These *apparatchiky* remained in control of the British party for the next twenty years.[8]

Pestrovsky demonstrated no less acumen in infiltrating the Conservative party, helped by an equally unscrupulous manipulator named Arthur Maundy Gregory. A homosexual wheeler-dealer, Gregory had made a fortune on commissions from brokering the sale of dukedoms, peerages, and honors to replenish Liberal party coffers during Lloyd George's postwar coalition administration. He remained untouched by a scandal in 1922 that resulted in changes in the law making it illegal to purchase titles by contributing to party funds.

A mere act of Parliament, however, was no obstacle to Maundy Gregory. This Oxford-educated son of a Southampton clergyman impressed the honors-hungry rich with an elaborate charade of extensive establishment connections. As publisher of the *Westminster Gazette* and proprietor of London's fashionably plush Ambassadors' Club, Gregory had both the facade and the facilities for continuing his profitable role as a middleman for the buying and selling of knighthoods or baronetcies. Nor was Sir John Davidson, the Conservative party chairman, above turning a blind eye to the law when it came to arranging substantial donations to Conservative party coffers.[9]

The potential for an explosive scandal increased, however, when Gregory began hiking his already steep commissions. His greed, evidently, finally persuaded the prime minister to act. Baldwin did not turn to the police or to the Secret Service but to Davidson, his trusted party chairman and adviser on the security services. Their strategy was simple and effective. A spy was infiltrated into Gregory's organization to obtain a list of his clients, all of whom were then excluded from the honors list.[10]

According to a cryptic footnote in Davidson's official biography, the "task of penetrating the Gregory organization was undertaken by A. J. Bennett." But the Tory M.P. for Nottingham, Albert James Bennett, whom Davidson had appointed assistant treasurer of the Conservative party in 1927, could not have carried out the operation alone. Robert Rhodes James, Davidson's biographer and the Tory M.P. for Cambridge, noted that "at Davidson's particular request" Bennett had "endeavored to conceal the identities of all individuals involved."[11]

The real reason for such high-level discretion emerges in a secret note that has come to light in Davidson's confidential papers. This reveals that in addition to A. J. Bennett, Davidson had enlisted the aid of Pestrovsky (Bennet) in his secret schemes.

Bennet/Pestrovsky gained access through his Comintern ties to Vladimir Bogovout-Kolomitzev, a former merchant from Odessa who became a go-between in back-channel commercial negotiations with prominent Conservative businessmen hoping to do a deal with Moscow. Bogovout had set himself up as a business entrepreneur with the profits of a loaded freighter on which he had escaped in 1917 to Constantinople. In 1922 he launched his Union for the Return of the Fatherland in Bulgaria, an organization that provided him with impeccable anti-Bolshevik credentials. But like the Hammers, Bogovout-Kolomitzev was a shrewd businessman who saw the opportunity for amassing personal wealth by facilitating Soviet trade with the West. His ambition was helped by his friendship with Leonid Krassin, Stalin's commissar for foreign trade, who let him in on a deal with the French bank used to finance the Soviet oil-export syndicate Smenovekhovets.[12]

This outwardly White Russian financier entered into a secret partnership with the OGPU, a fact known and publicized by the anti-Bolshevik émigré leaders in Paris. Bogovout managed to keep one step ahead of the French police, who were tipped off to his extensive Soviet connections. After the expulsion of the Arcos trade delegation from London, Bogovout-Kolomitzev became one of the go-betweens through whom Moscow sought to reestablish direct links with British industrialists willing to trade with the Soviet Union.

Among the prominent Tory businessmen who courted the assistance of Bogovout in the belief that they could trust a White Russian were Major Hugh Kindersly (later a director of the Bank of England), Sir Arthur Balfour, and the industrialist Ernest Remnant. Confidential information obtained from a Swiss source by author Richard Deacon suggests that a subsidiary role was played in these back-channel dealings with Moscow by Sir Arthur Pigou. This left-wing Cambridge economist had maintained his links with prewar Russian revolutionary contacts in Geneva.[13]

"While the idea was Pigou's, the names he gave us were simply those of suggested targets and the businessmen had no idea that Pigou had suggested them," this former member of the Soviet network, identified by the code name "Roger," told Deacon. "They were unconscious puppets strung along by Pigou, Bessedovsky, and Bogovout-Kolomitzev."[14]

Bogovout accompanied the British Industry Delegation to Moscow in 1929 (a trip made with the approval of Prime Minister Baldwin and his adviser J. C. C. Davidson) to discuss possible investment in a wide range of big industrial deals including oil drilling, construction of canals, and the building of the Moscow subway project. But none of the promised Soviet construction contracts materialized.

Bessedovsky, the acting Soviet chargé d'affaires in Paris, played a central role in the secret commercial negotiations with the British before his headline-making leap to freedom over the embassy wall in 1929. Although he provided valuable information to the British and French, he later cast his lot back with the Soviets by becoming Bogovout's business partner.

It was the role that Pestrovsky played as contact man with Bessedovsky and the secret commercial wheeling and dealing that proved an unexpected ticket of admission into the skeleton-packed closets of the Tory party. Evidence that Pestrovsky became a part of Davidson's plot to rid the Conservative party of the tiresome Maundy Gregory appears in Davidson's memorandum of November 28, 1929. There he emphasizes: "For his eyes only spell out the informant as either A. J. Bennett or A. J. Bennet, *taking great care to get the spelling of the surname correct* according to which one of the two it refers." Davidson, as Tory party chairman, took this decision because "it would be less likely to arouse comment than the use of any code name." That Bennet was indeed Pestrovsky is evident because "the same method of reference is currently being used in communications with Balfour, Remnant and Bogovout-Kolomitzev in Paris."[15]

Why did the Conservative chairman, of all people, turn to Moscow's man in London to help rid the party of Maundy Gregory's predations? Evidently Pestrovsky already possessed the information on the honors racket Davidson and Bennett needed because Soviet intelligence had been keeping tabs on Gregory ever since his leadership of the Free Ukraine campaign began in the early 1920s. Pestrovsky had succeeded in penetrating Maundy Gregory's organization and in learning of his homosexual connections in the political and Whitehall establishment. Among them were the intimate friends of Eddie Marsh and a number of leading Tory M.P.s. The potential for an explosive sexual scandal is why Davidson sought to neutralize Maundy Gregory. Moscow also saw the chance to kill two birds with a single stone. Not only did Soviet intelligence acquire useful blackmail information on the homosexual network, but with Maundy Gregory out of business, funding for the Free Ukraine campaign would dry up.[16]

Yet the best efforts of Pestrovsky and Davidson did not quite succeed in neutralizing Maundy Gregory. He persisted until 1933, when he was charged with trying to sell an honor to a naval officer. Even then, Davidson "brought pressure to bear on the authorities" to enable Gregory to plead guilty and retire to France on a comfortable pension after serving a brief prison sentence. Such plea-bargaining was unprecedented under English law. But Tories feared that Maundy Gregory would carry out his threats to implicate highly placed homosexuals. In addition, there was the danger that a prolonged trial might reveal the role played in the affair by Soviet intelligence. In fact, that appears to have been the greater concern. It was no coincidence that Maundy Gregory was not brought to book until four years after Bessedovsky's defection resulted in Pestrovsky's hurried return to Moscow at the end of 1929.

These clandestine channels of Soviet influence and disinformation to the British party, the sworn enemy of Bolshevism, survived the political crisis of 1929, when Baldwin and the Tories were defeated in a June election. The incoming minority Labour government formed by Ramsay MacDonald with Liberal acquiescence also brought the Soviets a bonus. Britain's second Labour Cabinet voted to restore Anglo-Soviet diplomatic relations in October 1929, the very same month that Wall Street stock prices crashed.[17]

This dramatic harbinger of the Great Depression was portrayed by Comintern propagandists as the beginning of final collapse of capitalism as prophesied by Marx. To the Communist party of Great Britain and its Marxist sympathizers, the financial shock waves were taken as a sure sign that capitalism was collapsing and that the new decade would usher in the long-awaited communist millennium. The Comintern issued instructions to step up propaganda and infiltration in British army camps and naval bases.

British security officials knew they were now facing a much greater threat. Even before the first members of the new Soviet delegation arrived in London to reopen the shuttered embassy in Chesham Place, both MI5 and the Metropolitan Police Special Branch faced the challenge of increased Soviet subversion. Unfortunately, their separately controlled organizations were short of manpower and resources.

"Communist efforts to tamper with H.M. Forces has increased and is still increasing," MI5 reported in February 1930, warning that these efforts, "if allowed to spread unchecked, will, in the long run prove disastrous to the Forces as a whole." These fears came dangerously close to materializing the following year, when the unity of the Labour Cabinet crumbled in the face of a severe fiscal crisis. Prime Minister Ramsay MacDonald and two ministers who supported his demand for massive cuts in government and service expenditures joined the Conservatives and Liberals to form an emergency national government. One of their first steps was to cut servicemen's pay. News of these cuts was met by a wave of protest among the sailors of some warships of the Atlantic Fleet based on the west coast of Scotland.[18]

INVERGORDON MUTINY was how the newspapers headlined what was in reality a minor and quickly suppressed revolt. But it rocked the Royal Navy. For the first time there was real alarm about the political threat to the empire's front line of defense. The right-wing press and parliamentarians reacted with a "Red Scare" outcry. The CPGB and the few Communists among the mutineers were slow off the mark and restricted to a belated agitation after the handful of ringleaders had been arrested. More important, the mutiny panicked foreign bankers.

After there had been a crippling run on the pound, the British government did what it had vowed never to do — it abandoned the gold standard. The economy reeled from the double blow. In a mood of high crisis, Ramsay MacDonald with Baldwin as his deputy appealed to the electorate to support the national government. The national government won a landslide majority in the October 1931 election, flooding the House with Tory supporters. The Labour party, deserted by its former prime minister, was cut back to a parliamentary rump. Despairing socialists began paying attention to the siren song of Communist propaganda.

In the wake of the Invergordon Mutiny, the Conservative-dominated national government had resolved to combine fiscal expediency with the need to increase internal security. The task of monitoring civil and military subversion was once and for all united, and MI5 was given responsibility for investigations "dealing with the Communist and foreign revolutionary movements." Captain Liddell and his Central Registry files came under new management. Scotland Yard's Special Branch continued to carry out the actual investigations on MI5's behalf, only now the Yard was directed by a unified organization, which, for the first time, could properly be described as Britain's "security service."[19]

General Kell's newly united forces did not underestimate the dimension of the new tactics of subversion being launched by Moscow. They knew that the OGPU had grown to be a vast empire within the Soviet state. It controlled the military forces guarding the Soviet Union's frontiers, plus the extensive prison system and labor camps. The Fifth Section of the OGPU Intelligence Division ran intelligence gathering and counterintelligence with the assistance of the Foreign Division. "Moscow Center," as it became known, controlled one of the most important organs of power and control in the Soviet Union. The twenty-five hundred OGPU officers at Moscow headquarters occupied "the whole district between the Lubianka and Srietenka." This was an area of several square blocks centering on the notorious prison complex in the heart of the Soviet capital.[20]

No one in the relatively tiny MI5 Cromwell Road headquarters, which was Britain's front-line command post in the secret war, can have underestimated the magnitude of the threat posed by the Soviet Union. But it is less certain whether they fully appreciated the threat developing within Oxford and Cambridge, the universities charged with grooming future proconsuls of the British Empire. The Soviets had developed an ambitious long-range plan to infiltrate Britain's governing classes by recruiting high-flying undergraduate Communist sympathizers as moles who would burrow their way up into the Establishment. A scheme that must rank with the Trojan horse as one of the most devious and successful stratagems of intelligence history.

The origins of this strategy were rooted in the important organizational change in the Communist intelligence apparatus that occurred after the 1927 Arcos raid. The Soviets had learned that the exposure of one spy ring must never again lead to their embassy. Safety measures were introduced by Mikhail Trilisser, the OGPU Foreign Division's founder and chief until 1930, who ordered his agents to build up an illegal *rezidentura*. The OGPU officers sent abroad to build up these secret networks no longer enjoyed diplomatic immunity. Armed with false passports, they concealed their Russian nationality by assuming the identity of a national in an occupation that could justify lengthy periods of residence in their assigned country of operation. These illegals were ordered to remain independent of the local embassy and Communist party. They established their own channels of communication with Moscow through mail drops, cutouts, and trusted couriers who were entirely separate from Comintern activities and the official diplomats.[21]

The *rezident* director of the Soviet underground in a foreign country ran his network of sources with the aid of two or more assistants, each of whom was an experienced staff officer from Moscow headquarters. They were the hard core of the illegal network or *apparat*, "close mouthed and on constant guard with almost everyone else." They operated through assistants who controlled two to five group leaders, most of whom were trained and trusted former members of the national Communist party. Their job was to maintain contact with the informants, known as "sources."[22]

The principal mission of the *apparat* was to recruit both high- and low-level government employees who were in a position to learn state secrets or otherwise aid the Soviet cause. Sources were rated according to three ascending categories. The *stukach*, or lowest grade of informers, were usually low-level government officials who provided information for pay. The *agent vliyaniya* (agent of influence) were reliable sources in foreign governments, business, the media, or academic institutions who did not spy for money. They were usually Communists or Marxist sympathizers who saw it as their duty to provide assistance to further the goals of the great socialist revolution. The *agent vliyaniya* have often been categorized as "fellow travelers," who declined official party membership to protect their careers or because they were not committed Communists. In the context of Cambridge, the *agent vliyaniya* could include either open Communists like Maurice Dobb or sympathizers like Arthur Pigou. In the American context, they were U.S. State Department officials in the Far East section who facilitated the growth of communism in Asia after World War II. *Agent vliyaniya* are regarded as being so pro-Soviet that their files in Moscow headquarters carry the stamp *nash* — literally "ours" — a term Soviet intelligence usually reserves for full-fledged agents.

The infiltration, or penetration, agents like Oldham and King, Blunt and Philby, were recruited under discipline and controlled by a Soviet intelligence service officer who was either an embassy legal or an illegal *rezident*. After the mid-twenties it was the exception for Comintern officials to be involved in running the agents, who, according to one Soviet defector consulted, were known as *proniknoveniye*.

Trotsky's expulsion from the Soviet Union in 1929 provided the OGPU Foreign Division with an additional reason to expand the underground tentacles of its overseas networks: Stalin increasingly relied on the OGPU to monitor the exile, who remained a potential focus of opposition. Until he was confident enough to order the elimination of his erstwhile rival, Stalin's suspicion fired his determination to be master of his own intelligence network.

Distrustful of the judgment of his subordinates, Stalin repeatedly warned his intelligence chiefs against "equations with many unknowns." He constantly urged them to acquire as many informants as possible to provide him with secrets obtained from locked dispatch boxes, ciphered communications, and the classified files of foreign governments. Stalin's obsession imposed a special mind-set on the KGB. Unlike Western intelligence operations, which sift important intelligence data from the mass of information legitimately available in newspapers, scientific journals, and records of parliamentary debates, the Soviets subscribe to the theory that *razvedka* — true intelligence — can be obtained only surreptitiously. OGPU's Foreign Division was therefore devoted to acquiring secret informants, undercover agents, and stolen documentation, while the Special Division intercepted and deciphered foreign codes and ciphers in addition to guarding the security of Soviet communications systems.[23]

The sharpest insider description of Soviet intelligence during the early Stalin era was provided by Leon Feldbin, who used the name General Alexander Orlov when he defected to the United States in 1938. During the five years he served in the uppermost ranks of Soviet counter-intelligence in Moscow, Orlov was involved in preparing intelligence training manuals and drafting top-level briefs for Stalin. Hungry for stolen secrets about foes domestic and foreign, the Soviet dictator insisted on having personal access to raw data. "An intelligence hypothesis may become your hobbyhorse on which you will ride straight into a trap," Orlov records Stalin as saying. As one of the heads of Soviet intelligence, Orlov recalled Stalin's penchant for dismissing as "dangerous guesswork" the estimates of his intelligence chiefs. "Don't tell me what you think," Stalin would interject. "Give me the facts and the source."[24]

Stalin's lust for obtaining secret intelligence endowed OGPU and its "organs" with unrivaled power, and he stepped up the pressure to expand the penetration of foreign governments. The primary target was Britain — the main adversary, in Stalin's eyes — where after a decade of effort, the number of Soviet spies infiltrated into the government was still too small to produce truly important secrets. The Foreign Office secrets and ciphers supplied by Oldham and King had been valuable, to be sure, but Moscow knew that these code clerks had no prospects of ever rising to the upper echelons of the British government. The OGPU tried to help its low-level infiltrators attain promotions, but as Orlov recorded, "the results were spotty and far from satisfactory." Thus, the Soviets needed to find a way of inserting trusted agents into the highest echelons of Western governments. These agents would have to have the right social and professional qualifications to make their way in the British ruling establishment. Once they were in place, their rise could be facilitated by dispensing good advice, covering their expenses for off-hours entertainment of colleagues, and even exercising the influence of trusted *agent vliyaniya* informants.

Not until "the early 1930s" — according to Orlov's account — did one of his fellow chiefs in Soviet intelligence "hit upon an idea which solved this most difficult problem as if by magic." He succeeded, we learn from Orlov, "because he approached the problem not only as an intelligence man, but as a sociologist." The "magic" plan was based on "the fact that in capitalistic countries lucrative appointments and quick promotion are usually assured to young men who belong to the upper class." The obvious targets for Soviet recruitment were therefore the "sons of political leaders, high government officials, influential members of Parliament." In Britain as in most European societies, privileges often brought promotion, and as Orlov noted, "it does not surprise anyone if a young man of this background, fresh from college, passes the civil service examinations with the greatest of ease and is suddenly appointed private secretary to a cabinet member and in a few short years assistant to a member of the government."[25]

Orlov was and is regarded by the Americans as a highly authoritative source on Soviet intelligence operations. While there seems no reason to doubt Orlov's assertion that the OGPU was the architect of the scheme, it has been pointed out that the Soviet Foreign Ministry officials at the time included Litvinov, Rothstein, and Ivan Maisky, the polished counselor to the Soviet diplomatic mission in London who returned there as ambassador in 1932. These men certainly would have made their contributions to the scheme. They would have endorsed the feasibility of the strategy and confirmed that the network of educational privilege in Britain focused on Oxford and Cambridge.

The Soviet blueprint for penetrating British government institutions also owes something to the patience inherent in the Russian national character. Years would pass before the young British penetration agents recruited at university proved themselves. The Soviets would also have recognized the need to allow for spillage and corkage of their university vintage. For each Blunt or Philby, there were many more undergraduates who were approached, only to fall by the political wayside or fail to meet the career goals set by Moscow. But as Orlov pointed out, there was no shortage of potential recruits. The increasingly disaffected political climate of the thirties encouraged the acceptance by the younger generation of what he termed "libertarian theories."[26]

According to Orlov, the plan was put into operation "in the early 1930s." The OGPU ordered their *rezidentura* to look for under-graduates who were "tired of tedious life in the stifling atmosphere of their privileged class" and who were responsive to a libertarian appeal "to make the world safe from Fascism and abolishing the exploitation of many by man." The undergraduates spotted and cultivated as pen-etration agents were also discouraged from joining the Communist party. They were advised they could be much more useful as members of a revolutionary underground.[27]

"The idea of joining a 'secret society' held a strong appeal for the young people who dreamed of a better world and of heroic deeds," Orlov wrote. "These young men hardly regarded themselves as spies or intelligence agents." Nor was solicitation couched as a brash demand to work for communism or the Soviet Union. It was something far more subtle and seductive. Anthony Blunt characterized his own recruitment as an invitation to join an "International Movement." The appeal of participating in global power was also a powerful inducement to Kim Philby. "It is a matter of great pride to me," he wrote, "that I was invited, at so early an age, to play my infinitesimal part in building up that power."[28]

The secret of the Soviet strategy, as Orlov recognized, was the "sublime idea of making the world safe from the menace of Fascism." This proved a powerful lure to young intellectuals adrift in the cynical political wasteland of the interwar years. "By their mental makeup and outlook," they reminded Orlov of the anti-tsarist Decembrists of the nineteenth century. They also restored to the Soviet intelligence service something of the "true fervor of converts and the idealism which their intelligence chiefs had lost long ago." Such was the fervor and dedication of this new breed of *proniknoveniye* that Moscow Center no longer worried about promotions for their new recruits. These "came automatically," as Orlov noted. [29]

Orlov makes it clear that the Soviets appreciated the advantages of tapping into homosexual networks, whose fraternities guaranteed both secrecy and multiple recruiting opportunities. He also indicates how the lines were cast into other European universities, but conditions at "Oxbridge" were especially favorable for the Soviets. And although Tom Driberg, as we shall see, was not the only Communist agent to emerge from Oxford, Soviet intelligence had a stronger presence at Cambridge. Thanks to the Comintern, they had in place a network of senior members, of whom Dobb was the most active. The GRU had its own line into the Cavendish, and Moscow had the sympathetic attention and interest of Cambridge scientists such as Bernal and Haldane. The seeds of Marxism were beginning to sprout in the Society of the Apostles, helping foster a Marxist attitude among the elite undergraduate intellectuals.

Cambridge was therefore the obvious place for the Soviets to start selection of the first ideological recruits for their novel program of deep-cover penetration agents — the so-called moles.

# "We Talk Endlessly in the Society About Communism"

Anthony Blunt deliberately confused the trail that should have led to the heart of the enigma: when the Apostles became adherents of dialectical materialism, which they equated with Marxism.

"I became a Communist and more particularly a Marxist in, let us say, 1935–36," Blunt said with remarkable imprecision when confronted with that pertinent question at the opening of his press conference in November 1979. His choice of words suggests a deliberate attempt to fudge, because, as a professional historian, he appreciated the importance of precise dates when making attributions on paintings. Blunt, moreover, gave an excuse for becoming a Communist that was equally vague. Trying to convey the impression that he was an elderly gentleman more sinned against than sinning, he inisted that by 1934 "all my friends — that is, an enormous amount of my friends and almost all the bright young undergraduates who had come up to Cambridge — had suddenly become Marxists under the impact of Hitler coming to power." This was a carefully rehearsed alibi.[1]

In 1972, however, Blunt had previously told his Courtauld students that "Cambridge had literally been transformed overnight" by "the wave of Marxism." He claimed that "the undergraduates and graduate students were swept away by Marxism" and that "during the next three or four years almost every intelligent undergraduate who came up to Cambridge joined the Communist party some time during his first year."

That Blunt's alibi was accepted at face value by the media is surprising: that it has remained largely unquestioned over the years is extraordinary. Still more incredible is Peter Wright's revelation that Blunt's assertions about Marxism in Cambridge were not followed up, or seemingly even challenged, by MI5 investigators after he first gave, in 1963, his hollow excuse for becoming a Communist in his secret confession to the intelligence service.

The credibility of Blunt's assertions that he did not come under Marxist influence until five years after his graduation was, however, questioned by George Steiner. In "The Cleric of Treason," a penetrating analysis published in *The New Yorker* a year after Blunt's press conference, Professor Steiner concluded that it was likely Blunt "became actively interested in and sympathetic to Communism as an undergraduate at

Trinity college." A longtime Fellow of Churchill College at Cambridge, Steiner explained that he came to his conclusion after a great deal of thought and that his reasoning had nothing to do with simple politics.[2]

"Political logic," Steiner explained to me, "is not the most reliable guide to explain why certain intellectuals in the thirties allied themselves to the Communist cause." But Steiner's contention that Blunt must have become a Marxist many years earlier than the "official" version claimed caused a minor storm at the Cambridge high tables. The obvious inference — though Steiner was too scrupulous to say so himself — was that some dons found his rationale politically embarrassing. Why? Because they too had been youthful experimenters with the Marxist dialectic?

Steiner's conclusion that communism was embraced by Blunt and his circle of Apostles while they were still undergraduates in the late 1920s was based on the presumption that a fastidious intellectual such as Blunt could not have come either lightly or quickly to embrace the dogmatic precepts of Marxist-Leninism. One of Steiner's preoccupations was to try to rationalize the process by which someone with Blunt's highly tuned academic mind could become an "out-rider to Stalinism." There had to be a more convincing explanation for such "radical duplicity, the seeming schizophrenia, of the scholar-teacher of impeccable integrity and the professional deceiver and betrayer."[3]

Another Cambridge academic who questioned Blunt's veracity was Lord Noël Annan, an authority on Britain's "intellectual aristocracy" — a phrase he coined in a seminal essay on the subject. Blunt's excuse that he became a Marxist only because "almost all the intelligent and bright undergraduates" were Communists between 1933 and 1937 was dismissed by Lord Annan as "arrogant rubbish." Annan emphasized that he was among the vast majority of undergraduates who never felt any inclination to join the party — even though he had arrived at King's in 1935, the year that marked the crest of the Marxist tide. Not only did Annan reject Blunt's assertion that Cambridge intellectuals "suddenly became Marxists under the impact of Hitler's rise to power," he also pointed out that the actual percentage of card-carrying Communists in his undergraduate generation was "very small."[4]

Blunt's cover story was believed only by those who did not know any better, who accepted the popular myth about the Marxist takeover of Cambridge. Investigators from MI5, such as Peter Wright, had less excuse than the journalists for being taken in by Blunt's mythmaking. They, after all, had access to the secret Registry records that showed how few Communist party members there actually were at Cambridge in the 1930s. Their suspicions should also have been aroused by Blunt's claim that Marxism hit Cambridge in 1933 as an overnight phenomenon. From the MI5 reports that have now been discovered in the U.S. National Archives, it is evident that Special Branch had been monitoring the academic Marxists for more than a decade!

While Blunt was not an overt revolutionary activist, he was associated with dons like Roy Pascal, who were members of the university Communist cell. It is difficult to accept that inherently suspicious counterintelligence officers really accepted Blunt's assertion that he was apolitical merely because he disdained vulgar proletarian protest. Blunt's brand of Marxism may have been far removed from such revolutionary activity as joining street demonstrations, selling *The Daily Worker*, or hissing the national anthem in the town cinemas, but this did not make him any the less a Marxist. However, he was first and foremost an academic who, like many dons, regarded himself as a member of the high priesthood of the intelligentsia. For many of these people Marxism's appeal was its aura of scientific rationality. This offered the opportunity for conceptual dissection, an essentially intellectual exercise that could be used to demonstrate superior knowledge and insight. The need to demonstrate his intellectual superiority over lesser mortals was important to Anthony Blunt.

"Blunt was someone who loved achieving power over people and institutions," Annan told me. His conclusion was formed of Blunt before the war and confirmed in the early sixties when he was a member of the London University selection board who rejected Blunt's chosen candidate for the chair of Fine Arts and Architecture. He also recalled the intractable director of the Courtauld with whom he dealt as provost of University College, London. Annan believes that Blunt's espousal of Marxism was intimately linked to his need for personal power and influence — and suggests that it was this quest that ultimately led Blunt into espionage. Blunt's conversation, said Annan, was a "mixture of charm, mischief making, subtle denigration, and a way of inferring that individuals act from base self-interest, or class-inspired motives."[5]

The first step in his career of treachery was the successful effort of Blunt and his allies in the Apostles to exploit "investigative Marxism" to capture the society. Annan, as a historian member of Cambridge's secret brotherhood, spoke frankly of the need to lay to rest the myths that have grown up around the much-maligned society. "It's all so long ago," he said, conceding that the apostolic oath of secrecy was to blame for much of the wild speculation. Many extreme theories about the role of the Apostles as a Soviet recruiting ground and a homosexual playground have proliferated because surviving members from the thirties were old men whose dedication to secrecy left them hamstrung when it came to dealing with aggressive newspapermen. Annan assured me that his own investigation has shown that despite the society's preoccupation with the "higher sodomy" before World War I, by the thirties only a minority were homosexual. The majority, by contrast, "rather prided themselves on their successes with the girls at Newnham and Girton."[6]

Noël Annan has an engaging manner. No one can accuse him of fumbling when it comes to dealing with journalists. A round-voiced and energetic member of the House of Lords, he is no stranger to controversy, having made his reputation as one of Britain's most outspoken postwar educationalists. In pencil-stripe suit and French cuffs, Annan in his early seventies looks more like a Tory banker in his fifties than one of the pillars of Britain's liberal intellectual establishment. Nor is he reluctant — as other Apostles have been — to engage in a frank and revealing discussion of Blunt and his influence on the society. It was soon apparent that he is as anxious to set the record straight as he is intrigued by the anomalies thrown up by the new documentation uncovered in the course of research for this book.

During our conversations, Annan registered his greatest surprise when I told him about a 1933 letter written to Keynes by Lord Victor Rothschild, who was elected to the Apostles at the end of 1932.

"We talk endlessly in the Society about Communism which is rather dull," Rothschild complained to Keynes. "We need your presence." The hitherto accepted view that politics was never discussed in the society can now be rejected. Rothschild's letter makes it plain. that by late 1933, when this letter was written, Marxism had become a staple preoccupation of the Saturday evening meeting.[7]

The discovery of this letter and a comparison with the full membership rolls as reconstructed from the surviving Apostles' minute book enables the role the society played to be properly understood. It is clear that the Apostles *did* discuss Marxism in 1933. Furthermore, they began their discussions of dialectical materialism several years earlier. In fact, it is now possible to chart Blunt's leftward turn as starting in the late twenties. It was then, despite the better judgment of Keynes, that the Apostles were lured by the intellectual pursuit of Marxism. Observing that the tendency toward communism was particularly strong among those whose intellectual ability marked them out for potential membership, Keynes — according to his official biographer — "attributed it to a recrudescence of the strain of Puritanism in our blood, the zest to adopt a painful solution because of its painfulness."[8]

Annan confirms that Keynes was indeed powerless to prevent the "marxisant brethren," as he categorized those who "had been influenced by a Marxist vision of the world" from capturing the society. Reconstructed membership records provide evidence that the radical faction began infiltrating the membership the year before Blunt's election in the late spring of 1928 — and this infiltration continued until his departure from Cambridge in 1937.[9]

That Blunt himself was not elected to the society until two terms into his second year was — as Annan points out — an indication that his "birth," as the Apostles referred to the secretive canvassing process that preceded election, was not an easy one. Just as good looks and intelligence were prerequisites for the birth of new members in the decade before 1914, Annan believes that being a "marxisant" became a qualification — although not an exclusive one — for election in the decade between 1927 and 1937. But discovering precisely what impact Marxism had on the society, he contends, is crucial to explaining how Blunt became a member and how he and his associates took over.[10]

The evidence that points to Moscow's future success is exposed by the analysis of the twenty-six Apostles elected between 1927 and 1937 (see Chart below). No fewer than twenty of these Apostles, or 75 percent of them, are identifiable as left-wing socialists, Marxist sympathizers, Marxists, or committed Communists. Fourteen of them, or more than half of all the new elections in this decade, fit into the broad category that Annan defines as marxisants. Of these, nearly a third became open or secret Communists. This, in a student body that was no more than a fraction of one percent Marxist.

## THE CAMBRIDGE APOSTLES 1919–1939

| No. | Name | Papers | Elected | College | Politics* |
|-----|------|--------|---------|---------|-----------|
| 259 | Penrose, A. P. D. | 4 | 29/11/19 | King's | |
| 260 | Spicer, R. H. S. | 3 | 6/3/20 | King's | |
| 261 | Sprott, W. J. H. (62 Secretary) | ? | 30/11/20 | Clare | |
| 262 | Penrose, L. S. | 9 | 30/11/20 | St. John's | |
| 263 | Braithwaite, R. B. | 18 | 26/2/21 | King's | Left Wing |
| 264 | Ramsey, F. R. | 10 | 22/10/21 | Trinity | |
| 265 | Rylands, G. H. W. | 7 | 25/2/22 | King's | |
| 266 | *Thompson, G. D. (63S)* | *13* | *10/11/23* | *King's* | *Communist* |
| 267 | Harmer, F. E. (64S) | 7 | 24/1/25 | King's | |
| 268 | Watkins, A. R. D. | 5 | 24/10/25 | King's | Left Wing |
| 269 | Lucas, D. W. (65S) | 11 | 7/11/25 | King's | |

| No. | Name | Papers | Elected | College | Politics* | |
|-----|------|--------|---------|---------|-----------|---|
| 270 | Robertson, D. H. | 1 | 15/5/26 | Trinity | | |
| 271 | *Watson, A. G. D.* (66&68S) | 19 | 29/1/27 | *King's* | *Communist* | *Int. MI5†* |
| 272 | *Proctor, P. D.* | 3 | 22/10/27 | *King's* | *Socialist* | *Int. MI5* |
| 273 | Blunt, A. F. B. (67S) | 11 | 5/5/28 | Trinity | Communist | Confessed Spy |
| 274 | Bell, J. H. | 13 | 17/11/28 | King's | Marxisant | |
| 275 | Crusoe, F. J. A. | 1 | 3/6/29 | King's | | |
| 276 | Lintott, H. J. B. | 3 | 30/11/29 | King's | Socialist | |
| 277 | Champernowne, A. G. | ? | 30/11/29 | Trinity | | |
| 278 | *Cohen, A. B. (69S)* | ? | *8/11/30* | *Trinity* | *Marxisant* | |
| 279 | Sykes-Davies, H. | 6 | 16/1/32 | St. John's | Communist | |
| 280 | Llewelyn-Davies, R (70S) | 4 | 30/4/32 | Trinity | Marxist | Int. MI5† |
| 281 | *Burgess, G. de. M. (71S)* | ? | *12/11/32* | *Trinity* | *Communist* | *Confessed Spy* |
| 282 | Rothschild, Lord (72S) | 2 | 12/11/32 | Trinity | Socialist | |
| 283 | Walter, W. Grey (73S) | 2 | 25/11/33 | King's | Marxisant | Int. MI5† |
| 284 | Collio, H. O. J. | 2 | 26/10/34 | King's | | |
| 285 | Champernowne, D. G. (74S) | 2 | 30/11/34 | King's | | |
| 286 | Hodgkin, A. | 1 | 22/2/35 | Trinity | | |
| 287 | *Straight, M. S. (75S)* | | *8/3/36* | *Trinity* | *Communist* | *Confessed Spy* |
| 288 | Humphrey, J. H. | 0 | 6/3/87 | Trinity | Marxisant | |
| 288 | Waterlow, J. (76S) | ? | 6/3/37 | Trinity | Marxisant | |
| 290 | Croadsell, G. B. | 0 | 6/3/37 | Pembroke | Marxisant | |
| 291 | *Long, L. H.* | 2 | *15/5/37* | *Trinity* | *Communist* | *Confessed Spy* |
| 292 | *Astbury, J. P.* | ? | *5/6/37* | *Christ's* | *Communist* | *Int. MI5†* |
| 293 | Bosanquet, R. G. (77S) | ? | 16/10/37 | King's | | |
| 294 | Hodgart, M.(79S) | 4 | 16/10/37 | Pembroke | Marxisant | |
| 295 | Rawdon-Smith, A. F. | 1 | 7/11/37 | Peterhouse | Socialist | |
| 296 | Kisch, O. C. | 2 | 13/11/37 | Trinity | | |
| 297 | Prince, P. D. V. | 2 | 22/10/38 | King's | | |
| 298 | Mayor, A. | 1 | 1/11/38 | Trinity | Socialist | |
| 299 | Luce, J. M. | 1 | 10/2/39 | King's | | |
| 300 | Noyce, C. W. F. | 0 | 2/5/39 | King's | | |
| 301 | Hobsbawn, E. (78S) | 1 | 11/11/39 | King's | Marxisant | |
| 302 | Wallich, W. | 0 | 11/11/39 | King's | | |

*As far as can be determined from contemporaries and documented sources
† Based on MI5 Investigations
?Unknown how many papers delivered

For Marxism to have become such a potent force in the Apostles, it must have put down strong roots in the 1920s. Despite the popular myths, the historical reality is that neither Blunt nor Burgess was the initiator of this powerful surge toward communism. Blunt was not by himself a sufficiently persuasive ideologue, and Burgess was not elected until November 1932, when the wave had begun to crest.

A prime mover of Marxism in the Apostles emerges from the membership lists, and the subsequent record of his professional career, as being a contemporary of Blunt's from King's College: Alister Douglas Watson. And he was aided and abetted by a senior Apostle who was his mentor: George Derwent Thompson. A classical scholar in 1922, who became an Apostle in 1924 and a fellow of King's in 1927, Thompson nursed a "hatred of capitalism."

Thompson's Marxism deepened when he taught at Galway University. An "inspiring" teacher and editor of a two-volume edition of Aeschylus's *Orestia*, he left Cambridge in 1937 to be professor of Greek at Birmingham University — where he was the organizer for the Communist party for many years. Significantly, Birmingham, a center for industrial and scientific research, emerges from later MI5 reports as being second only to Cambridge as a haven for academic communism. Thompson's proselytizing before and during World War II helped ensure that Britain's premier "red-brick" university became a refuge for émigré physicist Klaus Fuchs as well as Alan Nunn May, both of whom were to supply atomic secrets to the Soviet Union. Thompson's *Marxism and Poetry* (1946) made him the best-known British classicist behind the Iron Curtain. He later had to resort to Czechoslovakian publishers to bring out new editions of his works on Aeschylus when Cambridge University Press declined to keep his works in print.[11]

From the time of his election to the society in 1923, Thompson's passionate support for the Sinn Feiners had been at the heart of his radical influence on his fellow Apostles. An Irish grandmother had persuaded him to study Gaelic as a boy, and he passed his dedication to Irish nationalism on to Watson, his apostolic protégé.

Thompson's support for Watson's native intelligence accounted for his surprisingly early election to the society, at the beginning of his second term in January 1927. Watson had first become acquainted with Blunt in their first-year maths lectures. At Winchester College, Watson was remembered as being an awkward youth, whose prominent forehead and jutting nose emphasized his penetrating gaze. Although Winchester traditionally prided itself on its respect for precise scholarship, Watson was perceived by his fellow Wykehamists as a "dim and retiring figure."[12]

This analysis proved to be wrong, and the story of Watson's career remains untold. His intellect flourished in the liberal hothouse of King's. Unlike Blunt, he took firsts in 1929 for both parts of the Mathematical Tripos. After winning a succession of graduate studentships, he was elected in 1933 to a King's fellowship. His fellowship expired at the same time that World War II started and he joined the Admiralty as a temporary scientific officer. The brilliance of his work on radar and engineering designs led to his postwar promotion as senior scientific officer and an appointment in 1953 to the Admiralty's Submarine Detection Research Establishment.[13]

Watson's research contributed to the development of low-frequency sonar that was of vital strategic importance to NATO's ability to track Russian submarines. His work continued through 1967. Then, four years after Blunt's secret confession, MI5 investigators dug into Watson's background and learned that not only had his Cambridge Marxism led to a lifelong secret commitment to the Communist party, but surveillance showed him currently making contacts with KGB agents in London. Intensive interrogations and offers of an immunity deal similar to Blunt's failed to produce a confession. His interrogators were convinced that he had been a long-term Soviet agent. But since there was no evidence on which to bring an espionage charge, Watson was quietly shunted to nonsecret work at the National Institute of Oceanography until he retired in 1972. Ten years later he died of a stroke, taking his secrets to the grave.[14]

The Apostles' records show that despite Watson's brilliance as a mathematician, he produced only two papers as a Fellow. His contemporaries believed that his eclectic mind diffused his intellectual energies too widely. He appears never to have overcome his schoolboy resentment and his rebellious political enthusiasm for an independent Ireland. This was reinforced by his friendship with the Llewelyn-Davieses, a Cambridge family with connections to the university's "intellectual aristocracy" and a reputation for political crusading.[15]

Crompton Llewelyn-Davies had been one of the late-Victorian radical Apostles. His Irish wife, Moya (a close friend of Thompson), had been arrested in 1916 for her fervent support of the Sinn Fein rebels, and it cost her husband his senior civil-service post. Like many other Irish nationalists after World War I, other family members found a fresh outlet for their radical enthusiasms in support for the Soviet Union. By 1924 Margaret Llewelyn-Davies was the national chairman of the Society for Cultural Relations.[16]

Just as Blunt's adolescent obsession with modern art appears to have embodied his early revolt against established authority, so Watson's adoption of the Sinn Fein cause appears to have been a convenient flag of youthful rebellion against the ascetic regime of Winchester College.

Watson also had the type of fertile mind that throve on argument. For a time he found an outlet for his quest in endlessly didactic discussions with fellow Apostle Ludwig Wittgenstein.

"Ludwig is beginning, I think, to persecute poor Alister a little," Keynes, ever the watchful guardian over the younger brethren, wrote in a 1929 letter. But the seeds of a more scientific rebellion were already planted in the fertile mind of "poor Alister." His restless intellect was increasingly focused on the works of Karl Marx, and he began attending the meetings of the Moral Sciences Society and the Heretics. This brought one of the brightest Cambridge mathematicians of his generation into contact with J. D. Bernal and his followers, who had already decided that the best hope of mankind lay with the "scientific" society emerging in the Soviet Union. Under the guise of "investigative Marxism," Watson quickly became the most articulate proselytizer of Marxist faith among the Apostles. "To be a dialectical materialist means to think of things and our ideas of them, not as static, rigid, eternal entities, but as changing, developing, interacting," Watson wrote in an incisive defense of the Marxist approach published in the 1934 *Cambridge Review*. He boldly praised "the tactics of Lenin, which have converted Marxism into the 'official philosophy' so much hated and scorned. . . ."[17]

"I learned my Marxist theory at Alister's feet," Blunt admitted to MI5 investigator Peter Wright in 1966. This acknowledgment would appear accurate, and Watson's success as a mathematician, compared to his own first-year failure, may explain why Blunt respected Watson's intellectual ability and became his willing disciple. Blunt was also drawn to Watson's wide-ranging intellectual curiosity and artistic sensibility. Watson was exceptionally well read and possessed a keen aesthetic sense. The King's College bathhouse, according to contemporary witnesses, frequently echoed to his recitals of large portions of Milton's *Paradise Lost*. Watson was not homosexual, but there is ample evidence that he and Blunt were very close intellectually. In 1928 Watson was given top billing in the first issue of *The Venture* for his essay challenging those in the establishment who scorned William Blake's philosophy. Blunt, too, was a devotee of Blake, who held a place second only to Poussin in his pantheon of aesthetic heroes.[18]

Under Watson's tutelage, Blunt seems to have concluded that Marxism offered a scientific justification for a much broader assault on the social, political, and aesthetic underpinnings of British society. Blunt had already become imbued with the intensely rationalist philosophy current in France, and it should not be overlooked that in the thirties Gide and other French writers proclaimed the continuity of a European intellectual tradition that descended from Descartes via Diderot to Marx.[19]

Traditionally France had prized her intelligentsia more highly than the British, but in the thirties the French intellectuals found themselves locked out of the councils of government, political parties, and even editorial offices. As a result, they unfavorably compared their own lack of status under capitalism to the supposedly important role given the intellectuals in Russia — for in the Soviet Union the arts had been declared an integral part of the socio-historical order of the Marxist dialectic. The frustration of the intellectuals turned many to communism, which provided moral justification for their vociferous attacks on bourgeois capitalism. Similarly, Blunt and Watson imposed on the Apostles their own brand of intellectual Marxism, which appears to have reflected the same ambitions and the same deep frustrations.

Watson supplied the radical political theories, Blunt exercised his talent for manipulative intrigue, and the pair of them set about restructuring the Apostles. They raised the banner of Marxism in defiance of a tired, self-indulgent Bloomsbury liberalism of the past. They enlisted the support of Julian Bell to seize control of the society through the traditional authority of the junior Apostle to vet embryos. Their object — at least initially — seems to have been to overturn the authority of the older members of the society. Marxism became the convenient vehicle of intellectual rebellion against the powerful hold that Keynes and his Bloomsbury friends still exercised.

Blunt, as the only junior Apostle from Trinity, would also have been conscious of the need to break free of the dominance of a long run of Kingsmen. "Naturally you hope some of your intimate friends will be considered apostolic and your friends are likely to be from your college," Annan observed. "Hence the large number of Kingsmen. But what operated for King's also operated after Blunt's election." The record as we now have it does indeed attest to Blunt's success. Following his election, five of the next nine Apostles were from Trinity. But collegial loyalty appears to have weighed less with Blunt and Watson than the recruiting marxisant members.[20]

The first of the new Trinity Apostles was Andrew Benjamin Cohen, who became a member in 1930. Cohen was a historian and scholar from Malvern School, whose father was a former economic supervisor of Palestine and whose mother was the principal of Newnham College. Considered an energetic socialist by his contemporaries, Cohen later made his career in the Colonial Office. After wartime service that included helping organize supplies for Malta, he became a leading proponent in Whitehall for African nationalism. The Labour government appointed him governor of Uganda in 1949, and he was knighted in 1952. Following Blunt's secret confession, Sir Andrew was questioned by MI5 on his radical record and his Cambridge friends. Suspicion also clouded the final years of his distinguished career, but he had made no admission by the time of his death from a heart attack in 1968.

The pattern of apostolic elections, averaging two or three a year, suggests that two of Cohen's contemporaries, Hugh Sykes Davies and Richard Llewelyn-Davies, might well have been elected with him in 1930 — if there had not been objections from senior members. Since no apostolic elections took place in 1931 — a characteristic symptom of "birthing" difficulties, according to Annan — Keynes and his friends may well have tried to block the efforts of Blunt and Watson to recruit the left-wing faction. If so, their resistance collapsed in the spring and summer terms of 1932, which saw the election of Hugh Sykes Davies and Llewelyn-Davies. Both had by then graduated, and both were considered marxisants by their contemporaries. Davies became a member of the Communist party in 1937. A poet and writer associated with Empson's *Experiment* magazine, he later became a fellow of St. John's College. Shortly before his death fifty years later, he confirmed to author Richard Deacon: "It was Anthony Blunt who persuaded me to join the Apostles."[21]

Contemporaries have admitted that Llewelyn-Davies was one of the apostolic marxisants, but they dispute how far he traveled down the road to communism. Sir Isaiah Berlin, the distinguished Oxford professor, has publicly stated "on reliable authority" that Llewelyn-Davies eventually became a Communist. But there have been equally strenuous assertions that he never actually became a member of the party. Llewelyn-Davies made his reputation as an innovative town planner, who eventually became professor of Urban Planning at University College, London, a member of the House of Lords, and a member of the Royal Fine Arts Commission.[22]

Llewelyn-Davies's second wife, Patricia, had the reputation of being "a real left winger," as a Girton undergraduate in the mid-thirties. She was also a close friend of Blunt at Cambridge before her marriage to Anthony Rawdon Smith, another radical Apostle. After Cambridge she became a civil servant, divorced Rawdon Smith, and moved into Victor Rothschild's Bentinck Street flat along with Teresa Mayor (who became Rothschild's second wife), Blunt, and Burgess. After postwar duties in the Ministry of Transport and the Foreign Office, the second Mrs. Llewelyn-Davies stood for election a number of times as a Labour member of Parliament. She then became an outspoken champion of many radical causes, especially to do with Africa. Created a baroness in her own right by Prime Minister Harold Wilson, she was made chief Labour whip in the House of Lords during the late sixties.[23]

Lady Llewelyn-Davies has steadfastly refused to discuss with outsiders her friendship with Blunt, or her late husband's politics. At Cambridge her vivacious charm made her enormously attractive to her male contemporaries. To an even greater degree than Blunt, she is remembered for her mixture of charm, mischief-making, and the subtle way she inferred that individuals acted from base self-interest, or class-inspired motives."[24]

Hugh Sykes Davies confirmed that he and Andrew Cohen were "always in each other's rooms," making up what he termed "the inner circle of younger Apostles" who were "in constant contact with Llewelyn-Davies, Blunt and Watson." The society's membership roster (pp. 189–190) confirms the critical role played by this inner circle. It points up the hitherto unappreciated significance of the much-reproduced pictures of the six Apostles, including Julian Bell, incongruous in shapeless tweed knickerbockers. Only now does it become obvious that the six, who posed somewhat self-consciously for the camera of photographer Lettice Ramsay, are the ones who captured the Apostles for the Marxist cause.[25]

The pictures — apparently made in defiance of the apostolic secrecy rule — appear to have been taken during the early part of the 1932 Cambridge summer term after Llewelyn-Davies's election at the end of April. This explains the confident, smug expressions and the camaraderie of the group. They were clearly celebrating its triumph. The photographs seem to be a documentary record of the actual composition of the hard core of Blunt's marxisant Apostles.[26]

One influential left-wing Apostle who must have played a role in the group, but who did not appear in the picture because he had already gone down, was Dennis Proctor. He was elected the year before Blunt, three years after he came up from Harrow to King's. Proctor earned a first-class degree in economics and became one of the highest-flying civil servants of his generation. He started his career in Whitehall's corridors of power in 1929. The following year, he was made private secretary to Stanley Baldwin, the Conservative prime minister. Baldwin's son recalled that Proctor was on the "extreme left" but that proved to be no obstacle to his rapid rise in the civil service. Proctor served in the

Ministry of Health, and was a senior Treasury official when he abruptly resigned in 1951 shortly after the defection of Burgess and Maclean. After three years in Copenhagen with a Danish shipping company, he returned to London, resumed his career, and became a permanent secretary in the Ministry of Power. After receiving a knighthood, Proctor retired to become honorary Fellow of King's College.[27]

Following Blunt's confession in 1963, Proctor was investigated by MI5. He denied that he had ever been a party member or that the curious disruption of his Whitehall career had anything to do with the defection of Burgess and Maclean. Available evidence indicates that Proctor's involvement in the spy ring was probably peripheral. While he was almost certainly marxisant, he went down from Cambridge before that addiction led many of his contemporary Apostles to become full-blown Communists.[28]

New evidence has come to light that Roy Pascal, a Cambridge Fellow and not a member of the society, may have played a crucial role in effecting this transition. Pascal was second only to his mentor, Maurice Dobb, in promoting the Communist cause at Cambridge. In particular, he was responsible for converting George Derwent Thompson from Marxist to zealous Communist upon his return from Galway University to King's in 1934. Pascal had also been a friend and influence on Blunt since 1929, when they were both graduates in the Modern Languages Faculty and carrying out part-time teaching to supplement their research grants. Blunt took French supervision and Pascal held classes in German.[29]

Pascal's association with Blunt began, significantly it would now appear, just at the time that the apostolic marxisants were forging their plan for taking over the society. This move, according to Annan, was a characteristic Comintern ploy. "The Marxists wanted to capture things," he said, pointing out how the Cambridge Communists had also set out to take over the Socialist Society and the Union.[30]

Pascal had taken a first-class degree in modern languages from Pembroke College in 1927, and then won a Tiarks research scholarship. This enabled him to spend two years in Germany, working on his doctoral dissertation on Martin Luther and the social basis of the Reformation. The scholarship also unwittingly financed Pascal's deeper appreciation of Marxism. During his time in Munich and Berlin he saw at first hand the increasingly turbulent political struggle between the Nazis and Communists. By the time he returned to Cambridge, Pascal was a fervent Communist. His vigorously expressed politics alarmed some of the Pembroke dons, who argued that he was an unsuitable candidate for a fellowship. But he was elected despite their objections to join Dobb as a privileged senior member of the college. By now he was also a lodger at Dobb's small house in Chesterton Lane.[31]

Known as "Red House," it was the epicenter of Comintern activity at Cambridge. Here Dobb worked as a tireless propagandist of the Communist cause. He was a founding member and Cambridge organizer of the Society for Cultural Relations and the League Against Imperialism but he maintained links with the Marxist scientists at the Cavendish Laboratory. The "Red House," as we now know, had been under frequent surveillance by MI5 since the mid-twenties.

Pascal's pivotal role in the Cambridge Communist network owed as much to his marriage to Feiga "Fanya" Polianovska as it did to his association with Dobb. This darkly attractive Russian Jew had met Pascal at Berlin University, where she was taking a doctoral course in philosophy. "Fanya" was a dedicated Marxist whose revolutionary ardor was born of her experience of pogroms. Her "darkened childhood" in the Ukraine had been "branded by the anti-semitism of Tsarist Russia." That the Soviets granted her an exit visa to study in Berlin raises the presumption that her postgraduate work was not confined to philosophy.[32]

Fanya's marriage to Pascal coincided with the founding of the first Communist cell at Cambridge in 1931. Pascal and Dobb were the prime movers. Communist party headquarters detailed Clemens Palme Dutt, the Cambridge-educated botanist brother of the CPGB leader Rajani Palme Dutt, to become one of its eight founding members. A graduate of Queen's College, Dutt was "an expert on work among students," according to Dobb, who welcomed the participation of such "an able and persuasive propagandist." Among the other founding members of this cell were D. H. Stott, a psychologist, and an ex-miner Trinity undergraduate named Jim Lees, who became a friend of both Burgess and Philby.[33]

The Pascals assumed a pivotal role in the proselytizing activities of the Cambridge cell. Pascal spread the Marxist gospel in the Modern Languages Faculty and canvassed support from the left-wing members of the History Faculty for a series of Marxist histories under his own editorship. The project never came to fruition, but as the author of studies on the ideology of Marx and Engels, Pascal was the standard-bearer of a fervent brand of intellectual communism that he took with him to Birmingham University in 1939 on his appointment.as professor of German.[34]

Pascal was an "intellectual snob" and his wife "a very demanding and dogmatic woman, the type of central European who always took the view that England was very 'inferior,'" according to Professor Henry

Ferns, who came to Birmingham as professor of political science after the war and became an academic friend of Pascal's. Ferns, a Canadian who had become a Communist at Cambridge in the mid-thirties, told me that Fanya was the iron in her husband's political soul. She also had all the right qualifications for a full-fledged Comintern agent, as evidenced by her activities at Cambridge. Fanya became an activist with the Cambridge branch of the Anglo-Soviet Society, and was soon elected to the committee of an organization that was one of the principal links between the university and the Comintern in Moscow.[35]

Professor Ferns's most startling revelation was that just six weeks before Pascal's death in 1977, "Roy told me he had once been approached by Soviet intelligence, not to work for them but to recommend young people they might approach." Pascal assured Ferns he had demurred. "In such a serious matter as treason," he had declared, "individuals must decide for themselves."[36]

Yet Ferns did not fully accept that this would have been the response of Pascal, whose "special enlightenment through Marxism" made him overbearingly superior. "I don't doubt the truth of what he said," Ferns told me, "but somehow I found it hard to imagine Roy saying no to anyone as plainly as he suggested he had done to the Soviets."[37]

Whether or not Pascal actually became one of the Soviets' Cambridge talent scouts, the significance of the approach is that it shows the high degree of trust and confidence Pascal enjoyed. Although Pascal did not specify the year when the approach was made, Ferns agrees that by virtue of university and party seniority, it took place after 1931 and before 1935 — the year Blunt, by his own admission, became their Cambridge recruiter.

That Pascal, a Communist with a direct Comintern connection, was closely associated with Blunt before 1930 and was also responsible for converting Thompson, another senior Apostle, to communism is highly significant for two reasons:

First, it shatters the myth that Guy Burgess was the primary Marxist influence in the Cambridge Apostles.

Second, the approach to Pascal to become a Soviet recruiter himself is a clear indication that Moscow's blueprint for subverting undergraduates was already in operation earlier than the mid-thirties, as has previously been supposed.

# CHAPTER 11

# "A Clever, Dissolute
# Young Man"

The efforts of Dobb, Pascal, and the others in the Cambridge cell went well from the very beginning. They found a ready audience for their ideas, politics, and propaganda among an increasing number of undergraduates disillusioned by a capitalism that seemed to be crumbling under the weight of the worldwide depression. The far left, with its dreams of a Sovietized Britain, was particularly attractive to those who were angry at the Labour party's campaign failures and its cooperation with the Conservatives.

Kim Philby had come up to Cambridge in 1929 — three years after Anthony Blunt; Burgess and Maclean came up the following year, in 1930. While many student radicals took to the barricades and became open Communists — among them James Klugmann and David Haden-Guest — Philby, Burgess, and Maclean remained for the most part in the background. So did Blunt.

The man who became the best known of the Cambridge spies, Harold Adrian Russell Philby — nicknamed Kim, after the young hero of the Kipling novel — never joined the Communist party during his undergraduate career at Trinity.

Philby was the son of a Trinity-educated father who began his career in the Indian Civil Service. In 1917 he was transferred to Transjordan as an emissary and adviser to King Ibn Saud. According to a secret report given to the State Department in 1945 by the British, he was "soon at loggerheads with the Colonial Office" about pay and policy. He was dismissed in 1924 after he had "several times acted in deliberate violation of official policy." Turning his back on the British Empire, he settled in Jidda, becoming a Moslem and a member of Ibn Saud's Privy Council, where he was often able to influence the king in direct "opposition to British policy." With more historical justification than his one-time friend and fellow Arabist T. E. Lawrence, Harry St. John Philby really can lay claim to having played a leading role in laying the foundations for the modern state of Saudi Arabia.[1]

Kim grew up in the shadow of his often-absent father, whom he worshiped at a distance. At a very early age young Philby echoed his father's disgust for the British Establishment by declaring himself a Labour party supporter at school. He was remembered at Westminster as a stocky, taciturn youth with a pronounced stammer and a reputation as a hard worker. At school Kim did little to distinguish himself, but his academic ability proved impressive enough for him to win one of Westminster's three closed "exhibitions," or scholarships, to Trinity College. There, he recorded, "one of my first acts was to join the Cambridge University Socialist Society (CUSS)." But his ideological commitment appears to have been lukewarm. He said his stammer prevented him from making public speeches. Philby's plodding political dependability was rewarded in 1932 when he was appointed treasurer of CUSS. But there were already signs that what one Westminster friend referred to as "Kim's vaguely socialist ideas" were shifting farther leftward.[2]

Disillusioned with a dismal third class in Part I of the History Tripos, Philby switched to economics, a field of study that reinforced his radicalism. And he first met Guy Burgess under the aegis of Trinity's economics supervisor, Dennis Robertson, an old college associate of his father's and a homosexual confrere of both Burgess and Blunt. When Burgess and Philby met in Robertson's rooms in the fall of 1931, Burgess immediately fell for the contemplative, pipe-smoking youth. Philby was not homosexual, but if Burgess is to be believed, Philby's initial resistance crumbled before his overwhelming charm and persuasiveness. But even if Philby did succumb to Burgess's predations, it appears to have been a once-only encounter that made more impression on the sherry-time gossip of the Trinity homosexual clique than on Philby.[3]

The encounter was also too early in the Marxist enlightenment of Burgess to have had any serious political repercussions. Philby's own account describes how his political awakening, like that of so many of his generation, was the collapse of Ramsay MacDonald's government in 1931. After campaigning hard for Labour in Cambridge with John Midgely, a CUSS associate, Philby said he took the victory of the national government personally. "It seemed incredible that the [Labour] party should be so helpless against the reserve of strength which reaction could mobilize in times of crisis," Philby wrote.[4]

By contrast, Guy Burgess was not at this point deeply involved in the politics of the left. One of the myths that has grown up around this larger-than-life character is that he came to Cambridge from Eton as a revolutionary Marxist. At least, that is the way the Burgess-like character in the film *Another Country* is portrayed.

But the Cambridge record shows that Burgess did not become an active Communist until late in his final year as an undergraduate. He spent most of his first year with Etonian friends as a member of the reactionary Pitt Club, where a daily bottle of hock did not interfere with his ability to get a first in Part I of the History Tripos.

Burgess was a shameless exploiter of his boyish good looks. He made himself a sexual guide and erotic compendium for a regiment of contemporaries as well as male pickups from waiters to sales clerks. He was a witty libertine whose endless talk of his outrageous exploits offered a catharsis for those who indulged their homosexuality more furtively, fearing they could be clapped in jail for their inclinations. Guy's cheery devil-may-care self-assurance, his vitality, and his superficial maturity enabled him to provide convincing justifications for his actions and attitudes. He took particular delight in explaining how his aversion to women was the result of the trauma he suffered extricating his hysterical mother from under his father who, he claimed, expired in the act of copulation.[5]

Most of Burgess's close friends dismissed his dramatic story as a typical piece of Burgess embellishment, although his father, a retired Royal Navy commander, did die of a heart ailment in 1925 when Guy was barely thirteen. His mother, Evelyn Burgess, soon remarried a retired army colonel, John Retallack Basset, who made gifts of cash to curry favor with his already overindulged stepson. Defective eyesight had already liberated young Burgess from the harsh regime of the Britannia Royal Naval College, and he returned to Eton.

Guy Francis de Moncy, as he had been named as a tribute to his French Huguenot ancestors (Burgess was the English corruption of de Bourgeois) joined his younger brother Nigel at Eton. His schoolmasters later recalled him as a well-read, precocious pupil who had "something to say about most things from Vermeer to Meredith." Yet for all his charm and brilliance Burgess never made "Pop," the self-electing prefectorial elite of Etonian swells. The taint of homosexuality denied Burgess the prestige he felt he deserved and kindled a flame of personal rebellion that was fanned when his close friend David Hedley became school captain. Their friendship nevertheless endured, and Burgess's influence on Hedley continued at Cambridge, where neither disguised their shared sexual preference any more than their eventual ardent embrace of communism.[6]

Burgess was indeed a "kind of Figaro figure, ever resourceful in the service of others in order to manipulate them to his own ends." This was the judgment of his Oxford contemporary and close friend Goronwy Rees, who suspected that Burgess's "power of manipulating his friends" came because they were chosen "precisely because they were willing victims." Although not himself homosexual, Rees asserted that Burgess was usually the aggressive partner and "gross and even brutal in his treatment of his lovers." This insight was supported by their mutual friend Maurice Bowra, the eminent Oxford classicist and dean of Wadham College who was one of Burgess's many "victims." Bowra himself observed – not without a certain relish – that Burgess had "shit behind his finger-nails and cock-cheese behind the ears." This was in keeping with Burgess's prescription that sex with the working-class males, whom he referred to as "rough trade," was the ultimate remedy for releasing bourgeois homosexuals from their inhibitions.[7]

Burgess's interest in socialism developed during his second year, prompted, he said, by his study of nineteenth-century European history. But it is now apparent that his political education was also affected by his more left-wing associates in the Trinity Historical Society. One was J. P. "Jimmy" Lees, the ex-miner who was a founding member of the Cambridge Red Cell in 1931. (Lees was studying at Trinity on a trade-union scholarship.) Burgess was elected to the Historical Society committee in November 1931 – at the same meeting where Maurice Dobb addressed the members on communism, a talk followed by what the minute book recorded as an "animated discussion." Also attending that lively evening was Victor G. Kiernan, then a first-year Trinity historian who was to become one of the members of the Communist cell in Trinity, both as an undergraduate and a don.

The Trinity Historical Society, a heretofore uninvestigated forum, appears to have played an important formative role in inspiring Marxism in its members. The minute books reveal an increasing preoccupation with contemporary political issues. Through Lees, Burgess got to know David Haden-Guest, the son of a Labour M.P. and fellow Trinity undergraduate, who became his guide to dialectical materialism. Haden-Guest was a socialist when he abandoned his study of philosophy under Wittgenstein early in 1932 to spend two terms at the University of Goettingen. When he returned from Germany that autumn, after a spell of imprisonment for taking part in demonstrations against the Nazi party, Haden-Guest was a militant Communist. Burgess was sufficiently impressed by such personal dedication to spend much of his second year reconciling his own historical theories to the dialectical materialism in Haden-Guest's copy of Lenin's *The State and Revolution*. Burgess insisted that his conversion was "intellectual and theoretical" rather than an emotional issue of faith. His Marxism was not of the "Damascus Road" intensity that inspired Haden-Guest's willingness to die for his political beliefs on the Ebro front in the Spanish Civil War.[8]

Among the undergraduate Communists whom Burgess met through

Haden-Guest was James Klugmann, who had come up to Trinity on a modern-languages scholarship, as did his friend Donald Maclean, both from Gresham's School, in Norfolk. Gresham's, founded in the sixteenth century, was not a conventional public school. Its teams did not play other schools, and discipline was enforced primarily through an honor code that called for students voluntarily to report any transgressions. Among Klugmann's and Maclean's near contemporaries at school were the poet W. H. Auden, composer Benjamin Britten, and Sir Alan Hodgkin, a Nobel Prize–winning geneticist.

At Gresham's, Klugmann was a short, flabby boy who considered himself "one of Nature's rebels." Like many Jewish boys in Britain's public schools, he was regarded as "a clever oddity" with the brains to win all the scholastic prizes, but denied respect and authority by a prejudiced society. Klugmann decided to take revenge on the snobs in his final year by calling himself a Communist to annoy the authorities.

"I hadn't any clear idea, to begin with, what a good Communist really stood for," he recalled, "but having a very inquisitive mind, I soon remedied that." So he became his own Marxist mentor and the inspiration and guide for his friends. Maclean, anticipating strong parental disapproval, took care never to mention Klugmann or introduce him at home during vacations. Instead, the two met frequently to share Marxist politics in London pubs and cinemas during vacations.[9]

Klugmann was introduced to Burgess by Haden-Guest. The two became close friends, most likely toward the middle of 1933 when Burgess became an active member of the Communist circle. Through Burgess, Klugmann got to know Blunt socially, although the latter would also have supervised him in French. Klugmann was also responsible for introducing Burgess to his old school friend Maclean. Burgess was much taken with the tall freshman Marxist from adjoining Trinity Hall. With his customary predatory panache he was soon boasting that Maclean had been added to his list of conquests.

Burgess's later protests, that he was nauseated by the very idea of Maclean's "large, flabby, white whale-like body," do not jibe with contemporary recollections that they were often seen together, or that Maclean was a tall, athletically built undergraduate whose playful cowlick of dark hair accentuated his youthful good looks. As a college cricketer he was not regarded as homosexual. But there was nonetheless an effeminate quality to Maclean, whose diffidence hinted at sexual ambivalence. A *Granta* profile published in Maclean's final year provided some clues to his schizoid character. He chose Cecil, Jack, and Fred, "three dear little fellows," to characterize his multifaceted character.

Cecil, the effete side, was a mincing poseur in "blue velvet trousers" with a "*real* passion for flowers" and "delightful" figures on Greek vases. Jack was the rugger-playing Hawk's Club hearty with an eye for the "damn" fine waitresses at The George, while Fred was studious and preoccupied with distinguishing between the "material and the dialectic." Ironically, it was his latent homosexuality that came to the fore when Maclean, later in life, turned to the bottle to relieve the tensions of his double life as a spy.[10]

Cecil, Jack, and Fred had been a "pleasant game" at Cambridge, necessitated, as Maclean explained: "Because society demands it." After Maclean's father, the Cabinet minister, died of a heart attack in the summer of 1932, Klugmann remembers that he saw a good deal of Maclean, who "was cheerfully open now about his unreserved allegiance to the Communist cause."[11]

Maclean, however, was not a participant in a meeting of university Communist party representatives that Klugmann hosted at his parents' Hampstead home during the 1932 Easter vacation. Delegates from the London School of Economics, University College, London, as well as Oxford and Cambridge, gathered to hear Douglas Springhall, the national organizer of the CPGB, address the need for increased action. Some writers have made Springhall out to be the sinister mastermind behind the Cambridge spies, but he was too identifiable a Comintern figure for the OGPU. Springhall was an inspiring leader for the open Communists. "We simply *knew*, all of us, that the revolution was at hand," said Klugmann, recalling his heady emotion of the time. "If anyone had suggested that it wouldn't happen in Britain, for say thirty years, I'd have laughed myself sick."[12]

Among those who were intellectually sympathetic but not fully committed to communism at this time were Philby and Burgess. "It was a slow and brain-racking process," Philby wrote. "My transition from a Socialist viewpoint to a Communist one took two years." According to him, it was not until the summer of 1933 — with Dobb's encouragement — that he finally decided his life "must be dedicated to communism." To seal his faith he recalled how he spent his college prize money on the collected works of Karl Marx and set off on his motorbike for Europe to witness the struggle of Marxism against Fascism at first hand.[13]

Burgess also became a Communist in 1933, his final year as an undergraduate, and for a time threw himself wholeheartedly into revolutionary activities. He helped the Communist party foment a threatened strike by Trinity College waiters, addressed the Majlis Society of nationalist Indian undergraduates, and even booed the chancellor of the exchequer, Neville Chamberlain, at the annual Trinity Founder's Day Feast. Burgess also invited John Strachey to address the Trinity Historical Society in May 1933 on his forthcoming book *The Menace of Fascism*. This meeting, devoted to discussing communism as a historical alternative, attracted Philby and his fellow Marxist Apostle Richard Llewelyn-Davies as visiting participants.[14]

Uninhibited, outrageous, and articulate, Burgess was a blue-eyed schemer with "an inquisitive nose, sensual mouth, curly hair and alert fox-terrier expression," according to writer and critic Cyril Connolly. Burgess's prodigious intellectual energy was combined with a capacity to simultaneously shock and charm that captivated his Cambridge contemporaries. His good looks and irrepressible lasciviousness had caught the attention of two of Trinity's homosexual predators, Robertson and Blunt. Burgess's talent for biting caricature is plain to see in a drawing of a sardonic don in one of his surviving sketchbooks. Intimate friends believe this is Blunt, suggesting that it dates from the time he and Burgess had a homosexual love affair.[15]

Blunt was certainly intensely fond of Burgess, and his personal loyalty never wavered. Even after Burgess's flight to Moscow, Blunt stood up for his friend. He turned on those who had denounced Burgess after his defection by asserting, "Those people who now write saying they felt physically sick in his presence are very often not speaking the truth." Although he allowed that Burgess was "perverse in many ways" in his debauched later years, Blunt insisted he was always "a terrific intellectual stimulus."[16]

Blunt was nothing if not precise, but many appear to have misinterpreted the essential stimulus Burgess provided him in their long relationship. Burgess and Blunt did *not* share a lifelong sexual passion for each other, according to other bedmates. This is another myth that owes more to journalistic license and the demands of television producers than to the facts. Such evidence as there is confirms that their intimacy quickly outgrew the bedroom. This was in keeping with the character of Burgess and his insatiable sexual appetite. Burgess would not have acquired his reputation as the most notorious "homme fatal" of his generation if he had remained Blunt's bosom companion for long. Burgess had a peculiar talent for transforming his former lovers into close friends. To many of them, including Blunt, he became both father confessor and pimp who could be relied on to procure partners. Burgess devoured sex as he did alcohol — an overindulgence that suggests he was drowning a deep sense of sexual inadequacy.

For Burgess, communism was a call to arms against what he perceived as Britain's economic, political, and social injustices. His politicization was that of a disillusioned undergraduate of the thirties who yearned for revolutionary action. Blunt's communism, by contrast, was more esoteric, evolving as it had in the late twenties from a philosophic Marxist apostolic rebellion against the dominance of Keynes and the "milk-tea" liberalism of Bloomsbury. For Blunt, communism was not so much a political battering ram as a personal vehicle for fulfilling his quest for intellectual authority and secret power.

Burgess was fired politically in a way that Blunt never was: he blamed the British government for the country's economic and political decline, or what Annan called "an enfeebled capitalism in which managerial incompetence was not improved by doses of spurious liberalism." He also pointed out how Burgess regarded George Eliot as the greatest English novelist because he believed her characters reflected the suffocating morality of the Victorian middle class. Annan says that Burgess was "genuinely interested in ideas." He knew Burgess from prewar encounters at the Reform Club and from dinners the Apostles held in London. Annan recalls being surprised that Burgess looked him up when he traveled up to Cambridge to consult with the society's undergraduate secretary before the annual dinner of 1949 over which he presided. Annan was then a young don at King's. He recalls how Burgess chose to walk him up and down King's Parade, earnestly promoting the view that "Stalin had the most enlightened views on homosexuality" and that the stories of homosexuals being sent to Siberian camps were American propaganda. Annan, who is neither Communist nor homosexual, said that Maurice Bowra had coined the name "homintern" before the war and that Burgess's bizarre remarks to him reflected the preoccupation of Communist homosexuals with the fact that by 1949 their faith in Stalin had already been badly shaken.[17]

Burgess's erratic character and openly unconventional life make it most unlikely that Soviet intelligence would have chosen him as the mastermind of the spy ring they wanted to build at Cambridge. In 1932, the year in which it is most likely that the OGPU began its Cambridge recruiting in earnest, Burgess was not even a full-fledged Marxist. Charles Madge, a Communist acquaintance from Magdalene College, has confirmed that Burgess "cut me dead in King's Parade" in 1932 after Madge had joined the university Communist party. This is convincing corroboration of Burgess's contention that he did not become a party activist until the following year, although Burgess's Eton master Robert Birley, who visited his rooms during the summer term of 1932, was shocked at finding "a number of Marxist tracts and textbooks" along with "extremely unpleasant pornographic literature" on his bookshelf.[18]

In November 1932, when Burgess became an Apostle, he was a Marxist but not yet a Communist. Yet Blunt and others have successfully promoted the view that it was Burgess who converted them and the society to communism. A clearer reading of the facts and of the chronology leads to the obvious conclusion: It was the marxisant clique of Apostles — Blunt, Watson, Thompson, and the rest — who converted Burgess *after* he joined the society. This conclusion is reinforced by the letter that junior Apostle Victor Rothschild wrote to Lord Keynes. The head of the famous banking family complained that Blunt and the other Apostles talked "vehemently and endlessly" about "communism," which was "the all pervading topic."[19]

Lord Victor Rothschild had been elected to the Apostles at the same time as Burgess, in November 1932. He had come up to Trinity from Harrow that October, shortly before his twenty-first birthday, when he inherited a £2.5 million trust fund, a house in Piccadilly, and a Bedfordshire mansion, Tring Park. The banking fortune and country house, with its substantial art collection, had been established by Victor's grandfather, Nathan Mayer Rothschild, whose elevation to the peerage as the first Baron Rothschild in 1885 set the seal of social respectability on the English branch of Europe's most prominent Jewish banking family.

Rothschild had inherited his father's fascination with zoology, but his overbearing cleverness made him many enemies at Harrow. "Being intellectually precocious, no doubt unpleasantly so, I was frequently punished," Rothschild wrote, recalling that he was frequently beaten for being cheeky. When one of the senior boys threatened to report him for "lip" unless Rothschild agreed "to have a homosexual relationship" with him, he responded to the blackmail by reporting the boy to the housemaster.[20]

Rothschild won a scholarship to Trinity in 1930, but in deference to an appeal from his mother he gave up his studies at Trinity in 1931 to help manage the family bank through the financial crisis. But the young man quickly discovered he did not like banking and, after six months, returned to Cambridge to make his career as an academic in "a relaxed and perhaps somewhat unworldly atmosphere." At Cambridge his reputation for arrogance and a biting tongue had preceded him. But his darkly romantic good looks and willingness to charm led to his marriage in 1933 to Barbara Hutchinson, who moved with the Bloomsbury set. He shared with his friends generous hospitality, his love of fast sports cars, and his talent as a jazz pianist. Among the most loyal, he noted, was "a clever, dissolute young man called Guy Burgess with whom my mother got on very well."[21]

Through Burgess, Anthony Blunt also became one of Rothschild's close friends. "I first got to know Blunt a year after I went up," Rothschild wrote. "Like many others I was immensely impressed by his outstanding intellectual abilities, both artistic and mathematical, and by what for want of a better word, I must call his high moral or ethical principles." Rothschild credited Blunt, who "assisted me with my French from time to time," with helping him achieve the unusual distinction of being awarded a treble first in what he descrbed as "my contemptible Ordinary degree" in English, French, and physiology.[22]

An "excellent conversationalist and partygoer," Blunt was a welcome and frequent weekend houseguest at Tring Park. There he was able to impress his host with his insights into the Rothschild art collection. In fact, it was his rich friend's generosity that made it possible for Blunt to purchase a Poussin painting, *Eliezer and Rebecca at the Well*, in the spring of 1933. He had spotted the genuine hand of the master beneath the badly darkened surface varnish of a dingy painting on sale for £300 by a local art dealer. He had to ask Rothschild for the loan of a hundred pounds: He was given it outright. A MacNeice letter makes it clear the coveted Poussin was in his hands by April.[23]

The Poussin was Blunt's pride and joy. He told Alister Macdonald that to get it he had to ring up Lord Rothschild and tell him that he had found a "very interesting investment." Blunt told him what it was and how much it cost.

"Well, Anthony, you're not really talking about an investment," Blunt said, imitating Rothschild's booming voice. "What you mean is that you want me to buy it for you."[24]

Rothschild was a generous friend to Burgess, too, who became a favorite of his mother, the formidable Mrs. Charles Rothschild. At Tring, Burgess frequently crossed intellectual swords with Rothschild's aggressively brainy sister, Miriam. She was surprised to discover his total lack of debating ability.

"I used to argue with him, taking a conventional socialist line, while he wanted bloody revolution and was a self-styled Marxist," Miriam recalled. "On one occasion I reduced him to floods of tears and thereafter felt he was scarcely fair game and I hadn't the heart to bait him in general discussions."[25]

When recalling the Apostles in 1977, Rothschild said that he "rarely attended meetings" and did "not remember any emphasis on Marxism." But Miriam's recollection of Burgess's Marxism and Rothschild's complaint to Keynes about the society's discussions suggest something different. Whatever Rothschild recalls of this period at Cambridge, his letter shows that credibility must be strained to suggest that a new member, even one as articulate and persuasive as Burgess, could have single-handedly converted this elite fraternity of cynical Cambridge intellects to Marxism in a matter of months. The Rothschild letter goes a long way to demolishing the myth promoted by Blunt and others that Burgess was the First Man in the budding Soviet spy ring at Cambridge.[26]

Yet it is hardly surprising that Burgess emerges from a cast of gray dons with his role inflated into the central figure in the Cambridge spy ring. Journalists, writers, historians — even MI5 officers such as Peter Wright — appear to have succumbed to the myth that this Rabelaisian intriguer must have been the chorus master of the so-called Cambridge spy ring. But from what is now known of the priorities of Soviet intelligence in the early thirties, it is impossible to make a convincing case that the staid and calculating case officers at Moscow Center would have rated Burgess a potential leader. The OGPU would not have regarded Burgess's dirty fingernails, liquor-laden breath, and wild homosexual antics as sensible camouflage for an undercover agent. Even Burgess's instinctive grasp of Marxist dialectic, which was attested to by his many friends, could not have offset his drawbacks since Moscow was not looking for openly declared Communists. And his larger-than-life reputation was not the best qualification for an agent whose mission was to insinuate himself unobtrusively into the upper reaches of Britain's starchy Establishment.

Then there is the failure of Burgess to make the required grade for a Foreign Office or academic career. Although he was a senior scholar with a Part I first, his enthusiasm for communism in his final year left him unprepared for his Part II exam, which he flunked. An unspecified "illness" was the official reason for awarding Burgess a consolation *aegrotat* or pass degree in the summer of 1933. But Miriam Rothschild recorded that Burgess "collapsed in tears" in the examination room.[27]

Burgess's failure wrecked the glittering academic career or a top-grade entry into the civil service that he had so confidently predicted. Nevertheless, he had managed to impress G. M. Trevelyan, Trinity's regius professor of history. With the support of Robertson, who was a member of Trinity College Council, and Blunt, Trevelyan prevailed upon the college to offer Burgess a second chance with a research studentship that could lead to a prize fellowship. But the fickle Burgess made no effort to redeem his academic reputation. He abandoned his thesis on the English bourgeois revolution in favor of a Marxist interpretation of the Indian Mutiny, and after little more than eighteen months of postgraduate studies, Burgess gave up all efforts to become a don.[28]

Burgess's lack of persistence was confirmation of his deep-seated self-destructive impulses. Soviet intelligence was looking for recruits of sterner mettle. Moscow Center analysts were already applying the principles of psychology in their search for suitable spies. They knew that recruits to their secret world of undercover operations had to live under a state of psychological tension not dissimilar to schizophrenia. There is a dual reality for spies, who must function in the ordinary world without betraying their secret lives. Switching back and forth between these two worlds demands a cool character and prodigious mental power.

Even the most superficial personality assessment would have found Burgess wanting in several respects, in contrast to the coolly analytical Blunt. The role playing implicit in a spy's life was an important stimulant to Blunt, whose intimate friends repeatedly spoke of the powerful charge he derived from covert activity. This charge has been compared to the sexual stimulation experienced by the married man who takes a secret lover and has to resort to the same elaborate subterfuges as a spy — clandestine rendezvous, camouflaged communications, and elaborate alibis. In fact, Blunt's demonstrated ability to conduct a discreet sex life would have earned him high marks as a potential recruit for Moscow. Blunt was careful about his homosexuality. Even though the risk of arrest for sodomy was remote in the protected Cambridge environment, his controlled behavior was proof that he had made the psychological adjustment necessitated by his sexual orientation.[29]

In contrast to Burgess, who made passes at every man and delighted in astonishing his friends with graphic descriptions of his lechery, Blunt went to great lengths to conceal his homosexual activities from his mother and all but the most intimate of his Cambridge friends. This much is evident from the elaborate veil of secrecy in which he carried on his affairs with Julian Bell and Peter Montgomery.

One of the interesting discoveries about Blunt at Cambridge is that he seems to have delighted in encouraging ambivalent romantic relations with eligible young women at the same time as he pursued active relationships with members of his own sex. Of the several surviving women whose names Cambridge contemporaries gave as romantically linked with Blunt, only one was prepared to talk about her relationship with him.

"I was attracted to Anthony by his gentleness — he was one of the most gentle men I have ever known," Lady Mary Dunn said with a wistful smile as she recalled what it was that drew her to Blunt. Now a petite and perky widow in her late seventies, she is still elegantly attractive. When Blunt first met her in the summer of 1930, she was Lady Mary St. Clair-Erskine — the daughter of the Earl of Rosslyn — just out of her teens, with the boyish looks and enthusiasm that appealed to him. They became acquainted at a weekend house party at Tring Park. She was immediately attracted by the sharp intellect and keen sense of humor of the tall, thin young man who arrived from Cambridge in the company of the irrepressible Guy Burgess. There was much amusing talk over the dinner table and during the lazy afternoons beside the tennis courts. Both Rothschild and Blunt were good tennis players and she enjoyed partnering either of them in mixed doubles.[30]

Although she and Blunt flirted with each other, Lady Mary recalled kissing him only once. She was far too naïve, she said, to suspect he might be homosexual, and she put his reticence down to gentlemanly insistence on correct behavior. Lady Mary Dunn admitted she was "deeply fond" of Blunt, but was not certain how serious his attentions were until he invited her to accompany him to the Wimbledon Ladies' Final. After watching Helen Moody easily defeat Elizabeth Ryan, Blunt took Lady Mary to meet his mother at her cottage on Ham Common. He was very proud, she said, of the family's royal connections, but Hilda Blunt's home was "frugal and Victorian and certainly not the sort of house to entertain the queen to tea."[31]

The spartan discomfort of his mother's home had been a constant trial to Wilfrid, who complained of its drafts, hard chairs, prehistoric mattresses, barely glowing gas fires and lamps dimmed to save electricity. According to Lady Mary, Anthony was not in the least embarrassed by his frugal home. He seemed devoted to his mother, whom she found a "little woman, friendly and middle class in the sense she was determined to do everything *correctly*." At the same time Lady Mary felt that she was being vetted over the tea cups as a potential bride, and Hilda Blunt made no secret of her displeasure at finding that Lady Mary was a Roman Catholic.[32]

Later, when their friendship cooled, Lady Mary Dunn wondered whether it might not have been as a result of the disapproval of Blunt's mother. She put his implicit rejection down to a passing infatuation. But they remained friends, and she often saw him through the years — although her husband, industrialist Philip Dunn, made no secret of his distaste for Blunt, "because he was a pansy."[33]

At Cambridge, Blunt was often seen in the company of Jean Stewart, the daughter of the university reader in French studies. She was also a teacher in the Modern Languages Faculty. Blunt must have been fond of her because in 1931 he enlisted the aid of Louis MacNeice to try to get her a lectureship at Birmingham. "I broached your girlfriend to my own professor," MacNeice responded, "but he says that the French professor is all for having a man."[34]

A number of Cambridge contemporaries have emphasized that while they now have no doubt that Blunt was a member of the Trinity homosexual circle, he enjoyed the attentions of intellectual women. Apart from Jean Stewart, there was a certain undergraduate from Girton who boasted of her successful seduction of the gangling, aloof young don.[35]

Blunt, it seems, took special pleasure in carrying off the ultimate double bluff. His glacial self-possession would have impressed his Soviet assessors as much as his talent for organizing and manipulating his peers. He fitted the Soviet intelligence profile of the high-flying intellectual with a grudge against the British system and sufficient belief in the superiority of Marxist dialectic to betray his own society for the glory of contributing to the historic Communist experiment.

Moscow's plan to infiltrate the British Establishment depended on spotting potential recruits, particularly those who had demonstrated their ability to achieve rapid advancement. By October 1932, when Blunt was elected to a fellowship of Trinity College, he met many of the most important criteria that Soviet intelligence had set for its long-term Cambridge recruiter.

Blunt's teaching placed him in a good position to further the Soviet objective of penetrating the British Foreign Service. A good languages degree was an essential requirement for graduates hoping to do well in the Foreign Office examinations. As the Trinity don who supervised undergraduates studying French, Blunt could monitor the progress of the star candidates for the Modern Languages Tripos. Through the Marxist group in the Apostles and his friendship with Roy Pascal, who provided indirect contact with the university Communist party, Anthony could keep tabs on potentially successful undergraduates who were sympathetic to communism.

The testimony of General Orlov makes it very clear that Soviet intelligence wanted to avoid Comintern-type Communists. At Cambridge, then, the Marxist Apostles were an obvious target from which to select potential recruits. The secrecy of the society provided a perfect cover, while the elitism of the society ensured the patronage of highly placed senior members in the civil service, virtually guaranteeing graduating members good jobs.

I asked retired American intelligence officer Robert Crowley about the Soviet recruiting process. "Comintern-inspired activists were objects of acute disdain, because Stalin regarded them as Trotsky's children," he said. "Hair splitting intellectuals brimming with dialectics were not suitable agent material, as experience had proved their type very 'discipline resistant.'" Moreover, he emphasized, by the thirties, recruiting foreign nationals was very carefully monitored, with a rigorous procedure that followed a lengthy schedule before anyone was signed on as a Soviet agent.[36]

The induction process was organized in four distinct phases: Selection, Evaluation, Development, and Recruitment. The four stages could take a year or more to complete. Therefore, it can be stated with some certainty that Blunt was selected as a potential agent no later than 1932. This is based on the fact that we know he was acting as a Soviet-intelligence talent scout by 1935, exercising a supervisory role over Michael Straight in 1937, and that it was most unlikely that Straight would have been assigned to a foreign recruiter of less than a year's proven reliability and experience.

Blunt's initial recommendation may well have come to the OGPU *rezident* at Cambridge from one of the trusted *agent vliyaniya* in the university cell. Though the OGPU had a healthy disrespect for Comintern members as espionage agents, it nonetheless tapped them for such information as a list of dons who were Marxist sympathizers.

Discreet "tire-kicking" sessions, as Crowley calls them, would have been conducted in the course of normal social encounters. The Soviets took particular care to conceal their identity and interest from the candidates during the initial phase, which was designed to answer basic questions about the candidate. Where did he come from? Where was he going? What were his true political views? What were his motivations and aspirations?

A review of potential character strengths and weaknesses was essential to deciding whether the prospect exhibited the self-control and discipline necessary to become a secret servant of Moscow. In accordance with standard Soviet practice, the preliminary assessment was written up and passed on along the underground *apparat* to the Control Commission, which was usually the senior OGPU officer in the Soviet embassy.

Only if the candidate met with formal endorsement would the next stage in the review process begin. This involved sustained observation over a period of months by a second Soviet officer after a face-to-face encounter designed to conceal any links to other OGPU officers. The prospective recruit was given the impression that he was discovering a new friend. The second reviewing officer soon unobtrusively sounded out the prospect about his political values and willingness to act in the furtherance of shared Marxist goals. This procedure also involved a carefully devised charade to test the subject's cooperativeness.

In Blunt's case, it seems likely that the Soviets would have exploited his interest in art to elicit an article, critique, or essay for publication. A token payment would have been presented as certifying regard for his ability, but it was common practice to get a signed receipt both to establish the professional nature of a relationship and to provide incriminating documentary evidence to remind the candidate of his commitment.

"Flattery and status building were essential techniques of inflating the prospect's self-esteem and securing an ongoing relationship," according to Crowley. The sustained "playing" of a candidate always followed a set pattern, adjusted according to the personality of the prospect. "The Soviets are always careful not to disclose their real intentions during the evaluation process," Crowley explained. "That is why the candidate is passed along a succession of seemingly unconnected agents." The switching of roles and the introduction of new players had an important purpose: security. As Crowley put it: "The Soviet intelligence officers always need to keep uppermost in their minds the possibility of having to extricate themselves quickly and cleanly if their solicitations are reported to the authorities."

If the candidate passed all the tests, recommendation was passed on to Moscow Center. There, every piece of the accumulated biographical data was checked with the extensive files maintained in the central registry at Soviet intelligence headquarters. Contacts and family connections were reviewed for leads that might provide clues to the potential usefulness of the candidate. The Soviets placed great reliance, according to Crowley, on data they could double-check. Moreover, in Blunt's case it is now clear that Moscow records must have turned up what the OGPU reviewers would have regarded as two highly significant hits: the family association with the British royals and the Scawen Blunt connection.

We know that Blunt made no secret of his aunt's friendship with Queen Mary and of his own aristocratic Trinity friends, such as Prince Chula Chakrabongse of Siam, so there is every reason to suppose that this would have been picked up by the Soviets. An even more important family credential would have been provided by Theodore Rothenstein, who was then a ranking member of the Soviet Foreign Affairs Commissariat but who in 1907 had been a representative of the Bolshevik revolutionaries in Britain. His cover role was London correspondent for the *Egyptian Standard*, and Rothenstein had been in league with

Wilfrid Scawen Blunt, Anthony's black-sheep cousin, who was a vociferous campaigner for the independence of both Egypt and Ireland.[37]

This impression would have been reinforced by their attitude to Blunt's homosexuality. His carefully camouflaged appetite for male sexual partners, would have been regarded as a valuable potential asset. Thanks to Pestrovsky's involvement in the Maundy Gregory affair, Moscow Center would have an extensive file listing the homosexual contacts in the British Establishment. Blunt, as an Apostle with links to Eddie Marsh, would have been identified as a junior member of the homosexual network that extended into the very highest reaches of Whitehall.

General Orlov testified to the "considerable success" that OGPU agents had achieved extracting information from foreign diplomats "tainted with homosexual perversions." Soviet intelligence had concluded that "the biggest concentration of homosexuals can be found in the diplomatic services of Western countries." Blackmail offered a convenient mechanism for effecting control over homosexual informants who were instructed to approach their friends in the diplomatic corps. "The Soviet intelligence officers were amazed," Orlov declared, "at the sense of mutual consideration and true loyalty among homosexuals." The loyalty was ensured by the very fact that homosexual activity was a criminal offense. As British counterintelligence officers discovered to their cost too late, even those homosexual diplomats and government officials who refused inducements to treachery were still too fearful of exposing their illegal sexual habits to denounce those who made the approach.[38]

The final stages of Blunt's recruitment would have involved a series of carefully executed charades designed to discover his appetite for clandestine operations as well as measuring a repertoire of psychological attractions necessary to bring him under control. A typical test used by Soviet intelligence was to arrange a "meet" (a rendezvous in conspiratorial circumstances) that required a complicated approach route, secret recognition signals, and a contact agent who had to be approached in a particular way and at a predetermined time. The candidate would be kept under observation to confirm that he performed precisely according to orders — and to gauge the jolt to his composure when the contact man did not turn up or otherwise altered the routine. The Soviets also watched for evidence of hostile counterintelligence officers whose presence would be taken as a clear sign of betrayal by the candidate.

"The Soviets have a reputation for playing very sophisticated games to test recruits," Crowley explained. "But the missions were important only as elaborate tests of a candidate's ability to accept and carry out a mission spiced with a strong flavor of criminality." Performances were closely observed, and the reports on those prospects who passed a series of such tests sent on to Moscow headquarters for review by a team that included psychologists as well as case officers with experience in the British field. "Orlov made it very clear," Crowley stressed, "that the penetration plan developed by Soviet intelligence in the early thirties depended on a degree of expertise and professionalism that the Western intelligence services did not begin to match until after World War II." He calculated that with the resources of the *apparat* in Britain at the time, the Soviets could not have thoroughly vetted more than twenty Cambridge graduates, only a few of whom made a final short list.

Another likely candidate was his friend and fellow faculty member Roy Pascal, who was also supervising many of the same tripos candidates in German. Even though Pascal claimed to have rejected the role of recruiter, his proselytizing activities in the Communist cell opened up a second channel of influence on undergraduates to become more open Marxist sympathizers.

In contrast to Blunt's and Pascal's, the Marxism that was embraced by the undergraduate generation of the turbulent thirties, such as Burgess, had been crystallized by the shock of external political events. The lengthening dole queues and the spreading poverty of the Depression sharpened the political awareness of the new generation of Oxbridge students. So did firsthand accounts by contemporaries of the repercussions of Hitler's rise to power in Germany. But it was the decimation of the Labour party at the polls in October 1931 that raised the specter of a similar threat to social democracy in Britain.

Socialists blamed Ramsay MacDonald for the betrayal of his party, which many believed had effectively disenfranchised the working class. The British socialists were left in traumatic shock. Before 1931 the Labour party had appeared to be making steady electoral progress toward its goals of social reform. By 1932 the dream of achieving socialism in Britain through parliamentary democracy appeared so bleak as to be hopeless. As the Depression bit even deeper, it put into ever-sharper relief the glaring social inequality of British society. No single group was more deeply affected by left-wing sympathies than the disaffected and increasingly radical undergraduates of the privileged classes. Many were swayed by the persuasive Marxist sophistry of John Strachey, whose book *The Coming Struggle for Power*, published in 1932, was followed by *The Menace of Fascism*. The Oxford-educated son of St. Loe Strachey, the editor of *The Spectator* magazine, had once quipped that he had become a Communist as a result of "chagrin at not getting into the Eton cricket XI." Now he issued a rallying call to "the best intelligences" in Britain to join "the essential work of clearing the ground for the new order."[39]

Strachey's revolutionary rhetoric echoed that of the Communist party. It had always preached the futility of attempting to introduce socialism through parliamentary democracy. It now sought to exploit the human tragedy of the Depression to proclaim that the force of history was on the side of the revolution.

Marxism had acquired a fresh and urgent appeal to undergraduates such as David Haden-Guest, a Trinity contemporary of Burgess who had experienced the clash between Nazism and Communism at first hand. His arrest and imprisonment in Germany for taking part in an anti-Nazi rally endowed him with a reputation for action that made him the leading Communist proselytizer of the generation that came up in 1930. Among those Haden-Guest helped convert to communism were Burgess and his Eton friend David Hedley, Dennis H. Stott of Clare College, and a postgraduate Trinity student named Maurice Cornforth.

Haden-Guest also brought into the Dobb/Pascal Communist cell William Jackson "Bugsy" Wolfe, a Downing undergraduate biologist from a Jewish family in London's East End. Another scientist of Haden-Guest's generation with Communist sympathies was Alan Nunn May. He was a shy and introspective Trinity Hall undergraduate, who "managed to convey the distant impression of always being spiritually in the laboratory." His first class natural-sciences degree led to a career in nuclear physics. In the Communist-led Association of Scientific Workers, Nunn May became a leading activist and promoter of the Comintern's belief in the universality of science.[40]

Art, not science or politics, increasingly preoccupied Blunt during the 1933 academic year. He was not an undergraduate like Burgess, Philby, and Maclean. As a newly elected Trinity Fellow, he was particularly conscious of the need to display the gravitas of a senior member of the university. That he was already a Marxist is corroborated by his membership in the group of six like-minded rebels who had successfully hijacked the Apostles. Even if he was not yet a Communist, he was already well down the road to becoming one, according to the testimony of Goronwy Rees, an Oxford friend of Guy Burgess who encountered Blunt that year and became his close friend.

# CHAPTER 12

# *"I Saw Myself as a Spy"*

At his carefully staged press conference in 1979, Blunt appeared before the television cameras in a rumpled tweed jacket. On the only occasion when he was called to account for his treachery before the bar of British public opinion, the silver-haired old English gentleman offered the nation an offhand apology for what he admitted was his "appalling mistake."[1]

The cool condescension with which Blunt answered the reporters made their questions seem impertinent. And there was little evidence of penitence behind Blunt's mask of professional reticence. His invocation of the Official Secrets Act constraints was his excuse for being conveniently vague, particularly regarding the events that had overtaken him over forty years earlier when he had shortsightedly succumbed to appeals from his best friend: "to try to help anti-Fascism which was obviously the issue of the moment."[2]

"I think he is only telling the truth as far as his own conscience will allow him," Andrew Boyle told reporters afterward. As the author of *The Climate of Treason* (published in the United States as *The Fourth Man*), the book that had finally forced the government to disclose Blunt's treachery, Boyle was one of the few not taken in by Blunt's claim that he had not become a Marxist until the mid-thirties.[3]

Boyle told me that he had always known that the true story was very different. By nature a careful and diligent man, Boyle is a veteran radio journalist and prize-winning biographer of such British notables as Brendan Bracken, Churchill's press chief. Boyle earned the respect of highly placed sources as he painstakingly followed the elusive trail that led to Blunt.

"Various people had been dropping hints to me for some time," Boyle explained, "but I did not know precisely who did what until the summer of 1976." That August, he told me, marked his first meeting with a former senior officer of the British security services. "I told him that it was an amusing coincidence that my initials 'A.B.' happened to coincide with the name of the man at the center of my suspicions and inquiries," Boyle recalled. "My source didn't like my hint. He was clearly very disturbed. But he did warn me I would have to be very, very careful."[4]

From that reaction Boyle knew that his investigations were on the right track. But it was not until the following spring that he obtained confirmation from Goronwy Rees of Blunt's early involvement in the conspiracy. It was Rees who provided the name Boyle was looking for after a rendezvous in The Strand on the Green, a public house near Rees's home in the Thameside suburb of Turnham Green.

While crossing the road to Chiswick Common, Boyle recalled, he had been surprised when Rees drew him close and whispered, "Anthony Blunt." Rees made it clear that he knew Blunt was a Communist when he first met him in the early thirties. Rees told Boyle how he had lived to bitterly regret his encounter with "the man who had cast a long shadow over my life."[5]

Rees, one of the most brilliant Oxford undergraduates of his generation, had arrived at New College in 1928, a year after Blunt went up to Trinity. A ruggedly handsome Welshman, Rees was also blessed with a mental agility that enabled him to overcome the lack of a public-school education. His reputation as a scholar was secured by a first in modern greats, as the politics, philosophy, and economics course was known at Oxford. He then went on to win a coveted prize fellowship at All Souls in 1931.

As an undergraduate, Rees had become a "socialist and Marxist," in revolt against the very system of values from which he benefited. His rebellion, as admitted in his frank autobiography *A Chapter of Accidents*, had been encouraged by a deep sense of social inferiority. Dissatisfaction with the university's function as a "corridor" for privileged "ticket-holders" to the upper reaches of the class-ridden British Establishment led him to what he called "the Materialist Conception of History."[6]

In the twenties, Oxford undergraduate politics had yet to assume the dominating part it would play in the life of both the older universities in the following decade. A. L. Rowse, the literary historian, recalled coming up as a state-school scholar to the snobbish Christ Church in 1922 to find that there were only two other socialists in his college. When he became a fellow of All Souls three years later, Labour Club membership had increased to ten thanks to his proselytizing.

"Upon the new Russia now I base my hopes" was how Rowse recorded his youthful socialist fervor in his diary, "whatever happens to me in the future, whether I declare myself a Communist or not." In fact he never joined the party, but he told me that many of his contemporaries who did were inspired to do so by pacifism. He emphasized how the grim reminders of the World War I veterans scorched a profound influence on the left-wing idealists of his generation who were determined: "It must not happen again."[7]

Professor A. J. P. Taylor, one of the twentieth century's most prolific historians, was already a committed socialist when he came up in 1924.

He was soon enrolled as a Communist, although he "did not attach any importance to it" and remained a member of the Independent Labour party. In 1925 he visited Russia, which "still seemed full of revolutionary enthusiasm." Taylor recalls holding monthly Communist party meetings in Tom Driberg's rooms; curtains drawn and candles lit, with "Tom shuffling round the room in his dressing gown to the sound of a jazz record."[8]

Driberg brought a dandyesque quality to the Oxford Communist party. By combining homosexuality with communism, Driberg also contrived a double affront to social and political morality and a cover for the improbable role he contrived for himself. As the *Daily Express*'s successful society columnist under the nom de plume William Hickey, he used his openly declared Marxist views as camouflage for hiring himself out as double agent for both the Soviets and the British security services, eventually becoming a long-serving member of Parliament and a Labour peer.

Rees graduated from Oxford in 1930, *before* the major political upheavals of the decade. His communism and Blunt's therefore had nothing to do with saving democracy from Fascism. The motives that impelled Rees toward Marxist philosophy, as in Blunt's case, appear to have had more in common with intellectual snobbery than with direct political action. Both discovered in Marxism the attraction of a secret shrine of individual rebellion. Neither went about publicly declaiming his left-wing political beliefs and sympathy for the masses. Their inspiration seems to have been more opportunistic — the need to ensure their membership among the intellectual elite by becoming the clandestine outriders of the Communist revolution.

"I saw myself as a spy," Rees wrote — with perhaps more than intended significance — "dispatched on some desperate mission abroad whose success depended above all on disguising his identity by a process of protective coloration and on the thoroughness with which he adopted the manners and the customs of the country to which he had been assigned."[9]

The "ivory tower" rebellion of Rees and the Oxbridge intellectuals of his generation who became Marxists flourished at the end of the twenties because of the "peculiar condition," as Rees called it, of the English intellectual establishment. "To be a Communist, with the declared intention of subverting and destroying the fabric of existing society, was to occupy a respectable and respected position," Rees wrote. His contemporaries saw that "the difference between a communist and a liberal was merely one of those differences of opinion which arise between the best of friends and which both find mutually stimulating." This peculiar brand of late-twenties Oxbridge Marxism was founded on the assumption that it shared with liberalism the same humane and enlightened purpose: The only issue was the question of methods.[10]

Rees's strictly intellectual approach to communism bore many similarities to that of the Marxist Apostles like Blunt and Watson. It was to become even more closely identified as Rees became close friends with both Burgess and Blunt.

Burgess already enjoyed the reputation of being a brilliant Cambridge undergraduate when Rees first met him in Oxford in the summer of 1933. The occasion was a dinner party at which Burgess was the guest of Maurice Bowra, who was at that time infatuated with him. Burgess animated the dinner conversation that evening at the table of Felix Frankfurter, then a visiting professor from Harvard, who went on to become an associate justice of the U.S. Supreme Court.[11]

Later that night, as Rees and Burgess continued their discussion over whiskey in a deserted All Souls common room, Rees experienced Burgess's aggressive homosexuality. After deflecting his "tentative amorous advances," Rees decided that Burgess regarded sex as a game "which it was almost a duty to practice." Four years later, in 1936, during another whiskey-drinking session, Rees grew increasingly puzzled as Burgess lavished excessive praise on a review he had written of a sentimental book on the plight of the unemployed. Finally, Burgess came to his point. Choosing his moment carefully, and with a challenging look, he asked: "I want you to work with me, to help me." In response to Rees's question "Does anyone else know about this?" Burgess said he would give him one name only, that of Anthony Blunt. In *A Chapter of Accidents* Rees could not name Blunt for legal reasons. "I both liked and respected him, and with him I would gladly have joined in any enterprise," he wrote of this anonymous person. "I don't suppose he could have carried more weight with me." Since 1932, when he had met Blunt through Burgess, Rees had been close friends with the Trinity don. Burgess swore him to secrecy because it was "essential in this kind of work, that as few people as possible should know who is involved."[12]

Rees's account has been seen by many as confirmation that Burgess was indeed the principal recruiter of the Cambridge spy ring. To many sophisticated intelligence experts it proves the direct opposite. "There can be no doubt that Burgess violated all the established rules by making such a direct approach and then revealing Blunt's name," Robert Crowley emphasized. Not only was Burgess pointing to the man at the center of the espionage cell, he also betrayed the most basic security essential to all secret networks. "If Burgess had been under Soviet control he would have made an indirect approach," Crowley said. The standard operational procedure called for sounding out Rees through an intermediary, preferably one who had some hold over the potential recruit to prevent him from reporting the attempt to anyone else. In this case, it was Blunt who was using Burgess for the task.[13]

Whether or not Rees succumbed to the blandishments of his friends is a matter of debate. Although he admitted that he "was accidentally caught up in it," Rees — according to Boyle — denied "to the very end that he ever became a communist agent." But we now know that MI5 interrogators shared the doubts expressed to me by Rosamond Lehmann. After Rees told her about Burgess's approach, she asked the obvious question: "Did you agree to join him?" In response Rees only blustered and tried to confuse the issue. Her conviction that Rees was lying was reinforced when he threatened "to strangle her" if she told anyone.[14]

There is also the inescapable evidence that Rees had all the makings of a potential recruit. He was a Marxist and a restless intellectual rebel who had already abandoned his All Souls' fellowship to make a career as a journalist and write novels. But if he did join the conspiracy, there are indications — as will be shown — that Stalin's show trials shattered his convictions about the Soviet Union and that he had withdrawn his commitment by the time of the 1939 Nazi-Soviet pact. Rees served in British military intelligence in World War II and briefly in MI6 in Germany afterward. After the war, he never fully lived up to his early academic promise, although he was successively estates bursar of All Souls College at Oxford, and principal of the University College of Wales at Aberystwyth. In 1956, after Burgess and Maclean "reappeared" in Moscow, Rees authored a series of anonymous articles for *The Sunday People* that made thinly veiled allegations about Burgess and Blunt. The charges that blackmail and homosexuality had contributed to extensive Marxist penetration of the British security services caused a sensation.

"The explosion detonated by these articles was atomic," Lord Annan observed, "but the blast walls of the Establishment are so cunningly constructed that the person most hideously wounded was Rees." His friends deserted and condemned him for attempting to start a McCarthy-type witch hunt in Britain. Rees was eventually forced by what he claimed to be the "priest-and-professor-ridden" Aberystwyth to resign his principalship and turn to making his living as a novelist and free-lance writer. Fifteen years passed before he attempted a more detailed justification of his charges.[15]

In the spring of 1977, when Rees whispered Blunt's name to Boyle, he was still bitterly resentful at the Machiavellian intrigues of his Establishment enemies. "Goronwy's wife had just died," Boyle recalled, "and he was haunted by the belief that time was running out for him."[16]

It was. Two years later, when Boyle's book was published, Rees was lying in Charing Cross Hospital undergoing cobalt-radiation therapy for cancer. Two days after the prime minister denounced Blunt in the House of Commons, a newspaper reporter, hoping for a deathbed story, bluffed his way into the ward by posing as a Cambridge don. Rees was too ill to talk, and lapsed into unconsciousness shortly afterward.[17]

Rees rallied over the weekend and watched Blunt's press conference on television. He was so aroused by his former friend's unctuous denials that he asked for Boyle.

"Goronwy's son and daughter telephoned me that evening," Boyle remembered. "They said that their father had been so angered by Blunt's disingenuous press statement that he wanted to see me." The seventy-year-old Rees knew that his life was ebbing away and Boyle guessed that he still had something that he really wanted to say. Boyle found Rees's son and daughter at the bedside. "He was obviously gravely ill," Boyle said, "but despite the painkilling medication, Goronwy was absolutely lucid." He insists that Rees, although weak, talked clearly of his relationship with Blunt and Burgess.[18]

"At the time of our original meeting Guy was already an open Communist," Rees declared. "Blunt — no matter what he says now — was by then also a covert member of the party and, as a young don, a kind of Grey Eminence behind Burgess and other disciples, most of whom belonged to the Apostles."[19]

The picture of Blunt that emerged from Rees's deathbed confession was of a Volpone who exquisitely manipulated his friends through the agency of the Mosca-like Burgess. Rees did not realize the web of conspiracy he was entering in the summer of 1933. At that time, Blunt was already making a name for himself as the *Spectator*'s delightfully waspish art critic and had recently delighted in panning the annual summer show at the Royal Academy. "I found almost as little skill as soul," he had complained, reserving special contempt for the modern *genre* painters who portrayed "the pleasures of contemporary bourgeois life in a technique which aims, I imagine, principally at a tone of simple *badinage*."[20]

Lest there should be any doubt, Blunt had reminded his readers at the outset of the piece that the Communist uses *bourgeois* as a term of general abuse. It was evident to Rees that Burgess's friend shared their common enthusiasm for the efficacy of Marxist theory as a handy tool for criticizing British bourgeois art as well as social institutions. If there is any doubt as to whether Blunt could have been a Marxist at this stage of his career, the *Spectator*'s "Cambridge Correspondent" claimed that "the name of Karl Marx, if not on every lip, has stormed the august fortress of the *Cambridge Review*." Readers of the *Spectator* were informed that the Socialist Society was moving to the left and that Communists "comprised the intellectual side of undergraduate opinion." Whereas at one time the universities had regarded the outside world as "purely phenomenal," the unidentified *Spectator* Cambridge correspondent concluded, employing the Apostles' code words, "they are now, as Oxford has shown, not only prepared to discuss it, but even to treat it as if it were reality."[21]

The reference to Oxford was to the celebrated debate a fortnight earlier at which the Union had voted "That This House Would Not Fight for King and Country." The British press and public were shocked. The vote helped polarize Oxbridge undergraduates into two rival political camps: the patriots, who identified with the national government and the Buchmanite Moral Re-Armament movement, versus the pacifists and all those on the left, which included radical Christians, socialists, and the Communist party.

Antiwar councils sprang up and mounted exhibitions at the universities. The one at Cambridge in November 1933 coincided with the showing of the jingoistic film *Our Fighting Navy*. Left-wing undergraduates and their Communist allies protested against the film and a spirited clash broke out between them and patriotic groups organized by the college boat crews and rugger clubs. The pacifists came off worst in the brawl, but the damage to the Tivoli Cinema caused the management to lose its nerve. The showing of the naval film was then abandoned, making it appear that the pacifists and the left had won after all.[22]

This success encouraged the Socialist Society to join with the Student Christian Movement to carry a wreath in the Poppy Day or Armistice Day parade inscribed "To the victims of the Great War, from those who are determined to prevent similar crimes of imperialism." Even though the police insisted on the removal of the words "of imperialism," the hundreds of left-wing undergraduates who joined the parade on Saturday, November 11, came under constant attack from the hearties determined to prevent them from laying the wreath at the Cambridge War Memorial. The police made repeated baton charges to break up the fighting between the rival groups of jeering and shoving undergraduates. Julian Bell drove his Morris-Cowley with its bullnose draped with a mattress and Guy Burgess navigating. The mobile battering ram was pelted with tomatoes but kept moving forward.

The wreath was laid and the Cambridge left posted notice of its triumph in the *New Statesman and Nation* with Bell's article declaring that politics was "the only subject of discussion" and that "a very large majority of the more intelligent undergraduates are Communists, or almost Communists." The sons of Britain's leisured and educated classes, he claimed, had found that communism answered their need for "the moral equivalent of war." Bell ignored his own warnings about the need to beware "neurotic salvationism in our brand of Communism" by announcing to the world, "We are all Marxists now," a hyperbole inspired by the determination of the older activists not to be left behind by the new generation of undergraduates. A growing percentage of freshmen from the public schools had arrived at Cambridge station that October with heroic visions of leading the first charge in the Communist revolution in Britain.[23]

John Cornford was the outstanding left-wing leader of the 1933 freshman intake. His dark piercing eyes, square jaw, and swarthy handsome features were the raw material from which heroes were carved. The son of Francis Cornford, a Trinity classics don whose wife was a granddaughter of Charles Darwin, the charismatic freshman carried a double inheritance of the Cambridge intellectual aristocracy. John Cornford had become a Marxist at Stowe School before he won an open history scholarship to Trinity at the age of seventeen in 1932.

After two terms at the London School of Economics editing the *Student Vanguard* and taking time off to become a Communist with the Labour Research group, Cornford arrived in Cambridge. In his black shirt and dirty raincoat he cultivated the image of an austere party official tirelessly laboring for the revolution by organizing and recruiting new members. He injected a new sense of purpose into the Marxist membership of the two-hundred strong Cambridge Socialist Society, eventually effecting a Communist takeover by ousting the more moderate Labour supporters.

Cornford's arrival galvanized the older generation of Marxists such as Burgess and Maclean. Maclean was a very visible political figure at the Poppy Day demonstrations, according to Robert Cecil, who was then in his second year at Caius College. Cecil had become friendly in 1933 with Maclean and others who spent long hours discussing Marxism. One evening, after a prominent member of the Trinity cell made some arguments that seemed particularly persuasive, Cecil recalls coming to the conclusion that communism did indeed provide all the answers. But his conviction faded with his morning hangover, and as he put it, "nobody came to see me the next day on a follow-up mission." But Cecil continued his association with his left-wing friends including Maclean, with whom he walked for a short distance on a Hunger March in February 1934. It was shortly after this that he discovered for the first time that Maclean really was a Communist.[24]

"I went to Donald's room in Trinity a week or so later and was surprised when he told me he had spent the whole morning arguing with a Moral Re-Armer," Cecil said.

"Why you?" he asked Maclean.

"Because I'm a Communist and it would be a great feather in their cap if they signed me up!"[25]

Shortly after this, however, Cecil noticed that Maclean became less active in undergraduate politics. He appeared to be devoting himself to working for a first in his finals and his passion for cricket occupied any spare time in the summer term. His open Communist activities ceased. Some of his friends suggested that this was in response to the increasingly frequent visits of Lady Gwendolen Maclean, who was determined that her eldest son should finish his Cambridge career in a blaze of glory.

Cecil now believes that his Cambridge friend's sudden abandonment of communism was because Maclean was already coming under instruction from his Soviet recruiter. He cites a recollection of how Maclean's mother asked Donald if he was attending some political demonstration in London. Lady Gwendolen was immensely relieved when he told her: "Well, you must take me for a bit of a weathercock, but I've given all that up."[26]

Maclean also dropped his long-talked-about plans to go to the Soviet Union to do his bit for the revolution by driving a tractor or teaching English to Russian peasants. Instead, he concentrated on preparing for a career in the diplomatic service. Since this demanded he put his name down a year in advance for the Foreign Service examination and sign up with a crammer, Cecil — who would follow the same route the following year — is persuaded that Maclean must have come under some form of Soviet control during the summer of 1934.

Maclean had excellent prospects of achieving one of the OGPU's primary goals: the penetration at a high level of Britain's Foreign Office. Maclean's family connections and first-class degree considerably enhanced his chances of eventually becoming an ambassador. Soviet hopes were not disappointed the following year when Maclean placed in the top six of those who took the highly competitive Foreign Service examination. Later, before the interview board, Maclean brazenly fielded a question about his undergraduate Communist activities with the admission: "I did have such views — and I haven't entirely shaken them off."[27]

The Soviet determination to press their Cambridge moles into British government service offers an explanation of why Philby, a year earlier, had told his Trinity tutor that he was intending to sit for the Home Civil Service exams. He was patently unqualified because his degree, an upper second in economics and a third in history, would not have impressed a selection board looking for only the best Cambridge had to offer.

That Philby would even consider a Whitehall career *after* deciding to become a Communist suggests that he too had come under cultivation by the Soviets before he left Cambridge. Philby claimed in a 1988 interview in Moscow that he had already been "spotted" that summer by Maurice Dobb, who passed him on to a Communist group in Paris. This accords with Soviet practice and is further evidence of his actual recruitment the following year, after playing his small supporting role in what British Foreign Secretary Sir John Simon called "the mad little civil war," which erupted in Vienna during the winter of 1934.[28]

Philby claims he was sent by the Paris Communists to Vienna, a haven for European socialists. He made the journey on a motorbike bought with a graduation gift from his father. In Vienna he met Alice Kohlman Friedman, an engaging divorcée known as Litzi, who was a militant Communist in the Red underground movement that was cynically manipulating the Social Democrats who controlled the city. Tensions rose as the Austrian government coalition under Chancellor Engelbert Dollfus sought to establish its authority.

Confirmation that Philby was a "convinced Communist" in Vienna was provided by George Gedye, *The Daily Telegraph*'s Central European correspondent. When fighting broke out between the Social Democrats and the Austrian government troops in February 1934, Gedye discovered that Philby was a member of the Red underground unit known as the Kirov Brigade. Philby had appealed for his help in smuggling his fellow Communists out through the sewers to escape heavy government artillery fire. Kim married Litzi, and they made good their escape on his motorbike, their joint safety assured by Philby's British passport.[29]

Philby visited Cambridge shortly after his return from Vienna. Supposedly his trip was for the purpose of rallying the Socialist Society to help the Viennese left, the collection for their families actually being organized by Burgess. Philby claims that it was only after he returned to England that he was approached by a man who "was not a Russian, although working for the Russians," and asked if he would like to join Soviet intelligence. Significantly it was only *after* this visit that he dropped all his connections with the left. He then took a job as an assistant editor of the *Review of Reviews*, a struggling liberal periodical. This post now appears to have been the first stage in an elaborate exercise to camouflage his communism in the cloak of respectable liberalism.[30]

In his autobiography Philby states that at this time he was already under Soviet control, although not yet able to provide them with any useful information. He described himself during 1934 as "a sort of intelligence probationer" who wondered at "the infinite patience" of Moscow and that of his control officer, who made his weekly rendezvous in "one or other of the remoter spaces in London." His account suggests that despite his despondency, this period was a crucial part of the process of his education as an agent, since his unnamed control officer was free with "painstaking advice, admonition and encouragement."[31]

Both Maclean and Philby appear to have been spotted and taken through the evaluation and development stages of the Soviet-intelligence recruitment process during their final year at Cambridge. But they do not appear to have been brought under discipline and control until sometime after graduation. This supports the contention of American intelligence officers that the actual signing on of Soviet penetration agents in the thirties was conducted outside the country.

Such was the thoroughness of the Soviet vetting procedure and manipulation that it was very rare indeed for any candidate who made it to the final stage to withdraw. The new agent recruit was then invited to sign documents attesting to a willingness to act in subordination to Soviet authority, and the impression was given that any transgression would quickly be reported through a vast network of hidden informants. By exaggerating the extent of their underground networks, the Soviets also reassured their recruits that they belonged to a vast secret army.

Philby's account reveals just how successful was the spotting, evaluation, and development of the Cambridge recruits. "I did not hesitate," Philby wrote of his own recruitment in the preface to *My Silent War*: "One does not look twice at an offer of enrollment in an elite force."[32]

# CHAPTER 13

# *"The Bloody Sots Are Not Going to Have You!"*

"How, when and where I became a member of the Soviet intelligence service is a matter for myself and my comrades," Kim Philby wrote in 1968. Eleven years later, Professor Blunt took his cue from his Cambridge contemporary's self-serving autobiography.[1]

All that Blunt would admit to questioning journalists was that "anti-Fascism" prompted him to serve for two years as a Soviet "talent spotter" with no other duties. Guy Burgess was responsible for his enrollment to "help him with his work for the Russians." Blunt's memory was apparently not precise enough to say when this was, but he did "think it was just before the Spanish Civil War." When asked if he could recall the specific year, he was painfully equivocal.[2]

"No," Blunt replied, strangely unable to pinpoint one of the most important decisions of his life. "I could only say that I should think late 1935, early 1936."

That this was the same alibi Blunt had given sixteen years before to MI5 is clear from details Peter Wright supplied in his best-selling book *Spycatcher*. Other interrogators have confirmed that Blunt stuck to his guns and did not provide significantly more information about his actual recruitment than has already become public. They agree that Wright is correct in asserting "there was nothing like the wealth of detail we expected."[3]

Given Blunt's reticence, one surprising revelation to come out of Wright's memoir is the degree to which MI5 went along with Blunt's story that Burgess was the primary Communist recruiter of the Soviet agents in Cambridge. The acceptance of this alibi underscores both Wright's lack of training as a counterintelligence officer (he was trained as an expert in electronic surveillance) and the failure of MI5 as a counterintelligence organization. On the evidence we now have, it is clear that MI5 either never grasped the dimension, or chose not to reveal the fundamental mechanics, of the Soviet infiltration plan. Critics who have maintained healthy suspicion of the credibility of Blunt's confession have had their worst fears confirmed by reading *Spycatcher*. Wright's book suggests, however, that MI5 and the uninformed public believed in the overnight recruitment of Cambridge spies by a mysterious brotherhood.

Based on their extensive research and analysis, however, the Americans' knowledge of the history and mechanics of the covert operations of the KGB and its predecessors leads them to believe the Cambridge network could not have been masterminded simply by the Comintern. Washington's analysis indicates that it was the Soviet intelligence service, not the Comintern — of whom Stalin was inordinately suspicious in the early thirties — that recruited, directed, and controlled Blunt and his associates.

The CIA, like the KGB, has always recognized the importance of research and analysis. In the area of counterintelligence operations, both maintain highly trained analysts dedicated to this task. But the evidence in *Spycatcher* gives no indication that Wright — or anyone else in MI5 — exercised this critical function with anything like the skills and experience marshaled by the Soviets. Indeed, there is a somewhat amateur element in MI5's attempt to run down the Soviet moles by relying heavily on the collective wisdom of senior female staff in the MI5 Registry and the research department.

At least one former MI5 officer involved in the great mole hunt has told me Wright "cocked up" his two-hundred-hour-long effort to pry the truth out of Blunt. Wright's inside account, he said, reflects the faulty procedures of MI5 in permitting a relatively untrained officer to assume the burden for a major internal-security audit that failed miserably for want of professional research and analysis. (As we know now, and will discuss later, MI5 did not do a thorough research and analysis of the Blunt case until 1971.)[4]

That Blunt lied repeatedly becomes very clear from the significant differences between two public accounts he gave purporting to explain how and when he became a Communist.

In 1979 Blunt declared that he had "a sabbatical year's leave from Cambridge in 1933–34 and when I came back in October 1934, I found that all my friends ... had suddenly become Marxist." In an earlier 1973 article, "From Bloomsbury to Marxism," based on an "informal talk" to his Courtauld students, he wrote "quite suddenly in the autumn term of 1933, Marxism hit Cambridge. I can date it precisely because I had sabbatical leave for that term, and when I came back in January, I found that almost all my younger friends had become Marxist and joined the Party; and Cambridge was actually transformed overnight."[5]

These discrepancies must raise major questions about Blunt's truthfulness and underlying motives for giving conflicting accounts of when and how he became a Communist:

1. Why is there nearly a year's difference, 1933 or 1934, in the

supposed "overnight" conversion to Marxism of Cambridge undergraduates?

2. Why did Blunt in his earlier written — and therefore presumably
more considered — account state that his sabbatical leave lasted only
for the 1933 Michaelmas term that fall. But then, six years later, he gave
the impression that he was conveniently absent for the whole year when
Cambridge underwent its Marxist conversion?

3. What is the significance of Blunt's deliberate attempt in 1979 to
fudge the dates about which he had been so categorical in 1973?

Blunt told the reporters who questioned him that his sabbatical had
been spent "mainly in Rome and otherwise in south Germany." In his
article he was, however, more specific, asserting he had spent his
sabbatical in Rome, where Ellis Waterhouse, a Marlborough friend who
was also an art historian, was librarian at the British school in Rome.
"It was my first taste of the Italian baroque," Blunt recalled, noting
how they toured the sun-soaked heel of the Italian boot, studying the
architecture of the churches of Lecce. Waterhouse, before his death in
1986, confirmed Blunt's visit and also recalled that Burgess arrived in
Rome determined to talk politics.[6]

The actual record of Blunt's peregrinations between 1933 and 1934
can be pieced together from the surviving MacNeice–Blunt correspondence and Blunt's *Spectator* art reviews. The *Spectator* articles indicate
that Blunt remained in England without a major break until late August
1933. Then his articles shifted focus, starting with the Renoir exhibition
in Paris, then one on Riviera style — MacNeice had received a "nice
picture of the Casino" from Monte Carlo at the end of September —
and then a piece on the architecture of the Rhine and Danube in
November. This strongly suggests that he traveled through lower
Germany and Austria to Italy. In Rome Blunt visited the First Great
National Futurist Exhibition.[7]

By January 1934 Blunt was back in London in time to review the
Winter Exhibition at Burlington House. MacNeice's letters and subsequent gallery reviews show that Blunt remained in London until late
spring. Then he traveled to Munich; in June he went up through the
Black Forest to the medieval university town of Freiburg, where he
stayed with Dr. Walter Friedlander, a leading authority on Poussin. By
September he was back at Cambridge.[8]

The record shows that Blunt, who had plenty of time to prepare for the
press conference because the questions were known in advance, must have
been deliberately lying in 1979. The record shows that his sabbatical did
not take him out of the country for a twelve-month stretch. His earlier

account about being absent from Cambridge only for the first term of the academic year is therefore the more accurate version.

A major flaw in both of Blunt's accounts was his naming of James Klugmann, John Cornford, and Guy Burgess as the principals who influenced his decision to become a Communist. They were the "very powerful" and "very remarkable group of Communist intellectuals."

In his 1973 article, Blunt claimed that in the 1933 academic year in Cambridge, Klugmann, Cornford, and Burgess were the "individuals who dominated the movement." In fact, the record shows that Burgess *never* was one of the leaders of the Cambridge Communists. He had only just become a party member — but as a Pitt Club adherent with a taste for cultivating the wealthy and powerful. He was not accepted into the inner councils of the undergraduate Communist movement, even though he played a leading role with Julian Bell in the Armistice Day demonstrations.

Blunt also went out of his way to praise Klugmann. He described him as "an extremely good political theorist," who "ran the administration of the Party with great skill and energy and it was primarily he who decided what organizations and societies in Cambridge were worth penetrating."[9]

How did Blunt know this if he was not deeply implicated in the cell?

Blunt's statement reveals a familiarity with the inside workings of the Cambridge Communist party that is significant. To know how decisions were taken about penetration suggests that he and Klugmann must have been on very close terms.

When and for what reason could he have come to know James Klugmann, who was seven years his junior, not an Apostle, and by all accounts not especially interested in art. Blunt may have been his French supervisor, but the requirements of Klugmann's tripos studies hardly required passing on the secret decisions and planning of the university cell.

Did Blunt know this because it was Klugmann's job to keep him briefed, and did he — through Klugmann — exercise a sinister influence on the Communist cell?

What prompted Blunt to reveal his inside knowledge of the Cambridge Communist party just six years before he was publicly exposed as a Soviet spy? Blunt was still a member of the Royal Court and presumably anxious to avoid any tarnishing of his public reputation: Why then even reveal that he was once a Marxist?

Blunt's decision to publicly risk admitting a limited flirtation wth Marxism can only be explained by the pressing need to deny a larger guilt. The clue to what prompted his extraordinary action can be found in the statement made to me by British author Nigel West: that an internal MI5 reappraisal of the Blunt case had reached very disturbing conclusions.

In 1971 – a surprisingly late date, considering the secret confession made in return for immunity eight years earlier – Anne Orr-Ewing carried out the first in-house review of Blunt's secret confessions. Orr-Ewing, described as "one of the best" and an "extremely thorough officer" by Peter Wright, had become one of the leading forces of K7, the section investigating Soviet penetration of the intelligence services.[10]

According to another reliable informant, Orr-Ewing's report was unequivocal in declaring that Blunt had *never* told the truth – either in his 1964 confession or in his many lengthy debriefing sessions with Wright. But MI5 took no further action after the Orr-Ewing report. The obvious course would have been to begin a new round of tough interrogations to expose the inconsistencies and tax Blunt with his failure to tell the truth. Significantly, Wright – who retired in 1976 – does not mention the Orr-Ewing report in *Spycatcher*. So either he was not told of its conclusions – which seems unlikely in view of his long and close association with the report's author – or, more likely, he chose not to reveal failures in his interrogations of Blunt.[11]

Knowledge of Blunt's treachery was restricted to a handful of officers (including Wright), an indication of the extreme sensitivity with which the case was treated. The overwhelming need to keep the Blunt case under wraps appears to have influenced the decision to take no action on the Orr-Ewing report. Fear that forcing Blunt to recant might prompt him to "go public" might have been MI5's overriding concern. The damage that his revelations could do to any British government – not to mention to the already tarnished reputation of Britain's security services – apparently outweighed any information that might be gained.

Since Wright continued to call on Blunt until he left the service in 1976, he may, inadvertently or by design, have given some hint to Blunt of trouble ahead – either pressing certain questions too closely or increasing the frequency of visits.[12]

This would have tipped Blunt off that the "office" entertained fresh doubts about his story. On the eve of an illustrious retirement, he would have been especially anxious to remind the British government of the gentlemen's agreement that guaranteed his continued status as Sir Anthony and a Buckingham Palace courtier. What better way to make his point than a specific public reference to his involvement with the Cambridge Communists? That he chose to do so in a lecture and then allow publication in a magazine article must have made very plain his lack of concern about putting his youthful Communist indiscretions on the public record. Blunt also engineered his remarks to bolster the story he had already given in his secret MI5 debriefings.

At the same time Blunt reinforced the view that Guy Burgess was a kingpin of the Cambridge Communists. For the same reason, in 1979 he distorted the chronology, adding almost a year to the date when he claimed he had become a Marxist. This conveniently gave the impression that he could not have become a Communist until autumn 1934, *after* Burgess returned from his trip to Russia with Oxford Communist and fellow homosexual Derek Blaikie. According to Goronwy Rees's sensational articles in *People*, Burgess's recruitment had occurred that summer after "a long secret interview with Nikolai Bukharin, one of the most famous leaders of the Communist International."[13]

Rees's questionable assertion made it possible for both Blunt and the British government to promote the legend that Burgess really was the First Man of the Cambridge ring. This myth has gained credence over the years even though it does not jibe either with historical facts or with what is now known about Soviet recruiting methods. Bukharin could not have recruited Burgess in Moscow because by 1934 he held no official position in the Comintern; he had just been dismissed from the editorship of *Izvestia* and his authority diminished until his purge in 1938. Burgess, through Tom Driberg's "official" biography of him in 1956, actually denied that he had even met Bukharin. But even if, as Rees told Andrew Boyle, Burgess had also talked of meeting Ossip Piatnitsky, head of the Comintern Liaison Section, the Comintern was not responsible for recruiting agents in Cambridge.[14]

If for no other reason than Burgess's collapse in a drunken stupor in the Moscow Park of Rest and Culture, his visit could have done nothing to impress Soviet intelligence that he was a suitable candidate to become one of their Cambridge penetration agents. Nevertheless, Burgess's trip to Russia has come to be seen as a critical turning point in his career. He returned to Cambridge a changed man, more critical of the Soviet Union and retreating into the reactionary atmosphere of the Pitt Club. "He had broken with his Communist associates in 1934 in a manner that some of his friends found bizarre" was Michael Straight's recollection. But he does not say precisely when and admits that he "did not know that" at the time.[15]

Whether Burgess was responding to directions from Moscow Center or indirect control by a master closer at hand, his actions foster the notion that he returned from the Soviet Union as the First Man in the Cambridge network. Both Blunt and MI5 had good reason to reinforce that impression. Blunt wanted to dispel any suspicion that his own treachery could possibly have predated that of the now deceased Burgess. The British security services wanted to cover up from the government the investigative failures that were being revealed by the highly secret Orr-Ewing report.

Nor should it be forgotten that Moscow's agents also appear to have closed the recruitment of Kim Philby and Donald Maclean during the first half of 1934. So Blunt therefore may have had additional reason to say that he was out of the country at the very time when two of the most notorious Cambridge spies were inducted into the OGPU network.

Documentation leaves little doubt that the Apostles were already Marxist by 1932, so Blunt's assertion that he did not become a Communist until 1934 appears nothing more than a Machiavellian charade. His correspondence with Louis MacNeice offers additional evidence. There is a suspicious gap in the volume of letters from MacNeice between 1930 and 1931. The period covers the critical two years during which Blunt and Alister Watson were masterminding the marxisant take-over of the Apostles.

Despite indications of some earlier weeding by Blunt, the correspondence from 1926 to 1929 averaged fifteen letters a year; from 1932 through 1936 the average is eight, but for the years 1930 to 1931 *only three letters from MacNeice exist*. The contents of the surviving letters provide no hint of a rupture in intimacy on either side that could account for this mysterious hiatus.[16]

Since the correspondence is so consistent on either side of the gap, inadvertent loss appears a less likely explanation than deliberate destruction. For the letters that have survived do so only *by courtesy of Blunt*, who deposited them in the King's College archives in 1969 — ten years before his public exposure: He was in control. King's College archives also contain correspondence from Blunt admitting that he destroyed a letter from Julian Bell that, if his surviving correspondence is a reliable guide, contained references to Blunt's adherence to left-wing political views. This leads to the logical assumption that Blunt weeded out the MacNeice letters for the same reason, since any references to his Marxist leanings in 1930 or 1931 would have cracked his story that he did not become a Communist until 1934.

Blunt did not think to destroy another letter that gives a clue to the motivation and chronology for his life as a spy.

Shortly before Christmas, 1933, MacNeice wrote from Birmingham to tell Blunt that his university had just received the lavish Barber bequest to fund an art school and gallery and to endow a professor of fine arts. Blunt jumped at the opportunity. The letters over the next year show how seriously he pursued the post. In 1934 he submitted a set of glowing testimonials to Birmingham University from Gow and his influential friends. MacNeice also set about lobbying his fellow professors on the selection board, and his wife overcame her lack of affection for Blunt sufficiently to offer to pull strings with Kenneth Clark, a friend of her family, who in 1934 had become director of the National Gallery.[17]

Blunt journeyed up to Birmingham in the autumn of 1934 to write up an exhibition of English paintings at the City Art Galleries for *The Spectator*. He allowed his distaste for provincialism to get the better of his judgment, however. Not only did he question the attribution of two old masters but he also dismissed the "distressing style" of English sixteenth-century portraits as "mere furniture pieces" and labeled as "pathetic" a self-portrait of Sir Joshua Reynolds. Such carping evidently did not please the local Birmingham worthies who had loaned the pictures to boost civic pride.[18]

It was soon put around that Blunt was not even short-listed for the post. "The bloody old sots are, I fear, not going to have you," MacNeice wrote in November 1934, breaking the news that to Birmingham's "everlasting shame" the selection board considered his friend too young and inexperienced, despite their being "especially impressed by your testimonials." The Barber professorship eventually went to the director of the Dublin Gallery of Fine Art. To a Marxist determined to become one of the new wave of "scientific" art historians, such a snub would have been taken not only as a personal slight but also as an irrational insult from the fuddy-duddies who ran the British Establishment. Under an enlightened Communist regime, such an injustice would never occur.[19]

MacNeice appears to have provided another clue that dates his friend's Marxist conversion — and one Anthony was powerless to erase. In 1933 MacNeice published a biting short poem, "To a Communist," which likened the transitory appeal of intellectual Marxism to a pristine snow. "But before you proclaim the millennium, my dear,/consult the barometer." He does not name the person — clearly an intimate friend — for whom he intended this curious poem. But since MacNeice often used "My dear" as a form of address to Blunt in his letters, Blunt could have been the object of this highly personal meteorological admonishment.[20]

Although it will never be possible to establish precisely when Blunt was brought under Soviet control, all the circumstantial clues point to late 1933 or the first half of 1934. This would be in accord with Soviet intelligence's lengthy evaluation process before the actual closing of the contract and his functioning as a Cambridge talent spotter in the recruitment of Michael Straight in 1936. Since the consensus of American intelligence opinion is that the actual closing would have taken place outside England, it is likely to have occurred in the spring of 1934, when Blunt was traveling through France and Austria en route to Italy.

Also, Blunt's artistic interests may well have played an instrumental role in setting up his relationship with the Soviets. It is entirely possible that his induction was so arranged that it led Blunt to believe that he, not the Soviets, had initiated the process. Blunt implied direct access to "the highest circles in the Kremlin" in his recruitment of Michael Straight and was sufficiently self-important to defy orders to defect in 1951.[21]

An explanation of Blunt's inflated view of his status in Moscow could have come about if he believed he had volunteered himself for service with Soviet intelligence. Although it is possible that he could have simply been a "walk-in" like the Foreign Office clerk Oldham, it is more likely that it was his artistic pursuits that led Blunt to make an initial approach to a Soviet embassy, which the Russians later turned to their own advantage.

Such a scenario is probable because the early thirties saw the publication of the first catalog of the paintings looted in the Revolution from the palaces of tsarist nobles and merchant princes. Anatoli Lunacharsky, people's commissar of enlightenment and culture, had for years been battling against the policy instituted by Stalin and the Commissariat of Foreign Trade of secretly selling off parts of this priceless heritage of European old masters to raise hard currency. Lunacharsky, playwright and critic, was the official sponsor of the book *Selected Works of Art from the Fine Arts Museums of the USSR*, which listed the principal old masters hung for the public in state museums.[22]

There were a great many Poussins in the Soviet collections. So, publication of Lunacharsky's catalog in 1930 could have prompted Blunt, ambitious to establish his reputation as a "Poussiniste," to ask the Soviets for permission to study the Poussins in Leningrad and Moscow. Many of these works had previously hung in the private houses of Russian nobles and merchants and thus had not been readily accessible to scholars.

Such a request for visitation rights denied other scholars since the Revolution would have brought Blunt to the attention of Soviet intelligence. If he was already targeted or under evaluation, it would have reinforced their interest in him. In addition, the prospect of special access to the Poussins would have provided OGPU case officers with a hook for Blunt while leaving him with the impression that he was in control.

Christopher Wright, a former pupil of Blunt's and himself an authority on Poussin, confirms that even today dealing with Soviet museums is usually effected on a quid-pro-quo basis. "If I request photographs of paintings in their collection, I always anticipate being able to offer something in return," he told me. Wright also agreed that it was entirely possible that Blunt's early thesis studies brought him into contact with the Soviets, since the Leningrad Poussins represented the second largest body of the artist's work outside the Louvre.[23]

"It would have been impossible for Blunt to complete his thesis without access to this collection" is Wright's considered opinion. As it turned out, Blunt did not get to see the collection until his summer trip to the Soviet Union in 1935. This was a year before he was due to submit his thesis, by which time he had already embarked on a far broader study: an analysis of the artistic theories in the paintings of the Italian Renaissance. Blunt never accounted for switching away from Poussin to a more general focus, merely acknowledging that his studies "spread backwards into the sixteenth century." His friend and artistic mentor Andrew Gow could have influenced his decision. It was to Gow's "wide knowledge of painting of the Italian Renaissance, based on an extensive knowledge of the originals and a minute study of Berenson," that Blunt attributed his own standards of scholarship.[24]

Blunt himself provided another clue as to why he put aside his projected thesis: Poussin was a less suitable subject for Marxist analysis than the Renaissance. The pointer to this can be found in the revised version of his fellowship thesis that was finally published in 1940 as "Artistic Theory in Italy." In the Preface Blunt paid tribute to Antal for "instruction in a method, which has, I fear, been applied in an only too slipshod manner in this book and for many ideas on individual points."[25]

The "method," which Blunt was evidently reluctant to identify, was the Marxist analysis of art. Friedrich Antal was a leading exponent of the application of the principles of dialectical materialism to the study of art. He had arrived in London as an exile from Germany in 1934, and although he "had not at that time written much," he tutored Blunt "at great length verbally." Blunt also late admitted to being a devotee of the articles on the "general application of the Marxist theory to the arts" authored by Kligender, another German émigré.[26]

Marxism required Blunt to make "a complete reversal" of his aesthetic canon. "Art for Art's sake, Pure Form, went by the board totally," he would later recall. The Marxist theory of art derived from the "scientific" rationalization that because works of art were created by men who were the products of the society in which they lived, their artistic achievements must be determined by social and ultimately economic conditions. This required Blunt to go through some tortuous dialectical logic to make his aesthetic judgments on individual artists conform with the revolutionary tradition. As a result, Goya, despite his reactionary opinions, became a precursor of the nineteenth century's consciously revolutionary artists, such as Daumier and Courbet. Eighteenth-century artists such as Chardin became "semi-conscious social realists" who depicted the life of the bourgeoisie.[27]

According to the "gospel of St. Antal," the "progressive artists" of previous centuries were "all right," with Poussin in France and Rembrandt in Holland representing the progressive development of the bourgeoisie. Naturalism and Realism were the determinants of the Marxist aesthetic canon. Even the Impressionists fell under the critical logic of the true Marxist believers for falling into the trap of "optical effects," and Cézanne was condemned for "dehumanizing" art. Cubism had drifted away from contact with human life, and Surrealism was lost in a purely private maze of abstraction.[28]

Anthony Blunt's conversion to Marxism is apparent as early as 1933, when his weekly *Spectator* column on art began to echo his extreme socialist interpretation.

Despite the leaden proto-Marxist homilies, Blunt's early art pieces crackle with a provocative fire that makes his later academic writings appear desiccated. His youthful criticism was obviously designed to draw attention to his aesthetic virtuosity as he became a familiar presence at the London gallery openings. His criticism was always incisive, sometimes witty and often waspish, but always reflecting a dogmatism, increasingly Marxist in tone. Some of his judgments have proved to be sound: He had no doubt that "in two hundred years any authentic work by Picasso will be fought over by the directors of public collections." But his Leninist dogmatism corrupted his attitude to modern movements like Surrealism, which he castigated as "a style ill-suited to real greatness for which a high level of intellect is required."[29]

With mathematical precision, Blunt assigned all paintings to three categories: "those which produce an immediate effect of pleasure, which may wear off with time; those which produce at first practically no impression, but which closer acquaintance shows to possess considerable beauty; and those which produce no effect of pleasure at all on the spectator either immediately or after careful study."[30]

Blunt did not see art as an "activity entirely cut off from the other activities of life. If one believes that a painting is the product of a man and that it can only be fully understood as such a product," he wrote, "then it becomes important to know as much as possible about the man who produces the painting. The more we can fully understand his character, the more fully we can understand what he produces, whether it be in paint or writing."[31]

"Why must we all approach painting by means of that mysterious organ, the sensibility?" Blunt demanded in a *Spectator* polemic, "The Elect vs. the Rest," in which he clearly hinted at the roots of his Marxism. "Why is it wrong for those whose first interest is in the general human question and not in the refinements of aesthetics to approach paintings from their point of view," he asked, "and why should the pleasure which they finally derive from art be inferior to that limited enjoyment to which the purists' approach leads?"[32]

Rather than merely analyzing a painting through the technical achievements of the artist, Blunt saw it as his Marxist duty to "define the historical position of the artist, saying what influences went to form him, what kind of society produced him, and what other artists were influenced by him."[33]

Assembling the snippets of dialectic from Blunt's *Spectator* reviews reveals his progress toward an uncritical acceptance of full-blown Marxism, which holds that social and economic revolution chart the course of artistic development. "Each time society undergoes one of its great structural upheavals, the arts inevitably go through a parallel process," he wrote, noting how with the breakup of feudalism, "painting became a luxury and painters claimed that their art was liberal and they were intellectuals."[34]

The eighteenth-century academies in France and Britain were "perfectly appropriate to the social structure that produced them," a "symbol of that unity in the arts and letters which was to correspond with the political and religious unity aimed at by the centralizing power." But while he credited the Académie Française with the "extraordinarily high level of the arts," in that country, Blunt condemned Britain's Royal Academy for "satisfying the demands of a particular class." The defiance of its rigid bourgeois standards by the New English Art Club in the nineteenth century he likened to the struggle of Lutheranism against Rome. The Pre-Raphaelites were therefore, according to Blunt, the "Left Wing of English Art, challenging the accepted standards of painting as thoroughly as those of politics."[35]

By 1935 Blunt was firm in his belief that contemporary artistic movements were subject to revolutionary process. In times of social upheaval, he argued, the artist has a duty to reach beyond abstraction so as to give explicit expression to his ideals, making art "openly propagandist." Although he was careful not to label himself a Communist, his beliefs were increasingly implicit in such assertions as "Art is only valuable when it corresponds to the needs of society of its time."

The rising frequency of Blunt's use of the word *bourgeois* in slighting reference of the works of which he disapproved adds to the indications that by 1934 he could have declared that he was not only a Marxist ideologue, but also a full-blown Communist. Blunt had always considered himself a revolutionary when it came to art. In his case there were only a few short steps from debunking the aesthetics of bourgeois society to rejecting its political underpinnings and to a full acceptance of Moscow's invitation to treachery.

From his early childhood Blunt had felt a deep affinity for France. This attitude was nurtured at Marlborough and at Cambridge, where he was much influenced by his tripos studies of European cultural and intellectual traditions, to the point where his writings indicate a high degree of alienation from his British roots. In his attention to detail and concern with the logical particulars in his academic writings, Blunt reveals how much closer he was to French than to English academic traditions. Moreover, in common with the French intellectuals of the thirties, he may also have felt himself an outsider in society.

As an undergraduate Blunt set out to become one of the high priests of the art world. In Britain, however, this was not the best way to achieve the status, power, and respect he believed his superior intelligence rated. British society he regarded as hidebound by the "soullessness" of the philistines and smugly preoccupied with bourgeois values typified in the sentimental paintings of the Royal Academy summer shows patronized by the British social establishment.[36]

Professor George Steiner, who has studied the influence of communism on European intellectuals, suggests that the frustrations that afflicted Blunt were not uncommon in those years. Before the truth about Stalin's regime became known, wishful thinking and propaganda led many academics to a distant envy of the "philosopher priests" of the Soviet Union, who supposedly exercised their right to rule the masses by virtue of their special insight into the "scientific" principles of Marxism. This was no less true in the art world.[37]

"Blunt had arrived early at the conviction," Steiner concludes, "that great art, to which he ascribed preeminent value in human consciousness and society, could not survive the fragmented and anarchic and always modish government or private patronage and mass media trivialization."[38]

Most of the British intellectual and artistic community held in particular scorn the rise in popular culture after World War I. They saw the United States, especially through the impact of Hollywood films, as debasing English values and bringing about a society overly concerned with material gain. The crass American media tycoon bent on exploiting the mindless English-speaking masses became a common theme in the novels of Evelyn Waugh, plays, and literary criticism of the period.

The anti-Americanism that Blunt shared with many of his academic contemporaries was more than just the traditional British snobbism toward the colonials. The intellectuals were reacting to the worldwide ascendancy of the United States and Britain's concurrent economic decline and loss of prestige. The academic community — especially the dons at Oxford and Cambridge — saw it as their duty to stand guard over Britain's unique cultural heritage. Whether the issue was their own debate in the twenties over reforming the two older universities, the pollution of the language by Hollywood movies, the plundering of great works of art by transatlantic plutocrats, or any number of similar issues, the Americans had by the thirties become identified in the minds of many British intellectuals with an evil materialism that threatened their inheritance.

Anti-Americanism was a theme Blunt returned to time and again in his *Spectator* articles. Reviewing Thomas Craven's *Modern Art* in 1935, he found it "galling" to have to admit that "it had to be left to an American" to make the long-awaited "complete re-evaluation of all the movements in the arts during the last sixty years." He lamented that Britain had "become the inexhaustible storehouses upon which American wealth and lack of discretion have for decades been drawing." Forty years later he was vehemently outspoken about the need to halt the flow of artworks to the United States. As a member of the Reviewing Committee on the Export of Works of Art, Blunt wrote *The Times* in 1971 to condemn the selling of artworks from major British collections as a "sign of cultural barbarism."[39]

Blunt's early views on cultural barbarity would have been influenced by Maurice Dobb's reports of how the Soviet system venerated and promoted the arts. "Museums and galleries have been thrown open and increased in number," Dobb recorded of the "cultural revolution" he witnessed in Moscow. Artists' exhibitions toured the provinces and "at least half the tickets at theaters, operas and concerts are supplied at half price to the trades unions and factories."[40]

The supposed openness, accessibility, and importance of art in Soviet society contrasted favorably with the situation under capitalism, where governments were powerless to prevent American millionaires from buying up Western Europe's old masters to lock them away as investments in bank vaults, or to display them in private behind their mansion gates. This rosy view of the Soviet cultural utopia could have been a persuasive argument to a budding art historian whose career depended on gaining access to these works of art. Nor is it difficult to comprehend how an intellectual Marxist like Blunt needed little persuasion to believe that the best hope of preserving a common European heritage from what Steiner terms "prostitution in the money market" was by allying himself with a Communist system that not only promised but ostensibly did make public all private art collections — under the supervision of the intellectuals, of course.

"If western painting, sculpture, and architecture were to regain classic stature, they must do so under the control of an enlightened, educative and historically purposeful state" is how Steiner rationalizes the way Blunt might have come to believe in a central authority over the arts. The precedent for establishing such an authority owes as much to Plato's "guardians" as it does to Karl Marx. But in his belief that great art is of too universal a significance to be traded like stock certificates in a capitalist system, Blunt was evidently persuaded that the Leninist commissariat for art and the revolutionary ministry of culture in Mexico met the need for a modern-day equivalent of the Florentine Medicis.[41]

Steiner contends that the belief that "great art is not, cannot be, private property" played a crucial part in crystallizing Blunt's "contemptuous loathing for capitalism." It precipitated his slide from "undergraduate and salon Marxism into the practicalities of treason." Blunt's pact with Stalin's emissaries owed something to a common affliction among scholars that Steiner terms "odium philogicum." Consumed by their esoteric minutiae, the academic mind yearns for power and authority in the real world. Their bottled-up resentment normally surfaces in "the ad-hominem nastiness of a book review" or the "arsenic of a footnote."[42]

Yet, as Steiner emphasized, many British academics in the thirties became Communists, but only a very few committed treason in the name of Marx. Blunt was one of them. His "fantasies of virile action, those solicitations of violence, which bubble up like marsh gas from the depths of abstruse thought and erudition," Steiner theorizes, "must have made their contribution to treason and betrayal. What began as a misguided belief that a Communist regime held out the best hope for the survival of Europe's heritage eventually translated "into clandestine performance, into covert mendacity and, possibly, murder (the men and women Blunt tagged for Soviet vengeance in Eastern Europe)."[43]

# CHAPTER 14

# *"Then There'll Be Jam for All"*

As a Trinity don, Blunt may have concealed his role as a talent scout for Soviet Intelligence. But he seems to have made no effort to conceal his Marxism. There was really no need to; at Cambridge communism was acceptable, in some circles fashionable. Members of the undergraduate socialist movement remember the reverential tones in which Anthony's name was mentioned as one of the Communist dons.

"Blunt was well known in left-wing circles," recalled Leonard Miall, who was then a leading undergraduate politician reading law in St. John's. As a "right-wing socialist," Miall became president of the Union and chairman of the Cambridge Union Socialist Society Club in 1936. "Not everyone on the left was brave or foolhardy enough to become a card-carrying Communist," he noted. But as a *Spectator* reader, the future BBC foreign correspondent knew all about the Trinity don's Marxist views long before he first met him at an undergraduate party in 1935. Miall recalls the solicitude shown by Blunt, who warned him of the disastrous consequences of mixing gin and sherry.[1]

"Blunt was the sort of don you met regularly at undergraduate parties," according to Miall. He was frequently in the company of Burgess. Miall regarded it as somewhat unusual for a fellow of Trinity to mix so freely with undergraduates. "Except for King's, where fraternizing was normal, the dons tended to keep themselves apart socially," said Miall. Not until 1979 did he reflect that this unusually gregarious behavior was essential to Blunt's role as a Soviet talent scout.[2]

"While Blunt was not an active Communist," Leo Long said, "he was known to us in the Trinity cell as one of the senior members who were theoretical Marxists." A London secondary-school boy, the son of an unemployed carpenter, Long regarded himself as a Communist before he won the scholarship in modern languages that brought him up to Trinity in 1935.[3]

"My name had been passed to James Klugmann even before Blunt became my supervisor," Long insisted, explaining that his decision to join the college cell in his first year had nothing to do with Blunt's tutoring him in French. "I was a Marxist because I was against the inequities of society," Long said. To a solitary working-class youth, the social and political egalitarianism of the Trinity cell offered a unique opportunity to make contact with "Hons and Rebels" from the public schools, who might otherwise have considered themselves socially superior to a carpenter's son from Hackney.[4]

Two prominent Cambridge "Hons" who came up to Cambridge in 1934 and were "sucked into the prevailing Marxist vortex for a time" were the Hovell-Thurlow-Cumming-Bruce brothers. As the sons of a baron they managed to combine their membership in the Communist cell with foxhunting. Their brief flirtation with communism did not affect their careers. James, after studying law in Magdalene, rose to become a lord chief justice of appeal. His brother Francis, "reputed to sing the 'Red Flag' even in his bath" at Trinity, became Lord Thurlow after a distinguished career in the diplomatic service. Francis "admired and was rather awed" by Blunt's erudition but conceded that he "didn't like him much."[5]

A young man who turned out to be one of the most important figures in Blunt's life, an American named Michael Straight, came up to Trinity in 1934. Straight became a member of the college's Communist cell early in 1935, but he remained ignorant that the "very pale, very slender, very tall" don in Trinity was a Marxist. In retrospect, Straight is now convinced that from the day he first passed through the Trinity Great Gate, his politics and family ties had already marked him out as one of Blunt's future recruits.[6]

As the younger son of the late Willard Straight, a partner of the Morgan Bank who founded *The New Republic* magazine, and Dorothy Whitney, the heiress of one of America's great industrial fortunes, Straight represented potentially important connections and influence. His education in New York and England left him with schizophrenic loyalties that reinforced the powerful radicalism absorbed from his mother, a former suffragette who had campaigned for the rights of American labor unions. After Willard Straight's death she had married a penniless Englishman named Leonard Elmhirst and founded Dartington Hall, an experimental school in South Devon where Michael and his elder brother, Whitney, completed their education.

Dartington's "progressive" education, which put Freud above algebra, had stamped Michael with a fiercely impatient intellect. An intense dark-haired young man, he arrived at Cambridge with two novels and two volumes of poetry, all unpublished, determined, as he put it, to "gate-crash eternity" by making his reputation as a poet, not a Wall Street banker. Harold Laski was a family friend and arranged that before Cambridge Michael would study for a year at the London School of Economics where the socialist economist was the principal. Travel in India, participation in a Pittsburgh steel strike, and dancing

with a ballet company sponsored by his mother, had further nurtured
his restlessly impetuous temperament.[7]

He was preceded at Cambridge by his older brother, whose passion
for racing cars had made him a playboy celebrity. Whitney introduced
Michael to the Pitt Club, where he encountered Guy Burgess. Michael
quickly dismissed Guy as "an alcoholic adventurer, a name dropper and
a gypsy."

A month after his arrival at Cambridge, Straight was courted by a
different circle from that found around the Pitt's bar. He told me about
his undergraduate experiences as we sat in the spacious comfort of his
red-brick residence set among expansive wooded grounds in Maryland,
just over the District Line and a forty-minute drive from the White
House. Half a century has softened some of the aquiline intensity in his
features, but it has not subdued the earnestness barely held in check by
a patrician voice. The "torrential nervous energy" for which Straight
was noted as an undergraduate orator still bursts forth from time to
time in conversation, accompanied by a ferocious upward stare from
eyebrows that crease into his high forehead.

Straight can still recall the details of the chilly November evening in
1935 when two unexpected visitors came into his dreary Trumpington
Road digs. The evening was of long-considered significance to him, a
major turning point in his life. The two uninvited guests were the
leaders of the Cambridge Communist movement, undergraduate revolutionaries incongruously wearing the gowns and academic caps then
required for all members of the university after dark. Straight was
surprised and not a little flattered that two of his seniors should have
trekked so far from Trinity to see him. But he admitted that he had
been half expecting the call ever since he arrived.

"My name had obviously been passed down to the Trinity cell by the
Communists at the LSE, where I had been regarded as a 'C' prospect,"
Straight said, explaining that potential Communist converts were graded
on the amount of political persuasion needed to secure their loyalty. "I
was a C contact, which meant that I had lots of unanswered questions
and they would have to work on me.[8]

"One had a birdlike head and manner; his name was James Klugmann," Straight recalled. The other was John Cornford, whose "dark,
deep-set eyes" fixed Michael: "His entire body was taut; his whole being
seemed to be concentrated on his immediate purpose. Their objective,
Straight explained, was to recruit him for CUSC. He readily agreed.
CUSC was dominated by a Marxist core, and he guessed that it served
as an "antechamber" to the party itself. About one in four of its two

hundred members belonged to Communist cells. But he knew that the 1935 meeting of the Seventh World Congress of the Communist International had revised the attitude to other socialist parties and had called for a Popular Front to fight Fascism.[9]

The Socialist Society became Straight's point of entry into the Trinity Communist cell. He became a member "early in 1935," attending its weekly Thursday meetings, having fallen under the personal spell of John Cornford whose idealism he intensely admired, both as a poet and political thinker.

"The Communist movement in Cambridge had no name and seemed to me at the time to have no visible ties to the Communist party," Straight insisted. "We carried no little green cards in our pockets; we took no party assignments with us when we left Cambridge at the end of each term."

Later Straight was to discover that the Communist leaders in Cambridge took their orders directly from the London CPGB headquarters in King Street. Even though he "got along well with Harry Pollitt, the working-class leader of the British Communist party to whom, at James's urging, I gave as much money as I could without feeling the pinch," Straight insisted that he felt "no sense of loyalty to the party as such."[10]

Straight considered himself a "casual member" of Cambridge's best-led radical student movement, but he believed that his actions were directed "by my own free will." Notwithstanding, he drew a distinction between himself and those whom he regarded as the hard core of dedicated Communists. In contrast with his fellow comrades, who put party above self and pasted their weekly party-contribution stamps in their green membership books, he considered his commitment more an intellectual than a political creed.[11]

Straight took his cue from Victor Kiernan, whom Klugmann and Cornford had persuaded to become a Communist in 1934. To Kiernan, who became a graduate student in history and then a Trinity research fellow, Marxism was more than a political creed because it supplied the "right answers" and provided a philosophical base for his historical studies. He believed that Marxism "could lift us to a plane far above the Cambridge level."[12]

Kiernan, like Blunt, was an influence behind the scenes. It is evident from the minute books of the Trinity Historical Society that he was, with Burgess, important in giving a powerful leftward tilt to the group. "Harry" Ferns, another historian, recalls Kiernan as one of the two leading lights in what was "very much a Marxist debating ground with its emphasis on the economic interpretation of history."

There was a more shadowy tier to the Communist organization at the university. Soon after Michael Straight joined the cell on March 18, 1935, he noticed that Egerton Herbert Norman — who twenty-two years later mysteriously committed suicide in Egypt, where he was Canada's ambassador — ceased to appear among the dozen or so students at the regular Tuesday evening meetings. Klugmann explained that Norman would be working with the Indian students and "in our terminology became a mole." The word *mole* had yet to acquire its popular association with espionage. For "reasons of security" Norman had gone underground. An open Communist working among the Indian students would be sure to draw the attention of the Colonial Office. The Indian Security Police were receiving regular reports from MI5 on the activities of the Cambridge Marxists. Kiernan also became a mole when he took over the Indian work the following year, after Norman returned to Canada.[13]

According to Straight, other moles included the Italian Marxist economist Piero Sraffa, whom Keynes had brought over to Cambridge and who was in danger of deportation if his party affiliation was revealed, and John Cairncross, who was aiming for the civil service and could not therefore afford to be labeled as an open party member. A Union friend of Straight's at Pembroke had already stopped coming to meetings when he decided to make his career as a barrister.

Blunt was never himself mentioned as one of the moles by any member of the Trinity Communist cell. Dons were not supposed to involve themselves in undergraduate political activities. Maurice Dobb had nearly lost his fellowship over the issue of proselytizing. But Straight insists that this injunction did not cut Dobb's Communist activities, because he also encountered Dobb at meetings of the town cell. All Communist undergraduates had to join under party rules intended to prevent the Cambridge intellectuals from considering themselves an elite and to maintain contact with the lumpenproletariat.

Straight was certain that Anthony Blunt had no outward political commitments to either the Trinity or the town cell — or any overt relationship with Klugmann. That is why Straight was surprised to read, in 1973, the article "From Bloomsbury to Marxism," Blunt's statement that he was quite familiar with the leaders of the Cambridge Communist movement. By revealing that he knew so much about the inner workings of the group, Straight said that Blunt betrayed "an intimacy" with Klugmann that confirmed Straight's conclusion that Klugmann had been in league with Blunt and a "conscious spotter for the Soviet network." Straight found Blunt's appraisal of Klugmann to be "perfectly sound," but Blunt's insistence that Burgess was the third member who dominated the Cambridge Communists was "absurd." Burgess was "certainly not in any organized continuing way" considered by the Trinity-cell members to be one of the leaders.[14]

Clues that suggest Blunt may indeed have been acting as a secret Communist functionary in 1935 also appear in the political sympathies he expressed in veiled terms in *Spectator* articles under the pseudonym of "Your Cambridge Correspondent." In March 1935, for example, Blunt maintained that politics "now occupy the minds of the intellectuals here as completely as the arts occupied them seven years or eight years ago." Three months later Blunt reported the formation of the University Peace Council as "much the most important event" of the term.[15]

The supposedly politically naïve young don endorsed a pamphlet put out by a left-wing coalition because it "shows how easily the University was swept into an active co-operation in the last war, how unreflectingly propaganda was swallowed even by supposedly critical minds." Blunt urged the "importance of the contribution which Cambridge made in the matters of science" as the "very reason Cambridge is one of the places where resistance to them can be of serious effect." This, he stated, was especially important in view of "the extent to which war preparations are actually being carried on in Cambridge at the present day."[16]

Was it mere chance that his was precisely the line the Cambridge Commnists were promulgating? That it was not pure coincidence seems apparent from the increasing stridency with which Blunt repeated the message the following term.

"Politics, at the moment, dominate," recorded the *Spectator*'s correspondent in Cambridge in November 1935, facetiously complaining that "the menace of poppies on the 11th and the election on the 14th is almost more than our constitutions will stand." Blunt also noted the new "Popular Front" amity between the Socialist Society and the Labour Club. The socialists had "an audience of sixty to eighty to hear papers even on such austere subjects as Marxism and Science or Marxism and Economics." He forecast with evident satisfaction that "next term, perhaps, when the Red Menace has had time to corrupt the Freshmen," the socialists would dominate the Union for the first time.[17]

Blunt's cheering on of the Cambridge Communists from the sidelines of the *Spectator* became noticeably more strident after his return in 1935 from a summer trip to the Soviet Union. The organizers were Charles Rycroft of Trinity and John Madge, brother of the Communist poet Charles, who obtained free passage for himself by rounding up five others willing to pay the fifteen-pound Intourist fare for the passage by steamer to Leningrad and back.

"Anthony and I were making the journey in search of pictures and architecture," Wilfrid Blunt recalled. But since the group was "for the most part left-wing pilgrims to the promised land," according to his unsophisticated judgment, it attracted the special attention of MI5.[18]

On the same trip were Michael Straight and Brian Simon, another member of the Communist cell. Simon was to make a career as a leading educator and became a member of the Central Committee of the CPGB. Also on board was Charles Fletcher-Cooke, another Trinity man, a rising Union radical who later became a Tory M.P. He knew Blunt through their mutual friend Victor Rothschild. On board also was Michael Young, a sociologist from London University, a Dartington school friend of Straight. Two Oxford undergraduates were also in the group. Christopher Mayhew, a future Labour minister and lord, who was a former pupil of Wilfrid Blunt's at Haileybury, came with his friend Derek Nenk. The party sailed for Leningrad from the Pool of London on August 10, 1935.[19]

"Anthony never talked about politics, but it was clear to me he knew something about Marxist theory," recalled Charles Fletcher-Cooke. According to Straight, Blunt listened in silence to the shipboard seminars organized by Madge to rally their socialist expectations. They had packed "conscientiously shabby clothes" to meet an anticipated pro-letarian conformity. The lavatories on the ship were filthy, and eight of the passengers shared a cramped two-berth cabin.

"Freedom at last," one of the party exclaimed when they landed at Leningrad. There was no one at the landing stage to meet them, for their Intourist guide was still asleep. "We tried not to see the poverty, the squalor, the primitiveness that surrounded us wherever we went," Straight wrote. "We huddled inside our illusions, responding as Intour-ist intended we should to a dozen carefully staged interviews." From Leningrad they traveled by train to Moscow "hard class." Photographs of the Kremlin were forbidden, but the future Lord Mayhew remembers how he enlisted Blunt's aid to violate Soviet regulations: Blunt held his legs so that he could lean out of their room in the Moscova Nova at the corner of Red Square.[20]

According to Straight's recollections of what he termed "the summer pilgrimage," Blunt was mysteriously and repeatedly absent. Neither did Blunt join the group on a grueling two-day rail trip south to Kharkov and Kiev. Straight was shaken by witnessing the Red Guards firing their rifles to drive half-starved children from the tracks.

In his autobiography Wilfrid makes no reference to his younger brother's mysterious disappearance. Nor is it clear from his account whether he was with Anthony all the time. But he does provide confirmation that his brother must have obtained special privileges because, apart from a token visit to a Moscow shoe factory, the Blunts "managed to escape the organized tours of factories and the other wonders of the Soviet regime."[21]

Did Blunt spend all his time absent from the main party studying the Poussins in the Hermitage and the Pushkin Museum in Moscow, as Wilfrid maintained? It is probable that the extended absences so distinctly remembered by Straight provided the opportunity for Blunt to slip away from his brother and meet with officers of Soviet intelligence.

Straight also told the FBI in 1963 that Blunt left the ship for one day. He remembers taking a picture of Blunt and Fletcher-Cooke being lowered over the side in a boat to go ashore. The purpose was to visit a German medieval town on the Baltic coast. Straight told me that this was later confirmed by one of the MI5 officers who debriefed him in 1965.[22]

Charles Fletcher-Cooke did not recall the visit but says that he revised his views on Russia and socialism as a result of the trip and that he was later "cut" because of his lack of enthusiasm in his satiric article "Take Russher," which he wrote for the Trinity magazine.

Blunt's return to London aboard the merchant vessel *Smolny* on September 12 was duly noted by MI5 — as the records show the passenger manifest was scrutinized carefully by MI5. Particular attention was paid to this group because Harry Pollitt was aboard. The CPGB general secretary was returning from a conference of the Communist International in Moscow. They also met Nancy Cunard, who, Fletcher-Cooke said, "took a shine to Wilfrid Blunt."[23]

Questioned at the 1979 press conference about whether he had ever visited Russia, Blunt said he had made a "holiday" trip in either 1935 or 1936. He could not recall which year. "It was one of the ordinary Intourist visits," he said, implying that visiting the Soviet Union during the Stalin years was a common excursion for British tourists.

"It was not . . ." Blunt then hesitated — perhaps as he thought better of denying that there was any sinister purpose to the trip — and then concluded with: "I went with a group of enthusiastic left-wingers, mainly Communists, mainly undergraduates."[24]

*Spectator* readers had the benefits of Blunt's enthusiastic report of this trip a few weeks after his return in 1935. He found Leningrad to be a neoclassical marvel of a city. In spite of the "rather blown Baroque" of the Winter Palace that failed to rise above the "merely provincial Italian or German," there were a multitude of inspiring architectural gems including Sakharoff's quarter-mile-long Admiralty building. Nor did Blunt neglect the architectural achievements of the Revolution. "The best blocks of living houses in Moscow are extremely impressive," Blunt wrote, though he found that the rising Palace of the Soviets "threatens to look more like a giant Selfridge's wedding cake than a worthy monument to the October revolution."[25]

When it came to the revolutionary contribution to painting Blunt made no comment. But six months earlier he had described a small exhibition of Soviet art in Cambridge as leading him "to hope that Russian artists would soon emerge from the tiresome period of merely producing bad imitations of traditional bourgeois styles." In his view this was because "pre-revolutionary Russia left only the most horrible of traditions to its Socialist successors." Easel painting was "essentially bourgeois," and although Blunt did not find the result particularly attractive, he approved of the rejection of abstraction in favor of realism. He predicted that "the greatest achievements of Socialist art would be in decorative painting on a large scale — as was the case when painting was last a communal art in the middle ages."[26]

Marxism rather than Blunt's aesthetic sense had obviously influenced his judgment about the merits of Communist realism. This appears to have persuaded him that art should serve the revolutionary cause. This became clear in his review of an exhibition of anti-Fascist paintings by an Austrian artist. He declared the paintings' "nightmarish quality" became "chunks of reality" by exposing the horrors of the Nazi concentration camps.[27]

"The intellectual is no longer afraid to own to an interest in the practical matters of the world," Blunt announced. Within a month of his return from Moscow he was telling *Spectator* readers that "art has been on the wrong track since Impressionism and that the steady recession of art from nature and life has led to its reaching complete futility in the last abstractions of the Cubists and the intimate meanderings of the Surrealists." Blunt despised the highly burnished reveries of Salvador Dali and Max Ernst, which were enjoying a vogue in the London galleries. "Their belief that they are the true repositories of the orthodox Marxist faith is perhaps shaken but certainly not destroyed by the fact that the voice of Moscow constantly condemns them as heretical," he wrote.[28]

Blunt criticized surrealism as the "phase during which art under capitalism gradually destroys itself as the contradictions in the social system become more acute." Blunt thought that the proletariat needed heavy doses of socialist realist art of the kind produced by Diego Rivera and José Clemente Orozco. Their highly animated and vividly executed murals dramatized the political and social aims of the 1910 Mexican Revolution. Blunt also lavished praise on Lord Hastings, "a Socialist Decorator" whose "big mural at Marx House" was "more ambitious and in many ways more successful" than his paintings.[29]

"In a century or two communism may have produced its Raphael," Blunt declared, calling for "an art dealing with social problems of the day, an art more closely connected with life than any since medieval times." Just how far Blunt's commitment to Moscow had gone appeared in his review of the exhibition "Artists Against Fascism," in which he claimed that "the monstrous tyranny" of Nazi restrictions was not at all the same thing as the dictatorship imposed on the same artists in Russia. He dismissed the "good Liberal view" that all dictatorship of art was inherently evil because it crushed individuality. He argued that the Soviet ban on abstract art as "bourgeois" was "quite logical" because the function of abstract art was "to destroy bourgeois ideology." Since there was no bourgeois ideology in the Soviet Union, "what is irrelevant is also wasteful and therefore not to be tolerated."[30]

Blunt made no secret of his Marxism in Cambridge intellectual circles. "I knew perfectly well what his views were," Professor G. F. Wickens of Toronto University assured me. A Trinity freshman from a London high school, who came up in the 1935–36 academic year, Wickens read modern languages. Blunt supervised him in French while Pascal tutored his German. It is surely significant that Wickens quickly came to know from the way they both conducted their classes that they were Communists. "Pascal had a very clear intellectual grasp of Marxism," Wickens said. "Blunt didn't. He used to talk in catchphrases and was rather a lightweight when it came to Marxist theory."[31]

Wickens vividly remembers arriving for his first supervision and finding a lethargic-looking Blunt lounging on a sofa in a silk dressing gown. "Read your essay to me," he demanded. After Wickens finished, Blunt made no comment other than to offer him a glass of sherry. Wickens was appalled, looking back, on how little teaching he received from Blunt. Although fair in his academic dealings, awarding Wickens an "A" when it was deserved, Blunt was not encouraging. "You've got brains, you can write well and you work hard, but you realize that's not good enough," Wickens remembers Blunt saying. Aesthetic sensibility and taste were highly personal — a question of "background," really — and Blunt did not think his pupil had the necessary capacity.

"It was not so much intellectual snobbery, as social snobbery," Wickens recalled. "He made me feel I was a hardworking, grubby little bastard."[32]

Although sympathetic to left-wing causes, Wickens did not rate a place in Blunt's web of intrigue. Blunt's concern was not with recruiting the undergraduate foot soldiers for the party, but with spotting, cultivating, and passing on to Soviet intelligence those left-wing students most likely to succeed in making their mark on the governing establishment.

Michael Straight was a prime candidate. Blunt came to know him on their summer pilgrimage to Russia. As one of only four to get a first in Part I of the Economics Tripos in his freshman year, Straight was an academic high-flyer who had money and social position.

Although Straight was unaware of it, he was also under scrutiny for the Apostles by David Champernowne, a graduate left-wing economist of King's whose family happened to have been the former owners of Dartington Hall. It fell to Straight — in the absence of Maurice Dobb and the reluctance of Piero Sraffa — to defend the paper on Karl Marx's theory that Champernowne presented at a meeting of the Political Economy Club that October. Keynes responded to their dialectical efforts by saying that he had "read Marx, as if it were a detective story, trying to find a clue and never succeeding." Straight was taken aback.[33]

"It was the only instance that I had heard of a leading intellectual at the university challenging the new orthodoxy," Straight recalled. "I was shaken, but my political allegiance was unchanged."[34]

Straight's confidence was restored in November at a dinner with Anthony Blunt and Guy Burgess, arranged by James Klugmann. Straight was so "enthralled" and "flattered" by the "worldly brilliance" of Burgess and Blunt that when he returned to his rooms at half past eleven he had to put pen to paper. Writing to his mother, he confessed that he had "learned to love the Communist students, even if I don't love Communism itself"; he burned with "unreasonable and inexplicable" commitment as he tried to "describe the terrible significance of it all."[35]

Straight said that Blunt and Burgess had not appealed for his commitment to an international movement. "In no sense was it Russian expansionism or working for their intelligence service; that would have been entirely unacceptable," Straight told me. The vision they held out was that the world was at the dawn of a New Age. The old age was dying — disintegrating economically and socially.[36]

"Anthony and Guy made it appear that they had leapt from one age to the other," Straight said. "They were no longer representatives of a dying culture, but spokesmen for an emerging culture." Their cultural message to him was that Britain was dying and could not survive the Great Depression, the harbinger of the final crisis of capitalism predicted by Marx.[37]

Straight believed Blunt regarded it as a great tragedy that the Revolution had taken place in Russia, but in terms of power and leadership Moscow now had the leverage on the future. "They left that to Klugmann to explain," Straight continued, "but both he and Guy were convinced that the grand sweep of history would vindicate their decision to detach themselves from the past and work for the International Revolution."[38]

To any nineteen-year-old, the call to join a crusade that promised equality and social justice in place of a corrupt and faltering capitalist regime was a powerful motivation. For Straight, who already worshiped John Cornford and the Communist ideal he so intensely embodied, the appeal was irresistible. Only many years later did he reflect that Klugmann knew full well the extent of the personal bond that existed between them and had "reluctantly" decided to exploit it for the cause.

"Looking back," Straight said, "this was plainly the targeting of a potential recruit from the student Communist cell who was being turned over for inspection and cultivation by Blunt." He began receiving frequent invitations to the informal gatherings that Blunt held in his fine set of rooms above the cloistered colonnades of Trinity's New Court, in the shadow of the imposing Wren Library. Straight met Blunt's close circle of friends, among whom were Victor Rothschild and his lively first wife, Barbara.[39]

As Lord Annan has pointed out, a Marxist orientation was a prerequisite for election to the Apostles at this time, so it appears no coincidence that Straight was soon invited to become an Apostle. Straight learned that Blunt, Burgess, and Rothschild were among the active younger members, along with his sponsor, Champernowne.

At his induction meeting in Keynes's rooms on March 8, 1935, Straight was obliged to take "a fearful oath, praying that my soul would writhe in unendurable pain for the rest of eternity if I so much as breathed a word about the society to anyone who was not a member." As the only Apostle elected from his year, he assumed the traditional duties of the youngest member as secretary, keeper of the "Ark," and arranger of meetings.

"One must be very brilliant and extremely nice," J. T. Sheppard advised the new member. Straight found this King's don, who carried a cushion with him everywhere, rather childish and precious, but he did his best to comply by avoiding politics. The blasts of puritanical

Communist rhetoric that had brought sweat to the forehead of the junior Apostles three years earlier, and which Keynes, with fatherly indulgence, attributed to a youthful "zest to adopt a painful solution because of its painfulness," had subsided by 1936.[40]

"No Communist views were expressed in my presence, at least at society meetings," Straight insisted. Burgess made a point of traveling to Cambridge for the Saturday meetings because "he derived an almost sensual pleasure from the discussion of ideas."

Blunt seldom appeared, even at Saturday meetings. When he did speak, usually on artistic themes, he held forth at length. But Straight soon became aware that Blunt was trying to bring him under his influence. "He went out of his way to make himself a protector of mine and to make me indebted to him," Straight said, recalling how Blunt claimed to have intervened on his behalf in a row with the College Council in May 1936.[41]

Straight had been the first to sign a petition protesting that the Trinity servants received less than a living wage from the college. Called upon to explain himself to the fellows, he made the rounds of painful interviews amid rumors in the Senior Combination Room about his possible expulsion. The waiters eventually got their wage raise and Straight stayed. Blunt made a special point of dramatizing the role he had played in persuading the other fellows that Straight had been foolish rather than malign.

A few months later, at the Apostles' annual dinner in London, Blunt again made a move to manipulate Straight. It fell on Straight as the youngest member to make the first speech in praise of the Apostolic Spirit. Before the meeting Blunt urged Straight to give a hard-line address because the other speaker, a young Conservative member of the Treasury, was going to decry the politicization of the society.

Straight did not comply. To Blunt's obvious displeasure he made no full-blooded attack on the other speaker. Instead he hewed to a more moderate theme, explaining that while the Apostles of the past had reached their ideals through the endless discussion of a small group, and his generation was responding to the call for action of thousands, this did not necessarily mean they wanted to put deeds above deliberation. After Straight's call for reason, the Treasury man's anti-Communist diatribe fell flat. To Keynes it appeared that the Apostle from the Treasury had viciously attacked the integrity of another member of the brethren.

The whole affair was typical of what Straight called "Blunt's love of conspiracy and maneuver." What he did not know was that Blunt's attempt to set him up appears to have been another devious move in Blunt's long-standing feud with Keynes.[42]

A feud that was to backfire.

Blunt's thesis on Italian art was nearly complete in 1936, and he was in some doubt whether Trinity would elect him to a permanent fellowship when his four-year research fellowship expired the following year. This explains why he applied for a six-year open fellowship at King's College, instituted by Keynes, for studies in the humanities, social sciences, or natural sciences.

The release of Blunt's fellowship application, endorsed "Confidential and for the use of the Electors only," was finally permitted by the college authorities in 1988. It proves to be a very revealing document in which Blunt not only makes a rare admission that he received only a "second class" in the first part of the Mathematical Tripos, but it also confirms that he had been lecturing at the Courtauld since 1932. He taught "The Theories and Criticism of Painting," lectured on baroque architecture and painting as well as Mannerist painting, and also had given a course in Cambridge on French seventeenth-century painting for the Modern Languages Faculty.

The Harris Fellowship, Blunt told the King's electors, would provide him with the opportunity to turn his dissertation on "The Pictorial History of Painting" into a book. He claimed that he had already completed more than half of this project and would also carry out more research in southern Italy for his intended second book about baroque architecture. His referees were Walter Friedlander, who "spoke in the highest terms of Blunt's ability as a scholar as well as his fine personality," and George Constable, the Slade Professor of Art, who was struck by the candidate's "critical detachment and ability to consider both things and ideals with a fresh eye." He also observed that Blunt was "the type of man not suited to routine work of lecturing and teaching, but who works best and hardest when he has considerable freedom of movement and can arrange his own work." According to Dr. H. F. Stewart, the dean of Trinity — who, it seems, was independently consulted by the electors — Blunt was "a growing plant." Significantly, in Stewart's opinion, Blunt had already "reached the high point in art criticism." This he said was where his heart was rather than in teaching modern languages. Blunt had evidently been aware of reservations in the Modern Languages Faculty about his failure to pull his weight because, Stewart noted, "in the course of the last months" he had "developed a surprising ability to teach the French language, literature and to some extent history."

Blunt, it seems, made a very great effort to obtain the King's Fellow-ship. He was well aware of Keynes's influence and also worked hard to curry favor with him. A month before the electors made their final decision, the New Arts Theater, established by a trust sponsored by Keynes, raised its opening-night curtain to the full attention of the national press.

The production starred Keynes's Russian wife in the lead role of Ibsen's *A Doll's House*. In his *Spectator* review, Blunt described the first night as an occasion of "dazzling pomp" in which Lydia Lopokova enchanted everyone with her "tiny, twittering, highly successful Nora." Blunt then duly paid lip service to the simultaneous publication of Keynes's latest "epic on unemployment." Indeed, *The General Theory of Employment, Interest and Money* was to become the seminal work of twentieth-century economics. But perhaps because the General Theory infuriated Marxists such as Dobb, Blunt slightingly remarked that Keynes's new book "could be found lying about in the most unexpected rooms." The double-edged barb did not endear him to Keynes, whose original mistrust of Blunt at the time of his affair with Julian Bell had been confirmed when the Marxists took over the Apostles.[43]

When the King's electors met in March 1936 to consider the disser-tations, Keynes was openly hostile. He dismissed Blunt's work as "a lot of Marxist nonsense." Blunt was rejected. This was a bitter blow, the third time that Blunt had failed to meet the grade set by his fellow academics.

A few weeks later Blunt went off with Louis MacNeice on an Easter trip to Spain. The two old friends were both nursing wounded egos. MacNeice's wife had run off with an American from Oxford, "life was bloody," and he was so deeply in debt that Blunt had to pay for his steamship passage to Gibraltar.

In Spain the Fascists and the rightist Falange party were openly protesting the election of a Popular Front government of liberals, socialists, and Communists. MacNeice advised Blunt to tell their friends that they were going "to look at the churches before it is all burnt down." The civil war did not break out for three more months, but the political mood in Spain that March was as ugly as the weather: It rained continuously.[44]

"The Hammer and Sickle was scrawled all over Spain that Easter," MacNeice wrote. Blunt could barely contain his delight. "If Spain goes communist," he declared, "France is bound to follow. And then Britain, and then there'll be jam for all."[45]

During the two-week trip, as they toured churches and art galleries,

Blunt talked enthusiastically of the death of easel painting, with town halls and factories blooming with murals and bas-reliefs in concrete. Blunt's sanctimonious Marxism—preaching the "Categorical Imperative"—bore heavily on his more imaginative and free-thinking friend. Did Blunt make an all-out effort on the trip to persuade his old schoolmate to become a Communist? If so MacNeice resisted the overtures to join the Gadarene stampede that had sucked in Blunt and now beckoned his fellow left-wing Oxford poets Stephen Spender and W. H. Auden.

"The great danger of Marxist doctrine is that it allows and even encourages opportunism," MacNeice observed when he came to write about the trip with Blunt. "After a bit the Marxist, who is only human, finds such fun practicing strategy—i.e., hypocrisy, lying, graft, political pimping, tergiversation, allegedly necessary murder—that he forgets the end in the means, the evil of the means drowns the good of the end, power corrupts, the living gospel withers, Siberia fills with ghosts."[46]

"You always were so handy with the intellectual spanner," MacNeice wrote Blunt shortly after their return from Spain. As a poet, MacNeice was not born for dogma, and, as he wrote, "You can't feed Marx to an artist as you feed grass to a cow." After their return from Spain, he made one last effort to salvage his friendship with Blunt. Loading a sculpture made by a Birmingham friend, Gordon Herrick, into his car, MacNeice drove to Cambridge on May 5 believing that Blunt would help him sell the semi-abstract piece to Victor Rothschild.[47]

The highly polished stone *Cyclamen* was set up in Blunt's "coquettishly chaste room with white panelling and Annunciation lilies." Blunt protested that his Marxist convictions made it impossible for him to push the sale of a work that was primarily abstract. "Couldn't you get old VR to buy it to reduce his weight if nothing else?" Louis pleaded. "I didn't think that it's merely a decorative work anyway."[48]

Whether Rothschild shared Blunt's views about the *Cyclamen* is not recorded. Nor were Victor's socialist sympathies aroused because a working-class stonemason had labored to produce the sculpture in his spare time. MacNeice abandoned the effort to raise money for his friend's artistic effort.

"Cambridge was still full of Peter Pans, but all the Peter Pans were now talking Marx," MacNeice observed after an evening with Blunt's Trinity coterie. "Marxian purpose which, like early Christianity, promised self-fulfillment through abnegation, freedom through discipline. Young men flocked to the new creed just because it made demands on them and because, while it attacked human individualism, it simultaneously made the cosmos once more anthropomorphic."[49]

MacNeice was too much of a romantic to be a Communist revolutionary. The next morning, while Blunt was teaching, he decided to take his own revenge on Marx.

"I found a gin bottle in his room and drank myself blind before lunch; it seemed an exquisite outrage to the room and also to Dialectical Materialism," MacNeice wrote, adding that he had taken particular pleasure insulting "a very elegant evergreen don" before falling asleep among the dishes.[50]

"You see I am really much happier when drunk," MacNeice wrote to Blunt after driving back to Birmingham. He had given a lift to Guy Burgess and John Cornford, the latter to stand trial for causing an obstruction by distributing Communist pamphlets in the city center. "There is still hope for the human race," he wrote of Cornford, congratulating Cambridge for producing "the one chap of the whole damn lot of you who is going to be a great man." He told Blunt that Burgess, even though he "thought all the young men in the streets of Birmingham were queer," was "quite the nicest of your pals."[51]

Two months later, when MacNeice was in Iceland with W. H. Auden on a travel-book project, Blunt received a spoof postcard of a local boy with the suggestive message: "A donor who prefers to remain anonymous is sending a very pretty piece to King's this October. Impey's the name." Later that year Auden and MacNeice published a celebrated joint poem full of cryptic references to leading political figures and their friends, couched as a "Last Will and Testament." MacNeice had bequeathed Blunt "A copy of Marx and £1000 a Year/And the picture of Love Locked Out by Holman Hunt."[52]

This public flagging of Blunt's Marxism may have been the final straw for him. There are no more letters after October 31, 1936, and MacNeice makes no mention of Blunt after that date. But the poem's biting anti-Marxist cynicism about "the Comrades . . . who wanted to be at home with Stalin" suggests MacNeice's long friendship with Blunt foundered at this point.[53]

The Spanish Civil War had erupted in July with the revolt of the generals in Morocco led by Franco. To the intellectuals of all shades of left-wing opinion the issue was clear: Britain had a moral duty to help save the democratically elected Popular Front government from a rebellion engineered by the Fascist generals. But neither Prime Minister Baldwin nor the Tory press agreed. Nor, to the dismay of the left, did the French Popular Front government. It was left to the Soviet Union to send arms and technicians to help the government in Madrid. The war in Spain became the subject of bitter debate; the wedge between the left and right in Britain was driven deeper and deeper.

"The Spanish Civil War was felt to be a war of light against darkness" was how Stephen Spender described its impact on his friends. Spender was another of MacNeice's friends who had become a Communist. But he "gradually fell away from the Party," according to MacNeice, who may well have had Blunt's easy fanaticism in mind when he wrote that Spender "had not been born for dogma."[54]

John Cornford was the first Cambridge Communist to demonstrate that he was ready to lay down his life for his political beliefs. Abandoning his Cambridge mistress and his infant son by an earlier lover, Cornford rushed off to enlist in the Spanish army. His only qualifications as a soldier were his newly acquired double first, a copy of *Das Kapital*, and a volume of Shakespeare's plays. To his contemporaries this was in itself enough to transform the tousled Communist into a romantic hero.

"We buried Ruiz in a new pine coffin/But the shroud was too small and his washed feet stuck out," Cornford wrote in poems from the front that echoed, in less sentimental vein, those of another Cambridge war hero, Rupert Brooke.[55]

Julian Bell, David Haden-Guest, Tom Wintringham, Stephen Spender, and briefly Auden himself made the journey to the front line of what they believed was the battle between the forces of democracy and fascism. Some, like Spender, reported the war. Others, like Bell, drove ambulances, and still others, like Cornford, fought in the International Brigade. Mobilized with the aid of Communist organizations when the call to arms sounded from Moscow in December 1936, the socialist army that eventually numbered over 50,000 made a vital contribution to helping the Loyalists raise the siege of Madrid.

Within a year, as Russian troops arrived to enforce Moscow's own Communist goals, the International Brigade was subordinated to Soviet generals. Democracy was not on the political agenda that Stalin had drawn up for the reeling Popular Front government. The executions and intrigues in Spain and the relentless trials in Moscow as Stalin systematically purged the remaining opposition to his dictatorship took a heavy toll on the idealism of British intellectuals like George Orwell, Auden, and Spender. The anti-Fascist front of the left shattered over what Spender described as "a refusal on behalf of all but the most convinced ideologists to tell the lies required by the Stalinist communists."[56]

Anthony Blunt, immersed in the unemotional world of Poussin's painting and secure in his aseptically white intellectual aerie in Trinity, continued with his detached promotion of the Marxist theory of art.

"More and more, as I looked at these paintings," Blunt wrote of an Impressionist exhibition, "I was led to wonder: How did we ever believe in significant form, or whatever disguise we gave that theory, particularly when we had before our eyes such works as these?" He now believed that the "tragedy of Monet, as of so many inventors, was that he became entangled in the wheels of his own inventions and could never escape from them." Of an exhibition of Matisse drawings he wrote, "The vision which inspires them seems no longer to be one of the real world." Like those of Bonnard, who had become popular after the war, "they stuck just where they were, repeating over and over again a solution to the problems of painting which had made a fashion.[57]

"Since the War, everything has gone wrong," Blunt lamented. "A period of efficient and repetitive succulence was succeeded by one of slick and fluffy prettiness." Even Picasso (of whose paintings he had written as recently as 1934, "one feels oneself in contact with a great mind") was shrinking to pygmy size under Blunt's increasingly orthodox Marxist scrutiny. His abstraction had become "tiresome," Blunt wrote, although the "elements of emotionalism and ingenuity always fused in any works by Picasso" produced the "kind of painting which will appeal to those whose minds, like mine, are clogged in a love of the obscure and unusual but it is doubtful whether he has much to contribute to the development of painting at the present time."[58]

Since the Marxist canon demanded that art had to be socially useful, it also had to be realistic enough to convey a political message. Picasso, according to Blunt, failed to meet the criterion by running off into abstraction and surrealism, which he called "ingenious but empty cleverness." The dream had lost its vitality, Blunt declared, "and anyhow, are we to be contented with dreams?"[59]

Blunt's respect for the most important artist of the twentieth century was irrevocably shattered when he saw *Guernica*, which dominated the Spanish Pavilion at the International Exhibition in Paris in August 1937. The huge, nearly monochrome canvas with its jagged and screeching images of horror had instantly become one of the most celebrated visual statements of its time. Inspired by the artist's outrage at the destruction wrought by the civil war in his native land, Picasso had dedicated *Guernica* to the Spanish people. It memorialized the small Basque town that was reduced to rubble by the bombs of the Condor Legion sent by Hitler to hasten Franco's victory.

Blunt's immediate reaction to *Guernica* was a mixture of cynical disgust and dialectical disparagement. His words spoke no less eloquently about his own essential cold-bloodedness.

"The gesture is fine and even useful, in that it shows the adherence of a distinguished Spanish intellectual to the cause of his government," Blunt began his dismissive single paragraph on *Guernica*. With the chilling delusion of a Stalinist, he dismissed as "disillusioning" the one work that stands today, as it did in 1937, a testament to the inhumanity of war. "It is not an act of public mourning," Blunt wrote, "but the expression of a private brain storm which gives no evidence that Picasso has realized the political significance of *Guernica*."[60]

Over his lifetime Anthony Blunt admitted making a few errors. But this was one of his greatest. And he was forced to acknowledge it again and again. His shallow Marxist diatribe against Picasso left a blot on his reputation as a judge of art that lasted for years. Many years later Blunt tried to justify himself by asserting that he "was very much moved by it" but "horrified by it from a theoretical point of view." Although he was forced to admit the integrity and artistic significance of Picasso's best-known work, Blunt could never completely live down the accusations he made in the *Spectator* under the heading "Picasso Unfrocked."

"There is something pathetic in the sight of a talented artist struggling to cope with a problem entirely outside his powers," Blunt wrote. He poured scorn on Picasso's "obscene polyps, in mitre, coronet or mantilla" that "hack at statues, prance on tight ropes, ride on a charger which turns into a pig or Pegasus, pray to financial remonstrances, are tossed by bulls" with "arms, eyes, and head contorted in a scrawl of horror.

"Picasso should have seen more than the mere horror of the Civil War," Blunt railed on with the dogmatic indignation of a *Pravda* editorialist. The struggle in Spain was only "a tragic part of a great forward movement." The Revolution demanded optimism expressed "in a direct way and not with a circumlocution so abstruse that those who are occupied with more serious things will not have the time and energy to work out all its implications." Picasso had once been a "giant," but now, for Blunt "in a harsher glare, and up against more exacting standards, he appears a pygmy."[61]

Significantly, in the same *Spectator*, Goronwy Rees was attempting to make a pygmy of another of Moscow's onetime champions. In a review of André Gide's *Afterthoughts* — written after Gide returned from a disillusioning visit to the Soviet Union — Rees clearly set out to cast doubt on the accuracy of the second book the French philosopher had produced containing charges of grotesque abuses of Marxist ideals under

Stalin. The "indignation of a bitter enemy," he suggested, had tainted Gide's view of the Moscow trials. Rees was openly skeptical, going so far as to suggest that Stalin's bloody purge of his opponents was "historically necessary."[62]

Rees was then an editor of *The Spectator*, so it may have been no simple coincidence that he and his friend Blunt attempted to cut down two of the most prominent European Communist heretics. Blunt, through his expanding network, was proving his sinister capacity to serve Moscow's interest in ways that could not have been foreseen when he became one of the first of "Stalin's Englishmen." And he went so far as to give a clear indication of the ultimate reward he anticipated for this loyal service. In his January 1937 review of an exhibition of "masterpieces lost in the attics of our large and older feudal residences," he cast for himself the role as Commissar of Art and Culture in a Communist Britain.

"What a field day the Minister of Fine Arts will have," Blunt gloated, "when, after the Revolution, the State takes over all privately-owned paintings and collects the best in a central museum!"[63]

As a Marxist propagandist and a secret recruiter for Soviet intelligence, Blunt intended to ensure that by aiding the Revolution he also advanced his own career as a cultural overlord.

# CHAPTER 15

# "*Many a Fickle Makes a Fuckle*"

"Now, with my Party, I stand all alone," John Cornford had written before going into action as commander of the English Battalion of the International Brigade in Spain. On a rocky ridge above the Spanish village of Lopera on the Cordoba front, December 28, 1936, he made the ultimate sacrifice to his political commitment. The news that Cornford had been killed in action a day after his twenty-first birthday took a month to reach England. The donnish *Cambridge Review* said his death was "a bitter loss to English thought as well as to the undergraduates and working class of England." *Granta* mourned the passing of Cambridge's most heroic figure since Rupert Brooke as "the deepest experience of our lives." At a memorial meeting in the town a Communist party member from London referred to Cornford as "the finest type of middle-class comrade."[1]

Blunt's portrayal of Cornford in his 1973 article "From Bloomsbury to Marxism" as a "glamorous figure" and a "vehement orator" was a "travesty" to Michael Straight. He regards it as highly significant that Blunt chose to describe Cornford as "a highly emotional character" who "might have gone back on his Marxist doctrine." The gratuitous assertion that it was "appropriate" that he "should have gone to Spain to get killed" because Cornford was "the stuff of what martyrs are made of" was most revealing of all. "An incredible statement," Straight observed: "Only a hardened Communist functionary could have made a statement like that." Michael Straight had taken it upon himself to break the tragic news to Cornford's family and his lover, Margot Heineman. He also arranged for the care of Cornford's estranged girlfriend, Ray Peters, and her infant son, James. That the party might seek to make Cornford a propaganda symbol was no shock to Straight, but he was quite unprepared for the way that Blunt exploited his friend's death two weeks later, when he received a summons to Blunt's elegant rooms.[2]

"I assumed that he wanted to talk to me about the Apostles, or about Victor Rothschild's unhappy wife," recalled Straight. "Instead, he asked me what I planned to do when I graduated from Cambridge." Blunt listened to his hopes for becoming a British citizen and member of Parliament.[3]

"Some of your friends have other ideas for you," Blunt coolly told him. Then, with calculated reasonableness, he went on to explain that Straight's political activities might make it difficult for him to obtain naturalization. Since Britain was a declining nation, he suggested that Straight's talents would be better applied in the United States, which was destined to play a far larger role in world affairs. He should use his family connections in J. P. Morgan to make his future career in international banking.

"Our friends have given a great deal of thought to it," said Blunt. "They have instructed me to tell you that is what you must do." Straight recalled his surprise when Blunt identified the "friends" as "the Communist International." The implication was that Moscow had decided his mission was to provide them with inside information about Wall Street's plans to dominate the global economy. Blunt said he was instructed to help Straight prepare for this assignment by breaking all his political ties with the left. He was to use his grief at Cornford's death as a pretext for cutting himself off from the Cambridge Communists.[4]

Straight remembered how he sank deeper into Anthony's gray sofa as he tried to protest. It would mean abandoning his friends in the university Socialist Society and giving up the presidency of the Union that his recent election as secretary guaranteed. But Blunt undermined his resistance with an air of compassionate understanding and an obvious effort to sympathize with a predicament that required personal sacrifices to serve the cause. By implying that he was only acting for a mutual friend who wanted Straight to know he "regrets very much that he is not permitted to identify himself," Blunt gave Straight the impression that Burgess was Moscow's shadowy eminence. Straight weakened and agreed to the plan. But the very next evening he was back in Blunt's rooms, pleading for reconsideration. Blunt was sympathetic and promised to intercede with the "friend."[5]

"Sending the son of a J. P. Morgan banker to act as Wall Street agent of Moscow was the sort of bizarre plot that would have appealed to Burgess," Straight told me. The more he thought about it, the more it seemed an insane idea. "Anybody who knew anything about me would have realized that being a banker was the last thing I might want to do with my life. Unlike most undergraduates I did not have to worry about earning a living; the whole essence of my life at the time was Cambridge."[6]

A week later Blunt told Straight that Moscow had rejected his appeal. There was no choice but for him to return to the United States and go underground, even if he refused to become a banker. Straight says that he protested more strongly. Blunt never once raised his voice or lost his air of friendly authority. He simply assured Straight that he would make yet another plea on his behalf; this time it "would be considered in the highest circles of the Kremlin." Blunt implied that he himself would use a direct line of communication and that his appeal would reach Stalin himself. However, there was one condition. Straight had to stage his "breakdown" without further delay and cut his ties with the Communist movement. No more time could elapse if Straight's political retreat from the party was to be convincingly attributed to an emotional reaction to Cornford's death.[7]

"That was the bargain that was offered to me," said Straight. "I accepted it." He claimed that in his emotional state he simply lacked the will to stand up to Blunt's strong manipulative personality. "I did not subject Blunt's proposal to any rational analysis," Straight insisted. But by striking the bargain, he later recognized that whatever Moscow's reaction, he had lost the fight to determine his own future. Blunt's assault on his insecurity had exposed his own submissiveness. Had Blunt been didactic or doctrinaire, Straight admits that he might have found it easier to resist.[8]

"Anthony was, on the contrary, compassionate; he seemed as unnerved as I was by the sadness of the situation in which we found ourselves," Straight recalled, admitting that in the weeks following Cornford's death his defenses were down. "I wanted to be a martyr" was how Straight rationalized his capitulation, "I needed to sacrifice myself, as John had done."[9]

Straight's personal agonizing made it easier for him to stage a convincing charade of his breakdown. Under Blunt's tutelage he abandoned lectures and work and quarreled with the members of Trinity cell. He alienated his socialist supporters by advising them to vote for a Conservative candidate in the Union because he was not planning to return to Cambridge the following autumn. Only one of his friends, John H. Humphrey, guessed what was happening. He came around one evening to confide that Blunt had approached him too. Blunt later told Straight that Humphrey did not possess the dedication to communism sufficiently strong enough to survive going underground.

The full appreciation of his predicament made Straight fiercely determined not to let any of his other friends get snared in the same web. When Teresa Mayor — who later became Victor Rothschild's second wife — was being pressured to join the student Communist movement that spring, he exercised his veto, as chairman of the Socialist Society, against her enrollment. "I already had the veil lifted from my eyes by Anthony and I was determined not to let Tess get sucked in," Straight told me.[10]

By the end of the Easter term, Straight's personal crisis and the strain of faking a breakdown had reached the point where he could not stay on for the finals. Straight's mother was upset and pleaded that he reconsider. Blunt, Burgess, and Simon drove down to Dartington in April to offer their support. Blunt promised Straight's concerned parent that he would watch over her son. For his part Burgess drank too much whiskey, leered at the male dancers of the Joos Ballet, and infuriated Blunt by giving the clenched-fist socialist salute as they drove off from Dartington Hall.

Shortly afterward Straight sailed for America with his stepfather. Aboard ship he began to have second thoughts. He wrote to Blunt in desperation, offering to make over all his wealth to the party if he could escape from his commitment. Once back in Washington, Straight resolved to return to Cambridge after all. Blunt helpfully arranged with the Trinity bursar for Straight to have rooms in New Court near his own. Straight isolated himself from all his former friends in a desperate attempt to catch up with his economics studies for the finals. But if he intended to defy what he believed were Moscow's orders, he found Blunt prepared to exercise an additional psychological hold over him.

"My plea to be released had been reviewed by Stalin, so Anthony told me when I returned to Cambridge," Straight wrote in his autobiography *After Long Silence*. In his talks with me Straight said he had been able only to hint at Blunt's Machiavellian manipulation while the old spy was still alive. But after Blunt's death Straight could be franker. He explained that the web in which he was snared by Blunt was not woven simply around loyalty to Cornford's memory, but was also a cynical manipulation of a young man's emotional life and subtle sexual blackmail.[11]

A year before Cornford's death, Straight had fallen for Tess Mayor. In his own words, he was "stricken" with the "unearthly beauty" of Tess, who "had the gaunt nobility of Yeats's beloved Maud Gonne, and some of Maud Gonne's cold fire." He tried to press his affections on Tess in his rooms at Whewell's Court, but despite the sound of Mozart's concertos on the Gramophone and the reading of plaintive verses of Yeats's poetry, their love did not take fire, because, Straight concluded, "there was a knot within her that I could not untie."[12]

Frustrated, Straight turned to the ever-solicitous Trinity don for advice and consolation. The extent to which Blunt was already a master at putting people in his debt was evident from the solution he proposed: Straight should enter into a romantic liaison with the wife of one of his best friends, whose marriage was on the rocks. Not surprisingly, Straight was reluctant. But Blunt engineered a meeting between the two at one of his social gatherings. To Straight's surprise, the woman embraced him as they walked through the darkened cloisters of New Court and proposed they begin their affair right away. He rejected her advances, knowing that her husband was both possessive and jealous. But the woman did not take no for an answer. With Blunt acting as their go-between, she continued to pursue him as long as he was at Cambridge. Straight insists that Blunt repeatedly tried to push him into the affair although he knew Straight was involved with a German ballet dancer and had begun a serious courtship of Belinda Crompton, an American girl who was to become his first wife.[13]

"I regarded Anthony as a confidant. Now I realize he was only putting me deeper in his debt," Straight said. "He placed himself between me and the Crompton family and between me and _____ _____." Straight appears to have made his emotional life a hostage to Blunt, who used this leverage to insist that Straight continue seeing his friend's disconsolate wife.[14]

"She was desperate, genuinely in love with me, and I felt I had to be kind to her," Straight explained. He survived an attempted seduction under a blanket after a champagne picnic beside the Cam one May evening. But her husband's jealous rage on his return that night to find her reading Donne's poems by candlelight made Straight reluctant to see her again. Once again, Blunt prevailed. He said she was becoming suicidal. So Straight agreed to another meeting – but only in a London restaurant. Looking back, Straight cannot understand why Blunt went to such lengths to risk the wrath of her jealous husband. He speculates that not only did Blunt use the liaison to consolidate his hold over him, Blunt may also have been calculating enough to arrange an adulterous liaison for the husband to facilitate an eventual divorce, so putting another person in his debt.[15]

Blunt's manipulation of Straight also had another dimension. During his last two terms at Cambridge Straight rendered a further service to Blunt by "fathering" the "birth" election of a record intake of five new Apostles.

By 1937 the society's active membership had shrunk disastrously. Apart from Straight, the only other undergraduate member was Alan Hodgkin, a non-Marxist scientist who later was awarded a Nobel prize for biophysics. As master of Trinity at the time of Blunt's public exposure in 1979, Sir Alan Hodgkin sprang to the defense of the society in *The Times* by insisting that it was "quite wrong to suppose it was a kind of crypto-communist cell." But the apostolic record as it has now been reconstructed must cast considerable doubt on Hodgkin's assertion that the society was "basically an undergraduate debating society which had senior members come in."[16]

Straight confirmed that in February, before he renounced his left-wing views, as secretary of the society he was told by Keynes to summon all fourteen senior members for a meeting to discuss the urgent need for new undergraduate elections. As the youngest Apostle it fell to Straight to make recommendations. He recalled that he was so overcome by other matters that he simply put forward names of Marxist friends whom he considered apostolic. From among the circle who used to chant the "Internationale" and "Arise Ye Prisoners of Starvation" at his drinking parties, he selected John H. Humphrey and John Waterlow, both of Trinity, and Gerald Croadsell, who became a president of the Union. Within two weeks they were all members of the society.

"The ones I picked," Straight told me, "were people I knew, almost without exception, as active members of the student Communist movement." Keynes's resistance had evidently waned, because he considered the undergraduates "amateur Communists" who would grow out of their revolutionary ardour. But he had not calculated how skillfully the Soviet intelligence service, through Blunt, might exploit their ideological commitment. This was the case with Leo Long, an active Communist from Trinity. His recruitment was actively canvassed by Blunt and John Peter Astbury of Christ's, who was elected at the same time in the summer of 1937 as a result of Straight's recommendation. Astbury's brother confirmed that John Astbury was indeed an ardent Communist at Cambridge – a fact established by the records of the Cambridge Union, which show that he spoke on the losing side in favor of the triumph of the "dictatorship of the proletariat" and the "victory of the working class over Capitalism ... according to the principles of the Parties affiliated to the Communist International." Later, in January 1937, Astbury carried the House with him when he proposed an anticonscription motion that was Cambridge's equivalent of the famous Oxford Union "King and Country" debate.[17]

Fifty years later, Straight appeared quite proud of the achievements of the Apostles he fathered. Not only had his Cambridge friends proved a talented group, but with the exception of Leo Long, he pointed out, none of them had remained Communists for more than a short time. In fact, the records of subsequent elections reveal that the Apostles Straight fathered represented the high tide of apostolic communism. Since this group inevitably influenced the new elections, they ensured that the current of Marxism continued in the society right up until the outbreak of World War II, but after Blunt left Cambridge in 1937, the degree of emphasis on communism began to subside. However, Blunt used the Apostles in his own way, recruiting Leo Long, for one, into his wartime espionage network. And Blunt, according to Straight, approached at least one other member of this group. This is a convincing indication that Blunt regarded these Apostles as being in some way preselected when it came to recruiting potential Soviet agents.[18]

Straight drew my attention to the fact that four of his five fellow Communist Apostles appear with him in the historic photograph commemorating Haile Selassie's visit to the Cambridge Union at the end of May. Together with his Liberal allies, Straight was instrumental in marshaling left-wing support in the Union for making the emperor-in-exile of Ethiopia an honorary member. This anti-Fascist gesture demonstrated the Marxist ascendancy and provoked heated controversy.

The emperor's arrival was celebrated by a daring climber who fixed an Ethiopian flag on a King's College spire and by Michael Straight's Union speech of welcome, translated into impeccable French by Anthony Blunt. The Union's House of Commons-style oak dispatch box dwarfed the bearded Lion of Judah. He made no speech, but with an imperial flourish, he presented a gold-framed photograph of himself and signed the minute book to bring the evening's proceedings to a close. As he did so, the red glow of bursting rockets flickered through the Gothic windows onto the rows of undergraduates packing the Victorian debating chamber's leather benches.

The fireworks came from Victor Rothschild's house on the other side of the river, where a lavish farewell party for Michael Straight and his Union friends was already in full swing. Still in the white tie and tails customarily worn by Union officers, Straight headed off for the party. Union ex-president Leonard Miall remembers piling into Straight's Railton sports car and roaring over Magdalene bridge toward Merton Hall, the Rothschild residence.

"When we arrived, a vodka and caviar supper was being served on the terrace," Miall recalled. There was a Hungarian band in the floodlit garden, and Victor Rothschild was playing duets with the jazz pianist Cab Calloway. Straight recalls that he stayed only forty minutes, even though he was the guest of honor. Feeling tired and desperate, he left early to escape from Blunt's married friend.[19]

According to Miall the free-flowing liquor and the sylvan setting of the warm May night aroused Blunt's romantic passions. On a stroll with Charles Fletcher-Cooke, Miall recalls coming upon Blunt lying on a garden seat deep in the embrace of a male undergraduate from Pembroke.

"I wasn't surprised at all, because Trinity men had that reputation," Miall said. "Quite some time later I happened to take another walk, and there in exactly the same position was Anthony Blunt, this time embracing the wife of a don from Jesus."

This surprised and amused Miall. Later, Blunt appeared looking rather drunk in search of another vodka.

"Aren't you being a little fickle this evening?" Miall jokingly asked him.

"Many a fickle makes a fuckle," Blunt said, tapping his nose with his forefinger.[20]

Miall recalls that there were many hangovers round the table in the Union the next morning at the breakfast given in honor of the emperor of Ethiopia. Blunt did not attend either that function or the official photographic lineup that recorded the socialist ascendancy for posterity. But in the following week's *Spectator*, he applauded the culmination of a term when the Union, the bellwether of undergraduate opinion, had rejected rearmament, condemned British imperialism, and elected Haile Selassie its honorary member. "All of which shows that its heart is in the right place and rather solidly fixed there," Blunt wrote with unmistakable emphasis.

The swan song on which Blunt parted with Cambridge was a very public declaration of his Marxism in his contribution to "Art under Capitalism and Socialism," published that June in Cecil Day Lewis's book *The Mind in Chains*. Blunt's contribution to this strident collection of Marxist cultural essays was to proclaim that "in the present state of capitalism the position of the artist is hopeless" and to call on artists to "collaborate by arousing the proletariat to political consciousness and organizing it for the struggle." He quoted Lenin's axiom that "socialist culture will take over all that is good in *bourgeois* culture and turn it to its own ends." He anticipated the disappearance of paintings "as a unique private possession," and predicted the development of mural paintings in "communal buildings devoted to culture and recreation of the workers." Art was an offensive activity, Blunt contended, quoting Lenin's declaration: "Every artist . . . has a right to create freely according to his ideals, independent of anything. Only, of course, we communists cannot stand without hands folded and let chaos develop in any direction it may. We must guide this process according to a plan to form its results."[21]

With the publication of this astonishing declaration, Blunt had unmistakably and very publicly unfurled the red banner of his communism. There was an element of spite in this parting shot fired at the university that had once again rejected him. Blunt's failure to attain a permanent fellowship meant that, like Straight, he was reluctantly preparing to leave the ancient college that had been his home for eight years.

When Straight came to Blunt's rooms for the last time, he received the first indicator of the impositions that might be made on him as a result of his commitment to Moscow. Blunt arranged for them to meet in London a few days later. It was with a sense of foreboding that he picked up Blunt as arranged on a sweltering June morning in Oxford Street. The meeting in busy traffic shows that Blunt was taking precautions about being followed. Straight took his directions on a circuitous drive to what he described as a roadhouse on the Great West Road, somewhere near where Heathrow Airport is now located.

They made their way to the crowded swimming pool, where Blunt introduced Straight to a thick-set, dark-haired man that Straight remembered only as a "beefy Russian." Over a cigarette and a beer Moscow's emissary showed very little interest in the new recruit. Between plunges into the pool, the Russian reminded him to observe the rule about using the public telephone to avoid detection. "He was more like the agent of a small-time smuggling operation than the representative of a new international order" was the impression that Straight took away from this first meeting with a member of the Soviet intelligence *apparat*.[22]

When I asked Straight why he had not at this point abandoned his involvement, he reminded me of the influence that Blunt had established over him. Blunt reassured him this Russian was merely a "slab of beef" and the meeting an administrative detail. The Soviet, he said, was only part of a much grander and more elaborate scheme.

Blunt briefed Straight to be prepared to be on his own for some time when he returned to the United States. A new contact would be arranged as quickly as possible. He then asked Straight for a personal document. Straight took a drawing he had in his pocket, done in blue ink by his girlfriend, Belinda Crompton. Blunt tore it into two pieces and handed one back. The Soviet agent who made contact with him in New York would produce the other section, Blunt advised.

"I pretended to myself that the trap that I was in was merely an illusion," Straight said. He recalled how he tried to shut out all thoughts of Blunt during his voyage back to America. "I told myself that the ragged piece of a drawing that had been taken from me would never be thrust back into my hand."[23]

# CHAPTER 16

# "Too Much Hauteur
to Be a Charmer"

Blunt's use of the torn document and the meeting with the mysterious Russian after months of manipulating Michael Straight gives every indication that, by the spring of 1937, Blunt was acting as a supervisory agent of the Soviet intelligence service.

Yet at his press conference forty-two years later, Blunt brazenly invoked the Official Secrets Act to deflect a question about whether or not he had had direct dealings with the Soviets.

"There was not a man, an agent, no letter drops or anything like that?" asked one of the three handpicked reporters present. The reporter found it difficult to believe that Blunt had no direct contact with the Russians.

"I was eventually in touch myself," Blunt admitted. "I don't know with whom; I have no idea what his name was." When pressed, he said he was "trying to get his memory straight," but he supposed this might have been during the war. On how he communicated with the Soviets he replied: "I am afraid I cannot say."[1]

There was no challenge to these statements because his meeting at the swimming pool to present Michael Straight to the Russians was not then public knowledge.

Straight was correct in thinking that the "beefy Russian" was more interested in swimming than in talking to an unimportant agent. He was also most unlikely to have been Blunt's case officer, since his presence at an introductory meet with a prospect did not fit the pattern of security the Soviets usually imposed on their important controllers. Most likely he was a relatively lowly "legal" officer from the embassy detailed to carry out a preliminary inspection on the instructions from Blunt's control. And this leads to the all-important question: Who was Blunt's control? Who was his Soviet case officer?

At his press conference, Blunt insisted that the identity of this Soviet officer, along with the names of his other recruits such as Straight, was "an official secret." Whoever he was, and we'll discuss his identity later, he had to be a sophisticated, learned character.

Although Philby denied he was ever a member of "a Comintern cell," much has been made by the Cambridge spies, and by other writers, of their assertion that they were members of, or were run by members of, the Comintern. This was the post-1918 Communist International —

the organization that had been charged by Lenin and Trotsky with the task of binding the various Communist parties throughout the world into a disciplined, revolutionary force that would, one day, achieve the Bolshevik aim of worldwide revolution. The Soviet government had provided support for the Comintern. At the same time, however, the Soviets denied that the movement was anything other than a truly international organization of Marxist-Leninists, who voluntarily chose to associate with Soviet aims. In reality, it worked like this: After appropriate tutelage in the Soviet Union, the foreign representatives returned to their respective countries to propagate doctrine, enlist ideological recruits, mobilize demonstrations, and otherwise challenge and obstruct the functioning of national governments. These were the people to whom the term "Comintern agents" can be accurately applied.

Initially the Comintern had no intelligence function aside from the collection of data relating to local political and security considerations. But early in the twenties, the Cheka's counterintelligence chief, Mikhail Trilisser, began infiltrating his secret police into all levels of the Comintern. As a result, the direction and control of its covert mission began to change. Foreign members of the Comintern could carry out espionage and sabotage for Moscow much more easily than the Soviets could for themselves. Under the guise of Marxist education, the Comintern became an important pool of agent recruits for the Soviet intelligence and security organs.

The concept of an international organization devoted to the radical alteration of the world's ailing economic, social, and political structures — with the aim of elevating the status of mankind — had a broad appeal to many people. But Soviet communism did not. As Straight's account confirms, when Blunt made his recruiting pitch for the Comintern, he did not mean supporting a foreign state. Nor did dedication to Marxist principles carry an implication of treason. From the perspective of Soviet intelligence, however, the Comintern provided an appealing "false flag" for recruiting suitable prospects into the Soviet service. Once the recruits were in, they were in for life, like it or not.

After the Arcos raid, Soviet intelligence for many years relied on the so-called illegals — undercover agents with false passports and "legends" — to run their networks in Britain. This continued until the mid-1930s. Many of these agents were formerly Comintern members. The important thing to remember was that now it was the organs of Soviet intelligence, and not the Communist International, who ran them.

The OGPU had taken over effective control of the Comintern in 1932. Two years later Stalin reconstituted the OGPU as the NKVD — the Russian acronym for the People's Commissariat for Internal Affairs — what is today the KGB. In the period from 1934 through 1937, as Stalin's purges decimated the upper ranks of Soviet intelligence, the Comintern officers assumed a major role in foreign-intelligence operations. The clues given by Blunt during his interrogations all point to the recruitment of the Cambridge network by a member of Dzerzhinski's old guard when, by the thirties, these Comintern ideologues were all operating under NKVD control. By not making this distinction Blunt perpetuated a misleading myth and confusion as to who should be credited with originally recruiting and running the Cambridge agents. Until Blunt's confession became publicly known, there were two prime candidates for controller of the Cambridge agents: Samuel Cahan, Moscow Center's *rezident* in London, who was operating under diplomatic cover as first secretary of the embassy; and the longtime Tass representative in Britain, Semyon Rostovsky, who wrote under the name Ernst Henri.[2]

The case against either Cahan or Rostovsky as the Cambridge recruiter was their "legal" status as Soviet citizens with diplomatic positions. In the decade after the Arcos debacle, Moscow generally avoided using such people to run spy rings. Any exposure of their role in the chain of command would have jeopardized not only their official status but also Moscow's hard-won restoration of Anglo-Soviet diplomatic relations. Moscow Center would also have reasoned — correctly, as we now know — that Soviet officials in London were subject to intense scrutiny by British counterintelligence. And Soviet intelligence would not have risked exposing one of its most important underground operations to such close surveillance.[3]

"We were recruited individually and we operated individually," Philby has declared. But all the evidence points to his recruitment and control of the Cambridge agents by the same highly sophisticated illegal. Blunt admitted as much when he told MI5 that his recruitment by Burgess was orchestrated by a middle-class Eastern European whom he knew only as "Otto." Blunt described him as being "short with no neck and swept back straight hair." But despite being shown volume after volume from the extensive MI5 Registry of photographs of Soviet agents and suspects, Blunt never matched a face and name to this individual he vaguely recalled as being Czech.[4]

"For some reason, we were never able to identify 'Otto,'" Peter Wright of MI5 wrote, disclosing that two other members of the Cambridge ring, Philby and Cairncross, had told MI5 about their contacts with the mysterious "Otto" also without knowing or revealing his real name. During his "confession" to MI5 officer Nicholas Elliott in Beirut shortly before his defection in 1963, Philby said that "Otto" was a Comintern agent he had met in Vienna.[5]

Wright concedes he was never able to identify "Otto." Nor did anyone else in MI5 discover why Blunt and the other surviving members of the Cambridge network were so determined to preserve the identity of the mysterious Eastern European who between 1939 and 1940 was their mentor and link with Moscow.

What Blunt was doing to MI5 is what the fox does to the hounds: double back on his own trail and watch the pack rush by. First Blunt insists that he had been recruited by Burgess in 1936, which we now know to be untrue. Blunt also says that a man named Theodore Maly had recruited Philby, Maclean, and Burgess. Then Blunt denies ever meeting Maly because he had been recalled from England in "1936–37," so he had to be recruited by the mysterious "Otto." It is here that the fox doubles back on his trail, because there *is* evidence that Maly was in England after the date that Blunt gave. Furthermore, Maly was engaged in other espionage activities besides recruiting the Cambridge spy ring. The Registry file on Maly must have been thick and complex. He operated under a series of aliases, including the names of Paul Hardt and Peters. Maly also appears to have been the principal NKVD *illegal* operating in England from 1932 through 1937.[6]

Maly also fits exactly with Philby's assertion that the recruiter was "not a Russian but working for the Russians." One of the most remarkable non-Russian Comintern agents who ever served as undercover Soviet intelligence officers, Maly was a newly ordained Hungarian priest, who became a regimental chaplain with the Austro-Hungarian army when World War I broke out. Captured by the tsar's army on the Carpathian front, he was horrified by the starvation and disease in the prisoner of war camps.

"I lost my faith in God, and when the revolution broke out I joined the Bolsheviks," Maly once told a friend, explaining how service with the Cheka and Red Army during the brutal civil war against the Whites had hardened him. Like many of the foreign Communists who served Dzerzhinski, Maly played a key role in the burgeoning Soviet intelligence apparatus in the twenties. But Mikhail Trilisser recognized that Maly's real value to the *apparat* sprang from his passionate pride and his intellect and charm. Maly's ability to pass himself off as a cultivated European intellectual made it easy for him to recruit young left-wing Oxbridge intellectuals for the Soviets' secret global crusade.[7]

Early in 1932, using the alias of Paul Hardt, Maly arrived in London as an illegal resident with the immediate assignment of running King and

Oldham, the spies in the Foreign Office. When King was finally arrested in 1940, the payments made to his bank account led back to one of the key subsidiary operatives in Maly's network, Bernard Davidovich Gadar, another illegal Soviet agent. Moscow had established him in an appropriately nondescript company, a rag business in London's seedy East End, which served as a front. Gadar acted both as paymaster and communication point, while Maly assumed the role of a business representative who traveled extensively in search of waste linen.[8]

According to a friend who knew him in Moscow before he left for London, Maly was "a handsome, tall Hungarian with blue eyes and the charming smile of the naturally shy." By a strange quirk of fate, Maly's younger brother was making his career as a pianist. Theodore attended one of his brother's concerts in London, but shrank from making contact with his dead past. He was an articulate idealist in his mid-forties, and his dedication to his Communist beliefs was so complete that he willingly returned to Moscow in 1937 at the height of Stalin's purges, even though he knew he was going to his death. "They betray their own people," Maly explained before leaving England. "They will enjoy killing a Communist."[9]

It is not difficult to understand how Maly's inspirational faith made such a powerful impression on young Cambridge minds in search of a new God. Blunt told Peter Wright that Maly's "students worshipped him." Although Blunt claimed that his recruitment came too late for him to hear the message for himself from the blue-eyed Theo, Blunt later told Wright "on many occasions" that he would not have joined the cause if the appeal had been made to him by a Russian.[10]

Blunt's glowing and supposedly secondhand testimonial for Maly's abilities contrasts oddly with his inability to recall anything more about the mysterious "Otto" than his thick neck and swept-back hair. The evidence that Maly must have been the principal recruiter of the Cambridge ring is convincing.

First, there is general agreement that Maly recruited Philby and Maclean. If Blunt was recruited anytime between 1934 and 1937, then Maly had to have been the one to bring him in.

Second, from what is now known about Maly's career, he possessed the intellectual resourcefulness, engaging personality, and social sophistication that was needed to win Blunt's respect. It must have taken a person of extreme subtlety to mold, motivate, and direct Blunt's orientation to serve Moscow. His recruiter and initial controller confronted a formidable challenge as Noël Annan's definitive assessment of Blunt makes plain. Blunt, he wrote, was a "fascinator," who baited his conversation with "inside gossip" and had "too much hauteur to be a charmer." But he was more than fascinating. "He was a manipulator. He wanted more than most people in academic life to have his own way, appoint his own protégés and rule the roost."[11]

Arthur Koestler's inspiration for becoming a Comintern agent was his discovery in the sacred Marxist texts of the "mental rapture which only the true convert knows." By contrast, Blunt may never have responded to the spiritual appeal of communism, but Maly, a former priest who had served both the old and new gods, would have generated seductive echoes that rang deeply in the empty well left by Blunt's rejection of his religious upbringing. Maly would also have played upon Blunt's vanity by inflating the importance of the role that he could play in the grand international design for world communism.[12]

We have only Blunt's word that he was not recruited by Maly, but the fact is that Blunt was lying about when Maly left London. He actually remained as the NKVD's principal illegal agent n England until the early summer of 1937. Since Michael Straight's testimony shows that Blunt was acting as a Soviet agent in the spring of 1937, he could only have been operating at Maly's direction.

The most telling proof that Maly was still fully operational as late as April 1937 comes from the evidence of his involvement in the celebrated Woolwich Arsenal case. The rounding up of a Soviet spy ring in the all-important government-run armaments factory just down the River Thames from historic Greenwich Palace, has always been portrayed as one of MI5's most successful operations.

Ever since the Arcos raid, one of MI5's primary objectives had been to infiltrate agents into the Communist network in Britain. This assignment had been given to Maxwell Knight, a former merchant-navy officer who joined MI5 in 1925. Recognition of his own homosexuality and the suicide of his first wife had sharpened his sense of being an outsider.

Knight applied the field craft he had learned as a poacher in the salmon rivers of south Devon to his counterintelligence operations. The successes that established his reputation in MI5 began in 1930, when he recruited Olga Gray, a bright thirty-year-old secretary, to penetrate the head-quarters of Britain's Communist party. Her convent-school education, staunch Tory family background, and membership in the Ealing Ladies Hockey Club might have proved a liability in the self-consciously proletarian ranks of that group. But Knight, who acted as her coach and control officer for the next seven years, shrewdly calculated that the apparent rejection of her bourgeois past would provide a convincing cover.

Olga Gray's dedicated work as a volunteer for the Friends of the

Soviet Union and as a part-time typist for the Anti-War Movement
— both Communist fronts — eventually earned her the respect and
confidence of the general secretary of the CPGB himself. In 1934,
Harry Pollitt sent Gray as a courier to smuggle money out to the
struggling Indian Communist party in her sanitary napkins. On her
return, Pollitt asked her to join his full-time staff at party headquarters.
For the next three years Gray reported to Maxwell King from the heart
of the King Street headquarters of the CPGB.[13]

Percy Glading, a veteran British Comintern member, was especially
impressed with Gray's hard work and reliability. Glading had been
sacked from the Admiralty section of Woolwich Arsenal in 1928, after
MI5 learned of his involvement in the Indian Communist party's Meerut
conspiracy. He had then gone to Moscow to attend a Comintern
"university" where the practical curriculum consisted of training in
espionage and agitation techniques. Glading had returned to Britain
with orders to establish a clandestine network to obtain top-secret
military blueprints and armaments parts from his former employers at
the arsenal.

In February 1937, Glading asked Gray to set up a safe house that
could serve as a photographic workshop for copying documents. With
a hundred pounds to pay for a one-year lease, and Max Knight's
surreptitious assistance, she rented a basement flat at 82 Holland Park
Road. There in April she met the handsome "Mr. Peters." Glading told
her that "Peters" was an Austrian who had served as a captain in the
Russian cavalry after spending some time in a monastery. From Gray's
description of Peters, Knight had little difficulty identifying him as
being Theodore Maly.[14]

Gray did not see "Peters" again. He was briefly replaced by someone
she described as a "rather bumptious man," and, in August, Glading
brought "Mr. and Mrs. Stevens" to the flat and told Gray that she
would receive a five-pounds-a-week pay raise to act as their assistant.
Checking Gray's description of the "Stevenses" against Registry records, Knight was able to establish that they were a Romanian-born
Jewish couple, Willy and Mary Brandes.[15]

Recently recovered after gathering dust for nearly half a century, MI5
reports in the American archives reveal that the British knew from
their port records that the passports issued to the Brandeses had been
"unlawfully obtained." The Brandeses were identified as Soviet NKVD
illegals who had arrived in Britain in January 1937. At that time Willy
Brandes was using the cover of a traveling salesman for the Phantome
Red Cosmetics Company of New York and an agent for the Charak

Furniture Company. Both these companies were controlled by Americans of Russian descent.[16]

Olga Gray reported to Knight that when the Brandeses used the photographic equipment they instructed her to remain in the bedroom. But on October 21 she managed to obtain blueprint numbers from some photographic plates hung up to dry. Woolwich Arsenal records confirmed that these were top-secret plans for a new 14-inch naval gun. MI5 officers took up watch and tailed Mary Brandes to Hyde Park, where she passed a bundle to a gray-haired man later identified as George Whomack, an engineering foreman in the naval department at the arsenal.[17]

The trap had been sprung, and the British knew that they had two key NKVD agents in the bag. But no arrests were made! On November 2, Glading told Gray that the "Stevenses" were leaving for Moscow because their daughter was ill. He said they would "probably never return" and that there would be no work for her until Christmas. The Brandeses left for Paris on November 6.[18]

What is so puzzling about the Woolwich Arsenal case is that MI5 did not move in promptly to roll up the spy ring before the two Soviet agents most deeply involved left the country. Instead, MI5 waited until after Christmas, when Gray alerted them that Glading had resumed copying documents. On January 15, British agents tailed Glading and saw him receiving documents from Charles Munday, a government chemist from Woolwich.

At 8:15 on the morning of January 21, Glading went down into the lavatory at Charing Cross Station. There he handed over a parcel to Albert Williams, a Woolwich Arsenal carpenter. The police moved in and arrested them both as they made their way up the stairs to the station platform. Special Branch officers picked up Munday and Whomack a few hours later; and all were charged at Bow Street police station with offenses under the Official Secrets Act.

The trial of the Woolwich Arsenal spies made headlines in the first week of February 1938. The jury found Glading and all but one of his fellow conspirators, against whom charges were dropped, guilty. The judge handed out stiff prison sentences and praised the "extraordinary courage" of the patriotic blonde who was publicly identified for her own protection only as "Miss X." Olga Gray observed with bitter amusement how the popular press transformed her into a glamorously seductive counterspy, an overnight sensation. Max Knight was promoted to take charge of his own department, which mounted clandestine operations from an independent base in Dolphin Square, a block of luxury flats overlooking the River Thames.[19]

Fifty years later, the Woolwich Arsenal case does not seem to be quite the sensational counterintelligence coup it was made out to be at the time. Yes, MI5 succeeded in knocking out an important Comintern espionage operation, but only the British end of the ring ended up in jail. Not just one but at least three of four principal Soviet agents implicated in the ring managed to escape arrest. Some might argue that there was insufficient evidence in April to arrest Theo Maly for espionage. But at the very least he could have been arrested as he tried to leave Britain on his false passport. Moreover, six months later, when the time was ripe for MI5 to move against his successors, the Brandeses were also permitted to escape, even though MI5 had clear proof that they were involved in espionage.

Why were the Brandeses permitted to leave the country five days after MI5 received the warning that these top Soviet operatives were about to depart for Moscow? It has been suggested that MI5 watchers looked on helplessly on November 6, 1937, as "Mr. and Mrs. Stevens" loaded their luggage into a taxi at Fonset House in the Edgware Road and drove to Victoria Station. This revelation comes from Nigel West, a British authority on intelligence. West told me that there was a "debate," presumably between the senior MI5 officers involved, Guy Liddell and Knight, about the "advisability of allowing two Soviet agents to leave the country." Other writers have said that the arrests were not made because Knight was playing for time in the hope of catching even bigger fish. But West — on good authority — says, "Eventually it was decided that, since they both could claim diplomatic immunity if arrested, there was little to gain by taking them into custody."[20]

If this information reflects MI5's "official" justification for letting the Soviet agents slip away, it is made nonsense of by the recent recovery of the contemporary reports on the Brandeses' false Canadian papers. These show that MI5 cannot have been under any illusion that the couple had diplomatic immunity. The British knew by November that the Brandeses were Soviet *illegals* operating under the name of Stevens — a false "legend" unlawfully obtained in Canada.[21]

An investigation by the Royal Canadian Mounted Police in Montreal had produced sufficient evidence for the British to arrest Brandes on his way out of Dover and extradite him to Canada for prosecution on the criminal charge of fraudulently obtaining naturalization papers and passports. If MI5 officers were concerned about prematurely spoiling the stakeout on Woolwich Arsenal, they could have arrested the Brandeses on the false-passport charges at Dover without alerting the Soviets to the penetration of their ring.[22]

Yet MI5 was left to round up the small fry after a high-level decision allowed the big fish to slip through the net.

Why the Soviet spymasters were allowed to escape now becomes the important question: Chance, miscalculation, or deliberate tipoffs are the only possible explanations.

Chance or miscalculation may well have played a part. But to paraphrase one of Oscar Wilde's more abrasive aphorisms: To lose one spy may be regarded as a misfortune, but to lose both looks like carelessness. If MI5's failure was the result of carelessness or miscalculation, the very fact of its repetition — first Maly, then the Brandeses — suggests negligence, bungling — or worse.

Then there is the disturbing evidence given by the Soviet spy Wilfred McCartney at his post-Arcos trial ten years previously. He insisted under oath that the Russian embassy had received a timely tip-off about the Arcos raid. It was this that allowed them to remove the secret War Office document fed him by MI5 as the justification for raiding the Russian headquarters. But the possibility that some senior MI5 officer had tipped off the Soviets was as unthinkable in 1927 as it was in 1937. General Kell would have dismissed any suggestion that his handpicked officers and gentlemen would betray their country. But after Blunt, Maclean, Burgess, Philby, et al., it is surely not farfetched to consider the possibility that in the Woolwich Arsenal case the Soviets were tipped off, not once, but twice, that their principal London agent had been unmasked.

Was it pure coincidence that Maly left Britain a matter of days after Olga Gray reported meeting him to Max Knight? Why did Mr. and Mrs. Brandes flee the country less than a week after they were observed in a Hyde Park meet at which top-secret British naval plans had changed hands?

It can be argued that the abrupt departure of Comintern agents during 1937 was not exceptional. In that year Stalin's purge of his real and imagined enemies reached its bloody height. Operational failure, suspicion of Trotskyist sympathies, or non-Russian birth became death warrants or tickets to Siberian labor camps for many. Maly himself was under no illusion that his return to Moscow was other than a one-way trip. Perhaps he knew there was really no place to hide. His close friend Ignace Reiss, a longtime GRU agent, fled to Switzerland, but even there he was within the reach of NKVD assassins who killed him.[23]

Whether it was a recall from Moscow or a tip-off in London, the fact remains that the British let Maly and the Brandeses slip through their fingers. The evidence that Maly was instrumental in the foundation and running of the Cambridge network may explain why Blunt and Philby both went to great lengths to camouflage the fact that his role as their controller continued until his recall in the early summer of 1937.

The mysterious "Otto" has, according to a consensus of American intelligence officers, all the appearances of a classic disinformation ruse. "The invocation of 'Otto' as the omnipresent, though never identified, Soviet case officer is wholly consistent with the 'to be expected' conduct of a disciplined agent" was Robert Crowley's considered opinion. The reason, he argued, was that the Soviets always provided their agents with a well-rehearsed cover story based on information likely to be in the possession of their interrogator. Only when additional incriminating information has been disclosed will an agent under interrogation construct a new story based on what he has learned. And any new admission is designed to produce a sense of victory in the mind of the interrogator.[24]

Another tantalizing clue about Otto appears in Peter Wright's *Spycatcher* and points to the lengths to which Blunt may have gone to cover up the origins of his network. When Wright was first introduced to Blunt by Arthur Martin in 1965, so Wright could "play nasty to Arthur's nice," the first half hour was spent in a discussion "mainly about documents which Blunt removed from the Registry." No information is given about the documents, but the implication is plain.[25]

Even though the MI5 Registry data were supposed to be inviolable, at least one other case of the removal and destruction of files has now been reliably documented. In 1941 Max Knight personally removed reports on the disruptive personal behavior of a Royal Marine officer he wanted to bring into MI5. Any Soviet-directed cleanup carried out by Blunt and Philby — both of whom had access to the Registry files during the war years — would not have been limited to settling private scores. The extent to which they were able to doctor the records by removing or altering incriminating documents can only be guessed at.

This may be one reason why tracking down the truth about "Otto" proved so difficult after Blunt's confession in 1963. But, as Nigel West has revealed to me, the "sanitizing" of the Cambridge network files was not simply a matter of unauthorized deletions. "The MI5 files on Burgess and Maclean were all rewritten after 1951," West said, assuring me that his sources for this information were "absolutely reliable."[26]

"The first time that an MI5 file was altered, so far as I have been able to establish, was the Fuchs file," West said. In the late forties, the Registry records on atom spy Klaus Fuchs contained sufficient indications that the nuclear scientist might be a security risk. But nothing was done. To cover up the failure, MI5 records were doctored after the FBI produced the evidence that led to Fuchs's confession in 1950.

The Burgess and Maclean files as they now exist in MI5 — presumably the ones Wright relied on in 1963 — were, according to West, "manufactured" to remove any evidence of negligence. Under the direction of Guy Liddell, the files were completely reconstructed with the object of demonstrating that there had been no MI5 foul-up. West said that one of the purposes of the changes was to show that Burgess *had been under investigation* at the time of his defection. This simply was not true, according to West's source. This alleged investigation was mentioned in the 1955 White Paper issued by the British government on the missing diplomats.[27]

The "reconstituted" Burgess–Maclean file was presented as a peace offering to the FBI in an effort to "prove" that MI5's record was clear. But it was "all garbage," as West put it. He explained how Arthur Martin was sent to Washington in June 1951 with the file. The FBI, however, had been mounting its own intensive investigation, and was not taken in. When William C. Sullivan, J. Edgar Hoover's deputy director for domestic intelligence, read the offering, he exploded with indignation. He dismissed the MI5 report as "horseshit!" And an embarrassed Arthur Martin could only offer an uncomfortable smile.[28]

There is another twist to the story: What Arthur Martin and MI5 didn't know was that the FBI already had evidence pointing to Burgess's involvement in a high-level homosexual ring with disturbing Communist connections.

# CHAPTER 17

# *"Assisting Lord Rothschild"*

The FBI files on Burgess and Maclean reveal why the Americans were furious.[1]

The day after the news broke in the press about the disappearance of the British diplomats, the MI6 and MI5 liaison officers stationed at the British embassy in Washington went downtown to a meeting at FBI headquarters. Kim Philby and Geoffrey Patterson called on Robert J. Lamphere. The thirty-two-year-old Lamphere, a native of Idaho, was then the bureau's deputy chief of counterintelligence, and he recalls that it was an uncomfortable meeting.

"My discussion with Philby and Patterson went nowhere," Lamphere says. He was angered because he was convinced that MI5 had been keeping the results of its own investigations into Maclean from the FBI.[2]

Lamphere had every reason to be suspicious. In 1949 he had received firm evidence from signals intelligence sources in the U.S. Army showing that Moscow had a highly placed spy inside the British embassy in Washington in 1944. But the British seemed to drag their feet in investigating the matter.

"We decided that the British were holding out on us, and we decided to go after everyone we could find who knew anything about Burgess and Maclean." That was how Lamphere explained the massive FBI investigation that got under way *after* the FBI learned of the diplomats' defection at the end of May 1951. A secretary at the British embassy, who had worked with Burgess, was questioned and reluctantly disclosed that she remembered that Burgess had been in touch several times with the writer Christopher Isherwood.[3]

On July 16, orders went out by telegraph to the Los Angeles Bureau of the FBI. The following day one of its best field agents headed toward the Pacific Palisades to track down the expatriate British writer. Best known as the author of *Goodbye to Berlin*, the novel that inspired the musical *Cabaret*, Isherwood had come to America as a refugee from England in 1941 with the poet W. H. Auden. Brushing off the accusations of moral and physical cowardice made by their contemporaries who stayed to fight Hitler, these literary giants made no attempt in their new homeland to conceal their left-wing opinions, or their homosexuality.

"It was Christopher Isherwood who really opened up the whole can of worms," says Lamphere. With the sharp, cameralike focus with which he had limned the denizens of the Berlin underworld, Isherwood now portrayed for the FBI the decadence of prewar London's homosexual literary scene. Burgess, he explained, was pathetically desperate to be "in on everything significant." He also identified more than a dozen contacts who were under Burgess's influence or close friends of his.[4]

"The names of well-known writers like Auden and Spender leaped off the page when I read the report from Los Angeles," Lamphere recalls. The names are blacked out, however, in the copies released under the Freedom of Information Act. The bureau, it seems, is still bound by the secret Anglo-American intelligence agreement dating back to World War I that requires compliance with a formal request by the British authorities to withhold intelligence about British citizens. But sufficient textual clues survive, plus the tops and bottoms of letters missed by the censor, to make it possible to reconstruct the list of people that the FBI knew were close associates of Burgess.

"What we dug up alarmed and astonished us," Lamphere says. "We could not believe that the British would have allowed such people access to their diplomatic and security services."[5]

Deciphering these reports nearly four decades later, it is not hard to appreciate the sinking feeling they must have caused in FBI headquarters in July 1951. It would have been especially true in connection with one name that, surprisingly, survived the sanitizer's pen. Isherwood revealed that Lord Inverchapel was associated with Burgess in 1936. He was the British ambassador to Washington from 1947 to 1949, on whose staff Maclean served. More intriguing still is the discovery that Isherwood told the FBI that Burgess's closest friend was "a person named Tony." Not until his second interview did Isherwood recall that the mysterious Tony's surname was Blunt.[6]

"We did not at the time realize the full implications of all the names — or the Cambridge connection," Lamphere conceded after reviewing the FBI reports I showed him, the originals of which he had puzzled over thirty-seven years earlier. "We could not figure out how Inverchapel or Blunt fitted into the puzzle, or even Philby's connection to Burgess and Maclean. But we concluded that Philby had somehow been involved in their disappearance."[7]

The FBI then sent out agents to track down leads about anyone who might have been only remotely associated with Burgess and Maclean in the United States. The scale of the operation, judging from the pile of interview reports it produced, puts to shame the genteel and restricted investigation that was alleged to have been carried out simultaneously by MI5 in Britain. Had the British extended their sweep to include gas station attendants, restaurant waitresses, secretaries, and university friends who had contact with the missing diplomats as did the Americans, it must have exposed Blunt immediately.

By July 1951, as Lamphere confirms, even though the FBI did not have all the pieces of the puzzle, the agency knew that Burgess had associated with German Communists in a homosexual network whose connections reached into the highest echelons of the Foreign Office and Britain's security services.

Lamphere had the daunting job of preparing the briefings of this information for J. Edgar Hoover. Defaced though these briefings are by black-felt marking pens, a clear pattern emerges. At the height of Senator Joseph McCarthy's campaign against Communists in the U.S. government, the reek of sexual misconduct and left-wing chicanery on the part of Burgess and his Foreign Office friends must have fired Hoover's puritanical fury. The FBI could do little more than speculate about the Cambridge network: It did not matter that they suspected that MI5 was deliberately keeping them in the dark. The FBI played it straight. It methodically passed on what it had learned from Isherwood and the others to the MI5 liaison officer in the British embassy. These reports, for some obscure historical reason, were addressed to the British embassy using the code name SMOTH.[8]

"I suppose you could call us naïve — and in those days we were rather green about such matters," says Lamphere. But as he explained, Hoover had little choice but to put on a show of cooperation with the British intelligence services, whom he disliked and distrusted only marginally less than his new rivals in the CIA. But the FBI now had the hard evidence to prove that MI5 had made a determined effort to pull the wool over their eyes about the true significance of the defections of Burgess and Maclean.[9]

Within two months of Burgess's defection, Lamphere, with the help of his FBI colleagues in the Los Angeles office, had identified the key members of the prewar circle around Burgess and Blunt. They learned how the group frequented the Café Royal, the gilt and plush London restaurant that had been a favorite watering spot for Oscar Wilde. Isherwood said that he pitied Burgess, who drank too much and was "a confirmed social climber and pretty obvious in his tactics."[10]

Isherwood also told the FBI that high-ranking members of Parliament and diplomats were among Burgess's favorite targets. His allusions to "close friendships" left little doubt that a powerful undercurrent of homosexuality explained Burgess's association with Harold Nicolson and senior members of the Foreign Office such as Lord Inverchapel.

For the Americans, the most worrying of Isherwood's revelations was that Burgess had been a close associate of Lord Inverchapel. A Scot with florid features and a large nose, Archibald Clark Kerr was an eccentric in a career where eccentricity was usually a hindrance. But he had risen to the top despite his preference for bagpipes over bridge and the relaxing company of personable young left-wing intellects rather than diplomatic receptions. His peerage came with his appointment as Britain's envoy to Moscow in 1942. Five years later, when he arrived in Washington, his eccentricity caused unhappiness in the State Department and his Russian valet caused extreme discomfort to the director of the FBI.[11]

Robert Cecil, who came to know Inverchapel well, described him as a lonely but nonetheless genial superior. He had first met Clark Kerr in the Baghdad embassy before the war and later served under him in Washington. Like other senior members of the embassy staff, Cecil knew about his bedroom eccentricities.

"There was no doubt in my mind that he was bisexual," Cecil says. Inverchapel had taken a petite blonde Chilean woman as his wife, only to divorce her for desertion and then remarry her on his appointment to Washington. His Lordship's private secretary in Moscow had told Cecil that the ambassador's attitude to sex was: "If it moves go for it!"[12]

Cecil doubts that Inverchapel could have been a witting traitor. He did not have the right psychological makeup for a spy: "He was too sentimentally stupid about the Russians and too bluff to have been a mole like Philby." But Cecil concedes that Inverchapel's strong left-wing sympathies and cozy wartime relationship with Stalin would have made the British ambassador a very useful agent of influence.[13]

New evidence has come to light, however, that suggests that Inverchapel's naïve enthusiasm for the Soviet Union may have been more sinister than Cecil or the Foreign Office suspected.

In 1933, after the newly knighted Sir Archibald Clark Kerr arrived in Sweden, it is now known that he became an intimate friend of Stig Wennestrom. This Swedish air-force officer, although grounded by his lack of competence as a pilot, had taken on an astonishing career of espionage. When he was eventually unmasked in 1963, Wennestrom admitted he was a deep-penetration agent for Moscow and had secretly held the rank of major general in the KGB. Nor was Wennestrom the only known Soviet agent whom Inverchapel befriended in his career.[14]

While ambassador to China in the late thirties, Clark Kerr had become an enthusiastic admirer of Mao Tse-tung and the Chinese Communists. He also maintained suspiciously close personal links to the Soviet military attaché, who, according to a former member of Britain's legation, was a frequent late-night visitor to the ambassador's residence.

"Archie," as he was known to his friends, sponsored Günther Stein, a German journalist with Comintern connections, in his successful application for British naturalization papers. He also recommended him for journalistic assignments that enabled him to travel all over the Far East on the eve of World War II. U.S. Army Intelligence learned during its postwar investigation of Richard Sorge's spy ring that Stein had been a key member of the Red Army's Far Eastern GRU network.[15]

The amiable pipe-smoking ambassador never made a secret of his sympathy for the Soviet Union. He was given to lecturing his Foreign Office colleagues on this favorite topic and they tolerated his "steady passion for the Soviet Union," regarding it, like his bisexuality, as just another harmless eccentricity in a veteran diplomat.[16]

Yet even if Inverchapel was not a "spy" in the strict sense of the word, the evidence suggests that the Foreign Office blundered in its failure to appreciate that his sexual peccadilloes, and his favorable view of Russia, made him a major security risk. Whether the ambassador's passion for the Soviet Union was a clever camouflage for a more sinister purpose may never be known. But during wartime visits to London, he held parties for English intellectuals sympathetic to Russian writers. Soviet diplomats were guests at those receptions, as was Blunt's school friend Louis Mac-Neice and former Communist Stephen Spender. Inverchapel did not restrict himself merely to improving cultural relations. In 1944, he was a leading advocate in pressing the Foreign Office to accede to Stalin's demand for the forcible repatriation of all Soviet citizens.[17]

The rapport that Inverchapel established with the Soviet dictator cannot be attributed simply to a mutually shared devotion to pipe smoking or to huddling together in the Kremlin shelter during German air raids on Moscow. The ambassador was so cozy with the Soviet dictator that he secured the release from prison of a Red Army deserter whose sister was on the British embassy staff. Instead of facing a firing squad, Yevgeny Yost found himself presented — like some medieval serf — as a valet to Inverchapel when he left Moscow and returned to London at the end of 1944.

It was the presence of the Soviet valet, when Inverchapel arrived in Washington two years later, that raised eyebrows of State Department officials — and the hackles of J. Edgar Hoover at the FBI. Well past retirement age, Inverchapel owed his posting to his left-wing sympathies, which appealed to Labour Foreign Secretary Ernest Bevin.

"Inverchapel was no stuffed shirt, but he was a dead loss as our ambassador to the United States at this critical time in the Cold War," Cecil declares. The ambassador dodged the press corps, avoided official receptions, and upset the State Department. But it now appears that it was Hoover's concern about his valet, Yost — who had to be sent back to England — and the ambassador's high regard for Stalin that were instrumental in effecting Inverchapel's premature departure in 1949 on the diplomatic pretext of "ill health."[18]

Two years later, Inverchapel's former first secretary, Donald Maclean, defected. The FBI's suspicions about the ex-ambassador were then given a further dimension after Isherwood's revelations about his intimate friendship with Burgess, whose homosexual coterie had included a German expatriate named Rudolph Katz. "Rolf," as Isherwood referred to him, was an old friend from his days in Berlin in 1931. Stout, with fleshy cheeks and "thoughtful dark eyes," Katz was a Jew whom Isherwood described as being "an independent thinker and a very astute political analyst."[19]

On June 28, 1951, the FBI had tracked down Katz in New York. He was staying at the St. Regis Hotel on what he claimed was a business trip. Yes, he admitted he had known Burgess between 1936 and 1938, at which time they had fallen out, although he admitted receiving "infrequent letters" from Burgess afterward. Katz was careful to insist that he had no reason "to suspect that Burgess had been a member of a Russian espionage ring." He could think of nothing that led him to believe Burgess was "communistically inclined," although he was a strong supporter of the anti-Fascist Spanish Republicans.[20]

Katz was evasive about why he had left Britain in 1940. Inquiries to London revealed that Katz had been "ordered out of England due to homosexual contacts with British naval personnel." While his sexual predations may have gotten him into trouble with the British police, it was believed that Katz really crossed the Atlantic to Argentina to escape an internment camp for enemy aliens. In Buenos Aires he became the editor of a successful economic journal.[21]

We can now see, however, that what Katz told the FBI about how he had first met Burgess provided an important and hitherto missing link in the complex web of intrigue surrounding Blunt and his Cambridge spies. As reported to Hoover in the approved bureaucratic style: "Rudolph Katz advised that he met Burgess in England in 1936 when he was assisting Lord Victor Rothschild. Burgess was a social acquaintance of the Rothschild family."[22]

Heavy black ink erases the details of precisely what assistance a German Communist could have been providing the Rothschilds. But despite Katz's protestations that his relationship with Burgess had been "purely social," Isherwood had already told the FBI that "Burgess worked with Katz for a while in 1936–37 or 1937–38 in the publication of a magazine which devoted itself to surveys of economic and political matters." Since Katz had later run a successful investment and stock magazine in Buenos Aires, his association with Burgess in 1936 provides a clue to explaining why the Rothschilds regarded Burgess as a budding financial analyst — one of the most enigmatic of the myths at the heart of the Blunt affair.[23]

Michael Straight has always been puzzled, ever since Burgess revealed himself as a dedicated Marxist in the fall of 1935, exactly how Burgess's communism allowed him to accept the hundred pounds a month he supposedly received to act as investment counselor to Mrs. Charles Rothschild. This amount was four or five times more than Burgess's contemporaries might have anticipated earning. When Goronwy Rees heard that his friend had a job as "some kind of political adviser to the House of Rothschild," he found it "so bizarre that it introduced into Guy's career an element of farce which was to become increasingly prominent as the years went by."[24]

Thanks to Rudolph Katz, the myth of Burgess as a financial wizard now takes a different twist. Burgess, Isherwood confirmed, "collaborated with Katz in the publication of a financial paper in London." Even though Katz went out of his way to deny their association was anything but "purely social," it is significant that he told the FBI that Burgess had "a brilliant mind with a keen analytical outlook on political matters." It appears, therefore, that it was Katz who did the real work that allowed Burgess to claim that he was acting as an investment adviser.[25]

Why should Burgess have taken elaborate steps to camouflage Katz's role? One reason appeared in *The Daily Express* on June 14, 1951. As the first newspaper to break the story of the disappearing diplomats, Burgess and Maclean, the *Express* mentioned Burgess's friendship with the mysterious German. "Rolf Katz, a chunky man in his fifties," the *Express* disclosed, was "an important Comintern agent" who had "recently been in London from the Argentine."[26]

When the FBI interviewed Isherwood he was apprehensive. The McCarthy "hysteria" in 1951 encouraged him to play down Katz's Communist connections. He conceded that his old Berlin friend was "undoubtedly leftist" and might once have been involved in publishing a Comintern newspaper in Berlin. While Katz "at one time had probably adhered to the Communist party" Isherwood said he believed him to be a "sort of real old classical Marxist." Yet it is interesting to note that less than two years before, Isherwood had written in a travel book that Katz, whom he saw in 1947 in Buenos Aires, was "one of the very few people I have ever met who has really read, studied and digested Marx."[27]

The FBI had little difficulty penetrating Isherwood's smokescreen. They discovered that Katz was already an active Communist when he knew Burgess in London in 1936. German police and Gestapo records captured during the war confirmed that Katz, an economist, had joined the KPD (Kommunistische Partei Deutschlands) in 1921. His credentials also included his time as a correspondent for *Imprecor*, the journal of the Comintern. The KPD, which had received six million votes in the 1932 elections to the Reichstag, had been the third largest political party in Germany. But Moscow's orders forbidding its joining in a united front with the socialists emasculated the KPD in its bid to prevent the Nazis from taking over control of the German parliament the following year.[28]

Like most of the leading KPD activists, Rudolph Katz fled from Germany. He went to France in 1933. This was after Hitler had charged the Communists with setting the fire that gutted the Reichstag building on the last night of February. When the KPD leaders, Walter Ulbricht and Wilhelm Pieck, who became the postwar bosses of East Germany, arrived in Moscow, Stalin changed policies and called on all Communist parties to join in a united front against Fascism.

The Comintern leader who brilliantly succeeded in translating Moscow's Popular Front policy into a political and propaganda reality was Willi Münzenberg, a bearlike man who was the organizational genius of the KPD. MI5 records show that Guy Liddell had been tracking Münzenberg ever since the early twenties. At that time he came into prominence as the force behind the Workers International Relief. The success of this organization, known in party slang as "The Münzenberg Trust," spawned The League Against Imperialism. The headquarters of the Comintern operations were quickly reestablished in Paris. By May 1933, MI5 was warning the Americans that Münzenberg was back in business. This time Münzenberg's masterstroke was the creation of The World Committee for the Relief of the Victims of German Fascism. It launched an international juridical commission to investigate the Reichstag fire. These hearings at the Law Society in London, under Sir Stafford Cripps, a prominent Labour-party lawyer, exposed the Nazis' plan to make the Communists the scapegoats for the blaze.[29]

We now know that British agents were successful in penetrating Münzenberg's outfit. The following year they were able to alert the Americans that Münzenberg and his aide, Louis Gibarti, were en route to New York to address rallies in an attempt to establish a U.S. branch of the anti-Fascist front. It was a classic Münzenberg creation, skillfully window-dressed with an international committee of worthy non-Communist liberal and socialist figureheads. When the Spanish Civil War broke out, the front threw its support to the Republicans.[30]

Münzenberg had the popular reputation of being a "Red Millionaire," not in terms of money but in the remarkable power that he wielded in his organizations. He was "the grey eminence and invisible organizer of the anti-Fascist world crusade," according to Arthur Koestler, who worked for the French publisher of the so-called Brown Books that documented the "Hitler Terror." The actual author was Münzenberg's chief lieutenant, a Czech named Otto Katz (no relation to Rolf). This former avant-garde Berlin theater director had been a friend in Prague of the author Franz Kafka and had attended one of the Comintern schools in Moscow. By 1929, when he had earned Münzenberg's confidence, Otto was already a trained agent of the NKVD under orders to monitor Münzenberg.[31]

Otto Katz was a "smooth slick operator," a dark and handsome man who possessed what Koestler called a "seedy charm." It was particularly successful with women. Lillian Hellman, the American writer, encountered him in Spain and described him as a "slight, weary-looking, interesting man who moved in many circles." Otto's literary skills and facility with half a dozen languages made him indispensable to Münzenberg's proliferating organizations. Posing as "Ludwig Breda," an Austrian journalist, or as a French writer by the name of "André Simone," Otto traveled widely and stealthily as a contact man and fixer in European capitals. He helped Münzenberg organize the Reichstag countertrial, promoted the Republican cause in Spain, and organized the 1937 International Writers Conference in Paris. This literary circus, which E. M. Forster attended, demonstrated the solidarity of intellectuals in the Popular Front against Fascism and Nazism.[32]

As Isherwood explained it to the FBI, the success achieved by the Münzenberg–Otto Katz Popular Front stratagems made it "quite impossible" to understand the activities of the Popular Front in terms of the anti-Communist hysteria of the early fifties. Isherwood said that when Burgess and the "Auden Generation," as his friends became known, rallied to fight Fascism in the thirties, they gave little thought to Soviet motives. Not until the news of the Moscow purge trials began to leak out and they discovered for themselves how the Soviets had undermined the Spanish Loyalists, did Isherwood and Auden "realize that they had been duped in some of their so-called United Front activities."[33]

The consolidation of dictatorial powers by Stalin was signaled by the worst excesses of the purges that had begun with the Moscow show trials of Zinoviev and Kamenev in 1936, and the intellectual unity of the Popular Front was eroded. Münzenberg, too, was soon purged from his Comintern propaganda empire, a fall from grace that began with a dispute with Ulbricht and expulsion from the KPD in October 1937. The following year he broke with Moscow over Stalin's accelerating purge of the old Comintern guard. On Moscow's orders, Otto Katz had obediently attacked Münzenberg. A "most talented propagandist and intriguer" was how Katz was remembered by the left-wing journalist Claud Cockburn, who was no mean exponent of both skills himself. From 1938 Katz worked for Agence d'Espagne, assiduously promoting the Stalinist suppression of the Trotskyite POUM (Partido Obrero de Unificación Marxista), and he assisted in the liquidation of its leadership.[34]

MI5 concluded that Münzenberg's expulsion from the Comintern was no ruse, because the charges of Trotskyite contacts were "equivalent to political liquidation in the Stalinist movement." Undaunted, Münzenberg continued his anti-Nazi campaign through 1939, now with the support of the French government through a network of secret broadcasting stations. But macabre confirmation of Liddell's judgment call was to come three years later. Two French hunters found Münzenberg's decomposed corpse, with wire around its neck, under an oak tree in the forest of Caugnet a hundred miles southeast of Lyons. The former Red Millionaire had been last seen alive on June 20, 1940, with a group of several hundred refugees from an internment camp who were fleeing south from the German advance.[35]

State Department records seem to rule out Otto Katz's direct complicity in Münzenberg's murder: In May 1940 he had arrived in the United States with his wife, Ilse. After a brief stay, he spent the war years in Mexico. Using his cover as a journalist, he advised Lombardo Toledano, the Stalinist trade union leader, and carried out missions for Umansky, the Soviets' charge d'affaires.[36]

In 1946, equipped by the Russians with a Czech diplomatic passport, Otto Katz traveled via New York to London and thence via Berlin to Prague, where he joined the press department of the Foreign Ministry. As an agent of Soviet intelligence he was implicated in the 1948 murder of the non-Communist foreign minister, Jan Mazaryk, shortly after the Communists took control of the Czech government. But the Byzantine settling of old scores did not come until 1952, when Moscow ordered Otto Katz arraigned with Rudolf Slanský and a dozen Czech Communist leaders in a Stalinist show trial. Katz was hanged in a Prague prison yard on December 3, 1952, after confessing to being a "Trotskyist, Titoist traitor and enemy of the Czech people in the service of American imperialism."[37]

Yet Otto Katz appears to have played a useful role from the grave, since Philby and Blunt's references to a mysterious controller named "Otto" are clearly an identikit description of Otto Katz. There is no evidence that Otto Katz ever ran any Cambridge agent. His documented activities in Paris and Madrid rule him out of any role as the "missing" London controller of the Cambridge ring. American intelligence experts point out that by resurrecting a dead Soviet agent known to have made several trips to England, Katz was an ideal decoy.[38]

An even more enigmatic turn to the Münzenberg–Otto Katz saga was provided by Ellen Wilkinson, the feisty red-headed ex-Communist and longtime Labour M.P. from Jarrow. She encountered Otto in London when she was a member of the Commission of Enquiry into the Reichstag trial. She also knew Münzenberg well, because she had been an ardent supporter of his prewar anti-Fascist campaigns. In 1934, Otto accompanied Wilkinson and British peace campaigner Lord Listowel on a fact-finding tour of Spain. "Red Ellen," as she was affectionately known to her political friends and foes alike, was later education minister in the postwar Attlee government that included the Earl of Listowel as secretary of state for India. Before her death in 1947, Wilkinson confided that Münzenberg had once informed her that both he and Koestler, who escaped to England in 1938, had an enemy in the British counterintelligence service.[39]

The suggestion that some ranking MI5 officer might already have been working silently for Moscow as early as 1938 deserves attention. The MI5 records reveal that Otto Katz was known to be a key figure in the Comintern fronts. His Communist namesake, Rudolph – with whom Otto has often been confused – was permitted to reside in London until 1940. The ease with which the two Katzes and many of their German KPD associates were able to operate in Britain must raise questions about MI5's surveillance. What is particularly puzzling is the revelation that in 1933 the British Cabinet *was* alerted to the danger of subversion by the Communist activities among the German refugees fleeing to England. MI5 – we now know – received plenty of warnings from MI6 agents on the Continent about those who were likely to continue their KPD loyalties and activities in Britain.[40]

No less an authority than the minister responsible for MI5, Home Secretary Sir John Gilmour, advised the British Cabinet of "a risk that the influx of refugees from Germany may include a certain number of

Communists." He promised that immigration officers would exclude "any who are prominent." But the subsequent success achieved by Soviet intelligence through its agents in England before and during the war is a telling indictment of the failure of Britain's counterintelligence service through lack of resources, negligence — or more sinister reasons.[41]

It was not just the two Katzes; there was another German Communist party member in London, a Jew of Polish extraction named Jürgen Kuczynski. His instructions came from KPD leader Ulbricht. He had only recently joined the CPGB, which should have given MI5 cause for concern, since Olga Gray, its agent in King Street party headquarters, regularly reported on all new members. Kuczynski then began teaching at the London School of Economics, and even managed to obtain a government post as a statistician. One of his contacts was Klaus Fuchs, who came to England to continue his physics studies at Bristol University. Fuchs was eventually granted citizenship and given a top-security clearance to work on the British atomic-bomb project, although it has been claimed that in 1934, MI5 opened a file on him because of his KPD associations.[42]

If MI5 — as now seems beyond dispute — knew that Fuchs and Otto Katz were Communists, the assumption is that if only because of the name, they would have opened a file on Rudolph Katz. As a Marxist economist and KPD activist, with a record as a Comintern journalist, Rudolph Katz, like Otto Katz, according to FBI files, had contacts high up in the Establishment. So it is unlikely that Rudolph Katz could have remained in London without coming to MI5's attention.

Piecing together what the FBI learned from Isherwood, it is clear that Burgess's association with the expatriate Rudolph Katz provided him with the convenient claim to have been a financial adviser to the Rothschilds.

It is a matter of record that despite Burgess's efforts, the weekly financial newsletter failed through inaccurate forecasts and lack of subscribers. Even Rothschild's astute sister, Miriam, has admitted that she very much doubts that Burgess's advice can possibly have been worth his large fee because she recalls that he was "out of his depth" in financial matters. "I never got the impression he was remotely interested in the gold standard," she stated, "or knew much about share movements."[43]

This suggests that the role Burgess played as her mother's financial adviser might have been a convenient cover. As Miriam Rothschild recalled, Burgess was only one of the many people whom her mother, who did not believe in giving charity by lump-sum gifts, "assisted or supported by periodic and regular payments." Burgess himself never provided a clue about how long the salary continued. But until he joined the BBC in October 1936, he did not have any regular income with which to support his lavish life-style, one that involved suppers in the Café Royal and frequent trips to the Continent. So for more than a year and a half, Burgess was supported by the Rothschilds. The question therefore arises, if Katz was the financial analyst, what service was Burgess providing?[44]

An important clue is provided by Rudolph Katz himself: He told the FBI that Burgess "was helping a group of individuals who were acting as consultants to Winston Churchill, and that Burgess's field was Russia and India." What is most significant is that Katz tried to draw attention to Burgess's role as a consultant to senior members of the Conservative party. But in 1935–36, it was not Churchill to whom Burgess was offering advice.[45]

One of the single most bizarre elements in the quixotic career of Guy Burgess is that while he was a secret Marxist, and a salaried consultant to the Rothschilds, he also became a member of the pro-Hitler right wing of the Tory party. And when he failed to obtain a post in the Conservative central office, through his friendship with Harold Nicolson, with his many connections in the Establishment homosexual network, Burgess succeeded in infiltrating himself as the secretary and personal assistant to a newly elected, right-wing Conservative M.P. Captain John Robert Macnamara was a thirty-year-old ex-guards officer who had won the plum seat of Chelmsford for the Tories in the November General Election of 1935. He shared Burgess's sexual tastes, and the latter, acting the role of the servant who is really the master, served as his political counselor and procurer. Through "Captain Jack," Burgess met Macnamara's financial sponsor, the Venerable J. H. Sharp, the heir to a Dundee jute-mill fortune, who had taken holy orders. He was then the Church of England's arch-deacon in southeastern Europe. He also was homosexual and he suc-cumbed to the boyishly irrepressible Burgess.[46]

In the spring of 1936, the trio set off for the Rhineland, accompanied by Macnamara's friend Tom Wylie, a young official in the War Office. Ostensibly they were escorting a group of pro-Fascist schoolboys to a Hitler Youth camp. But from Burgess's uproariously bawdy account of how his companions discovered that the *Hitlerjugend* satisfied their sexual and political passions, the trip would have shocked their sponsors – the Foreign Relations Council of the Church of England.[47]

Macnamara was not, however, simply another member of the post-World War I generation of Cambridge homosexuals like Christopher

Isherwood and John Lehmann, for example, for whom the muscular blondness of the Nordic males had a powerful erotic appeal. Captain Jack was an outspoken advocate of improving relations with Hitler. He was one of the parliamentary members of the Anglo-German Fellowship. He was also a member of the Link, a less reputable pro-Nazi fringe organization that had been founded by Admiral Sir Barry Domvile when he retired as director of Naval Intelligence in 1930.[48]

The Anglo-German Fellowship was not, like the Link, simply a refuge for the extremist fringe, although many of its members, such as Captain Archibald Maule, the M.P. for Ramsay, belonged to both groups. The Fellowship was an influential and well-organized pressure group with direct connections to powerful men in the British press, banking, church, and government. Sponsored and financed by a group of leading Conservative businessmen, it boasted the support of three directors of the Bank of England and the backing of fifty members from both houses of Parliament. Its well-heeled members enjoyed lavish receptions at the German embassy and at banquets bedecked with swastikas in the fashionable Mayfair Hotel.

The Anglo-German Fellowship attracted members of the Prince of Wales's set. The future Edward VIII was known to have strong pro-German sympathies. So it was not surprising to find that his close friend, and later his personal secretary, Major Edward "Fruity" Metcalfe, frequently attended the Fellowship dinners. Metcalfe's wife, Lady Alexandra, was a member of the pro-Fascist January Club, to which many of Sir Oswald Mosley's supporters belonged. Lady Emerald Cunard, Mrs. Ronnie Greville, Lady Londonderry, and Lady Astor were also among the more prominent society hostesses who openly expressed admiration for Hitler and Mussolini during dinner-table conversations.[49]

"If only the Chancelleries of Europe knew that his speech was the result of Emerald Cunard's intrigues, themselves inspired by Herr Ribbentrop's dimple!" diarist and Tory M.P. "Chips" Channon once mocked after hearing about allegedly pro-German remarks by the Prince of Wales in November 1935. Lady Cunard, a "twittering bejewelled bird," flattered her guests with the impression that her drawing-room gossip influenced foreign policy because she had introduced Mrs. Wallis Simpson to Dr. Hoesch, the German ambassador.[50]

The Anglo-German Fellowship dinners and meetings were made part of their social calendar by Lady Cunard and Mrs. Greville as they vied with one another in their invitations to German aristocrats. Not since the balmy days before World War I had so many of the leading names in the *Almanach de Gotha* appeared together at the London dinner tables.

The Duchess of Brunswick, the daughter of the exiled kaiser, the Prince and Princess von Bismarck, and a slew of counts and barons sipped champagne with the emissaries from Berlin. The Nazi leaders were quick to seize the initiative and exploit the fascination of London society for aristocratic Fascism. They responded quickly to the call from one Conservative M.P. "to advertise the merits of Germany's internal and foreign policy." Trips to Germany to take in a Nazi rally at Nuremberg or attend the 1936 Olympic Games in Berlin became a fashionable pastime for the smart set of London. They entrained for Germany with the same excited enthusiasm with which their undergraduate sons were making their uncomfortable pilgrimages to Moscow and Leningrad.[51]

One new recruit to the Anglo-German Fellowship who did not go to Germany was Kim Philby. He had joined the Fellowship in 1936, but not because of admiration for Hitler. He became a dutiful supporter of Anglo-German reconciliation at the direction of his Soviet masters. His new role was to obtain information and hide even deeper his Communist past. With the assistance of Burgess, who as Macnamara's aide was a familiar figure in the Fellowship offices, Philby was introduced to Lord Mount Temple and Lord Redesdale, for whom he was soon ghosting speeches and articles. The glamorous banquets he attended while editing the Fellowship's magazine were a strange environment for the four-pound-a-week subeditor of a foundering Liberal monthly. But his friends, amazed that his political allegiances should have careened so far to the right, were fobbed off by Philby's explanation that he was doing it for money. His marriage with Litzi was on the rocks; so it was no surprise to those who knew him that within a year he would take off for Spain to cover the civil war from the Nationalist side.[52]

Ironically, most of the leading Conservatives and businessmen Philby encountered in the Fellowship had joined because they feared communism. While their children paid tribute to the struggle against Fascism being waged by the Soviet Union and the Spanish Loyalists, their fathers saw Hitler and Nazi Germany as a bulwark against the spread of the Red Revolution from the East. In much the same way as the Society for Cultural Relations with the U.S.S.R. served as a front for furthering Stalin's objectives with the younger generation, the Anglo-German Fellowship helped shape their parents' appeasement of Hitler.

This generational schizophrenia was very much to the taste of Guy Burgess. To former left-wing Cambridge friends who expressed surprise at his newfound enthusiasm for the Nazis, Burgess shrugged off his interest with the evasive comment that "one may as well see whether there is anything in it."[53]

Goronwy Rees, who renewed his own friendship with Burgess after returning from a spell in Vienna and Berlin in 1935, was not fooled, however. Rees was skeptical about Burgess's assertion that only an alliance of the extreme right could save Europe. "It was as if Guy, like a deep-sea diver, had plunged into the great ocean of communist dialectics and come up with the weapons which enabled him to demonstrate the precise opposite of what he had previously believed and now professed to deny," Rees wrote. He surmised later that Burgess invented an "intellectual defense" for the transformation in his way of life, which, in reality, "he had made for quite other and more practical reasons."[54]

Rees was correct in assuming there was some deeper reason for Burgess's turnabout. In one respect, however, Burgess remained unchanged. His quick ear for gossip and adaptive mind were useful attributes for a mole. But it was Burgess's special charm and taste for homosexual philandering that propelled him, in a matter of months, into the unsuspecting arms and confidences of some of the principal pro-German members of Parliament.

So successful was Burgess at penetrating the Anglo-German Fellowship that it has always been assumed he could have been acting only under the direct orders of Moscow. This is an accusation that, interestingly enough, Burgess himself rejected. He denied that he went to Germany in 1936 as a Communist agent or that he was under Communist direction. He asserted — through Driberg — that such a suggestion was "particularly wide of the mark."[55]

Burgess had many reasons to lie about many things. But this denial — made some twenty years later, from Moscow — has a ring of truth about it. The Soviets had already planted Philby, a controlled and disciplined agent, deep into the Anglo-German Fellowship movement. So it makes sense that Burgess may have been dropping a very broad hint that in 1936 he was operating in the same right-wing milieu as Philby, but under the direction of someone else.

If the Soviet NKVD did not recruit and direct Burgess to become a mole in the right wing of the Conservative party, who did?

The evidence pointing to the identity of Burgess's sponsor begins with two clues. The first was provided by Rudolph Katz when he told the FBI in 1951 that he met Burgess while "assisting Lord Rothschild." The second appeared in the biographical apologia written by Burgess's friend Tom Driberg, which derived from extensive interviews with Burgess in Moscow. In *Guy Burgess: A Portrait with Background*, there is a reference to how "the house of Rothschild had been deeply disturbed by Hitler's accession to power." In truth, the Jewish banking dynasty could not fail to be sensitive to the growing Nazi threat in the 1930s. But it was the appearance of pro-Germans among the city's merchant bankers and business interests, who worked together with right-wing Tories for a rapprochement with Hitler, that was most alarming to the Rothschilds.[56]

As a potential bulwark against Bolshevism, Hitler was one thing. The increasingly hysterical anti-Semitism of the Nazis was something else. The Rothschild family shared, with other leading members of the Jewish establishment in England, the hope that subtle persuasion in Whitehall would win Jews the right to settle in Palestine.

The Rothschilds were also concerned that their hard-won social status, as accepted members of Britain's ruling class, might be endangered if they openly backed the Zionist call for an independent state of Israel. Their influential friends were quietly working to get the British government to accept Palestine as a homeland for Jewish refugees fleeing Nazi persecution. And they knew they were tiptoeing on a slippery high wire spanning the chasm between national loyalties and political compromise. At the time, most people in Britain regarded the Holy Land as a part of their global empire, administered by London under a mandate from the League of Nations.[57]

Foreign Secretary Lord Balfour might have given official recognition to Zionism in 1917, but for the British government, it remained a matter of lip service rather than action. The Balfour Declaration that called for a Jewish homeland had been addressed — more for protocol than practical politics — to the Second Lord Rothschild, from whom Victor was to inherit his title in 1937. James de Rothschild, Victor's cousin, who was Liberal M.P. for Ely, had inherited from his branch of the family the financial underwriting of a large number of Jewish cooperatives in Palestine. But attempts to expand those settlements in the interwar years had led to greater friction with the Arabs and made Whitehall increasingly reluctant to honor the spirit of the Balfour commitment. By 1936, the Rothschilds had every reason to worry about the ominous news from Germany. Their fears increased when the Anglo-German Fellowship proclaimed the "immense potential significance" of the growing ties between the Conservatives and Hitler. Consequently, countering the spread of Nazism became as important for the Rothschild interests, and their London Bank in New Court, as it was to dispossessed Jewish members of the Comintern like Rudolph Katz.

The Rothschilds were no strangers to the necessity for a private intelligence network. They had been using such a sophisticated operation for more than a century. The founding father of Britain's Rothschild dynasty, Nathan Mayer Rothschild, had ensured his financial success by organizing a faster and more extensive spy service than the British government's. In 1815, his couriers followed Wellington's armies — which his loans helped finance. The Rothschild agents also spied on all the fractious European courts. Their mission was to collect and transmit to their employer timely intelligence reports regardless of the expense. He also established a courier-pigeon post to and from the Continent. Nathan Rothschild was therefore the first in London to receive news of Napoleon's defeat at Waterloo, and this information enabled the House of Rothschild to make a killing on a jittery London Stock Exchange awash with rumors of a French victory.[58]

Since private intelligence was an essential element of the Rothschild business operation, what better cover could they give their latest recruit in 1935 than to characterize Burgess as an investment counselor and dispatch him as their private spy to monitor the Anglo-German Fellowship? Information about threats to the House of Rothschild resulting from secret deals between British sympathizers and the Third Reich would more than justify the hundred guineas a month paid to Guy Burgess.

Victor Rothschild had implicit faith in his Cambridge friend because he, like Blunt, knew of Burgess's true loyalties. But Burgess's volatile enthusiasms would help persuade his right-wing friends that he had recanted his earlier Marxism. His homosexual appetite would prove an exploitable talent when it came to sharing the bed of a pro-German Tory well placed to pull strings and advance an ambitious young man's career. Nor should it be forgotten that Rudolph Katz, with his own extensive network of homosexual and Comintern contacts, also contributed to Rothschild's private intelligence network that, at the time, shared with Stalin a common enemy: Hitler.

Blunt, who was as close a friend of Rothschild as Burgess, may well have had a hand in staging and scripting the game that Burgess had embarked upon. Blunt was "the clever young English historian who had a kind of pupil-and-master relationship with Guy, from whom he imbibed the principles of the economic interpretation of history." This was the thin disguise that Rees, fearing a libel suit, gave Blunt in his autobiographical recollection of the odd coterie who used to meet of an evening in the flat Burgess rented in Belgravia.[59]

The eye-bursting red, white, and blue decor of Burgess's rooms overlooking the plane trees of Chester Square anticipated Pop Art. But it was not for artistic or patriotic reasons that Burgess chose the patriotic colors that he said were the only ones "any reasonable man could live with." It struck Rees forcibly that it had been a "very strange collection" of men who had gathered in a room often submerged by the debris of the previous night's drinking bout and stinking from the saucepans of congealed garlic-flavored porridge on which Burgess sustained himself at home. They were all, he said — not excepting himself — "to some degree infected with Marxism."[60]

Kim Philby, about whom Burgess "always spoke in terms of admiration so excessive that I found it difficult to understand on what objective virtue it was based," was, according to Rees, also a visitor. But it is likely that Philby was not a frequent presence. To associate too often and too closely with other members of a spy ring would break the rules of security that Soviet intelligence instilled in its disciplined agents.[61]

Philby justified his 1936 association with Burgess because of their shared participation in the Anglo-German Fellowship. But such meetings were impossible after February 1937, when Philby left for Spain to report on the war from the Nationalist side. This was the first test of his cover story and the right-wing contacts he made among the Fellowship. MI5, when it was investigating him, blundered by assuming that his trip was sponsored by the *Times*. The record shows that he did not become an accredited correspondent until May 1937 and a simple check of his bank records would have shown that he did not have the means for "gallivanting around Spain" for any length of time.[62]

Philby proudly admitted that "the enterprise had been suggested to me, and financed by, the Soviet service." His assignment was to use his cover as a journalist to provide intelligence from the Nationalist side, and he carried his code on a tiny piece of edible paper. For two and a half years Philby carried out his mission, supplying his Soviet contacts in France with military and political information and keeping the *Times* readers informed about the war. His fellow correspondents believed that his dispatches often unfairly promoted the Nationalist cause. None of them guessed that he was zealously following Moscow's orders. His career as a Soviet agent was almost terminated on New Year's Eve, 1937, when a shell from a Russian cannon hit a car full of journalists. Two of his companions died, but Philby, although wounded, survived to be decorated personally by Franco with the Red Cross of Military Merit.[63]

To recuperate from wounds to his head and arm, Philby was ordered to France for a brief rest. It was on a visit to Paris early in 1937 that he met up with Burgess who had also — according to Philby — helped replenish his funds.

When Philby went to Spain, by a curious coincidence, Donald Maclean was attached to the Spanish desk of the Western Department of the

Foreign Office. Although Maclean lived less than a mile from Chester Square in a small flat in Chelsea on Oakley Street, there is no record that he ever visited Burgess. Rees, however, does recall that he met Maclean on a yachting weekend on Southampton Water. He had heard Burgess talk admiringly of Maclean, whom he had seduced at Cambridge. But Rees disliked the young man, whom he found "rather superior."[64]

Rees also took an instant dislike to another of Burgess's close friends: a "grossly obese Central European," who was a correspondent for *Imprecor*, whom he only knew as Ignatz. This can only have been Rudolph Katz — not Otto Katz as so many have wrongly assumed, from an error originating in a confusion of their Christian names.[65]

Another member of the circle was a "working-class ex-chorus boy," whom Rees called Jimmy. In reality, his name was Jack Hewit. Jackie, as he was known to the group, was the son of a Tyneside tinsmith. A tubby boy with glasses, Hewit was teasingly called "Porky Suet" by his schoolmates. His overprotective mother died when he was twelve and his father intended to apprentice him to a plumber. In 1932, at the age of fifteen, he left home to come to London to fulfill his boyhood ambition to become a dancer. After a succession of jobs as a hotel page boy he managed in 1936 to get into the chorus line of *No No Nanette*.

The first time Hewit saw Burgess was one night outside the stage door. He was waiting in a parked car. Hewit thought Burgess was attractive, but that evening Burgess did not even introduce himself — he was waiting for another male member of the cast. Now in his seventies, Hewit is a genial teddy bear of a man who talks with undisguised affection and gratitude about Burgess when recalling that he actually met him for the first time in the War Office.

The incongruity of the encounter still amuses Hewit. He told me how, hungry and low on cash, he picked up a Hungarian one evening in a Whitehall pub called the Bunch of Grapes. Instead of offering Hewit a dinner, the man invited him to a party. Hewit, assuming that a party meant food, accepted. He was surprised when they walked up Whitehall to the War Office. The man pushed the doorbell and Hewit found himself in the flat of Tom Wylie, the resident clerk.

"What on earth is all this," Hewit recalls asking himself as he was introduced to a smoke-filled room of twenty men who were all drinking and "my dearing" each other. It was the conversation that fascinated Hewit. He could not follow a word of it, because they were talking a kind of upper-class shorthand like a Noël Coward sketch. Hewit knew at once he had stumbled into the upper reaches of London's homosexual demimonde. The nineteen-year-old working-class lad was so overwhelmed by it all, he quite forgot his initial dismay that there was nothing to eat with the liquor flowing as freely as the outrageous conversation.[66]

Among the crowd he recalls being introduced to Brian Howard, who was made up to the eyebrows and in full gush. Hewit found him a "real pansy, a stereotype Empress who 'my deaaared' everybody to death." He also met Anthony Blunt, who talked so quickly that he was not sure what it was about. Hewit observed with cheerful self-effacement: "I am sure if I had the brains to take it in, it would have been like going to a University lecture."

Burgess he recognized and found even "more attractive" than the night he had seen him outside the South London theater. To Hewit's relief and delight, Burgess came to his rescue when a fat man began to paw him and make himself objectionable. "A big fat man, an enormous lump" was how Hewit described the German who had introduced himself in heavily accented English as Rolf Katz. Burgess offered to drive Hewit home, but instead took him to the Chester Square flat that he was to share with Burgess for the next four years.[67]

"Guy was a very amusing companion. He was not ashamed to take his boyfriends everywhere," Hewit said. "He had this fixation about working people and he wore them like some men wear badges." Hewit did his best to keep up appearances, tidying up the flat, making sure Burgess bathed, cleaned his fingernails, and put on clean shirts, but despite these efforts, he said, "Guy always looked like an unmade bed."

In return, Burgess, who called Hewit "Mop," tried his best to waken his literary tastes, encouraging him to delve into Jane Austen and Mrs. Gaskell. These Hewit recalls enjoying, but he rejected Burgess's attempts to educate him politically. He told Burgess that Thomas Paine's *The Rights of Man* was rubbish and that he couldn't afford to be a socialist. "We never talked politics again." Their domestic arrangements were never easy. Burgess was an insomniac who regularly took Nembutal sleeping tablets at night and Benzedrine pills to wake up in the morning.

Burgess, according to Hewit, was "promiscuous to a degree." His infidelity was the cause of "very, very frequent rows," which often sent Hewit over to Blunt's bed-sitter in Palace Gate for consolation. "I'd arrive saying I was going to kill Guy," Hewit recalled, explaining how Blunt would always calm him down. Blunt and Burgess were extremely close and together they always managed to patch things up with Hewit. He found Blunt kind and considerate and admired his wicked sense of humor. He felt sorry for the ordeal that Blunt went through later when he was publicly exposed. He sent a note from Majorca, where he was at the time, inviting Blunt to come and stay for a rest. Blunt had evidently not lost his sense of humor, because a note arrived back saying that he hoped Hewit's invitation was for "a rest" and not "arrest."[68]

Hewit does not recall precisely when he moved in with Burgess but thinks it was sometime in late 1937. He recalls meeting at the flat on several occasions with the anti-Nazi diplomat from the German embassy whom Rees wrote about as being a frequent visitor to the Chester Square menagerie and another key player in the conspiratorial group.

This was Baron Wolfgang von und zu Putlitz. A member of Ambassador Leopold von Hoesch's staff at Carleton House Terrace since 1934, Putlitz was the son of a Junker and heir to an ancient Prussian lineage. He was a career diplomat in the German Foreign Service and took an immediate dislike to the Nazi regime when Hitler came to power in 1933. By his own admission he began passing information to the British in "the autumn of 1937."[69]

Records in the State Department archives confirm his value to the British Foreign Office. They suggest, however, that Putlitz might have become a mole even earlier. And there is every reason to believe that he served London *and* Moscow.

Putlitz wrote a carefully constructed memoir with the approval of the KGB some twenty years later. In it he claims that only after Ribbentrop arrived as German ambassador to London in 1936 did he begin furnishing confidential reports to Sir Robert Vansittart, the permanent head of the Foreign Office. He remained one of the key sources for what became known in the Foreign Office as "Vansittart's Private Detective Agency" after he was posted as a counselor to the 1938 German legation at The Hague.[70]

Putlitz's cover was blown by the Germans during the Phony War after they had penetrated British intelligence in the Netherlands. In November 1939, they learned about Putlitz when they kidnapped the senior MI6 officer, Major Richard Stevens, and his undercover British associate Captain Sigismund Payne Best, after luring them to a rendezvous on the road to Venlo near the German border. Fortunately for Putlitz, his ambassador entrusted him with the task of decoding an eyes-only cable from Berlin that was intended to seal Putlitz's fate. With his manservant Willi Schneider, Putlitz "disappeared." Using a secret radio transmitter to call for a rescue plane, they flew to England before the Gestapo caught them.

Shortly after Dunkirk, in June 1940, Vansittart tried to arrange American visas for the baron and his companion to prevent their being confined in one of the internment camps set up for enemy aliens during that summer's invasion scare. An unusual plea was made to the American ambassador, Joseph Kennedy, that Putlitz "had rendered him [Vansittart] invaluable services." But the State Department refused to grant the visas because the Gestapo had not taken the usual reprisals against Putlitz's family in Germany and this raised suspicions that he might be a Nazi undercover agent.[71]

A ten-day landing permit in New York for Putlitz and his manservant, en route to Jamaica, was all they were permitted. The State Department also instructed the FBI to conduct round-the-clock surveillance as soon as the two exiled Germans landed. Hoover's men reported that instead of trying to meet known German agents, Putlitz and his companion spent their time making contacts of a rather different nature while "patronizing places frequented by homosexuals."[72]

State Department records confirm that Putlitz *was* part of an extensive network of informants that Vansittart had built to keep the Foreign Office informed about developments in Germany — intelligence that he shared with a select circle outside the government, including Winston Churchill. Confidential information supplied by Dutch diplomats shows that they knew that Putlitz was "collaborating with British intelligence" by using his "so-called servant to maintain the risky contacts and pass on the information."[73]

American suspicions about Putlitz were aggravated by Hoover's undisguised aversion to homosexuals. So despite appeals to Vansittart from Putlitz's American friends, he was never permitted to reenter the United States. Obliged by "financial misery" to remain in a Jamaican internment center for three years, Putlitz finally received official permission to return to England in January 1944. After working under close surveillance for the Political Warfare Executive, preparing anti-Nazi broadcasts, in 1946 the baron was finally allowed to return home to Kiel as a translator in the British occupation zone. With his family estates in the East under Soviet control, he was penniless. He taxed Vansittart about his penurious condition in a letter complaining that his fellow Germans regarded him as a traitor. Worse, he warned his "old friend" of the dangers in store for the "alien" and misguided British occupation.

"Things are drifting into a state which will be fatal not only to me but also to you," Putlitz wrote Vansittart, without explaining his cryptic warning. Vansittart failed to come to the rescue of his now-discarded agent. With no hope of an influential position in the new Federal Republic of Germany, Putlitz turned to his other masters and the Soviets finally let the baron come in from the cold.[74]

On a snowy January day in 1952 Putlitz finally exposed his true Communist colors and took the one-way ride on the S-Bahn from West Berlin to settle in East Germany. It was just six months after the defection of Burgess and Maclean. Doubts about his true loyalties, and his links to the Cambridge moles, were clarified five years later when he published his memoirs. They contained an effusive tribute to Burgess, who had by then reappeared in Moscow, saluting him for his courageous defection, which showed his disgust with Britain's "final and total dependency on the United States." Burgess, he claimed, was "one of the first young Englishmen I had ever met who seemed really to have made a study of Marx."[75]

More surprising was Putlitz's unexplained tribute to "Mr. Anthony Blunt, whose kindness and understanding I will never forget." At the time of his book's publication, this slighting reference to the surveyor of the queen's pictures, who had just been knighted, must have mystified everyone but Blunt himself. What MI5 made of it is still an official secret. But it seems that the KGB intended to remind Sir Anthony that his primary loyalty was to the occupants of the Kremlin rather than to the reigning monarch in Buckingham Palace.[76]

It was not the first time that Putlitz had been involved in sending a "valentine." What is now clear is that he was a crucial, if minor, player in the events that led to the abdication of King Edward VIII.

Over the years, the Soviets had maintained a discreet line to Prime Minister Baldwin's right-hand aide, J. C. C. Davidson, via Anatoli Baykolov, or Baikaloff, as he was known to MI5. Supposedly a "mild liberal" White Russian, this foxy London journalist made himself an expert on Soviet affairs. In this capacity he acted as an adviser to the General Council of the British Trades Union Congress. But Baykolov's true mission was to maintain a close liaison with prominent right-wing Tories. He proved to be a powerful influence on Kitty Atholl, the Scottish Conservative. She moved so far to the left in her campaign against the government's nonintervention policy in Spain that she became known as the "Red Duchess."[77]

Yet as early as 1933, a warning had been sent to MI5 by the Russian émigrés in Paris that Baykolov was working for the Soviets. MI5 ignored these warnings and continued to use him as a clandestine channel of communication. Liddell, according to recently discovered letters to Vansittart, remained in contact with Baykolov until 1951, believing him to be a reliable source of information. Whether Liddell ever suspected that Baykolov was a double agent whose primary loyalty was to Moscow — or if Liddell knew and concealed it — remains unclear. But his long association with Baykolov adds yet another question mark against one of MI5's veteran counterintelligence officers.[78]

Meanwhile, new evidence has come to light that Moscow did not hesitate to activate the Baykolov back channel when it believed Moscow's interests could be served.

This appears to have been the case on January 30, 1936, the day King George V died. There was a widespread concern about the pro-German sympathies of the new king, Edward VIII, and members of his entourage such as Lady Cunard. It was feared that Edward's coronation would accelerate a rapprochement between London and Berlin. There is evidence that the Soviets activated the Baykolov connection to pass word of this danger, which was already worrying Britain's prime minister. The Soviets were getting their information from inside the German embassy via their mole Putlitz and it seems they tipped Baykolov to alert Davidson that Wallis Simpson was a putative German agent.

MI5 must have known that the new king's mistress, Mrs. Ernest Simpson (she was not yet divorced), was a frequent visitor to the receptions at the German embassy, thrown for the Anglo-German Fellowship by Ambassador von Hoesch. And it was through the Baykolov back channel that Davidson learned just how friendly Mrs. Simpson was with the German ambassador. Davidson's source was, after all, the same one through which he had obtained the damning information that helped sink Maundy Gregory's honors racket.

Davidson's personal, unpublished papers reveal the reasons for his concern. The king had been consorting with Ernest Simpson's wife at the same time he had sponsored Simpson's membership in the Masons. To ensure Simpson's election, the king had stated that he was not involved with Mrs. Simpson, a lie, and Simpson was apparently going to take action against the king on the grounds that the king was breaking his Masonic vows by having an adulterous affair with Wallis Simpson. There was the added complication that the king intended to marry Mrs. Simpson, which would make for an impossible situation. In a most-secret memorandum dated February 14, 1936, Davidson wrote: "I am quite convinced that Blackmail sticks out at every stage. H[is] M[ajesty] has already paid large sums to Mrs. S[impson] & given valuable presents. I advocate Most Drastic steps if it is true that S. is an American but if he isn't the situation is very difficult. The Mason vow is very clear. The P of W got S. in on a lie & is now living in open breach of the Masonic law of Chastity because of this lie he first told. So Mrs. S. who is obviously a golddigger has obviously got him on toast. . . ." The most important line in Davidson's memo, however, is the last, which sets forth the real problem: "Mrs. S. is very close to Hoesch and has, if she likes to read them, access to all Secret & Cabinet papers!!!!"[79]

This latter problem, together with the king's pro-German sympathies, can only have hardened Baldwin's attitude to Edward from the outset of the abdication crisis. It must therefore have been no little relief that on Good Friday Ambassador Hoesch was found dead on his bathroom floor.

Rumors ascribed his sudden death from a weak heart to execution by the Gestapo. His valet believed that Hoesch had committed suicide with a drug overdose. But his death now appears to have been suspiciously coincidental after Davidson's terse recommendation that "Most Drastic steps" be taken in the Simpson affair. Both the British and the Soviet governments had pressing motives for removing Hoesch. This raises the intriguing possibility that the back-channel liaison with the Soviets could have resulted in a contract with the NKVD on Hoesch.[80]

All such speculation aside, it is established fact that Blunt, Putlitz, and Katz were involved intimately with Burgess while he was in Rothschild's pay.

What puzzles intelligence experts is the unusual evolution of the Cambridge Soviet agents who flouted all the rules of good security by keeping such close company with one another. Only in Burgess's case is it explicable since in 1936 he would have been acting for the Rothschilds and was not yet a full-fledged Soviet agent.

It now seems plausible to conclude that Blunt was running Burgess as a subsidiary agent in much the same way that Blunt had involved Michael Straight. This would have advanced Blunt's standing with his Soviet masters, and it would provide Moscow with the information that Burgess was obtaining from the Anglo-German Fellowship at no additional effort or risk to its own operation. It also appears to have compromised Victor Rothschild, who was the unwitting sponsor of an extension of an NKVD network.

# CHAPTER 18

# *"It Was All a Bit of a Lark"*

Evidence now available leads one to the conclusion that Burgess did not come under the direct control of Moscow Center until 1939, years later than had previously been accepted.

Soviet intelligence exercised extreme care in picking its foreign penetration agents, and quite apart from his lack of career qualifications, Burgess was an undisciplined dilettante compared with Kim Philby. Before being sent to Spain, Philby managed to work his way into a position of influence in the Anglo-German Fellowship hierarchy, but Burgess never achieved an office in the Fellowship. On the contrary, Burgess's contacts were personal: as the "secretary" to an eccentric homosexual right-wing M.P. Moreover, by the spring of 1936, when Philby was still beavering away, writing the Fellowship's pro-German press releases and speeches, Burgess abruptly left the organization to try out as a journalist with *The Times* of London.

The reason Burgess gave Goronwy Rees for leaving Captain Macnamara's employ was: "He really was *too* absurd." When viewed alongside the story Rees told about how Burgess tried to recruit him, this contradicts the popular myth that he was already a Soviet agent. That Burgess blundered by making a direct approach to Rees is strong evidence that he was certainly not the mastermind of the ring. Worse, by revealing Blunt to be a Comintern agent, Burgess was breaking a fundamental tenet of Soviet undercover operations. Together they provide convincing evidence that Burgess had not yet been brought under discipline or NKVD control.[1]

The portrayal Burgess gave to Rees of Blunt's being an *éminence grise* is evidence, moreover, that Blunt was running Burgess as a subsidiary free-lancer. This explains many of the discrepancies in the case. It suggests how Burgess's usefulness was brought to the attention of the Soviets. With Blunt serving as the channel of access for the gossip that Burgess picked up, Moscow Center used the intelligence he provided while remaining safely insulated from any debacles that might result from his volatile enthusiasms.

During Blunt's final year (1935–36) as a don at Cambridge, the right-wing political and Whitehall circles into which Burgess was insinuating himself made him an increasingly useful source. Much of his intelligence came from the secretive homosexual network that maintained its "special" friendships with politicians and bureaucrats in the

French capital. Edouard Pfeiffer was one of those contacts — and he proved to be one of the most valuable sources Burgess met while working for Macnamara.

Pfeiffer was a former secretary general of France's right-wing Radical-Socialist party. He was a political *confidant* of the party's leader, Edouard Daladier, a taciturn university professor who, as the son of a provincial baker, was well qualified to lead this fractious alliance of *petite bourgeoisie*, *fonctionnaires*, and peasant landowners. Only once did Daladier lose his grip on a ministerial office in France's years between the wars. He had been premier twice for the unstable Popular Front coalitions of the Third Republic. And when the musical chairs of coalition politics thrust him into office again, in April 1938, Daladier and the British prime minister, Neville Chamberlain, joined in an alliance to pressure the Czechoslovakian government to give the Sudetenland to Hitler.[2]

Pfeiffer was an arch-intriguer "who would not normally respond to anything except the grossest kind of appeal to self-interest." Surprisingly, he became an ardent supporter of appeasement, and, as one of Daladier's *hommes de confiance*, he served as the principal secret negotiator with the French right.[3]

As a connoisseur of homosexual decadence, Pfeiffer had few equals, even in Paris. As an officer of the French boy-scout movement, his private life was devoted to the seduction of youth. Burgess discovered all this when he first visited Pfeiffer's apartment in Paris and found a group of men in full evening dress watching Pfeiffer play table tennis with a naked young man serving as the net. While Pfeiffer deftly flicked Ping-Pong balls over the youth's athletic thighs, he explained to Burgess that the young man was a professional cyclist, who just happened to be a member of Jacques Doriot's pro-Hitler Popular party.[4]

Burgess found Pfeiffer's combination of conspiratorial politics and homosexuality irresistible. They became intimates, and Pfeiffer often turned up at Burgess's flat in Chester Square whenever he was in London. Rees recalled how he often encountered a "peculiarly detestable Frenchman who seemed to me to smell of every kind of corruption."[5]

Thanks to Pfeiffer's inside gossip, Burgess was soon better informed than the Foreign Office about the Machiavellian maneuvering of the French government. Burgess was to find himself uniquely well placed to exploit his private line into the French Cabinet because, in October 1936, he landed a job with the BBC. He was always suspiciously vague about how he pulled off this coup, especially after having failed to get onto the *Times* staff. Earlier writers have believed that Burgess moved as a response to Moscow's orders to find a job in one of Britain's major

communications institutions. But this does not fit in with his other
desperate, and simultaneous, attempt to become a correspondent for a
French newspaper. Through his friend Pfeiffer, Burgess was contributing articles to a "controlled" right-wing newspaper financed by Otto
Abetz, a German who later was appointed as the Nazi regime's ambassador to occupied France. Burgess's efforts led to a month's trial in May
1936. But as a *Times* subeditor it took less than four weeks for Burgess
and the *Times* newsroom to realize that they were totally ill-suited for
each other. During his probationary work with the newspaper, Burgess
made the acquaintance of Roger Fulford, a member of the newspaper's
editorial staff.[6]

Fulford was another member of London's literary homosexual circuit.
During the war Fulford would become an MI5 officer, recruited,
significantly, by Roger Hollis, the future MI5 director who was later
suspected of being the Soviets' most senior mole in Britain's intelligence
services. Hollis had just returned from China and was trying to become
a *Times* journalist that November 1936.[7]

Hollis, like Burgess, was also turned down by *The Times*. Within a
year, however, Hollis managed to get into MI5. Fulford not only kept
in touch with Hollis, whom he had known from their days at Worcester
College, Oxford, in the late twenties but, in 1940, was himself recruited
into MI5 by Hollis, who was then a rising member of F Section,
responsible for monitoring the activities of the Communist party in
Britain. Fulford therefore represents a direct link between Burgess and
Hollis that has been overlooked.

Curiously, Wright makes no mention of Fulford. He also appears to
have overlooked another clue linking Burgess to Fulford, who was later
knighted for political services to the Liberal party. The archives of the
BBC reveal Roger Fulford as a prewar friend of Burgess. Furthermore,
Fulford made frequent BBC broadcasts after Burgess had become a
"Talks" producer.

BBC documents have recently become available that clarify the
importance of Guy Burgess as a potential Soviet agent after his appointment to the BBC in October 1936. Most accounts, including the internal
MI5 investigations seen by Wright, have taken at face value Burgess's
own story of landing his job at the BBC. Burgess said it was the result
of telephoned references to a senior executive from two fellow Apostles:
G. M. Trevelyan and J. T. Sheppard.[8]

It will not be possible to establish precisely how Burgess arrived at the
BBC until the Confidential Staff Archives are opened to researchers after
being sealed for seventy-five years. But from other files, it appears likely

that he prevailed on his friend Harold Nicolson for a strong recommendation. Nicolson had already established his reputation as an accomplished broadcaster, and through his Foreign Office connections, he had influential contacts in the BBC. But the person actually responsible for appointing Burgess was George Barnes, the deputy director of Talks.[9]

Barnes, like Burgess, was another Cambridge man. He joined the BBC in 1935 from the Cambridge University Press. Like Burgess, he also had been a Dartmouth cadet and had graduated from King's in 1925. He then taught at the Royal Naval College before returning to Cambridge as assistant secretary of the university press. Barnes, moreover, must have known all about Burgess's communism since Burgess had lodged in his house.

"George Barnes was greatly impressed with Burgess as being a young man bursting with ideas," says Lord Annan, who also points out that Burgess was very friendly with Barnes's pretty young wife, Anne. (Burgess was adept, as Rosamond Lehmann attested, at turning his boyish charms on married women.) At least two people who knew the Barnes family have pointed out that the Cambridge gossip was that Barnes was one of the few men who successfully kept a boyfriend and a mistress at the same time.[10]

This could have given Burgess a secret hold over Barnes. It also allowed Burgess to share Barnes's circle of friends, Cambridge radicals who included John Hilton, the unconventional professor of industrial relations.[11]

Hilton, whose steel-rimmed glasses accentuated his eaglelike countenance, was a former mill mechanic. He had risen by dint of his prodigious intelligence to become assistant secretary and director of statistics at the Ministry of Labour. An ardent trade unionist, Hilton had been cold-shouldered out of a college fellowship by the condescending Cambridge dons who resented a self-educated, working-class professor being thrust upon their university. Hilton accepted the snub and created a loyal following of enthusiastic left-wing undergraduates. His enormous appeal derived not merely from his firsthand experience of trade unions and proletarian life but from his tireless efforts to establish social clubs to help the unemployed.

Hilton was also one of Britain's first national radio celebrities, whose success began in 1933 with a series of talks on industrial relations. He was a natural broadcaster. His *This & That* series, based on his talks to the unemployed clubs, ranged from tips on pensions to international affairs. The huge amount of mail that flooded in confirmed that — for the first time — the BBC had reached a large working-class audience.[12]

Although Hilton was not a Marxist in the political sense, his champion-ship of the "little man," the unemployed, the John Bull in a cloth cap and hobnail boots, appealed to Cambridge Communists such as Straight who were striving to identify with the working class. Burgess knew and admired Hilton, who was a frequent guest in the Barnes household. Later, during the war, Burgess would become one of Hilton's producers.

The surviving internal BBC correspondence between Barnes and Burgess confirms that they both shared Hilton's views. Unlike Burgess and Blunt — whom it is clear from BBC records that Barnes also knew — Barnes was never openly a Marxist, either at Cambridge or during his long career at the BBC (for which he received a knighthood for the part he played in televising the coronation of Queen Elizabeth II). Broadcasting one's political views was forbidden, but the records of the Talks Department confirm that Barnes invariably took Burgess's point of view whenever politics intruded into the talks he was producing. He appears to have been Burgess's mentor and backer. He not only monitored Burgess's progress during the three months that Burgess spent at the BBC staff training school but quickly promoted him to be a producer in the Talks Department.

If Barnes was the alter ego of Burgess as a broadcaster, one of the beneficiaries of the relationship was Anthony Blunt. He was one of the first speakers Burgess brought before the microphone in June 1937 after the completion of his training. The messages Blunt exchanged with Barnes about his proposed broadcast on the Sistine Chapel suggest that the deputy director of Talks and Blunt were already on familiar terms.[13]

Blunt would later broadcast for Burgess on many occasions, thereby adding to his reputation as a wide-ranging authority on art. It is particularly significant that in the course of their preparations for a series on modern art, which was interrupted in 1939 by the outbreak of war, Blunt and Barnes agreed to devote time to the influence of contemporary paintings on the industrial community of Preston and among coal miners. This approach to art was very different from the erudite studies of Poussin and Philibert Delorme that Blunt was then pursuing at the Warburg Institute Library. It is also instructive that he used his commentary on "Spanish Painting" in January 1939 to slip in a political slant that provided yet another clear indication where his political sympathies lay: far to the left of the government-approved BBC line. Describing how the Loyalists had sent masterpieces of art from the Prado museum to Switzerland to save them from the ruthless hordes of Franco, Blunt observed: "I think we can imagine the Ghost of Goya watching with approval the saving of his work."[14]

British listeners were unaware that the supposedly spontaneous talks and discussions broadcast by the BBC were then carefully scripted and approved by the government. The censors might have missed the importance of Blunt's remarks, but they could hardly have escaped notice by the Foreign Office. Despite the BBC's jealously guarded tradition of impartiality, the corporation's records for the first time reveal that the government exercised tight control over the producers. And the Foreign Office exercised vetting rights over all scripts referring to international affairs. They could censor, request changes, and ban discussion on sensitive topics — even veto certain broadcasters.

The Spanish Civil War was a specially sensitive area for the British government. Burgess and Blunt would have congratulated themselves on their small triumph in broadcasting derogatory references to Franco and the Fascist victors. The ability of Burgess to subtly influence and color BBC broadcasts became more apparent in 1938, a year that saw Europe teetering on the brink of war. Hitler, by annexing Austria and then demanding the return of the German-speaking Czechoslovakian territories, succeeded in bluffing his opponents in the diplomatic poker game. Unnerved and divided, the British and French governments retreated in a policy of appeasement as they tried to dignify their position at the bargaining table at Munich in September 1938.

Burgess — thanks to his French homosexual connections — managed to play a winning hand for himself. He found the key that would admit him and Philby into the British intelligence service via the back door. But it was Pfeiffer who became the ace in Burgess's hand.

There is a curious inconsistency in Burgess's account of how and when he came to have access to the secrets of the French Cabinet that were his first intelligence coup. Burgess has always been taken at his word when he claimed his coup occurred in 1936. The evidence, nonetheless, indicates that it was really 1938. This date, as will be seen, is very significant in determining which year it was that Burgess was most likely to have become a full-fledged Soviet agent.

According to what Burgess told Driberg, it was in late March 1936 when, on a trip to Paris, he discovered that the French had come within one vote of going to war with Hitler. But this story does not fit the historical record — or Burgess's claim that it was Pfeiffer who obtained the details of the French Cabinet's deliberations directly from Edouard Daladier.[15]

Daladier was *not* a member of the French government in March 1936. The French records *do* show, however, that on March 11, *1938*, as minister of national defense and war in Premier Camille Chautemps's

Cabinet, Daladier *did* argue strenuously for military action against the Anschluss — provided the British agreed to participate. The following month Daladier came back into power as premier in the Cabinet reshuffle precipitated by the Austrian crisis.

This greatly increased the value of the connection Burgess maintained with Pfeiffer. Also to be considered is the assertion by Rees that Pfeiffer was a member of the dissolute group in Burgess's flat who were "all to some degree infected by Marxism." This suggests that the Frenchman was transferring some loyalty to Moscow. That inference was also hinted at by the respected political journalist, André Geraud, who was accused by Pfeiffer and a former French Comintern official of undue hostility to Russia that same year.[16]

All this increases the probability that it was March 1938 and not March 1936 when Burgess obtained from Pfeiffer the "detailed and graphic account of the discussions within the Cabinet and the positions taken by its various members." On his return to London he passed it on to "a friend" who was "a distinguished novelist, who happened to work for the Secret Service." A few days later Burgess effectively became an MI6 agent when that same friend paid him a sum of money "sufficient to cover his Paris expenses."[17]

Burgess admitted that the Pfeiffer connection opened the door for him to become an MI6 informant. With the exception of James Bond's creator, Ian Fleming, distinguished novelists were a rare breed in Britain's intelligence services at that time. So Guy's "giveaway" reference makes it possible to identify his MI6 friend as David Footman, already an accomplished writer of fiction. His second novel, *Pig and Pepper*, was a literary *succès d'estime* in 1936, after he had published *Balkan Holiday* the previous year.

A mousy, scholarly man with a very dry sense of humor, Footman was — like Blunt — the Marlborough-educated son of a Church of England cleric. After graduating from Oxford and winning a Military Cross in World War I, he obtained a post with the Levant Consular Service. In 1935, he transferred to Section I of MI6, the Secret Intelligence Service, the political division. As was customary, his cover was as a member of the Foreign Office, and he became a Russian expert. His intense study of the Soviet Union surfaced in a series of books on communism and Russian history that were published in the postwar decade before he retired to pursue his interests as an Oxford don.[18]

Just before the outbreak of World War II, Footman had become one of MI6's acknowledged experts on the Soviet Union. This makes it surprising to learn that he did not enjoy the complete confidence of his contemporaries. Sir Patrick Reilly, a Foreign Office colleague and a wartime assistant to SIS director Sir Stewart Menzies, cryptically referred to Footman as "emphatically not a man to commission any study of Stalinist policies."[19]

Just how Burgess became acquainted with Footman is unclear but the initial contact could have been made through mutual friends in the left-wing London literary scene. Once the introduction was made, however, Footman became one of Burgess's most valuable contacts and he was instrumental in getting both Burgess and Philby into MI6. Suspicions are raised when Philby deliberately alludes to Footman as being "a strong ally" at the time of his 1944 coup to take over the Counterintelligence Section. Footman's early association with Burgess, and his later alliance with Philby, cause doubts about Footman's integrity. In 1953 — just two years after Burgess defected to Moscow — Footman retired from MI6 to pursue his Russian studies as a fellow of St. Anthony's College.[20]

"I don't think Footman was ever given a completely clean bill of health," a wartime member of the Foreign Office told me. He said that after Blunt's exposure, he had asked Sir Dick White whether he ever knew where he stood with Footman. "No, I wish I had," the former director of MI5 and MI6 ruefully admitted.[21]

The most unequivocal pointer to prewar collusion between Burgess and Footman is Burgess's invitation to Footman to participate in broadcasts about literary and travel subjects. The BBC Talks Department records also reveal that Burgess was unusually careful to deal with Footman through his literary agents. Such a formal approach stands out in contrast to the old-boy network he used to approach his other guest speakers. By the spring of 1938, Burgess was regularly passing on to Footman intelligence obtained from the French Cabinet via Pfeiffer. That May, Burgess became a subcontractor for MI6. One of the assignments was Konrad Henlein. A former gymnastics teacher and leader of the Sudeten German party, Henlein provided Hitler with the excuse for making his bid to occupy the northern part of Czechoslovakia. He came to London in May with instructions on how to hoodwink the British government with his demand for independence and denial that he was "acting on instructions from Berlin."[22]

Burgess told his boyfriend Hewit all about Henlein. Because of his switchboard experience, Hewit was to substitute for the telephone operator at the Goring Hotel, where the leader of the Sudeten Germans was lodging.

"It was all a bit of a lark," Hewit told me, recalling how he monitored all of Henlein's calls. After "work," he said he then met with Burgess and David Footman at a pub in Westminster near the St. James's underground station that served the Broadway Buildings that were MI6's headquarters. Hewit said that he felt "used" by Burgess, who had pressured him into becoming an unofficial secret agent. Their relationship had already cooled because of Burgess's generosity in "lending him out" to friends who were in need of a lover. Burgess then added insult to injury by returning from a holiday trip to Cannes with his mother and a "very attractive seventeen-year-old boy named Peter Pollock in tow." The *ménage* left Hewit feeling neglected. In August 1938 he packed his bags and went off to Belgium with Christopher Isherwood. With his German boyfriend barred from entry to Britain, Isherwood recorded that he now found Hewit to be "desirable as well as companionable" because he had once had sex with the beloved Heinz.[23]

Henlein's mission to London succeeded despite Hewit's telephone monitoring. The Sudeten leader had fooled the distrustful Vansittart, who reported to Neville Chamberlain's Cabinet that he found Henlein "a wise and reasonable man." After telling a group of Conservatives, including Churchill and Harold Nicolson, that the only thing the Sudeten Germans wanted was their autonomy from the repressive Czechs, Henlein had returned to Prague via Berlin. There he personally reported to Hitler that his mission had been a success and that Britain was indifferent to the fate of the Czechoslovaks.[24]

The British Cabinet may have been hoodwinked by Henlein, but Burgess was not. In his capacity as a BBC radio producer he hoped to alert the country to the danger of failing to face up to Hitler. He planned a series of talks on "Aggression in the Mediterranean."

Burgess also embarked on a less public mission that summer. In his spare time he was shuttling back and forth to Paris as a courier. He appears to have been serving several different masters, among whom, significantly, were the Rothschilds. At the same time he was liaising with Pfeiffer, on whose behalf he claimed to have received secret letters for "a man of title closely linked with the Prime Minister." This reference was to Viscount Halifax, who had become foreign secretary in February 1938, when Anthony Eden resigned after learning that Neville Chamberlain was bypassing the Foreign Office in trying to engineer a rapprochement with Mussolini.[25]

The prime minister, who distrusted the hard-line anti-Fascist Vansittart, preferred to negotiate his deal for Mediterranean appeasement through his confidant, Sir Horace Wilson, who had opened up a private channel to Rome. This was done via Sir Joseph Ball, the Conservative party's research director who, thanks to his pro-Fascist friends in the Anglo-German Fellowship, had already established his own direct lines to Count Grandi, the Italian ambassador.[26]

Into this Machiavellian web of diplomatic intrigue the homosexually-inclined Ball introduced his protégé, Guy Burgess. Burgess knew how to cultivate such a confidant. He later revealed that he, too, was acting for "an unofficial intelligence organization which supplied information not only to Neville Chamberlain but to Sir Horace Wilson, head of the Civil Service and Chamberlain's *éminence grise.*" Burgess was now in his element in these furtive maneuverings, working for no fewer than three masters.

As a courier for the Rothschilds he acted as the go-between for Chamberlain and Daladier as they plotted their appeasement of Hitler. Their communiqués about how to secure peace at any price were written in the third person and signed by subordinates. Burgess disgustedly referred to their letters as "the communications of a confused and panic-stricken patriot to an ignorant provincial ironmonger." He was fully aware of their contents because he fed the correspondence to a third party. This was MI6, who monitored the secret traffic between the British and French premiers for Sir Robert Vansittart, the watchful head of the Foreign Office.[27]

Whenever Burgess undertook a courier mission to Paris, he stopped off at a "safe house" — a flat that MI6 maintained in the St. Ermin's Hotel — conveniently near the Broadway headquarters of the Secret Intelligence Service. An MI6 officer "took photostatic pictures of the letters," and Burgess helped him translate them because "his French was not very good." Burgess proudly claimed responsibility for having destroyed one letter he was given by Pfeiffer to carry to Chamberlain because it protested the mobilization of Britain's fleet at the height of the Munich crisis at the end of September.

Burgess, although he was careful not to brag about it, also must have been passing this information about the secret British and French exchanges to the Soviets. The question is: Did he pass the information through Blunt? Or by 1938 was he also a trusted, disciplined NKVD agent — and, if so, how was he controlled?

Here again, it is interesting to find that Blunt seems to have done his best to confuse the picture. According to Wright's account, Blunt insisted that in 1938 their espionage ring was supposedly "out of touch and apparently abandoned" following the recall of their controller "Otto" to Moscow. This, as has been shown, does not square with the MI5 records that indicate that "Otto" was a nonexistent control, a fabrication for disguising the fact that Theodore Maly, the original founder-controller of the Cambridge ring, had not left Britain until the summer of 1937 — a year after his supposed recall by Moscow.[28]

Furthermore, Blunt told Wright that it was Burgess and Philby who reestablished contact with the Soviets through Litzi Friedman. The first Mrs. Philby, supposedly a "longtime European Comintern agent," he claimed had passed messages through Edith Tudor Hart (the wife of Dr. Tudor Hart, a prominent member of the Communist party) via "Bob Stewart, the CPGB official responsible for liaison with the Russian embassy." But Blunt's explanation does not hold water because: (a) Philby's own account demonstrates that he was in direct contact with the NKVD in Paris from the spring of 1937 onward and (b) MI5 had already penetrated the headquarters of the British Communist party.[29]

Wright reports that Blunt later confessed that it "had always puzzled him that the Cambridge ring was not detected at this point." Now that we have the documentation on the Woolwich Arsenal case, showing the extent to which Olga Gray and Maxwell Knight's other MI5 agents had burrowed into the inner sanctums of the CPGB, it becomes apparent that Blunt's contrived puzzlement was a highly sophisticated double-bluff. According to American intelligence experts, Blunt's perplexity was the typical ploy of a well-briefed long-term Soviet agent. By expressing puzzlement, Blunt was hoping that MI5 would begin revising its previously rock-solid conclusions.[30]

Apparently the trickery worked. Wright stated that MI5 "had always assumed the Ring had been kept entirely separate from the CPGB apparatus," but now "it appeared that we had missed the greatest CPGB secret of them all." As we can see, however, the claim that the ring was run through British Communists until 1940 does not fit the facts. The agent-running operations of Soviet intelligence were undoubtedly disrupted by Stalin's purges of the old Comintern/NKVD group that included Theodore Maly. But the frequent trips that Blunt *and* Burgess made to France right up to the outbreak of the war in 1939 would have enabled them to keep in touch with NKVD control officers in Paris. This would not have been nearly as risky as communicating directly with the Russian embassy in London through the CPGB as Blunt claimed he did.[31]

The BBC's records reveal that Blunt and Burgess often arranged to be in Paris together in 1937. While this is, of course, no proof that either communicated with the Soviets while in the French capital, it seems to be no coincidence that Blunt stayed at the Hôtel Récamier on the Place Saint-Sulpice. This discreet left-bank pension happened to be a short walk from the tightly shut gates of 79 Rue de Grenelle, which a brass plate engraved with a hammer and sickle discreetly identified as being the Soviet embassy.[32]

Paris, as MI5 records and Philby's account confirm, was the principal European base of operations for Soviet intelligence during the Spanish Civil War. Surveillance of the Russian embassy by the French secret service was complicated. The embassy was located (in or near) the warren of narrow back streets of the Latin Quarter. The French capital boasted a far larger number of both *legal* and *illegal* Soviet agents on the ground than did London. This arrondissement included both the Soviet embassy and the Sorbonne university, plus the Café de Flore and the Deux Magots, which were the best known of the artists' cafés serving as meeting grounds for a whole generation of young French intellectuals under the spell of André Malraux and his followers. Malraux, the dominant Communist philosopher, polemicist, and passionate champion of the Spanish Loyalists, was credited with converting more young people to communism than Marx ever had.

When Donald Maclean arrived in Paris toward the end of 1938, he moved into a left-bank apartment and became an habitué of the two famous cafés in the shadow of the Romanesque tower of Saint-Germain-des-Prés. By day the formally attired young diplomat diligently waded through official paperwork in the British embassy across the river. By night he shunned his fellow diplomats to join the Bohemian crowd that gathered at the marble-topped café tables.

The Left Bank was also home to Münzenberg's shadowy empire of Communist-front publishing houses, propaganda factories, and relief organizations. The myriad of safe houses tucked away in the Parisian student quarter, where all-night comings and goings attracted little attention, enabled NKVD officers to move in and out of the nearby Soviet embassy to clandestine meets and recruiting operations.

It is perfectly possible to believe that Moscow Center found it advisable to run the Cambridge agents from Paris after Maly's recall from London in the summer of 1937. That was, after all, where Philby implies that he was controlled from while in Spain. With Maclean also in the French capital in 1938, and with Blunt and Burgess making frequent trips across the Channel to Paris, it would have made sense for Paris to administer Soviet operations in Britain.

Without the French police records that disappeared during World War II, it is not possible to identify the recruiter, or establish precisely when it was that Burgess signed on with the NKVD. Conversations with American intelligence officers with extensive contacts in the DST, the French counterintelligence bureau, produce a scenario that has to take into account the extreme selectivity and caution of the NKVD between 1937 and 1938 (when Yezhov was purging the organ of its old Comintern agents). Burgess, they believe, was managed by trusted NKVD officers in the Soviet embassy in Paris, who cultivated him as a "source" rather than as an agent. They would have encouraged him to think he was nominally under Blunt's direction — until such time as Moscow Center had established his access to vital information and his willingness to submit to their discipline and control.[33]

This would not have precluded the Soviets from using Burgess for missions of the kind Philby revealed that he ran in 1937, to "replenish my funds." This was the probable destination for the "bundles of bank notes" that Goronwy Rees "caught sight of stuffed away in the indescribably untidy cupboards" of Burgess's flat in Chester Square. One of these "replenishment" runs for Philby may have coincided with the trip that Burgess made to Paris in the early summer of 1937 when he accompanied Rees to a conference of the Writers' International. He was present when Burgess delivered "Marxist literary lectures to two well-known communist writers, from whom he differed only in his greater fidelity to the party line." Since Burgess had tried to persuade Rees to join him as an underground Comintern agent, Rees was left wondering why someone who had "advertised so loudly his breach with communism" should risk blowing his cover by actively participating in a Communist-front organization.[34]

This outspokenness and lack of discretion can be interpreted as further confirmation that Burgess was not under Soviet control in 1937. His eagerness to participate in the "impassioned revolutionary oratory" of the Writers' International also brought him into contact with Münzenberg's operatives. Senior MI5 officials have been credited with believing that Burgess must "have learnt a lot" from these contacts because they were "tremendously good operators."[35]

Still, it is unlikely that Münzenberg was the contact through whom Burgess supplied Moscow with the information Rees said he obtained from Pfeiffer. It is more likely that Burgess passed it on through Blunt, or directly to a Soviet embassy official in Paris. According to Rees, Burgess had also been given an underground contact and "maildrop" in London. He described him as a Russian with whom Burgess made contact "at regular intervals" in a café in the East End of London. It is thought that this was Davidovich Gadar, the Soviet illegal whose legitimate business as rag merchant had served as a front for Maly's paymaster and mail-drop address.

Burgess developed a liking for Chinese food that may well have resulted from his many trips to the East End in the summer of 1938. Friends would later recall for MI5 investigators how they would accompany Burgess to a Sunday dim sum lunch at an unfashionable Cantonese restaurant on Mile End Road. They noted how their host excused himself on occasion, left the restaurant and slipped across the street to push an envelope through the letter box of a seaman's outfitters.[36]

As the Czechoslovakian crisis deepened and Moscow's need for information from the secret exchanges between Daladier and Chamberlain increased, so did Burgess's appetite for steamed dumplings. The importance of what Burgess was able to pass on to Moscow is apparent from his bold assurances to Rees that Daladier would never fight for Czechoslovakia. This was important news for Moscow, because the Soviets, like the French, had a mutual defense treaty with the Czechs. And Daladier had made it quite plain to Chamberlain that France would stand by its pact only if the British joined the guarantees against Germany. According to Burgess, the British government "was well aware of this." Whitehall had no intention of making any commitment. What is more, Chamberlain and Daladier, who distrusted Stalin more than Hitler, sought to dissuade Czech President Eduard Beneš from giving credence to the Soviet Union's last-minute offer to unilaterally come to the aid of Czechoslovakia if Germany attacked.[37]

When Britain's seventy-year-old prime minister was preparing to bargain with Hitler at Munich in 1938, Burgess made his own move. Thanks to his clandestine trips he already knew what the outcome of this search for "peace with honour" would be. So he tried to use his position as a BBC producer to turn public opinion against Chamberlain's appeasement policy. He had an effective weapon at his disposal, a BBC series entitled *This Week*.

The topical current-affairs program had proved an enormous success. Ambitious members of Parliament wined and dined Burgess for the privilege of receiving an invitation to appear on his shows. Burgess had already acquired the reputation of a magician whose ideas, polishing of scripts, and careful coaching could make radio personalities out of the most pompous parliamentarians.

It was to his friend Harold Nicolson that Burgess turned as the member of Parliament most qualified to provide what were the only topical commentaries broadcast by the BBC at the time of Munich. Burgess hoped to create a public protest while Chamberlain and Daladier, nudged by Mussolini from the sidelines, secretly agreed to pressure President Beneš into accepting the dismemberment of Czechoslovakia.

Egged on by Burgess, Nicolson tried to condemn Hitler's blackmailing diplomacy. But the Foreign Office demanded that the proposed script be heavily censored. Barnes, Burgess's friend and mentor, as deputy head of Talks, acted as intermediary in the rancorous dispute. In the end, all that Nicolson could do was to deliver his talk "in a voice of ironic gloom." He and Burgess then headed down Regent Street from the BBC to the Café Royal where they found their literary friends already drowning their "tears in England's shame" in large quantities of alcohol.[38]

A week later, on the eve of his fateful flight to Munich, Chamberlain made an apologetic broadcast. In a reedy, croaking voice he advised the British people that it was "horrible, fantastic, incredible" that they should be digging trenches and trying on gas masks because of what he called "a quarrel in a far-away country between people of whom we know nothing.[39]

Burgess decided that Nicolson should not give up. The next day he sent a rallying reminder on BBC notepaper to his friend at the House of Commons that was significant for its overtly indiscreet pro-Soviet sympathies. Citing a "semi-confidential authority," Burgess said that Hitler was going to propose an Allied Conference "excluding Russia." He urged Nicolson "to do exactly as you did in your talk about Czechoslovakia ten days ago."[40]

It was too late.

Forty-eight hours later, Chamberlain returned to Heston aerodrome. Before a swarm of reporters, the smiling but gaunt prime minister, clutching his umbrella, triumphantly waved Hitler's signature on the ruinous scrap of paper that he declared guaranteed "peace in our time."

Burgess knew better than his countrymen that Chamberlain had brought neither peace, nor honor, back from his sell-out to Hitler. Furthermore, the recently released BBC records reveal that he planned to play an intrusive propagandist role in a series of "scripted" discussions about the Mediterranean. Although he did not originate the idea, Burgess claimed he had "chosen" the topics to "illustrate the chronic danger of Fascist aggression that formed the real background of the wars in Abyssinia and Spain." When instructing his anchorman, E. H. Carr, he sought to draw his attention to the Foreign Office fears that too much attention was being focused on the sensitive issue of Anglo-Italian rivalry. He also took great care to dstance himself from any association with Comintern propaganda by observing that "the Third International (though not I suppose, strictly the Soviet Government) was, I think pretty busy in Spain."[41]

Burgess later told his BBC colleagues how he had telephoned the

Soviet ambassador for his advice at the height of the Munich crisis. Ivan Maisky, he claimed, had urged him to go and see Churchill "to call on him in the name of the Youth of Great Britain, to intervene." Whether it was the Soviet ambassador or his own whim that prompted him to drive down to Kent, Burgess *did* visit Churchill at his country home in Chartwell to discuss the Mediterranean broadcasts.[42]

A staunchly outspoken opponent of Chamberlain's policy of appeasement, Churchill had originally accepted an invitation, then declined to broadcast during the Munich crisis. He complained that the Foreign Office would never permit his harshly critical words to go out over the air. The memorandum filed by Burgess after his visit reveals that Churchill believed "he would be even more muzzled in the future since the work of the BBC seemed to have passed under the control of the Government." Burgess's admission that "as a matter of courtesy" the Foreign Office was, indeed, allowed to see scripts "on political subjects" did not persuade Churchill to change his mind.[43]

It was a Saturday morning and Burgess picturesquely claims that "like Balbus" he found the gruff elder statesman, trowel in hand, building his famous orchard wall. Evidently impressed by the eloquence of the young BBC producer's conviction of the ominous inevitability of war, Churchill presented Burgess with a leather-bound copy of his speeches, *Arms and the Covenant*. He inscribed the volume: "To Guy Burgess, from Winston S. Churchill, to confirm his admirable sentiments. September 1938."[44]

Churchill's book became a cherished possession of Burgess. One of his "party pieces" was to relate a highly embellished account of his close and warm relationship with Britain's wartime leader. "If I ever return to a position of responsibility and power and you wish to help me just bring the book along," Burgess would claim Churchill said when bidding him farewell, adding the assurance: "I shall never forget."[45]

These statements may have been more imagined than real, just as Burgess claimed that he was fired from the BBC a short time after because of his series of broadcasts on Spain. His idea for *From Both Sides of the Line* would have brought left-wing speakers to the microphone. This was, apparently, unacceptable. But the BBC records that are now available for inspection do not bear out his claim, although he did apparently run into difficulty by putting forward J. B. S. Haldane for a broadcast on the subject.[46]

Burgess also claimed that after leaving the BBC he received an invitation to join Section IX of MI6 after serving the organization on a free-lance basis. But the truth, as it has recently come to light, is that he was invited to become a producer for a highly secret clandestine broadcasting operation, which the government conjured into being at the end of 1938 to wage a secret radio war against Hitler. No comprehensive records of the innocuously named Joint Broadcasting Committee exist in the British archives. The historian has to search hard even to find a reference to the small organization that was headquartered at 71 Chester Square, a few doors away from Burgess's flat. So secret were the Joint Broadcasting Committee's activities that even as late as 1985 the few surviving members of its staff were receiving "official" visits from MI5 staffers trying to establish who ran it and what its real function was.[47]

The MI5 people appeared most concerned, nearly half a century after the JBC was set up, that it might have fallen under the control of Burgess and his Communist friends. There can be few more glaring examples of how the traditional rivalries in Britain's secret services interfered with the efficient conduct of intelligence, because the JBC was given its birth by MI6.

The JBC had grown from the determination of the Foreign Office that a British prime minister's conciliatory words could counter the bellicose speeches of Hitler. But to broadcast directly into Germany was in contravention of the 1936 international conference that banned "the systematic diffusions of programs or communications which are intended for listeners of another country." The SIS had already engineered the transmission of Chamberlain's speeches on the Munich crisis over Radio Luxembourg. Broadcasting mainly popular music, this commercial operation was one of Europe's most listened-to stations and the British government had paid for the air time through the secret agency of the Travel and Industrial Association of Great Britain.[48]

The belief that Hitler could be influenced by the German population led the Foreign Office to look for alternative ways to expand such clandestine broadcasting operations. The JBC came under the aegis of Major-General Laurence Douglas Grand. He liked to describe himself as Director of Fortifications and Works at the War Office. Grand was a tall, mustachioed man, whose already dashing impression was accentuated by the red carnation he always wore in his buttonhole. He had been appointed in March 1938 to head up MI6's Section D. The designation of his new outfit was officially derived from "D for Destruction." It might more accurately have stood for "Dirty Tricks," since the unit's assignment was to prepare ways for "attacking potential enemies by means other than operations of military force." The caveat imposed on D Section was that none of its operations were officially sanctioned to go into operation until war broke out.[49]

In the aftermath of Munich, however, Grand's masters in the Foreign

Office decided that they did not have to wait until the balloon went up to start clandestine propaganda broadcasts into Germany in defiance of the International Broadcasting Convention. Accordingly, respectable public figures – including Harold Nicolson and his fellow M.P. and banker A. V. Hambro became members of an eight-man board of public worthies operating under the nominal chairmanship of the Earl of Rothes. The JBC's director and prime mover was Hilda Matheson. As the BBC's first director of Talks, and former secretary to Lady Astor, Matheson already had the establishment and broadcasting contacts to execute Grand's directive. Her instructions were to set up a "Goodwill Committee" that was nominally independent of the government to "prepare programs for use in neutral countries, but aimed primarily at a German public."[50]

The facade of respectability implicit in the Joint Broadcasting Committee's Chester Square address, and its notepaper headed by Big Ben guarded by two lions, was deceptive as to its origins and purposes. Even Burgess, who was not known for his discretion, insisted that the JBC's purpose was merely "to get British propaganda on American networks." That may have been the cover story, but so secret was it kept that until the outbreak of World War II the JBC's funds arrived in gold sovereigns, and Grand used the alias of Douglas in his meetings with the JBC staff. It was he who held responsibility for arranging the production and transmission of the programs destined for Germany. Grand selected Burgess for this task – on the recommendation of Harold Nicolson and his MI6 friend David Footman.[51]

Burgess appears to have been the main fount of ideas and principal producer of clandestine programming. In compiling the careful assembly of propaganda talks, variety shows, and hit records, he was assisted by Paul Frischauer, an Austrian refugee, and his wife, who were members of an anti-Hitler group in London. Burgess's admission that one of his German-speaking British broadcasters was Stephen Haggard suggests that he turned to members of Blunt's circle for talent. Haggard, whom he described as "a brilliant actor and a passionate anti-Fascist," was an *amour* of Blunt's brother, Wilfrid, whom Anthony had also known.[52]

Since the clandestine operations of the JBC are still considered so sensitive that its records are virtually nonexistent, it is not clear precisely how these broadcasts were put out. What is known is that at least some of Burgess's programs, recorded on large shellac discs, were taken by couriers to European commercial stations such as Radio Luxembourg. But there is a tantalizing reference in one Foreign Office docket about a prerecorded message of the prime minister's that was to be prepared "for smuggling into Germany" for broadcasting from one of the "mobile units inside Germany." Just how Grand and MI6 managed to organize such facilities under the noses of the Gestapo is still a closely guarded secret.[53]

The operation may well have been modeled on — and may even have utilized — the existing facilities of the underground anti-Nazi broadcasting networks operated by Hitler's old party comrade Otto Strasser and his associates. One of their clandestine stations calling itself Die Deutsche Freiheitwelle operated from a large Buick sedan until someone tripped over its aerial wire and reported the car's license number to the Gestapo. There were other secret transmitters in Czechoslovakia and France, where Willi Münzenberg contributed to the "Freedom Station" that was beaming anti-Nazi propaganda into Germany under the secret sponsorship of the French government. Burgess said later that he made a clandestine visit to Lichtenstein to investigate the possibility of setting up an underground radio station in Vaduz. It is believed that he made direct contact with Münzenberg and other members of the Communist underground during the many trips he made in the first six months of 1939, and that they made full use of the recorded propaganda programs he produced.[54]

Whatever the means used to put these programs out, Burgess at last was able to fully use his talents in waging the clandestine war against Hitler. And only now that the real function of the Joint Broadcasting Committee has been uncovered, is it possible to understand why the instrumental role Burgess played in one of Britain's most hush-hush operations earned him such a high position of trust in the secret service. So sensitive was the job that Burgess did for MI6 in the JBC between 1939 and 1941 that any reference to it has been excised from the FBI files in Washington at the request of the British government.[55]

The cloak of official secrecy still shrouds details of operations that Burgess betrayed to the Soviets. But there is little doubt that his JBC role in MI6 had also made him a potentially valuable agent to Moscow. With an "official" excuse to travel all over Europe, he demonstrated his usefulness on courier and liaison duties. During the early months of 1939, while Franco's forces were winning Barcelona and recognition from the British government, Burgess headed south from Paris to the French border town of Saint-Jean-de-Luz, where he met the war-weary Kim Philby.

The Soviets were already cutting their losses and abandoning the Spanish Loyalists. Philby, however, had been told by Moscow to remain in his reporter's job. He stayed in Spain until July 1939, doggedly reporting the tide of Fascist military victories for the readers of *The*

*Times*, with little to console him but the affections of his attractive mistress, Bunny. The vivacious Lady Frances Lindsay-Hogg's marriage to her aristocratic matinee-idol husband had ended in divorce and Bunny was always ready to welcome Philby to her Canadian father's villa, on the outskirts of Saint-Jean-de-Luz.[56]

Burgess was able to offer little more than encouragement to Philby, who must have been heartened — and not a little envious — to learn from him how he was rapidly advancing his career in the British secret service. That this meeting took place during the critical months of 1939 suggests that it must have been held at the direction of Soviet intelligence. As a member of MI6, Burgess would now have been regarded as a very valuable asset by Moscow Center. It is likely that it moved very rapidly after Burgess joined the JBC in 1939 to convert him from a regular "source" to a controlled agent.

The important transition in Burgess's relationship with the NKVD could well have taken place during the visit to Philby. The latter seems to have always been fully aware of the status of his fellow Cambridge agent's links with Soviet intelligence. But it is doubtful whether either Philby or the NKVD would have been reassured had they known that Burgess's sexual indiscretions had led to his arrest in a public lavatory by the London Metropolitan Police only a few months earlier. Burgess had escaped the charges of importuning an illegal sexual act by protesting that he had been reading *Middlemarch* while answering a call of nature. He said his reading had been interrupted by the arrival of an indecent note slipped under the stall partition by an unseen hand. Burgess claimed with indignation that he had promptly returned the offensive document to its sender before returning to the pages of his novel.

Had they known about it, Moscow Center would have found Burgess's story less amusing than the Café Royal coterie who shrieked with laughter when they found out how Burgess had "met his Waterloo" in a public lavatory at Paddington railway station. Blunt, who would certainly have been told about the incident, may not have seen it as in either of their interests to report the arrest to the Soviets. It would have been an unpleasant reminder that he, too, was not above running the risk of a similar arrest by soliciting homosexual partners in public lavatories.[57]

For despite what Blunt told Wright, it is clear that both he and Burgess were under direct NKVD control in the months leading up to World War II. This is plain from Blunt's admission to Nigel West in the year before his death that, at the end of 1938, he had tried to obtain a commission in the Officers' Emergency Reserve. This move, he explained, was his response to the instructions of his Soviet controllers to position himself to infiltrate either the military or civilian intelligence organizations should war break out.[58]

Since Christopher Blunt had already enrolled as a member of this particular reserve branch of Britain's part-time Territorial Army, Anthony asked his younger brother, who was then working in the City, for help. Anthony's embarrassment that he had involved his brother in a recommendation to the War Office was enormous when his application was flatly rejected.[59]

Goronwy Rees also joined the same 90th Field Regiment of the Territorial Army. This suggests that despite his protestations of patriotism, he, too, was responding to the same directive. Rees had no difficulty getting a reserve commission, despite his openly professed Communist sympathies. Blunt made a great fuss of assuring West that it was Burgess to whom he turned for reassurance that once war broke out, there would be many opportunities for complying with Moscow's instructions.[60]

Blunt's repeated statements that it was Burgess who was the organizing genius of the Cambridge network now appear to have been intended to throw MI5 off the scent. What is obvious is that his own failure to get into the Territorial Army in 1938 reveals that someone in the War Office was fully cognizant of his background.

This proved not to be true a year later, when Blunt joined the army's intelligence section.

# CHAPTER 19

# *"I Can Trust No One!"*

Blunt and Burgess were in the south of France on a motor tour when the newspaper headlines of August 23, 1939, caught their attention. The news from Moscow was that Hitler and Stalin had signed a nonaggression treaty. The two men cut short their tour and hurried home.

For the diplomats in London and Paris this alliance came as a devastating blow. Britain had joined France on March 31 that same year in unilaterally guaranteeing Poland's sovereignty. Two weeks later, newly promoted Soviet Foreign Minister Vyacheslav Molotov formally proposed a triple alliance against a German attack. British and French diplomats had been shuttling to and from Moscow ever since to hammer out the terms of an acceptable treaty. But suspicions of Moscow's motives, and a deep aversion to any alliance with communism, snarled the negotiations. Meanwhile, Stalin was equally suspicious of his potential Western allies and had begun making secret overtures to Berlin.

The clamor of Hitler's saber rattling presented the British and French governments with "brutal truths." That is what Churchill called them in a House of Commons debate on the stalled Russian alliance. "Without an effective 'Eastern front,'" he declared, "there can be no satisfactory defense in the West, and without Russia there can be no effective Eastern front."[1]

Chamberlain and Daladier fumbled disastrously. Their dallying over the Soviet proposals, and their refusal to send a high-level delegation to Moscow, persuaded Stalin that neither Britain nor France meant business. He later told Churchill how he decided "the British and French governments were not resolved to go to war if Poland was attacked, but they hoped the diplomatic lineup of Britain, France and Russia would deter Hitler." As Stalin told the British prime minister in Moscow in 1942: "We were sure it would not."[2]

Stalin had struck one of the most cynical diplomatic bargains in history. In return for a ten-year nonaggression treaty, he and Hitler agreed in a secret protocol to carve up Poland and the Baltic states. As Stalin would brag to the Russian people in a radio broadcast shortly after Hitler reneged on the treaty two years later: "We secured peace for our country for one and a half years as well as an opportunity of preparing our forces for the defense if fascist Germany risked attacking our country in defiance of the pact."[3]

The treaty was seen as a devil's pact by many British people, and it caused real consternation on the left. The trauma was especially severe for those in the Communist party and their sympathizers. Goronwy Rees was typical of those Marxists who broke immediately with the Communists over what he saw as "the treachery of the Soviet Union." He wrote that he noticed how even the normally unshakable Burgess was in "a state of considerable excitement" and appeared "frightened" when he arrived back in London. But when Robert Cecil asked Blunt during an interview in 1981 whether they were all shaken by the Nazi-Soviet pact, Blunt burst out with laughter.[4]

"Guy and I were not at all upset because it was just what we thought was going to happen," Blunt said with assurance. He and Burgess believed the orthodox view, that Daladier and Chamberlain had been trying to push the Russians into war with Germany and the pact had been Stalin's only way out. "We argued that it was simply a tactical necessity for Russia to gain time," Blunt said, echoing the standard Stalinist platitude that "it gave them time to rearm and to get stronger to resist." But he did concede that when they heard the news they turned the car around and headed back for England without a moment's hesitation.[5]

"We came back immediately to London because we knew that war was about to break out," Blunt told Cecil. Then he admitted that the person who was most upset was Rees. That Burgess had abandoned his car at Calais — "one of the possessions which he values most in the world" — implies that Blunt and Burgess had rushed back to England to prevent Rees from defecting, but he proved recalcitrant. He believed that "one might as well entrust the interests of the working class to a rattlesnake."[6]

"I never want to have anything to do with the Comintern for the rest of my life," Rees told Burgess, adding: "Or with you, if you really are one of their agents." If Rees had been a part of their conspiracy up to that point — as Rosamond Lehmann and others firmly believe — they now ceased to regard him as trustworthy.[7]

Cecil found it strangely significant that Blunt chose to dramatize the issue by asking him to go into the bathroom at this point, proceeding to turn on all the taps.

"I think that other room is bugged," Blunt breathed to Cecil over the rush of water. "I want to tell you that Rees was one of us and this was the time he quit."[8]

Cecil said the whole performance was most odd. It puzzled him why Blunt should be so concerned about making the admission. Not until Cecil read *Spycatcher* some six years later did he appreciate that Blunt had not made this admission during any of his interrogations with Peter

Wright. Confirmation that Rees was more deeply involved in the conspiracy than he had ever admitted is evidenced by his statement that Burgess pressured him "to forget about the whole thing." Burgess refused to be satisfied until Rees assured him that he would "never mention it again." A short time later, Rees donned his Territorial Army uniform and reported for duty on the London docks when, as Blunt and Burgess had so confidently predicted, Hitler launched an attack on Poland.[9]

On September 3, 1939, Chamberlain, his voice cracking with emotion, announced on the BBC that Great Britain would honor its commitment to defend Poland and "we are now at war with Germany." The prime minister's declaration created a tricky problem for Blunt and the other members of the Cambridge network. They had to keep a low profile while *The Daily Worker* did an about-face on instructions from Moscow: The new party line was that the British, French, and Polish governments were responsible for starting the hostilities. Communists who had previously been antagonistic to appeasement were now obliged to adopt what MI5 described as "a policy of mild opposition to what they termed 'Britain's Imperialist war.'" This discredited the party in the eyes of many on the left. The security services therefore wisely decided not to "molest the Communists at present."[10]

From the day war broke out until the Soviets became Britain's allies two years later, in July 1941, Blunt and his fellow conspirators in the Cambridge network were guilty of a truly serious crime. A six-hundred-year-old statute decreed that a British subject who was "adherent to the King's enemies in his realm, giving them aid and comfort in his realm or elsewhere" was guilty of the capital offense of "High Treason." If Blunt had lived only two centuries earlier, he would have lost his head to an executioner's ax.[11]

As soon as the fighting broke out, Blunt resumed his efforts to get into intelligence. He was responding to orders from Moscow to find a position in which he could best serve its interests. Since his lack of army service and previous rejection by the War Office precluded a direct entry into Military Intelligence, he took an alternative route.

The BBC issued an appeal for linguists to volunteer for a special wing of the Corps of Military Police. Blunt responded promptly, volunteering because of his fluency in French and German. He filed multiple applications to different departments in the anticipation that the War Office would be too inundated by emergency paperwork to run more than the most cursory checks with MI5. Blunt would claim later that because of a bureaucratic foul-up he was both "accepted and rejected by the same post."[12]

Blunt tore up the letter of rejection, kept the one of acceptance, and on September 23, 1939, he reported to Minley Manor. This, and the neighboring Mytchett Barracks, near Aldershot, were the headquarters of the Corps of Military Police and its offshoot, the Field Security Police. There he submitted to the indignities of basic military training that he had despised at school: relentless drill, kit inspection, and scrubbing the floors of the uncompromisingly bare barrack huts. Blunt could take some comfort that he was not the only academic to endure the rigors of basic training among the pine trees of the Hampshire heathland some seventy miles south of London. Other volunteers included his Cambridge contemporary, Enoch Powell, who had left his professorship of Greek at Sydney University to enlist; and Malcolm Muggeridge, who had abandoned Fleet Street and who described the advertisement for linguists that brought him into the five-week course as "calculated to assemble as sorry a company as could possibly be imagined" by their exasperated drill sergeants. His fellow recruits included modern-language teachers from grammar schools, unfrocked priests, and "contraceptive salesmen who had roamed the world."[13]

This diversity of talent was "fairly routine material" to Brigadier John Shearer, who commanded the basic-training establishment. His recruits received only the most rudimentary lectures in gathering field intelligence. The program presupposed the current campaign would be fought under the same conditions as the Western front of World War I. There was no discussion of military secrets: The recruits were told only what MI5 and MI6 stood for, not how they operated. Yet it is significant that someone in the War Office now decided that Blunt's background of Marxism made him a potential security risk for even this minimal indoctrination in intelligence.[14]

Three days after Blunt arrived at Minley Manor, Brigadier Shearer summoned him to inform him that the War Office had ordered him out of the training course because of "a rather adverse report." At breakfast that morning, Shearer explained to other staff officers that Blunt was being withdrawn because he had been a Communist at Cambridge.

Blunt reported as ordered to the War Office. There he faced questions from Major Kevin Martin, the deputy director of Military Intelligence. According to Blunt, MI5 had come up with a "trace" against him in its Registry records. Martin told Blunt that there were "two items on his file," Cecil said. The first was his trip to Russia. Blunt explained this away by pointing out that he had gone to study paintings in the company of Fletcher-Cooke and his brother, for whom there were no MI5 traces. The second trace referred to the three articles he had written for the

Communist-leaning *Left Review*. These he fobbed off, doubtless relieved that his Marxist essay in *The Mind in Chains* had been overlooked.[15]

Fortunately for Blunt, Major Martin was not very astute. Nor were the MI5 traces thorough. Martin might otherwise have been familiar with the former *Spectator* art critic's frequent Marxist disdain for "the unstable position of an apparently decaying civilization," and his preference for populist socialist realism typified by Soviet painters who portrayed "peasants going out to a collective farm, or in the Red Army marching past Lenin's tomb." By 1938, Blunt's openly expressed views on the need for state direction of art were dictatorially Stalinist. He saw a need for what he called "individualistic" artists to "straighten out" by discovering a "common interest" with the proletariat — as had the Mexican muralist Diego Rivera.[16]

Even if the more subtle Marxist nuances of the art criticism had escaped Major Martin's attention, as well as that of the less artistically literate members of MI5 such as Guy Liddell, they had not been missed by Blunt's masters in Moscow. That is evident from the remarkable change in Blunt's writings. From over fifty articles and reviews in 1938, his output shrank to less than a dozen pieces in 1939. Blunt's appointment that April to London University as a reader in the history of art attached to the Courtauld Institute may have increased his sense of gravitas. But it does not account for the dramatic shift in emphasis and subject of his writings.

By giving up his regular art column for *The Spectator*, he had reduced the parade of his Marxist opinions. Such recondite subjects as "The Triclinium in Religious Art" or "A Poussin-Castiglione Problem" did not lend themselves to a discussion of socialist realism. Suddenly Blunt was confining his commentaries to the specialized journals, such as that published by the Warburg Institute, whose circulation was restricted to scholarly art historians. But he could not hide what he had already published. If Blunt had been confronted by someone in the War Office other than a Philistine such as Major Martin, there is good reason to believe they would have been more difficult to hoodwink. This particular deputy director, as Blunt was later to admit with wry amusement, was a pushover.[17]

"Major Martin had no use for MI5 and was very happy to send me back to Minley Manor," Blunt told Cecil with a wry smile. His esoteric Marxist aesthetics lavished on "Dalou and the Worker's Monument" in a pro-Communist magazine had no military significance for Martin, who was more impressed by Blunt's academic record. Martin was also confronted by a self-possessed young man whose aloof prefectorial authority was the essence of the "officer-and-gentleman" quality that the British army regarded as essential for leading men into battle. As Cecil emphasized, the decisive factor was that the army had found itself desperately short of French-speaking officers at exactly the moment when General Gort's 158,000-strong British Expeditionary Force was being dispatched to northern France.[18]

Burgess had been correct. He had predicted the year before that the war would give Blunt his break. Nor is it surprising that Blunt went straight from the War Office to Burgess's apartment to celebrate achieving the first step in becoming a part of the British intelligence apparatus.

Promoted to captain, Blunt was assigned command of the 18th Section of the Field Security Police. One of his lance corporals, Alan Berends, recalled how he appeared one day "'fully armed from the brow of Zeus' and looking very military with his swagger stick." On December 9 the unit embarked for France to assume the policing of the Boulogne sub area of the British Expeditionary Force command. Their unit was armed with rifles and equipped with thirteen motorcycles. Blunt was issued a revolver and a small Austin to serve as his staff car, driven by his batman, Private Hunt.[19]

"I worked with him more closely than the rest of the section back in Boulogne who spent most of their time censoring the mail of leave-bound troops," Berends said. He told me how one of the captain's more interesting duties involved the local prostitute population, which mushroomed overnight when many of the cafés installed a girl in the back room to supplement the overextended services of the one municipally licensed brothel in Boulogne. Concern about the medical and security risks involved Blunt in a plan to open a second official facility. But despite his command of the French language, he was unable to overcome obstruction from the town councilors and the café proprietors.

When Berends was sent on detached duty to the port of Dunkirk, Blunt drove up in his Austin once a fortnight to see him. It was on one of these trips that he was appalled to find that his lance corporal had never tasted an oyster. He insisted on taking Berends out to lunch, ignoring the military impropriety of the difference in ranks.

Over a plate of the succulent shellfish Blunt got on the subject of Impressionist painting. His grasp of the subject jogged Berends's memory.

"Suddenly the penny dropped and I looked him in the face and said, 'You're *Tony* Blunt!'" Berends told me he was very indignant. "Blunt knew no more about the army than I did, and I could not think how he had become a captain."[20]

As Berends explained it, the command did not exactly overtax the military skills of either the tall, austere captain or his men. Their task was to guard against espionage and sabotage and to prevent the morale of the troops from being destroyed by enemy infiltration.

"There was really no intelligence work at all," Berends stated emphatically. Their time was spent preventing the troops from taking uncensored letters on leave to England, or liaising with the four different French police forces, whose protocols and rival sensitivities Blunt appeared to understand very well. Berends cannot recall the so-called "spy hunts" cited by some other writers. He assured me that the most dramatic incidents were preventing friction with the local populace and filing the once-weekly report to BEF HQ in Arras.

Blunt spent five months of the Phony War in France, carrying out the most mundane duties. The most important thing he could achieve was the assurance that with each passing month of military service he was increasing his chance for a really important intelligence posting once Hitler attacked France and the shooting war began.

Lord Victor Rothschild had also volunteered for military service. However, he was not posted to a humdrum unit of the Field Security Police. Rothschild's brains, financial contacts, and scientific talents had been quickly snapped up by MI5. His task was to prepare a series of secret reports on "German Espionage Under Cover of Commerce."[21]

Rothschild was attached to B Division of MI5. Its deputy director, since 1931, had been Captain Guy Liddell. From an organization report prepared for the Americans in August 1940, it is clear that Liddell, even before his promotion that May as head of the Counter-Espionage Investigation Division, exercised more authority, more continuously and with more detailed knowledge of Communist activities, than any other officer of MI5.

According to this document, Liddell had responsibility for many key areas: "Counter-Espionage, Enemy and Neutral. Commercial Espionage, Sabotage. Communications, Censorship Liaison. Leakage of information and Examination of aliens arriving in the UK." His responsibilities overreached and overlapped with those of others, including F Division's. This was the Subversive Activities Section that monitored "Internal Security in H.M. Forces and Government Establishments, Left and Right Wing Movements, Pacifists & New Politics and Social Movements." It was F Division that Roger Hollis joined in 1938. He was assigned to the unit that monitored subversive Communist activities.[22]

The MI5 records show that Liddell had acquired the most intimate picture of Communist subversion in Britain since the early twenties.

More often than not, it is his signature that appears on the reports about Communist activities and individuals; he often carried them personally to trusted officers of the U.S. embassy in London. And it was to Captain Guy Liddell at the secret MI5 mailing address — Box 300, Parliament Street P.O., London SW1 — that the State Department sent data and answers to queries from FBI records.[23]

In March 1938, Liddell embarked on the *Queen Mary* to make his second visit to the United States to discuss "matters of mutual interest." London advised the chief of the European Affairs Division in Washington to "put him in touch with Mr. Hoover of the Department of Justice." The letter of introduction portrayed the MI5 officer as being "our friend in Scotland Yard who has contributed much useful information to us, including the secret information which led to the discovery of a spy plot."

Liddell's own report on the trip, recently discovered in a private British archive, reveals that he never met with Hoover. The FBI director was "out of town." But he did meet with one of Hoover's assistants to discuss the "spy plot." This was the Rumrich case. It had come to light as a result of MI5's intercepting a suspiciously large number of letters with foreign postmarks sent to the Scottish widow of a former German National. (This is, in itself, revealing confirmation of the extent to which MI5 would go to arrange to monitor mail after a tipoff from the local police.) In the case of Mrs. Jessie Jordan, it turned out that German intelligence officers in Hamburg were using her address to communicate with Gunther Gustave Rumrich, an American army deserter in New York. His letter of January 17, 1939, was signed "Crown," and disclosed his "little coup" — a crude plot to kidnap the commander of the U.S. Army base at Fort Totten, New York. MI5 alerted the U.S. military attaché in London about the plan.[24]

When Liddell arrived in the United States he learned that Rumrich had been arrested. The subsequent investigation revealed him to be a rather inept part of a large Nazi espionage operation that ranged from a brazen attempt to obtain a code machine from Agnes Driscoll, the Navy Department's leading code breaker, to "the crudest attempt" to "suborn" naval and military personnel for information about aircraft carriers and the defenses of the Panama Canal. The FBI investigations also revealed that Rumrich had been passing his information to officers and crew members of the German liners on the Hamburg–New York run. The FBI told Liddell that its investigation concluded that "nearly 80 percent" of the information obtained by the German intelligence service in the United States was being sold to the Japanese for "a very high figure."[25]

The German consulate in New York appeared fully aware of the activities of undercover Abwehr and Gestapo agents. They were running an underground network controlled by Kitty Moog, the mistress of a Manhattan stamp dealer, Dr. Griebel. ("This stamp dealing business is well known to us as a cover for espionage," Liddell added with a touch of satisfaction in his memorandum on the case for MI5.) Liddell was impressed by "the thoroughness" of the FBI investigations, noting how espionage cases in America were handled under Section 32 of the Federal Code, which was "not nearly as wide as our Official Secrets Act." He was also struck by the results of the surveillance of Griebel and Moog—who "were quite ready to incriminate anybody except themselves"—which resulted in their exposing more than twenty other members of the network. This had been accomplished by intercepting Griebel's mail and "using a dictaphone to obtain details of his [telephone] conversations with other members of the gang."[26]

What is clear from American and British records is that Liddell's trip to the United States had a specific purpose: His mission was to persuade America to reconsider its earlier rejection of the British suggestion that there be an official exchange of information on Nazi and Fascist problems. The exchange would be similar to that "in force on Comintern affairs." The State Department had objected because of "practical difficulties."[27]

Liddell reported to London that these "practical difficulties" were "obviously" bureaucratic. The American armed forces had been "clamouring for years for the necessary funds to set up a counter-espionage organization." Moreover, the FBI was definitely "anxious to establish a liaison with us, which could cover not only Soviet, German and Italian activities, but also those of the Japanese." It was the State Department that was determined to "keep the strings in their own hands." State did not want to "let the soldiers and policemen loose on their own." Liddell concluded that State feared being led "into deep water politically, and there may be awkward repercussions in Congress."[28]

As a result, liaison with the U.S. authorities was "not altogether satisfactory," according to Liddell. The State Department had a "tendency to cut out anything of a delicate nature and to edit the FBI reports from a political angle." Thus he advised shifting the liaison program on espionage matters to the British military attaché in Washington and to the FBI because of the "very close contact" he had established with "Mr. Hoover's organization" in Washington and New York.[29]

Whitehall decided to go along with Liddell's strategy. At the end of the year, Captain Sir James Paget was posted as the passport-control officer to the British consulate in New York. This was the standard cover used by MI6 officers overseas. After a tactful interval, we find Liddell suggesting to the American embassy in London that "a number of small matters with which neither you, nor ourselves, would want to be bothered" could be dealt with better if Paget liaised directly with the FBI and State Department in Washington. It was only when Paget started making direct contact with the FBI through U.S. Military Intelligence that the diplomatic fur began to fly.[30]

On September 5, 1939, two days after the outbreak of war in Europe, a strongly worded protest reached First Secretary Herschel Johnson at the embassy in London. James C. Dunn, State's Adviser on Political Relations, touchily expressed his concerns about the "delicacy and gravity of the present international situation." He "desired" therefore that MI5 be advised that "information should continue in the regular channels established many years ago and now embodied in your informal memoranda to me." The matter was "taken up informally," and the British issued "appropriate instructions" to the head of their New York consulate. Dunn, who jealously believed himself to be the State Department's "Mr. Intelligence," had won the first round. (Eventually he would lose this bureaucratic battle with Military Intelligence and the FBI for exclusive control of this vitally important information.)[31]

It was ironic, therefore, that it was State Department bureaucracy that blocked Dunn's trading a U.S. residency permit for information from one of the most knowledgeable Soviet intelligence officers ever to defect to the West. Samuel Ginsberg, better known as Walter Krivitsky, had begun his career in the GRU prior to transferring to Soviet Intelligence. Before defecting in 1937 Krivitsky had been the principal NKVD underground *rezident* in Holland.[32]

An intense, intellectual, and quiet-spoken man, Krivitsky had been posing as an Austrian bookseller in The Hague. It was a perfect cover for his clandestine job as "chief of the Soviet Military Intelligence for Western Europe," as he explained it. He was the possessor of many of the most closely held secrets about the Soviet networks and penetration agents in Britain and the United States. Marked for assassination by the NKVD, he had received police protection from the French in return for information. But he had no guard when he reached New York in December 1938, and he found that he was shadowed by members of the local Soviet consulate whom he knew well as former NKVD colleagues.[33]

Krivitsky made a number of visits to the State Department, but he failed to secure legal immigrant status when Ruth Shipley, of the Passport Division, and Raymond Murphy, of the Soviet section, concluded he was holding back too much information to be trusted. Krivitsky said as much to his attorney, Louis Waldman, but he added that there was good reason for his reticence. According to Waldman: "He said that there was no use telling the American government anything in confidence, because it was so sloppy about security, and so honeycombed with agents, that everything he said the first time had got back to Moscow in 48 hours."[34]

Facing penury and deportation, Krivitsky took the advice of fellow Russian exiles, including the journalist Isaac Don Levine. He contracted to write for *The Saturday Evening Post* a series of articles at $5,000 per article in an attempt to alert America to the menace of "Stalin's Secret Service." A month after war broke out in Europe, Krivitsky agreed to testify before the House Committee on Un-American Activities in return for a halt in the threatened deportation proceedings. He exposed the Soviet Trade Mission, Amtorg, as one of the principal cover organizations of the NKVD, and claimed that it had "agents planted in all institutions, governmental and industrial" in the United States (including the armed services), but he was still disappointingly unspecific. He explained that he would withhold total exposure until the State Department granted him resident status. The committee supported his claim, and he went into seclusion to await the fulfillment of his request.[35]

Krivitsky may have withheld much information from his articles and testimony, but he had confided to Levine and Louis Waldman some vital nuggets relating to Soviet agents in key positions in the British government. With Britain fighting Hitler, who was now Stalin's ally, Isaac Don Levine, like many Jewish Americans, believed it his duty to pass on the information to the British. Through Loy Henderson, an assistant secretary of state, an appointment was made for Levine on September 3 with the Marquess of Lothian. At first the aristocratic ambassador was inclined to dismiss the warning that "at least two fully fledged Soviet spies were in the inner sanctums of the British government." But Henderson intervened to suggest that it might be wise to run a routine check. Krivitsky had identified one agent as being "a code clerk in the secretariat of the Cabinet," a man named King. He did not know the name of the other, but described him as being "a member of the Council of Imperial Defense." He also referred to another traitor in the Foreign Office "whose name was Scottish and whose habits were Bohemian."[36]

Lothian's ciphered telegram bearing Krivitsky's news reached the desk of the permanent head of the Foreign Office the following morning. "Very unpleasant" was how Sir Alexander Cadogan noted it in his confidential diary, "which seems to fix us a line on the 'leaks' of the past few years."[37]

Cadogan's comment is revealing. It shows that the Foreign Office had been aware of serious leaks but had been unable to track them down. Now MI5 moved swiftly. Although there were no code clerks in the Cabinet office with that name, one of Krivitsky's suspects was quickly identified as being Captain John H. King of the Foreign Office. On September 15 Cadogan's diary reveals that the counterintelligence chiefs of MI5 and MI6 were putting King and another suspect, whose initials were "O.K.," through a "Third Degree" examination. Robert Cecil points out that the involvement of rival counterintelligence organizations indicated the extreme seriousness of the situation. "The Foreign Office regarded MI5 officers as little better than policemen in big boots," he told me. "They were always unhappy whenever they were involved in internal investigations. Cadogan had to keep the dirty laundry in-house, if possible."[38]

"Looks pretty black against King," a worried Cadogan wrote in his diary. "Very disturbing; shall have to have swift and discreet action at the right moment."[39]

The suspects had been suspended from their duties and sent on sick leave. King's apartment and that of his girlfriend, Helen Wilkie, were searched and their bank accounts investigated. King had already confessed to receiving money over the past six years from a Dutch agent of the Soviets: Henri Pieck. Whatever an MI5 "Third Degree" interrogation involved, it produced the desired results. On the evening of September 25 Cadogan reports receiving the news that MI5 had decided "to jug him" that night. "There is no doubt he is guilty — curse him — but there is no absolute proof," Cadogan noted, adding cryptically, "They are on the track of Mrs. (. . . .)" This appears to be a reference to King's girlfriend. Sure enough, a safe-deposit box in Helen Wilkie's bank in Chancery Lane held a stash of large-denomination notes (£5 and £10 notes were large denominations in prewar England). The records of their serial numbers at the Bank of England showed that some had been issued to the Moscow Narodny Bank in London. Another £500 was traced to Bernard Davidovich Gadar.[40]

Confronted with this evidence, King confessed. But he claimed he had never handed over Foreign Office code books. On the strength of his admission of guilt, he was quickly tried and convicted *in camera* before Mr. Justice Hilbery in No. 1 Court, Old Bailey, on October 18, 1939. Wartime regulations permitted the government to impose a publicity blackout on King's trial and his ten-year prison sentence.[41]

Since no details of the case were published, for the next seventeen years the Foreign Office denied there had been any internal spies. Not until 1956, when Isaac Don Levine testified before the U.S. Senate, did the truth begin to emerge. Levine's claim that Krivitsky's evidence had resulted in King's execution led to questions in Parliament. To avoid embarrassment, the British government issued only a brief statement on the case. Yes, a low-grade code clerk had been caught spying for Moscow. But Captain King had not been executed as Levine claimed; he was still living in England. The affair was played down. There was no discussion of how long King had been a spy, or what information he might have passed to the Soviets.

MI5 was so determined to keep the significance of Krivitsky's revelations secret that it also hushed up the involvement of the second spy and possibly a third suspect at work in the Communications Department. These startling facts emerge from the unpublished secret passages in Cadogan's diaries. They indicate that MI5 also investigated two other officials, O.K. and another. There was not enough evidence to make them stand trial, but Cadogan records that they were nevertheless sacked for "irregularities." The damage was so great that Cadogan decided the Foreign Office had no option but to try to rebuild the security of its Communications Department from the ground up — starting with an entirely fresh cipher staff.[42]

The Cadogan diaries do not reveal, nor has the Foreign Office ever admitted, that this monumental breach of security actually began ten years earlier, when King's fellow code clerk Andrew Oldham walked into the Soviet embassy in Paris.

The reluctance to explain the anomalies arising from the King case is one of the more puzzling skeletons in the MI5 closet. Surprisingly, not a single reference to King or Krivitsky surfaces among the secret communications exchanged between Liddell and the U.S. embassy in London. Nor is Oldham mentioned. And there are no fresh clues provided by Nigel West whose book *MI5* relies on inside sources. In fact, West goes out of his way to state: "None of Krivitsky's revelations were relevant to Burgess, Maclean, Philby or Blunt." Yet Krivitsky had been vindicated, so it is surprising that what appears to be an "official" line is echoed by Christopher Andrew. Citing Lord Gladwyn as his authority, Andrew asserts that Krivitsky's reference to "a young man in the Foreign Office of good family" was too vague to have enabled MI5 to uncover Donald Maclean in 1940.[43]

Gladwyn Jebb, as a rising young diplomat, was in 1939 private secretary to Sir Alexander Cadogan. It was in this capacity that he met Krivitsky early in 1940. Yet when I interviewed him in 1982, he was carefully vague about why Krivitsky was believed to be so valuable an informant that the British government offered to send a destroyer, or submarine, to bring him to England for a full debriefing by MI5. According to his friends, Krivitsky was extremely reluctant to risk the transatlantic trip. It was not the threat of U-boats that worried him, but the fear of betrayal or assassination by Soviet agents in Britain. By mid-December, however, he agreed to make the voyage and he arrived in London on January 19, 1940.

The responsibility for Krivitsky's interrogation lay with Brigadier A. W. A. Harker's B Division of MI5, which had authority over counter-espionage investigations. Harker was, by all accounts, a military figure-head rather than a leader. One colleague recalled him as being "a sort of highly-polished barrel which, if tapped, would sound hollow (because it was)." It was his experienced deputy, Guy Liddell, who had charge of the day-to-day operations. Gladwyn Jebb, who sat in on some of the discussions and saw the final MI5 reports on Krivitsky, recalled that Lid-dell was "intelligent and introspective." These were precisely the qualities needed to deal with the jumpy NKVD defector, who knew how deeply the NKVD had tapped into the Whitehall machine.[44]

Liddell assigned Jane Sissmore, a former barrister and one of MI5's most sympathetic officers, to the delicate task of debriefing Krivitsky. Their conversations continued for three weeks. Sissmore was already well versed in the makeup of Soviet espionage networks. Her former colleagues credit her with doing a superlative job of extracting a mass of information from a not always cooperative subject. Nigel West suggests, however, that beyond showing that Soviet intelligence had "well established agents in a position to transmit the contents of all Foreign Office documents," Sissmore's report, "Summary of Interviews with General Walter Krivitsky," dated January 1940, was *not* especially informative.[45]

Other writers disagree. Seven years before West began his "revelatory" investigations, Brook Shepherd had quietly and systematically interviewed intelligence officers on both sides of the Atlantic. He asserted that in three weeks of "skilled and systematic debriefing," Krivitsky had identified ninety-three agents around the world of whom "no fewer than sixty-one were named by him as operating in the United Kingdom itself, or directly against British interests elsewhere."[46]

Krivitsky was also able to confirm names of the principal illegals who had operated in London, including Pestrovsky, Maly and his subagent, Gadar, and Arnold Deutsch, who had been briefly active until his recall in 1937. They were among the twenty-six whom Krivitsky named as being members of the NKVD *apparat*. Six were legal spymasters in the Soviet embassy or trade mission, and twenty were illegals working under varying nationalities, backgrounds, and professions. Their job was to run the thirty-five agents who were actively engaged in espionage against Britain. Of the sixteen British nationals Krivitsky named in this menacing category, eight were active in left-wing politics and the trade-union movement, six were civil servants, and two were journalists.

According to Brook Shepherd's inside source, only half of these names were new to MI5. Immediate steps were taken to "neutralize" them, but none were ever prosecuted or their identities revealed. What then was the extent of MI5's knowledge of Soviet penetration in 1940?

From the wealth of reports passed to the State Department about American Communist activists studying in British universities, it is clear that MI5 and Special Branch had not overlooked the academics. Cambridge had long been a focus for Special Branch surveillance. In his final years as a Trinity don, Blunt had not been shy in peddling his overtly Marxist view of art to a public audience that ranged from the readers of *The Spectator* to the Left Book Club, which had been founded, in 1936, by the socialist publisher Victor Gollancz, not to mention his contribution to *The Mind in Chains* in 1937.

The reports in the U.S. archives can be only the tip of a large iceberg of MI5 surveillance documentation. From the considerable volume of British reports filed under the 800 "B" (for Bolshevik) classification, many bearing Guy Liddell's signature, it does not appear that MI5 was neglecting the potential Communist subversives at home. The warnings were perfectly clear, including an eloquent *cri de coeur* written by a twenty-seven-year-old civil servant that had appeared in the Christmas 1937 issue of *The Spectator*.

The anonymous writer had graduated from Oxford a year after Blunt. He proclaimed that it was the gospel of Marx that "inspires both the righteous indignation of the very young, conscious of the need for sweeping away the filth and decadence of capitalism in decay, and also the reasoned allegiance of the man of thirty who realizes that only the victory of communism will safeguard all that is worth safeguarding in the society of today." The logic of events in Spain, Germany, and China dictated that "only communism is able to organize the scattered forces of peace to prevent the world being given over completely to the horror of totalitarian war."[47]

That such a strident affirmation of Communist loyalty should be made by someone who was working in the heart of the British government ought to have given MI5 cause for alarm. If a serious investigation had been mounted to discover the identity of the author, it might have uncovered another nest of Oxbridge Communists in the Whitehall machine. For among the Cambridge graduates who divided loyalties in varying degrees with Moscow, we now know that Andrew Cohen was then in the Colonial Office, Dennis Proctor was in the Treasury, and John Cairncross and Donald Maclean in the Foreign Office. Although they had gone underground and the identity of many of their sympathizers remains concealed to this day, at least one other Oxford graduate, Jenifer Fischer Williams, has admitted to being a secret party member when she joined the Home Office in 1938.[48]

Until the British government releases the MI5 reports, it will be impossible to know with certainty whether Liddell investigated, ignored, or dismissed these warnings that Communists were rising to influential positions in Whitehall.

Yet it was claimed later by Liddell's supporters that when it came to Anthony Blunt and the Cambridge agents, Krivitsky was painfully vague. While he made reference to at least two high-ranking Foreign Office spies, he could name no names. Krivitsky had recognized papers from the Imperial Defense Committee's reports of 1937, which he claimed to have read in Moscow before his defection. But this was not a direct pointer to Donald Maclean. He was only one of many Foreign Office officials who had access to them. Nor did the Scottish name point directly to Maclean, although an exhaustive check might have revealed that he had been living in a Bohemian quarter of Paris since arriving in France.[49]

Philby further muddled what is publicly known about Krivitsky's evidence by alluding in his Soviet-approved autobiography to a "nasty little sentence," presumably in Sissmore's January 1940 report, which said that "Soviet intelligence had sent a young English journalist to Spain during the Spanish Civil War." He also "recalled the statements of Krivitsky" which mentioned a Foreign Office recruit "of good family who had been to Eton and Oxford," whom the Soviets recruited in Europe in the "mid-thirties" and who was "an idealist working without payment."[50]

Again this clue did not lead directly to Maclean. He had neither attended Eton nor been to Oxford. But Philby acknowledged that when he was in Washington in 1949, a Foreign Office investigation that matched known leaks against Krivitsky's shadowy candidates produced a list of "perhaps six names," including Maclean's. But as Richard Deacon has pointed out, the "high-ranking" Scotsman of Bohemian tastes recruited in the mid-thirties was unlikely to have been Maclean, who had only just entered the Foreign Office. A more likely candidate was the bisexual, bagpipe-playing ambassador, Lord Inverchapel, who had developed a "fixation" for the Soviet Union when posted to Stockholm in 1934.

A year after Krivitsky went to London for his interrogation he was discovered by a chambermaid in a seedy Washington, D.C., hotel with a bullet in his head. His "suicide" could not have come at a more convenient moment. The next day the Soviet defector had been scheduled to resume his testimony on Capitol Hill.

The secrets that Krivitsky took to his grave with his "suicide" on February 10, 1941, have yet to be admitted by the British, who are evidently acutely aware of the potential for embarrassment they could still cause. Perhaps this explains why the self-appointed "official" historians of British intelligence continue to dismiss Krivitsky's significance.

According to Peter Wright, when he checked the still very secret file on people named by Krivitsky, he was quickly able to pinpoint a Captain Charles Howard Ellis as having given information to both the Germans and the Soviets via the émigré connections of his White Russian wife. What had sparked Wright's interest was that Philby had been through the files before Wright, at a time when Philby was the head of Section IX, the counterintelligence section of MI6.[51]

"Who is this man Ellis? NFA (No further action)" was what Philby had written in the margin on the file. This puzzled Wright because, at the time, Philby's office in 1945 was just down the corridor from the one occupied by the same Ellis. Not only had Ellis apparently given the Germans the MI6 order of battle at the outbreak of the war, he had also warned the Germans that the British had tapped into the private conversations between Ambassador von Ribbentrop and Hitler's office in Berlin. Another treasonable act attributable to Ellis was that he was responsible for the Venlo incident of November 1939, mentioned earlier, when the Germans captured two high-ranking British intelligence officers near a Dutch border town. Even more worrisome was the fact that, during the war, Ellis had been the deputy to Sir William "Intrepid" Stephenson's operation in New York.[52]

It was the conclusion of Wright and the Fluency Committee, set up in 1964 by MI5 and MI6 to investigate Soviet penetration, that Ellis could well have been an undercover agent for thirty years: first with the GRU before the war and later, after Philby saw his file, blackmailed by Philby into spying for the KGB. The case is all the more astonishing because of (1) the apparent ease with which Philby was able to cut off any investigation into Ellis, and (2) the fact that Wright had obtained a partial confession from Ellis. But Ellis suffered from heart trouble, and Maurice Oldfield, the new head of MI6, preferred to give Ellis the benefit of the doubt because it "was all long ago and best forgotten."[53]

After all, one is talking about going back to when the intelligence organization was leaderless. At the time of the Venlo incident, Admiral "Quex" Sinclair, who had been head of MI6 since 1923, had just died of cancer. His chosen successor, Colonel Stewart Menzies (pronounced Mengies), had been the head of Section II (military) and had been deputizing for Sinclair during his illness. Menzies, however, was not formally appointed as the new "C" by the prime minister until November 29, two weeks after the Venlo incident.

A forty-nine-year-old ex-Etonian and Life Guards officer, Menzies had an aristocratic wife and mother. He was a London clubland figure who hunted with the Duke of Beaufort's pack near his country home in Wiltshire. He was a prominent member of the Turf and St. James's clubs and had even been known to hold MI6 meetings in White's. One colleague recalled Menzies's "maniacal fondness for security." It was a sorely needed virtue as 1940 opened with revelations of fresh disasters in the Foreign Office.[54]

On January 26, a report was made to Cadogan that "secret documents" had leaked to the German government from the Central Department of the Foreign Office. This is the only reference to what must surely have been another major breach of British security. Cadogan confessed bitterly in his diary entry of January 26, 1940: "I can trust *no-one*."[55]

The fresh alarm did, however, convince him that security was a major priority. Ten days later the Foreign Office named its first security officer, a retired diplomat named William Codrington. But he had no salary or assistant, and the post had little real impact until a fully staffed Security Department was established after the war.

At the start of one of the most crucial years in Britain's history, the Foreign Office was in turmoil because of spies and leaks. This contrasts with a glowing presentation prepared for the Americans barely six months later. Labeled STRICTLY CONFIDENTIAL, the report emphasized the success of British efforts "to ferret out and counteract the purposes and activities" of subversive groups. The report was transmitted to the State Department in August 1940 with the "wholehearted co-operation" of MI5, and the thirty-page report, which was recently uncovered in the U.S. National Archives Regional Center at Suitland, Maryland, is a masterpiece of bureaucratic wishful thinking. It sets out the full extent of British secret-service operations, though in a way that has never been officially acknowledged.[56]

This report owes its genesis to the new prime minister, Winston

Churchill, who recognized that the Battle of Britain in the air was only a preliminary round in a desperate struggle. His rhetoric in the House of Commons had rallied the nation. But it was not enough to hurl back the threatened German invasion. His three-month-old coalition government had to woo from the Roosevelt administration the military, economic, and political support that was being withheld by a resolutely isolationist Congress.

Churchill was so anxious to secure the means with which to keep on fighting Hitler that in return for fifty overage destroyers, he was offering more than just British territory to be used for U.S. naval bases. The files suggest that by offering a blueprint of the British security service, Churchill may also have intended a larger trade-off of secret intelligence. Sir Eric Holt-Wilson, who for twenty-eight years was chief of staff to MI5 director General Kell, was even "willing to go to America to assist in the setting up of a centralized organization if such a move was considered desirable." This was a shrewd offer. Holt-Wilson and Kell had just been retired on the advice of Churchill's new Security Executive, which had been established in May 1940 to coordinate "all security activities" and to prevent "overlapping and omissions." Lord Swinton, a War Cabinet member who was the Lord President of the Council, had been named chairman; Joseph Ball, Burgess's close friend, was his deputy. (Ball had been responsible for getting Burgess into MI6.)[57]

"The English have done a very smart thing in connection with counter-espionage, which might well be copied by the United States," was how the U.S. embassy in London reported the offer to Washington. First Secretary Johnson considered himself "privileged to reveal" the deep secret with which he had been entrusted on his promise that it would be kept "absolutely confidential by the American Government."[58]

"I am told that this information has been given to few Britishers and has never before been given to the representative of a foreign government," Johnson wrote, somewhat wide-eyed at the secrets revealed to him by MI5's longtime deputy chief Holt-Wilson: "Unknown to the British public, unknown to the newspapers, and unknown even to most of the Government officials," he continued, "there has been in existence for 31 years an elaborate organization for the detection and prevention of the activities of foreign governments." He went on to reveal that the security service had grown from four officers and half a dozen clerks in 1914 to "between 250 and 300 people now in the Service, of whom more than 100 are officials [sic]."[59]

According to the U.S. report on MI5: "The scope of the organization can be seen from the fact it now embraces 300 Chiefs of Police — 250 from Great Britain and Northern Ireland and 50 from the Empire." Senior officers of the British security service had assured Johnson that "absolute secrecy" was the key to their success. "They declare that no British newspaperman has ever discovered the true scope of their organization," Johnson added, noting that MI5 was the "only counter-espionage activity which is ever mentioned in the newspapers." Further-more, the press reports of recent spy cases confirmed that neither the British people, nor German intelligence, had "any inkling" of the extent of the security service: "Apparently the public is completely unaware of the existence of the super mchine of which MI5 is only one cog."[60]

The "super machine" that was the British security service relied on a "centralized control" that embraced the army and navy intelligence services and MI5, plus links that reached out through the police chiefs into the network of constables all over the British Isles and the police forces of the empire. The reach was therefore truly global. It supplied information for the "central index of suspicious persons," which was one of the "major activities" of the security service. The Registry index contained "the name of every person ever suspected in any part of the world of anti-British activity — a total of 4,500,000 names."[61]

The index in the Registry was the heart of MI5. The Americans were assured that it was "used freely" by British industry and government departments. Before a man could get a job in an airplane factory, "his name must be cleared through the register." The same applied to "employees of all government departments, even down to messengers."[62]

This window dressing may have seemed essential to impress the Americans about Britain's vaunted security apparatus. But the truth was something different. The super machine, which Churchill hoped to export to the United States, was breaking down. Blunt and Philby were about to be recruited into the British intelligence apparatus because of inadequate vetting — or preexisting high-level penetration by the Sovi-ets. As the summer months of 1940 were to prove, the super machine of British security was as futile a defense for England as was France's vaunted Maginot Line.

Exporting the Revolution: Cambridge undergraduate "special constables" (above) volunteered to fight the general strike in 1926. The Metropolitan Police (below left) guard the Arcos offices on May 12, 1927, during the raid on the nerve center of the Soviet Union's subversive operations in Britain that was masterminded until his death in 1926 by Feliks Dzerzhinski (below right) who founded the Cheka, the predecessor of the KGB.

KING'S COLLEGE ARCHIVES

JOHN HILTON

Aesthetic Rebel: Clifford Canning (above left) was the principal mentor of Anthony Blunt at Marlborough College. In Blunt's farewell portrait given to his friends, the school prefect (above right) chose an unconventional but characteristically authoritative pose. The studied aesthete (below) posing in a very unmilitary "wopsical" sun hat during OTC (Officer Training Corps) camp.

JOHN HILTON

Image Making: Blunt forged his successful "Anonymous Society" with Louis MacNeice and John Hilton (above left), together with the handsome rugby-playing "hearty" Michael Robertson (in striped tie, above right with Hilton). Blunt's artistic efforts (below left) won him no accolades for painting, but his mathematical ability was rewarded with a scholarship to Trinity and prize books shared (below right) with classmate John Hilton.

"Bloomsbury un peu passé": Rosamond Lehmann and her brother, John (left), with Lytton Strachey at Ham Spray. Blunt with fellow Apostles Donald Lucas and Julian Bell (below). Jean Stewart, the daughter of the dean of Trinity, and her friend were frequent female companions to camouflage Blunt's 1929 homosexual affair with Bell. Lettice Ramsay's celebrated photograph of the marxisant Apostles (bottom) celebrating their "capture" of the society shows (left to right) Richard Llewelyn-Davies, Hugh Sykes Davies, Alister Watson, Anthony Blunt, Julian Bell, Andrew Cohen.

"University is really rather amusing": So Louis MacNeice, the Oxford Aesthete (top right) wrote. Cambridge boasted the flamboyant homosexual John Tresidder Sheppard of King's "performing" (top left) with Lydia Lopokova, the ballerina wife of John Maynard Keynes. Andrew Gow of Trinity (above left) cultivated Blunt's artistic sensibilities, while Anthony flirted with Lady Mary St. Clair Erskine (center). Peter Kapitza, (above right) the brilliant Soviet physicist, was another prominent Trinity don who enrolled Blunt's fellow Apostle Alister Watson in his famous scientific discussion group.

Cambridge Contemporaries: Blunt, as a Trinity don caricatured by Burgess (right). Active Communist party dons Maurice Dobb and Roy Pascal (opposite, top left and center) were "spotters" for the Comintern. Their task was facilitated by liberal Bloomsbury intellectuals opposed to Fascism such as E. M. Forster (opposite top right). The prime targets for moles were disaffected undergraduate Marxists such as Donald Maclean, Guy Burgess, and Peter J. Astbury (opposite, middle), not charismatic revolutionaries like John Cornford (opposite, bottom left), who recruited Michael Straight (opposite, bottom center) into the Trinity Communist cell. Straight, however, talked Teresa Mayor (opposite, bottom right) out of joining the party; she later became the second wife of Blunt's Apostle friend Victor Rothschild (below).

Popular Fronts: Edouard Pfeiffer (above left), the Machiavellian French politician and homosexual contact of Burgess, intrigued with the Communist "fronts" in Paris promoted by Willi Münzenberg (above center) and his one-time aide, Otto Katz (above left). The Popular Front of the late thirties forged an alliance of socialists and liberals against advocates of Fascism like Sir Oswald Mosley (below right) and aristocratic supporters of Hitler such as Prince Philip of Hesse, shown (below left) with Princess Mafalda, daughter of King Umberto of Italy, Mussolini's supporter.

The Royal Connection: Blunt knew Prince George, Duke of Kent (above left) on the London homosexual network. But it was on his secret mission to Germany in 1945 for King George VI that he discovered the true extent of the intrigues involving the Duke and Duchess of Windsor, who met Hitler at Berchtesgaden in 1937 (above right). Noël Annan (below left), who served in 1945 with the British Control Commission in Germany, suspected Leo Long (below right), whom Blunt had run as a subagent for the Russians. Goronwy Rees (below center) also served with army intelligence but always denied passing information to Blunt.

The American Connection: FBI investigations launched before the end of World War II exposed the pattern of Communist infiltration in the United States. Testimony of penetration in Washington was provided by Elizabeth Bentley and Hede Massing (above left) and Whittaker Chambers (above right). It is now clear that decrypted Soviet cipher traffic played a critical part in extracting a confession from physicist Klaus Fuchs (below left) in 1949. The same source also helped expose the atomic espionage network operated by Ethel and Julius Rosenberg (below right with fellow accused Morton Sobel), but the FBI was not allowed to introduce the Venona decrypts at their controversial trial and subsequent execution.                    NATIONAL ARCHIVES

The "Missing British Diplomats": Anglo-American relations were soured and Foreign Secretary Herbert Morrison (above left with Ambassador John Foster Dulles) was embarrassed by the defection of Burgess and Maclean. The weekend before they left, Burgess had visited his old Trinity and wartime MI5 friend Kemball Johnston (left) and reminded him of his Marxist sympathies with a sketch of Stalin (below left). Philby (below right) brazened his way through his 1951 interrogations to be completely exonerated in 1955.

I wonder what Kemball is thinking? *G.B.*

"The Uninvestigated Mole in MI5": Guy Liddell (above left) was a gifted child cellist, whose musical career was terminated by army service in World War I (center), after which he joined Special Branch and became the longtime head of MI5 counterintelligence (above right). Maurice Oldfield (below center) told American contacts shortly before his retirement as head of MI6 that Liddell was his prime suspect and should have been thoroughly investigated. Analysis of the prewar MI5 records supports that suspicion. But MI5 investigators — including Peter Wright (below right) — considered that the former deputy director-general had to be blameless of any complicity, conceding only his "unfortunate" friendship with Blunt (below left).

# CHAPTER 20

# *"Keep That Man Out of the Office"*

On May 10, 1940, the German assault on the West promptly disposed of the Maginot Line. On the same day Winston Churchill began his "walk with destiny" as Britain's pugnacious wartime prime minister. (A month earlier the German invasion of Denmark and Norway had ended the Phony War, and Chamberlain's ineffective leadership collapsed.) But within five days of taking office, the new prime minister found himself facing military disaster.

Resistance in bombed and battered Holland collapsed. Queen Wilhelmina and her government escaped to England in a destroyer. Then the French army broke on the Sedan salient on May 14 and an avalanche of German armored might burst out onto the plains of northern France. Three panzer divisions raced for the French coast to isolate the retreating British Expeditionary Force that was withdrawing from Belgium to reinforce the battered French army now falling back on Paris. Covering the retreat for *The Times* was Kim Philby, who was evacuated through Blunt's sector in Boulogne.

Captain Blunt received the alarming news that the Germans had broken out and were heading for Boulogne. The equanimity with which he received the message astonished the men of his platoon. "In April 1940, we had been disarmed to equip the troops in the Norway campaign," Alan Berends explained. Except for a single rifle and Blunt's revolver, the 18th Field Security Section had no weapons to defend themselves.[1]

On May 15 the platoon was split up. Berends and two other lance corporals who spoke Flemish left for General Gort's Tactical Headquarters. That was the last they saw of their languid commanding officer. But Lance Corporal George Curry, who remained with the platoon, recalled that his thirty-three-year-old captain remained studiously untroubled.

In truth, the commanding officer of the 18th Field Security Section was fast asleep in his billet when the Germans arrived on the outskirts of Boulogne on May 25. "It was only when we got a call from someone in the navy back in Dover telling us to get out fast that we decided to do so," Curry said, adding how he had "to go and dig Blunt out of his billet." Six of the platoon elected to make their escape via Dunkirk, but Blunt and the other six men managed to find a lone boat packed with explosives intended for the demolition of harbor installations. "The ship didn't have time to unload before we got away," Curry observed wryly. Their precarious position atop all the high explosives, while German planes bombed and strafed all around them, was relished by Blunt. His sangfroid left an indelible impression on his men.[2]

Yet Curry believed there was something unnaturally calculated about Blunt's glacial coolness under fire. His demeanor appeared to have had more to do with a cold-blooded intellect bent on testing itself to the limit than with bravery in the accepted sense. His disregard for his own safety was not personal courage directed to any heroic military objective. According to Christopher Blunt, who was also among the 300,000 allied soldiers rescued from Dunkirk's bomb-torn beaches, after they were reunited in England, they "had a giggle" about their hair-raising escapes.

According to his brother, Anthony was not only "very relaxed about his predicament" but "talked constantly" of how he had waited until the last moment to drive his staff car off a pier so that it would not fall into enemy hands. Blunt's peculiar psychological makeup was such that he needed to remind himself — and others — of his steel nerves. Just as a weight lifter needs constant exercise to stay in tone, Blunt's intellectual iron-pumping seems to have been a psychological necessity to maintain his sense of superiority over ordinary mortals.[3]

That summer, the dogfights of the Battle of Britain etched their surrealistic patterns in the skies over southern England. In the House of Commons, and over the BBC, Churchill's bulldog rhetoric rallied the nation with his call to fight the expected German invaders on the beaches, streets, and hills — and never surrender.

In the lecture room of the Warburg Institute, appropriately attired in his army uniform, Dr. Blunt resumed lecturing as the avenues of his beloved Paris echoed to the goose-stepping Nazi victory parades. His subject was François Mansart, the architect of that city's most graceful sixteenth-century churches and formal residences. Blunt reminded his class of London University students that "present circumstance" made it "impossible to visit any of the buildings," but they ought not to forget the debt civilization owed to Mansart, whom he called a "paradigm" of the classical style.[4]

The determination to combine art with his military duties gave Blunt's war effort a schizophrenic quality. On the one hand, he was preparing his Cambridge thesis, "The Artistic Theory in Italy," for publication. It bore a surprising dedication to Guy Burgess in acknowledgment of "the stimulation of constant discussion and suggestions on all the more basic points at issue." On the other hand, he was heeding Moscow's instructions to find himself a post in the British intelligence services.[5]

Blunt knew that any direct approach might attract a rebuff because of the negative traces he knew might exist against him in the MI5 Registry. But a high-level personal introduction, and his nine months of army service as an officer in the Field Security Police in Military Intelligence, should be credentials enough. He could also count on some help from Burgess, then working for Section D of MI6.

Since the outbreak of war, both MI5 and MI6 had expanded rapidly by recruiting some of the best intellects from Oxford and Cambridge as well as the legal professions. There were other friends of Blunt's now in the service who could be relied on to put in a good word for him on the old-boy network.

One of the most prominent was Lord Victor Rothschild who had joined MI5 shortly after the war began in 1939. His claim to have merely given up his Trinity fellowship and biophysical research into the fertilization of frog eggs to concentrate on countersabotage does not do justice to his remarkably versatile career as an intelligence officer.[6]

A July 1940 report, newly discovered in the U.S. Archives and signed by Rothschild, shows that he was originally brought into MI5 as an investigating officer in the Commercial Espionage unit of Division B. (Only later did he transfer to the countersabotage section, where he won the George Medal in 1944 for dismantling a German time-bomb device concealed in a box of Spanish onions.)[7]

Just how Rothschild came into MI5 has never been revealed, but his sponsor appears to have been Guy Liddell, who was then B Division's deputy director. A recommendation from Burgess may also have persuaded the B's director of the need to tap into the Rothschilds' network.

Access to extensive commercial intelligence data helped Rothschild make a unique contribution to MI5's efforts to counter German espionage operations in Britain. It was his investigation that revealed "a number of undertakings," which were "either controlled by persons of German origin or have strong German connections," who were "in a position to conduct espionage on a large scale and in departments vitally connected with our war effort." Rothschild advised the adoption of "drastic action" to curtail "a system of espionage which is so extensive and so subtle and so difficult to combat" that in his view it could prove "an important strategic factor in the conduct of the war."[8]

The magnitude of the danger facing Britain from commercial espionage early in the war appears in the detailed analysis Rothschild made of one of the most important sectors of British industry: machine tools.

He found this to be heavily dependent on German suppliers and their agents, who had infiltrated the business. The only prudent solution was for the Ministry of Supply to transfer its business to American machine-tool manufacturers.

Rothschild's report must have made a great impression with Liddell, because he sent Rothschild himself to the U.S. embassy to alert the Americans. This suggests not only his regard for Rothschild, but the authority he exercised as the head of B Division after Churchill's shakeup of MI5 in May 1940 put him in charge of counterespionage.

Rothschild had both Liddell's respect and access to him and thus could easily draw his attention to Blunt's abilities. Blunt admitted at his 1979 press conference that his recruitment, "like all of that kind" was "done simply" on the basis of personal recommendation. "Someone who was in MI5 recommended me," he stated. "I was recommended." What is more, he confirmed that his referee on the old boy network was well aware of his open Communist convictions.[9]

Ever since, the fear of libel action has obliged writers to make careful allusions to an anonymous MI5 officer who recommended Blunt. This despite Blunt's 1981 interviews with Robert Cecil, confirming Blunt's embarrassment in using his close friend Rothschild to write the necessary letter of recommendation.[10]

"That Rothschild had become acutely sensitive about his relationship with Blunt is understandable because he had originally recommended Blunt for recruitment into the Security Service and had introduced him to Guy Liddell" was the assertion made by Nigel West in *Molehunt*. "This was a matter of record within MI5 and was known to a great many of his former colleagues, some of whom had mixed feelings about Rothschild."[11]

Lord Rothschild did not press West with his threatened libel suit. But Rothschild's friends still protest that he has "been wrongly accused of being responsible for bringing Blunt into MI5." Indeed Rothschild has let it be known that he "now has proof that MI5 has no letter showing that he introduced Blunt into MI5."[12]

After such vigorous denials, I asked *Molehunt*'s author whether he still stands by his assertion that Rothschild was instrumental in getting Blunt into MI5. Now a Conservative member of Parliament, Rupert Allason, who writes under the pen name of Nigel West, confirms "absolutely" his original account. Like Robert Cecil, he is one of the few people outside Britain's security service to have interviewed Blunt before his death. Furthermore "West" explained that he does not make his case on what Blunt said, but on his own face-to-face talk with Rothschild.[13]

The interview, said West, took place at Lord Rothschild's invitation, in his impressive London house in St. James's Place in January 1987. West had told Rothschild that he knew from a very reliable inside source that it was his letter of recommendation to Liddell that constituted "the first page of Blunt's personal file" in the MI5 records.[14]

"That's very interesting, I would like to see it," Rothschild responded, because he "could not remember" writing such a letter. He challenged West, who, he said, he "knew had worked for MI5" to produce it.

"I am not denying that I introduced Blunt to Guy Liddell," Rothschild told West. "In fact, I'll tell you a funny story about it." He then related how Liddell, his B Division boss, had asked him to arrange a meeting with Blunt "to look him over." That tête-à-tête took place, shortly after Blunt's escape from France, at the three-floor London maisonette that Rothschild and his first wife, Barbara, then occupied on Bentinck Street. (Liddell insisted that he be introduced as Captain Black.) Liddell was a keen amateur art collector and got on famously with Blunt. Halfway through the evening it became apparent that Blunt's appointment with MI5 was a foregone conclusion because, as Rothschild told West, Liddell dropped the charade and identified himself, much to the amusement of all present.[15]

According to West, after this personal introduction, subsequent vetting was a mere formality. The right school and college were an almost automatic guarantee of acceptance during MI5's rapid expansion to meet the demands of war. By the end of 1939, its dramatic growth necessitated moving out of the overcrowded office building in St. James's to Wormwood Scrubs, a forbidding-looking Victorian prison in North London. The four-foot-thick walls may have provided adequate physical protection for the secrets of the extensive Registry files until an incendiary bomb forced their evacuation to Blenheim Palace near Oxford in September 1940. Vetting admitted some startlingly indiscreet new members to the premises.

"You know anyone could come into the Scrubs and put up a sign saying he's starting a new section to cover this and that," Liddell had joked in 1939. Anyone, that is, who had been to the right public school and Oxbridge college. Little attention seems to have been paid to the political reliability of these new recruits. Vetting was so lax, for example, that shortly after Blunt's admission, the notorious aesthete Brian Howard was engaged to report on Fascist sympathizers among the upper-class London nightclub set. The "beautiful Peter Pollock," the boyfriend Burgess had picked up in Cannes, was also living it up in the Dorchester on an MI5 expense account. His mission was to "keep an eye on aliens — particularly Hungarians."[16]

Blunt, however, was seriously determined to make an efficient secret-service officer — even if he was serving two masters — when he joined D Division in the late summer of 1940. For the first two months, Blunt served Brigadier I. H. Allen in that part of the division that an organizational chart designates as being concerned with "General Military Security Problems." Although D Division was somewhat remote from the real center of MI5 operations, this was a logical appointment, given Blunt's previous army experience in the Field Security Police. But his desk job was also in the section that handled the security of Britain's armaments factories, ports, and armed services.

Rothschild's disclaimer in all this has been to point out to his friends that Blunt "joined a section remote from Rothschild's work." But it is now clear from Rothschild's 1940 MI5 reports that, far from having no connection with Blunt, the two may have had a close liaison.[17]

This was because Rothschild's work for B Division had exposed a dangerous lack of security in Britain's factories, especially the machine-tool industry. And Blunt had joined the section that, among other security responsibilities, supervised the very factories that were the biggest users of machine tools.

As for Soviet intelligence, there was an additional bonus in having Blunt work for Brigadier Allen. The wartime organization chart reveals that Allen was also responsible for supervising the work of C Division. This was the outfit that carried out security vetting, euphemistically described as the "Examination of Credentials" of civilians and military personnel in "key positions."[18]

Although Blunt would complain about routine paper-pushing during his first two months in MI5, he had access to valuable data to pass on to his Soviet controller. He had a near-photographic memory, so had no need to copy documents or make notes that would make him vulnerable to any security searches. On the one occasion when he did take secret papers out of the office, he was stopped by the police, who, much to his relief, failed to spot the incriminating documents. This close call was a salutary lesson. Blunt never again removed papers. He thenceforth relied on his memory to carry information to his Soviet control officer.[19]

At his press conference, Blunt took care to be evasive about the identity of his Soviet control officers and how they communicated. His excuse was that "these are things which ought not to be discussed." But when pressed, he conceded that he had been in touch with a member of the staff of the Soviet embassy in London after joining MI5 in 1940. In subsequent private conversations with Nigel West, Blunt was less reticent. He said his first wartime controller used the code name

"George." In 1940, he was replaced by a Soviet embassy official named "Henry." Evidently MI5 never succeeded in identifying "George's" diplomatic cover.[20]

In 1963, during debriefing interrogations, Blunt did identify "Henry." From visa photographs of the wartime Soviet legations, he picked out Anatoli Gorski, who served as a first secretary and who arrived in London in 1940 and left four years later for Washington. Gorski, who was also known as Anatoli Gromov in the United States, is the most likely candidate for the wartime control officer of Blunt and the other leading Cambridge moles.[21]

In resorting to its old practice of employing legals in the Soviet embassy to run its foreign agents in the wartime emergency, the NKVD had to offset the advantage of exercising more direct control against the increased risk of more direct surveillance. Operatives who passed themselves off as diplomats were already known to the "watchers" whose job it was to tail them for MI5. This required elaborate precautions by both the agent and the control officer in establishing their meets.

Blunt told West that "Henry" and he never had any problems, even though they used to rendezvous on a regular basis. Blunt gave the impression that he met his control every week, more often than not in the smoke-filled saloon bars of public houses. Golders Green and East End bars were particular favorites of the Soviets. The long journey to these outer London suburbs required trips by subway and bus, which simplified the roundabout routes and doubling back required to shake off any tail. Blunt's military uniform made him inconspicuous among so many others in the packed wartime bars, and the blackout made it easy for them to slip away into the night undetected.

After a couple of months "Johnson," as Blunt was code-named by Moscow Center, received instructions from "Henry" to seek a position closer to the heart of MI5 operations. Liddell was "terribly susceptible to flattery," according to one of his wartime officers, and he was carefully cultivated by Blunt. The two men toured the London galleries with Blunt advising Liddell which pictures to buy. Before long Blunt was made Liddell's personal assistant in the B Division directorate.[22]

Blunt's diligence and attention to detail impressed Liddell. He gave Blunt the task of reporting on the efficiency of the watchers who tailed MI5 suspects. This enabled Blunt to go through all the reports and warn the Soviet embassy how best to avoid the surveillance of its diplomats. Unfortunately for Moscow, its agent "Johnson" proved too diligent. Blunt's growing influence over the director of B Division, who increasingly deferred to him, ignited the resentment of Margo Huggins, Liddell's longtime secretary.

A straitlaced woman, Huggins objected to the smooth-talking intruder not because she suspected his motives but because she found her own influence with Liddell threatened. She sought an ally in Dick Goldsmith White, the deputy director of B Division. The former Oxford scholarship student and Commonwealth fellow was himself interested in art and confessed to having enjoyed Blunt's polished conversation and civilized camaraderie. But he could not help but notice how his Cambridge contemporary went out of his way to single him out in the canteen for a chat. Blunt, he recalled "made a general assault on key people to see that they liked him."[23]

White resented the way that Blunt "cultivated Liddell as a way of protecting himself." White did not suspect his colleague of treachery at the time. But he knew all about the academic snobbery of homosexual Oxbridge aesthetes. He could hardly have failed to see through Blunt, whose refined vices were familiar to White from his years at Christ Church, where he had counted himself among the hearties through his extracurricular passion for athletics. Nor was White any stranger to intellectual superiority, since the members of his own college irritated members of lesser foundations by parading their arrogance and referring to Christ Church snootily as "The House."

White was neither an intellectual, political, nor social snob. A mild-mannered, studious undergraduate, he had no taste for the revolutionary politics that afflicted so many of his contemporaries. Nor was he less intellectual than his peers, as is confirmed by his exhibition in history to Christ Church, followed by postgraduate studies at the universities of Michigan and California. As a result of his firsthand experiences in the United States, White had begun his career as a public-school master possessed with a pro-American sympathy and understanding that was unusual for most Englishmen. He regarded the decline of Britain's power and the steady rise of the United States — which caused resentment in so many of his contemporaries — as part of the historical process.

Despite his ramrod bearing, White's patient understanding and quizzical eyes are more evocative of the musty classrooms of the public school where he began his career. Even Philby paid him the grudging compliment of admitting White's "gifts for chairmanship." His fundamental good sense and knack of avoiding departmental fights were the qualities that would eventually lead Sir Dick Goldsmith White, KCMG, KBE, to the top of both MI5 and MI6.[24]

The chance encounter that had transformed the reflective schoolmaster with a talent for mediation into Britain's most respected spymaster was the result of a shipboard meeting with one of Liddell's officers in 1935. An invitation to join B Section the following year made him the youngest member on Liddell's staff. He was promptly dispatched to Germany for nine months to prepare him for his first major task: monitoring German businesses in London. With this professional grounding in MI5 operations, he was groomed and ready to move into the post of deputy director when Liddell was promoted to head B Division in May 1940.

White's skill at soothing ruffled feathers restored tranquillity in Liddell's office. Blunt was transferred to B(1)b and put in charge of maintaining surveillance on the foreign embassies in London.

The redoubtable Miss Huggins, however, did not assert her authority over the director fast enough to save the life of a Russian mole whom the British had run for seven years on the Politburo staff in Moscow. He was a school friend of an MI6 officer named Harold "Gibby" Gibson, who had been educated in prerevolutionary Russia. While Gibson was in Moscow in 1933 he had been able to persuade his friend, who was then working in the private office of Anastas Mikoyan, that his disenchantment with Stalin could be repaid by espionage. Shortly after Blunt's arrival in B Division in the fall of 1940, this valuable inside source in Moscow dried up.[25]

Charged by Wright with silencing "Gibby's spy" during his interrogation twenty-five years later, Blunt made no effort to deny his responsibility. "He was a spy," he snapped back with icy disdain: "He knew the game; he knew the risks." For a brief instant Blunt dropped his mask, and Wright glimpsed the ruthless professional agent who had proved his worth to the NKVD.[26]

But Blunt was not the only Cambridge mole to start paying rich intelligence dividends by mid-1940. Donald Maclean was reestablished at the Foreign Office in London after a hair-raising escape from France with his wife. He had hurriedly married Melinda Marling, his American student girlfriend.

When Maclean reported for duty at the Foreign Office, he was not assigned, like the rest of the embassy officials, to the French Department. Instead he was put into a newly formed General Department. This section dealt with economic warfare, handling issues such as shipping, contraband, and the international repercussions of Britain's decision to impose a naval blockade of German seaborne trade. Maclean's more ambitious colleagues considered such concerns very low-grade duties. But such technical data was of immense value to the Soviets.[27]

Meanwhile, Burgess was also feeding "Henry" information from MI6, plus the nuggets he gleaned from his MI5 friends. Burgess was now a vital player in the NKVD game plan. This was not so much on account of the value of the intelligence he was supplying, but because he was uniquely placed as a gatekeeper to ease the admission of Philby and other agents into the British intelligence services.

Burgess's shadowy activities in the Phony War as producer for the Joint Broadcasting Committee proved a convenient cover for pursuing an independent liaison with members of the European Communist underground. Among the contacts he mobilized into his clandestine broadcasting network for infiltrating illegal literature and broadcasts into Germany were Edo Fimmen of the international seamen's union, and Willi Münzenberg, who was operating radio stations under the secret sponsorship of the French government. In his own carefully guarded words, Burgess said that he spent 1940 "buzzing about doing a lot of things."[28]

Among the "things" Burgess is known to have done were talks with ex-President Beneš that were transferred to records and parachuted into Czechoslovakia for broadcast by the clandestine radio transmitters. Another was to persuade Rosamond Lehmann that it was "her duty," as one of the English writers whose work was well known in France, to broadcast to the French people.

"I can see him now trudging through the snowflakes with a diplomatic bag on his shoulder," Miss Lehmann recalled. An unseasonable snowstorm had greeted them in Paris in March 1940. She had no doubt that Burgess was on an official mission as they checked into the Hôtel Crillon. But then he mysteriously vanished. "Nobody knew where he was, or why I had come," she said after finding that no one at the French national broadcasting center knew anything about why she was there. Feeling that the city was already in the grip of a "tense despair," she flew back to London the next day by herself.[29]

Burgess was given too long a rein by Major Laurence Grand. But after war broke out Grand's attention switched from propaganda to the sabotage operations he and his staff had been planning. As a result, Section D ballooned with staff until, by July 1940, Grand's "Dirty Tricks" department of 175 outnumbered the main body of MI6 by almost two to one. Yet none of Grand's ambitious schemes for disrupting the German iron-ore supplies from Sweden and the barges carrying oil supplies from Romania up the Danube materialized. Detonating the cliffs of the Iron Gate gorge proved as impractical as Burgess's plan for starving the Germans into defeat by setting the wheat fields of Central Europe ablaze with incendiary-carrying balloons.[30]

After the fall of France cut Burgess off from his European radio network, he became one of the principal ideas men in Section D. The sprawling nature of the empire that Grand had built enabled Burgess to exploit its inconsistencies and confusion to recommend his friends for jobs. His first success was to get Kim Philby into Section D by skillful lobbying with Grand and other War Office and MI6 contacts. He even contrived to attend Philby's second and final vetting interview, which took place with Marjorie Maxe at the St. Ermin's Hotel. Afterward, Philby reported for duty to Burgess's office, having handed in his resignation to *The Times*.[31]

According to Philby, Burgess was known by the initials DU, in accordance wih the standard MI6 practice of assigning alphabetical administrative designators to its staff. Each section head was identified by the appropriate section letter. In this case Grand was referred to as D. His subsection heads were DA, DB, and so on. That Burgess was number twenty-one in the Section D pecking order is an indication that he had only recently achieved official status in the MI6 hierarchy. It was a reflection of Burgess's respect for Philby — and his sense of mischief — that he refused to make Philby DU-1, which would have institutionalized his assistant status. Instead Philby was known as DUD.[32]

It was not, as Philby admitted, "the ideal starting point for what I had in mind." His first objective had been to join the Government Code and Cypher School. This was the top-secret code-breaking center at Bletchley Park, where a team of brilliant Cambridge mathematicians turned cryptanalysts were already beginning to penetrate the mysteries of the German Enigma codes.[33]

A "mutual friend" had introduced Philby to Frank L. Birch, a former history don at King's College whose World War I service with the cryptanalysts in Room 40 at the Admiralty led to his recall to the GC&CS in 1939. Since Birch was a BBC broadcaster, it is possible that it was Burgess who effected the introduction. But to Philby's fury — and the dismay of his Soviet controller — he was turned down. According to Philby, this was because Birch "could not offer me enough money to make it worth my while." But it is more probable he was rejected because his father, St. John Philby, was then regarded as a pro-Nazi sympathizer.[34]

According to Philby, there was "Nothing Recorded Against" his name in the MI5 Registry. So when Burgess recommended him for a job in Section D, only the most cursory check was made into his background credentials. But once admitted to MI6, DUD soon proved himself to be anything but for the Soviets. He was soon able to pass on to "Henry" the important administrative details of MI6. He also convinced Grand that what his outfit needed to become really effective was a school for civilian saboteurs. Burgess took the credit, but it was Philby who in July 1940 turned his friend's "riot of ideas" into a series of cogently argued memoranda that resulted in official approval for establishing a training school for saboteurs in the secluded Brickendon-bury Hall estate in Hertfordshire north of London.[35]

Philby and Burgess were appointed members of the staff of what they jokingly called "Guy Fawkes College" which was set up in July 1940 under Commander F. T. Peters, a genial naval officer who had known Burgess's father. Its first class consisted of a motley collection of twenty-five trainee saboteurs including Norwegian fishermen, a Breton onion seller, a Belgian cavalry officer, and a group of young Spaniards. These veterans of the guerrilla war against Franco did not take kindly to lectures from Philby on the necessity for setting a short dynamite fuse. "We double it to be quite safe," one of these eighteen-year-old *dinamiteros* told him knowingly. "That is why we are still alive."[36]

Burgess, meanwhile, hatched a plot too Machiavellian to ascribe to any Soviet control officer. He proposed to Harold Nicolson, now the parliamentary secretary to Alfred Duff Cooper, the minister of information, that Burgess and his Oxford friend, Isaiah Berlin — a fellow of New College and a fluent Russian speaker — were uniquely qualified to be the press attachés to Sir Stafford Cripps, the ascetic left-wing Labour M.P. whose appointment as ambassador to the Kremlin had just been announced.

Nicolson's recommendation, coupled with a convenient bureaucratic silence from the Foreign Office and some fast talking by Burgess, enabled him to set off with Berlin for the United States at the end of June. Their plan was to travel by way of San Francisco across the Pacific to Vladivostok and on to Moscow. But it came unstuck when they reached Washington. A cable arrived from the Foreign Office making it very plain that Cripps had most strenuously objected to the pair.

Burgess had suffered a setback, but he was infinitely resourceful and made the best of his time in Washington by renewing contact with Michael Straight.

Straight had recently married his Cambridge sweetheart, Belinda Crompton. They were living in a rented home across the Potomac in Alexandria, Virginia. At their house on Prince Street, Straight had already played host to a string of distinguished left-wing English visitors. Auden had dropped in on his way to self-imposed exile in New England in February. The following month, Sir Stafford Cripps stopped by on his way back to London from his mission to Delhi.

Then Esmond Romilly, one of the most colorful of all the British hons. who became rebels, arrived for a short stay with his wife, Decca, who was expecting their first child. Winston Churchill's renegade nephew had joined the Communist party while still at Wellington, from which he ran away after founding *Out of Bounds*, a radical magazine of public-school rebellion. He then joined the Loyalists in the Spanish Civil War. Romilly had caused another sensation by eloping with the younger sister of Lady Diana Mosley, the wife of the self-styled leader of the British Fascists. Romilly and Straight were "good friends" by the time he joined the Royal Canadian Air Force later that year to continue his personal crusade against Hitler. Romilly lost his life when his plane was shot down over the North Sea in December 1941.[37]

According to Straight, Burgess was the least welcome of his British visitors. During their lunch at the Little Garden Tea House, Burgess went out of his way to remind his fellow Apostle of the pact that he had made before leaving Cambridge. "I am completely out of touch with my friends," Burgess said. "Could you put me in touch?"[38]

Straight says that Burgess was sounding him out to see "whether he was still cooperating" with the Soviet intelligence service. But Straight did not tell Burgess that he had had contact with a Soviet agent. Nor did he rise to the bait that evening, after Burgess had invited himself to supper at the Straight residence. The topic came up after Burgess had insisted on cataloguing his sordid excursions with Pfeiffer to the male brothels of Paris.[39]

When Straight disclosed the details of Burgess's 1940 visit to FBI investigators (twenty-three years later, in June 1963), he admitted that he had felt unable to report either this meeting, or the contacts he had been having with agents of the Soviet intelligence service that began in December 1937.[40]

The first contact had been made by telephone when the caller identified himself as Michael Green and conveyed greetings "from your friends in Cambridge University." Straight told the FBI that he "sensed immediately it had originated with Anthony Blunt." He was then living at his mother's apartment on Park Avenue in New York City. He had approached Edward Stettinius of United States Steel while "looking around for a job." This was after he and a friend from Cambridge, John Simmonds, had spent most of the summer and fall chauffeuring Roger Baldwin, the head of the American Civil Liberties Union, on a speaking tour of the United States.[41]

The call from Green Straight said he had been apprehensively hoping would never come ever since he left Cambridge. Nevertheless, he "made arrangements with Green for a personal meeting which was consummated."

Michael Green shook his hand warmly with a firm grip. Although he apologized for having "mislaid" his half of the torn blue-ink drawing of Belinda that Blunt had retained a year before, he introduced himself by using the "verbal parole" (passwords) Straight had been given.

Straight later told the FBI that Green was in his early thirties, a dark-haired "chunky" man with a flattened pugilist's nose. They had "a couple of meetings" in New York. Straight remembered they had walked through Central Park and visited the zoo. He said that Green made no demands "but endeavored to study and appraise him and appeared to have prepared topics and lines of conversation to test his thoughts and points of view and to shape his mind." He said that he was "usually witty and given to making puns."[42]

Green was obviously Russian, although Straight was impressed that he spoke English fluently. From his "inexpensive" American-cut suit — which was a half size too small — and bureaucratic manner, Straight assumed he was posing as an American businessman. From FBI photographic records he "immediately and positively" identified Green as William Grienke.

Declassified FBI files characterize Grienke as Straight's "Soviet Intelligence Service (SIS) handler." Straight himself stated that he did not believe Green trusted him and did not regard him as a "dedicated Communist." This he felt may have been because he insisted on maintaining his friendship with Roger Baldwin and his sister's pro-tsarist drama teacher, which caused Green/Grienke annoyance and displeasure.

Straight had moved to Washington in the spring of 1938 and through his connection with Eleanor Roosevelt, the president's wife, was given an unsalaried assignment under Herbert Feis, who was then an economic adviser to the State Department. He told the FBI he "was sure" he had told Green of his plans, which perhaps explains why the Soviet intelligence-service officer phoned him. They had "three or four meetings" in Washington "at intervals of approximately one a month" at Washington restaurants during which they "discussed topics of current interest." In his autobiographical memoir, Straight said that Green suggested he could assist him by taking "interesting" documents home from the State Department "to study."[43]

According to the FBI records, Straight admitted that he furnished Green with a memorandum on "Economic Consequences of European Rearmament," which he had prepared for the secretary of state. He also conceded that on one occasion he met Green by car and passed over "two official State Department documents" that he had not prepared. Straight insisted these were "not highly classified," although he admitted they were "not for public consumption and may have borne the classification Confidential." He recalled how on this occasion he had dropped his Russian handler off in the vicinity of the Soviet embassy "so he could have copies made," and then picked him up later.[44]

Green had been careful not to disclose his own address. But since he had discussed the possibility of setting up an insurance business in Baltimore or Philadelphia, Straight told the FBI that "the thought occurred" to him that Green probably lived in Philadelphia. Green had once provided Straight with a Brooklyn telephone contact whose name was Alexander Koral, but he had never had occasion to call the number. Nor was Straight able to identify the FBI photographs of Koral as anyone he had ever seen. But he did identify FBI pictures of one Zalmond David Franklin. This former Communist member of the Abraham Lincoln Brigade, with a "background of service for the KGB," was a young Jewish man from New York whom he met sometime during "1939–40" with a written questionnaire about Cabinet appointments and political questions. Straight declined to cooperate with Franklin. Nor did he help another unidentified Soviet agent who approached him later, whom he described as looking like a "Czech ski instructor."[45]

Straight also told the FBI that during the period when Green remained out of touch with him, he had been contacted by a Solomon Adler in the summer of 1938. Adler turned out to be an associate of Solomon Lichinsky, the man whom Elizabeth Bentley was to link in 1948 to the Soviet espionage ring in the State Department. Adler told Straight to "lay low," that he would be recontacted, and that he had been referred to him as "a Communist in the Department of State" by a radical co-worker named Donald Stephens, who had been a friend of Straight's mother.[46]

Green eventually reappeared. He continued to contact Straight after he had left the State Department early in 1939. Straight told the FBI that Green was "dissatisfied" with his departure from government service but "mollified" when he "invented" the possibility that he was hoping to get a job at the War Department. Straight's decision to turn down a permanent position in the Office of the Economic Advisor to work for the Department of the Interior, Straight says, was influenced by his resistance to Green's continuing pressure to hand over more classified government documents to the Soviets.[47]

Tommy "The Cork" Corcoran and his associate, Benjamin U. Cohen, counsel for the National Power Policy Committee, were two of Roosevelt's New Deal cronies. With Europe heading for war, Straight jumped at the opportunity to write speeches for the president, the Cabinet, and the liberal leaders of Congress. The speeches were "non-classified," so Straight felt less constrained in handing over to Green his anti-Stalinist attack on the Nazi-Soviet pact, together with "four or five other commentaries" prepared for the Department of the Interior. But his main job was speechwriting. He hoped that his words might make some contribution to a shift in America's stance from neutrality toward an active participation in the struggle against Hitler.[48]

This put Straight, on matters of policy, at loggerheads with the official Moscow position of supporting Hitler. The 1940 appearance of Burgess in Washington therefore only increased Straight's discomfort. So, after driving Burgess back to Washington that night, Straight told his wife that he had been having contacts with an emissary of the Soviet Union. In response to her understandable concern, he says he promised to break off contact with Green. And it was in response to her appeals that Straight left the Department of the Interior soon afterward to get away from Washington and spend time with his family in Wyoming. When he returned in August and obtained a position as assistant to James Dunn, the chief of the State Department's European Division, he was careful — as he told the FBI — not to let Green know about his new post. His Soviet handler, as a result, did not attempt to contact him again until after he had left the State Department, in May 1941.

Burgess, it seems, had overplayed his hand, not only with Straight but with Whitehall. After returning to London, his brainchild, the "Guy Fawkes College," was closed down and merged with the Special Operations Executive (SOE). Burgess was transferred with Philby to SOE headquarters at 64 Baker Street. With Grand no longer his sponsor, the undisciplined Burgess soon found himself without a job. He fell "victim to bureaucratic intrigue," as he explained his sacking in November to Philby — who anticipated the same fate. But to Philby's surprise he was appointed to SO1 (radio and propaganda operations) as an instructor. His field, propaganda techniques, eventually became the Political Warfare Executive at Woburn Abbey, where the future Labour party leaders Richard Crossman and Hugh Gaitskell worked with Sefton Delmer and his team of German expatriates (later to include Baron von und zu Putlitz), waging the "black propaganda" war of leaflets and radio broadcasts against the Nazis. It was part of Philby's job to liaise with Woburn, but he spent the first part of 1941 languishing — as far as his secret mission for Moscow was concerned — in Hampshire at SOE's Beaulieu training establishment.[49]

Philby was eventually rescued from the SOE backwater to which bureaucracy had assigned him by Tomas Harris, who emerges as one of the most enigmatic characters in the whole Cambridge network. He was a friend of Burgess, and either on his own or on Philby's urging, Burgess had persuaded Grand to appoint him to the staff of Brickendonbury Hall as "a sort of glorified housekeeper, because he and his wife Hilda were inspired cooks."[50]

Harris was a year younger than Blunt and had a devotion to the arts that was both passionate, practical, and profound. Unlike his Cambridge friend, however, Harris was a gifted artist, sculptor, engraver, and ceramicist. (His talents had secured him a scholarship to the Slade School of Art at the age of fifteen.) His striking Mediterranean features were accentuated by his swept-back hair, beaky nose, and intense dark eyes. Evidently Blunt had made his acquaintance, when he was a fellow of Trinity, through his father, Lionel Harris, whose Spanish Art Gallery in Mayfair dealt in the works of Velásquez and Goya. Harris had been one of the first dealers to recognize the importance of El Greco at a time when few in England appreciated his masterpieces. Lionel's gifted son Tomas was brought up amid considerable family wealth and educated in Spain — where his mother was born — which accounted for the idiosyncratic spelling of his first name.

A gregarious and brilliant man, Harris was known to his friends simply as Tommy. The suggestion by one of his wartime colleagues that the handsome Harris might have been bisexual is hinted at in Blunt's effusive tribute to "one of the most complete human beings I have ever known." Blunt even went so far as to compare Harris's paintings to those of van Gogh. Among the leading members of the Cambridge agents, Harris was unusual in that someone who was such a close personal friend of Blunt and Burgess also struck a chord with Philby. It is surprising that Philby, whom his wartime colleague Malcolm Muggeridge described as having an "allergy to nearly all things intellectual and spiritual," was to write of his "close and highly prized friendship" with the "brilliantly intuitive" Harris.

Such effusive tributes from two self-confessed Soviet spies give good reason to believe that Harris was deeply involved in their web of conspiracy, the more so since they were written some years *after* his death, when their own part in the plot was known to the authorities. Blunt engineered and wrote a glowing entry for his friend in the *Dictionary of National Biography* — the bibliographic equivalent of a memorial plaque in Westminster Abbey.

Circumstantial evidence and new documents suggest that Harris was another Soviet mole whom the Cambridge ring conspired to infiltrate into the security service by the back door. The most specific charge was made by a former member of a Soviet network in Switzerland. Intelligence authority and author Richard Deacon quotes his informant as saying that Harris first made contact with the Soviets while he was studying in Rome in the early thirties. The source, code-named "Roger" by Deacon to protect his confidentiality, insisted that Harris's recruiter was an underground Italian Communist who was also an art dealer in the same INSA network as the Swiss informant.[51]

This accounts for Harris's rather surprising decision to become an art dealer rather than a full-time painter. Spain became his most profitable hunting ground and perhaps it was not coincidental that he was traveling extensively and buying up Spanish art during the civil war at a time when the Soviet "advisers" to the Loyalists masterminded the systematic stripping of monasteries, churches, and castles of their art treasures.

Stalin's orders were that the Spanish comrades on the Loyalist side had to pay for the "fraternal aid" received from Moscow. Besides carting off all the gold bullion held by the Spanish National Bank, Soviet intelligence was using unsuspecting art dealers in Paris and Brussels to sell off the looted Spanish paintings. One of these was alleged to be Alexander Zelinski, the White Russian father-in-law of Charles Howard Ellis, the MI6 officer who later confessed to passing information to the Abwehr. Soviet defector Georgi Agabekov was employed by one of these White Russian art syndicates, which in the summer of 1937 arranged for him to be sent to France to help suppress the shipping of the looted Spanish treasures across the Pyrenees border.

Harris, it seems, was part of the same network of French and Belgian dealers who were raking in handsome profits as middlemen selling the Spanish artworks looted by Soviet agents. He was seen by a friend of Ellen Wilkinson, the British Labour M.P., at one of the high-mountain inns in the Pyrenees in July 1937 talking with Agabekov. Shortly afterward, Agabekov disappeared on one of the mountain trails, the presumed victim of an NKVD retribution murder.[52]

Twenty-seven years later, Harris was himself to die in curious circumstances. On January 27, 1964, his new Citroën DS suddenly left the road and hit a tree while taking a gentle bend on the road east of Palma, Majorca. No apparent cause was ever found to explain the accident. It appeared inexplicable to his wife, who survived the crash, and to the local Civil Guard. It was midafternoon, the road was dry and her husband was neither drunk nor speeding on the route they both knew well.[53]

That Harris was held in such high regard by both Blunt and Philby

— whose eldest son's education he paid for — inevitably raised questions about the wealthy art dealer's real loyalties. It appeared doubly suspicious that Harris died so soon after Philby's defection and Blunt's confession. Not until fifteen years later, when Blunt's public confession aroused the intense interest of British reporters in the fate of his close friend Harris, was there any independent effort made by British intelligence to investigate the crash in which he died. But the trail had long grown cold.

The publication of *Spycatcher* in 1987, however, revealed that Peter Wright never got around to interrogating Harris before his untimely death. The "official" verdict of his former MI5 colleagues gave Harris the benefit of the doubt. But this convenient decision to let him rest in peace appears to owe a good deal to an official unwillingness to admit another major Soviet penetration.

There is no question that Harris had contributed to one of the most successful military operations in Britain's history. He was one of the organizers of the successful "Double-Cross" operations in which Abwehr agents operating from the Iberian peninsula, who had been turned, misled the Germans over the Allied plans for the invasion of France in 1944. But the question that remains unanswered is whether Harris was also working for the ultimate victory of the Soviet Union.

Flora Solomon, who had known (since 1937) that her longtime friend Philby was an underground Communist, remained convinced to her dying day that Harris was another Soviet agent. She also believed that her 1962 confession to MI5, which finally exposed Philby's treachery to the authorities, also contributed to the chain of events that caused Harris's death.[54]

The Solomon story provides another connective thread in the tapestry of treachery woven by Blunt and Philby. Flora was the daughter of a banker named Grigori Benenson, whose wealth enabled him to surmount the stigma of being Jewish in Czarist Russia. He was one of the backers of Alexander Kerensky, whose government was overthrown by the Bolsheviks in 1917. After fleeing to England in 1917, Flora married Colonel Harold Solomon, whose family was prominent in the Jewish community in London. During the thirties she was an active promoter of Zionism, a cause that involved her with many prominent British socialist leaders.

During a trip to Palestine in 1923, she met the eleven-year-old Kim Philby and his father at her parents' house in Jerusalem. She encountered Philby again, eleven years later, on his return from Vienna with his vivacious Jewish bride. From her Viennese housekeeper, Solomon learned about Litzi Friedman's communism, but this did not concern someone as passionately anti-Nazi as Solomon, who was a sympathizer and friend of left-wing intellectuals. John Strachey and the Stafford Crippses patronized her salon. For a time she employed Auden to tutor her son and he, or Philby, often brought Burgess to her large house in Addison Road.[55]

Solomon carefully avoided giving the impression in her autobiography that she had gone out of her way to cultivate Philby. But Arthur Martin, who was later to debrief her, suspected that the widow Solomon — her husband had died in 1930 — had developed an intense romantic attachment for Philby. Given her "hard left" sympathies and strong Zionist allegiance, her claim that she did not know about his pro-Nazi sympathies and involvement with the Anglo-German Fellowship seems incredible.

Solomon's own account hints at a maternal attraction to the "gentle charm" of the well-mannered Philby, who "mingled easily" with her socialist friends. She found Philby's stutter attractive, and a strong bond developed between them. But, according to Philby, she was also "hard left" and she mothered the dedicated young Communist twenty years her junior. That much is clear from her admission that just before he set off for Spain in the spring of 1937, Philby revealed to her that he was secretly working for the Comintern. He would not have confided in her, or asked her to join him in "important work for peace," if he — and his controller Theodore Maly — had not been supremely confident that Solomon would not betray him.[56]

Solomon says she declined the invitation not because of her Russian capitalist background but because she was too busy saving the persecuted Jews of Europe. The following year, during one of his trips home from Spain, Philby evidently tried again to recruit her. This time he appealed to her maternal instincts by revealing that he was in "great danger." She, for her part, was left in no doubt that he "was still associated with the Communist Party."[57]

On this visit Philby, then estranged from his Litzi, met the woman who became his second wife, Aileen Furze. Solomon was then a staff director of Marks & Spencer, the department-store chain run by her Zionist friends Simon Marks and Israel (later Lord) Sieff. (They had given their blessing to bringing Jewish refugees into the organization.) Philby felt an instant attraction to Aileen, who was one of Solomon's principal assistant managers. When he returned to London from France in May 1940, he moved into a flat with Aileen, where they lived together as man and wife.

Flora Solomon saw a good deal of Philby when he was in SOE. Its London headquarters was two floors above the corporate offices of Marks & Spencer in Baker Street. In 1945, when Philby finally married Aileen,

Flora Solomon was one of the witnesses at their wedding at the Chelsea Registry Office. The best man was Tomas Harris. But Solomon did not come forward to reveal what she knew about Philby's Communist past when he came under public suspicion after Burgess and Maclean's defection. She might have done so if she had known that Philby had written to Burgess, telling him that in desperate straits he could go to Solomon for help, because she knew all about his secret life. Blunt later admitted he had discovered and pocketed this incriminating letter while he was "assisting" MI5 in its search of Burgess's London flat in 1951.[58]

Fear of setting off a McCarthy-type "witch hunt" was what Solomon said had restrained her from exposing Philby in 1956, when his loyalty was at the center of the "Third Man" parliamentary row. But the death of her old assistant, Aileen, whom Philby abandoned with his children when he went as a journalist to Beirut, and the strident Arab bias of his *Observer* articles, finally killed her remaining affection for him. Her love for Israel proved greater than her old socialist loyalties.

"The thought occurred to me that Philby had, after all, remained a Communist," Solomon wrote ingenuously of her mounting distress at the pro-Soviet tone of his dispatches. In August 1962, during a reception at the Weizmann Institute, she told Lord Victor Rothschild of her concerns. Rothschild had close connections with Mossad, the Israeli intelligence service, and she knew that Philby had been a wartime colleague of Rothschild's in the British intelligence services because they had worked together in Paris.[59]

"How is it that *The Observer* uses a man like Kim?" Solomon demanded of Rothschild. "Don't they know he's a Communist?" She insisted that he "must do something about it." Rothschild appeared startled, but said he would "think about it."[60]

When Solomon returned to London, she received a call from Rothschild asking her to meet him at his London house along with a member of the security services. She was hesitant, but eventually agreed. The interview took place at Rothschild's London house.[61]

Flora Solomon was a "strange, rather untrustworthy woman," according to Wright, who monitored the interview conducted by Arthur Martin with a hidden microphone at Rothschild's house. He said they were both convinced that Solomon "never told the truth" about her relations with Philby, even though she "clearly had a grudge against him." The implication was that she was much more deeply involved and knew more than she had admitted. Why else had she not come forward to tell the authorities all she knew six years earlier?

The two MI5 officers interpreted Solomon's curious behavior as implying that she had shielded Philby because of some deep loyalty; possibly, they reasoned, he had once been her lover. There may have been a more sinister explanation.[62]

As Wright reveals, Solomon flatly rejected Martin's suggestion that she appear as a witness if Philby was brought home to stand trial. She said she feared what the Russians might do to her family. MI5 suspicions that Solomon was more deeply implicated than she cared to admit increased when she named Harris as a co-conspirator of Philby's. She would give no evidence for this, only insisting that "those two were so close as to give me an intuitive feeling that Harris was more than a friend."[63]

Solomon could not have known that it was Harris who had been instrumental in rescuing Philby from operational oblivion in SOE. It was Harris who made a point of inviting Philby to the receptions at his home in Chesterfield Gardens so that he could meet Dick Brooman-White, the head of the Iberian unit of MI5's B Division. In September 1941, when Brooman-White was transferred to set up an Iberian unit in Section V of MI6 (Counterintelligence), Harris — who was promoted to B(1)g in MI5 — lobbied on the old-boy network for Philby's appointment to this new section. The move to Section V proved to be the breakthrough in Philby's career. Within a decade this secret Soviet agent was being tipped as the future director of Britain's foreign-intelligence service.[64]

Just how Harris himself managed to jump to MI5 has never been properly accounted for. Burgess, who was responsible for obtaining Harris's semi-official MI6 status, had no direct office contact with Liddell. Yet while Burgess's hoped-for appointment to MI5 was black-balled by the personal animosity of the director, Liddell approved Harris — an unqualified and noncommissioned member of SOE — for a direct transfer right into B(1)g, the heart of MI5's principal operational division.

Harris could not have made the change without the approval of B Division's director. It is significant that not only was Harris a close friend of Blunt's, but his move was made while Blunt was working as Liddell's personal assistant. The director of B would have been susceptible to Blunt's pointing out his friend's artistic qualifications, in addition to his special knowledge of Spain. This must have played a crucial role in persuading Liddell to take Harris aboard since, up until then, his only demonstrable ability in government service had been as a cook-housekeeper. It would have flattered Liddell's vanity as a collector of pictures and china to add another art adviser to his staff.

*       *       *

Blunt and Harris found it easy to cultivate the artist *manqué* in Liddell. Throughout the war, he was a frequent guest at the Harris home. The Mayfair mansion that served as his father's gallery was a veritable museum. Velásquez paintings and Goya drawings competed for attention with tapestries and furniture as fine and rich as those of any castle in Spain. Guy Liddell and other senior members of the secret intelligence fraternities were frequent guests at lavish parties thrown by hosts who were able to ignore the normal frugalities of wartime rationing.

In the cliquish British intelligence service, the "Chesterfield Garden Mafia" represented a powerful network that continued long after the war with Liddell's attendance at the Harrises' Garden House salons. Harris, who worked in the Iberian unit under Dick Brooman-White, easily found a niche in MI5 for his sister, Violetta, as a Spanish-speaking officer in Section B(1)a. Harris's friends were a remarkable group of young, Oxbridge-educated secret-service talent. Blunt and Rothschild, along with Liddell's brother, David, and his immediate superior, Brooman-White, were from MI5. And Philby's Westminster friend Tim Milne, and Peter Wilson, the future chairman of Sotheby's, provided the connections into MI6.[65]

The Harris "Mafia" enabled Blunt to introduce new recruits into the security service on a social basis. Nor were they all brought in as potential moles. His old Marlborough friends John Hilton and Alastair MacDonald, both of whom transferred to MI6, served with loyalty and distinction. But Guy Burgess, whom Blunt tried his best to get Liddell to accept as a full member of the service after his rejection by SOE in November 1940, was flatly rejected. Impressed though Liddell was with Blunt, he was fastidious when it came to MI5 and he had been unfavorably impressed by Burgess's unsavory reputation and light-fingered intelligence free-lancing for Sir Joseph Ball in Chamberlain's secret exchanges with the French at the time of Munich. "Keep that man out of the office," Liddell had cautioned his staff on several occasions, "and don't leave anything lying about if he does get in."[66]

"Liddell thought that Burgess was a disgraceful figure," Dick White confirmed. "He did not approve of the goings-on that were associated with Burgess. He told everyone in MI5 that no one was to have anything to do with Burgess."[67]

When it became clear to Burgess that he would not find an official welcome in the bosom of MI5 as Harris had, he rejoined the BBC as a Talks producer. But, as Blunt's closest friend, he proved impossible to keep out of MI5's corridors. His brother, Nigel, and his wife had been taken into the "office." Nigel Burgess, after service with an antiaircraft battery, joined F Division under Roger Hollis, where he worked with Blunt's left-wing friend, Kemball Johnston, monitoring the activities of the Communist party. Although Burgess was officially persona non grata, Christopher Harmer, another wartime recruit to B Division, remembers how he "was always in and out of the 'office.'" He had the impression that Burgess was "a great friend of Liddell," who, he says, was "indiscreet" and "talked a lot out of school."[68]

Liddell must have relaxed his ban on Burgess. It is now known that MI5 continued to exploit his talents as a homosexual intriguer to tap sources in the various London embassies. One of those contacts was a Communist diplomat from Switzerland, "Orange." Sir Dick White has conceded that MI5 *did* receive useful information from agent "Orange" through Burgess. However, White insisted that Blunt "never ran GB [Guy Burgess] as an agent." It seems logical, then, that Liddell must have authorized the use of Burgess as an MI5 free-lance agent.[69]

"Intellectual spiv" and adept charmer though Burgess was, he could not have bulldozed himself back into the good graces of B Division's director without the help of his many friends. Blunt and Harris were his most influential advocates, but it was another friend, Victor Rothschild, who permitted Burgess to install himself in the London maisonette in Bentinck Street, which was conveniently close to his job at the nearby BBC Broadcasting House.

So much sensationalism has grown up about the ménage that coalesced around Burgess and Blunt that their wartime living quarters have become synonymous with a homosexual bordello serving as a viperous nest for Soviet spies. The truth, as far as it can be established from eyewitnesses, suggests that, like all scandals, this one has been exaggerated in the telling.

Lord Rothschild had the three-story maisonette at 5 Bentinck Street. It had been constructed in the mid-thirties above the ground floor offices of *The Practitioner*, a doctors' magazine. When the London Blitz began in September, Rothschild and his pregnant wife, Barbara, decided to retreat to the country. Although the Rothschild lease ran out at the end of 1940, the flat was convenient and had an excellent bomb shelter in the basement. So he offered it to Anthony Blunt and their mutual friends Teresa Mayor and Patricia Rawdon-Smith, who had just been bombed out of their Gower Street flat. The lease was too expensive for three of them to manage on their own, so Blunt suggested Burgess share it. *The Practitioner* said that having four people's names on the lease was like "signing up a football team," so it was Mayor who took on the responsibility.[70]

In 1941, Mayor began working for Rothschild at MI5 as his secretary/personal assistant, and she was to marry him after his first marriage to Lady Barbara ended in divorce in 1946. Patricia Rawdon-Smith née Parry was estranged from her husband. After her divorce she would marry Richard Llewelyn-Davies, a close friend of Blunt and a fellow left-wing Apostle of her former husband's.

Blunt, with his knack of taking care of details, managed the accounts. The quartet sorted out their living arrangements to share the kitchen and sitting room on the first level for general entertaining. Blunt took the bedroom and dressing room on the second floor, sharing the bathroom with Burgess, who had the other bedroom down the corridor. The two girls shared the top floor. An Irish maid, Bridie, came in to clean and cook for whoever was in that evening. The bomb shelter was a great attraction for visiting friends and many of them stayed overnight.[71]

"Everyone at Bentinck Street was a friend of Lord Rothschild," Jackie Hewit told me. He said that Mayor and Parry knew all about Blunt and Burgess. They were aware that Blunt was sleeping with Hewit and that Burgess and some of his friends were bringing boys back to the flat. Burgess used to partner Parry at the big dances around London; Mayor helped Blunt prepare the manuscript for his book on François Mansart.[72]

According to Hewit and others, Rothschild was a visitor to Bentinck Street. He could not have been unaware of its homosexual ménage, since he knew that Blunt had moved Hewit into his dressing room on the second floor as a permanent resident in the autumn of 1940. He remained as a part of the Bentinck Street household, pooling his wartime ration book for the mutual benefit of the entourage until late 1944, when his army unit was posted to the Continent after the liberation of France.

Hewit had attached himself to Blunt rather than to his old lover Burgess. This arrangement worked to his advantage because Anthony kept his room "like a monk's cell" whereas, down the corridor, "you had to step over the mess" to get into Burgess's room. He was, in any case, never sure who would be found in Burgess's bed. "If Guy fancied someone, he'd go up to him in the street and proposition him," Hewit explained. "His theory was that any man between the ages of seventeen and seventy-five was haveable." During all the time he lived in Bentinck Street, he can remember that Blunt had only one person ever stay with him: his friend from Cambridge, Peter Montgomery.[73]

"Anthony was always much closer physically to Peter than to Guy. I suppose you could describe them as long-term lovers," Hewit said, insisting that the very idea that Blunt and Burgess had any physical relationship was "absolute rubbish." Despite what others have speculated, Hewit asserts that in all other respects but the sexual, Burgess and Blunt were "Mutt and Jeff." His statement carries the conviction of someone with intimate experience of both men.

"Guy achieved the excitement in his life that Anthony would have liked to have if he had been as liberated. I could see that he got a great deal of vicarious satisfaction listening to Guy's endless sexual talk," Hewit observed. "And how Guy would talk, he had no hang-ups about himself or other people."[74]

Burgess used to meet him regularly at his "haunt" — the Reform Club — and then they would go to the Gargoyle. This late-night club owned by the Honorable David Tennant, former husband of actress Hermione Baddeley, was the preferred wartime hangout of the London theater and literary crowd. Another favorite with Burgess was Le Boeuf sur le Tôit, a risqué bar in Soho's Orange Street, where Nell Gwyn once plied her ancient trade. Its owner, Teddy Ashton, filled it with antiques from his Piccadilly shop. He needed no excuse to take over the piano to lead wildly outrageous choruses of the bar's famous ditty, which began "Boeuf sur le Tôit is a rendezvous/Where you see the aristocracy drinking itself to death/With the lesser lights of democracy who never draw a sober breath." Blunt found the atmosphere "altogether too camp," according to Hewit, who accompanied him one night to the bar that was rumored to be one of the best spots in town to pick up lonely GIs on a London furlough.

Yet for all Burgess's one-night stands and homosexual banter, Hewit says indignantly, far too much has been made of Goronwy Rees's spiteful charge that the Bentinck Street flat had "the air of a high-class disorderly house, in which one could not distinguish between the staff, the management, and the clients." Hewit insists that Rees was only an occasional visitor and may have been inspired by Burgess's raunchy boasting to charge: "Civil servants, politicians, visitors to London, friends and colleagues of Guy's popped in and out of bed, and then continued long and absorbing discussions." Hewit insists that this was a totally fabricated description of one of his own birthday celebrations. These and other Bentinck Street parties were always "perfectly respectable" because there were always so many people from the "office" present. The party could never have turned into the orgy Rees described. Hewit also contends "there was never enough alcohol at Bentinck Street in wartime — even the pubs sometimes ran short."[75]

If there has been an exaggeration in people's recollections concerning sexual revelry, there can be no doubt that the political hue of this exotic wartime salon was deepest red. John Strachey was for a time a resident before he joined the RAF. According to Hewit, Burgess said that Richard Llewelyn-Davies, another marxisant Apostle, whose wartime duty as an architect was with the LMSR railway company, was like the-man-who-came-to-dinner. He was a regular visitor who finally moved into the top-floor flat in 1943 when he married Patricia Rawdon-Smith. Rothschild lent them a stable flat at Tring, where they lived after 1945 when their daughter was born.[76]

Another frequent animator of the Bentinck Street salon, especially when it came to arguing (after Hitler's attack on Russia) that the bomber offensive should be ditched in favor of opening a second front, was J. D. Bernal. A wartime scientist with Combined Operations, the Communist sage of prewar Cambridge was, as Hewit personally noted, a "great friend of Tess and Anthony." It was his presence that so forcibly struck Malcolm Muggeridge, another Cambridge graduate who had briefly succumbed and then rejected the lure of Marxism after a spell as a journalist in Moscow in the twenties.[77]

After his one and only visit to what he described as "this millionaire's nest" in Bentinck Street, Muggeridge — then a junior member of MI6 — felt himself "morally afflicted." A heavy air raid going on contributed to his discomfort at finding himself in the company of Strachey, Bernal, Blunt, and Burgess — "a whole revolutionary *Who's Who*" as he aptly put it. He found it corrupting to be sheltering in "so distinguished a company — Cabinet Minister-to-be, honored Guru of the Extreme Left-to-be, Connoisseur Extraordinary-to-be, and other notabilities all grouped round Burgess, Etonian mudlark and sick toast of a sick society." Rubber bones from the doctor's office were available to bite on if the tension became unbearable. To Muggeridge the atmosphere was not so much a conspiracy as "decay and dissolution." It was, he noted, "the end of a class, of a way of life."[78]

To Jackie Hewit, the soldier with a working-class background, the Bentinck Street gatherings were far from being dissolute. "I was meeting people, who as far as I was concerned, were absolutely exceptional and absorbing it like blotting paper," he said. Hewit says that he dismissed all their talk about the struggle to save the downtrodden working class as "fake." He frequently told Burgess and Blunt that it was "absolute rubbish" to talk about Marxism when the country was fighting for its survival.[79]

On occasion, Maclean was a wartime guest. And Philby dropped in whenever he was in London. Rosamond Lehmann recalls meeting him during her one visit. Another member of the inner circle, according to Hewit, was Tommy Harris, whom he described as "very macho, an absolute sweetie, very close with Anthony and Guy." Other members of MI5, including Patrick Day, who worked alongside Blunt in B(1)b, and Geoffrey Wethered, were familiar faces in Bentinck Street. This may well have been because their chief, Guy Liddell, was one of the most frequent and welcome guests.[80]

Liddell's seemingly close involvement with the exotic coterie at Bentinck Street would later raise serious suspicions over whether or not he had also been sucked into Blunt's conspiracy. These are strengthened by Hewit's admission that the "quiet and gentle" head of B Division was "definitely not a partygoer." This suggests that the company revolving around the homosexuality and Marxism of Blunt and Burgess must have had a strong personal attraction for Liddell, who was now leading the private life of a reclusive bachelor. It has been suggested that it was the former rather than latter that attracted him, and that the breakup of his marriage had left him lonely and vulnerable after his wife left him to go to the United States in 1936.[81]

"If anything Liddell was a 'voyeur,'" Hewit says, "not in the strictly sexual sense, but he enjoyed the company of homosexuals like Guy and Anthony. He was amused by the repartee and reveled in the interplay of personalities."

Liddell may well have succumbed — as Sir Joseph Ball and Harold Nicolson had — to Burgess's uncanny ability to detect the homosexual weakness in older men. And Liddell's susceptibility to charm and flattery could, as one MI5 officer observed, lead to indiscretions — especially among members of his staff. The plain fact that one of the most important directors in the British secret service had been drawn into the heart of Blunt's coterie must have given cause for some self-congratulation at NKVD headquarters in Moscow.

More astonishing is that Liddell could have been so unsuspecting of the dangers of compromising his status. He must have been aware that the flagrant homosexuality of the Bentinck Street ménage exposed its male participants to serious criminal charges — even in wartime. Yet the head of B Division appears to have had no reservations about spending much of his off-duty time with Blunt, Burgess, and their male friends. It seems that Liddell's dislike of Burgess was a smokescreen directed mainly to impressing his deputy Dick White and his colleagues at the office. Off duty, he liked nothing better than to let his hair down in Burgess's outrageous milieu. Hewit says Liddell shared his passionate enthusiasm for the music hall. He would join them to the Metropolitan in Edgware Road one week, and Chelsea Palace of Varieties the next, on a regular basis. Blunt rarely accompanied them. His preference was for more serious pursuits.

Liddell, as Hewit told me, also knew that Hewit was being used as a free-lance agent for B Division. "In a sense, I was working for Anthony, even though I was not officially attached to MI5," Hewit said, explaining how in 1940 he had found himself transferred to the War Office from the Royal Artillery regiment in Essex to which he had been posted. Thanks to Blunt and Liddell, Hewit was reassigned just in time to prevent him from being sent overseas to North Africa.[82]

"As an army officer Anthony was entitled to a batman," Hewit said, recalling how "striking" Blunt looked in his uniform. "But," he added cryptically, "I was not assigned to London just to shine his boots and webbing."

When asked precisely what he did do for Blunt, he became coyly evasive. The assignments he was sent on for MI5 were still official secrets. "I suppose you could say that I was a decoy," Hewit added enigmatically, although he admitted that he played a part in helping Burgess and Blunt arrange for "Orange," the Swiss diplomat, Eric Kessler, to become an MI5 informant.[83]

Hewit confirmed that he had a "normal job" at the War Office during the day, and only worked "social hours" as an MI5 free lance. Blunt would assign him certain "targets," who, it appears, were probably homosexual foreign diplomats. He was, he said with a knowing smile, "a sort of middleman," who occasionally accompanied Blunt whenever he took the night express from King's Cross to Newcastle or Edinburgh. This was to do with providing a military escort for the couriers of the foreign embassies in London as they shuttled their diplomatic pouches to and from the sea- and airports in the north of England.[84]

It was Robert Cecil who shed light on these missions. In the spring of 1941, Cecil's diplomatic career led to his appointment as assistant private secretary to Sir Alexander Cadogan. He arrived in the Foreign Office early one morning during the darkest days of World War II and came face to face with Blunt, whom he had last seen six years earlier in Trinity Great Court. So complete was Blunt's transformation, Cecil did not immediately identify the smartly turned-out army officer with the aloof Trinity don he knew at Cambridge.

"I came into the anteroom to Cadogan's office to find a distinguished-looking military officer enthusiastically engaged in an animated conversation with Peter Lockersley," Cecil recalled. "Who the devil was that?" he asked after the strangely familiar figure had left the office. His colleague, Cadogan's other assistant, explained that it was Major Anthony Blunt from MI5. He had just "had an incident with one of the foreign governments' diplomatic bags." Cecil could not have been more astonished.[85]

"Anthony was effervescing over this absolutely hair-raising incident he had just been through," Cecil vividly recalled. "But what struck me forcefully was that at the same time he was as cool as a cucumber and obviously immensely enjoying the whole business."

The tricky business was gaining covert access to the contents of the diplomatic bags of various Allied governments-in-exile. These included Poland, Holland, and Denmark, as well as the neutral countries of Spain, Switzerland, and Sweden.

"It was not an easy job, and it required iron nerve and split-second timing." Blunt acted as the commander of the military escort that accompanied foreign couriers during their journeys to and from ports and airfields where ships and planes could still make the trip in relative safety to the other non-Axis countries.[86]

To gain the trust of the couriers, decoys like Hewit plied them with alcohol, or even arranged for appropriate sexual consolation during the long journeys that were made in locked compartments on blacked-out trains. When the couriers had been distracted or lulled into a drunken stupor, Blunt supervised the discreet removal of the diplomatic pouches. They then were passed to a specially trained assistant in another sealed-off compartment. He carefully slit open the stitches. The papers were taken out and photographed. The pouches were then skillfully stitched up again with identical threads and, with their official seals still intact, were slipped back into the courier's compartment.

The timing of these intricate operations did not always go smoothly. In the event of a slipup, it fell to Blunt to try to persuade the courier that the diplomatic pouch had not been tampered with. It was his job to use blackmail, or any other means at his disposal, to persuade an alarmed dupe not to make a formal report. Blunt could be extremely persuasive and was usually successful. But MI5 was under orders to alert Cadogan's office on any of these close calls so that the Foreign Office was ready to issue the appropriate denials. That was what Blunt had been reporting to Lockersley that morning.

"I was impressed by the effervescence and the incredible sangfroid of the man," Cecil told me. "Although I never witnessed him chatting up the queen, I knew from my own experience what a consummate act he could put on." Other sources say that is why the queen "would not hear an ill word spoken about him until his public exposure." Blunt's sheer nerve and ability as an actor is why, Cecil said, "MI5 and the Foreign Office believed for so long in his integrity."[87]

Yet during the war, in Cadogan's office, Cecil also observed the ruthless side of Blunt's character that he described as "ice cold." It left him wondering what sort of man could be so unhuman as to have betrayed so many lives — not to mention sovereign nations — to the Soviets. Blunt's extensive contacts with his Warburg patrons, such as Saxl and Wittkower and the other émigré European art historians, ought to have aroused his compassion for those who had been forced to flee from Hitler. His rifling of the diplomatic secrets of wartime refugee governments of countries like Poland, Latvia, and Czechoslovakia would have enabled him to pass the names of those opposed to Moscow on to the Soviets.

"Anthony showed not a shred of sympathy for the refugees from the occupied Baltic states and Eastern Europe," Cecil told me. With all the bitterness of a betrayed colleague, he added: "We now know that he either exploited their misery in order to make them work for the Russians, or if they would not, then he was bloody well ensuring that Stalin knew who was on his side and who was not."[88]

This information was invaluable when the Soviets rang down the Iron Curtain on Eastern Europe. Speaking from his unique vantage point as the assistant private secretary to the Foreign Office's permanent under secretary, Cecil attaches special importance to the note of December 23, 1943, in Cadogan's diary that says: "4 (pm) Blunt." This, Cecil says, is a telling indication of just how high Blunt had risen in the intelligence hierarchy. "No other representatives of MI5 were received by Cadogan while I was in his office," Cecil assured me, "except the director general, Sir Charles Petrie, and his deputy, Guy Liddell."[89]

# CHAPTER 21

# Thwarting a "Need to Know"

The night of May 10, 1941, saw the most savage German air raid of the war. That night the Luftwaffe tore into the heart of London, and incendiary bombs ignited more than two thousand fires. Three thousand Londoners died or were wounded. It was days before the Fire Brigade brought the fires under control.

Jackie Hewit has vivid memories of that awful night. He was driving home with Burgess and Blunt when a police roadblock stopped them on the road that crosses Hampstead Heath on the outskirts of the city. From this high vantage point, five miles northwest of St. Paul's Cathedral, they had a grandstand view of the raid, with the dome of the cathedral rising above a sea of spreading flames.[1]

The shells fired by the antiaircraft batteries that surrounded London added to the shriek of falling bombs and the clanging bells of distant fire engines. Overhead, golden mushrooms of flak burst in a dark sky crisscrossed by icy-white searchlight beams. There was a terrifying awesomeness to the devastation, but Blunt remained detached. It was as if he were in some Olympian gallery studying the details of one of the demonic *Last Judgments* painted by Hieronymus Bosch.

"The worst attack was the last," Churchill wrote later. The bombing was particularly hurtful for the prime minister because incendiary bombs had consumed his beloved House of Commons.[2]

The up side was that the air-raid sirens in Britain's beleaguered capital did not wail again for months to come. This was a blessed relief to Hewit and the other residents of Bentinck Street who prayed for temporary relief. But Blunt possessed secret knowledge that the blitz had ended. He already knew that Hitler had ordered the Luftwaffe's bombers to airfields in the east of Germany and Poland.

There was only one interpretation to put on this information: The Soviet Union was about to be attacked by Germany. The sources from which the Joint Intelligence Committee had assembled its estimates ranged from diplomatic rumors circulating in the U.S. and other friendly embassies, to MI6 sources, including a reliable Abwehr mole named Paul Thümmel. But it was the code breakers at the GC&CS establishment at Bletchley Park who provided the definitive evidence.[3]

Their decrypts of German military Enigma traffic provided the basis for Churchill's personal message warning Stalin on April 3 that panzer divisions were massing in Poland. The prime minister cited a "trusted agent" to disguise his source for the information. But he was certain that the Soviet leader would "readily appreciate the significance of these facts." Nor was this the only occasion when Stalin, at the prime minister's insistence, received a warning of the accelerating German military buildup on the Russian border.[4]

From mid-May on, the Enigma intercepts revealed Luftwaffe bomber and fighter squadrons transferring from France to the airfields in Poland at a rapid rate. It was a decrypt from this source that disclosed on May 8 the German code name for the operation: Barbarossa. A recently supplied American "Purple" decoding device had enabled Bletchley Park to eavesdrop on the reports radioed to Tokyo by the Japanese ambassador in Berlin. Although Hitler did not trust his Axis pact partner with the actual date, a cable on June 4 from Japan's embassy in Berlin alerted Tokyo that the Germans were ready to strike.[5]

"Hitler has made up his mind to have done with Soviet obstruction and intends to attack her," Britain's Joint Intelligence Committee advised when it met to weigh up the intelligence picture on June 12, 1941. "It remains our opinion that matters are likely to come to a head during the second half of June." The next day Churchill approved Foreign Secretary Anthony Eden's decision to tell the Soviet ambassador of the British estimates of the imminent German offensive — with the offer to send a military mission to Moscow.[6]

That is why the recently published volume of the official history of British intelligence in World War II asserts with finality that there is "no truth in the much-publicized claim that the British authorities made use of the 'Lucy' ring, a Soviet espionage organization, which operated in Switzerland, to forward intelligence to Moscow."[7]

It is now clear that the Soviet espionage network in Britain kept the Kremlin privy to the same intelligence that Churchill and the JIC were sending Moscow. This provided irrefutable evidence of the German mobilization of 180 army divisions, 8,000 tanks, and more than 3,000 aircraft along the Soviet–German border. Moscow should not have been taken by surprise when the invasion began shortly before dawn on June 22, 1941, with a cataclysmic artillery barrage along the 1,800-mile front.

Despite all the official and unofficial warnings Stalin received, he was powerless to prevent the mechanized German tidal wave from engulfing the Red Army in European Russia. But this was no fault of Anthony Blunt and the other members of the so-called Cambridge spy network, who had systematically conspired to betray Britain's most valuable strategic intelligence asset: Ultra.

Admission to the "Ultra secret" — as the wartime Enigma signals intelligence or SIGINT has become known — was jealously guarded and controlled by the MI6 director, Stewart Menzies. The overall direction of the code-breaking operation at the Government Code and Cypher School was under C's fiat. His authority derived from the Foreign Office's responsibility for the "Golf Club & Chess Society," as the Bletchley recruits irreverently referred to their establishment. That so many of the best cryptanalysts were brilliant chess players was a tribute to the judgment of Dillwyn Knox, the veteran World War I code breaker and former King's fellow who remained chief cryptographer until his death in 1943. By then the joke had played out because of the redesignation of GC&CS as Government Communications, Head-quarters — GCHQ, a name still carried by its vastly expanded present-day successor at Cheltenham in the south of England.

The intelligence derived from the decrypts that Knox and his Cambridge eggheads produced in an ever-increasing flow was the fount of Menzies's authority. Hardly a day passed during the war when he did not personally carry the more important code-breaks in a buff cardboard box to the prime minister. Intelligence, especially the horse's mouth kind gathered from German radio traffic, concentrated immense power in C's hands. He was as determined to preserve his control over what Churchill called the "geese who laid the golden eggs and never cackled" from his rivals in the armed services, as he was to protect their secrecy.[8]

Menzies, who had a fetish for code names, had originally ascribed this "absolutely reliable" source of intelligence to a notional German agent code-named "Boniface." Later it became "CX," until the Admiralty replaced its "Hydro" with "Ultra" in June 1941. This had a certain ring of authority that stuck. Soon it was used extensively to apply to all Axis SIGINT. Despite its changing nomenclature, an immutable security governed Ultra. Theoretically, only C had full access to all the decrypts. These he circulated in condensed and paraphrased form to the prime minister, plus about thirty others in Whitehall who were involved with the higher direction of the war and intelligence effort.[9]

Dick White has confirmed that he and his chief, Guy Liddell, were fully aware of Ultra. Blunt was never officially a member of the exclusive circle. But he had no need to be because, from 1941 on, he was working in a unit of B Division that devoted itself to making assessments of enemy military intelligence and therefore received and examined most of the important German Enigma decrypts. This was B(1)b, whose head was a distinguished barrister, who later became a high-court judge, Helenus "Buster" Milmo. He was a Trinity College contemporary of Blunt's; so was another Cambridge barrister, who became a lord justice of appeal, Edward B. Stamp. Two left-wing Oxonians, the lawyer Patrick Day and the philosopher Herbert Hart from New College, completed the formidable analytical brainpower available to the section.[10]

Herbert Hart, who had "unlimited access" to all Ultra derived from decrypts of the Abwehr traffic, married Jenifer Fischer Williams in 1941. A quarter century later, she would admit to MI5 investigators that she had been an underground member of the Communist party while working in the Home Office. She claimed that she gave up her Communist affiliation before her marriage, and that the loyalty of her husband, who later became professor of jurisprudence at Oxford, was beyond reproach. Jenifer Hart was another Bentinck Street regular. So was Patrick Day, whom Blunt in 1945 had invited to take over Tess Mayor's share in the maisonette.[11]

There is evidence that the Soviets had also recruited a separate Soviet spy network from left-wing Oxford intellectuals. After interrogating Mrs. Hart, Wright strongly suspected that it overlapped Blunt's Cambridge agents. At any rate, B(1)b, as the clearing house for Ultra German intelligence-service reports would have been of intense interest to the Soviets. According to Christopher Harmer, then a junior officer in B Division, it was Professor Hart's task to analyze all those decrypts coming in from Bletchley. Who shared Hart's office? Blunt![12]

There is general agreement among wartime MI5 veterans that Ultra was an open secret to Blunt because of the ever-increasing volume of raw intelligence data that flowed through the office he shared with Hart. Until the end of 1941, Blunt fed "Henry" material culled from these decrypted Abwehr ciphers. And at Bletchley, Oliver Strachey digested the raw intelligence into summaries. With the panache worthy of his deceased brother Lytton, he designated them "ISOS" — Intelligence Source Oliver Strachey.

Blunt must have seen ISOSes, realized their importance, and alerted Moscow that Bletchley had broken the cipher keys unlocking the Abwehr and Security Police Enigmas. This breakthrough enabled the British to monitor the communications of the German military-intelligence service, and it produced a flood of data ranging from the reports of secret agents to military-intelligence assessments. ISOS Ultra proved especially important for Moscow because the traffic contained reports from Abwehr units attached to the German armies invading the Soviet Union.[13]

Ultra ISK, so designated to honor Dilly Knox, who had broken the Abwehr Enigma, also provided the British intelligence services with the opportunity to develop what became one of the most successful and secret counterintelligence operations of the whole war. What evolved into the Double-Cross operation had begun shortly after Dunkirk. Finding that the English Channel, Britain's "moat defensive," cut them off from information needed to prepare for Operation Sealion, the Germans took alternative measures to obtain intelligence for their projected invasion of Britain. They tried to infiltrate agents: dropping them by parachute, or landing them from submarines, or introducing them from neutral countries, such as Spain.

"Either we could have treated it as a simple security problem and apprehended and executed every agent that we could lay our hands on," noted one of the British organizers, "or we could have turned round some at least of the agents we caught, let the Germans think that they were still at large and working for Germany." A nine-page draft report on "controlled enemy agents" is unsigned, but it appears to have been written by a senior MI5 officer, conceivably by Masterman himself. It also helps reinforce the contention that Dick White was responsible for the original idea of turning captured German spies into double agents.[14]

The operation proceeded slowly at first because, as the report noted, "we still thought that there might be competing uncontrolled agents who could check up on ourselves [sic] and who might expose them [sic] if they reported anything which was demonstrably untrue." Between the autumn of 1940 and the end of 1941, the report discloses that some twenty-five double agents were recruited after they were captured.[15]

"Very slowly we came to the conclusion we did, in fact, control virtually the whole of the German system in this country," declared the British report. Once that was apparent, "all double-agent activities came to be based in the later stages on this assumption." The program went into high gear in January 1941 when the "Twenty Twenty" Committee — so-called from the pun on the XX symbol for a Double-Cross — was established under the "Wireless Board." It brought together representatives of the two intelligence services, the navy, army, and air force under J. C. Masterman, an Oxford don with extensive personal knowledge of Germany. The choice of this self-deprecating historian was influenced by Dick White, whom Masterman had tutored at Christ Church twenty years before. A tall, finely chiseled figure who had been an outstanding undergraduate athlete, Masterman ran the Double-Cross Committee with the finesse of an Oxford tutorial. He combined a rigorous intellectual authority with tea and buns at the committee's weekly meetings.[16]

Of the six key objectives that Masterman set for the Double-Cross, the most important was to control the German intelligence system in Britain. As the report makes plain, by feeding the Germans "a good deal of true information," they kept the Abwehr satisfied and the Germans sent "less and less spies over." At the same time the British "did at least know what information the Germans had and what they did not."[17]

Apart from the revelations about the "personalities and methods" of the Abwehr, and providing a channel for deception, Double-Cross also produced valuable intelligence of the Germans' operational intentions. This raised alarm that the Germans might be considering bacteriological warfare as a result of information from the double-agent G.W. – a Welsh Abwehr recruit by the name of Gwilym Williams. According to the report,"GW was asked about the water supplies in Wales and how these water supplies might be poisoned."[18]

The report also reveals previously unknown secrets of the Double-Cross operation. For example, the code books issued to the German agents, and updated on a regular basis, brought enormous benefits for the code breakers at Bletchley Park. According to one GC&CS cryptanalyst, "'Garbo's new cipher had saved him nearly six months' work." The report also reveals that some agents, like "Treasure," were kept going "merely to act as a crib to GC&CS, after their value as agents had otherwise ceased."[19]

Other secrets exposed by the report were Plan Midas and Plan Dream. These two deceptions successfully fooled the Germans into contributing £85,000 toward the British war effort. Midas involved the invention of a "wealthy but chicken-hearted Jew who required money lodged in his name in New York," to whom the Germans paid money to fund their agent Wulf Schmidt whom the British called "Tate." In Dream, a "certain Spanish fruit merchant paid over sterling to 'Garbo' in return for pesetas handed over to nominees in Madrid."[20]

While Masterman's committee set guidelines and monitored the information that was fed to the Germans by their turned agents as "chicken-feed," MI5 officers under the direction of the head of B(1)a conducted the actual running of the spies. Its head was Colonel T. A. "Tar" Robertson, a clever graduate of Sandhurst military academy, who had abandoned his army career for counterintelligence work and had been a partner with Liddell in B Division since 1933. Eventually Robertson's group turned some 120 operatives into Double-Cross agents.

Not all the agents were pliant subjects. "As early as 1940 one agent throttled his guard and attempted to escape on a motor bicycle with a canoe lashed behind it," the report reveals. Fortunately he was recaptured before he reached the Channel coast. If he had reached France, the escapee would have blown the whole Double-Cross operation and very possibly the Ultra secret, too. The incident confirmed that handling these controlled enemy agents – or CEAs – demanded considerable intellectual effort, insight into the psychology of human nature, and an unusually high degree of cunning.

"For this reason the case officer was always instructed to live the life of the agent so far as he could; to steep himself in the lifestyle and thoughts of the agent; to make a careful psychological study of him, and to introduce every sort of confirmatory detail which would convince the Germans that the agent was free and working honestly for them."[21]

One of the MI5 officers who demonstrated a supreme ability when it came to handling his double agents was Tomas Harris. He was responsible for managing "Garbo," a Spanish hotel manager named Juan Pujol García, whose fictitious British network helped fool the Germans about the D-Day landings in what turned out to be one of the most important deceptions of the war.

The bizarre names assigned by the British to their Double-Cross agents, such as "Bronx," "Giraffe," "Scruffy," and "Treasure," reflected the equally bizarre range of occupations — in these cases: diplomat's wife, French army officer, Belgian seaman, and émigré Russian vamp — from which the Abwehr recruited its would-be spies. One of the most notorious was "Tricycle," a Yugoslav adventurer by the name of Dusko Popov, who was ordered by the Abwehr in 1941 to spy on Pearl Harbor.

Popov has become the center of a popular myth, largely as a result of his own writings. In these he charged that FBI Director Hoover was so indignant at his flagrant womanizing that he did not take him seriously and so failed to inform the U.S. Navy of the Pearl Harbor espionage target that he had been given by the Germans. Hoover's neglect, it has been argued, contributed to the success of the Japanese attack on December 7, 1941. But in 1984, as the result of renewed accusations, the FBI conducted an exhaustive internal investigation and produced evidence that made it clear that Popov, in his book, misstated the obviousness of the reference to Pearl Harbor — it had been given the same emphasis as the other sixteen items on his brief. Documentary confirmation was found, moreover, that proved Hoover *had* immediately forwarded all of Popov's material to the appropriate U.S. military intelligence agencies in Washington.[22]

The British, however, regarded "Tricycle" and "Garbo" as two of their most reliable double agents. They had used their own initiative and, after first approaching the Germans, came and offered their services to the British and were put in touch with MI6 representatives. The other CEAs had been picked up sneaking into Britain when intensive interrogation weeded them out from legitimate European refugees.

Blunt worked closely with Tar Robertson's case officers running the double agents. So he knew all the secrets of the Double-Cross operation. Another of Blunt's Cambridge friends associated indirectly with Double-Cross was Lord Rothschild, who was running a small section known as B(1)c to counter German sabotage operations. Many of these involved bombs that originated from the same Abwehr operatives who dispatched undercover agents to England from the Iberian peninsula.

According to Hewit, Blunt made frequent trips down to MI5's interrogation center at Wandsworth in the early part of the war. His analytical abilities and languages made Blunt a valued assistant at the debriefing of potential German agents and in deciding who could be turned. During these sessions Blunt also found the opportunity to provide some direct assistance to these Soviet agents. Unfortunately, only after the war was it realized — in both London and Washington — that some key German agents in the Double-Cross operation were really Soviet-run Triple-Cross agents.

One of the "triples" was Natalie Sergueiev. Lily, as she preferred to be known, was a striking auburn-haired French girl whose father was a Russian. Only after the war was it realized that she had been inducted into the Soviet network by her uncle, Nicolay V. Skoblin, aide to her other uncle, former czarist General Yevgeny Miller. Skoblin was a turncoat in the Paris-based White Russian veterans' organization. According to Natalie Grant Wraga, Skoblin's wife, the singer Nadezhda Plevitskaya, was responsible for his becoming an NKVD agent in the network that she bankrolled in the 1937 assassination of General Miller. Skoblin, it seems, also "doubled" as an undercover informer for the Sicherheitsdienst, the German Secret Police, and his SD connections enabled Lily to get herself recruited by the Abwehr under the code name "Tramp." She distinguished herself as the only female spy in German service during World War II who was trained and trusted to operate a clandestine radio.[23]

It was under the code name of "Treasure," however, that Sergueiev achieved her great wartime success. She was recruited into MI5's double-agent operation by Tomas Harris after she contacted the British consulate in Madrid in August 1943. Major Donald Darling of MI9 interrogated Sergueiev before she was flown to London by way of Gibraltar. His job was to filter out Axis infiltrators, and he was suspicious to learn she had worked for the Germans since 1940. He later recalled that it "didn't make sense" that the Abwehr had waited so long to send her on a mission to England. But even before Sergueiev reached London using the code name "Mary Tremaine," she had the sponsorship of Tommy Harris, who, as head of MI5's Iberian unit, had her flown to

England. Despite Darling's reservations about her integrity, Sergueiev was quickly indoctrinated as a member of the Double-Cross operation.[24]

Masterman states that Sergueiev did not belie her British code name of "Treasure." But he concedes that she "proved exceptionally temperamental and troublesome." It later became necessary for MI5 to send an operator to run her transmitter. Not until long afterward did American intelligence sources discover that "Treasure" was really of value to the Soviets, to whom she passed "detailed plans of American-British operations in the closing stages of the war." In 1977, author Richard Deacon discussed Sergueiev with Darling shortly before he died, and the former MI9 officer recalled that he had been uneasy when he interrogated her, especially about her connection with Harris. He "was very surprised indeed that she should already seem to know the man who was to be her case officer in London."[25]

The Deacon interview took place before Blunt's exposure, so Darling did not make the link between Harris and Blunt. But it is obvious now that the detailed knowledge Blunt obtained of Double-Cross could have helped Soviet intelligence infiltrate other triples like Sergueiev into the operation. Postwar CIA investigations of other British wartime anti-Nazi agents recruited from émigré communities in Europe revealed many who had been working for the Soviets.

Undoubtedly the most valuable function Blunt performed during the early part of the war was to keep Moscow posted — through his control officer at the Soviet embassy — about the eavesdropping on the German intelligence services. He was also in the unusual position of being able to update and check this information with British assessments of the German Order of Battle.

This information was passed along through Leo Long, who now occupied a key position in military intelligence. Long, a fellow Communist Apostle, had been cultivated by Blunt at Trinity. He had spent a year, after graduating in 1938, teaching in Frankfurt. In the wartime call-up he enlisted in the Oxford and Bucks Light Infantry, and when the chance came to use his languages to obtain a posting with military intelligence, Long jumped at it. He said that the army was so desperate for German linguists that no one bothered to ask about his politics. It was "purely accidental," Long assured me, that he obtained a commission as a second lieutenant in the army intelligence corps.[26]

Long was also insistent that it was an "equally accidental thing" that he was posted to MI14 in December 1940. He claimed that Blunt did not know that he was working in this sensitive section because he had "lost touch with him when I was called up." So, when they happened to meet in the bombproof basement at the War Office, where the staff of MI14 worked analyzing the steady stream of SIGINT that came in on the chattering banks of teleprinters, Long says that "it was a genuine surprise" to Blunt.[27]

"This was not a preplanned thing, this was an accident," Long stressed. The encounter, he agreed, had taken place in 1941 when Blunt arrived on "lawful business." Just what brought an MI5 officer primarily concerned with foreign diplomatic missions into the army-intelligence office that made the detailed analysis of Oberkommando Wehrmacht dispositions, Long could not say. Nor was he able to recall precisely when this "chance" confrontation with Blunt took place. Yet it was obviously a critical moment in his life, since Blunt "took up where we left off before," proposing that Long pass on to Blunt top-secret German intelligence.

"I can't remember, it was around that time," Long said, pausing for a long time when I asked whether Blunt approached him before the German invasion of Russia. His deliberately evasive answer suggested that this was not the first time that he had been asked to clarify this crucial point. Blunt was always careful to insist that he had not passed anything of value to the Soviets *before* Churchill announced his offer of an alliance to Stalin in the mutual fight against Hitler on June 21, 1941.[28]

"Any man, or state, who fights on against Nazidom will have our aid," the prime minister promised. He had no idea how reassuring this BBC broadcast was for Blunt and his network. They now regarded themselves as "double patriots," conveniently forgetting that up until that day they had been "double traitors." Instead of betraying their country to Stalin, who also happened to be Hitler's ally, they now saw themselves as fighting Hitler for King and Country *and* as proxies of the Soviet Revolution.[29]

Long dismissed the issue of when he betrayed official military secrets to Blunt as a "meaningless question." It did not appear to concern him whether the Soviet Union was an ally or not. Blunt, he said, was aware of his political sympathies when he asked him for "every piece of information that could be useful to the Russians."[30]

Long was so defensive about recalling whether he had begun passing information to Blunt before June 22, 1941, that he gave the clear impression that his treachery predated Britain's alliance with the Soviet Union. He had, it seemed, been similarly elusive when interrogated by MI5 after Blunt had exposed him in 1963. Peter Wright thought that he lacked the class of the other Apostles. He found Long an "officious, fussy man with a face like a motor mechanic's," whose "superior" take-it-or-leave-it account did not tally with Blunt's.[31]

It is not known precisely what Blunt told MI5 about the information he received from his tame subagent in MI14. But according to Long, they met on a weekly basis, usually at lunchtime to avoid suspicion, in a pub in Portman Square, or at a snack bar called Rainer's on the corner of Jermyn Street, which was conveniently midway between the War Office and the MI5 offices in St. James's. He would pass under the table a handwritten report that he described as a "sort of boiled-down version of the weekly departmental appreciation."

It incorporated *all* the intelligence sources available to MI14. But Long was adamant that he did not give Blunt notes of the raw Ultra. His claim that he was "too concerned about protecting the security of the source" sits oddly with his willingness to trust Blunt with some of the most sensitive military intelligence in the whole of the War Office. His repeated assertion that he did not pass on Ultra intelligence because it was "too hazardous" seems to confirm that he began feeding his weekly summary to Blunt in the spring of 1941 when there was justification for fearing that Stalin might leak it to Hitler. He also said that Blunt never showed much interest in his reports; he assumed that Blunt did not know just how extensive the Ultra decrypts were because Blunt never had anything to do with military operations.

"I saw all the German army and air force Ultra," Long admitted. He said he had access to the Abwehr decrypts "only insofar as they related to military operations." In any case, he said, "there was no point in passing that on because he knew MI5 was receiving all the Abwehr material.[32]

"Looking back on it, I suppose I come out of this as a rather weak-kneed and useless sort of individual," Long said, blaming "torn loyalties" for his treachery. "Blunt never tried blackmailing or bullying me, because we shared a deep belief in the Communist cause." He conceded that he had no doubt that his breach of military regulations may have amounted to treason. But he pointed out that it was not only the dedicated Communists like Blunt who felt that not enough intelligence was being given to the Soviets after June 1941.

"I was not one of those officers who said 'Oh God! we cannot give away our secrets to anyone'," Long said, recalling, in an attempt to justify his actions, what he called the "long debate about how much information should be given to the Russians." His wartime colleague in military intelligence, Noël Annan, recalled that Long could be "very dismissive" about anything that did not coincide with his views. This was the same arrogance that he shared with Blunt and other Communists, a belief that their cause justified putting the survival of Britain at risk.

Annan has no sympathy with the argument that Long and Blunt were justified in taking matters into their own hands to provide the intelligence that saved the Soviet Union. This was a governmental function Annan contends. He regards their actions as "monstrous" because, if the Germans had captured information revealing the Ultra secret, history shows that it could have cost the Allies the war.[33]

Furthermore, the Enigma decrypts revealed by July 1941 that the Germans were reading several Soviet codes and ciphers. This was the persuasive argument that C put to the prime minister for not sending Ultra intelligence to the Russians. But Churchill ordered the British Military Mission in Moscow to alert the Soviets to the insecurity of their cipher and pass on military information "provided no risks are run." As a result C established a system for vetting the telegrams drawn up by the three service intelligence directorates for their Soviet opposite numbers and attributing the information to "a most reliable source."[34]

Over the next three years, the amount of Enigma traffic that reached Moscow varied according to the prime minister's concern for providing warning of German offensives and dispositions to help the hard-pressed Red Army stave off defeat. "Has any of this been passed to Joe?" Churchill would note in red ink, nudging the MI6 chief and the services into providing the Soviets with more information. Although a naval Enigma machine was given to the Russian navy in July 1943, the British were understandably reluctant to put their most precious Ultra asset on the line for a surly Soviet ally. Stalin treated all Allied requests for German intelligence with suspicion, and never made good on any of the promised sharing of military information as had the United States.[35]

We know now that it was because of their agents such as Blunt that the Soviets had no need to cooperate. Nor was Leo Long the only member of the Cambridge network who kept Moscow supplied with intelligence from the code breakers at GCHQ. Under interrogation in 1963, Blunt named John Cairncross, who had left the Treasury in 1940 to join the strong Cambridge contingent at Bletchley.

Like Long's, his intellectual communism had fused with his working-class background. Cairncross had left Britain after falling under MI5 suspicion in 1951 as a result of papers containing Treasury information that were found in Burgess's flat and identified by his Trinity College contemporary Sir John Colville. But it was not until 1964, when Arthur Martin confronted him with Blunt's accusation, that Cairncross finally confessed to his wartime spying at GCHQ's Bletchley Park establishment, Station X.

Cairncross was originally assigned to Hut 3 where most of the

Luftwaffe Red traffic was assessed. But because this Enigma contained much army information, Cairncross had free access to the more than 250 translators, analysts, and filing clerks who worked in shifts around the clock, processing the Wehrmacht intercepts in a sprawling group of buildings known collectively as Hut 6. (Bletchley Park had collected so many of the best Cambridge brains—including eleven fellows of King's College, Cambridge—that "Little King's" was the nickname they gave to the wartime establishment.)[36]

Cairncross may not have been a brilliant mathematician like Hugh Alexander, Gordon Welchman of Sidney Sussex, or Alan Turing. But his Trinity College credentials and first-class degree in modern languages were a laissez-passer among the analysts, who included the pick of the prewar crop of the university's classicists, linguists, historians, and mathematicians. It was the twenty fellows from Cambridge who supplied most of the collective brainpower that was responsible for cracking the German Enigma traffic. The gregarious red-haired Cairncross was one of the university family, so to speak, and would have been privy to the confidences shared over meals in the Bletchley canteens and common rooms. He would have had no difficulty keeping abreast of the gossip and passing it on to the Cambridge agents' controller "Henry." Through Cairncross the Soviets would have known the precise details of Dilly Knox's success with the Abwehr cipher, and about the development of the world's first electromechanical computer by Alan Turing. These *Bombes*, which sparked and sputtered through thousands of numerical calculations a minute, were primitive by modern standards, but they dramatically speeded up the laborious task of processing the Enigma decrypts.[37]

No evidence has yet surfaced to suggest that the Soviets obtained the actual secret of these first computers, or of their more elaborate vacuum-tube successor known as Colossus. But Cairncross was well placed to obtain technical data from Turing, whose vulnerability to blackmail because of his homosexuality made him a security risk. These pressures eventually contributed to Turing's suicide in 1954, following his arrest and conviction under Britain's sexual-offenses act.

Turing's left-wing undergraduate activities would also have been played upon by Cairncross. Letters discovered in King's College archives reveal that Turing was not quite the "apolitical person" he has been portrayed to be. As his Cambridge Communist contemporary, Cairncross would have known all about the mathematical genius's involvement in what Turing described to his mother as the "rather communist" student Anti-War Council. He had also joined the November 1933 Armistice Day demonstration (in which Burgess and

Maclean took part), and he had seriously considered making a pilgrimage to Russia that same year.[38]

Cairncross was Moscow's most valuable mole at Station X. Once inside GCHQ, Cairncross confessed to Arthur Martin, he had copied and passed on Ultra documents and data over a period of nearly four years. However, the details of his confession remain locked away in MI5's most secret files.

What we do know is that the Russians considered Cairncross important enough to provide him with the money to purchase a small car. This made it easier for him to make his weekend meetings with "Henry" in London on a regular basis. A car would also serve as a convenient and mobile safe house for debriefing and passing data. So pleased was Moscow Center with the intelligence received from Cairncross that after the decisive battle of Kursk in the spring of 1943, "Henry" relayed a special commendation for the contribution Cairncross had made to the Red Army's decisive victory. Cairncross also admitted supplying the Enigma decrypts that contained the Luftwaffe dispositions. He also told Peter Wright and Arthur Martin in 1964 in Paris and Rome that he was congratulated on supplying the information that enabled the Red Army to destroy hundreds of German planes on the ground.[39]

These incomplete glimpses of Soviet gratitude that Cairncross chose to provide are a measure of the importance and quantity of the intelligence to which he had access between 1940 and 1944. That he occupied a key position of trust in the Ultra operation for such a long period must make Cairncross one of the most important of all the Cambridge spies. Nor, by his own admission, was he the only mole in GCHQ. During meetings with Martin and Wright, Cairncross "burned" four other agents. Their names have not been disclosed because they are still alive. Three turned out, on investigation by MI5, to be suspects, but there was not enough evidence to proceed against them. The fourth, according to Wright, was cleared.

Wright was convinced that Cairncross remains a committed Communist and was fully aware that he was immune from prosecution on the Continent where his debriefing took place. So it is unlikely that he revealed any more than he — and the Soviets — considered necessary to provide a credible cover story after Blunt had named him in his confession. Given the methodical thoroughness of Soviet intelligence operations, it is certain that Moscow Center had other moles in place at Bletchley Park, on whom they could rely for Ultra data. Otherwise Cairncross would not have been permitted to transfer to Section V of MI6 in 1944.

After working briefly on German counterintelligence, Cairncross moved to the Balkans Division. There he capped his golden career as a Soviet mole by reinforcing the efforts of his Cambridge contemporary, James Klugmann, in helping the Communist takeover of Yugoslavia. Despite his open association with the Communist party, Klugmann had managed to join SOE on the strength of his Serbo-Croatian languages. He was assigned to the Balkans Division headquarters in Cairo. His responsibility for communications with the Yugoslav partisans enabled him to help undermine the anti-Communist General Mihailovich and promote the cause of Tito — Josip Broz — as the eventual leader of the resistance to the Germans.[40]

The extent of Cairncross's treachery shocked Arthur Martin. But Cairncross insisted that it was not Blunt who had recruited him as a spy and introduced him to the Soviets, but Klugmann. He said that his principal control officer while he was at GCHQ was Anatoli Gorski, the same Soviet embassy official who ran Blunt, Burgess, Philby, and Maclean. That "Henry" appears to have run all the Cambridge agents suggests that Blunt must have played some behind-the-scenes supervisory role.[41]

Unlike Klugmann, who was an openly identified member of the Communist party, Blunt emerges as something more than a wartime source and a recruiter of other Cambridge agents. He was assigned by "Henry" to run Long as a subagent. Long told me that he had dealt only with Blunt and never met directly with any Russians. Obviously Moscow Center placed a great trust in Blunt, who, the evidence now shows, also managed for a time both Burgess and Straight. That Blunt jealously guarded this authority is clear from what he told MI5 about another Cambridge man whom he discovered making an attempt to recruit Long.[42] Once again, analysis reveals that most of the connections ran through Blunt, who, when under interrogaton, had no hesitation about betraying both Long and Cairncross to prove his full cooperation with his interrogators. He admitted that he had run Long throughout the war. He had even made an unsuccessful effort in 1946 to arrange for Long's transfer into MI5, writing a recommendation and canvassing Dick White's support![43]

Apart from Long and Cairncross, Blunt named five other contemporaries who could have been spies. But as Wright lamented, Blunt "always pointed at those who were either dead, long since retired, or else comfortably out of secret access and danger." In the vernacular of espionage, Blunt succeeded in the classic tactic of offering up sacrificial small fry who had long since become "burnt-out cases."[44]

Blunt himself nearly fell victim to a similar burning by the inadvertence of his Soviet masters in 1941. Ever since he had joined B(1)b in late 1940, one of his standing instructions from "Henry" was to help identify the MI5 moles in Britain's Communist party. He spotted one, code-named "M8" in a routine report on the CPGB that he probably saw in Liddell's office. From a reference to a book that had been written by "M8," Blunt deduced and passed on to his controller that this particular informant was Tom Driberg, then a *Daily Express* journalist.[45]

Driberg was one of MI5's most reliable sources inside the CPGB. He had been run for years by Captain Maxwell Knight, who was conducting countersubversion operations from his headquarters in Dolphin Square. It was his female infiltration agents who had rooted out the Communist spy ring in Woolwich Arsenal in 1937, and obtained the conviction in 1940 of Tyler Kent, an American embassy code clerk, for passing copies of Churchill's secret telegrams to a pro-Hitler group of Russian émigrés.[46]

Knight became suspicious that it had been someone in MI5 who had leaked that Driberg was a secret informer after Driberg had been perfunctorily informed by a Fleet Street "comrade" that he was "no longer a member of the Party." Blunt was even angrier than Driberg. He protested to his Soviet controller over the clumsy handling of the affair that had jeopardized his own position.[47]

There might have been more serious trouble for Blunt if Knight's standing in MI5 at the time had not been so low because of the imprisonment of Benjamin Greene, the former private secretary of Ramsay MacDonald. Greene was released after becoming the focus of a public storm over the misuse of the 18b Defense of the Realm regulation that had enabled the government to lock him up with Nazi sympathizers such as Sir Oswald Mosley. The affair had damaged Knight's credibility within the security service. Thus his reports on Communist infiltration went largely unheeded by Liddell.

"I am sure M never suspected Blunt," Joan Miller, Knight's assistant, confirmed. She wrote nonetheless that it was "rather odd really as he had several protégés at Cambridge before the war and certainly knew all about the Apostles." Could Knight have been as well informed about the Cambridge Comintern as Miller asserted? Given what is now known about Special Branch monitoring of the university Communists in the twenties, it is not impossible.[48]

"Max didn't like Blunt — and he didn't want to work with him," recalled Knight's deputy, John Bingham, later Lord Clanmorris. "He used to say that he wouldn't have that 'bugger' round the section." Liddell's reaction was not so much a recognition of Blunt as a potential spy, but a distrust that too close an association might expose his own vulnerability. And other wartime MI5 officers have confirmed that Blunt always paid close attention to Knight and the infiltration activities he ran semi-independently from B Division: Blunt had a remarkable sense for nosing out and blocking those who threatened him.[49]

Joan Miller also recalls how Knight's memorandum on Communist subversion, "The Comintern Is Not Dead," was rejected flatly by Roger Hollis, the head of F Division, with a dismissive comment that it was "over-theoretical." Hollis's attitude adds to the suspicion that he too was a Soviet mole. But even Guy Liddell opined that "M was allowing his personal distaste for Communism to swamp his judgment." As a result, the Driberg incident passed without a full-scale investigation by Knight's section that might have discovered the truth. It is also certain that Blunt alerted the Soviets that MI5 had installed secret microphones in the CPGB's King Street headquarters.[50]

Yet despite Blunt's warnings, the CPGB failed to appreciate the scale of MI5's surveillance operation. Knight's agents were instrumental in trapping Douglas Springhall, a veteran of the Spanish Civil War and a longtime member of the CPGB Central Committee. He was monitored in 1942 trying to extract information from Olive Sheehan, a Customs and Excise clerk at the Air Ministry. When arrested, she disclosed that Springhall had told her, quoting a source in the security service, that the British were withholding vital intelligence information from the Russians.

In April 1943, MI5 watchers tailed Springhall to a meeting with his source, who turned out to be Ormond Uren, yet another Communist Cambridge graduate. A Hungarian speaker, Uren had transferred as a temporary captain from the Highland Light Infantry to the Hungarian section of SOE in May 1942. At his in camera trial, Uren denied having any direct links with the Soviets. But he confessed to passing details of SOE communications and policy for Eastern Europe to Springhall to demonstrate that he was a "sincere believer in Communism." Uren received a seven-year jail term. Springhall, who was also charged with trying to steal the secret of the newly developed jet engine, was also tried in camera and sentenced to seven years' imprisonment. He then suffered the ultimate indignity of expulsion from the Communist party.[51]

Once again Moscow Center had burned its fingers by hooking its espionage operations too closely to the Communist party. Blunt could only have been wryly amused at the self-congratulatory mood within B Division after the successful convictions of Uren and Springhall. There must have been a certain grim satisfaction in knowing that MI5 had eliminated only one of the minor moles.

Of all the agents in place when the Japanese attacked Pearl Harbor on December 7, 1941, not even Blunt was to advance to a position of such trust and influence as Kim Philby. Reflecting on Philby's astonishing accomplishments during his debriefing with Peter Wright, Blunt attributed his comrade's success to their different outlooks on life: "He only ever had one ambition in life – to be a spy."[52]

After languishing in SOE's backwater for more than a year, Philby jumped at the opportunity to join MI6 to "get away from the Rhododendrons of Beaulieu." As previously argued, there is good reason for believing that Tomas Harris had sinister objectives in canvassing so hard for Philby on the old-boy network. And it is ironic that it was the resolution of a dispute between MI5 and MI6 that gave Philby his chance to insinuate himself into the heart of the latter. The historic rivalry between the two organizations had been thrown into stark relief by the Double-Cross operations. The success of MI5's "controlled enemy agents" depended on information furnished by MI6. Apart from Ultra ISK and the ISOS summaries of Abwehr signal traffic, British MI6 agents operating in Spain and Portugal were important pointers to the targets the Germans wanted to infiltrate. But interservice rivalries died hard – even when fighting a common enemy.[53]

MI5 complained that Menzies and his lieutenants treated their opposite numbers like poor relations: They jealously restricted the flow of intelligence. A particular target of Liddell's was Felix Cowgill, who in January 1941 had succeeded Colonel Valentine Vivian as head of Section V – the MI6 counterespionage operation. Cowgill held steadfastly to the belief that his opposite numbers in B Division were entitled only to such information as pertained to its own internal-security mission. Liddell, however, demanded access to all the information that came across Major Cowgill's desk.

Like Vivian, Cowgill represented the contingent in the counterespionage section of MI6 who had begun their careers in the Indian Police. They owed their loyalty to "Ve-Ve," as they called him, who emphasized his authority as C's deputy chief by signing himself DCSS in a distinctive shade of red ink to distinguish himself from ACSS, his archrival, Colonel Claude Dansey, Menzies's assistant chief of staff. Dansey, who headed the espionage section of MI6, was an incurable snob. He recruited his spies from the more select London clubs. The result was a deep internal division among the professionals in MI6 and the wartime intake of academic amateurs. This gave rise to a good deal of cynical amusement among these younger officers, who included the writers Malcolm Muggeridge and Graham Greene, and their Oxonian academic friends in MI5, Stuart Hampshire and Hugh Trevor-Roper.

The prewar professionals "sometimes regarded the war as a dangerous interruption of the Service" was how Trevor-Roper, Oxford's future regius professor of history, scathingly wrote of his painful wartime experiences in MI6. "There were the metropolitan young gentlemen whose education had been expensive rather than profound, and who were recruited at the bars of White's and Boodle's by Colonel Dansey," the future Lord Dacre complained. They were frequently at odds with "the Indian policemen who were recruited, through the Central Intelligence Bureau in New Delhi, by Colonel Vivian."[54]

While Menzies's two deputies sparred with barbed memos and administrative maneuvers, Cowgill remained the staunchest of Vivian's "Indians." He had been Vivian's assistant in the Directorate of the Central Intelligence Bureau in New Delhi. In February 1939, he had returned as Vivian's deputy in the counterespionage section. Cowgill was an acknowledged expert on the Comintern. His firsthand experience of dealing with Communist subversion in India had taught him the need for security if he was to preserve his new fiefdom from external and internal poachers. For a long time he held out against Liddell's demands.

Only through the tactful intervention of Dick White, Liddell's diplomatic deputy, was a resolution reached in the bitter territorial dispute between MI5 and MI6. The compromise proposed in the autumn of 1941 had the blessing of Sir David Petrie, who had been brought out of retirement to head MI5, an appointment that helped smooth Cowgill's ruffled pride. He had been plucked from the Calcutta Special Branch ten years earlier and made Petrie's assistant when Petrie was director of the Central Intelligence Bureau of India. Thus, a deal was struck in which Brooman-White transferred from MI5's Spanish desk to head a separate Iberian group in Section V. His role was to liaise with Tomas Harris, his former deputy, who became his opposite number in B Division. Harris then worked assiduously to get Philby into MI6.

Cowgill confirmed to me that Philby was first recommended for a post in the Iberian group "via Harris and Brooman-White." He said Harris claimed to have known Philby in Spain. Since Section V was given a "No Trace" background slip from the MI5 Registry files, an approving chat with Vivian, who had known Philby's father in India, was sufficient to get him the job.[55]

Cowgill first encountered Philby when he arrived at Section V's wartime headquarters at Glenalmond, one of a pair of neighboring country houses on Lord Verulam's estate near St. Albans, twenty miles north of London. His first impressions of Philby were favorable. The new recruit was efficient and effective. He did not complain about putting in long hours. But Cowgill was a stickler for enforcing the "need to know" principle. He suspects that by working late, Philby was able to flout office security rules by familiarizing himself—and his Soviet controller—with the contents of the Central Registry files of MI6, which were located in offices adjacent to those of Section V, in the house known as Praewood.

Philby later paid a backhanded tribute to Cowgill's "fiendish capacity for work." Mrs. Cowgill, who was also working as a temporary staff member, "carding and filing" in the Registry, remembers how she used to organize late suppers at their flat for them both. Philby, however, spitefully dismissed his wartime superior's "slender" intellectual endowment, his lack of imagination, and his possessiveness, which Philby claimed made Section V "like a hedgehog position." When I brought up Philby's charges twenty years later, Cowgill, an intelligent and careful commentator, suggested that his former assistant's nastiness resulted from Section V's emphasis on "need to know."[56]

Cowgill was also an authoritarian who despised the office politics and intrigues that were a daily fact of life in the fractious MI6. On the other hand, Philby, the *apparatchik*, loved them and cunningly exploited the conflicting rivalries. He prided himself on being one of the few people who dared to beard Dansey in his office, thereby disarming him of his weapon of choice: "the barbed little memo, which created a maximum of resentment to no obvious purpose." He skillfully played off the assistant chief's hatred of the "timorous" Vivian, while pretending to side with Cowgill and the Indian policemen against the amateurs. He picked his sides carefully, no doubt aware that some of his Oxbridge contemporaries knew too much about his undergraduate communism. Many years later, Trevor-Roper would acknowledge that he "knew of Philby's Communist past." But he insisted that it "never occurred to me, at that time, to hold it against him" because "our superiors were lunatic in their anti-Communism."[57]

That Trevor-Roper did not expose Philby owes as much to his own hostility to MI6 as an institution as to his failure to discern from Philby's "congenial" conversation that he adhered to a quietly fanatical brand of communism. Malcolm Muggeridge, on the other hand, purged of communism in Moscow during the late twenties, took it for granted that Philby was "vaguely leftist." But even he records that he was taken aback when Philby told him that "Goebbels was someone he felt he could have worked with." This he found unsettling. It was, he said, evidence of his colleague's attraction for buccaneering, womanizing, and violence. He believes it to be the explanation for Philby's "otherwise unaccountable love for Burgess and tolerance of his unlovely ways."[58]

While Philby was playing up to Cowgill, he smugly admitted he had also "cultivated MI5 assiduously." His own account leaves no doubt that he succeeded in charming his principal target: Guy Liddell. In contrast to his scathing remarks about Cowgill, Philby praised the "subtle and reflective mind" of the head of B Division. He described Liddell as the "ideal senior officer for a young man to learn from." Philby seems to be congratulating himself on luring the "deceptively ruminative" Liddell into a trap already baited by Blunt and Harris. Nor could he resist gloating over the success of his deception. He sardonically declared how he had "rejoiced at Liddell's discomfiture" at losing the MI5 directorship in 1946 to Sir Percy Sillitoe, a senior officer in the police force, and a person the recently installed Labour Cabinet considered to be "safer."[59]

Philby had good reason to gloat. Once he had won the confidence and trust of the director of counterintelligence, both MI5 and MI6 were wide open to Soviet infiltration. Hewit's testimony has made it plain that Liddell was not merely a casual guest in the eclectic social circle that treated Bentinck Street and Chesterfield Gardens as a saloon bar for off-duty intelligence officers. Liddell's weekly forays to Chelsea and to the London music halls in the company of Hewit and Burgess — whom he had supposedly banned from the office — suggest that he derived emotional as well as intellectual stimulation from the "homosocial" entourage.

Liddell's former security-service colleagues to a man — and a woman — fiercely reject any suggestion that Liddell might have been trapped by homosexual tendencies into becoming a traitor. What cannot be denied, however, is that he made himself very vulnerable by seeking solace in the male companionship to be found at Bentinck Street. The fact is that Liddell was suffering deep emotional scars caused by the desertion before the war, by his wife, Calypso, for her American half brother. The ensuing battle for custody of their children, which resulted in the dissolution of their marriage in 1943, is enough to give pause to a professional counterintelligence officer.[60]

For the soon-to-be-divorced head of an operational division of the British secret service to mix socially with a homosexual coterie was not only curious, it ran serious risk of misinterpretation. That Liddell sought the company of Burgess and Hewit on a weekly basis for several years gives ground for suspecting that something more than a "love of the music hall" motivated his choice of off-duty companions. The valid suspicion remains that Liddell placed himself in a situation in which he could be compromised.[61]

American intelligence analysts familiar with the long history of Soviet sexual "honeytraps" point out that Moscow Center would not have ignored the chance to exploit the inclination shown by Liddell for homosexual company. These intelligence experts, who have no need to defend a colleague's reputation, believe that Blunt exploited Liddell's friendship to compromise him. The experts also point out that Liddell had chosen to ignore — if he had ever asked about — the evidence of Blunt's intellectual adherence to Marxism. Moreover, as a frequent visitor to the Bentinck Street ménage, he could not have missed the left-wing tilt of so many of Blunt's friends any more than he could have been ignorant of their overt homosexuality.

The Liddell case has an unsatisfactory conclusion for the historian. There are no documents available showing what Liddell's response was when it became known in 1951 that Burgess and Maclean were Soviet agents. (As discussed earlier, we know that MI5 did not have a significant research and analysis capability at the time.) All we have for the record are statements by Liddell's faithful colleagues that his failings were those of "incautious" friendship and "unfortunate" wartime association with homosexuals. But the logic of the situation, as the historian charts it, leads to the conclusion that Liddell's associates could say nothing else. To do so would have put their own actions and decisions at risk. Was this logic sound?

I flew to Washington in 1987 with the documents I had discovered on the matter to consult with a former senior member of American counterintelligence, who was personally aware of the events related above. I put my question to him. He paused in deep reflection before he answered. "I'd prefer not to comment on this," he said. "I know what I know, and I see no point in opening old wounds that would only benefit the KGB and hurt my friends."[62]

# CHAPTER 22

# "Recommended to the Service"

As the year 1942 drew to a close, the tides of war were changing in favor of the Allied cause. The American navy had won the crucial battle for the control of the Pacific at Midway in June. The British Eighth Army soundly defeated Rommel that October in the battle of El Alamein and, with the help of the newly arrived Americans, was forcing the Germans to begin their retreat from North Africa. In November, the Red Army launched its counteroffensive against Stalingrad, marking the beginning of the end for Germany's hopes to win the war.

While the average infantryman fighting from hill to hill might not have had an appreciation of the new direction the war was taking, the political leaders in the capitals of the world were aware of what was happening. So were Blunt, Philby, and Burgess. It was time to start planning for the future, for what would happen after the war ended.

In his spare time, when he was not engaged in his program of opening courier bags, Anthony Blunt was working in his chosen field. Already a London University reader in the history of art, he had been made deputy director of the Courtauld Institute and was preparing the first catalog of the drawings in the royal collection at Windsor Castle.

Guy Burgess was back at the BBC as a successful talk-show producer, and was trying to work his way upward in the monopoly that controlled all broadcasting in Great Britain.

Kim Philby was to stay on doing what he did best: intelligence. With Liddell neutralized, Philby had already enhanced his reputation as an effective administrator by establishing a close liaison with MI5 while serving as head of the section running for Iberian operations at MI6.

Philby's trick was "letting others assume they understood quite well what he thought or intended," said Malcolm Muggeridge, who encountered him during his wartime service in MI6. "He gave the impression always that he was a man of integrity" was how another of his SOE colleagues described him. "A man who could be trusted." Philby's ability to elicit the confidence of his superiors, his mastery of detail, and the cool skill he displayed at interdepartmental meetings impressed not only Cowgill but Valentine Vivian, C's vice-chief, and Menzies himself.[1]

Philby prided himself on his ability "to sniff the breezes of office politics" and play on the conflicting personalities and rivalries within

MI6. He maneuvered against Cowgill in 1943 by discreetly mobilizing the Section V staff in favor of moving back to London from their irksome isolation in St. Albans. Their new headquarters would be in Ryder Street, just two minutes from MI5, thereby achieving the "propinquity" between the two operations so long desired by Sir David Petrie and politely resisted by Cowgill and Menzies.[2]

Section V's return to London also made it more convenient for direct access to Blunt who was still running the operation that rifled the diplomatic pouches leaving London. Philby's connection with this highly successful operation is evident from his revelation that the Soviet embassy was the only foreign government immune to the activities of Blunt's team. This was not simply because Russian paranoia led to the employment of two couriers to guard their diplomatic pouches, but because of a rumor — perhaps put about by Blunt himself — that the diplomatic bags of the Kremlin were booby-trapped with "bombs designed to obliterate the inquisitive."[3]

What Philby does not admit is that the move of Section V back to London, done against the better judgment of Cowgill, enabled Philby to meet with his Soviet controller more easily. Just as he was anxious to impress his superiors in MI6, Philby was even more concerned to prove to Moscow Center his ability as an agent. The amount of sensitive intelligence to which he had access was steadily increasing; all was relayed rapidly to Moscow via "Henry."

To serve two masters Philby had to work long hours. This willingness to burn the midnight oil impressed Cowgill as much as the efficient management Philby brought to running the counterintelligence activities of the Iberian unit. Philby had come to the attention of Menzies by reporting to the Joint Intelligence Committee, in June 1942, the clues he unearthed in the Abwehr Ultra that revealed a German scheme to monitor the Strait of Gibraltar with undersea sonar devices. Thanks to Philby, the potential threat to Operation Torch was thwarted before the November Anglo-American landings in North Africa. As a result, his responsibilities were extended to include counterintelligence activities in North Africa and Italy.

When Cowgill visited the United States a short time later, he assigned Philby to deputize for him. This was a sign to Philby's colleagues that he was on the ladder for rapid promotion. So too was his membership in the Athenaeum, the club preferred by bishops and the upper echelon of Whitehall civil servants. His rise in the MI6 hierarchy enabled Philby to be more than a simple conduit of information for the Soviets. He was now also able to act as an "agent of influence," taking decisions that worked in favor of Moscow rather than the other Allies. In the summer of 1943, for instance, he used his authority to block the circulation of a report that argued, from clues in the Abwehr Ultra, that some German army officers were preparing to put out peace feelers to Churchill and Roosevelt. It was not in the interests of the Soviet Union to encourage a separate peace that would leave Russia at the mercy of Hitler.

Philby's rise in MI6, fortuitously for the Soviets, coincided with the arrival in London of the first echelons of American intelligence officers. These were the men in General William O. "Wild Bill" Donovan's Office of Strategic Services (OSS). Philby was presented the opportunity he was waiting for: to secure his reputation with Washington. At the end of 1943, he succeeded by staking his reputation on the judgment of Allen Dulles, the future CIA chief, who in 1943 was the OSS representative in Switzerland. This put him into conflict with C's pompous deputy, Claude Dansey, who had dismissed as too obvious a plant the suitcase full of documents that Dulles said had come from the Foreign Ministry in Berlin. After Dansey's haughty rejection, Philby checked the documents with the cryptanalysts at Bletchley who compared them to the intercepted messages sent by the German military attaché in Tokyo. They quickly and enthusiastically confirmed the authenticity of the Dulles haul — much to the chagrin of Dansey who had regarded the Americans as amateurs poaching on his Swiss preserve.[4]

Since June 1942, when the OSS established its X-2 counterintelligence operation under James R. "Jimmy" Murphy, Donovan's former assistant, the Americans had been trying to negotiate an exchange of information and personnel with MI6 and MI5. The British — especially Liddell, Dansey, and Menzies — resisted. They feared that the Americans would commandeer their Ultra-based empire, so they stalled by suggesting that the admission of untutored and unsuitable OSS amateurs would risk upsetting the security of counterintelligence operations.

The British went out of their way to impress the Americans with how MI5 and MI6 handpicked their officers by a ritual steeped in the social mystique of England's old-boy network. According to a contemporary report prepared for the OSS, the process by which English gentlemen obtained posts in the secret service had more in common with raising Thoroughbred racehorses than with clandestine operations.

The Americans were told that His Majesty's Secret Service could not risk the wrong kind of chap making an application. Suitable candidates had to be "initially recommended to the service by friends already in the service or by particular alumni of the service designated for this purpose because of their experience in the types required and because of their appropriate situation in life." This was the job of former MI6 and MI5 officers who acted as talent scouts "in the British universities." In practice the dominance of Oxford and Cambridge produced "young men with unusual qualifications of language and travel."[5]

It was explained to the OSS how candidates were observed "over a long period of time, examining their intellectual abilities, their social stabilities, and their loyalty." Nothing so vulgar as a direct approach was ever made by MI6 spotters for "security reasons." Recommended candidates were therefore "generally contacted by recruiting officers not overtly connected with the British services themselves." MI6 admitted that it sometimes recruited an older candidate from "the ranks of men already in another branch of government service whose abilities and loyalties have been tested." But the regular army contributed "almost not at all to recruitment."[6]

Further evidence of the degree to which Britain's ruling establishment deluded itself, even at the height of the war, that family connections and the old-school tie could guarantee national security emerged in a confidential report by the War Cabinet's panel that investigated staff "Engaged on Secret Work." This recommended that temporary staff had to be vetted by MI5, stressing the "need for secrecy in dealings with the Security Service." Established civil servants were "rarely put under any sort of scrutiny." Nor should they be submitted to such indignities. Only if they were "transferred to appointments involving MOST SECRET work" was a vetting necessary, and then due weight would be given to "personal recommendations from persons whose judgment can be relied on and who have close acquaintance with the candidate."[7]

Liddell passed these War Cabinet recommendations to the American embassy in June 1942.

There is a bitter irony that the Soviet intelligence service had already exploited the old-boy network in which the British placed so much trust. The MI6 objections, moreover, that the OSS lacked the system they considered so essential to ensuring the security of a secret service, were also unfounded. The majority of the senior officers in the OSS were self-selecting Ivy Leaguers like Donovan. A large number were graduates of Yale, whose collegiate system had traditionally maintained close links with Cambridge, while Harvard men considered themselves spiritually closer to Oxford.

The soft-spoken X-2 chief, Murphy, did not hail from either Yale or Harvard. But he was instrumental — after some high-level lobbying on Downing Street by Donovan — in negotiating a joint operating agreement with MI6 in May 1943. It took six more months before the

OSS reached a similar arrangement with MI5, but by early summer the first contingent of four American officers, and four secretaries, arrived at the St. Albans headquarters of MI6's Section V. (The original group was to expand within two years to more than three hundred European-based counterintelligence officers.)

A quarter of a century later, Philby, writing under the disparaging eye of the KGB in Moscow, described the American arrivals as a "notably bewildered group." But neither he nor his Soviet masters at the time underestimated the implication of the OSS involvement.

Somewhat to Philby's surprise, Cowgill continued to hold back information from the professionals in the FBI, even though Section V indoctrinated the OSS officers, who were, in the words of one of them, "a bunch of ignorant bums" compared with Hoover's men. The quip was ascribed to Norman Holmes Pearson, one of the four OSS men assigned to MI6. The remark would have been delivered with the engaging good humor of this poet and English-literature lecturer from Yale who would also make a joke about belonging to an organization with an "Oh So Social" acronym.

Whatever sour twist Philby found it convenient to give Pearson in his book, the X-2 wartime reports show that Pearson quickly struck up a close working relationship with Cowgill. Section V issued new red stamps marked TOP SECRET to replace the MOST SECRET British classification. Full access was given to Pearson's liaison team, who were working on the MI6 agent operations, and ISOS and ISK Ultra material. Pearson reassured Philby they had "come to school." But in Pearson's appointments diary the name "Philbee" appears too frequently to be an accidental misspelling. Pearson seems to have enjoyed mischievously mocking the stuffed-shirt earnestness displayed by the rising young deputy head of Section V. His relationship with Cowgill, whose downfall Philby was instrumental in engineering, was altogether more rewarding.[8]

"I was always able to talk to you easily and directly, without the flourishes of a gavotte which other tunes demanded" was how Pearson paid tribute to the "mutual respect" that developed into close friendship between the Yale academic and the former Indian policeman. During our discussions, Cowgill recalled for me the twinkling eyes and warm manner of the "professor," whose somewhat birdlike appearance was accentuated by a limp caused by tuberculosis of the hip. While not himself a Rhodes scholar, though many of his British colleagues took it for granted that he had been one, Pearson had studied at Oxford. So even when promoted to head up the X-2 organization in London, with the code name "Saint," Pearson carefully underplayed his role as the affable Yankee intruder. His diary suggests that the chefs at Prunier's and the Connaught, whose virtuosity with meager wartime rationing only an American officer's pay could afford, helped Pearson win over the senior officers of MI6 and MI5.[9]

Pearson was also admitted to the innermost secrets of Double-Cross as an ex-officio member of the Twenty Committee. Masterman also accorded the head of X-2 the unusual privilege of a desk in his office in MI5 headquarters on St. James's. Pearson's hip ailment precluded him from making the two-minute bicycle ride to Ryder Street, where his office, 22-A, was just down the corridor from Philby's.[10]

The OSS obtained the priceless "fruits of many decades of counter-espionage experience," Pearson would report later. "Furthermore, the British offered to train American personnel in the techniques essential to the proper use of all categories of their records." Within two years, the OSS "gained full access to the experience and extensive files of both the internal and external experience of the British counter-espionage services" and was "treated as an independent equal."[11]

Pearson could take much credit for that success. As the astute manager of the Anglo-American wartime counterintelligence liaison, he showed MI5 and MI6 how to submerge suspicions and rival interests in a "great adventure" of counterintelligence cooperation that provided the United States with the training and data that helped lay the foundation for the postwar CIA.

It was one of Pearson's former students at Yale who joined the X-2 team at Ryder Street and became the leading theorist of American counter-intelligence strategy. James Angleton, an English-literature graduate of Yale and an accomplished poet, had been drafted into the army from Harvard Law School in the spring of 1942. Looking for a military career that would stimulate his intellect, he volunteered for the OSS, where his outstanding performance at the OSS schools and training course impressed Murphy. He assigned Angleton the Italian desk in his Washington headquarters on the strength of the young man's experience of Italy, where his father had been vice-president of the National Cash Register (NCR) subsidiary in Rome. He joined the X-2 team in MI6 after the agreement on full cooperation with the British in 1943.

Pearson put the rake-thin young American in charge of Italian affairs for X-2. A brooding theoretician, Angleton had already become intrigued by the problems of counterespionage and security. He amazed his British colleagues by moving an army cot into his Ryder Street office, the better to concentrate on developing his belief that counterintelligence could be made into a science. The key, he concluded from close analysis of Ultra's application in MI6 operations, was penetration — a conviction reinforced by his future experiences on the ground as OSS chief in Italy.[12]

It became a central axiom of Angleton's theory that penetration was essential to achieve the manipulation necessary to deceive an enemy by forcing him into an unreal world. When Angleton became the CIA's chief of the counterintelligence staff in 1954, he finally had the chance to test his theories of deception and penetration in a global contest with the KGB at the height of the Cold War. He was fully cognizant that obsessive suspicion was one of the dangers inherent in his theories. The constant testing and analysis necessary to guard against enemy infiltrations of false information, or suborning, could lead the contestants, as Angleton himself once graphically acknowledged, into "a wilderness of mirrors."[13]

We can see from the X-2 reports how Angleton's analysis of counterintelligence, based on Britain's Double-Cross operations against the Germans, shaped his perceptions of the Soviets. Nor could he ever forget in later years the humiliation of having been duped by Philby, his wartime colleague at Ryder Street. The true dimensions of the deception that Philby helped the Soviets work against the Americans at the height of the Cold War has never been discussed publicly. But the revelations contained in the epilogue of this book explain why Angleton would never underestimate the Soviet talent for infiltration. His experience in wartime Britain taught him how vulnerable even the most supposedly secure counterintelligence service is to clandestine penetration.

That was the lesson Angleton would draw from the British failure to realize that their own secret service might be subject to penetration. He found this especially ironic, given the British achievement in completely taking over and controlling the Abwehr's network in England. A recently discovered X-2 report on the "Theory of Counter Espionage," which reflects Angleton's thinking even if he was not the author, declared that the "ideal situation had come close to being achieved" by the wartime British secret service. The "incalculable benefits" of the "Most Secret Source material" — principally Ultra — had been the key "to the innermost recesses of the enemy's espionage system [that] enabled the British (and later the Americans who shared the secret) not only to obtain a constant and increasing flow of up-to-date-information on the organization of German intelligence and its officials, but also to keep track of agent activities in the United Kingdom, western Europe, and to some extent, indeed throughout the world." According to the report, whose author was clearly in a position to know: "Thousands of individuals became known and their movements, actions, and even thoughts were recorded." By virtue of Ultra, "Counter Espionage operations could often be conducted with great confidence, and with the assurance that the enemy was being fooled."[14]

Why, when they had triumphantly penetrated the German intelligence operation, did the British secret service, or even X-2's cerebral theorist Angleton, not conceive of the possibility that MI5 or MI6 might themselves be similarly fooled? The answer lies in the trap into which the British had fallen: overconfidence at their own success. A contributory factor was the concentration of all counterintelligence resources on defeating the Axis, and the assumption that the Soviet threat had been eliminated by the fifty-year Anglo-Soviet treaty of friendship and alliance in which both nations had pledged not to interfere in the other's internal affairs.

It can be argued that Liddell, as director of MI5's counterespionage division, should have been more skeptical. He should have known that it would take more than a scrap of paper to turn the devious old Bolshevik enemy into a trustworthy ally despite the campaign for Britain to open a "second front" in Europe to relieve the strain on the Red Army. Nor should it be forgotten that Liddell was making frequent appearances at Bentinck Street, as well as spending weekly nights out with the persuasive Burgess, who never concealed his admiration for the Soviet Union.

Burgess had been among the first of the BBC producers to submit proposals for shows on Russian themes. Shortly after the German invasion, the BBC and the Foreign Office were still debating whether it was safe to broadcast the "Internationale." But Burgess put in a full raft of suggested topics.

The BBC archives reveal that after consulting John Strachey and Professor Bernal, Burgess presented his suggestions, "put down hastily, as the problem is urgent," he reminded his superiors. He bubbled over with ideas that displayed the astonishing depth of his knowledge of Russian literature, from "Lenin's favorite passage" in *War and Peace* to Ilya Ehrenberg and the satires of Zoshchenko. He urged the BBC to reverse the broadcast ban on Professor Haldane so that he could talk about Soviet science. He proposed Christopher Hill, a Marxist who was a fellow of All Souls, as the "best authority in England" to give talks on Russian history.[15]

When it came to speaking about art, Burgess put forward the names of Dr. Kligender and Dr. Blunt. "Neither are Communists," he emphasized for the benefit of the head of Talks. This was knowingly disingenuous. Kligender was the émigré German art historian whose theories had shaped Blunt's own Marxist aesthetic interpretations. But Burgess knew that before anyone could sit before a BBC microphone during the war, he had to receive MI5 clearance. It was the producer's responsibility to find out whether or not this had been given.

This was especially significant in regard to Hill. Burgess identified him as a Communist in an official BBC communication. The future master of Balliol College, Oxford, has claimed that he did not tell anyone that he was a member of the Communist party. He says he just assumed the authorities must have known of his left-wing views when he joined the Field Security Police before transferring to SOE in 1940. Subsequently, Hill was appointed to the Northern Department of the Foreign Office, where he had access to sensitive papers on relations with the Soviet Union. He was obviously in a position to influence crucial policy decisions. Hill, who made his reputation as a Marxist academic, has declined to say whether he was a secret or open Communist. He has also strenuously denied he ever infringed the Official Secrets Act, or found a conflict of interest between his Marxist beliefs and his wartime government work.[16]

That such an open Marxist, albeit a distinguished Oxford historian, could be recruited for secret government work on the old-boy recommendation of Sir Robert Lindsay, then master of Balliol, is a reflection of a serious lapse by MI5. That Burgess mentioned Hill as a Communist in 1941 suggests that MI5 must also have known, otherwise Burgess would not have alerted the BBC. Nor would he have put Hill's name forward to the BBC Talks Department if he had had any doubt that clearance could be easily arranged through his MI5 contact. The Oxbridge Communist network had, it appears, a direct line to someone inside MI5 other than Blunt (who, by 1941, was no longer in C Division) able to deal with vetting Registry files.

A clue to where the other moles might have tunneled in the apparatus emerges in the dismissive treatment of Max Knight's memorandum on the Comintern's future threat. Knight was one of the few members of B Division who had not dropped his guard. He continued to warn of undiminished Soviet subversion. But his voice was often drowned out by comments from F Division, where Roger Hollis and his assistants were responsible for assessing the threat from the Communist party. It is now evident that Hollis arrived at his decisions on the advice of two assistants whose own Marxism meant that they may have been far from disinterested parties.

One was Roger Fulford, Hollis's longtime college friend, who had also been associated with the London "homintern" network of which Burgess was a member. Another was Kemball Johnston, a Trinity contemporary of Blunt's. According to his eldest son Johnston hated the Establishment throughout his life. "You could not get much further left than Father," he said. This view was confirmed by Johnston's Trinity roommate, Peter Fairbairn, whose lifelong friendship with Johnston began at Summerfields prep school and continued through Eton, where Johnston — a scholar — refused to join the OTC. His antiestablishment rebelliousness made him a member, with John Lehmann, of the so-called "Second Bolshy Election" at Britain's most famous school — the first was fomented by Cyril Connolly and Eric Blair (George Orwell). Like Orwell, Johnston was a Utopian schoolboy socialist but by the time he came to Cambridge he was never openly political and devoted his enthusiasms to playing tennis. It was after his confrontation with Hitlerism in Germany in 1934 that he became sympathetic to Marxism, even though his daughter told me that he was never a member of the Communist party and that he became thoroughly disillusioned with the Soviet Union long before the end of his life. Johnston worked for BBC Scotland before becoming a barrister who specialized in commercial law. Like Goronwy Rees and many other Marxist sympathizers, Johnston joined the Territorial Army as a personal commitment against the British government's deal with Hitler at Munich in 1938. But illness kept him from being sent to France when war broke out, and he missed Dunkirk. In September 1940, Kenneth Younger, an old Etonian contemporary, who was in B(1)a, recommended him for an MI5 posting. He became an assistant to Hollis in F Division, where he took part in counterintelligence operations against German agents who landed in East Anglia and a chef of the Dorchester Hotel who was suspected of being a spy. It was during his wartime service with MI5 that he grew close to Burgess and Blunt, who became godfathers to Johnston's second son: Guy Anthony.

According to Johnston's daughter (a Cambridge historian), Blunt would later tell her father that he had indeed considered him at one time a potential Soviet recruit. But she says that her father was too independent-minded to have ever been a witting spy. It may be that Blunt and Burgess obtained information from him unwittingly. In the light of the suspicions of disloyalty that were later to surround Roger Hollis, it is significant that other MI5 officers have confirmed to me that Johnston was not the only member of F Division who was known to have Marxist sympathies long before the Soviet Union became Britain's ally.

This surprising MI5 tolerance of Marxists had its limits, however. The risk of being caught and charged with espionage was greatest to anyone who had direct links to the Communist party. That was because

Knight was as ardent a pursuer of Communist subversion as of German fifth columnists. He also had the advantage of running a semi-independent network, which, after the Driberg incident, kept its secrets more closely within its Dolphin Square headquarters. Blunt, whose cover was nearly blown by the careless use of information he obtained from Knight's reports, would have advised his Soviet controller of the need to steer clear of any connection with the deeply infiltrated Communist party. That is why it is most unlikely that the SOE officer, Captain Ormond Uren, who was arrested in June 1943, along with the Communist party National Organizer, Douglas Springhall, for offenses under the Official Secrets Act, had anything to do with Blunt's agents even though Uren happened to be another Cambridge graduate.[17]

The Uren/Springhall espionage case provided a warning jolt. Menzies was sufficiently concerned to order Vivian, his assistant chief and adviser on security, to conduct an investigation to see if anyone in MI6 had party connections.

Vivian made his report just about two months after Uren's conviction. His conclusions were sufficiently unsettling to send Menzies hurrying in to see the permanent under secretary of the Foreign Office.

Friday, August 13, 1943, was not a good day for Lord Cadogan, according to his terse diary entry: "'C' about Communists in his organization." The line, which was carefully excised from the edited version of the diaries approved by the Cabinet Office in 1971, confirms that even as the marriage with the American OSS was being consummated, Menzies knew of Communist penetration.[18]

In the absence of Vivian's report, which is still classified Secret, it is impossible to be certain about the extent of the damage Vivian discovered. However, Air Vice-Marshal Sir James Easton, who succeeded Vivian as C's assistant in 1949, but who was not in MI6 at the time, believes that David Footman became a prime suspect. Author Anthony Cave Brown quotes him as saying that Menzies never revealed why or when he came to suspect Footman, who had been the resident Soviet expert in the Political Section of MI6 since 1935.[19]

"C had a bee in his bonnet about Footman," Easton recalled. He said that "even almost a decade later, whenever we were discussing possible security risks, C would state: 'And don't forget to see to it that Footman's name is on the list.'" If Footman was a suspect in Vivian's 1943 investigation, why, it seems pertinent to ask, was he permitted to remain in MI6 until nearly ten years later?[20]

The answer appears to be that Vivian's investigation was neither as thorough nor as far-reaching as Cadogan's diary entry has led others to believe. Cowgill cannot even remember any major inquiry or internal flap about security in 1943. As the MI6 counterespionage chief, he would certainly have known if any senior officer was under investigation. That not even the slightest whisper of suspicion was raised toward Philby leads Cowgill to suppose that C must have been referring to a relatively low-level inquiry that led to one dismissal in Section V. This was of a secretarial-grade assistant, whose schoolmaster husband turned up as a member of the Scottish Communist party on MI5 Registry records.[21]

What is clear is that the Uren/Springhall espionage case, and the investigation that resulted in the dismissal of a secretary, should have reminded the directors of both MI5 and MI6 of the continuing threat of subversion. If the 1943 investigation put Philby and Blunt on their guard, it also bolstered their confidence. Vivian's failure to identify any major penetration would only have served to reinforce Menzies's conviction that the old-boy network had once again proved its value by keeping Communists out of the officer ranks of MI5 and MI6. A combination of relief, complacency, and loyalty implicit in family connections made it impossible for anyone to conceive that such products of the system as Blunt and Philby might be untrustworthy.

Yet a very different attitude prevailed when it came to foreigners. Distrust and suspicion were the reflexive responses of the British security-service officer — even to close allies, as the American OSS contingent had discovered in 1943. The French were to be even more resolutely cold-shouldered the following year when concerns for security heightened as the Allied invasion of France drew near. In April 1943, the prime minister learned that members of the French National Committee, some of them known to be Communists, were on their way to England to work with the Allies on intelligence preparations for the landing in the south of France. He was enraged. Menzies and Petrie went to Downing Street and reiterated for Churchill the dangers demonstrated by the Uren/Springhall espionage case. They evidently found it expedient to exaggerate the thoroughness and expedition with which they were pursuing other Communist suspects in Whitehall, because an urgent telegram was fired off from Downing Street to the British representative in Algiers.

"I suppose you realize that we are weeding remorselessly every single known Communist from our secret organizations," the prime minister curtly told Duff Cooper. "We did this after having to sentence two quite high-grade people to long terms of penal servitude for their betrayal, in accordance with the Communist faith, of important military secrets. If therefore the French Committee or any representatives sent here are infected with Communism, they will certainly not be made party to any British or, I expect, American secrets."[22]

The prime minister, like his security-service directors, was blissfully unaware that Soviet agents were already deeply involved in the secret Overlord strategy. Dozens of British counterintelligence officers obtained secondments to Eisenhower's staff to play leading roles in planning and overseeing the elaborate security and deception operations at Supreme Headquarters Allied Expeditionary Force (SHAEF). The SHAEF headquarters was at Norfolk House, a red-brick office block in St. James's Park, conveniently close to both Section V of MI6 in Ryder Street and MI5 headquarters at the top of St. James's, plus the gentlemen's clubs of Pall Mall. SHAEF records show that competition for the posts was particularly keen among the younger uniformed members of the Pall Mall network, who counted heavily on their public schools or aristocratic titles to get in. For example, the skimpy résumé submitted by a young peer, who was a lieutenant colonel in a prestigious regiment, gave more prominence to Eton than to his knowledge of French, German, Swedish, and "practically everywhere in the world." This was evidently sufficient to make him a "desirable candidate for SHAEF intelligence.[23]

Another young lieutenant colonel who found a plum appointment at SHAEF headquarters was Christopher Blunt. The U.S. Army files reveal that he became one of the principal officers in the censorship office. This came under the Counter-Intelligence Division of G-2, where Colonel Dick White, Liddell's deputy in MI5's B Division, was deputy to Colonel Sheen of the U.S. Army. Many of Anthony Blunt's other acquaintances from MI5 and MI6 had moved into Norfolk House. It is likely that his recommendation played a part in getting his younger brother into the organization. SHAEF headquarters directories reveal that British officers dominated and controlled the Supreme Allied Command's intelligence establishment in the run-up to D-Day.

One of the potentially disastrous results of this jobs-for-the-boys approach was to let Anthony Blunt — and therefore Moscow — into another of the greatest secrets of the war. This negated all the elaborate security precautions intended to keep the Soviets from learning in advance the actual invasion date and the target beachheads for the Allied invasion of Normandy. While it was not in the Soviet interest to prejudice the invasion, Churchill had good reason not to communicate the date and real targets to Stalin. The code breakers at Bletchley had ample evidence from the German Ultra intercepts that the Germans had broken some of the Soviet military-cipher systems.

Despite all precautions, the secret of D-Day was leaked to the Kremlin. Philby knew it; so did Blunt. According to William Cavendish-Bentinck, both men knew a secret considered so vital that Allied officers – even in MI5 – had to receive special clearance for D-Day planning material stamped BIGOT. As the wartime chairman of the Joint Intelligence Committee that provided the analyses and forecasts on which Churchill and the British Chiefs of Staff based all their decisions, Bentinck remembers that Blunt attended several of his meetings. "He struck me as being rather a dull dog," Bentinck recalled. He insisted that he never once suspected Blunt or Philby, who also sometimes attended the JIC sessions. Blunt also told Robert Cecil that he had gone to "one or two" JIC meetings "while he was working for SHAEF."[24]

Yet Blunt was never officially part of the SHAEF intelligence establishment. This comes from Sir Dick White, who was himself one of the senior officers in the setup. A search of all the recently declassified G-2 and G-3 SHAEF records confirmed the authority of his statement. While there are many documents identifying Colonel Christopher Blunt and his activities in the censorship division, there is not a single memorandum, assignment, or telephone number for Major Anthony Blunt.[25]

How then did Blunt get into SHAEF and act as a representative at the Joint Intelligence Committee? This had puzzled Cecil. He pressed Blunt on this point during his interviews with him. The answer he was given fits the facts, because on April 24, 1944, in order to impose the maximum security precautions, all diplomatic mail was subject to search and censorship.

"Anthony said that he found himself out of a job at the end of April. The suggestion was made, he could not remember by whom, that he should help out with the D-Day deception scheme," Cecil told me. "Since he was already a uniformed member of MI5, which was heavily involved through the Double-Cross operation, he was 'lent' to SHAEF. It was in this capacity that he attended one or possibly two JIC meetings."[26]

Blunt talked so enthusiastically about his work for SHAEF that Cecil concluded he must have hugely enjoyed his part in the deception. The idea was to persuade the German High Command that the main target of the D-Day landing was the Pas de Calais area rather than the Normandy coast of France. Code-named Fortitude South, the elaborate and minutely constructed deception operation had been under way since the beginning of the year. Dummy landing craft were assembling in the ports of the Thames estuary and the region was sprouting inflatable tanks, canvas trucks, and wooden guns. Radio traffic was rerouted to convey the impression that the First U.S. Army Group (FUSAG), under

General George C. Patton, supported by Canadian and British divisions, was assembling and training in the fields of Kent and Sussex for an assault over the shortest cross-Channel route. While this phantom invasion force grew in the east, the real concentration of Allied military might was gathering in Hampshire, Dorset, and the West Country ports for the actual invasion two hundred miles down the French coastline from the Pas de Calais.[27]

Unlike most deception operations, history shows that Fortitude South succeeded in achieving its threefold objectives: to "induce faulty strategic dispositions"; to "deceive enemy as to target date and target area"; and to "induce faulty tactical dispositions during and after NEPTUNE by threats against the Pas de Calais." Lieutenant Colonel H. N. H. "Noel" Wild, a British Army intelligence officer who was the chief of the Ops B subsection of SHAEF G-3 (Operations Division), directed the implementation of one of the biggest deception operations in military history.

The most sensitive component in the Fortitude plan was the use of controlled enemy agents to feed misleading information about Patton's forces in southeast England. (The original intention was that SHAEF would establish a Special Agent Section to direct the CEAs (controlled enemy agents) before the Overlord landings, and it would also pick up and run the "stay-behind" agents the Germans would leave in their rear as they retreated through France.) As the American records reveal, there was "a certain amount of disagreement" over who should control this activity. Eventually agreement was reached: Special Counter-Intelligence operations in France would be run by the SCI units co-ordinated under Section V of MI6, with a pool of American and British case officers. This provided an important incentive for Philby to make his move to take over Section V as soon as the Allied troops had hit the beaches.[28]

After the bickering subsided, the Double-Cross Committee retained final control of the pre–D-Day deception information sent by its agents in Britain. To provide the necessary liaison with MI5's B(1)a Division, which ran the CEAs, Major Christopher Harmer — Blunt's Marlborough contemporary — joined Ops B at SHAEF. According to Colonel R. F. Hesketh, who was in charge of the Special Means Section, there was a "strict rule that there should be no direct contact between the SHAEF deception staff and the agents themselves." Instead, it was the MI5 case officers who came to Norfolk House for briefings on the doctored intelligence that the double agents radioed to their Abwehr contacts.[29]

In the early summer of 1944, the ISOS intelligence provided by Bletchley confirmed that the Abwehr believed that the double-cross agents known as "Garbo" and "Brutus" were their most reliable sources in England. Juan Pujol ("Garbo"), and a Polish airman named Roman Garby-Czerniawiski ("Brutus"), were therefore selected as the main mouthpieces for Special Means. Also involved were many of the other double agents being run by MI5 officers under T. A. Robertson — to promote the Fortitude deception directly to the Germans. "Garbo" was run by Blunt's close friend Tomas Harris, while "Brutus" was run by the Honorable Hugh Astor, a friend of Christopher Blunt's. So it is not surprising to find that Blunt arrived at SHAEF to collaborate with Harris and Astor."[30]

According to what Blunt told Cecil, his special responsibility was to play commander of the 4th Canadian Armored Division. Using the elaborate Fortitude South plan as his guide, he worked out of the Ops B war room at SHAEF headquarters with its large map of the dispositions of Patton's phantom FUSAG forces. By advancing the flags representing the Canadian tanks and men from their notional training camp at East Grinstead in Sussex to concentration at their embarkation port of Dover during May, he devised credible sightings for the reports that Harris and Astor had their agents relay to the Germans.

To reinforce this deception, Blunt and Harris had "Garbo" "invent" a subsidiary agent who supposedly operated in the Dover area. This agent was a disaffected Welsh nationalist seaman, code-named "Donny." He provided a steady stream of sightings of American and Canadian troops assembling in the vicinity of England's principal channel port. His reports continued even after Allied troops had landed on the Normandy beaches on June 6, 1944. This contributed to the German High Command's decision to recall divisions already on their way south, in anticipation of a second and bigger operation taking shape in the Pas de Calais.[31]

Blunt's work at SHAEF headquarters lasted only from the end of April through June 1944. But he told Cecil that he was very proud of his contribution to the masterpiece of deception that guaranteed the success of D-Day. Blunt seems to have been paying himself an indirect compliment when he paid tribute to the "extraordinary imaginative power" of Tomas Harris, who was "one of the principal organizers of 'Operation Garbo.'" The value of the operation according to Blunt, was that it had been "described by a senior military commander as worth an armored division." Blunt was upset by the lack of credit given to Harris by Masterman in his "Double-Cross" book. So Blunt used this as the pretext for penning the memorial to Harris in the *Dictionary of National Biography* that also lauded the supposedly great contributions he had made to British artistic culture.[32]

No one disputes that deception was Blunt's forte. There is no surprise among those who knew him that he probably derived as much pleasure from helping deceive the Nazis as he did from passing on the secrets of D-Day to his Soviet controller. In this context, it is significant to note that Anatoli Gorski, the case officer for the leading members of the Cambridge ring since 1940, did *not* transfer to the Soviet embassy in Washington until July 1944. It has always been assumed that Gorski — otherwise known as Gromov, who later became head of the KGB's First Directorate dealing with Anglo-American territories in the fifties — followed Donald Maclean across the Atlantic when he was promoted in March 1944 to become the first secretary of the British embassy in Washington.[33]

An explanation for Gorski's four-month delay in following Maclean to the United States was the importance that Moscow attached to monitoring the D-Day operation. The Soviets were reluctant to risk disturbing the direct channels of communication with Blunt as long as he remained at SHAEF headquarters. Gorski's departure from England in July also happened to coincide with the end of Blunt's stint with the Fortitude team at Norfolk House. It was then that Boris Krotov, another Soviet embassy official, replaced Gorski as the high-level agent runner in London.[34]

Blunt evidently did not get on warmly with Krotov, his new controller. During his interrogations with Wright, Blunt portrayed Krotov as a technocrat, in contrast to his more individualistic prewar controllers. This was a reflection of the methodical professionalism demanded of agents by Lavrenti Pavlovich Beria, who succeeded his chief, Yezhov, as director of the NKVD in December 1939. A Georgian, like Stalin, Beria ruled for fifteen years with a unique combination of ruthlessness and administrative efficiency that restored order and coherence to Soviet intelligence operations after the disruptions caused by the purges.

Beria completed the elimination of the Chekist old guard, replacing them with a younger generation of dedicated Stalinists. A rigorous program required all agents of the NKVD Foreign Department, known as the INU (Inostrannoye Upravlieniye), to undergo a two-year espionage training course covering everything from political indoctrination to codes and the practical exercises of meeting contacts. By 1944, the NKVD's primary internal-security function required the creation of a subsidiary Commissariat for State Security, known as the NKGB. By the end of the war the People's Commissariat (NK) designation was dropped in favor of Ministry for State Security (MGB) and Ministry of Internal Affairs (MVD). It was not until Beria had been arrested and shot, after an abortive attempt to seize power after Stalin's death in 1953, that the mighty empire of fear he had created was finally broken up. This reorganization gave birth to the Committee for State Security — the KGB (Komitet Gosudarstvennoy Bezopasnosti).

The cold dedication of the new breed of Soviet technocrat agent did not impress Blunt. Minutely detailed demands relayed from Moscow contrasted with the urbane relationship the Cambridge spies had once enjoyed with Theodore Maly and "Henry." By the summer of 1944, Soviet operations in London were being run with ruthless mechanical efficiency to gather quality intelligence from Stalin's Englishmen. Expectations were raised. Beria knew that his Cambridge agents were now rising high enough in the British government apparatus to satisfy Moscow's demands.

While Maclean was en route to the United States, and Blunt and Philby were passing on the secrets from SHAEF, Burgess was in the process of moving to a more productive position. After two years of incidental intelligence gleaned from hobnobbing with M.P.'s who took part in *The Week in Westminster*, which Burgess produced for the BBC, his influential friends had still failed to overcome the "fixed and strong dislike to the man" held by William Haley, the new BBC director general.[35]

On June 4, 1944, Burgess resigned his dead-end post of Talks producer at Broadcasting House to take up an appointment in the press department of the Foreign Office. It was a more rewarding monitoring post for picking up the high-level government intelligence that Krotov wanted. But the most cheering news that summer for Beria's Foreign Department chief in Moscow was not that the NKVD now had another of its British undercover agents inserted into the Foreign Office, nor the opening of a second front against the Nazis. It was Krotov's report that Philby, as its chief penetration agent, had a good chance of being chosen to head MI6's renewed assault on communism in postwar Europe.

Anticipating the coming struggle, Sir Stewart Menzies revived the anti-Soviet operations of MI6 shortly after D-Day. According to Felix Cowgill, the SIS files on Communists had "been on ice" since he completed sorting them in August 1939. C turned to the rival intelligence service for help. He arranged for the transfer of Jack Curry, a veteran of Liddell's counterintelligence staff, to start up Section IX with a skeleton staff. The new outfit was reinforced by the addition of Jane Sissmore Archer, one of the most experienced anti-Communist officers in MI5. Her task was to begin updating the dormant Communist files of Section V(v) in preparation for renewed operations against Moscow's espionage and subversion in Europe after Hitler's final defeat.[36]

"It was C's idea that the anti-Soviet operations would be run by

Section IX, which would absorb the staff of my Section V after the dissolution of its wartime establishment" was how Cowgill explained the proposed reorganization. (He was particularly anxious to correct the impression conveyed by other accounts — including Philby's — that as head of Section V he was to preside over a merger with Section IX.) It was IX that would then take up Britain's battle against postwar Communist subversion in Europe by drawing on Section V (v)'s experience. This included the Double-Cross agents and the network of underground agents in Lithuania, Latvia, Estonia, Poland, Czechoslovakia, and Hungary. The intention was that those nationals, whom MI6 had recruited for the struggle against the Nazis, were to be the front-line forces in the fight against the Soviet occupiers of Eastern Europe.[37]

Felix Cowgill was originally designated as the commander to lead that campaign. His outstanding record of wartime counterintelligence success with ISOS, which had identified 3,575 enemy agents, in addition to his extensive prewar anti-Communist police work in India, made him the obvious choice to head Section IX. But although Cowgill's fetish for internal security, and his strict adherence to the "need to know" principle, had protected Ultra and ensured the success of the Double-Cross operation, it had also made an enemy of Valentine Vivian. And unknown to Cowgill, his most dangerous rival was his seemingly dutiful and hardworking deputy: Philby began conspiring against his unsuspecting chief as soon as he realized that Curry, who was deaf and near retirement age, was only a stopgap head of Section IX.

"For the next few weeks, virtually all my discussions with my Soviet contact concerned the future of Section IX" was how Philby recounted working out his strategy with Krotov. Moscow Center was intimately involved in ensuring that its man in MI6 undermined Cowgill's authority. Krotov directed Philby that he "must do everything, but *everything*" to ensure his becoming head of Section IX. Philby was the supreme organization man and calculating subordinate. His repeated assertions that he attempted to "demur" because he disliked "office intrigue" is patently disingenuous in the light of his role in manipulating Liddell.[38]

Philby followed Moscow's orders to the letter. He subtly played on the enmity between Vivian and Cowgill with "the greatest care." He impressed Vivian with his efficiency, and using the ear of Christopher Arnold-Forster, the vice-chief's staff officer, he inflamed the long-running dispute between MI6 and MI5. He encouraged Arnold-Forster to approach Liddell — no doubt with the connivance of Blunt — with a damaging litany of Cowgill's intransigence. Vivian told Philby, with a wink, that it was a "real eye-opener." Philby then stirred Foreign Office antagonism against his boss, who had become embroiled in a heated dispute with Hoover over the lack of confidentiality with which the FBI director treated intelligence supplied by MI5.[39]

There were plenty of opportunities for Philby to work his plan because Cowgill had put him in charge of Section V when he himself went to the United States in June 1944. As a result of his position as acting head of Section V, Philby had access to the full dimension of Allied counter-intelligence secrets in the critical weeks leading up to D-Day.[40]

Ironically, Philby appeared more reticent about briefing his boss than the Soviets when Cowgill returned to London just three days before the Allied troops went ashore in France. When Philby arrived that evening at their flat for a late briefing, Mrs. Cowgill suspected that something was up.

"Philby was hedging, and his stutter, which he put on when he was in trouble, was worse than usual," Mrs. Cowgill recalled. "I remember saying to Felix after Kim left, 'That man is after your job.'"[41]

Felix Cowgill dismissed his wife's warning, knowing that she had taken a personal dislike to his deputy. Mrs. Cowgill explained that she had grown very close to Philby's common-law wife, Aileen. She had taken over her London flat in Drayton Gardens when Section V moved on to Ryder Street from St. Albans. She was a frequent visitor at the Philbys' grand house — rather too grand, she now realizes, for Philby's meager salary — in Chelsea, where she went in the daytime to keep Aileen and her four children company. Mrs. Cowgill tried to avoid Philby, whom she described as "callous" after hearing from Aileen how he had once walked over her after she had fallen and was lying on the kitchen floor.

"I thought that was a terrible thing to do," Mrs. Cowgill said, "but Aileen, who was very, very fond of Kim, thought it all rather a joke."[42]

Mrs. Cowgill's intuition proved correct. Philby was already preparing to walk over her husband to get his job. By September 1944, while Cowgill was on a trip to Belgium, arranging for Section V's Special Counter-Intelligence units to operate behind the lines of Montgomery's advancing 21st Army Group, Vivian's report on Section IX landed on Menzies's walnut-inlaid desk. It came out strongly against Cowgill as head of the anti-Soviet operations of MI6, and recommended that Philby should be Curry's successor in Section IX. Menzies moved without waiting for Cowgill to return. He summoned Philby and told him he was to take over Section IX immediately. For the first time he called him Kim. Then C even gave him Vivian's memorandum — which Philby had already seen but nevertheless pretended to read. Insidiously using his "I-hope-I-am-not-speaking-out-of-turn-sir" approach, Philby then asked for — and quickly obtained — written approval of Philby's appointment by the MI5 chief, Sir David Petrie, plus Petrie's promise of full cooperation.[43]

When Cowgill returned from Brussels early in October, he was confronted by a fait accompli. Realizing that Philby's appointment to Section IX had effectively cut him out of the job he believed he was better qualified to take on, Cowgill resigned after a stormy confrontation with Menzies. Philby's friend Tim Milne, who had succeeded Philby as head of the Iberian desk in Section V, assumed responsibility for the whole section.

"I never saw Philby again," Cowgill said. The residual bitterness about the whole episode was evident in the deliberate way Cowgill told me how he "handed over" to Milne on January 18, 1945, before taking up an assignment with the British Control Commission in Germany. He took some comfort in the letter of consolation he received from Norman Holmes Pearson. The head of the OSS X-2 mission in London wrote of his "numbness at the pit of the stomach" upon officially learning that his friend was no longer in charge of Section V. The organization was "in all truth your creation," wrote Pearson. Furthermore, he told Cowgill, he was speaking for his boss, James Murphy, in assuring him that "American counterespionage owe[s] its maturity to your education." After nearly two months of delay, Cowgill responded to "this most comforting letter," which he had "not dared to answer" before because "words fail to rise to the occasion."[44]

Philby, meanwhile, had impatiently assumed command of Section IX by drafting a charter of operations, for C to sign, giving his outfit the responsibility for "the collection and interpretation of information on Soviet and communist espionage and subversion in all parts of the world outside British territory." Menzies himself, Philby noted with pointed satisfaction, added the rider that "he was on no account to have any dealings with any of the United States services."[45]

While there is evidence of C's disenchantment with Colonel Donovan's efforts to open independent links with Soviet intelligence, and to use the OSS for clandestine operations against the British Empire in India, the actual record does not show such a severing of Anglo-American counterintelligence links as Philby and others have suggested. Pearson continued to have exchanges on the most sensitive cases, as revealed by his December 1945 summary of the amalgamation of Section IX and Section V to become the Counter-Intelligence Section of MI6. Six months later Pearson's successor was dining with Philby's deputy, Milne, who disclosed that the new counterintelligence chief wanted X-2 to be the "channel for American liaison for counterintelligence matters."[46]

Philby's mischievous assertion appears to be yet another reflection of the Soviet strategy to drive a wedge between the wartime allies. But as he assumed the burden of his new anti-Communist duties, Philby was increasingly confronted with having to deal with American interests. MI6 and the OSS jointly operated the Special Counter-Intelligence units that were operating in the rear of the Allied advance through France and the Low Countries. They were uncovering, and deploying, as double agents a growing number of German stay-behinds to act as CEAs and feed false information to the retreating forces of the Wehrmacht. Some of the best of these agents were later discovered to have been originally infiltrated into the Abwehr by the Soviet intelligence services — a fact that Philby must have known as he made frequent trips to SHAEF counter-intelligence headquarters in Paris in October 1944.

Malcolm Muggeridge, then an MI6 agent attached to De Gaulle's Services Speciales, knew from a secret directive from London about Section IX. But he found his reports detailing the growing Communist infiltration of the French government machine were dismissed as "so much poppycock" by Philby, who was contemptuous of his sources of information. Muggeridge recalls how on one visit, Philby took him to an expensive dinner in a Left Bank restaurant and then, as he talked about his new responsibilities, insisted on walking up the Boulevard Saint-Germain to the Rue de Grenelle.[47]

"I realized without any particular amazement, that we were making for the Soviet embassy," Muggeridge recalled, vividly describing the bizarre scene that took place in front of the large stone building with its impassively tall blue wooden gates and shuttered windows. "How are we going to get in there?" Philby kept saying as he shook his fists and regaled his astonished junior colleague with the difficulties of penetrating the Soviet embassy. He told Muggeridge that he saw "no chance of planting a servant when all the staff, down to the lowliest kitchen maids and porters and chauffeurs are imported from the USSR and sometimes in reality hold quite senior posts in the Soviet *apparat*."[48]

In the sober light of the next morning, Muggeridge concluded that too much wine and cognac had ignited the bizarre display that Philby had staged for his benefit. Graham Greene had already turned down Philby's offer of a job in his new section. Muggeridge reasoned that Philby was hoping to persuade him to stay on in MI6 because he had become an outspoken anti-Communist since his days as a green left-wing British journalist in Moscow. But Muggeridge did not entirely trust Philby.

Although Muggeridge enjoyed Philby's company, he described him as "one of nature's *farouches*," and a "wild man." The histrionics in front of the Soviet embassy were not the only unsettling incident that had occurred during Philby's October visit to Paris. Muggeridge had arrived with Lord Rothschild shortly after the liberation of the city, when the priceless ornaments, French furniture, and art treasures of his gilt- and marble-encrusted mansion were being brought up from the basement, where they had survived the German occupation.

"Hitlers may come and go but Rothschilds go on forever," the ancient concierge philosophically remarked as he organized the mansion as Rothschild's billet. Records in the U.S. Army files — some of which were withheld at the request of the British government — confirm that "Col. Ld. Rothschild" operated from the Rue Petrach offices of 105 Special Counter-Intelligence attached to SHAEF advanced headquarters.[49]

When Philby came to Paris he, too, was put up at the Rothschild mansion on the Avenue de Marigny. Over dinner one evening, a bitter argument broke out among them about the Soviets' right to have full access to Allied intelligence. It was Rothschild, Muggeridge recalled, who led off the discussion of whether Moscow had been supplied with everything that SHAEF knew from Ultra about the German order of battle. Rothschild knew how extensive this intelligence was because he had access to it on a day-to-day basis as it came into SHAEF headquarters.

Muggeridge reminded his host that some caution was legitimate because, in 1940, Stalin had been passing intelligence to Hitler. The British and Americans had to be on their guard against treachery. The debate grew heated. Philby joined in. "He spluttered and shouted that we were duty bound to do everything in our power, whatever it might be, to support the Red Army," Muggeridge said, recalling that he insisted that this included risking the security of the Ultra secret.[50]

Rothschild became highly indignant that the Russians were not getting all the information, and, as a dedicated opponent of communism and a loyal MI6 officer, Muggeridge remembers, he suddenly found himself like a skeleton at a feast. He would later conclude, incorrectly, that Philby's treachery began during his trip to Paris.[51]

Philby, as Muggeridge reminded me, was not the only member of the Cambridge ring to use the Rothschild mansion as a high-class billet in the months after the liberation of Paris. Both Burgess and Blunt came and stayed shortly afterward. When Rothschild's former personal assistant from MI5 arrived for a week's visit, she found it highly amusing that the two notorious residents of the Bentinck Street flat had already been guests in the Avenue de Marigny mansion.

Kitty Muggeridge still enjoys chuckling over how her cousin Tess Mayor, the future Lady Rothschild, had wickedly quipped to Malcolm: "How nice to have the buggers in the house again!"[52]

# CHAPTER 23

# "Most Secret Matters"

What exactly Anthony Blunt did in Paris that September 1944, and for the remaining months of the war, has been the subject of considerable speculation. His MI5 superior Sir Dick White, who was then deputy head of SHAEF counterintelligence, has stated that Blunt was "not really" with *his* outfit. At the same time, White acknowledges that Blunt did not come to Paris "purely as an art historian," who had been "brought in by the fine arts people in London after the invasion to come over to Europe to try to find some of the works of art stolen by the Nazis."[1]

It is curious that Blunt's name appears nowhere in the records of the special Monuments and Fine Arts section (MAFA) of SHAEF that was established in May 1944. With the rank of lieutenant colonel, Leonard Woolley, the archaeologist who had won international renown as the excavator of the cradle of Western civilization at Ur in Mesopotomia, had taken the responsibility for recruiting the British contingent. He brought together many of the country's leading art historians, including Blunt's school friend and lifelong professional associate Ellis Waterhouse. Their mission was to follow the Allied armies and survey the state of Europe's ravaged cultural heritage.[2]

Woolley wanted Blunt's help. "The officer I would prefer and could most strongly recommend as a capable man, a first rate German speaker and out of the top drawer as an art historian, is Major Anthony Blunt, now serving with MI5," Woolley wrote the SHAEF MAFA German Section. He had "spoken to Major Blunt, who promised to make strong representations to his C.O. but did not hold much hope that he would be released." Woolley pleaded with Colonel Bridge to do "anything you can to help us get the services of this officer." Despite the high regard of the art world for Blunt's professional abilities, Woolley could not get him released from MI5.[3]

The inference to be drawn from Woolley's communication is that MI5 considered Blunt too valuable to release as head of SHAEF's German art mission. But as Blunt admitted later, his work with the London diplomatic couriers was already over when Woolley made his request. Instead, Blunt appears to have tipped off his Marxist art-historian friend Professor Kligender to offer himself as a substitute. The expatriate German art historian, however, was politely advised in August 1944 not to "hold out very much hope" for the job. The xenophobic War Office was unwilling to commission civilians when it was "able to obtain men from various military organizations."[4]

The official record and the recollections of Blunt's MI5 superiors, White and Hesketh, seem to confirm that there was no pressing military demand for Blunt's services that legitimately should have kept him from Woolley's outfit. This suggests that Blunt spent the final months of the war on some other jobs of special intelligence so sensitive that no official records exist.[5]

In unraveling the mysteries behind Blunt's actions, it is now possible to see exactly how these missions provided him with a gilt-edged "insurance policy" that later would protect him from prosecution should it be learned he was a Soviet agent. To use the word *blackmail* may be melodramatic, but it seems obvious that what Blunt knew — secrets that caused Prime Minister Churchill and Buckingham Palace to exert all their powers to keep them hidden — were the trump cards in Anthony's deadly game of espionage.

So highly classified were Blunt's actions at the end of the war, claims Peter Wright in *Spycatcher*, that even MI5 was forbidden to pry into its details thirty years later. This Wright discovered when he assumed responsibility for interrogating Blunt in 1965. He discovered, to his surprise, that Buckingham Palace was already aware that there was a confessed Soviet spy in its midst. Michael Adeane, the sovereign's private secretary, assured him "in the detached manner of someone who wishes not to know very much more about the matter," that the queen "has been fully informed about Sir Anthony, and is quite content for him to be dealt with in any way which gets at the truth."[6]

One matter, however, the queen absolutely did not wish discussed — even within the British security service. This was "an assignment he [Blunt] undertook on behalf of the Palace — a visit to Germany" that he had made at the end of the war.

"Please do not pursue the matter," Adeane directed. "Strictly speaking it is not relevant to considerations of national security." In the hundreds of hours that Wright subsequently spent with Blunt, Wright dutifully avoided discussing the German trip.

"I never did learn the secret of his mission at the end of the war," Wright said, observing foxily that the Palace had become adept in the "difficult art of scandal burying" over several centuries, whereas "MI5 have only been in the business since 1909."[7]

Wright's statement in 1987 provides the first authoritative confirmation from an MI5 source that Blunt spent the last months of his wartime service on some highly secret personal mission for the king.

Professor Hugh Trevor-Roper had dropped the same hints a few days after Blunt's exposure in 1979. The former regius professor of history was seconded in 1945 by Dick White to his counterintelligence group at SHAEF and his familiarity with captured German records enabled him to write the first major postwar study of Adolf Hitler. Trevor-Roper was therefore regarded as speaking authoritatively — if somewhat indiscreetly — when he told a reporter from the *Sunday Times* how he ran into Blunt at the St. James's MI5 headquarters as Blunt was reporting to Guy Liddell on his mission.[8]

Trevor-Roper gathered that Blunt had been sent to Germany on the orders of King George VI to retrieve documents that were believed to be in the hands of the royal family's many German relations. According to Trevor-Roper, the main objective had been the long and intimate correspondence that Queen Victoria maintained with her eldest daughter, "Vicky," who in 1858 married Frederick III of Prussia and became the mother of Kaiser Wilhelm II. The king, and particularly his mother, Queen Mary, who had corresponded with her German relatives and been a frequent visitor in her youth to the Hesse castles that were now in the U.S. Army's zone of occupation in the Frankfurt area, were fearful that the intimate secrets of Britain's royal family could fall into unscrupulous hands — even making headlines in the American press.[9]

According to Blunt, his mission had been successful. Trevor-Roper recalled that Blunt made a special point of telling him that among the massive collection of royal letters he had discovered one from a court official who had called on Karl Marx. So it was obvious that Blunt had made himself familiar with the contents of these papers. Blunt also told Trevor-Roper how he dined one evening in grand style at a German castle that appeared untouched by the privations of war. Twenty people had sat down to a magnificent six-course meal served by liveried footmen behind every chair.[10]

The *Sunday Times* reporters had difficulty persuading the reluctant eighty-three-year-old Prince Wolfgang of Hesse to talk with them. But when they did, he confirmed that Sir Owen Morshead, then the royal librarian from Windsor Castle, and Anthony Blunt, had driven up one day in the spring of 1945 in a military truck. He was not precise about the date, but it was sometime after the troops of General George S. Patton's Third Army had arrived in the village of Kronberg in the last week of March 1945.

It must have been late April or early May 1945, since Prince Wolfgang mentioned that their massive nineteenth-century palace was already functioning as a GI rest camp. The British party had first been to

Schloss Friedrichshof, five kilometers away, only to be redirected to the townhouse in the shadow of the old Kronberg castle to which the Hesse family had been unceremoniously evacuated by the Americans.

The royal librarian produced a letter signed by King George VI requesting his distant cousin's permission to remove sensitive royal papers to Britain for safekeeping. But this was technically a matter for the Landgrave of Hessen, the titular head of the family — Wolfgang's twin brother, Prince Philip. The former Nazi state president of Hessen and lieutenant general in the Storm Troops had fallen out of favor with Hitler after Mussolini's capitulation, when he was sent to Flossenbürg concentration camp. His wife, Princess Mafalda, had died in Buchenwald in an American air raid. Prince Philip survived the camps, only to face another period of captivity as one of the wanted Nazi leaders.[11]

A hurried family conclave concluded that the princes' seventy-two-year-old mother, Princess Margaret, would give her written approval for the removal of what Prince Wolfgang claimed were over a thousand documents. They were part of the family archives stored in packing cases in the attic of the schloss. Armed with this information, Blunt and Morshead returned to their army truck and drove up the five miles of winding road that went through the Hesse estate.

The dark tower of the Friedrichshof that broods over the wooded slopes of the Taunus Mountains above Kronberg bears an uncanny resemblance to Queen Victoria's beloved Balmoral castle in Scotland. The castle that Princess Victoria built for herself reflects her mother's taste for the wooden-beamed Scottish baronial style with its entrance hall and corridors cluttered with paintings of her English royal relations. Now restored, it is run by the business-minded Hesse family as the Schloss Hotel. Guests who can afford $1,100 a night can stay in the Royal Suite used by Queen Victoria when she visited the Friedrichshof to stay with her "Dearest child" on April 26, 1895.[12]

In one of those strange congruences of date, it was half a century later — probably to the week — when Blunt and Morshead drove their two-ton army truck up to the stone portico emblazoned with Tudor roses. They entered bearing the warrant signed by Queen Victoria's grandson, George VI, and endorsed by her granddaughter, the Princess of Hesse. But their unique authority, according to Prince Wolfgang, did not impress Captain Kathleen Nash of the U.S. Women's Army Corps. She was in command of the rest camp. She did not have the authority, she said, to relinquish control over papers that were now the property of the U.S. Army.

With characteristic verve, Blunt resorted to subterfuge. While Morshead and the soldiers accompanying them headed up to the attic to locate the two packing cases of documents described by Prince Wolfgang, Blunt took on the intractable Captain Nash. After considerable argument he persuaded her to telephone U.S. Army headquarters in Frankfurt. Meanwhile the crates had been brought down and loaded onto the waiting lorry. The irate WAC captain emerged from her office too late to stop Blunt and Morshead from driving off with their haul.

The successful execution of this mission for the House of Windsor created an unexpected setback for their royal cousins. Prince Wolfgang remained convinced to his dying day that the episode led directly to what *The New York Times* was to call "the greatest gem theft in modern times."[13]

Until the emissaries of the king of England arrived on her preserve, the WAC captain was as oblivious as any other wartime volunteer from the rural heartland of Wisconsin might be to the significance of the Hesse-Kassel family in the intermarried tree of European royalty. But Nash's friend Colonel Jack Durant, an army flyer, was a savvy graduate of Georgetown Law School. Together they reasoned that the schloss might contain more royal documents that might fetch a high price from American newspaper editors. A tip from one of the German bartenders led them to a bricked-up subcellar. Inside they found the cache of fifteen hundred bottles of wines of ancient vintage and, buried beneath the stone floor, a lead-lined wooden box containing the Hesse family jewels. The chest also contained engraved silver items, a Bible with royal signatures, and nine volumes of original letters to the queen-empress from her daughters. The collective value of the diamonds, emeralds, rubies, and pearls in the tiaras, necklaces, bracelets, and rings was, in 1946, conservatively estimated at over $3 million.[14]

"We first decided we would turn them in," Captain Nash stated in her confession. "Then we thought we could take only a few pieces and then we decided we would take the lot." She and her friend Durant pried the jewels from their irreplaceable antique settings to smuggle them back to the United States with the aid of a U.S. Army major and a corporal, who joined the conspiracy for a 25 percent split of the loot. The Hesses did not discover that their priceless heirlooms had been stolen until April 1946 when they tried to retrieve their jewels on the eve of the marriage of Princess Sophie, the sister of Prince Philip of Greece, who the next year became the husband of the future queen of England. As fate would have it, Durant and Nash, now in the United States and honorably discharged from the army, were planning their own nuptials.[15]

On May 28, Kathleen Nash and Jack Durant became man and wife in Chicago. Their wedding added a romantic twist to the "Kronberg Heist" headlines when the story broke after their arrest by military police a week later. The bulk of the Hesse treasure was recovered from a luggage locker at the railroad terminal. The glitter of huge canary-yellow diamonds and flawless green emeralds on the baize tables in the Pentagon hearing room added sparkle to the discomfiture of the U.S. Army, which had recalled the newlyweds to active duty to face court-martial for looting. They were both found guilty under the Eightieth Article of War and were sentenced to jail.[16]

The headlines added to the embarrassment of the House of Hesse-Kassel and its royal English Windsor cousins because the U.S. Army arrested Prince Philip of Hesse on April 29, 1945, after liberating him from Dachau concentration camp. The SHAEF intelligence records indicate that, as target number 53 in the Nazi hierarchy, the former president of Hessen-Nassau had a high priority in the Ashcan operation that rounded up several thousand alleged German war criminals for interrogation. Although he did not face trial at Nuremberg, Philip of Hesse was only one of the ex-kaiser's relations to have fallen under Hitler's spell. He was an S.A. general and, until 1943, one of the most sycophantically Nazi of the German princes. His wife was the daughter of King Umberto of Italy. For this reason Hitler used him as a special mediator with Mussolini at the time of the Austrian Anschluss, and again during the Czechoslovak crisis. His success as an intermediary, and the Führer's belief in the importance of blood ties, made Prince Philip the obvious choice to mediate with the Duke of Windsor, with whom he shared the distinction of being a great-grandson of Queen Victoria.[17]

This revelation was made by Prince Wolfgang to the *Sunday Times* in 1979. While he hesitated to confirm that Prince Philip had been an intermediary for Hitler, he described the role as "unofficial" mediation. This he said was "not proper mediation in the true sense of the word" but discussions conducted with King Edward VIII through his youngest brother, George, Duke of Kent. The Hesses, like the Windsors, were haunted by the 1918 murders of their Romanov aunt, uncle, and cousins by Bolshevik revolutionaries who supposedly hurled them alive down the Alpaeresk mine shaft or gunned them down in the bloody cellars of Ekaterinburg.[18]

This fear of the Soviets followed King George V to his deathbed. When Edward came to the throne in 1936, Hitler concluded that the time was ripe to attempt a rapprochement with the British through their new and impressionable monarch. Like his youngest brother and closest confidant, Edward had a great affinity for Germany. Despite his popular image as a champion of the unemployed, Edward was a fierce anti-Communist. He believed that the Nazis had saved Germany from the Revolution. "Every drop of blood in my veins is German," he once said, reflecting his love for the homeland of his royal predecessors.[19]

A Germanophile and an authoritarian at heart, Edward admired Hitler's leadership, which he contrasted with the inability of his own ineffectual ministers to resolve Britain's economic woes. So Hitler had no difficulty maintaining a private channel of communication to Edward, both while he was king and later, after he abdicated, as Duke of Windsor, through his royal cousins Philip of Hesse and Karl Edward, duke of Saxe-Coburg-Gotha.

Coburg, who was a schoolfellow of Edward's at Eton, was rewarded for his devotion to the Führer with an appointment as a senior officer in the Sturmabteilung. It was no accident that this ranking officer of the notorious Nazi stormtroopers was a frequent visitor to London. He was actually closeted with the new king during the first critical hours of Edward's reign in January 1936, when the German army was in the final stages of its preparations to move into the Rhineland. It must have been a great relief for Hitler to learn from his royal emissary that he could defy the Versailles treaty. There would be no risk of military intervention from the British government because of the new king's "sincere resolve to bring England and Germany together."[20]

King Edward, it now appears, was intent on developing a "nonofficial" British foreign policy toward Germany. He intended to orchestrate it personally with the Führer, via his cousin. Coburg said on his return to Berlin that Edward requested that he "visit him frequently in order that confidential matters might be more speedily clarified in this way." Edward appeared ready to overstep constitutional restraint if necessary. "Who is King here, Baldwin or I?" he testily reminded Coburg. "I wish to talk to Hitler, and will do so here or in Germany. Tell him that please."[21]

The immediate clash with Baldwin came not from Edward's determination to engineer a rapprochement with Nazi Germany but from his affair with the twice-divorced Wallis Warfield Simpson over which he went down to defeat in a constitutional battle with Prime Minister Baldwin that summer. This was a setback to Hitler's grand design for making Britain his ally. Hitler had regarded the king as "a man after his own heart and one who understood the *Führerprinzip*, and was ready to introduce it into his own country." There were still, however, plenty of arrows in Hitler's quiver. One of them was Mrs. Simpson herself.[22]

The ambitious and chic Mrs. Simpson had been courted by the

Anglo-German Fellowship and Hitler's ambassador to London. After the abdication, when King George VI denied her the title of Her Royal Highness, the scene was set for a long and bitter feud. Hitler promptly turned it to his advantage by inviting the Windsors to visit Germany. "The duke accepted the invitation because he wanted to compensate the duchess by giving her the experience of a state visit," Sir Dudley Forwood told me, recalling how the king had told him he wanted "every possible step" taken to dissuade his brother from making the trip.

The private visit, billed as the first stage of an international tour to study labor conditions, caused consternation in Britain when Nazi propagandists made it a triumphal two-week showcase of royal approval. To the astonishment of his erstwhile subjects, their former king was photographed with Göring and Goebbels — even giving what appeared to be his version of the stiff-arm Nazi salute. The Duke of Coburg orchestrated the attentions of party bigwigs and the duchess was treated royally by the cheering crowds and addressed as Her Royal Highness at banquets.

The high point of the Windsors' visit was the Führer's invitation to his Berchtesgaden hideaway in the Bavarian Alps. Hitler insisted on using his personal translator Paul Schmidt. This irritated the duke, according to Sir Dudley, who recalled that the duke repeatedly spoke in fluent German. But both ex-king and Führer were careful to avoid promises in the informal talks in which Windsor stressed his understanding of the Germans as a result of his family and blood ties. But even this took on a sinister significance. "The duke was never able to forget that he was abdicated royalty and of no importance compared to what he had been," Sir Dudley said. "I think he may have thought that his wise counsel might sway the Führer from confrontation with England." As *The New York Times* commented, the duke's tour "demonstrated adequately that the Abdication did rob Germany of a firm friend, if not indeed a devoted admirer, on the British throne."[23]

The duke was too loyally pro-British to be compromised, according to Sir Dudley, but *The New York Times* pointed out that he had been "very critical of English politics as he sees them and is reported as declaring British ministers of today and their possible successors are no match for the German and Italian Dictators." Sir Dudley also concedes that the duke was prey to "manipulators" like Charles Bedaux, the American-born "time-and-motion" millionaire who had lent the Windsors his château at Candé for their wedding and had become part of their entourage. Bedaux had engineered the German visit through Nazi connections that became known in 1942 when he died in mysterious circumstances after his arrest as a Vichy undercover agent by Free

French forces in North Africa. The British confiscated an attaché case of documents in which Bedaux was alleged to be carrying a U.S. Army intelligence file. Its contents might have shed light on the shadowy intrigue that so compromised the embittered ex-king.[24]

There seems no doubt that the Windsors became the center of a German plot because of the attempt to suborn Sir Dudley Forwood. "The outcome of this war is probably clear to you," Bedaux conspiratorially told Forwood over dinner at Claridge's a day after hostilities erupted in September 1939. "I can assure you that when the result does take place, I will look after you and see you get a good post." Forwood left the duke's staff, but he agrees that Bedaux was a "clever manipulator" and the Windsors had "no idea what a four-letter man he was." They were easy prey for a conspiracy. The private diary kept by Windsor's faithful equerry, Major Edward Metcalfe, reveals the degree to which Bedaux was an intimate member of the Windsor entourage during the Phony War. "Fruity," as the faithful but pedestrian retainer was known, did not put as much trust in Bedaux as his royal master did. "He knows too much," Metcalfe wrote suspiciously. "He hinted at Berlin being one of those places," Metcalfe observed just a month after war broke out — adding, as if to reassure himself, "He beats me, but he is my pal!!!"[25]

What is now clear is that Bedaux was close to Ribbentrop and his emissary, Otto Abetz, whom the French police expelled from Paris in 1939. (Abetz returned to settle old scores as Germany's much-despised ambassador to Vichy.) Captured documents reveal that Bedaux's mysterious peregrinations were an integral part of the web of shadowy "peace maneuvering" that preoccupied the Berlin Foreign Ministry — and the secret services — of Britain, France, Italy, and Germany during the Phony War. The evidence that Bedaux was a channel of communication between Windsor and Hitler appears in the January 1940 communication to Germany's undersecretary for foreign affairs, Baron Ernst von Weizsäcker, from the German ambassador in The Hague.

"Through personal relationships I might have the opportunity to establish certain lines leading to the Duke of Windsor," Count Julius von Zech-Burkesroda reported, explaining that the duke was not "entirely satisfied" with the role he had been given as a member of the British Military Mission. "Also there seems to be something of a *Fronde* forming around W[indsor] which for the moment of course still has nothing to say, but which at some time under favorable circumstances might acquire a certain significance." Windsor's significance, it seems, was already appreciated by Hitler.[26]

Because he was a trusted major-general on the staff of the British Military Mission, with access to the most senior officers in General Maurice Gamelin's headquarters, Windsor had comprehensive and detailed intelligence on the Allied order of battle, plus the French defensive dispositions. He also demonstrated a sound grasp of the alarming military deficiencies of the western front as shown by two still-classified, highly critical reports that he prepared for the British staff. To prepare these assessments, the duke had to have knowledge of Plan D. This plan required the British Expeditionary Force (BEF) to advance northward in the event of a German invasion of Belgium — a move that both Windsor and the German High Command foresaw would expose a catastrophic weakness in the Ardennes sector north of the Maginot Line.

The Ardennes was precisely the sector where General Guderian's XIX Panzer Group burst through on May 10, when Hitler unleashed his offensive in the West. This fact raises the possibility of a connection between the Duke of Windsor's activities at Allied GHQ and the German decision of February 1940 to scrap their original attack plan in favor of a bold drive through the Ardennes to the Belgian coast so as to cut off the British forces. The connection becomes clearer now that we know that when the duke was not at the front rallying the troops, and bracing himself with frequent halts for "kettly" (his infantile jargon-word for fresh-brewed tea), he was back in Paris dining in the best restaurants with an entourage that more often than not included Charles Bedaux.

Published accounts and diaries of the Windsor circle report that the duke was an opinionated, compulsive, and indiscreet talker at the dinner tables of the Ritz. His hefty tabs were usually left to Bedaux to settle. If, as now seems indisputable, Bedaux was in the pay of the Germans, their investment paid off. The connection is reinforced because, throughout the Phony War, Bedaux made frequent trips to his office in Holland — and it was the German ambassador in The Hague who identified the duke in his reports to Berlin as being the source of important military intelligence.

On February 19, Zech-Burkesroda cited the "D. of Windsor" as the origin of detailed information on how the British and French planned to deal with a German invasion of Belgium from the "exhaustive discussion at its last meeting" of the Allied War Council. By comparing Allied and German records, it is now possible to develop a convincing case that an intelligence leak leading back to the Duke of Windsor may well have played a significant part in prompting Hitler to order his generals to change their battle plan. The revised strategy was one the German High Command considered risky. But the Führer was vindicated when it succeeded five months later, cutting off the BEF at Dunkirk and starting the snowballing rout of General Gamelin's traumatized French army.[27]

Whether Windsor contributed wittingly or unwittingly to the disasters that led to the fall of France, the evidence of captured German Foreign Office documents suggests that he played another, more knowing role in the subsequent plot to use him as a pawn in Hitler's bid to bluff Britain into suing for peace. Even the British Foreign Office acknowledged "the backwash of Nazi intrigue which seeks now that the greater part of the continent is in enemy hands, to make trouble about W[indsor]." But not until after the war, when the German records fell into Allied hands, was it appreciated just how deeply Windsor and his wife were involved in the intrigue. The remarkable collection of telegrams in the German Foreign Office Windsor file shows that the plot began on June 23, two days after the Windsors arrived in Madrid after fleeing France. For the next seven weeks, German emissaries assiduously courted the duke, first in Madrid and then in Lisbon. The operation was masterminded by one of Reinhard Heydrich's ranking SD agents, Walter Schellenberg, who told Windsor to "hold himself in readiness" for a starring role in Hitler's master plan. "Germany," the Windsors were told, "is determined to compel England to make peace by the use of all methods and would be prepared in such an event to pave the way to the granting of any wish expressed by the Duke and Duchess, in particular with respect to ascension of the English Throne by the Duke and Duchess."[28]

The cables reveal that the Germans had high hopes when the Windsors went to Portugal, after British pressure to do so, that the presence in Lisbon of the Duke of Kent for the jubilee celebration would prove a decisive factor. "The Duke is toying with the idea of dissociating himself from present tendency of British public policy by a public declaration and breaking from his brother [King George VI]," Eberhard von Stohrer, German ambassador to Spain, advised Berlin on July 23. The Germans continued their unrelenting and subtle pressure on the Windsors. Emissaries who ranged from businessmen to housemaids arrived with warnings of intrigues against them by Britain's secret service agents, and hints of changes in the British constitution over which "the Duchess in particular became very thoughtful." They also tried persuading the duke and duchess to return to Madrid under German protection, and Schellenberg made elaborate plans to stage a "kidnap" of the duke and duchess during a hunting expedition.[29]

"The Duke hesitated right up until the last moment," Stohrer reported to Berlin. An ocean liner was held for him in Lisbon until August 1. Only after Churchill's emissaries, led by the Windsors' former legal adviser, Sir Walter Monckton, persuaded the duke to accept a less-than-glamorous wartime role as governor general of the Bahamas was the episode closed. According to the German reports, "his legal adviser was once again able to exert his influence." He convinced the Duke that the "possibility of peace did not exist at the moment." If Windsor acted contrary to the British government's directions, as the duke explained it to the emissary of Berlin, he would "let loose upon himself the propaganda of his British enemies which would rob him of all prestige for the moment of possible intervention."[30]

Shortly before embarking on the American steamship *Excalibur* for Bermuda en route to the Bahamas on August 1, the duke and duchess attended a farewell reception. It was given by their Portuguese host Dr. Ricardo Espiritu Santo e Silva, a banker who was reported to be friendly with the Germans and whom the duke assured of his "deepest sincerity and expressed admiration and sympathy for the Führer." Moreover, Windsor said, "he could, if necessary, intervene from the Bahamas," and "promised to remain in constant contact" with "a code phrase on receipt of which he would immediately return."[31]

Germany's ambassador to Spain had played a key role in the month-long drama. He confirmed that Schellenberg had "reached certain agreements which are to facilitate a resumption of relations with the Duke." This the duke put into effect as soon as he reached Bermuda on August 15, when he telegraphed Silva "asking him to let him know as soon as action is necessary on his part."[32]

When these telegrams came to light five years later, they caused consternation at Buckingham Palace. "King fussed about Duke of Windsor File & captured German documents," Cadogan recorded in his diary on October 25, 1945. But that was not the reaction of the British army officer who had tumbled on this most confidential material in the German Foreign Office records five months earlier.[33]

"Drinks all round!" is the penciled congratulation that appears at the end of Lieutenant Colonel Robert Currie Thompson's report on how he tracked down thirty boxes of microfilms. They included "the most top secret German Foreign Ministry papers containing a complete account of Germany's foreign policy and doings from 1933 to 1944, and including correspondence and records of conversations between Hitler and Ribbentrop on the one side and Mussolini, Franco, Laval, Molotov and Japanese and other personalities on the other, also reports by ambassadors and ministers on the most secret matters." Thompson was the leader of the British Foreign Office File Team involved in Operation Goldcup. This was the code name given by the Combined Intelligence Operations Section to the tracking down of the important records of the Reich dispersed over Germany for safety. (In April 1945 the American army had already recovered the main body of Foreign Ministry records, estimated at 170 two-and-a-half-ton-truck loads, as they were being sent to safety in the Harz Mountains of central Germany.)[34]

Preliminary sorting at the temporary Allied documents center at Marburg revealed that some of the most important sections of the record were missing. Quite by accident, Thompson ran into Karl von Loesch, a Foreign Ministry translator, who had told the Americans who captured him that he had had charge of the most secret papers but had destroyed them on orders from Berlin owing to "a sudden Allied advance." But when confronted by a British officer — "a somewhat rare specimen in Thuringia" — Loesch revealed that he had been at school with Churchill's son-in-law, Duncan Sandys. He then explained that a microfilm set of the ministry's most confidential papers had been made in 1943 by Ribbentrop. This had survived. He offered to lead Thompson to the grounds of the schloss above the village of Schönberg, an estate some twenty miles from Mülhausen. Since this part of Thuringia was allocated for the Russian zone of occupation, Colonel Thompson wasted no time driving with Loesch to the spot where they found the cans of microfilm buried under a tarpaulin in a ravine.[35]

Among the thousands of page-images in those thirty rolls of microfilm was an extensive collection of papers covering "German-British Relations," including a thick dossier on the Duke and Duchess of Windsor.

The potential dynamite in these documents quickly reached the ears of General Eisenhower. He later described how he "had them thoroughly examined by Ambassador Winant and by my own Intelligence Staff." Under the terms of the inter-Allied agreement *all* captured German records were technically held as joint property of the British, Americans, French, and Russians. Eisenhower, however, decided he had to make an exception in the case of the Windsor file. Later, he sought to justify his decision to hand the papers over to the British, saying his advisers had conveniently concluded that "there was no possible value in them, that they were obviously concocted with some idea of promoting German propaganda and weakening the Western resistance, and that they were totally unfair to the Duke."[36]

When Prime Minister Clement Attlee received the file he concurred. The documents had "little or no credence." Their publication "might do the greatest possible harm," he advised former Prime Minister Churchill, who was given the sensitive file for his comments.[37]

"I earnestly trust it may be possible to destroy all traces of these

German intrigues," Churchill urged. He had been one of Edward's most outspoken parliamentary supporters in the abdication crisis nine years earlier and, despite the events of 1940, still had great affection for the king he had lost.[38]

Despite this high-level conspiracy to "edit" the documents, Ribbentrop's microfilms had a charmed existence. They survived intact this second order for their destruction and became available to the Allied historians responsible for compiling the German Foreign Office documents. An objective assessment of the Windsor papers' true significance came when the historians decided to include that part of the file dealing with the exchanges of the German ambassadors in Spain and Portugal. Publication was scheduled for 1954.

The German papers on Windsor therefore resurfaced to haunt Churchill at a most inconvenient moment: He was back in harness at Downing Street at the head of a new Conservative government. A month before the June 1953 coronation of Queen Elizabeth II, there was every reason for concern. He intervened directly and sent a "Secret and Personal" letter to President Eisenhower, urging "My dear Friend" to "exert your power to prevent their publication." The episode was of "negligible historical importance" in Churchill's view. Inclusion of the telegrams in an official publication would "leave the impression that the Duke was in close touch with German agents and was listening to suggestions that were disloyal." Eisenhower replied, promising he would investigate but "I do not know exactly what it is possible for me to do." Churchhill was recovering from a slight stroke and "Ike" sent his "earnest prayers" for his old friend's "early return to full and vigorous health."[39]

When neither the American president nor the French government appeared willing to bury the past, Churchill appealed to the Cabinet. He disclosed that the late King George VI had seen the file and insisted that if "publication could not be avoided," his brother the duke be given "timely warning." But Churchill's Top Secret memorandum of August 1953 that circulated to the Cabinet reveals that the Nobel Prize-winning chronicler of the war was thwarted by the historians.

The British editor in chief, the Honorable Margaret Lambert, threatened to resign if there was any government interference with the Anglo-American agreement of June 1946 guaranteeing its historians the right to "select and edit" the documents they desired and to publish them "on the basis of the highest scholarly objectivity." Churchill was partially successful in his fallback position: to delay publication for possibly "ten to twenty years on the grounds that these papers, tendentious and unreliable as they should undoubtedly be regarded, would give pain to the Duke of Windsor and leave an impression on the minds of those who read them entirely disproportionate to their historical value." The volume of German documents containing the Windsor telegrams did not appear until 1957. Then it included the caveat about its being a "necessarily much tainted source" and the assertion that the Duke of Windsor "never wavered in his loyalty to the British cause."[40]

One of the Allied historians who had no doubt about the historical veracity or value of the German Foreign Office material was Donald Cameron Watt, now Stevenson Professor of International History at the University of London. He confirmed that by 1948 more than four hundred tons of documents had arrived from the Allied Documents Center in Berlin for analysis under the more secure conditions of the Rothschild mansion at Whaddesdon Hall in Hertfordshire. Watt believes he was the first historian to see the Windsor section of the German Foreign Ministry files, including all the exchanges that took place in Spain and Portugal in 1940.

"Everything was there which we thought should have been there, with one exception," Watt observed. The exception, he said, was the record of the Windsors' meeting with Hitler at Berchtesgaden. This struck him, and the other historians, as being particularly odd because the two groups of Duke of Windsor material and the file on Edward as king had been kept in the same file record. Yet even without the Berchtesgaden record, the documentary evidence makes it difficult to avoid the conclusion that the duke was not as unwilling a participant in the German intrigue as Churchill and his other defenders have tried to make out.

Was the duke really unwavering in his loyalty to the British cause? An objective reading leaves an uncomfortably wide margin for suspicion. The Windsors were embittered royal exiles. They were isolated by what they believed to be continuing rebuffs from Buckingham Palace and Downing Street. But they were too easily persuaded to enter into negotiations — if nothing more — with the emissaries of Hitler. Their justification may have been a misguided belief that by helping to make peace, Windsor was freeing Germany to deal with the Soviet Union. The duke undoubtedly believed he was helping save the empire — and the world — from being overrun by the Communist menace. Nor was he alone among his countrymen in believing that despite its totalitarian unpleasantness, Nazi Germany was Britain's natural ally.

Under Britain's ancient law, treating with the king's enemy in the hour of Britain's mortal peril must surely have been high treason. But for his unique royal status and Churchill's indulgence, it seems that the duke came perilously close to committing this most serious crime. Further evidence to reinforce this charge comes from American intelligence agents who monitored the Windsors' activities in the Bahamas during the war. These reports confirm that the duke made good on his promise to Hitler to "remain in constant contact" while the Windsors struggled to come to terms with the "rust and discomfort" of the governor's mansion overlooking the tranquil emerald waters of Nassau Bay.

Suspicion continued to hover over the Windsors in their palm-fringed backwater. This explains the surprising number of FBI and U.S. Navy intelligence "enemy agent" category reports filed under "Windsor, Duke and Duchess of" that document their suspicious activities and those of their Bahamas coterie. The prime suspect was Axel Wenner-Gren, the Swedish millionaire blacklisted by the British and American governments for trading with the Axis. He arrived in Nassau harbor in his magnificently appointed yacht *The Southern Cross* shortly after the Windsors.

Most British historians with whom I have discussed this documentary evidence still loyally take the view that the duke and duchess were more sinned against than sinning. But John Loftus, a trial attorney who worked in the U.S. Department of Justice, has assured me that the Windsor FBI documents so far declassified represent only part of an even more substantial file on the Windsors. As the special investigator who coordinated the search for Nazi war criminals living in the United States, he was armed with a security clearance that enabled him to see classified material still held by the FBI and CIA. Loftus spent more than two years combing thousands of still-secret files and interviewing agents involved in wartime counterintelligence against the Nazis.

"Purely by accident I came across an 'Eyes Only Attorney General' file on the Windsors," said Loftus, who is an Irish Catholic graduate of Boston Latin School. He served as an army officer before simultaneously obtaining a master's degree in public administration and a law doctorate, then joining the Office of Special Investigations in 1979. His systematic search of all the Top Secret files pertaining to American knowledge of Nazis had taken him up to the sixth floor of the Justice Department building on Pennsylvania Avenue in Washington D.C., where there is a locked vault containing the most confidential records.[41]

Loftus explained that because he had the proper security clearance, it was only necessary for him to add his signature to the others on the cardboard cover sheets to obtain the *still* unclassified complete FBI dossier on the Windsors.

"It contained a bureau precis of the British and American intelligence reports on the duke and duchess," said Loftus. He was surprised to read J. Edgar Hoover's report that surveillance confirmed the Windsors were indeed considered a major threat to Allied security. Hoover recommended their internment for the duration of the war. Although the U.S. government did not take this drastic step — presumably in deference to Churchill and to avoid embarrassment to the British royal family — the files reveal that Hoover brushed aside demands from the duchess herself to stop censoring her mail and telephone communications.[42]

Loftus also recalls seeing in this highly secret Windsor file a report that while Edward was still on the throne, he had been in the process of setting out the basis of a deal with Hitler. The origin of the intelligence was obscure, but considered reliable by the U.S. State Department. As part of the "nonofficial" foreign policy that the king was promising, he would see to it that the British government turned a blind eye on German intentions to annex Austria and Czechoslovakia and move into the Balkans against French interests, in return for Hitler's protection of British interests in Poland. Without the documentation itself and without checking the reliability of the source, there is, of course, no way of judging the degree to which Edward's 1936 signal to Berlin of his "sincere resolve to bring England and Germany together" might have encouraged Hitler on the road to Munich.[43]

The final verdict of history is not yet in on the role played by Windsor. Churchill's unprecedented action in 1945, and then again in 1953, to suppress part of the German Windsor File, and Buckingham Palace's injunction to Peter Wright in 1967 against questioning Blunt about his mission to Germany, all suggest an extraordinary and continuing effort to keep a skeleton of substantial dimensions nailed up in the Round Tower of Windsor Castle, where the Royal Archives are kept.

Whatever bones of the Windsor/Hitler intrigue are still secreted in the Royal Archives, there can be no doubt that King George VI must have personally charged Anthony Blunt in 1945 with the delicate task of gathering up those remaining in the various castles of his royal German cousins. That it was an extensive operation lasting several years is now evident from revealing correspondence from the royal librarian. A memorandum of 1947 from Owen Morshead, which turned up in an obscure Foreign Office file on captured German records, finally provides the documented confirmation of their secret mission to collect the Hesse documents from Schloss Friedrichshof.

The file describes how Blunt and Morshead were still on their royal magpie mission in August 1947. This time they flew to The Hague. Their hunt was prompted by a still-classified memorandum from John Wheeler-Bennett, later official biographer of George VI but then editor in chief of the captured archives of the German Foreign Office. It seems

he came across a reference in these files to the role played in the
Windsor saga by Kaiser Wilhelm II, whose son Friedrich Wilhelm and
his wife, Cecilie, were both used by Hitler as royal intermediaries. The
old kaiser had died in 1941, but Haus Doorn in the Netherlands, where
he spent his exile, still contained his private papers and possessions.[44]

Morshead's report on their return to the king's private secretary, Sir
Alan Lascelles, specifically notes that "no documentary material was
found." But they did locate the kaiser's Garter insignia, and Blunt did
spot a Cosway painting of the Duke of Clarence, whose "proper home
is in the Royal library at Windsor." Blunt suggested the king make a
personal request for Queen Wilhelmina "to quitely"[sic] permit the
transfer of certain items to England. A month later, Morshead noted
the king's delight that the British ambassador in The Hague had quietly
retrieved the Garter and picture. The memorandum concludes with a
revealing paragraph that not only alludes to the Kronberg mission, but
suggests that even the king had doubts about the legality of possessing
the Hesse papers that were now securely locked away in the Round
Tower of Windsor Castle. Morshead wrote:

"The King expressly told me that we only hold them on the same
footing as we hold the things which I brought back from Frankfurt, i.e.
if the German Family in the future want them back . . . well, we have
no title to them; we hold them in security for them, over here in
England till things are settled."[45]

Morshead does not specify what it was that he brought back from
Frankfurt. But the reference to the mission to Schloss Friedrichshof in
the spring of 1945 is clear. Since it is a matter of public record that
Captain Nash and her boyfriend discovered the hidden gems and the
bound volumes of Queen Victoria's letters, the Doorn memorandum
reinforces the conclusion that the papers Morshead and Blunt collected
had even greater importance and more contemporary significance.
Prince Wolfgang confirmed that before she died in 1954, Princess
Margaret of Hesse requested, and received from Windsor, her mother's
correspondence and "other papers." Prince Wolfgang and the surviving
members of the family have kept discreetly silent about whether Philip
of Hesse's papers were among those returned — and if so, whether they
contained the records of his role as an intermediary for Hitler with the
Duke of Windsor and his brother the Duke of Kent.

Indirect corroboration that the Hesse archives *did* contain documents
relating to the Duke of Windsor's communications with Hitler also
comes from the former Justice Department investigator John Loftus.
He told me that it was after he had read the Top Secret FBI Windsor

file "late in '79 or early '80" that he interviewed two former U.S. military intelligence officers from the SHAEF T-groups attached to Patton's forces. His interest now fired up by the potentially high-level British–Nazi connection, Loftus inquired whether they had come across any documentary evidence. One of the officers confirmed that he had indeed seen references to communications between the Duke of Windsor and Hitler. He had discovered them in what he described as a "villa that was owned by a close relative of the duke which was occupied as an American officers' club."[46]

My own research confirms that the relative mentioned by Loftus's source must have been Hesse. The prohibitive expense of occupying the Schloss Friedrichshof full time had obliged Princess Margaret and her sons to live since 1925 in the expansive villas they had built in the wooded glades north of the main courtyard of the castle. This officer also told Loftus that shortly after he had reported his discovery, the British arrived to collect the highly embarrassing papers. The record shows that the Allied T-group officers in Operation Goldcup reported directly to SHAEF main headquarters.

The organizational charts show that Lieutenant Colonel Dick White was deputy head of counterintelligence in the G-2 organization, which was heavily staffed with MI5 officers. Another future MI5 director, Major Martin Furnival Jones, was in charge of Evaluation and Dissemination under White. Thus, it is obvious that any discovery of the Hesse-Windsor documents would have resulted in the relaying of the news by the most secure channels to King George VI and the prime minister. They would have recognized the need to act swiftly and secretly to prevent these documents — and any others like them — from falling into American hands. Deciding their fate presented less of a problem than effecting their retrieval from under the noses of inquisitive U.S. Army intelligence officers. Since they were private papers and not government documents, according to Professor Cameron Watt, they were justifiably removed to the security of the Royal Archives, because they were not covered by the inter-Allied agreement.[47]

The involvement of the royal archivist was a prerequisite. But Owen Morshead, although he had served with distinction in World War I, was well into his fifties and needed the assistance of an experienced intelligence officer. With his proven finesse for removing documents from diplomatic pouches, plus the confidence of his MI5 colleagues at SHAEF HQ and lack of official attachment, Blunt was the obvious man for the job. He was already an internationally recognized art authority and the OSS Art Looting Investigation Unit established in late 1944 by Norman Holmes Pearson's X-2 OSS counterintelligence group provided him with a ready-made cover for the secret royal mission.[48]

Dick White's reference to Blunt's post–D-Day involvement with looted art appears to corroborate that looted art was the convenient cover for the secret operation to scoop the royal documents. Nor, it seems, was Kronberg the only target of Blunt's mission. Prince Wolfgang was adamant that the six-course dinner Blunt recalled for Trevor-Roper could not have taken place at the Friedrichshof, which was already a U.S. officers' club. But even allowing for exaggeration, it is conceivable that such an elaborate affair was laid on for the royal emissaries of King George by the Hesse-Kassel cousins at one of their residences at Darmstadt or Wolfsgarten. Ellis Waterhouse recalls Blunt joking about returning to Windsor Castle and having to keep Queen Charlotte's crown in a chamber pot overnight. If Waterhouse remembered the item correctly, then Blunt retrieved this diadem at some royal residence other than Kronberg. For when Blunt went to Kronberg, the Hesse jewelry was still safely stowed in a lead box buried in the wine cellar of the Friedrichshof.[49]

Still unanswered is the enigma of what Blunt was doing between August 1944 and April 1945, the earliest date at which he could have been in Kronberg. How many months did he spend on other missions before he went to Germany to retrieve royal letters and jewelry? He was always adamant that he was not made surveyor of the king's pictures as a quid pro quo for his secret mission. Even if we take Blunt at his word, it is significant that the press announcement that appeared on April 27, 1945, *backdates* his appointment to the first of the month. In a curious blunder that must have given both Blunt and Soviet intelligence some cause for wry amusement, one London paper reported that Blunt "works in the British newspaper published in Russia."[50]

While the Soviets preferred that Blunt continue to serve their interests by remaining in the British intelligence services, his appointment to the Court was the first indication that he was determined to resume his artistic career. One of the most astonishing features of Blunt's schizophrenic life is that he had allowed neither his wartime duties, nor his spying for the Russians, to interfere with his relentless pursuit of his artistic aims. As the deputy director of the Courtauld, he continued lecturing and writing throughout the war whenever his MI5 duties permitted — even though the strain of two jobs plus his undercover work had taken its toll.

Blunt's iron constitution flagged in 1942. Mental exhaustion and physical illness forced him to retreat on medical leave to the Northern Ireland home of his Cambridge friend Peter Montgomery. But after a few weeks of rest, Blunt returned to London to resume his punishing schedule. And he still found time to produce learned commentaries for *The Journal of the Warburg* and *The Burlington Magazine* at an average rate of four a year, ranging from a discourse on Blake's pictorial imagination to the landscapes of Nicolas Poussin.[51]

Since 1943 Blunt had been devoting much of his off-duty time to Windsor Castle. In the reverent silence that reigns behind the mullioned windows of the Royal Library, he spent hour upon hour peering through his magnifying glass cataloging old-master drawings. Even before his scholarly book on five hundred French drawings was published two years later, to universal academic acclaim, his painstaking study had brought him to the attention of the royal household as an obvious candidate for surveyor of the king's pictures.[52]

The post, created by Charles I, the greatest of Britain's royal art patrons, involved maintaining and cataloguing the huge collection of more than five thousand pictures and hundreds of pieces of furniture and porcelain that the Crown had acquired for its palaces from Tudor times. Since 1934, the appointment had been reluctantly held by the director of the National Gallery, Sir Kenneth Clark. The Oxford-educated millionaire's son, whose reputation as an art historian was built on his stylish writing, had been dragooned into the job by King George V, who was known to be more interested in his stamp collection than in paintings.

Clark claimed he was "too obstinately committed to aesthetic values to give up my time to second-rate limners of royalty." Yet following the accession of George VI in 1937, he struck up a rapport with Queen Elizabeth, later the Queen Mother, who became an attentive pupil, admirer, and lifelong friend. With Benedict Nicolson, the son of Harold Nicolson, as his deputy, Clark had supervised the packing and removal of the royal treasures for safe storage at the outbreak of the war.[53]

Clark, an urbane connoisseur, got on surprisingly well with Blunt, whose bent was to dissect art mathematically. They had both served on the same exhibitions committee of the Royal Academy before the war, and it seems both believed in an aesthetic responsibility toward the common man that meant the inevitability of socialism. Although Blunt was now disguising his political convictions, Clark had written at the start of World War II that socialism was "the only solution." True to his egalitarian beliefs, he had persuaded the king and queen to commission paintings of the Blitz by contemporary artists. But as the war approached its final year, Clark was tiring of his responsibility for the royal collection, technically the private property of the sovereign being "held in trust for the nation." The return of the collection from the safety of the mountain caves in Wales raised the need for a cataloging and restoration program that Clark had neither the time nor the inclination to oversee.

The task was tailor-made for Blunt. He saw, and grasped, the chance to profit from his reputation as Britain's most promising young academic art historian. By diligently pursuing the laborious work of producing the first comprehensive catalog of the royal drawings at Windsor, he marked himself for preferment. He knew that he could count on Kenneth Clark's recommendation, and he cultivated Gerald Kelly, president of the Royal Academy, who spent most of the war as a semipermanent guest at Windsor Castle, completing the state portraits of the king and queen. An ebullient Irishman, Kelly's witty conversation made him a welcome guest at the royal dinner table during the dark days of the war — and some of his fellow members of the academy noted with interest how Blunt made a point of becoming his close friend.[54]

Apart from Blunt's professional qualifications, there were the ties of blood, family, and school on which he could advance himself with influential members of the royal household on whose advice the king relied. Blunt claimed distant kinship with Queen Elizabeth (he was her third cousin, their common ancestor being George Smith, the M.P. for Selsdon in 1792), and throughout his career at the Palace, remained a favorite guest at her table. He patiently deferred to her untutored interests in painting. According to one reliable account from the sixties when she was queen mother, Her Royal Highness delighted in gently deflating Blunt by having him perform the role of an elephant in her favorite after-dinner charades.[55]

One of Blunt's strong supporters was the royal librarian, Sir Owen Morshead. He was also an old Marlburian and pre-World War I Cambridge graduate, as well as a confidant of Queen Mary. As the matriarch of the House of Windsor, she avidly read books about art, and regarded herself as something of an expert on the vast artistic collection.

"Queen Mary was an enthusiastic collector, though her taste was for objets d'art rather than paintings," Blunt would later acknowledge. What he tactfully omitted was that this daunting matriarch was accustomed, to the dismay of her hosts, to exercise the ancient royal prerogative to "collect" bibelots from dealers and the country houses of friends. Until Queen Mary's death in 1952, Blunt took great care to defer to and remain on good terms with her. She returned the compliment by slipping into the Courtauld from time to time to hear him lecture on her favorite painters. She always insisted on the minimum of formality. But her large maroon Daimler, anachronistic Edwardian parasol, and veiled toque hat made it impossible for her to arrive and depart unceremoniously.[56]

Blunt's royal patron subscribed to *The Burlington Magazine* and counted herself among his most devoted students. When he wrote of a Venetian painting "lost" to the royal collection, she triumphantly remembered it had been hanging all the time in a dingy corridor of Holyrood Palace. The affectionate regard in which Queen Mary held Blunt made an indelible impression on Jackie Hewit. He said that each Christmas a small personal gift would arrive for Blunt from Marlborough House. When she sent a "reticule" that she hoped "Dear Anthony" would find "useful," it became an enormous joke among his homosexual friends — the queen mother had given the regal Blunt what appeared to be a handbag.[57]

Although Queen Mary's "reticule" was an unintentional blunder, it was certainly known at the Palace that Blunt was a homosexual. His fellow art historian, Ellis Waterhouse, insisted that "everyone knew about Anthony's personal habits" by 1947, when Oliver Millar, Blunt's eventual successor as surveyor, was appointed to be his assistant. Waterhouse said the parents of the twenty-four-year-old former Courtauld student "were very worried that he would be working alongside such a notorious queen as Blunt." According to a former British SOE officer who frequented Windsor Castle, even the guardroom used to crack jokes about the need for "backs to the wall" if Blunt was about.[58]

Homosexuality was not a drawback when Blunt started to work his way into royal favor. Membership in the royal household has traditionally provided homosexuals with the same comfortable security as the cloistered enclaves of an Oxbridge college. This applies not just to the courtiers upstairs, but also to many members of the male staffs in the royal palaces.

It was the present queen's cousin, the late Lord Mountbatten, who tartly dismissed criticism that his naval servant was homosexual: "Of course — all the best valets are." As one distinguished royal biographer pointed out: "Many of the footmen and butlers are homosexual because they have to put in long hours for relatively low reward." This source also assured me that older members of the royal family even preferred the attentiveness shown them by homosexual courtiers like Blunt. Their lack of family commitments, willingness to partake in the whimsical royal after-dinner parlor games, and their biting gossip about the upper crust of British society made them sought-after companions.[59]

The rule is to "know but not openly acknowledge" the important role that homosexuals have always played as royal retainers. Yet while the amorous adventures and marital infidelities of the junior members of the House of Mountbatten-Windsor make newspaper headlines, there is still a strict taboo on gossiping about the homosexual networking that operated in the glittering prewar London circle. Those in the know claim that it revolved around Edward, the Prince of Wales, his younger brother, George, the Duke of Kent, the queen's brother, David Bowes-Lyon, and their cousin Lord Louis Mountbatten. The principal players are dead and cannot deny stories that they were observed making discreet visits to the London pubs where guardsmen were for rent. But some of those who knew them are still alive. Before and during the war, they have assured me, a pub called the Packenham was the favorite haunt of Blunt and the royal set in pursuit of illicit male sex.[60]

"I want to be like the boys at the Packenham and go about whackin' 'em and stickin' my jack in 'em." According to Robert Harbinson these were the first lines of a bawdy ballad that celebrated the notorious pub in Knightsbridge that was conveniently close to Whitehall, Buckingham Palace, and the barracks occupied by the Household Cavalry and the Guards. This unashamedly bisexual author, who writes under the name Robin Bryans, recalled his own visits to the Packenham as one of Blunt's intimate circle, which he joined after Guy Burgess picked him up at Oxford early in 1944.[61]

"You see, Anthony was very, very proud of his royal connections," Harbinson contends. He talked frankly about his personal experiences, producing letters and family trees that mapped out the web of interlocking friendships that connected Noël Coward, and London's theatrical homosexuals, to the Foreign Office network that included Burgess's friend Harold Nicolson, to the country-house homosexual circuit into which Blunt was introduced by Peter Montgomery. In turn, this enabled Blunt to plug in to the special friendships associated with the royal set.[62]

Harbinson was insistent that it was important to take into account Blunt's prewar association with the Duke of Kent, the black sheep of the royal family, who was killed in an RAF crash in 1942. Even Palace biographers have acknowledged that the tall, fair-haired duke had what, today, would be called a drug problem — not to mention a series of amorous entanglements until he was persuaded to settle down and marry Princess Marina of Greece in 1934. The Duke of Kent's handsomeness attracted partners of both sexes, according to Harbinson, who says he possesses letters that reveal how Lady Bridget Parsons broke off her liaison with Prince George after discovering he was sleeping with a male relative.

Much of what Harbinson told me appears to be gossip that can never be substantiated. But it contains some hard facts. It is recorded that Blunt met the Duke of Kent, who was five years his senior, through his Trinity College contemporary Prince Chula Chakrabongse. Blunt was anxious to make his reputation as an art historian, and Prince George had inherited his mother's interests and established himself as a discriminating connoisseur who spent lavishly on paintings, the most significant being the Altieri Claudes that Admiral Nelson had brought to England. Whether Blunt was ever amorously involved with Queen Mary's wayward youngest son, as several of Blunt's intimates believe, there is now no way of proving.[63]

Bizarre though some of Harbinson's theories may be, those that could be checked mesh with the established record. When I made inquiries, I discovered that many of Harbinson's more exotic assertions about the degrees of homosexuality in the Palace network were discreetly confirmed by reputable authorities who knew of the matters through their official positions or personal contacts. They, too, are of the opinion that Blunt would not have hesitated to exploit his personal connections, or knowledge, in preparing his way to become a trusted member of the royal household.

Blunt's appointment as surveyor of the king's pictures was, on the face of it, a curious career move for an intensely ambitious art historian. While it brought prestige and responsibility, it was a job that Kenneth Clark said involved too many pointless duties and was excessively demanding in terms of time. Ellis Waterhouse recalled how he "thought it was an insane thing for Anthony to do." His attitude prompted Blunt to admit to him after his exposure thirty-three years later: "You know, Ellis, the only time I thought you might ever suspect me was when I became surveyor."[64]

Now it is clear that Blunt's acceptance of the post was not, as Waterhouse thought, simply because he thought the prestige would enhance the Courtauld. Blunt's main objective seems to have been that he needed to persuade his Soviet masters that he could withdraw from MI5 and continue serving them by resuming his career as an art historian. To have been able to do this was a unique achievement because those who joined Stalin's underground service were expected to make a commitment to serving Moscow for life. But Blunt shrewdly realized that, as a member of the Court, he could position himself as able to serve as an informant for Moscow from an even loftier position in the British establishment.

The British sovereign, by virtue of constitutional authority, has the right to — and does — read *all* the most important state papers and consults with Cabinet ministers on a weekly basis. History shows that dictators like Hitler, on the basis of their own Byzantine court intrigues, misinterpreted the real influence and power of the British monarchy and aristocracy. This misunderstanding applied with even greater force to Stalin and his intelligence chief, Beria. Neither had any conception of the mechanisms of constitutional democracy, and their Soviet regime was run with a despotic absolutism that few of the tsars could equal.

"From 1945 I ceased to pass information to the Russians," Blunt declared publicly in 1979. The reason he gave was his loss of conviction that the Soviet regime "was following the true principles of Marxism." However, a curious slip suggests he did not finally decide that the Kremlin was no longer the repository of the true faith until *six years* after his supposed break with Moscow. For he added: "By 1951, anyhow, I realized that this was totally false." Blunt also tried to give the impression that handing in his notice to the Soviets was no more complicated than resigning from an ordinary job. "It just happened," Blunt told the reporters, "They realized I was no longer interested."[65]

Blunt's assertions are dismissed as disingenuous by the American intelligence community. They know from their experience in debriefing other KGB defectors that such a mutually agreed unilateral withdrawal is so unusual as to make Blunt the unique exception to the rule in the history of Soviet intelligence operations.

"Blunt's departure from the security service at the end of the war cannot be viewed as an act of spontaneity on his part," contends Robert Crowley. "Breaking with Moscow is never easy. It is usually effected only if the agent defects or confesses. There is no evidence that Blunt did either. In his case, the Soviets had too many coercive levers that could have been used to force him to continue." So, Crowley reasons, Blunt would have been allowed to take up the Palace appointment only after it had been examined with great care "both by his Soviet controller and his senior officers in Moscow Center."[66]

The Soviets did permit Blunt to leave MI5. This leads to the presumption that they already had another agent in place in the British security service. While American and British intelligence officers differ on some aspects of the Blunt case, the consensus of those I have consulted is that Moscow Center would have sanctioned Blunt's 1945 move from MI5 only if two conditions were satisfied:

(1) Moscow already had in MI5 another agent — or agents — of equivalent seniority and access.

(2) Blunt convinced Moscow that he would continue providing high-level intelligence about the British government.

Leaving for later analysis the contentious issue of who took over from Blunt as the principal mole in MI5, Blunt would have had no difficulty satisfying his Soviet controller as to the second condition.

"Blunt had good connections at Court and no doubt he exaggerated what he could make of these," Robert Cecil emphasized. "Without concluding that he had any link with the homosexual royal circle, it seems clear that his ability to chat up people and relay their gossip would have enormously impressed his controller and his bosses in the Kremlin."[67]

Even before Blunt accepted the post of surveyor, his access to the Palace and SHAEF headquarters would have made him aware of the cover-up of the Windsor affair. This information would have been an additional bonus for the Soviets, to whom he certainly disclosed the contents of the Hesse files, plus the contents of any other incriminating documents that he scooped up on his secret missions to Germany. While it may be true that the royal appointment was offered to Blunt *before* he set off with Morshead for Kronberg, the end of April announcemen, which backdated his appointment to the first, may reflect the refusal of his Soviet masters to agree until *after* he returned with the incriminating Hesse documents.

Once Blunt gained knowledge of the explosive royal secret, it became his gold-plated insurance policy. Even if his espionage was uncovered, Blunt would argue, his crime paled before the enormity of Windsor's wartime activities. And given the lengths to which the British government was willing to go to cover up these activities, Blunt would have been able to make a convincing case that he had a cast-iron guarantee against ever being publicly exposed. The Kremlin must also have appreciated that, in the Palace, Blunt could also provide a safety net for the other Cambridge agents. No one Blunt had recruited could ever be brought to public trial in Britain without implicating Blunt. Again, to expose Blunt would threaten the Windsor secret. Eighteen years later, when the royal insurance policy had to be cashed in because Michael Straight burned Blunt with the authorities, the policy proved to be pure gold. It protected Blunt and his subsidiary agents from public disgrace for another sixteen years.

So Blunt's insistence that he did "absolutely nothing" for the Soviets after 1945 can now be rejected as "totally untrue." By his very presence in Buckingham Palace, Blunt assisted Moscow's schemes. So were his assertions about working for MI5 merely "tying up loose ends."[68]

"Even in the pursuit of his career as the royal art historian, Blunt continued to be regarded and occasionally employed as a trusted former security-service officer who maintained excellent informal relations with a number of senior serving officers," contends Crowley. "The most compelling argument against his having abruptly quit the Soviets is the important role he played in the pre-official search of Burgess's flat, and the advice and guidance he offered the security service in their investigations of the flight of Burgess and Maclean."[69]

In 1945 Blunt was highly respected. And it was not only the Soviet intelligence service that was anxious for him to find a way of staying on. His position of trust at the Palace enhanced rather than hindered his continuing close association with his former friends in MI5. Blunt admitted that he met "one or two of them socially, over a drink" including Dick White and Guy Liddell. "By that time I was also going to the Travellers' Club, and he [Liddell] was a member so I used to go and meet him there," Blunt said.[70]

Blunt's claim to have broken formally with both MI5 and Soviet intelligence is also disputed by Leo Long. In 1946 Blunt unexpectedly dropped in on Long at 21st Army Group headquarters, forty miles southwest of Hanover at Bad Oeynhausen. Long was then serving with the British Control Commission, a job he said he took rather than return to intelligence work in London for MI4 following his hospitalization. He had been injured when his jeep overturned near Le Havre during the Normandy landings. Long told me he had come to Germany to get away from what he called "the spying business." But if this was so, then he ended up in the wrong job. Long was on the staff of the organization that included Felix Cowgill. Their job was rounding up Nazis and weeding out Communist subversives to set the stage for returning the British zone of occupation back on the road to political normalcy.[71]

"I was under the impression Blunt was on some hush-hush mission from MI5 headquarters in London," Long said. "As director of operations in intelligence, I was the obvious man for him to contact." He recalls driving Blunt to "some castle." But Long does not know much more about the mission. Nor, he insisted, did Blunt put any pressure on him to provide secret information, although, he admitted, he "had access to most Allied intelligence reports."[72]

One of the inconsistencies in Long's story is that he admits that Blunt persuaded him to apply for a post in MI5. When he was later interrogated by Peter Wright, Long said Blunt had written out his recommendation. Although his candidature was rejected, Blunt had canvassed and obtained the backing of Dick White — a letter of recommendation that later caused the future director of MI5 and MI6 considerable discomfiture. Long then moved to Düsseldorf to continue his intelligence work for the Control Commission. He ducked behind the Official Secrets Act when I asked him precisely what he had been doing there. But he insisted it had nothing to do with the Russians. Wright, who was privy to the details of Long's job, did not believe him. He says that Long's repeated denials of contact with Blunt, or any other Soviet agents, was "rubbish."[73]

Noël Annan, who was then serving in Germany as a colonel in the Political Division of the Control Commission, also has his doubts. Annan says he found Long was suspiciously "opposed to anything which helped the Christian Democrats," whose leader, Konrad Adenauer, was prepared to accept the political division of Germany.[74]

According to Nigel West, the real function of Long's job was to infiltrate agents behind the Iron Curtain, but "his efforts were largely nullified by his then undiscovered dual role as a Soviet spy."[75]

More evidence is coming to light from the U.S. Archives that suggests that the full story has yet to be told. It appears that Long was a link in a major Cold War plot to infiltrate Soviet agents into the U.S. intelligence services with the connivance of their other moles in MI5 and MI6. This conspiracy, for which we now have the first documentary evidence, was so immense that its dimensions were not fully appreciated for another twenty years.

# CHAPTER 24

# *"An Enormous Amount of Influence"*

The defeat of Hitler was only a matter of months away on February 4, 1945, when the Big Three leaders arrived at Yalta for a summit meeting in the imperial splendor of the Livadia summer palace. The British and American leaders faced a dilemma: how to prevent a resurrection of German power without leaving the Soviet Union dominant in Europe.

The Yalta Conference for the first time brought Winston Churchill face to face with the painful reality of the new superpower politics. Britain no longer commanded top-dog status at the conference table. The prime minister found Roosevelt deaf to his entreaties about the need for military guarantees to prevent communism from rolling over Poland and Eastern Europe. When and where the Iron Curtain would descend on postwar Europe was going to be determined by the Soviet Union and the United States.

The president, ill and with his powers of concentration visibly in decline, focused his remaining energy on winning Stalin's commitment to launch the United Nations. According to the prime minister, his old American ally was "behaving very badly" by distancing himself from the British delegation. He was accepting on trust Stalin's verbal guarantees of Polish sovereignty. "He won't take any interest in what we are trying to do," Churchill complained to his aides.[1]

"Sombre indeed would be the fortunes of mankind if some awful schism arose between the Western democracies and the Russian Soviet Union," Churchill reported to the House of Commons after his return from the Crimea. While he was uneasy about Stalin's keeping his "solemn agreements" of free elections in the German-occupied nations liberated by the Red Army, the prime minister publicly took comfort that: "The United States has entered deeply and constructively into the life and salvation of Europe."[2]

Military muscle and industrial resources, and not the geographic silt of the imperial adventure, defined the postwar era. But for more than a decade — until the debacle at Suez in 1956 — the British government refused to face the reality Churchill had acknowledged in 1945. "Britain fondly imagined she had won the war. She had not," declares historian Noël Annan. "America and Russia had won the war. Britain had merely, in her finest hour, not lost it."[3]

By the end of World War II the British government had also ceased to be the primary target for Soviet penetration. The United States became the major objective of Soviet clandestine assault.

"An Iron Curtain is drawn down upon their front," Churchill warned Harry Truman, the new American president, on May 10, 1945, barely forty-eight hours after the official celebration of victory over Germany. Could Stalin be trusted to keep his word now the Red Army held a line from the Baltic to the Adriatic that occupied half of Europe? Before the question could be answered, Churchill was swept from office by a landslide Labour victory. So he was unable to influence the resolution of these concerns at the Allied conference in Potsdam that July.[4]

We can now see that Churchill's fears about what could happen behind the Iron Curtain were tragically ironic. At the very moment when the dropping of two atomic bombs on Japan brought the global conflict to its shattering climax in August 1945, a veritable brood of Soviet moles were roaming undetected in the corridors of Whitehall — and, as we shall see, also in Washington. Three of the original Cambridge recruits had done credit to their alma mater by rising to positions in the British governing elite. Blunt was untouchably ensconced behind the throne of the British monarch (with Guy Liddell, now deputy director of MI5, effectively compromised and in his pocket); Philby was in charge of anti-Soviet operations in MI6 and grooming himself for C's office; and Donald Maclean was the first secretary of the British embassy in Washington.

Stalin's Englishmen could now ensure the Kremlin an inside track on Anglo-American foreign policy. This access was doubly secured by Donald Maclean and Guy Burgess, who, in 1945, managed to satisfy a selection board that he should be taken into the permanent establishment of the Foreign Office. When Clement Attlee's Labour government took office, Burgess became personal assistant to Hector McNeil, a young Scottish socialist M.P. and journalist friend from BBC days. McNeil was an aide to the His Majesty's minister of state for foreign affairs. While Ernest Bevin approached Moscow with the rugged skepticism of a tough trade-union leader who had successfully fought Communist infiltration, the fact that Burgess was in his outer office gave Stalin the advantage.

According to Filip Vasilievich Kislitsyn, who at the time was a cipher clerk in the Soviet embassy in London, Burgess was one of the most productive spies the Soviets were running. Ten years later, when Kislitsyn was with the Soviet legation in Canberra, he told Vladimir Petrov, his senior MVD officer, how "Burgess was bringing out briefcases full of Foreign Office documents, which were photographed in the Soviet embassy and returned to him."[5]

When Petrov sought asylum in Australia in 1954, he provided a sworn affidavit about this for the American embassy. It explains how well Kislitsyn knew the London embassy case officer responsible for Burgess. He "used to return with muddy clothes after his meetings, which evidently took place at some obscure country rendezvous." Kislitsyn, who was in London from 1945 through 1948, recalled how he used to encipher "the more urgent information and cable it to Moscow." The rest he prepared for dispatch by courier in the diplomatic bag. Back in Moscow in 1949, Kislitsyn specialized in English until his appointment to the KGB's First Directorate and the responsibility for "a special one-man section" of top-secret archives.[6]

"This section was devoted solely to the great quantity of material supplied by Maclean and Burgess," Kislitsyn told Petrov. "Much of it had not even been translated or distributed to the ministries concerned, but Kislitsyn used to show particular files and documents to high-ranking officials who visited his section for the purpose."[7]

Apart from his role as Soviet spy, the garlic-chewing Burgess was also an "agent of influence." Despite the slovenly dress that infuriated the exacting Foreign Office mandarins, his position papers — invariably coffee-stained and embellished with doodled cartoons — were persuasive, skillfully argued and subtly designed to manipulate the outcome of policy issues in a way that favored Moscow. Burgess, however, was by no means the only agent of influence among his Cambridge contemporaries.

These agents were just the tip of the Soviet penetration effort to come to fruition from prewar recruiting. (Only in the KGB archive in Moscow are the complete files that could tell us for certain how many spies, agents of influence, and sympathizers the Soviet intelligence services had infiltrated into government on both sides of the Atlantic by the end of World War II.)

What we know now is that in Whitehall, in the Colonial Office, a fellow Apostle, Andrew Cohen, began to play a critical role in molding the views that set the stage for the dismantling of Britain's empire in Africa. In the Treasury there was Dennis Proctor, and in the Admiralty, Alister Watson, also a member of the society, worked on top-secret devices for submarine detection. Alan Nunn May, the nuclear physicist then working in Canada on the Manhattan Project, was providing Soviet agents in Canada with samples of enriched uranium used in the Hiroshima bomb. Another Communist of the same Cambridge vintage, the Canadian-born Egerton Herbert Norman, was a rising diplomat in Canada's External Affairs Ministry attached to the staff of General Douglas MacArthur in Tokyo.

In the spring of 1940, Herbert Norman returned to complete his doctoral thesis on "Japan's Emergence as a Modern State." After completing his Harvard doctorate in May, Norman returned to the Canadian External Affairs Ministry. His career as a diplomat began with a posting to Japan in 1940 as third secretary of the Tokyo embassy. Eyewitness testimony suggests that these two former members of the Trinity cell were also enmeshed in the circle of Communists and their close sympathizers who were involved in far-eastern affairs.

Professor Karl Wittfogel testified that he knew Norman in 1937–38 as being a member of "a small Communist study group" of Columbia academics. Norman also had contacts with Chi Ch'ao-ting, a Moscow-trained Comintern agent associated with the American Friends of the Chinese People. Dr. Chi, who went to Chungking in 1941 as an economist in Chiang Kai-shek's Ministry of Finance, was a secret protégé of Chou En-lai under whom he served as a high official in Mao Tse-tung's Communist regime.[8]

Philip Jaffe, a Communist and a businessman who made his fortune in greeting cards, would also testify later that Herbert Norman was "certainly a very close fellow traveler" to whom he had been first introduced in1935 by Chi Ch'ao-ting. According to Jaffe, Dr. Chi acted as "the leader of the Far East Group of Communists operating on the East Coast of the United States" who "corrected our ideological mistakes."[9]

According to Jaffe, another "intimate friend" of Chi's was Frank Coe, also a Canadian, who gravitated to the U.S. Treasury Department. Another member of the Harvard circle suspected of being a Communist was Far East faculty member Dr. John K. Fairbank. A wartime OSS adviser and future Harvard professor, Fairbank denied the accusation.

Records of the Senate Judiciary Committee show that Jaffe had been "confidentially assisting the Internal Security Subcommittee since approximately 1951." He corroborated testimony that Norman was in the Communist network cell at the Institute of Pacific Relations, an organization that the executive of the Communist Party of the U.S.A. regarded as being "the Little Red Schoolhouse for teaching certain people in Washington how to think with the Soviet Union in the Far East."[10]

The Institute for Pacific Relations, headquartered at 125 East Fifty-second Street in New York, was an international group established in 1925 to promote public and governmental awareness of the economic, political, and cultural affairs of the nations of the Pacific rim. Ostensibly representing the liberal left, its organization was that of a classic Münzenberg Communist front. An international secretariat made up of prominent Asian scholars, politicians, and businessmen acted for branches that contained Communists and their sympathizers. There was a section in Moscow. One of the representatives of the British branch was Günther Stein, the Shanghai journalist with NKVD connections and links to Mao Tse-tung's American eulogist, Agnes Smedley.

"The IPR itself was like a specialized political flypaper in its attractive power for Communists" was the conclusion of a U.S. Senate investigating committee, which in 1952 reported that "a remarkably large number of Communists and pro-Communists showed up in the publications, conferences, offices, institutions of the IPR, or in letters and homes of the IPR family." In the words of the majority report, the "effective leadership" of the institute had diverted that organization's "prestige to promote the interests of the Soviet Union in the United States."[11]

The effective leadership of the Institute of Pacific Relations and its journal *Pacific Affairs* was handled by an executive committee under the secretary general and his allies: Edward C. Carter, Frederick Vanderbilt Field, and Owen Lattimore. All were alleged to have Communist sympathies or affiliations. Congressional testimony linked Lattimore, a Johns Hopkins University academic, to the same Communist cell as Philip Jaffe and Frederick Vanderbilt Field. Lattimore denied these accusations although Luis Budenz testified that he was present in 1937 when the CPUSA chairman laid down that Lattimore was to be "given general direction of organizing the writers and influencing the writers in representing the Chinese Communists as agrarian reformers. . . ." Lattimore would deny the accusation and coin the term "McCarthyism."

When I interviewed former IPR assistant Andrew Roth, he told me the institute's role was to influence American policy in the Far East "in a certain direction." Born in Brooklyn of Hungarian émigré parents, Roth graduated from City College and worked for Jaffe at the institute in the summer of 1940. (He had obtained his master's degree from the School of Far East Studies at Columbia University.) Senate investigators later alleged that Roth "was known to be a Communist" by the time he received his naval commission two years later. Roth denied this. "We were pro-Chinese and liberal left," Roth declared.[12]

Four days before Pearl Harbor, Roth enrolled in the navy and attended a Japanese-language course at Harvard the following year. He became a lieutenant attached to the Office of Naval Intelligence in Washington. Roth told me that he maintained his close connections with IPR while in the navy because he wanted to write and Jaffe was the editor of its *Amerasia* magazine, who was assisting with his magnum opus calling for extensive postwar reforms in Japan.

Another name to be linked with the IPR was that of Michael Straight, who had broken away from the Soviet network by quitting his State Department job in May 1941 to become Washington editor of *The New Republic*. He also involved himself with liberal causes, including the American Peace Mobilization and the North American Spanish Relief Committee. Because of his close friendship with John Cornford, the war in Spain held emotional ties for Straight, whose sister-in-law had married Gustavo Durán, a pianist and composer, who had been a Loyalist officer in the Spanish Civil War.[13]

Straight's involvement with what the FBI regarded as "a number of organizations of varying degrees of Communist and non-Communist sympathies" prompted J. Edgar Hoover to authorize "extremely discreet inquiries" into his activities and those of *The New Republic*. The FBI case file on Straight quotes an article, "Muddled Millions, Capitalist Angels of Left-Wing Propaganda," that appeared in *The Saturday Evening Post* in February 1941. This named *The New Republic* and *The Nation* as the two journals that had "given the most aid and prestige to the Communists in this country." The FBI estimated that the Straight family trust had subsidized *The New Republic* to the annual tune of $100,000 and that what the report characterized as "these Communistically inclined publications" had "benefited from the Straight fortune to the extent of approximately $2,500,000."[14]

That an American capitalist fortune should fund left-wing propaganda evidently galled J. Edgar Hoover. His vexation intensified at the end of 1941 when the Straight family lent money and support to the promotion of the Free World Association. Its declared objective was "to promote the cause of justice, democracy and human freedom in the USA and throughout the world." The Free World Association attracted the support of many distinguished liberals, politicians, and internationalists. But it had all the trappings of a Communist front. Although the FBI detected "no known members of the CPUSA" in the organization, careful monitoring of its meetings and publications led to the conclusion that its "general tenor" was pro-Communist.[15]

The FBI had good reason for its suspicion because Louis Dolivet played a central role in the Association and its related publication, *World*. Dolivet has always denied these suspicions, but FBI, State Department, and Military Intelligence records support congressional testimony that he was a former associate of Willi Münzenberg. Dolivet's real name was Ludwig Brecher. Accompanied by Pierre Cot, a French

deputy and suspected Soviet spy, Dolivet arrived in New York from
Marseilles in the summer of 1941 on a refugee visa. Cot and Dolivet
spoke fervently about peace and freedom, enlisting the support of Alan
Cranston in the Office of War Information, Nelson D. Rockefeller —
and Michael Straight, who invested $250,000 in *World*.[16]

Straight introduced Dolivet to his sister, Beatrice. Notwithstanding
that the charismatic Hungarian looked like Beethoven and, according
to FBI records, was living with an Irish-American movie director's
daughter, he wooed and married Beatrice in Des Moines, Iowa, in
November 1941, taking care to initial his signature in the wedding
register "L.B." Fired by Dolivet's Free World philosophy and the
January 1942 signing by the Allies of the Declaration of the United
Nations, Straight began writing and speaking on his vision of the
postwar world organization.[17]

"The New Deal is more dynamic than Fascism and more revolutionary than communism," Straight declared in March 1942 at a dinner that
marked the tenth year of the Roosevelt administration. The significance
of that statement did not escape conservative newspaper columnists.
They pointed out that Straight's radical pronouncement followed hard
on *The New Republic*'s assertion: "Known Communist sympathizers are
again finding it relatively easy to get Government jobs." The following
month, *The New Republic* carried Straight's attack on the FBI for "still
hounding union leaders, while, on the New York waterfront, Axis agents
have no trouble signing on as stevedores."[18]

Hoover could not ignore this affront to the integrity of the bureau.
FBI records show that in February 1942 its investigation of Straight
was given a more sinister designation: "Internal Security-R[ussian]."
The cover sheets show that Straight shared the same case file with
another person. The censor's pen conceals the other name, but from a
letter count and other references to that individual's activities, the file
suggests that it was Straight's mother, Dorothy Whitney Elmhirst, a
lifelong champion of liberalism and socialism.

Straight's ardent championship of a radical New Deal philosophy
encouraged the Soviets to make a fresh effort to reclaim his services.
After an interval of two years, in the late summer of 1942 when he was
back at the family's Old Westbury estate, Straight received a telephone
call from "Michael Green" (Walter Grienke). Twenty-one years later,
Straight would tell the FBI how he took the Long Island Railroad from
Westbury to Jamaica Station. While driving around the suburbs of
Queens for "an hour or more," Straight renewed his acquaintance with
the Russian described in the bureau records as his "Soviet handler."

Straight could not recall any "requests or discussions," but said only that it was a general conversation about what he was now doing.[19]

Green urged Straight to meet with Earl Browder, the leader of the CPUSA. Straight was then in the final stages of finishing a book about how the United Nations should deal with the collapse of colonialism in a postwar world that would urgently need a global policy of relief and reconstruction. He told the FBI that he did not meet Browder until the publication party of *Make This the Last War* in January 1943. He also explained how he had contacted Maxim Litvinov, the Soviet ambassador, to inform him about his forthcoming book, which advised Moscow to "stop paying lip service to democracy or another great war was inevitable." Green, he said, was also given a memorandum summarizing his arguments.[20]

Straight also told the FBI that he had at least one other meeting with Michael Green at a New York restaurant called Longchamps. Also present was a woman named Helen whom he understood to be Mrs. Green. He did not question this at the time because they "comported themselves as a happily married couple." Straight's FBI file notes that either at this or an earlier meeting, "at the request of Michael Green," Straight had supplied letters of accreditation for a Swedish woman journalist and for Mark Julius Gayn. (The journalist was later identified by a defector as a Soviet agent, and Gayn, a Chinese expert with IPR affiliations, was arrested in the *Amerasia* case.)[21]

The FBI was particularly anxious to fix the date for Straight's final meeting with Michael Green. He agreed that it must have occurred after November 24, 1942, because that was the day Straight registered for service with the U.S. Army Air Corps. This decision, Straight said, was prompted both by Michael Green's renewed attention and by the birth of his son that October. He reiterated to the FBI his hope that military service would enable him to "avoid subsequent contacts" with the Soviets.[22]

The FBI records also disclose that in December 1942 Straight attended an Institute of Pacific Relations conference held at the Canadian resort of Mont Tremblant in Quebec. Since one of the invitees was Egerton Herbert Norman (he returned from Japan in August 1941 aboard the liner *Gripsholm* with other repatriated Allied diplomats), the conference brought together two former members of the Trinity Communist cell. Straight, however, cannot recall whether he met Norman at Mont Tremblant.

Although the Communist parties were playing down their commitment to violent revolution, the FBI provided the U.S. attorney general with a list of proscribed organizations, including Communist fronts, membership in which made applicants unsuitable for government work. The IPR was not yet on the list but was soon to be implicated in raising support for Mao Tse-tung's struggle to overthrow the government of Chiang Kai-Shek.

Accompanied by Owen Lattimore, Henry Wallace embarked on a fact-finding visit to China in June 1944. The Nationalist demand for a billion dollars more in aid had opened a policy rift in the State Department. Veteran China hands in the Far East Division, led by Stanley Hornbeck, who supported the loan, were resentful of the lack of support for, and the increasing criticism of, Chiang Kai-shek by the "pro-Chinese liberals." This faction was arguing for U.S. support of the Yenan regime and raising suspicions that Chiang might deflect the aid from the war against the Japanese to reopen the civil war with an attack on the rival Communist forces of Mao Tse-tung.

Central to this strategy was persuading Roosevelt and the American people that the Russian-backed-and-equipped People's Army and its leaders were not really Soviet-style Communists. Wallace's diary reveals that Currie and Fairbank had successfully convinced the vice-president that the Chinese Communists "were agrarian reformers." Owen Lattimore, who spent part of the war in Chungking as an adviser to Chiang Kai-shek, denied he had ever described the Chinese Communists as "agrarian reformers." But that was the impression he gave by his portrayal of Mao's regime as a "peasant party" that was responsible for the "most positive step yet taken in China by any party away from dictatorship and towards democracy."[23]

On his fact-finding mission to the Communist headquarters in Yenan, the vice-president naïvely volunteered to negotiate a settlement between the rival Chinese leaders. Mao took the cue. He talked with the American representatives about his admiration for democracy. He hinted at the need for "free enterprise and foreign capital in China." Even Soviet Foreign Minister Vyacheslav Molotov joined in the "window dressing" by scornfully calling the Chinese "margarine Communists," saying they had "no relation whatever to communism." The popular press in America quickly echoed the new theme.[24]

"For the foreign reader it is somewhat confusing that this Chinese agrarian reform movement is called 'Communism,'" *The Saturday Evening Post* told its audience. "Communism in China is a watered-down thing today." In the State Department, John Stewart Service, another of the "pro-Chinese liberals" with IPR connections, wrote of Mao's New Democracy, contrasting his rosy view of the Yenan regime with the corrupt and intractable Nationalists. With sympathizers in the Roosevelt administration and a supporting chorus of popular propaganda from pro-Communist writers such as Agnes Smedley and Günther Stein, Mao began preparations for the final leg of the Long March that would take the Communists to power.[25]

The expulsion of the Nationalists from mainland China four years later ended with a search for scapegoats in Washington. The notion that infiltration of the Roosevelt and Truman administrations could have been responsible for the "loss of China" fueled the flames of the anti-Communist outcry. Historians still furiously debate what portion of the blame — if any — lies with Washington as opposed to the inherent corruption and military incapacity of the Nationalists. The Senate committee that investigated the Institute of Pacific Relations in 1952 concluded, however, that the institute and its alumni in the administration were the "vehicle used by the Communists to orientate American far eastern policies toward Communist objectives."[26]

The orientation, it is now clear, also involved what can be called espionage. *Amerasia* was an "obscure little magazine" linked to but published independently by the institute. Edited by Philip Jaffe, it was radical in tone and remarkably well informed. Too well informed, the OSS decided in February 1945 when the magazine printed an article on the Nationalist Chinese army that was a virtual paraphrase of a secret OSS report only two months old.

An investigation led, on the night of March 11, 1945, to an OSS surveillance team picking the lock on the *Amerasia* office door. They found the premises "literally strewn with Confidential government documents." The case was now turned over to J. Edgar Hoover. Armed with a warrant, the FBI raided *Amerasia* and seized some one thousand clearly classified government documents, including papers from the State Department, Naval Intelligence, OSS, and British Intelligence. The FBI arrested six suspects, among them Philip Jaffe, the editor; Mark Gayn, a liberal journalist; Andrew Roth, then a lieutenant in the Office of Naval Intelligence; and his State Department liaison officers: John Stewart Service and Emmanuel Larsen.

Conspiracy to violate the espionage act was the charge against the *Amerasia* group. There was an immediate outcry. Newspapers portrayed the raid as a flagrant attempt by the FBI to curtail freedom of the press. The Roosevelt administration backpedaled furiously to avoid an explosive political issue. For security reasons, the contents of the Navy and State Department documents were not disclosed to the grand jury, which refused to indict three of the defendants, including Service. The government dropped espionage charges against the others, who then faced lesser counts of "conspiracy to embezzle, steal and purloin" government property. No mention was made of communism in the *Amerasia* case. Roth was released on a motion by the government. Jaffe's defense was that he had "transgressed the law" only "from an excess of journalistic zeal." This plea did not prevent his conviction, but it obviously impressed the judge, who imposed only moderate fines because the magazine was "a losing proposition financially."[27]

The reluctance to prosecute Roth and the other State Department employees became a club for Senator McCarthy five years later when he belabored the Truman administration for burying the *Amerasia* affair to cover up the Communist infiltration of a Democratic administration. But recently declassified records of FBI phone taps of New Deal influence peddler Tommy Corcoran show that he worked the coverup. As one of Chiang Kai-shek's American lobbyists, Corcoran had Truman's blessing to try to "fix" the *Amerasia* affair to avert "a Dreyfus case." The fear was that the disclosure of Chiang's corruption might rouse Congressional opinion against the Chinese Nationalists.[28]

The *Amerasia* case, however, exposed the depth of infiltration in the Roosevelt administration. It provided evidence that secret government documents were being stolen by a group with Communist affiliations. On his discharge from the navy after the *Amerasia* affair, Roth left the United States for good. Now a British citizen, he is publisher of a parliamentary gazette whose volumes line the walls of his basement office in the shadow of Westminster Abbey.[29] Jaffe, on the other hand, stayed in the United States and later defected from the Communist cause to become an informer on his associates.

Declassified FBI records dating from the autumn of 1945 reveal an extensive network of Communists in government. The files identify twenty-seven officials suspected of involvement with a Soviet espionage network in Washington. The list covered some half-dozen departments and agencies. It named seven from State, including Assistant Secretary Alger Hiss; eight Treasury officials, including Assistant Secretary Harry Dexter White; three officers from the Pentagon; more than two OSS officers; and a Justice Department official.[30]

More than a hundred names were given to the FBI by Elizabeth Terrill Bentley when she began telling of her eleven-year career as a Communist and underground Soviet agent on November 8, 1945. A plump and rather dowdy graduate of Vassar College, then in her forties, Bentley had joined the CPUSA in 1935 while studying for a master's degree in Italian at Columbia. She said she was motivated by her revulsion against Fascism when she accepted orders to go underground in 1938 and take directions from Jacob Golos, her Russian-born control officer. He operated using the cover of World Tourist Inc, an Amtorg-related corporate front in New York. When Bentley's involvement with Golos blossomed into a full-blown romance, she learned that as a member of the Control Commission of the CPUSA, he was one of the ranking Soviet intelligence agents in America.[31]

Bentley used the code name "Helen" while she worked for Golos as vice-president of the corporate subsidiary U.S. Service and Shipping, founded with $20,000 supplied by Moscow and channeled through Earl Browder, the national chairman of the CPUSA. Ostensibly its business was sending freight packages to Russia. But, like its predecessor World Tourist, Bentley told the FBI, it was purely a "cover firm for Soviet espionage." She described how she had been a courier between Golos and underground Communist networks in the government. According to Bentley, "by far the most valuable" source of information was a network in the Treasury Department. Nathan Gregory Silvermaster, a Russian-born Jew and underground Communist, she testified to be its leader. He used the basement darkroom in his home to photograph documents supplied by the other members of his ring.[32]

Bentley sometimes had more than forty rolls of filmed documents to bring back in the knitting bag she carried on her fortnightly train trips to Washington.

Bentley obviously possessed considerable authority in the Soviet underground *apparat*, and after Golos suddenly died of a heart attack in 1943, she took his place. For almost a year she directed both the Silvermaster group, plus a second network established by Victor Perlo in the War Production Board. But in the fall of 1944, she received instructions to hand over both groups to the direct control of a Soviet officer. Bentley claimed to the FBI that there was a third network in the State Department. She said that her Soviet contact had also alluded to the existence of a fourth group, but she learned no more than this.[33]

The significance of Bentley's testimony was that it corroborated and illuminated many details another defector from the same GRU network had omitted. This was David Whittaker Chambers, who three years earlier confessed to the authorities. The behavior of this pudgy man, whose corn-fed appearance concealed a foxy intellect, puzzled the bureau's Soviet Espionage officers when he first approached them in May 1942. His Dostoevskian belief in his personal mission complicated the task for his interrogators and damaged his credibility as a witness for the prosecution.

A dropout from Columbia Law School, Chambers had abandoned the law to become a Communist journalist. He joined the CPUSA in 1925. In 1932, while he was editor of *New Masses*, he was recruited for "underground work." He served as courier and manager of a GRU-linked Washington Communist network until 1937, when Stalin's purges aroused in him "a profound upheaval of spirit." He broke with the party in 1938. Fear of reprisals prevented Chambers from coming forward until 1939, but with the encouragement of Isaac Don Levine, Chambers gave Assistant Secretary of State Adolf Berle a list of his Communist contacts within the administration.[34]

Berle's memorandum on the "Underground Espionage Agent," which contained an outline of Chambers's allegations of his involvement in a Communist network of New Dealers, arrived on President Roosevelt's desk at a most inopportune moment. Its potential for destroying Roosevelt's unprecedented bid for a third term — at the very moment he was stretching the Constitution to bring America into the war against Hitler — prompted Berle to bury the report and not to send it to the FBI for another four years.

When Hoover obtained Berle's report in 1942, the FBI questioned Chambers, but did nothing more about him until 1945. They did not act on the information Chambers provided because he was, by turns, furtive and revealing. Chambers refused at first to elaborate on his original disclosures until he had received indemnities against prosecution for himself and others he might name. Hoover rejected these conditions as unacceptable. Chambers then tried to portray his activities as Communist infiltration rather than Soviet espionage. No doubt mindful of the twenty-year jail term under the Espionage Act, he did not reveal until 1948 — five years later at the hearings of the House Un-American Activities Committee — that he had evidence in the form of filmed State Department documents and a handwritten memorandum from Harry Dexter White, which he had secreted, as an insurance policy, in the shaft of a dumbwaiter at his wife's sister's home in Brooklyn.

Chambers also revealed that he operated under the direction of "J. Peters — "a Hungarian émigré by the name of Alexander Goldberger. His mission was to build a network with the help of Communist sympathizers who had entered the economic and social agencies set up under the New Deal. Starting with the Communist group in the Department of Agriculture, Goldberger's ultimate objective was "to penetrate the 'old line agencies,' such as Navy, State, Interior etc."[35]

Aided by his fellow Communist Nathan Silvermaster, then an economist with the Railroad Retirement Board, Chambers obtained from the Treasury briefcases full of official documents for photographing. Harry Dexter White was the principal source. A graduate of Stanford and a Harvard economics teacher, White had once considered going to Moscow to study. Instead he became assistant secretary to Henry Morgenthau at Treasury. He was the architect, along with John Maynard Keynes, of America's postwar fiscal policy and the International Monetary Fund. He had also played an influential role in shaping the original Carthaginian peace proposal, known as The Morgenthau Plan, that would have reduced Germany to a permanent pastoral state.[36]

White may not have been a member of the party, according to Chambers, but he was a "fellow traveller." He "enjoyed being of the Communist Party but not in the party and not subject to its discipline." So far as Alger Hiss was concerned, Chambers testified under oath that Hiss was a member of the Communist cell established in Washington by Harold Ware.[37]

Hiss's background was similar to that of most of the Cambridge Communists. He came from an affluent Maryland family and began his career with the educational privileges of the post-World War I American Ivy League generation. After graduating Phi Beta Kappa from Johns Hopkins University, he attended Harvard Law School, where he became a protégé of Felix Frankfurter and clerked for Justice Oliver Wendell Holmes before joining the Department of Agriculture. The Depression had encouraged Hiss, like his British counterparts, to a certain sympathy with the intellectual adherents of Marx; he had also been drawn into a group of crusading radical intellectuals in the International Juridical Association, two of whom joined a Communist cell.

Hiss made the most of the war and established himself as a wunderkind, rising fast and high to become one of the youngest assistant secretaries in the State Department. His grasp of how policy was made in Washington meant he was an important member of businessman Edward Stettinius's department. (Stettinius succeeded Cordell Hull as secretary of state on the eve of the November 1944 Dumbarton Oaks Conference that prepared the administrative foundations for the United Nations.) Hiss played a prominent role at the Yalta summit and, as acting secretary general of the 1945 meeting of the U.N. in San Francisco, seemed destined — because of strong Soviet support — to become, at the age of forty-one, its first permanent head.

But when it came to Communists in strategic positions in the government, Bentley attested that it was Harry Dexter White and Lauchlin Currie who were "two of our best ones" in the administration. She portrayed these two as having "an immense amount of influence. They knew people and their word would be accepted when they recommended someone." On one occasion, Bentley said, Currie had sent word to Moscow via White that the United States was about to break the Soviet codes.[38]

Bentley dutifully relayed this warning to Golos, whose own superior in the NKVD *apparat* was Gaik Badalovich Ovakimian, the *rezident* in the New York Amtorg office. In partnership with Vassili Zubilin, the second secretary of the Washington embassy, Ovakimian, it was later established, had directed Soviet intelligence activity in North America since the early thirties. Ovakimian, known to the FBI as "the wily Armenian," had faced arrest in May 1941 on charges under the Smith Act, which required agents of a foreign government to register with the attorney general. The charge was a technical one, but the opportunity for the FBI to roll up the Golos network was lost when Ovakimian returned to Russia in exchange for six Americans detained by the Soviets.[39]

When Zubilin returned to Moscow in July 1944, his replacement directed Bentley to hand over control of the Silvermaster and Perlo networks to two Soviet intelligence officers. She knew one of them as "Al." From FBI photographs Bentley established "Al" to be Anatoli Gromov, who had used the cover name "Henry" when he controlled the Cambridge agents in London. Gromov's decision to strip Bentley of her authority contributed to her decision to defect: In August 1945 she first reported to the FBI office at New Haven in her home state of Connecticut.

In a series of debriefings that ran through November, Bentley had no difficulty identifying "Al." She also picked out from the photographic files two other Soviet agents with whom she had been in contact: "Margaret," who was Olga Borisovna Pravdina, an employee of Amtorg, and her co-worker, "Lisa," who turned out to be Elizaveta Zubilin, an experienced NKVD agent-runner and the wife of Vassili Zubilin.[40]

Bentley's account was given more credence when she turned over to the Bureau the $2,000 obtained from her meeting with "Al" on October 17, 1945. She subsequently arranged another meeting with the Russian, this time under FBI surveillance, on November 21. But Hoover's hopes of using his tame defector as a double agent evaporated when she received no instructions from "Al." Gromov, it seems, had become suspicious. A few weeks later he returned to Moscow.[41]

Even if Bentley had failed to trap a top Soviet spymaster, she had named more than a hundred individuals with connections to Soviet espionage, of whom twenty-seven were government employees. She also stated that she learned from Golos that he was running an English agent in New York with the code name "Benjamin," an officer with William "Intrepid" Stephenson's British Security Co-Ordination from 1941 to 1943, who allegedly passed to the Russians a manual on Scotland Yard surveillance techniques and other papers.

The FBI was primarily interested in Bentley's Washington contacts. Of those she named, the FBI decided that fifty-one individuals were of "sufficient importance to warrant investigative attention by the Bureau." The fact that only four of Bentley's names had appeared in the information supplied up to then by Chambers, confirmed that he had provided the FBI with a very incomplete account.[42]

Bentley had no hard evidence to support her staggering story. But documents confirming the extensive reach of the Soviet networks in North America soon came from an unimpeachable source: a defecting GRU cipher clerk at the Soviet embassy in Ottawa.

Igor Gouzenko had been responsible for encrypting most of the confidential traffic of both Ambassador Georgy Zarubin and the military attaché, Colonel Nikolai Zabotkin, who was head of the GRU networks in Canada. When Gouzenko defected on September 5, 1945, he walked out of the embassy with a carefully selected sheaf of secret cables and pages from Zabotkin's handwritten diary. These Russian files provided the most conclusive proof yet obtained in the West of the extent to which the Soviets had breached the security of Canada, Great Britain, and the United States. The Royal Canadian Mounted Police carried out Gouzenko's debriefing; officers from the FBI eventually assisted them. The Bureau discovered at first hand that Zabotkin's network extended beyond Canada. They uncovered another GRU network centered in Los Angeles and run from Ottawa via an illegal named "Ignacy Witczak," who was a teacher at the University of Southern California.[43]

It was a cable ordering Zabotkin to "take measures to organize the acquisition of documentary materials on the atomic bomb" that caused the most alarm in Washington. The instructions were intended for one of four scientists whom Zabotkin controlled. The physicist's code name was "Alek." Zabotkin's cable of July 31, 1945, alerted Moscow that he had "worked out conditions of a meeting with Alek in London" because the scientist had been recalled to fly to England in September to take up an appointment at King's College.[44]

This information enabled M15 to identify "Alek" as the Cambridge scientist Dr. Alan Nunn May. Although Nunn May had never joined the party, he had made no particular secret of his Communist leanings. For a shy experimental physicist, he was remarkably outspoken during the first year of the war, when he came out in favor of the Moscow line with his public protests against the "imperialists' war." Notwithstanding such obvious manifestations of his sympathies, M15 cleared Nunn May in April 1942 to join the Cambridge team working on the top-secret Tube Alloys atomic-bomb project. In January 1945, Nunn May again received M15 clearance when his old Cavendish mentor, Professor Cockcroft, brought him to Montreal to work under him at the Atomic Energy Division of the Canadian National Research Council. Nunn May had access to the Chalk River heavy-water facility and the Chicago Metallurgical Laboratory, plus other facilities of the Manhattan Engineering District, where the atomic bomb was being assembled by the U.S. Army Corps of Engineers.[45]

One of the most worrying of the Zabotkin cables brought by Gouzenko revealed that "Alek" had supplied him with a sample of uranium 235 and the thin platinum membrane used in the enrichment process. Alarm about the extent of the breach that the Soviets had made into the Manhattan Project brought Canadian Prime Minister Mackenzie King hurrying to Washington for a top-level meeting on September 30 with President Truman and Secretary of State Dean Acheson. Anatoli Yakolev, the Soviet vice-consul in New York, was identified as the focus of atomic espionage in the United States. But Truman — at the request of Prime Minister Attlee — cautioned against premature action until full investigations had been conducted.

"I was expecting something like this," Nunn May said when he was taken into custody and charged on March 4, 1946. His arrest came a few days after thirteen Canadians were detained by the Royal Canadian Mounted Police on charges of espionage. Nunn May pleaded guilty and received a ten-year prison sentence.[46]

One of the thirteen Canadians arrested as a result of Gouzenko's revelations was Israel Halperin, a mathematics professor at Queen's University, Kingston, Ontario. Although subsequently acquitted of conspiracy charges, Halperin's notebook contained several references to Herbert Norman. The FBI began inquiries at Harvard about the ex-Cambridge Canadian, who was then a liaison officer on MacArthur's staff in Tokyo, with the rank of minister.[47]

The FBI found of greater importance the information supplied by Gouzenko that appeared to confirm the accusations of Chambers and Bentley about Alger Hiss. Gouzenko claimed that Zabotkin's deputy, Lieutenant Kulakov, had told him in May 1945 that the Soviets had an agent "who was assistant to the then Secretary of State, Edward R. Stettinius."[48]

This startling statement was appended to the report that Hoover sent to the White House on November 25, 1945. It set out in much greater detail the preliminary warning he had given on November 8 that "a number of persons employed in the Government . . . have been furnishing data and information to persons outside the Federal Government, who are in turn transmitting this information to espionage agents of the Soviet government."[49]

The FBI already had put the twenty-seven individuals named in Hoover's report under surveillance, including phone taps where authorized. But of all the names, those of Harry Dexter White and Alger Hiss gave President Truman the most cause for worry. The other senior White House official Bentley named — Lauchlin Currie — was not on the list because he had left government service. Roosevelt had died in April 1945, and a month after moving into the White House, Truman let it be known that he was "very much against building up a Gestapo" in the FBI. Now Hoover was telling him that two of his senior officials might be Soviet agents. Truman, who came to the presidency with no knowledge of Communist conspiracies, was skeptical. He chose to take no immediate action. Truman allowed White's nomination as executive director of the International Monetary Fund to go ahead for Senate approval.[50]

Hiss, then the director of Special Political Affairs, found a fierce defender of his integrity in the secretary of state. Another graduate of Harvard Law School and a Frankfurter protégé, Dean Acheson was cast in the same idealistic New Deal liberal mold as Hiss, alongside whom he had worked in the State Department when both were assistant secretaries. As the son of a privileged family and a graduate of East Coast educational establishments that had reared the American governing class, Acheson — like his contemporaries in Britain — just could not believe that Communist traitors could bloom in their carefully groomed elite plot.

The FBI investigations corroborated Bentley's claims about White; surveillance of White revealed he had extensive contacts with Silvermaster, whose house had a photo lab in its basement. But unlike Gouzenko, Bentley had brought no documents to support her charges. "They just plain did not want to believe us," as Robert Lamphere, a Midwesterner who at the time was a Soviet espionage officer in the FBI told me with characteristic bluntness. "They," he said, were the White House and Justice Department officials who pointed out that there was little except Bentley's allegations on which to base a prosecution. The final strategy, according to Lamphere, was to put "hundreds of agents in the New York and Washington field offices" into "an intensive surveillance of all those named." Emphasis was placed on the need for cautiously building up cases to avoid allowing those under suspicion to cover their tracks.[51]

"Operations were supposed to be very discreet," says Lamphere, "but when you put full-time physical surveillance on so many people, as we did in November and December 1945, it was bound to be blown." He also believed that Hoover's reports to Truman, despite their top-secret status, were quickly leaked to suspects. Although no steps were taken to force resignations, others might have become aware that they were under suspicion when they learned in 1946 that their government employment was "terminated due to reduction in force."[52]

The bureau soon learned that the Soviets were alerting their Washington networks. This information surfaces in the FBI records released to Michael Straight. The transcript of a 1975 interview of Straight reveals that he learned how Bentley had, in "late 1945," identified Straight's Soviet contact Michael Green as Grienke, and that by "early 1946" the Soviets began warning their contacts of the danger and "advising them of what action to take to avoid being implicated."[53]

Was it possible, the FBI wanted to know, that "Green contacted him early in 1946 to warn him of the disclosures of Bentley?" Straight "excluded this completely." He insisted that he "didn't see Green after 1942".[54]

Lamphere told me he remembered that the New York field office received "definite playback" from reliable informants "within a month or two" that the Soviets were passing the warning around their networks. They were instructed to take precautions by breaking off their contacts and keeping their mouths shut.[55]

"I still believe that if we had been allowed to move in right away we could have got the corroborating testimony that would have enabled us to get a successful prosecution against White and many of the others on that list Hoover sent to the White House on November 25," Lamphere told me. He recalls the exasperation felt by him and his fellow agents that an opportunity was slipping away. He also acknowledged that he was "second-guessing" the decisions made by many of his old friends, principally Bill Harvey, the FBI's resident counterintelligence expert.

"Experience in later espionage cases suggests that with as many suspects as we had in 1945 we could have found one or two who might have broken ranks under close interrogation to give us the confessions we needed to implicate the rest," Lamphere asserts. He points out that the secret of successful interrogation is to move in, "right bang," taking the subject by surprise "when he is not ready for what's coming." The time to have moved in, he contends, was immediately after Gouzenko's defection, when the Soviet intelligence apparatus in North America was in a state of shock and no one on the other side knew how much the FBI had learned from Gouzenko and other defectors.[56]

Lamphere said that by 1947 the suspects knew the FBI did not know that much. So when the Justice Department finally put Bentley before a federal grand jury in 1947, it was a signal to the subpoenaed witnesses, such as Harry Dexter White, that the FBI had no hard evidence against them.[57]

Forewarned and forearmed that they faced only Bentley's unsupported allegations, the defense attorneys confidently attacked her as a liar. As a result, no indictments were returned against any of those named by Bentley. Instead, the grand jury shifted its focus and, in July 1948, returned twelve indictments against the leaders of the CPUSA for alleged violations of the 1940 Smith Act.

Within weeks, the public was reading about the sensational revelations of the "Red Spy Queen." Following Bentley's testimony on Capitol Hill, the Communist takeover of the Czechoslovakian government and the Soviet blockade of Berlin set the stage for another Red Scare of the type that had spread across the United States in 1920. The president had laid down the so-called Truman Doctrine, promising American economic and miltary aid to check the advance of Soviet influence in Europe. Now, his decision to get tough on communism at home as well as overseas was influenced by the popular reaction to J. Edgar Hoover's "Red Fascism" speech in 1946. The FBI director had also taken his case to the public and warned that "at least 100,000 Communists were at large in the country." The "disloyalty of American Communists is no longer a matter of conjecture," Hoover told a cheering gathering of American veterans in San Francisco. The administration tried, and failed, to defuse the charge that the Democrats were soft on communism with Truman's 1947 executive order introducing a loyalty check for federal employees.

Michael Straight knew personally that some of those whom Bentley and Chambers testified about were members of the Washington underground Communist network. He later told the FBI that Lauchlin Currie had given him "many stories" for *The New Republic*. "My fear and sense of guilt," Straight recalled of his emotions during the 1948 hearings, "were secret, shared by no one."[58]

Why, FBI officers asked Straight in 1963, had he not contacted them in 1948 instead of waiting another fifteen years to volunteer his story? He replied that he had "considered doing so on many occasions but was afraid." Straight said that he "could not bear the publicity of the hearings and trials, with the resultant injury to his wife and children."[59]

Straight was also agonizing over his old Cambridge loyalties. His FBI records confirm that this conflict came to a head when he traveled to England "on personal business" in 1946, shortly after leaving the U.S. Army Air Force. On this trip — which in his book written twenty years later he sets in 1949 — he said he saw Burgess for the first time since he summer of 1940. He attended the annual dinner of the Apostles in a private dining room of the RAC Club. Straight recalls in his book that he became embroiled in a row over Czechoslovakia with Eric Hobsbawn, a rising Marxist historian. Blunt, who witnessed the dispute from the far end of the room, came up when the dinner was breaking.[60]

"Guy and I would like to talk to you," Blunt announced in his courteous but clipped manner. "We'll meet you here tomorrow morning."[61]

The next day their discussion became bitter when Straight accused the Soviet government of endangering the peace over the issue of the atomic bomb. Burgess questioned the motives of the American government. Straight "told both of them that he had grown up and was completely disillusioned with the communist movement." This made them "hostile and tense." Blunt, who up until this moment had been silent, suddenly intervened.[62]

"The question is," he said, "are we capable of intellectual growth?"

"Exactly," Straight replied, getting up to leave. Burgess looked at him intently and asked: "Are you still with us?" Straight said he was not. In answer to the question of whether he was "unfriendly," he replied: "If I were, why would I be here?"[63]

Straight admits that he still had to come to terms with his past and gave "a weak evasive answer" of the sort he "habitually gave" when he "faced a confrontation of any kind." Blunt appears to have known only too well how to manipulate Straight's complex psychological predicament. Despite what he described to the FBI as a "confrontation" with his Cambridge recruiter, his continuing silence was all but guaranteed by the apostolic oath. As articulated by E. M. Forster, it put loyalty to friends before country. In his often misquoted statement, he said: "If I had to choose between betraying my country and my friend, I hope I should have the guts to betray my country."[64]

After another meeting with Straight the following year, which included lunch at the Savoy in London, Burgess would have been able to reassure Blunt and Yuri Modin, their new Soviet controller, that their secrets were still safe. If Straight was not "with them" he was certainly not "against them" either.[65]

The first test of Straight's commitment to the bond of apostolic secrecy came with the 1948 House Un-American Activities Committee hearings. He was torn between his journalistic commitment to the truth, his family duty, and his loyalty to old friends. The result was an agonizing compromise. As editor of *The New Republic*, he decided that even if he could not go to the FBI about his peripheral involvement with the Communist underground in Washington, he had a commitment to his readers to support — if not explain — the truth.

"In general we believe that the outline of Elizabeth Bentley's story is largely accurate," Straight declared in a signed editorial. It cost him the disdain of many of his New Deal liberal friends. His stand was supported by his wife, who was then under analysis with Dr. Jennie Welderhall as part of her training to be a psychiatrist. Welderhall's husband was an Australian named Hall who happened to be attached to the British embassy in Washington. Straight later told the FBI that his wife, Belinda, "had furnished the names of Anthony Blunt and Guy Burgess to her analyst . . . as two individuals engaged in underground Communist activity in order that the information could be passed on to Mr. Hall and the British government."[66]

Robert Cecil, who was first secretary at the embassy until 1948, has confirmed that such a warning would have been relayed to the chief of security or the head of chancellery. At one point that post was held in an acting capacity by Donald Maclean; but he evidently had no need to intervene to prevent a report from reaching London. Dr. Welderhall decided not to relay Belinda Straight's warning to her husband because "it would have disrupted the work [the analysis] we were doing." Furthermore, Dr. Welderhall recalled that it was only Burgess, not Blunt, whose name was discussed in their analysis sessions.[67]

The House Un-American Activities Committee (HUAAC), the permanent successor in 1946 of the Dies Committee, which had investigated internal Nazi and Communist subversion before the war, was already warming up for its self-appointed mission to purge the federal bureaucracy of Communists. It planned well-publicized hearings aimed at weeding out "Reds" in the Hollywood film industry. Encouraged by carefully orchestrated leaks to legislators from J. Edgar Hoover, Richard Milhouse Nixon and the Republican politicians on the committee sought to remedy the failure of the judiciary to deal effectively with the reality of Soviet penetration. On July 31, 1948, Bentley sat at the witness table. A packed committee room heard her tell, for the first time in public, a staggering tale of infiltration and subversion.

The star turn came when Whittaker Chambers sat in the spotlight to corroborate Bentley's account. Characterized by Nixon as the "reluctant witness," this self-confessed ex-member of the Communist underground was led through a penetrating cross-examination to implicate Hiss and White in the conspiracy.

When White came to the stand, he parried Nixon's questions skillfully. Although he was recovering from a heart attack, he issued a steady stream of denials and eloquent appeals to the "American creed" of free speech. Three days after he appeared before the committee, on August 16, 1948, White died of a second and fatal heart attack.

When Alger Hiss appeared at the witness table he was dignified and suavely confident as president of the Carnegie Endowment for International Peace. Hiss appeared before the committee two days after Chambers finished his testimony. He firmly denied all Chambers's allegations. He conceded only that he dimly remembered Chambers when Chambers was using the alias of George Crosley to "soft touch" him for a loan for a secondhand car. The polished, self-confident ex-diplomat then threw down the gauntlet by daring the man he had called a "deadbeat" journalist to repeat his charges outside the privileged sanctuary of the hearings.

Chambers promptly did so on a radio show. And when Hiss sued for libel, Chambers led FBI investigators to the dumbwaiter in Brooklyn and the yellow foolscap pages in White's handwriting. From the hollowed-out center of a pumpkin on the pumpkin patch on his Maryland farm, he retrieved a film he said he had kept for ten years as a "life preserver" against possible revenge by the Communist underground. The film contained notes of the confidential State Department reports. Chambers alleged Hiss had produced these for him on his Woodstock typewriter. The documentary evidence that Chambers had withheld so long from the FBI transformed the case, although the delay led some to doubt its credibility.

Since Hiss had denied under oath that he gave any government information to Chambers, he was called to account for perjury. A grand jury returned an indictment on two perjury counts in December 1948. The first trial ended in an eight-to-four hung jury in July 1949.[68]

At the second trial in January 1950, a former Soviet spy runner confronted Hiss and the jury. She was Hede Massing. This former GRU/NKVD undercover agent in the Soviet-American *apparat* had made a full confession to the FBI in 1947 about how she had taken over Chambers's network after he broke with the party in 1938. Her eyewitness testimony describing a confrontation she had with Hiss in 1935 over cell member Noel Field (who had vanished behind the Iron Curtain in 1949) made a strong impression on the jury. Hiss was convicted of perjuring himself as to whether he had known Chambers, not over whether he had lied about passing on government information. Notwithstanding, he received a stiff five-year prison term — and he continued to protest his innocence after his trials and conviction roused the press to fury.[69]

(Ever since his conviction, Hiss has steadfastly maintained that he was framed on the perjury charge and that he was never involved in any form of Communist conspiracy.)

On September 23, 1949, the president stunned the nation with the announcement that the Soviets had exploded an atomic bomb. The news that the United States had lost its military supremacy, which most Americans took for granted as their stipend from World War II, was compounded the following month when Mao Tse-tung proclaimed final victory in the Communist takeover of China. Seven months later, the Cold War turned into a hot one in Korea.

The Communist infiltration that Joe Citizen seized on as the convenient collective scapegoat for these foreign-policy disasters was given demagogic volume by Senator Joseph McCarthy. Even before U.S. troops went into action under the U.N. flag to drive the North Korean army back across the 38th parallel, this obscure and undistinguished junior senator from Wisconsin had launched a crusade against domestic communism. In a fiery speech he charged that the State Department harbored over fifty Soviet agents.

It mattered little to McCarthy that the Tydings Committee, which had investigated these allegations, had called them unfounded. At a time when GIs were being killed by Communist bullets, the reprise of the testimony of Elizabeth Bentley and Whittaker Chambers helped McCarthy spark a holy war against the Red Menace. It led to what historian Barbara Tuchman termed with deft insight a "tawdry reign of terror."[70]

Formerly secret Senate investigatory records confirm that J. Edgar Hoover — as was long suspected but always denied — had provided the ammunition for McCarthy's campaign in its early stages. But former FBI officer Lamphere confirms that Hoover eventually withdrew this clandestine support when the senator ran amok and "began to tar it up," oblivious to the damage he was doing to counterintelligence operations and the democratic fabric. It was too late by then to prevent the damage done by the venomous fallout of McCarthyism. The hearings polluted the political debate and served as a smoke screen to cover Soviet intentions. Counterintelligence officers like Lamphere and his colleagues in the Soviet Espionage section of the FBI deplored Senator McCarthy's "witch-hunting" approach as fervently as those who proclaimed themselves champions of constitutional rights.

"McCarthy's star-chamber proceedings, his lies, and his overstatements hurt our efforts," Lamphere explained. "McCarthy's approach and tactics hurt the anti-Communist cause. It turned many liberals against legitimate efforts to curtail Communist activities in the United States, particularly in regard to government employment of known Communists."[71]

In weighing the historical record of those times it must not be forgotten that "McCarthyism" is a political epithet and not a legitimate defense. In uncovering the patterns of Soviet networks, neither counterintelligence analysts, nor historians, have to adhere to the strict rules of evidence that apply to the protection of individual liberty in a court of law. McCarthyism is not therefore a valid rubric for dismissing a vast body of corroborative testimony that confirms the known blueprint of Soviet-directed subversion.

When evaluating the recently released congressional investigatory records, and the testimony of scores of witnesses in both public and private executive sessions, historical judgments must ultimately be made by weighing the balance of probabilities. While giving due consideration to the dangers of relying on "guilt by association," the political associates and beliefs of an individual cannot be ignored.

"If X is a member of the Communist Party, he is more likely to commit espionage for the benefit of the Soviet Union than he would be if he were not a member of the Party," Professor Herbert Packer postulates in his perceptive analysis *Ex-Communist Witnesses*. "Thus stated, the proposition is a truism, but it is a truism that cannot be ignored. Absent other evidence, a charge of espionage activity carries more weight than it would if there was no such evidence. . . ." Even at the height of the furor over McCarthy, it is significant that *The Nation* — the magazine that had championed the American intellectual left through the Depression — was not insisting on evidence that could sustain the rigorous "test of guilt" that would be applied in criminal courts: "Impartial observers should ask themselves whether sufficient credible evidence has been presented to lead reasonable men to conclude that the accused individuals were spies for a foreign power."[72]

Historians and writers continue to take opposing sides in the debate over the credibility of Elizabeth Bentley. And there are no easy rules for judging whether possibilities are probabilities, or when probabilities become certainties. But of one central factor in the equation there can be no doubt: Moscow *did* target the U.S. administration for penetration. The historical argument therefore becomes one of evaluating the degree of its success.

Moreover, as Lamphere and other intelligence officers have emphasized, U.S. Army code breakers provided the key to checking the accuracy of at least part of Bentley's evidence. The breaking of the wartime Washington-Moscow cables, the so-called Venona traffic, gave positive corroboration that the Soviets were indeed receiving information from the American agents who were inside, and outside, the U.S. government. The Venona intercepts are still yielding information, so none of the intercepted signals have been officially released. But Peter Wright revealed in *Spycatcher* that one of the messages refers by cryptogram to a Soviet agent who traveled back from Moscow to the United States in the same aircraft as Ambassador Averell Harriman.

"I began to receive this confirmation of Bentley's testimony sometime after 1948," Lamphere told me. But he was never permitted to use it as corroborative evidence — even in the highly contentious case of Ethel Rosenberg, who was also identified in a Venona decrypt. The decrypts were — and still are — a highly classified military-intelligence secret.

What is now known about the corroboration that Venona gave to Bentley's original testimony must add authority to the 1953 report of the Senate Judiciary Committee's subcommittee that investigated "Interlocking Subversion in Government Departments." After a new round of hearings, its report catalogued the awesome extent of the Soviet penetration operation. According to the evidence in the committee's records, those involved in the secret Communist underground included an executive assistant to the President of the United States; an Assistant Secretary of the Treasury; a United States Treasury attaché in China; a leading member of the Office of Special Political Affairs for the State Department; a key official of the International Monetary Fund; a top member of the Latin American Division of the Office of Strategic Services; a member of the National Labor Relations Board; a secretary of the National Labor Relations Board; a chief adviser to the Senate Sub-Committee on Civil Liberties; a senior member of the Statistical Analysis Branch, War Production Board; and a leading member of the National Research Project of the Works Progress Administration.[73]

"How many priceless American secrets had been conveyed to Moscow through the tunnels of the American Communist underground will never be known," the report advises. "The fact that documents were accumulated by unauthorized persons has been well established," it continues, citing the OSS, Navy and State Department files recovered in the FBI raid on the offices of *Amerasia* magazine.[74]

The blueprint of Soviet penetration was made clear by Bentley, Chambers, and Budenz: "All of the Government employees exposed by these witnesses were threads in this design." The report explained how the prewar target for Communist penetration had been the New Deal agencies managing the economic-recovery programs. During the war the target had shifted to "such wartime agencies as the Board of Economic Warfare, the Federal Economic Administration, the Office of Strategic Services and the like." Then, toward the end of the war, the infiltrators were "operating in the foreign policy field," and after 1945 "gravitating towards the international agencies."[75]

The Senate Judiciary Committee report establishes that the modus operandi of the Communist networks in the U.S. government was not simply espionage but also acting as agents of influence:

> They colonized key Committees in Congress. They helped write laws, conduct congressional hearings, and write congressional reports. They advised Cabinet members, wrote speeches for them, and represented them at intergovernmental conferences. They staffed interdepartmental committees which prepared basic American and world policy. They traveled to every continent as emissaries and representatives of the American people. They attended virtually every international conference where statesmen met to shape the future.

Noting that "almost all the persons exposed by the evidence had some connection which could be documented with at least one — and generally several — other exposed persons," the committee stressed its findings of an "interlacing combination" of Communist networks in government:

> They used each other's names for reference on applications for Federal employment. They hired each other. They promoted each other. They raised each other's salaries. They transferred each other from bureau to bureau, from department to department, from congressional committee to congressional committee. They assigned each other to international missions. They vouched for each other's loyalty and protected each other when exposure threatened.

Concluding that there was evidence of "4 Soviet espionage rings operating within our Government," the committee cautioned that "only 2 of these have been exposed." It found, too, that there was a characteristic common to all those who had been exposed: "Virtually all were graduates of American universities. Many had doctorates or similar ratings of academic and intellectual distinction."[76]

The Senate Judiciary report in essence confirms that Soviet intelligence turned the same deep-penetration strategy against the United States as it had used against Britain. Both penetrations depended on the recruitment of ideologically committed members of the university-educated elite. The number of Harvard graduates in the American networks parallels the dominance of Cambridge graduates in Britain. There was, moreover, a transatlantic crossover between the two networks in at least two known cases: Egerton Herbert Norman and Michael Straight.

In contrast to their operations in Britain, where the vigilance of MI5 and Special Branch ruled out the exploitation of the CPGB by the NKVD after 1927, Soviet infiltration and control of its moles in the U.S. government was facilitated by the openness of American society and the CPUSA. Until Bentley defected from the *apparat*, the FBI underestimated both the scale and objectives of the Soviet assault.

"We knew with absolute certainty that Moscow had long directed the American Communist party," Lamphere said. But the major mistake, he believes, was Washington's naïve acceptance of the Russians as friendly wartime allies, and the concentration of the FBI's domestic counter-intelligence effort against the Germans and Japanese.

"It was not until Bentley came to us in 1945," says Lamphere, "that the FBI realized the extent to which the Soviets had used the American Communist party members to build up their penetration network behind our backs."[77]

This is difficult to comprehend, since the confidential State Department records prove that MI5 had been supplying the Americans with top-secret reports on Soviet subversion since the early 1920s. This leads to a crucial question: Why was the FBI so taken by surprise when it learned that the United States government had become the prime target for Soviet penetration?

Two possible answers are immediately self-evident. First, in 1945 the various American intelligence services were involved in a battle for turf. The OSS was being shut down; the CIA had not appeared on the scene. British information on Communist subversion was no longer being channeled via the State Department for dissemination to all the intelligence agencies in Washington. Instead, it was coming to Hoover from his good friend Guy Liddell of MI5. And Hoover was trying to preempt the postwar counterintelligence scene for the FBI. This theory is substantiated by an OSS report from London to Washington that discussed Liddell's trip in early 1946 to the United States.

"It should be pointed out that Captain Liddell has been for years a close friend and great admirer of the FBI, and during this trip spent most of his time in Washington with FBI officials," the senior OSS representative in London cable headquarters. Liddell, in his new capacity of deputy director of MI5, had "spent a great deal of time with Mr. Hoover and Mr. Ladd of the FBI," according to Lieutenant Commander Scott. The main subject for discussion, according to Scott, was the impending reorganization of the U.S. intelligence services: The FBI director gave Liddell the impression that it was "a definite possibility that they would take over all Counter Intelligence."[78]

The second answer is that the Americans really shouldn't have been surprised by the extent of the Soviet penetration into the American government. British counterintelligence, which had been keeping track of Soviet subversion inside England until the war, was also being made to look foolish — even to the point of having Soviet infiltrators moving up to positions to run British counterintelligence. Here was Guy Liddell advising J. Edgar Hoover about Soviet penetrations, and Liddell did not know what was going on in his own shop. Or did he?

# CHAPTER 25

# *"He Had His Best Man on It"*

"It has given me great pleasure to be able to pass the names of every MI5 officer to the Russians." Anthony Blunt made this off-the-cuff comment during a preretirement chat with Colonel T. A. Robertson in November 1945.

"It was an electrifying remark," recalled Robertson, a bluff man with piercing blue eyes who is not given to overstatement. "I couldn't keep it under my hat. I must have told Guy Liddell."[1]

While Blunt had a reputation for cynical humor, Robertson's account makes it plain that he *did not* take the astonishing statement simply as a mischievous jest. The very nature of the remark appears to have been deliberately contrived so that Robertson, an ex-army officer and stickler for security, was forced to relay it in confidence and verbally to his chief. That Blunt should risk such a statement indicates that he could rely on a personal defense from Liddell, the head of B Division. Other counter-intelligence experts view the remark as being a deliberate "testing of the circuit" by Blunt before he retired from full-time service with MI5.

Liddell never took any formal action as a result of Robertson's report, so Blunt had reassuring proof that his friend really was a trustworthy protector. This asset would become immensely valuable in later years.

Had it not been for the Labour government and its suspicions about MI5 dating back to the notorious Zinoviev letter, Liddell would probably have become its director general. But Prime Minister Attlee, distrusting an internal appointee, brought in Percy Sillitoe, former chief of the Kent Constabulary. As an outsider, he never settled in comfortably as director general at Leconfield House, the postwar headquarters overlooking South Audley Street, a block away from Hyde Park. The former police chief never fathomed the subtleties of the network of school and college loyalties that bound MI5 together. And during Sillitoe's tenure, it was silently acknowledged that the deputy director, Liddell, was the indispensable power behind the throne. As director of B Division, he had built an empire within the heart of the organization. It was Liddell who had forged close personal ties with the mighty J. Edgar Hoover and the American intelligence community. Above all, Liddell possessed another attribute that Sillitoe lacked: a personal network that reached through the clubs of Pall Mall and St. James's, providing the MI5 directorate with the informal contacts with the civil service that were essential for the smooth functioning of the security service.

When Sillitoe moved into Leconfield House on April 30, 1946, Blunt was moving out. In the six months since his formal retirement, Blunt had been popping in and out of the office, handing over his various projects. And for the next five years, his mournful face was never absent for very long from the inner sanctum of the deputy director. Blunt was never too busy lecturing at the Courtauld, or with his duties at the Palace, to give advice or carry out free-lance missions for Guy Liddell.[2]

Just how many of these private missions had to do with art and how many with intelligence is impossible to judge. But Liddell, according to Sir Dick White and others, was a passionate collector of paintings. With his friend's lofty position at the Palace, Liddell now had even more opportunities to indulge his hobby—and Blunt saw to it that he was on the VIP guest list for all the Royal Academy functions.

The most glittering postwar exhibition—and arguably one of the most important that Blunt ever organized—was the Royal Academy's winter exhibition that opened in October 1946. By all accounts Blunt played an instrumental role in persuading King George VI to lend truly spectacular items from the royal collection. It was the first opportunity the public had ever had to see some of the masterpieces from Buckingham Palace and Windsor Castle. More than a third of a million people packed an exhibition that offered a magical escape from the coal rationing and power cuts that marked the cruelest winter of Britain's drab postwar austerity. One of the first admiring visitors was Queen Mary. She recorded in her diary: "The pictures looked lovely and were well hung by Mr. Blunt and the Committee, all the rooms were filled."[3]

Liddell also regarded Blunt as an adviser for his own picture collecting. While this may help explain the power that Blunt continued to hold over his wartime MI5 chief, it appears that he brought Liddell something considerably more valuable than intellectual companionship. In February 1944, Christie's auctioned an unattributd painting of two heads from the collection of the Earls of Carlisle. Shortly afterward, the painting passed into the Liddell family collection. But now its value was dramatically increased because Blunt had identified it as a fragment of a long-lost Poussin painting of the *Adoration of the Golden Calf.* Its authenticity, however, came to be hotly disputed, except by Blunt, as the result of X-ray analysis conducted in the Courtauld laboratories by Professor Stephen Rees-Jones. "He would only accept my findings if it suited him," Rees-Jones allowed, recalling that when Blunt became the institute's director in 1947, "he ruled it like a medieval court."[4]

As surveyor of the king's pictures, Blunt played the role of deferential courtier in Buckingham Palace. But at the Courtauld, he was an autocrat. He moved himself—and his male lovers—into the director's two-bedroom flat. From atop this elegant Robert Adam-style house, overlooking the leafy oasis of Portman Square north of the bustling shops of Oxford Street, for the next twenty-five years Blunt invoked his undisputed authority over staff and students. Former students still recall the deferential hush that overtook the corridors of the institute whenever the footfalls on the magnificent marble spiral staircase announced the descent of the director, his gown billowing out over a formal gray-flannel suit.

Blunt treated the Courtauld staff as his household retainers. This came as a surprise to the long-serving librarian of the institute, Lillian Gurry, who was one of those who "thought it a joke for a Communist to get a royal appointment." But the director quickly earned recognition for the Courtauld and for himself by his prodigious output of articles, books, and lectures stressing the historical and social context of art, and he gave up the Marxist clichés—along with the red ties that Gurry had remembered him wearing before the war.[5]

As a full-fledged professor of London University, Blunt was not content. He determined to transform the Courtauld into the main center for artistic studies in Britain. When he became director, the institute's reputation was that of a genteel and undemanding finishing school for the sons and daughters of the wealthy, or for those going into the antiques trade. This he quickly changed. Under Blunt's directorship a rigorous teaching curriculum and a carefully managed admissions policy turned the Courtauld into a postgraduate center with an international reputation. By the time he retired twenty-five years later, Blunt could pride himself on having nurtured a host of graduate students who, by the time of his death, were gravitating into the top directorships and plum curatorial positions of Britain's leading art galleries, museums, and auction houses.[6]

In a grand design to propagate his view of art history, Blunt took a leaf out of the Soviet book. Just as the momentum of his privileged education and contacts had carried him into the upper reaches of the British *governing* establishment, Blunt set about using the institute to groom ideological devotees of his theories who, he believed, would eventually take control of the British *art* establishment.[7]

To achieve his ambition of stamping the art world with the imprimatur of his scholarship, and building an unparalleled network of influence, it was vital that Blunt preserve the secret of his clandestine allegiance to Moscow. Ironically, during his last months as a full-time MI5 officer Blunt discovered that a couple of defecting Soviet intelligence officers stood between his potentially illustrious career and a very long prison sentence.

Here was an unpleasant reminder of just how fragile the cover of the Cambridge moles really was. Unlike most Soviet spies, they had not operated through a series of insulated cells. The principal members of Blunt's network were not only known by their wartime associates in MI5 and MI6 to be friends, but each member's treachery was known to the others. Each realized that exposure of one would immediately cast suspicion on the rest, a risk enhanced by Burgess's bizarre behavior.

The first threat to Blunt was Konstantin Volkov's attempted defection in August 1945. This Soviet intelligence officer did not make it clear whether he was KGB or GRU when he first walked into the British consulate in Istanbul. He said only that he was the local Soviet consul-general. He claimed he had worked in the "British Department." In return for £27,000 and a safe defection, he offered impressions of keys for filing cabinets in Moscow and a key to a flat where he had left a suitcase full of documents. As an token of good faith, Volkov returned a few days later and gave John Reed, a British Foreign Office official, a "shopping list" typed in Russian. Volkov insisted that his request to defect not be communicated to London by telegram, because, he said, a number of the British diplomatic ciphers had been broken.

Reed's rough-and-ready translation of the shopping list in part read: ". . . files and documents concerning very important Soviet agents in important establishments in London. Judging by the cryptonyms[the code names in secret cables between London and Moscow] there are, at present, seven such agents, five in British Intelligence and two in the Foreign Office. I know, for instance, that one of these agents is fulfilling the duties of Head of a Department of British Counter Intelligence."[8]

Unfortunately for Volkov, although Reed's report reached London a week later by diplomatic pouch, Sir Stewart Menzies regarded the matter as one of "such delicacy" that he summoned Kim Philby and insisted that he handle it himself. As head of Section IX, which had by now swallowed up Section V and controlled all the Soviet counter-intelligence operations in MI6, Philby read the report from Istanbul and immediately recognized the danger it posed to himself and the other members of the Cambridge agents.

"I stared at the papers rather longer than necessary to compose my thoughts," Philby would write later. "The only course was to put a bold face on it." Philby managed to persuade C to let him handle the matter by flying to Turkey, as we have seen. Meanwhile Philby alerted his Soviet controller, Boris Krotov, who had taken over the running of the high-grade agents from Anatoli Gromov, who was now in Washington.[9]

To give Moscow time to arrange for the "repatriation" of its would-be defector, Philby delayed his flight to Turkey. By the time he reached Istanbul, nearly two weeks later, the Turks reported that Volkov and his wife had been flown to Moscow strapped to stretchers.

Philby returned empty-handed to London. But he stopped off briefly in Rome to touch base with James Angleton, who was then the American counterespionage chief in Rome. Menzies accepted Philby's inadequate report and the specious rationalization that Volkov's nervousness must have betrayed him during the three weeks it took MI6 to respond to his offer. Philby was then permitted to keep Volkov's shopping list in his own safe. Thus he kept it away from the Registry and from those who might have considered it worthy of more objective analysis.[10]

Volkov's report was not examined again for six years — until suspicion fell on Philby after the Burgess and Maclean defection in 1951. Then it seemed that Philby was the obvious suspect fingered by Volkov as the man who was "fulfilling the duties of Head of a Department of British Counter Intelligence" because, in October 1944, Philby had only recently become head of Section IX of MI6.

In 1965, a retranslation of Volkov's original Russian list was made at the request of mole-hunter Peter Wright. This was done by Geoffrey Sudbury, a fluent speaker of Russian, from GCHQ. This translation revealed that Reed had mistakenly omitted the words *otdela* ("section") and *upravleniya* ("directorate") from his original translation. What Volkov had actually tried to tell the British, according to this interpretation, was that "one of these agents is fulfilling the duties of head of a *section* of the British Counterintelligence *Directorate*."[11]

The new translation made it unlikely that Volkov was pointing to Philby, because "Counterintelligence Directorate" was how the Soviets customarily referred to MI5; Philby was in MI6. The correctness of this new evaluation was confirmed by three more Soviet defectors: Igor Gouzenko, Vladimir Petrov, and Anatoli Golitsyn.[12]

If Volkov's mole was not Philby — or any section head in MI6 — who was he?

The term "fulfilling the duties of" suggested to Sudbury and Wright that, whoever he was, he must have been "acting head" of some section in MI5. Wright considers the obvious candidate to be Roger Hollis. As head of F Division, which monitored political parties, Hollis held the rank of assistant director until early 1947 when he took over C Division, which made him a full member of the MI5 directorate. But if Volkov's information was tracked back to 1943, the identification could equally well apply to Roger Fulford, the deputy head of F, who assumed the responsibilities whenever Hollis was absent recuperating from his recurrent bouts of tuberculosis.[13]

However, if by "fulfilling the duties" Volkov meant that Moscow's agent was simply doing the job of a division chief, which made him ex officio a member of the MI5 directorate, then it could have been any one of five candidates — including Guy Liddell.

Philby's personal response in 1945 was commensurate with his belief that Volkov was pointing at him. But he may have known better by the time he wrote his KGB-sponsored account in 1968. Significantly he devoted a whole chapter to the Volkov affair, reinforcing the impression that he was the Soviet agent identified by Volkov.[14]

What Philby's account does not reveal is that one of the five Soviet agents in the British intelligence services on Volkov's shopping list was stationed at the time in Persia. The serious candidate was Robert C. Zaehner, who ran the MI6 counterintelligence operations out of Tehran during the war. (Goronwy Rees also named Zaehner to MI5 in 1951 as one of Burgess's friends whom he suspected of being a Soviet agent. He repeated his accusation to Wright in 1965, but offered no firm proof.) Zaehner seemed a likely suspect. He had links to Cambridge, having spent a year at King's College (where Rees alleged he became a secret Communist), before returning to Oxford in 1937 to pursue his studies in Persian. In 1940 Zaehner had been part of a group of brilliant, left-wing Oxford academics, which included his Marxist contemporary Christopher Hill, who trained for operations associated with SOE against the Baltic States. When the operation was canceled, Zaehner returned to Oxford, but his command of Middle East languages led him into MI6 in 1942, and out to Persia where his wartime operations took him behind Soviet lines.[15]

When Wright's mole hunt caught up with Zaehner in 1965, he was Spalding Professor of Eastern Religions and Ethics at Oxford and a very distinguished fellow of All Souls. Zaehner denied ever having been a traitor. His tearful reaction to Rees's accusations persuaded Wright that Zaehner must be innocent. Wright's account suggests that his conclusion was influenced as much by the sheer obscenity of impugning the honor of a mild-mannered fellow of All Souls as by Zaehner's speculation that one of his local recruits, by the name of Rudi Hamburger, suspected at the time of also dealing with the Soviets, was a more plausible candidate for Volkov's MI6 agent in Persia.[16]

Was Professor Zaehner unjustly accused, or did Wright too hastily exonerate the professor? The answer may never be resolved satisfactorily. Most of the prewar Oxbridge graduates who were suspected after Blunt's interrogations of some degree of wartime treachery as a result of their youthful Communist sympathies were distinguished members of the Establishment. Most knew that their cases had grown too cold for any successful investigation and prosecution without a full confession.

What is so striking about the Volkov list, and the information supplied a month later by the defection of the GRU cipher clerk in Ottawa, is that both cases produced such seemingly clear indications of massive Soviet infiltrations into MI5 and MI6. Yet both cases seemed to be quickly buried with no action taken. In MI6, Philby, who was in control of all counterintelligence operations, stifled any further investigation by locking the Volkov file in his personal safe. But MI5 handled the case of Igor Gouzenko. That *neither* service made any serious attempt in 1945 to respond to the evidence of Soviet penetration is astonishing. Either the "mental equipment" of Sir Stewart Menzies — and of his opposite number in MI5 — was as truly "unimpressive" as Philby claimed — or the Soviets had a stronger grip on the British intelligence apparatus than anyone appreciated at the time.

The failure to respond to similar items of evidence was so dilatory that it can be argued that the Soviets not only controlled the counter-intelligence chief of MI6, but also a ranking officer in MI5. More importantly, this officer was *not* Anthony Blunt, because the evidence about another Soviet agent in MI5 came from an impeccable GRU source: Igor Gouzenko. The stocky, twenty-six-year-old Red Army cipher clerk had smuggled out the GRU cables that led to the arrest of the atomic spy Alan Nunn May, exposed Soviet espionage rings in Canada and the United States, and provided MI5 with some startling information about cipher traffic he had seen two years earlier in Moscow.

When Gouzenko gave his secret testimony in February 1946 before the Royal Canadian Commission, he recalled that the GRU ran two agents who had the similar cryptonym of "Elli." (American intelligence sources confirm that this was not an unusual Soviet practice.) In these instances, Gouzenko knew one agent was male. The other he knew was female. But since they operated on different sides of the Atlantic, there was little room for confusion.

One of the cryptonyms had appeared in a telegram from Moscow on August 24, 1945. This castigated Gouzenko's chief, Colonel Zabotkin, for giving Ambassador Zarubin a "report on financial credits" which "had uncovered the identity of our source on the objective ELLI."

Gouzenko identified this female "Elli" as Kay Willsher. She confessed later to the Royal Canadian Mounted Police that she had indeed supplied information to the Soviets while working in the office of Malcolm MacDonald, Britain's high commissioner in Ottawa.[17]

"There is some agent under the same name in Great Britain," Gouzenko said; but he did not know who it was. Unlike the female "Elli" — whom the RCMP designated "Ellie" to avoid confusion — Gouzenko could not produce any documentation on the use of the male cryptonym. Nor is it clear from the Gouzenko files that have been declassified to date just how much detail he gave the commission about the male "Elli." But seven years later in a May 6, 1952, memorandum to the head of the RCMP's Special Branch, Gouzenko insisted that he "was not told by somebody, *but saw the telegram myself* [his italics] concerning the person" (the male "Elli").[18]

Gouzenko recalled that in "the latter part of 1942, or the beginning of 1943" he had been working the night shift at the cipher branch of the GRU headquarters in Moscow. He was sharing a worktable with Lieutenant Lubimov, a former student friend of his from the Moscow Architectural Institute, which they had both attended before joining the Red Army. Gouzenko explained how they "quite often showed each other interesting telegrams." On this particular night, what aroused their interest was a cable referring to a GRU agent named "Elli" who was "one of five of MI." He was obviously a very important source, because "personal contact with this man was avoided." The telegram referred to arrangements for collecting information supplied from him at a *dubok* (the Soviet intelligence nomenclature for a dead drop) in a graveyard "in a split between the stones of a particular tomb."[19]

This particular cable struck Gouzenko and his friend as being so "unusual" they had a "short talk about it." Lubimov told Gouzenko that he had seen previous telegrams about the same agent, from which he had learned: "This man has something Russian in his background." Another cable from Moscow that Gouzenko recalled translating two years earlier in Canada reinforced his belief that this male "Elli," who apparently was contacted only by *dubok*, and only every one or two months by the GRU in Britain, must be a very high-ranking MI5 officer.[20]

The second message was a warning to the Canadian-based Zabotkin to take extra care because "representatives of British 'Greens' [counterintelligence] were due to arrive in Ottawa with the purpose of working with the local 'Greens' [RCMP]." According to Wright's investigations, this cable appears to have coincided with Guy Liddell's secret visit to North America in 1944, providing additional corroboration that the leak must have been coming from a highly placed Soviet source in MI5.[21]

No exhaustive attempt was made to uncover the identity of the Soviet agent in "five of MI" until 1965. The Wright investigation then uncovered the cables about Gouzenko's revelations that were sent to London by Peter Dwyer. Dwyer was the MI6 representative in Washington who had flown to Ottawa to help in debriefing Gouzenko. The cable containing the information about a spy code-named "Elli" was dated September 18–19, 1945. According to Wright, it was the only one of the entire series of telegrams that had four folds dirtied along the edges as if it had been stuffed into a pocket. Philby had also initialed and dated it — but *two days after* it had come into his office.

Analysis of the cable-traffic logs of the Soviet embassy in London revealed a dramatic increase during the week that ended on September 22. One of these undeciphered cables sent to Moscow on September 19–20 stood out. It had been sent with the most urgent priority. Moreover, the GCHQ cryptanalysts found that a count of its number groups corresponded to the approximate length of the verbatim telegram with the grimy folds about the male "Elli." Since it had been sent by the Soviet intelligence section, it appeared to be the message that alerted Moscow to the news of "Elli" that Philby had received the day before from Canada. A search for high-priority messages going the other way yielded only one that could be Moscow's reply.[22]

Wright says that by late 1965, a "determined attack on his message" finally succeeded in breaking out the plaintext:

> Consent has been obtained from the Chiefs to consult with the neighbors about STANLEY's material about their affairs in Canada. STANLEY's data is correct.

Wright recalls that at first he thought there was a mistake. "Stanley" was clearly Philby's cryptonym. But why, he wondered, did Moscow Center's reply suggest that it doubted the warning passed on by its senior mole in MI6? The answer soon became obvious: Beria's MGB (the KGB's immediate predecessor) truly did not know about the GRU spy in MI5 code-named "Elli." Therefore the "Chiefs" — the Soviet Politburo — authorized consultation with the "neighbors" — the GRU. The subsequent flurry of cables on the Moscow to London circuit was commensurate with urgent instructions to step up security.

The 1945 Soviet signal traffic suggested that Gouzenko's revelations about the mole in MI5 caused a major flap in Moscow Center. But this was not confirmed until Wright's investigation in 1965 because twenty years earlier, neither MI5 nor MI6 had the key to break the Soviet cable traffic. Air Commodore James Easton, whom Menzies brought into MI6 as the successor to his assistant chief of staff, Colonel Claude Dansey, confirmed that C *did* know about Gouzenko's male "Elli" in 1945. "He told me about it at our first meeting and raised it with me regularly afterwards," Easton has stated. "Since Colonel Vivian was the chief of internal security, I raised 'Elli' with him, and Vivian responded that 'he had his best man on it.'"[23]

The best man was Philby.

When Easton summoned the head of Section IX to his office, Philby said "*he* had *his* best man on the job." This was Tim Milne, whom Easton described as Philby's "closest friend and deputy in counterespionage." Milne was "fairly consistent in the view that the suspect was not in SIS [MI6] at all but in the Security Service."

According to Easton, C thought David Footman was the only possible suspect in MI6, and he naturally preferred to believe Gouzenko's assertion that the spy was in MI5. Milne shared that view. C told Easton that "there were a number of politically doubtful characters in MI5, including the head of the counterespionage division, Guy Liddell, who had some very rum friends."[24]

This disparaging reference to Liddell by C could be significant. But then again it might simply have reflected the bad blood between MI5 and MI6 rather than any serious suspicions. After all, it was C who agreed to Philby's proposal that instead of sending him to Canada to interview Gouzenko about "Elli," MI5 should undertake the mission.

Moscow Center evidently regarded Gouzenko as a far more serious threat than Volkov had presented a month before. This time, Krotov evidently instructed Philby to remain in London where he could monitor the progress of the investigation. So instead of making the trip to Canada himself, Philby persuaded C to get MI5 to send Roger Hollis, whom Philby described as his "opposite number" in charge of the "section investigating Soviet and Communist affairs." This was not completely true. Hollis appears to have been a somewhat surprising selection for a mission that seemed more appropriate for a senior member of MI5's B Division, which handled counterintelligence, or C Division, which handled security. Hollis spent most of the war monitoring political subversion and was hardly an experienced counterintelligence officer.

The justification Philby gave in his book was that he and Hollis "never failed to work out an agreed approach . . ." when they served on the Joint Intelligence Subcommittee dealing with Communist affairs.

Another plausible explanation for choosing Hollis was that Philby's Soviet control wanted it arranged so that the MI5 officer who went to Canada would not dig too deeply into Gouzenko's allegations.[25]

Hollis's surprisingly shallow "Elli" investigation was later taken as further evidence that he could have been a Soviet agent in MI5. He was also "violently anti-American," according to Sir William Stephenson, whom Hollis saw when he reached New York. Stephenson's biographer goes so far as to say that Stephenson so distrusted Hollis that he wired London: "Sending your man back by next available transport."[26]

The records show, nonetheless, that Hollis did go to Ottawa, where he and Peter Dwyer attended high-level briefings with the Canadian external affairs minister on Nunn May. The diary of Mackenzie King contains a September 23 entry noting Hollis as saying: "The Russians have got a lot of information on the atomic bomb." Also as early as 1946, Hollis made a second trip to Ottawa and personally questioned Gouzenko. According to Gouzenko's account, his three-minute session with "the gentleman from England" was so brief that there was not even time for them to sit down.[27]

Wright confirms that Gouzenko's information was given very little credibility in Hollis's 1946 dispatch from Ottawa or in his later report. If "Elli" existed at all, Hollis apparently suggested that he might have been a member of the Double-Cross Committee. When Gouzenko was shown the Hollis report on him in 1972, he described it as an "old gray mare," charging that it was so full of lies and distortions that it was deliberately faked to destroy his credibility.

"If the report was written by Hollis, then there was no doubt he was a spy," Gouzenko insisted. "I suspect Hollis himself was 'Elli.'"[28]

Gouzenko's story was convincing, and while not final proof, it persuaded Wright in 1965 that he had pinpointed the identity of the mole in MI5. Further evidence seeming to point to Hollis came from another Soviet defector, a lieutenant colonel named Yuri Rastvorov who fled from the Soviet embassy in Tokyo in 1953. He told the CIA how Lieutenant Skripkin, a former friend of his, had tried to defect to the British in the Far East in 1946, but his plan was blown. On a trip back to Moscow to collect his wife, Skripkin betrayed himself to MGB officers posing as MI6 contacts, was tried and shot. An examination of the Skripkin records revealed that Hollis had handled the case in F Division and that he had ordered the files buried away in the Registry without taking any investigative action. When they were first examined in 1954, following Rastvorov's report to the CIA, it was thought that Philby was the culprit.[29]

What is truly astonishing is that MI5 appears to have taken no steps before 1965 to mount any far-reaching investigations into the evidence of Soviet penetration. This is curious because Wright disclosed that the office diary of Liddell — code-named "Wallflowers" by Wright, who countermanded an order for the diary's destruction by Hollis — *did* take note of the Hollis and Dwyer reports on Gouzenko to the extent of recording his thoughts on who the spy "in five of MI" might be. Liddell's speculation about "Elli's" identity is still more intriguing, given that he seems to have done nothing about looking into the affair. He relied on the disparagement of Gouzenko by Hollis, who was a long way from being the best-qualified counterintelligence officer to make such a dismissive judgment.

That Liddell, the head of counterintelligence, on the eve of his promotion to deputy director of MI5, failed to order a full investigation into prima facie evidence of high-level Soviet penetrations of British Intelligence is suspicious. Liddell knew more than anyone else in MI5 about Soviet intelligence objectives and penetration operations. His failure to act when the alarm bells were sounded by Gouzenko evidently surprised Anne Last, one of MI5's most dedicated research officers. After the Burgess and Maclean defection in 1951, Last set to work with Evelyn McBarnett to compile a handwritten book on all the cases that pointed to evidence of systematic Soviet penetration of MI5. They discovered that Maxwell Knight had minuted warnings throughout the war that he was sure a Soviet spy was operating in the upper reaches of the service, but no action had been taken. They also discovered that Gouzenko's allegations had been filed away to gather dust.

"People didn't believe him," Evelyn McBarnett assured Wright when, in 1963, she showed him Gouzenko's allegations in Last's secret analysis book. "They said he had got it wrong. There couldn't be a spy inside MI5," McBarnett told Wright.

Menzies evidently shared the same belief. In a reorganization of MI6, Philby became head of a newly designated R5 anti-Soviet counterintelligence section. C also put him down for a "gong" for his wartime work. Philby became a member of the Order of the British Empire in the 1946 New Year's Honors Lists. A story that has gained wide currency is that he invited James Angleton, who happened to be in London on leave at the time, to attend his investiture. After the ceremony he supposedly made the remark: "You know, what this country needs is a good dose of socialism." This piece of folklore is not true; it was denied by Angleton, and the January investiture was canceled in 1946 because the king was ill. But Angleton did have his doubts about Philby. Nor was he the first American intelligence officer to become suspicious of Philby. The unofficial OSS representative on the Double-Cross Committee, Norman Holmes Pearson, learned from John Masterman that he should be circumspect in his dealings with Philby.[30]

Philby's phenomenal run of luck ran sour over his marital affairs that same year. When he had joined SOE in September 1940, he had claimed Aileen Furze was his wife. But he had not married her, although they lived together for the next six years as man and wife. But in 1946, Philby, as one of the rising stars of MI6, realized that his marital irregularity could be a stumbling block to his career. So he made a clean breast of it to Colonel Vivian, the head of MI6 security. He also revealed that he was divorcing his first wife, Litzi Friedman, who had left him in 1938, to marry Aileen. The private ceremony took place in September at the Chelsea Registrar's office. Philby invited only his two intimate friends, Flora Solomon and Tomas Harris, as their witnesses.[31]

The price Philby paid came when Vivian ordered a routine check on his first wife. The Registry files revealed that Litzi Friedman had been living with an Austrian Communist, a suspected Soviet agent named George Honigmann, who in 1945 had moved to Berlin. As a matter of course, Menzies learned of Philby's transgression. Normally a stickler about these matters, such was the esteem that Menzies held for Philby's talents that he did not think it necessary to order a follow-up on why Philby's former wife had run off with a Communist. At the same time, Menzies and Vivian realized that Philby's false declaration about Aileen Furze could be a potential embarrassment — perhaps even lead to questions about the Communist connections of the head of anti-Soviet operations. So they decided to post Philby out of the country as the MI6 station chief in Turkey.

"Philby must have had rather a pleasant, interesting, and extended holiday, for we did not use Istanbul much while he was there," Easton observed. This is the impression that Philby himself conveyed in his book, suggesting that he spent much of his time on expeditions to Mount Ararat as cover for running agents across the Soviet frontier. But it is now clear that Philby also rendered more valuable service to the Soviets than tipping them off about minor British operations.

It began during the war when the Turkish intelligence service offered hospitality to defecting Soviets. One of their prize "guests" was Ismail Akhmedov, a GRU officer who had slipped away disguised as a Turk. A fluent speaker of Turkish, he had eluded his pursuers and studiously avoided contact with British intelligence because he harbored an inherent distrust of the British. But in 1948, the Turks finally persuaded

Akhmedov to meet with the representative of the His Majesty's Secret Intelligence Service.[32]

"Philby was successful in getting from me the names of several hundred officers and engineers associated with me," Akhmedov later admitted. These were people still inside the Red Army who, he believed, might be sympathetic to an approach from the British. Not until after Philby's defection to Moscow in 1963 did Akhmedov understand why the British MI6 officer had not seemed interested in 1948 in his own GRU background and career. Philby's Soviet masters were more interested in learning the identities of other potential defectors. The sickening realization that Akhmedov had been tricked into betraying so many of his friends was later to give him many sleepless nights.[33]

The full extent of the damage done by Philby in his two years in Turkey will never be known. But since the early days of the century, Istanbul had been a way station for European agents playing the "great game." After World War II, it served as an important crossroads for British and American intelligence operations directed at the Soviet-occupied Balkan countries and southern Russia. Since MI6 had no grounds for suspicion, Menzies believed Philby was now ready for one of the most important assignments in MI6: liaison with the United States.

After receiving the telegram from headquarters in August 1949, Philby records that it took him "less than half an hour" to make up his mind to accept the Washington post. The final decision was not his to make, although he says he accepted it "without waiting for confirmation from my Soviet colleagues." But it did not need second-guessing for him to realize that Moscow Center would share his view about the "irresistible" lure of the American job.[34]

"At one stroke," Philby wrote, his appointment as liaison officer to both the FBI and CIA "would take me right back into the middle of intelligence policy making and would give me a close-up view of the American intelligence operations." His statement that the Washington-based intelligence organizations "were already of greater importance" than those in London can now be seen as a tongue-in-cheek affirmation that the Soviets must have sustained their high-level penetrations of MI5 and MI6 *despite* Philby's overseas posting.[35]

The timing was highly opportune for the Soviets. In late summer, 1947, Congress had passed the National Security Act, which established the Central Intelligence Agency under the National Security Council "to advise the President with respect to the integration of domestic, foreign and military policies." The new agency absorbed its precursor, the Central Intelligence Group. This was an uneasy stepchild of the

Departments of State, War, and Navy that the Truman administration had established by executive order the previous year to inherit the functions of the disbanded OSS. But J. Edgar Hoover had not succeeded in making the FBI the principal U.S. counterintelligence authority. He did, however, connive with Truman to ensure that the former OSS chief William Donovan did not become head of the CIA. That post went to a compromise candidate, Roscoe H. Hillenkoetter, an amiable admiral who authorized the CIA's first covert operations against the Soviet Union. They consisted of a radio transmitter for broadcasting to the Soviet bloc and a fleet of balloons for showering Eastern Europe with propaganda leaflets.[36]

Amateurish though these first operations were, the Cold War was heating up. By 1949, the rapidly expanding CIA posed a growing threat to the Soviet Union. The "unlimited potentialities" open to Philby in Washington enabled him not only to act as a monitor for the Soviet intelligence service but also to assist with the infiltration of the CIA's European operations.

"I thought to myself, what a decent fellow," Air Vice Marshal Easton recalled after Philby told him of the birth of his fifth child and his anticipation of the rewards of having "two rows of heads diminishing in size at the dinner table." When Easton briefed Philby on his Washington assignment, which was to redress the balance of British cooperation in favor of the CIA and away from the FBI, Easton insists there were no grounds to doubt Philby's loyalty when he departed for Washington in September 1949.[37]

Philby anticipated problems with Hoover. Of far graver anxiety was his briefing with the "formidable" Maurice Oldfield, as Philby describes the counterintelligence officer who had taken over his old post as head of R5, the anti-Soviet section of MI6. Oldfield indoctrinated Philby for the first time into the top-secret Anglo-American investigation then under way to track down the person who had been leaking to the Soviets information from the British embassy between 1944 and 1948 and the atomic bomb data from Los Alamos.

It did not tax Philby's ingenuity to guess that the British embassy spy was his old Cambridge contemporary Donald Maclean. More significant was the fact that Philby knew within two days, from his Soviet contact in London, that Moscow also knew about the FBI investigation. This Soviet contact was later identified as Yuri Modin, an embassy official who succeeded Boris Krotov. He was also in touch with Burgess and Blunt. Philby records that he had "been nagged for months" by his Soviet control officer in Istanbul to find out what the British were doing about the Washington embassy investigation. That they had already learned of the new danger to their deep-cover moles is yet more evidence that "Elli" "in five of MI" was keeping Moscow fully posted.[38]

What Philby learned from Oldfield was that the alarm bells for this high-level penetration had not been sounded this time by a Soviet defector who could be disparaged. They came from the most reliable source of all, SIGINT, the proverbial horse's mouth. The 1943 Britain/USA agreement, which provided "a full exchange of the cryptographic systems, crypt-analytical techniques, direction-finding, radio interception and other technical communications matters," had been extended, in 1947, by a secret pact still unacknowledged by either government and known by its acronym UKUSA (United Kingdom–United States Security Agreement). This continued the wartime arrangement for pooling SIGINT gathering and the resultant cryptanalysis of Soviet cipher traffic. When this most secret of all agreements was made, no one in the United States suspected that the Soviets had in Philby a direct line into the British intelligence service. As one American intelligence officer put it, the UKUSA agreement was "like opening up a party line to Moscow Center."[39]

The worldwide collection of Soviet traffic by the United States, Britain, Canada, and Australia had the cover name Operation Bride. And despite the impression some British writers convey, the U.S. Army made the first significant breaks in the traffic that the British and Americans code-named Venona.

When Robert Lamphere arrived at FBI headquarters in 1947 to establish a counterintelligence office covering the Soviet satellite countries, he found locked in a safe in the espionage division a few pieces of paper with fragmentary decrypts from the MGB messages sent in 1944–45 by the Soviet consulate in New York to Moscow Center.

Lamphere knew little about codes and less about ciphers, but he took the mostly blank pages and vowed in his words "to do something about them." He gathered together all the information he could obtain from the Gouzenko case. Gouzenko's knowledge of how the GRU encrypted and used its "one-time pads" provided a valuable insight into how the MGB used its similar system. The messages were first encrypted from a code book into five-digit groups. Low-priority cables were sometimes sent out in this form, but most important messages went through a second encryption process in which their five-digit groups were added (by "false addition") to a random sequence of five-digit groups used only for that message — hence the description "one-time pad."[40]

Theoretically, the enciphered message was decodable only with access to an identical cipher pad. Use of a separate additive sheet for each message endowed the one-time pad with a near-impregnable security. But cipher clerks were fallible; so was Russian bureaucracy. Sometimes a careless code clerk enciphered two messages with the same pad.

The code breakers of the U.S. Army Security Agency (ASA) had been given a head start because in November 1944 OSS chief Donovan had purchased from the Finns some 1,500 pages from a partially charred MGB code book that had been recovered on a battlefield. In a dubious and misguided display of international probity, Secretary of State Edward Stettinius had insisted on returning the originals to the Soviets in 1945. Fortunately, Donovan had defied orders and copied them. Meredith Gardener, a cryptanalyst and linguist with ASA, used the old code book to tackle some duplicates of the cables sent by the Soviet consulate in New York.[41]

When Lamphere began making his fortnightly trips to Gardener's office at ASA headquarters across the Potomac in Arlington, progress was painfully slow. "We started with very, very fragmentary information," Lamphere told me, "trying to read between the lines while the code breakers worked on the messages." The major breakthrough came after the FBI's New York field office answered Lamphere's request for help by sending him a large bundle of documents. The material dated back to a carefully executed break-in the FBI had mounted on the New York offices of the Soviet Purchasing Commission.[42]

"When I got the material it was mostly in Russian, and it was like searching for a needle in a haystack," Lamphere explained. "I had no idea that it would turn out to be a gold mine." Even when Gardener, a normally withdrawn and dour person, called up and excitedly summoned Lamphere to Arlington Hall, he was still doubtful anything major had come up.[43]

"You can't believe what you've given me here," Lamphere recalled Gardener saying. "It was the only time I ever saw him smile," Lamphere said, recalling how the army code breaker explained that the FBI haul included plaintext messages of the enciphered cables already intercepted by the Americans. Most valuable of all was the discovery that the trade mission had received a set of one-time code pad additives that duplicated those sent to the MGB agents in New York — the result of a bureaucratic foul-up in Moscow. With three parts of the cryptographic puzzle in his possession, Gardener explained in his shy way that he had hit the jackpot: He had been able to re-create the plaintexts of several enciphered messages.[44]

From the time of this breakthrough in the spring of 1948, Lamphere began to acquire a steady stream of fully and partially decrypted Soviet reports of their intelligence networks in the United States. Working with the FBI case file for 1944, and drawing on his own knowledge of the Russian émigré community in the United States, Lamphere was able to fill in some of the gaps and develop leads that led to surveillance and arrests of Soviet operatives.

Within a year a spy ring involving Judith Coplon, a political analyst in the Foreign Agents Registration section of the Justice Department, and her contact, Valentin Alekseevich Guibitchev, a Russian attached to the Soviet U.N. mission, were arrested and charged after FBI agents caught them in the act of transferring documents. The FBI was to lose its case against Coplon because it had arrested her without a warrant. But while Lamphere was suffering Hoover's anger at this setback, he had fresh leads developing from Gardener's code-breaks. Eventually they resulted in the exposure of the Soviets' most important espionage rings.

Initially the new code-breaks led nowhere. The first clue that would later tie the Rosenbergs in to the notorious atomic espionage case emerged from a single reference in a Soviet cable to a woman with the forename of Ethel. She was involved in a technological spy ring operating among a group of Communist sympathizers and former classmates at City College, New York. Another lead came from a fragmentary series of decrypts that indicated someone in the British embassy in Washington had been providing the Soviets in New York with copies of high-level cable traffic between the United States and the United Kingdom.

Lamphere obtained copies of telegrams exchanged in the late spring of 1945 between Churchill and Truman. From them Gardener established a word for word translation of some of the Soviet messages — even down to their identifying cable numbers and dates. In the fall of 1948 Lamphere told the Washington representatives of MI5 and MI6, Peter Dwyer and Dick Thistlethwaite, about these developments. As it happened, this was shortly after the source of those leaks — Donald Maclean — had departed for a new posting at the British embassy in Cairo. Since October 1944 he had been a model of diplomatic efficiency as the first secretary in Washington, and this had led to his appointment a year later as acting head of chancellery — which included access to the code room.[45]

In 1948 neither Lamphere, nor the British, had any reason to suspect Maclean. But the decrypts revealed that someone in the embassy was leaking very high-grade information to the Soviets. According to Lamphere, both Dwyer and Thistlethwaite were "startled by this revelation, as well they should have been."[46]

Anglo-American communications at the highest level during the closing days of World War II had clearly been compromised — and might still be at risk. It was decided to launch an urgent investigation, and the two British representatives agreed to provide a list of possible suspects. The security damage implied by several of the Soviet cables was so serious that Lamphere expected immediate action. But when nothing happened for a week, then a month, he became concerned.

"I just couldn't believe it, but I was busy working with the Coplon case and had the other leads breaking all around me," Lamphere recalled. "I tended to say to myself: 'What the hell's the matter with them that they are not getting anywhere!' Then I'd get on with those cases that I could do something about."[47]

Lamphere concedes that the FBI often ran up blind alleys during those days. But he still does not believe that MI5 or MI6 had any excuse for failing to provide the FBI with a short list of possible embassy suspects. His frustration became so intense at one point that he considered unilaterally asking the State Department to help in trying to get such an investigation going. Lamphere contends that if the situation had been reversed, with a spy in the American embassy in London, the FBI would have been working around the clock to establish, from a roster of embassy staff and the records, who could have seen the cables and what their movements were. Yet to his amazement, months passed, and his British opposite numbers had still not produced a list of suspects.

"Every month or so, when I inquired about it, I would be told that there was no new information, but that MI5 and MI6 were still working on finding that possible spy," Lamphere recalled. It was strictly British business, but Lamphere explained to me how he kept up the pressure on Thistlethwaite and then on his replacement, Jeff Patterson. He found it hard to accept the repeated "no progress" reports during the year that passed before Philby arrived in Washington in October 1949 to take over as the new MI6 liaison officer. His predecessor, Dwyer, had been a clever and witty "horse trader" for information, according to Lamphere. But Philby's immediate "lack of friendliness" struck him forcefully. When Lamphere asked why there were no leads about the identity of the embassy spy, Philby said it was not the direct responsibility of MI6.

Lamphere did not realize of course that Philby knew who the spy had been. Nor did Lamphere know that Michael Straight's wife had tried to alert the embassy, via her psychiatrist, Dr. Jennie Welderhall. But for reasons of professional etiquette, she decided not to pass on the information that Guy Burgess was a Soviet agent. Had the message been relayed, the Cambridge connection would have been an obvious pointer to Donald Maclean as the spy in the British embassy. However, since Belinda Straight delivered her warning during the summer of the

House Un-American Activities Committee hearings *at the very time Donald Maclean was acting Head of Chancellery*, he would not have passed the message on to the Foreign Office.

In his book, Philby goes out of his way to heap scorn on the FBI, which, he says, "was in sorry shape when I reached Washington." He blames its record of failure, which he calls "conspicuous," for not catching Maclean or Burgess. The KGB evidently designed Philby's account so that his readers would disparage the bureau and congratulate their hero master spy for so easily pulling the wool over the eyes of the FBI and the "nice pudgy native of Ohio." But there was nothing ineffectual about the relentless way Lamphere pursued Soviet agents. He was one of the most frequent users of the UKUSA arrangement whereby the FBI exchanged information with MI5 and MI6 by addressing memos to SMOTH, the acronym for the British intelligence office in Washington.[48]

Lamphere is adamant that he never stopped reminding the British about the case. And the evidence now available certainly confirms that London's failure to identify Maclean — and consequently to implicate Burgess and Philby in the same Soviet network — before May 1951 was not because of any failure on the American end. The real culprit could only have been the GRU mole in MI5 who ensured that the investigation crawled forward at slower than a snail's pace.

The MI5 file on the investigation into the spy in the British embassy remains after nearly forty years, officially secret. But Lamphere is not the only American counterintelligence expert to have assured me that there is really no excuse for the incompetent way in which MI5 handled the case. Lamphere points out that MI5 knew from an absolutely incontrovertible source that during 1945 at least one senior member of the staff in the elegant colonial mansion on Massachusetts Avenue was a Soviet spy. The information may have been incomplete, but as Lamphere points out, by 1949 the clues that should have made Maclean the obvious suspect had piled up. The clincher was his weekly trips via New York to Massachusetts where his wife Melinda was staying at her mother's. These weekly trips coincided with the dates of the Soviet cables transmitting the Anglo-American conversations to Moscow.

"MI5 was not a very efficient outfit," Lamphere told me. "One of our criticisms of it was that there were too many case officers sitting at desks who had no real experiences of field investigations." He recalls that this was the prevailing attitude in the FBI at the time. He believes that this was one factor that held up the Maclean investigation. Another factor was the "bad faith" of the British, an issue that still disturbs

Lamphere. He had suspected for some time that Patterson and Philby had lied to him about there being "no progress" in the investigations in London. He reiterates that an embarrassed Arthur Martin had told him about this appalling breach of faith when he flew to Washington in June 1951 with Sir Percy Sillitoe to try to end the bad feelings left behind by the Burgess and Maclean defection.[49]

Was a Foreign Office embargo the true reason that MI5 had kept the FBI in the dark for so long about the Maclean investigation? Lamphere finds it as hard to believe today as he did in 1951, when Martin handed him the specially prepared MI5 memorandum on the Maclean investigations. Nigel West assured me that authoritative sources in MI5 all know that this memorandum was deliberately "manufactured" under the direction of the MI5 deputy director to conceal London's astonishing failure to conduct any prompt and serious investigation of the embassy spy.[50]

It is a curious, but nevertheless consequential, fact that the failure to investigate — and therefore the responsibility for organizing the coverup over Maclean — can only be attributed to B Division, whose head was none other than Guy Liddell. Moreover, there is good reason to believe that nothing would ever have been done about the embassy spy case had it not been for another code-break. Again, this was the result of Lamphere's and Gardener's efforts. This break revealed that Dr. Klaus Fuchs had supplied most of the secrets of the atomic bomb to Moscow agents.

Lamphere's investigation into the possible leakages of atomic secrets resulted from the White House's announcement, on September 23, 1949, that the Soviets had exploded an atomic bomb of their own. The stunning news that the Russians had nuclear weapons a good five to ten years earlier than the best military intelligence estimates prompted J. Edgar Hoover to take action. He ordered Lish Whitson, the head of the FBI Espionage Section, to call a special meeting to determine if the Manhattan Project had been penetrated in the United States. It was already known that the Cambridge scientist Alan Nunn May had breached the Canadian end of the project; that he had stolen a uranium sample and passed on a critical item of technology in the form of a piece of the barrier material that was used in the gaseous-diffusion method of enrichment.

Meanwhile, Gardener had provided Lamphere with a newly deciphered 1944 MGB decrypt containing references to the gaseous-diffusion process. Lamphere dropped everything to work on this message. With the help of a friend in the Atomic Energy Commission, he located the original paper of which the message was a summary. The second part of the decrypt dealt with the agent, or messenger, who had provided the information, and the two parts together, according to Lamphere, confirmed beyond any reasonable doubt that the MGB in New York City "had had an agent within the British mission to the Manhattan Project."[51]

The prime suspects were: Rudolf Peierls, another scientist whom Lamphere declined to name, and Dr. Klaus Fuchs, the author of the paper on gaseous diffusion. A search of the files produced significant derogatory information only on Fuchs. The first was from a Gestapo file from 1933, which identified Fuchs as a Communist: The Germans had considered him dangerous enough to issue a warrant for his arrest. The second derived from Fuchs's name in the notebooks of Israel Halperin. The Canadian scientist had been charged — but not convicted — of acting as a GRU agent on evidence supplied by Igor Gouzenko four years earlier.

Lamphere could not be absolutely certain of the identity of the Soviet agent in the Manhattan Project, but he was so sure it must be Fuchs that he set out his reasoning, along with the evidence, in a top-secret letter addressed to SMOTH at the British embassy.

This time the British responded within a few weeks that they too considered Fuchs to be the prime suspect. But since there could be no question of ever revealing the Venona decrypts in court, the only way to get the evidence to convict him of espionage was to coax a confession from him. William Skardon was the best interrogator in MI5. His first interview with Fuchs took place on December 21 at Harwell, which the nuclear scientist had joined in 1946 as head of the Theoretical Physics Section. With patient but wearing questioning, Skardon, a deferential but infinitely persistent former policeman, gradually wore down the physicist, whose high forehead made him a living caricature of the egghead scientist. On January 24, 1950, Fuchs confessed to his espionage and to his double life, which he described as being in a state of "controlled schizophrenia." Six months later Fuchs pleaded guilty at the Old Bailey to a four-count indictment under the Official Secrets Act. The brief thirty-minute trial ended with the judge sentencing him to a fourteen-year prison term.[52]

Fuchs's admission of guilt spared the British government from trying to obtain a conviction when not even an in camera jury could be allowed to learn of the political and intelligence secrets implicit in the Fuchs case. That was the problem confronting the FBI when Lamphere followed up a lead given by Fuchs that finally uncovered the identity of the mysterious Ethel.

Fuchs had identified a Philadelphia chemist named Harry Gold as one of the contact men with the Soviets. Gold led investigators to

David Greenglass, a U.S. Army machinist who had worked on the atomic-bomb casing at Los Alamos. In turn, Greenglass incriminated his brother-in-law, Julius Rosenberg, as one of the principals in the Soviet spy ring in New York. Rosenberg denied he was in the service of the Soviets, but other Venona decrypts tied him to two of his former Communist college friends, Max Elitcher and Joel Barr, whom the cables had revealed as feeding technical information to the Soviets.

Julius and Ethel Rosenberg, and the rest of their group, were arrested in 1950. Indictments followed for their conspiracy to transmit classified military information to the Soviet Union. But none of the convincing circumstantial evidence contained in the Soviet cable traffic could be revealed by the prosecution at the lengthy and controversial trials that ended in stiff jail terms for their associates and the death penalty for the Rosenbergs. It took nearly three years to exhaust the appeals process. No pardon saved the Rosenbergs from the electric chair. They went to the execution chamber still protesting their innocence. In the minds of many Americans they became martyrs and sacrificial victims to McCarthyism.

Klaus Fuchs, the scientist who supplied the Rosenberg network with the secrets of the atomic bomb, emerged from a British prison in 1959. He returned to nuclear research in East Germany, a national hero and a member of the Communist Party Central Committee. Arguably, MI5's failure to pick up the blatant trail of clues about his treachery ranked alongside the treason of both the Rosenbergs and Fuchs.

"Traitor by courtesy of incompetence" is how *The Times* of London headlined Dr. Fuchs's obituary notice on January 29, 1988. What is now plain is that the degree of incompetence shown by MI5 in the Fuchs case was so devastating as to be criminal. There was a mass of evidence showing that after Fuchs had fled Germany in 1934, he had maintained his connections with the exiled KPD Communists in England.

Even more astonishing was why MI5 gave Fuchs clearance for top-secret work in 1941, when Fuchs had made no secret of his Communist activities in support of the exiledGerman KPD run by his friend Jürgen Kuczynski. At Bristol University in 1934, Fuchs had been active in the Friends of Soviet Russia and the Society for Cultural Relations with the Soviet Union. A reticent man who attracted the nickname "penny-in-the-slot-Fuchs," Fuchs's communism was apparent to those who knew him before the war at Edinburgh University, where he worked in Max Born's laboratory. Nor did Fuchs make any secret of his beliefs during his 1940 stay in an internment camp on the Isle of Man and later in Canada.[53]

Yet a year later Fuchs was brought back to England. Cleared by MI5, he joined the team at Birmingham University led by Otto Frisch and Rudolf Peierls, who were working on the top-secret Tube Alloys atomic-bomb research. It was their 1940 memorandum on a "super bomb" that led to the establishment of a committee of scientists known as MAUD, which endorsed the British effort to develop the uranium-fission bomb. Peierls, who was aware of Fuchs's student communism, was at first directed to "tell him as little as possible." But by October 1941, Peierls requested and received from MI5 "definite clearance" for Fuchs's admission to the full Tube Alloys secret so that he could work on the gaseous-diffusion process.[54]

Nor was there any MI5 objection the following year when Fuchs achieved British naturalization. It was said that police inquiries by the chief constable of Birmingham failed to turn up any open Communist associations. It is difficult to believe that MI5, who we know had closely monitored the student Communists at Cambridge, was not by then aware that the GRU had made Birmingham University another of its prime targets because of its extensive scientific and engineering research. The faculty and student body at Birmingham hosted a strong Communist organization and even before the war had become the refuge for many of the Cambridge Communist activists, including Professor Derwent Thompson, Blunt's friend Roy Pascal, and his militant Marxist wife, Fanya.[55]

It was also MI5 that gave Fuchs his clean bill of health to transfer to the Manhattan Project at the end of 1943. Security was a U.S. Army responsibility, but in March 1944, Hoover received assurances from MI5 that it had thoroughly vetted all the members of the British mission. Therefore there was no suspicion of his trustworthiness when, in August 1944, at the personal request of Professor Rudolph Peierls, Fuchs transferred to the heart of the Manhattan Project — the assembly and design laboratory at Los Alamos. After attending the early conferences that laid the theoretical groundwork for the hydrogen bomb, and working on preparations for the atomic-bomb test at Bikini Atoll in 1946, Fuchs returned to England in July of that year.

Even though Nunn May had admitted he was a Soviet spy, MI5 evidently did not see fit to check either its own or the captured Gestapo files later on when Fuchs became head of the Theoretical Physics Section and deputy scientific director of Harwell. This burgeoning, top-secret government research station near Oxford was supposedly dedicated to the peaceful development of nuclear reactors. In reality, Britain had assembled its own team of scientists and engineers to clandestinely develop its own atomic bomb after being cut off from U.S. atomic secrets when Congress passed the McMahon Act in 1946.

Had it not been for Venona and the FBI, Fuchs's career as a physicist might have continued until, like Blunt, he was rewarded with a knighthood. But in contrast to Blunt, after exhaustive interrogation by Skardon in 1950, Fuchs made a full confession *without any offer of immunity*. He admitted that since 1941 he had been in touch with a Russian he knew as "Alexander" — otherwise Simon Davidovitch Kremr, secretary to Moscow's military attaché in London and a senior GRU agent runner. In the autumn of 1942, "Alexander" passed Fuchs on to a new control officer he knew only as "Sonja." She was Ruth Kuczynski, the sister of Jürgen, who, in preparation for her deep-cover mission in England, had married a Briton named Len Beurton. Sonja had come from Switzerland in 1940 to set up the family home in Kidlington near Oxford.

Sonja was no ordinary illegal. She had achieved the rank of a GRU major while married to her first husband, Rudi Hamburger. After serving Soviet Military Intelligence dutifully for many years in Shanghai, she went to Montreux, where in 1938 she recruited Allan Alexander Foote, after carefully giving him the impression that she was abandoning communism and espionage for a quiet family life in England. This brawny Yorkshire Communist stayed behind to play a part in the so-called "Lucy Ring" that was run by Rudolph Roessler, an expatriate German living in Lucerne. Before she left Switzerland for England, Sonja had divorced Hamburger, who went to Turkey, where Zaehner claims he was employed by MI6 during the war.[56]

Operating out of Kidlington, Sonja ran a stable of spies from her cottage, which was not far from MI5's wartime outpost at Blenheim Palace. For over a year she rendezvoused with Fuchs — usually at Banbury, the nursery-rhyme market town midway between Birmingham and Oxford. She transmitted his written reports to Moscow in cipher via her radio with its aerial strung out in her loft. The ever-resourceful Sonja had smuggled the radio set into Britain with some of its key components concealed in her children's teddy bears. Complex mathematical equations that she could not encode went to Kremer at the embassy for transmission by the diplomatic pouch.

A damaging indictment of the failure of the wartime counter-intelligence effort mounted by MI5 against Soviet infiltration is Peter Wright's revelation — from his inside knowledge of the case file — that Sonja's importance did not become clear *until 1972*. Only at that late date did a sophisticated computer analysis break open a large batch of GRU messages code-named HASP. These had been transmitted by the Soviets from Britain during the war and intercepted by the Swedes, who passed them to the British in 1959. These decrypts yielded literally dozens of cryptonyms of British scientists and journalists who fed intelligence of military value to the Soviets during the war. Among them was the Cambridge-educated cinema specialist Ivor Montague and J.B.S. Haldane, the biochemist who, during the war, worked on secret projects for the Admiralty. Most revealing of all was the series of messages relayed by Kremer, the GRU *resident*, describing his meetings with Sonja.[57]

Wright says: "Kremer's messages utterly destroyed the established beliefs." The conventional wisdom in MI5, based on the authority of Alexander Foote, who defected back to the British in 1947, was that Sonja had given up her spying when she left Switzerland. But the traffic emanating from the Soviet embassy in 1941 proved beyond doubt that Sonja was running a bevy of agents *before* she began handling Fuchs. The Hasp traffic contained not only details of the payments Sonja made, but the times and durations of her own radio broadcasts.[58]

The number of those messages suggests that there was a good chance that even such a careful clandestine transmitter as Sonja's would have been picked up by the MI5 department known as the Radio Security Service (RSS). Its mission was to scan the broadcasting frequencies to monitor and track down any illegal radio transmission. Churchill, after 1941 when Stalin became an ally, had embargoed any attempt to eavesdrop on the Soviet embassy. But what turned out to have been a rash prime ministerial injunction never applied to the illegal transmissions of undercover agents of Moscow. The odds are that Sonja's transmissions were picked up and duly reported.

If so, who in MI5 failed to authorize action against this most active of Soviet spies? Still more curious is Sonja's failure to leave England for sanctuary in East Germany in 1947 when, after Foote's defection, two MI5 investigators arrived on her doorstep to interview her. One was the ace interrogator William Skardon. Yet even after Sonja's cover had been blown, she did not depart for East Germany until 1950. This was *after* Fuchs made his full confession, in which he named *Sonja* as his Soviet controller![59]

Even more curious is that Sonja was never, at any time, put under surveillance by MI5, either during or after the war. Yet Soviet defector Walter Krivitsky had, according to a reliable source, tipped off the British in 1940 that Kremer was the GRU *resident* and the presumption was that any sustained tailing of him must have revealed his contacts with Sonja.[60]

The conclusion must be either that the redoubtable Sonja was unbelievably lucky, or that MI5 was incredibly incompetent — or that the GRU agent had an invisible GRU ally *inside* MI5 who was senior enough to deflect both the wartime investigation of the radio messages and any postwar investigation. None of Blunt's wartime work for MI5 could have provided him with the access, or the authority, to bury RSS reports or stop investigations of such obvious leads. Nor was he in a position to arrange Fuchs's clean bill of health for top-secret atomic work, or to provide the protection that it seems Sonja received until 1950.

According to the debriefing that Fuchs gave the FBI after he confessed, he did not contact Sonja on his return to England because he did not know where she was. Nor was he successful in carrying out the instructions to contact his old friend Jürgen Kuczynski, given him via Harry Gold, the Rosenbergs' sub-agent. Fuchs broke all the rules of tradecraft and approached Johanna Klopstech, whom he knew earlier to be a Czech KPD refugee. FBI records show that from 1940 she had been under MI5 surveillance as a "dangerous" Communist. This approach ran the risk that the British watchers would pick him up. Klopstech put Fuchs in touch with a new Soviet agent whom he met six more times, until early 1949, in London pubs and from whom he accepted £100 for information — presumably from Harwell, relating to the British atomic-bomb project.[61]

Ironically, the Russians, thanks to Fuchs, probably knew more about Britain's top-secret race to build its own atomic bomb than did the Americans. It was not until May 1948 that a member of the U.S. Atomic Energy Commission on a visit to Harwell discovered that the research reactors he saw there had been designed to produce plutonium and *not* power!

Another curious twist to the Fuchs-Sonja case is contained in Professor Robert Chadwell Williams's carefully documented study of the Fuchs case, which cites evidence from a former MI6 officer that suggests that the atomic spy *did* neet Sonja again in 1947. If this source is reliable — and the British government is covering up another skeleton — it raises the possibility that from 1947 onward, the authorities *knew* that Fuchs was a Soviet spy. Nor is it inconceivable that it was the deep-cover Soviet mole "Elli" who had a hand in protecting Fuchs from exposure. Another plausible explanation is that any espionage Fuchs carried out was believed to be less important than harnessing his considerable talents as a physicist in Britain's secret race to build her own bomb.[62]

After the 1949 explosion of the Soviet bomb, espionage considerations took second place to Britain's race to join the exclusive nuclear club. Fuchs himself told the FBI that after he returned to England, his GRU contact was less concerned with manufacturing details than with how to calculate the potential yield of a nuclear explosion. In the eyes of

Prime Minister Attlee, and the half-dozen Labour Cabinet members who had secretly authorized the £100 million atomic-bomb project without parliamentary approval, the possession of nuclear weapons was Britain's ticket to retaining her status as one of the Big Three powers.[63]

Was the culmination of MI5's blunders over Fuchs a devious foreign-policy gamble that was unwittingly aided by the Soviet mole in the British security service? The history of counterintelligence suggests that in the wilderness of mirrors such concatenations are not impossible. There is good reason for believing that if the FBI had not intervened and presented the incontrovertible evidence of their so-called Foocase files, MI5 would never have moved against Fuchs.

The same deduction of either criminal negligence, or complicity by officers of MI5, can be drawn from the case of Bruno Pontecorvo, the Italian nuclear physicist who had worked in the Paris laboratories of the unashamedly Communist scientist Pierre Joliot-Curie in 1940. After the fall of France, Pontecorvo headed for the United States. In 1943 he joined the British atomic-research team in Canada, eventually working on heavy-water research alongside Nunn May at the Chalk River facilities in Ontario. The RCMP relied on assurances of a British security screening of Pontecorvo that had never taken place! Nor did any derogatory information surface from his Communist past when he transferred to Harwell in 1949 and was granted British citizenship. He underwent security clearances no fewer than six times by UKAEA officials who relied on data supplied by MI5.[64]

Pontecorvo had originally hoped to work on nuclear energy in the United States. But the FBI, suspicious of his past, had arranged for a discreet search of his American home and found incriminating Communist documents. This information was passed in 1949 to the MI6 officer in Washington: Kim Philby. He suppressed the file, but alerted his Soviet controller. Pontecorvo was then tipped off by the Soviet underground network in Britain and induced to defect. As one of the few scientists with an intimate working knowledge of the reactor technology necessary to produce lithium deuteride, Pontecorvo was a valuable asset for the Soviets' H-bomb project. His damning FBI report did not come to light until after Pontecorvo ended up in Moscow.[65]

The news that Pontecorvo was behind the Iron Curtain did not break for over a year, but his "assumed defection" had occurred barely six months after the trial of Klaus Fuchs. To the FBI it was another security disaster for the British. Whether it was another success for "Elli" was not clear. But because of the remarkable similarities to the Fuchs case, an immediate investigation by MI5 into the adequacy of its vetting procedures would have been in order. But there is no evidence that Liddell, who in his capacity as deputy director bore the ultimate administrative responsibility, ever considered ordering a full investigation.

This second damaging breach, and the stalled investigation into the Soviet spy in the British embassy in Washington, should have raised a major question mark about the competence of MI5. What is even odder is that Liddell, despite his long track record in counterespionage, did not order a major review, or internal investigation, into security-service vetting procedures.

The chronic incompetence of the British secret services did not contaminate the FBI alone. The CIA was soon to suffer similar symptoms that could be attributed only to an astonishing run of bad luck — or to infection from too close an association with MI6.

The first American organization afflicted was the Office of Policy Coordination (OPC). Though it sheltered under the umbrella of the CIA, OPC was not yet an integral part of the agency. The OPC was a euphemism for all covert action programs, i.e., psychological, international organizations, paramilitary, political and economic activities and propaganda. It was set up in 1948 to run anti-Soviet subversion operations on a worldwide basis under the direction of the Department of Defense. The OPC head was Frank Wisner, a prematurely balding, self-important forty-three-year-old who had acquired a taste and talent for covert activity while serving in the OSS with distinction in Istanbul and the Balkans. His aim was to take a leaf from the Comintern book and turn the weapons of subversion and infiltration against the Soviets and their satellite regimes.

Turning the tables on the Bolsheviks was a dream that had preoccupied British intelligence in the immediate aftermath of the Russian Revolution. But the revolutionaries in Moscow had proved to be more devious and cunning than anticipated. MI6 had been badly burned in the early twenties when its agents, including Sidney Reilly and Robert Bruce Lockhart, had been trapped by the cleverly contrived plots of "The Trust," one of the more deadly brainchildren of Dzerzhinski's fertile scheming.

Stewart Menzies, then a rising star of MI6 in the thirties, had covertly channeled British funds and support to anti-Bolshevik organizations that included General Aleksandr Pavlovich Kutepov's Combat Organization to act as an irritant to the Soviets. Many groups of dispossessed and disaffected Byelorussians — who adopted exotic code-names such as the Prometheus Network, the Intermarium Program, and the Abramtchik Faction — were already penetrated by the Soviets before World War II broke out, when the Abwehr recruited the leaders and members in 1939 to the German cause. Two years later, when Germany invaded the Soviet Union, many Ukrainians rallied under Stefan Bandera in the Russian Army of Liberation that was organized by the SS. The leaders of the anti-Bolshevik factions, now avowed Nazis, became Hitler's puppet governments in Byelorussia and the Ukraine.[66]

In 1945, when these groups were once again pushed toward the West by the tides of Soviet victory, Menzies's dream was revived. Despite their Nazi records, C believed that their supposed anti-Communist zeal, inflamed by the Soviet takover of Eastern Europe, would make them ideal mercenaries for launching an underground war against the Communist bloc. Many of the surviving members of Intermarium, Prometheus, and the Abramtchik, along with an ill-assorted band of Caucasian separatists, Albanian monarchists, and anti-Tito Yugoslavians, were secretly funded and reemployed by MI6. A united front known as the Anti-Bolshevik Bloc of Nations (ABN) was formed by the merger of three constituent groups: the Organization of Ukrainian Nationalists (OUN) from the Ukraine and Polish Galiacia, the Prometheus League representing Poland and White Russia, and the Intermarium Confederation, which claimed to represent the old Catholic states of the Austro-Hungarian Empire. The Americans were also separately rallying Soviet-bloc exiles into a Committee for a Free Europe, nominally a privately funded operation that included Allen Dulles, who would later become head of the CIA, and Dwight D. Eisenhower.[67]

How best to employ the combined resources of the ABN, funded primarily by the British, became a matter of secret debate inside MI6 and the Foreign Office. In 1948, a Russian Committee, under Gladwyn Jebb, was set up with the declared objective "to liberate the countries within the Soviet orbit by any means short of war." With the shining example of Anglo-American successes with "Double-Cross" German agents in mind, counterintelligence officers in Britain and the United States seized on the idea that there was an underground army of émigré East European nationalists ripe for recruitment and infiltration into the Soviet bloc to foment revolution and unrest.

President Tito's break with Stalin in 1948 encouraged the British and Americans to believe that an opportunity for successful covert operations existed in the Balkans. The target selected was not Yugoslavia, but the mountainous country to the south, Albania. The Americans accepted the Foreign Office's Russian Committee proposal for a plan "to detach Albania from the Soviet orbit."[68]

When Philby arrived in Washington — where his duties included liaising with Frank Wisner at OPC — he participated in the strategy meetings for the Anglo-American covert operation to use Albanian émigrés to overthrow the Communist government there. Malta would be the forward base for an operation for which the Americans supplied the finances and logistical support from their Libyan air-force bases. "Kim was the one who made all the operational decisions," recalled George Jellicoe, a member of the British planning team. Alluding to the bitter wrangling that went on between the British and Americans, Philby archly states it was "perhaps surprising that the operation ever got off the ground."[69]

Lives and Anglo-American goodwill would have been saved if Philby had *not* applied his talents to pulling the disparate operation together. But by alerting the Soviets to every one of its operational details, he ensured the failure of the entire operation — from the first night in October 1949 when the initial boatloads of British-trained agents landed on the rugged Albanian coastline. In what Philby vaingloriously characterized as a rehearsal for the CIA's Bay of Pigs operation twenty years later against Cuba, the British and Americans continued to send infiltrators across the border and parachute their agents into Albania until November 1950.

"The bands of criminals who were dropped in by parachute or infiltrated across the border," Albania's Communist leader, Enver Hoxha, later boasted, ". . . came like lambs to the slaughter." One of Stalin's most loyal client dictators, Hoxha seized on the aborted Anglo-American operation to whip up a reign of terror that secured his oppressive Communist rule in the most impoverished country in Europe.[70]

Philby encouraged laying the blame for the Albanian debacle — with some justification — on inadequate security at the émigré training bases in the Mediterranean. But others besides the perennially suspicious Hoover were beginning to wonder if there were more sinister reasons than sheer bad luck to explain why every operation against the Soviets involving the British had turned sour. The suspicion began to grow in the months after the termination of the Albanian adventure, especially after another Venona code-break gave the FBI an additional important clue to the source of the 1944 leak at the British embassy. By late November or early December 1949, Lamphere knew that the spy's code-name was "Homer" and that he had made weekly trips to New York throughout 1944 to meet his Soviet contact.

"This information should have dramatically shortened the list of possible suspects," Lamphere contends. "Yet when I pressed Jeff Patterson [the MI5 liaison officer] to come up with such a list, he'd report back that London said there was 'nothing new' on the investigation."[71]

Whoever was sitting on the investigation in MI5 must have realized that the latest "Homer" information from Washington had narrowed down the choices. The FBI could not be stalled much longer. Hoover's concern was growing that MI5 was paralyzed by incompetence. This might lead to Hoover's own investigation. If the Americans discovered the identity of "Homer," it would be more difficult to contain the damage and would start a hunt for the MI5 officer responsible for two years of inactivity.

The development about "Homer" arrived at the Foreign Office just at the time that Patrick (later Sir Patrick) Reilly assumed responsibility for intelligence and security and the chairmanship of the Joint Intelligence Committee. He has gone on record as stating that it was this information, received "at a fairly late stage," that enabled him to cut down the list of suspected officials, ranging from code clerks to first secretaries, from thirty-five to nine. "The investigation of these people," Reilly explained, "was a long and tedious job, and so it was not surprising that for a long time MI5 had nothing to report."[72]

Lamphere nonetheless finds it difficult to believe that it took Reilly and MI5 another year to winnow down the short list of nine candidates to pinpoint Maclean. Lamphere says "Homer's" frequent train trips to upstate New York would have been a simple matter to check and connect to Maclean, who made weekly visits to his wife, Melinda, at the Dunbar family farm. Lamphere believes that the FBI could have tracked him down if MI5 had only seen fit to provide either the long list of thirty-five or the short list of nine. To this day, Lamphere still cannot understand why the British kept the FBI totally in the dark about the investigation.[73]

Sir Patrick Reilly begs to differ. He is on record as insisting that it is "pure fabrication" and "totally untrue that the Foreign Office told MI5 not to inform the FBI that Maclean had been identified." Furthermore, Reilly contends, Sir Percy Sillitoe was absolutely determined not to put a foot wrong with Hoover, since he had had such a lot of trouble with the latter over the Fuchs and Nunn May cases. Therefore, Sillitoe had "kept Hoover informed with special messages which were sent over for special security through MI6 and therefore, of course, through Philby."[74]

"I was in charge of the American FBI investigation in the "Homer"-Maclean matter, and I would be glad to swear to this in a court of inquiry, or court of law, that we in the FBI were never informed of the identification of Maclean until after his flight," Lamphere wrote to me after reading Reilly's 1986 letter to British historian Dr. Anthony Glees. "I was also told by Arthur Martin that it was Foreign Office pressure and the sensitivity of the investigation which caused MI5 to hold out on us.

HE HAD HIS BEST MAN ON IT

Whether Martin was telling me the truth is something I have no way of knowing, but I can imagine with the troubles in the Fuchs matter only a year old, both the FO and MI5 might have been afraid that Hoover might leak to the U.S. press something about the investigations."[75]

Even if the Foreign Office prevented the FBI from learning that the hunt for "Homer" was narrowing down, "Elli," the mole in MI5, and Philby both knew all about it, as did Moscow Center. The Soviets might well have considered it prudent to have Maclean's control officer in Cairo alert him. If Maclean learned about the Venona messages, this would explain why his behavior in Cairo suddenly became increasingly erratic in the early spring of 1950. His bouts of drinking worsened in their violence and frequency. On May 8, 1950, Maclean broke into the apartment of a woman who worked at the American embassy, drank her whiskey, and smashed up the furniture. The American ambassador lodged a formal complaint. The Foreign Office recalled Maclean to London on sick leave and urged him to seek psychiatric counseling.

Surprisingly, George Carey Foster, who was then Foreign Office head of security, stated that "Maclean was not under suspicion" when he was sent home "for what was considered a nervous breakdown." That there was considerable confusion at the British end of the "Homer" investigation appears confirmed by the decision, after he had had six months of sick leave, to offer Maclean the appointment as head of the American department at the Foreign Office in November 1950. Maclean gratefully accepted. He bought a large house in the village of Tatsfield, an hour and twenty minutes from London by commuter train.[76]

The Foreign Office decision must have been only marginally less explicable in 1950 than it appears with the full knowledge of hindsight. Given the facts as they were known to MI5 in the fall of 1950, it still adds up to near-criminal negligence. By then Maclean was — or ought to have been — on the short list of nine suspects. Nor did it require much investigative foresight to see, from the Fuchs case, that Maclean was an obvious target.

Yet no one, either in MI5 or the Foreign Office, appears to have taken note that from 1945 on, Maclean had been the U.K. representative on the Combined Policy Committee that shared information on atomic research. From late 1947 he was the committee's secretary, enabling him to pass the minutes of meetings discussing classification policies and strategic reserves of uranium directly to the Soviets. In his official capacity he also received a pass that allowed him unescorted access — at all hours — to the Atomic Energy Commission's headquarters.[77]

The Foreign Office — presumably with MI5 acquiescence — not only permitted but actively encouraged Maclean to take over the American desk. He may have left his career as a future ambassador in the wreckage of a Cairo apartment, but he was still a valuable Soviet spy. Thanks to the clannishness of the Foreign Office, Maclean continued for another six months to supply Moscow with valuable information on Anglo-American foreign-policy decisions during the first crucial months of the Korean War.

The degree to which His Majesty's Foreign Office protected its own was nothing short of amazing in the cases of both Maclean and Burgess. The most outrageous breaches of diplomatic etiquette and propriety had not brought the irrepressible Burgess anything more than a reprimand. As a member of a subcommittee convened during the 1948 U.N. General Assembly in Paris, Brian Urquhart, an assistant to the secretary general of the United Nations at the time, vividly recalls his encounter with Burgess at meetings attended by the foreign ministers of Britain, Greece, Bulgaria, Yugoslavia, and Albania, "the latter being eminently conventional, old-fashioned Communists." They were even more outraged than the Western diplomats by Burgess's appearance one evening "drunk and heavily painted and powdered for a night on the town." According to Urquhart: "When I mentioned this episode to Sir Alexander Cadogan, the head of the British delegation, he replied icily that the Foreign Office traditionally tolerated innocent eccentricity."[78]

There was, it seems, a limit even to the Foreign Office's toleration of such eccentricities. Shortly afterward, Burgess was moved to the Far Eastern Division where he helped influence Britain's decision to recognize Mao Tse-tung's Communist takeover of China in the summer of 1949. The 1955 British government white paper on the Burgess-Maclean defection sought to belittle the damage the diplomats had done. But judging by the evidence of Burgess's initials on Foreign Office documents declassified under the thirty-year rule, he avidly devoured a vast range of top-secret information during the critical period running up to the outbreak of the Korean War. What he was able to pass on to the Soviets ranged from military-intelligence reports from General MacArthur's headquarters in Tokyo to Joint Intelligence Committee assessments reflecting Anglo-American intelligence about the disposition of forces in Korea.[79]

Burgess's career as an increasingly outspoken member of the Far Eastern Division came to an end after his autumn 1949 trip to Gibraltar and Tangier. It turned into what Goronwy Rees described as a "wild odyssey of indiscretions," insults to the local MI6 representative, and homosexual drunkenness that left him either brawling or singing in a loud voice at bars: "Little boys are cheap today/Cheaper than yesterday." The protests reached the Foreign Office even before Burgess returned to London. But because he was a protégé of Hector McNeil, George Carey Foster decided to give him one more chance. So instead of getting the sack, which he expected, Burgess was posted, with the rank of second secretary, to the British embassy in Washington.[80]

The appointment was even more extraordinary given Burgess's well-articulated dislike of U.S. global policies, and his ill-concealed loathing of all things American, which he shared with Blunt and the other Cambridge agents.

"Guy, for God's sake, don't make a pass at Paul Robeson" was the advice Burgess said he was given by those who warned him to avoid discussions about communism, homosexuality, and the color bar in the United States. The occasion of his celebrated remarks was the bon voyage celebration Burgess threw for himself in July 1950 at his second-floor flat in Lower Bond Street. Packed into the main room, according to Goronwy Rees, was an odd assortment of strange bedfellows including Jackie Hewit, back in residence as housekeeper; the secretary of state for Scotland, Hector McNeil; Guy Liddell, the deputy director of MI5; and "two working-class young men who had obviously been picked up off the streets that very evening." The old wartime Bentinck Street crowd showed up in force, led by Patricia Parry, Lady Rothschild, David Footman, and Anthony Blunt.

"The only connection between us was Guy," Rees observed. "I remember thinking that the oddest thing about the party was that no one seemed to think there was anything odd about it at all."[81]

Yuri Modin, Burgess's Soviet control officer, was — for obvious reasons — the one missing link in the festivities. But Moscow Center cannot have been pleased at the prospect of this particular agent exhibiting all the symptoms of going wildly beyond prudent control and landing up in Washington, when they knew that the FBI were closing in on Maclean. Because the Cambridge agents knew each other, Burgess was becoming a wild card, an errant joker with the potential to self-destruct — and to take the whole pack with him.

That same sense of unease must have flashed through Blunt's mind. We now know that it concerned Philby, because he accepted responsibility for putting Burgess up as his houseguest in Washington.

"This posed a problem," Philby wrote, perhaps reflecting the arguments he deployed to convince his own apprehensive Soviet control officer after he had received Burgess's letter announcing his arrival. "In normal circumstances it would have been quite wrong for two secret operatives to occupy the same premises. But the circumstances were not normal. From the earlier days our careers had intertwined. . . . Our association was well known, and it was already certain that any serious investigation of either of us would reveal the past links. It seemed that there could be no real professional objection to him staying with me."[82]

The welcome that awaited Burgess at the British embassy on Massachusetts Avenue in the sticky heat of early August 1950 had all the underlying tension that might presage an afternoon thunderstorm sweeping up the Potomac from Chesapeake Bay. With his Soviet controller's assent, Philby took Burgess into his confidence about the steady progress of the "Homer" investigation. This was a measure of the Soviet concern about how Maclean and the other members of the network would deal with the eventual demise of the Cambridge ring.

Time was running out. The FBI was forcing the pace on the Foreign Office. Within a matter of months, possibly weeks, Maclean would be interrogated as a suspected Soviet spy. Philby and the other members of the network would no longer be able to count on protection from what he characterized as "a genuine mental block, which stubbornly resisted the belief that respected members of the Establishment could do such a thing."[83]

# CHAPTER 26

# *"Something Quite Horrible"*

Guy Burgess arrived at the British embassy in Washington during the first week of August 1950. His official duties as second secretary included serving as an alternate member of the British delegation on the Far East Commission, the eleven-nation U.N. body set up in December 1945 to monitor the terms by which Japan fulfilled her obligations under the treaty of surrender. State Department officials who worked with Burgess on the War Criminals subcommittee recalled the "odor of liquor" on his breath and his "very poor personal appearance in contrast to the usual type of person associated with the British embassy."[1]

In another official capacity, as liaison officer to the Department of State, Burgess had access to American policy makers and their sensitive documents. He was, therefore, able to pass on to the Soviets much valuable information during the critical opening months of the Korean War when General Douglas MacArthur drove the invading North Korean army back to the Yalu River and was pressing the Truman administration to allow him to carry his counteroffensive across the Yalu and into China.

Blair Bolles, a member of the Foreign Press Association, who had dealings with Burgess in Washington, told the FBI of Burgess's deep concern that "the United States might try to control the Chinese situation." Bolles guessed Burgess was a homosexual, because he took as a "personal affront" the attitude of some congressmen "towards homosexuals in the State Department." Burgess always drank heavily during their meetings at the Washington Press Club. He made no secret of his anti-Americanism, and he was "very restless and agitated and had a feeling that the United States was headed for doom."[2]

When he was drunk, Burgess was prone to make a pass at any convenient male drinking companion. But he *never* betrayed his Communist sympathies to a single Washington acquaintance. Robert Rusmore, another writer, was one of those who remembered having to fend off his unwelcome homosexual advances. He could recall only one occasion, in September 1950, when Burgess became "psychotic" and complained that the "Western world was very muddled and said he would like to get away from it." Burgess pined for the trappings of the British Establishment, and he never missed an opportunity to express his disgust for the uncouth and ill-mannered Americans. Still, he shamelessly cultivated the bluebloods of the Metropolitan Club in hopes of an invitation to join Washington's select establishment.[3]

One aspect of American life that meshed with Burgess's own passions was the nation's love affair with the automobile. He quickly acquired an imposing twelve-cylinder 1941 white Lincoln convertible, which he drove with wild abandon. One of the first trips he made in his new pride and joy was to New York, where he looked up Valentine Lawford. Although the former British diplomat was a fellow Cambridge graduate, the two had never been close, but Burgess insisted on taking him for a spin around Oyster Bay, during the course of which he seemed despondent and said he was "thinking of leaving the Foreign Office."[4]

In November 1950, Burgess's spirits were temporarily revived when he was given the task of showing the capital to Anthony Eden, who wrote: "Truly I enjoyed every moment of my stay in Washington." An Etonian bond united the elegantly dressed future Conservative prime minister and the disheveled second secretary with his grubby fingernails and his distinctive blue-and-black-striped old-school tie, his only concession to sartorial respectability.

Burgess's habits, the unkempt hair, frequent intoxication, and dirty nails, did not escape Dr. Wilfrid Basil Mann, a British nuclear physicist. He had worked on the atomic-bomb project in Canada in 1943, and since 1948 had been at the embassy as Ministry of Supply liaison officer with the CIA on atomic-energy intelligence. Burgess occupied the office diagonally opposite his, in the small main chancellery, causing Mann to note him as "the uncouth character who sported a battered duffle coat." Burgess purposely kept his own door ajar and sought any excuse for a chat. He considered himself an accomplished caricaturist, and he gave Mann a wicked lampoon of Bertrand Russell contemplating the recent atom-bomb test at Bikini atoll. Although it was already inscribed "to Julian," Burgess scribbled a new dedication to Mann.[5]

Philby and Geoffrey Patterson, the MI6 and MI5 liaison officers in the embassy, occupied adjoining offices on the same corridor with Philby's secretary, Esther Whitfield. A matronly Foreign Office spinster, Whitfield had been in the MI6 office in Istanbul, where she first encountered Burgess on his visit to Turkey in 1948. She lived with the Philby family in the frame house at 4100 Nebraska Avenue in northwest Washington, where Burgess had taken up residence in the basement. According to her, the adult members of the household knew all about his nightly forays.

The FBI file on Burgess makes it plain that Inspector Roy Blick of the Washington Metropolitan Police Vice Squad also knew about Burgess. Blick kept tabs on the Washington bars and rest rooms where Burgess sought out homosexual companionship. The threats of eviction with which Philby faced Burgess whenever he brought male companions back to the family home were never carried out. Philby knew that his own security depended on keeping an eye on his wayward partner in crime. Miss Whitfield also seems to have taken the scene in stride, showing amused tolerance of the rumors put about by Burgess that she was his office romance. But she vigorously denied that her friendship with Burgess ever extended to telling him about the progress of the "investigation to identify Maclean."[6]

What Whitfield did not know was that her boss was keeping both Burgess and Moscow abreast of the developments in the "Homer" investigation. By December 1950 it became apparent that Patrick Reilly, the newly appointed Foreign Office undersecretary with special responsibility for security and intelligence matters, was taking steps to resolve the case. The unease about events beyond their control in London added to the psychological pressures on Maclean's two co-conspirators in Washington. In turn, this caused considerable concern in Moscow Center, because the unique history of the Cambridge agents made each highly vulnerable to the exposure of a single member.

The errant behavior of Burgess took a dramatic turn on January 19, 1951. He started taking a perverse delight in upsetting the leading members of the U.S. counterintelligence community. On that particular evening, the Philbys were hosting a dinner at home for the CIA's chief Soviet espionage specialist, Bill Harvey, and his wife. Also invited were James Angleton, who was later to become the agency's counterintelligence chief, and his wife, Robert Lamphere, from the FBI Soviet Espionage Section, Robert Mackenzie, the regional security officer of MI6, and Dr. and Mrs. Mann. As they sat down to dinner, only Philby knew that the basement beneath them contained the photographic apparatus with which he copied the top-secret Anglo-American intelligence reports on Chinese dispositions in Korea. Philby had been routinely supplying these to the Soviets, along with whatever information he gleaned during his meetings with deputy CIA director Allen Dulles, and his weekly sessions at Harvey's Restaurant with James Angleton.[7]

If Philby had chosen that evening to confess he was a spy, the consternation of his guests could have been scarcely less dramatic than that caused by the appearance around 9:30 of Guy Burgess. Uninvited, and visibly the worse for liquor, Burgess arrived and insisted on drawing a highly unflattering caricature of the wife of the guest of honor, transforming her prominent lower jaw into a "battering ram."

"I've never been so insulted in all my life," Mrs. Harvey shrilled, and she stormed out of the house with her equally angry husband. Mann told me how he and Angleton escaped outside to walk around in the relief of the unseasonably warm January night. When they returned half an hour later, they found the normally composed Philby sitting in tears on the sofa, wearing shirt sleeves and red suspenders. Burgess insisted that Mann join him in celebrating his coup against the pompous Harvey with a bottle of Scotch in the kitchen. After downing a tumblerful of whiskey, Mann decided he dare not risk driving home because Ambassador Sir Oliver Franks "had a reputation for being tough on traffic offenses."[8]

When Mann returned to pick up his car around ten the next morning, he discovered, to his amazement, Burgess and Philby in bed together, downing a bottle of champagne. "I got the impression that Philby and Burgess were enjoying the situation immensely," Mann remembered. He told me that he did not think they had spent the night together. But he was sufficiently disturbed by the homosexual overtones of the situation to report his uneasiness to Lieutenant Commander Eric Welsh, his MI6 superior at the Atomic Energy Directorate of the Ministry of Supply, when he returned to England a few months later. But Mann received a brushoff from Welsh. It made him feel an "outsider" to raise "doubts about the strange behavior of a senior officer of MI6." The following year, when Mann returned to take up an appointment at the National Bureau of Standards, he told the story to Angleton, who submitted it in a formal report for the file. Looking back on the celebrated dinner party more than thirty years later, the former CIA counterintelligence chief said that had he known in 1951 about the episode he could have "changed the course of history."[9]

Angleton's cryptic comment appears to confirm that while he was increasingly uneasy about Philby, the CIA had no solid grounds to suspect him in the spring of 1951. Nor is there any evidence in the declassified FBI files to suggest that Philby's house was bugged, as some have suggested. But the FBI records intriguingly suggest that there was some surveillance on Burgess at this time, probably by Blick's men, because the standard bureau euphemism "information of known reliability" was used to report the fact that Burgess was seen on two occasions escorting a striking platinum blonde and in the company of Russians eating at the Old Balalaika Restaurant in downtown Washington.[10]

Former CIA officers familiar with the nuts and bolts of Soviet espionage networks operating in the United States in the early fifties believe it unlikely that Moscow Center would have risked using such a public and well-observed locale for meeting Burgess. Washington was a much smaller town than it is today, with far fewer restaurants, and as far as the Soviets knew, crawling with officers of both the FBI and the local police. The main beachhead of the *apparat* was New York, where the large Soviet delegation to the United Nations provided diplomatic cover for a small army of GRU and MVD agents.

Until the end of November 1950, Burgess, as a British delegate to the Far East Control Commission, also had an official pretext for frequent trips to New York. These provided a convenient opportunity for meeting with his Soviet control officer and it allowed him to act as a courier for Philby, too. But the FBI files show that these visits continued even after the ambassador's unhappiness with Burgess's performance cost him his post with the Japan commission. Subsequent investigation of hotel and telephone logs revealed a remarkable regularity in his monthly trips. Burgess would arrive in New York on Friday night, check into the Hotel Sutton, and return on Sunday or Monday to Washington.[11]

Burgess was in New York from Friday, December 10, to Sunday, December 12, 1950; from Saturday, February 3, to Monday, February 5, 1951; and then again from Saturday, February 10, to Monday, February 12. His final trip recorded by the bureau was from Saturday, March 17, to Monday, March 19. The close correlation to the sequence of events leading to Burgess's recall and the ongoing "Homer" investigation in London suggests that the main purpose of these visits was to meet with his Soviet control.

Philby's uncharacteristic tearful collapse on the night of January 19 and the champagne tête-à-tête in bed with Burgess the following morning appear also to be directly related to the realization that the Foreign Office was stepping up its efforts to trace the 1944 spy in the British embassy. They both knew that Moscow would have to find a way to get Maclean out of England before the Foreign Office turned the case over to MI5 for surveillance and interrogation.

There appears therefore to be special significance to the fact that Burgess made *two* back-to-back weekend trips to New York in February. Both Burgess and Philby were under increasing strain as they pondered what to do about Maclean. Moscow Center was, we now know from the affidavit of defector Vladimir Petrov, equally concerned. Kislitsyn, who was then a member of the First Directorate of Information, responsible for running agents in the Anglo-American territories, told Petrov how he attended a conference called by the First Directorate chief, Colonel Raina, which Anatoli Gorski (Gromov) also attended. As Maclean's contact in New York during 1944, and the one-time London controller of the Cambridge agents, Gromov understood the peculiar difficulties they faced in rescuing Maclean without blowing the entire network. According to Kislitsyn's account, the "perils of the proposed operation caused much misgiving, and many plans were put forward and rejected."[12]

The ruthless arithmetic of Colonel Raina added up to the fact that Maclean was blown; and that made Burgess expendable. His usefulness as an agent was coming to an end. His instability threatened the star Cambridge mole, Philby, who might still succeed to the directorship of MI6, providing he could be sheltered from the impending storm. To divert suspicion from himself, Philby tells us how he gave the "Homer" case a "nudge in the right direction" by drawing attention to the 1940 claim by Walter Krivitsky that the Soviet spy in the Foreign Office was from Eton and Oxford. Although Maclean had been to neither, Philby took credit for helping narrow the list of suspects from nine to six, and he wrote: "The disconcerting speed of later developments suggested that the idea must have been relatively new."[13]

Whether Philby — as he later claimed — or Moscow Center decided to use Burgess to effect Maclean's defection, it is evident that Colonel Raina in Moscow gave his final approval to the strategy before the February 12 meeting in New York. In another two weeks Burgess successfully brought about his recall to Britain without arousing suspicion. He accomplished this by exploiting the well-known aversion of Sir Oliver Franks for British diplomats getting ticketed for motoring offenses. A recall in disgrace was virtually guaranteed because of the speeding tickets Burgess received on an official embassy mission to deliver a speech entitled "Britain: A Partner for Peace" at an international-relations conference during the first weekend of March 1951, at The Citadel college in Charleston, South Carolina.

The FBI files confirm that Burgess deliberately and calculatingly set out to get himself ticketed for breaking the speed limits. To compound the offense, he put a hitchhiker named James Turck behind the wheel of his white Lincoln as he headed south from Washington, through Virginia and the town of Fredericksburg on Thursday, March 1.

"All during the time Mr. Burgess kept telling me to step on it," Turck told the FBI. He also admitted that he spent the night with Burgess. Turck said that Burgess assured him that his DPL license plates guaranteed him freedom from arrest after a Virginia state trooper stopped the Lincoln near Woodbridge doing over 90 mph. Later on, while overtaking an army convoy near Ashland on route 301, they were doing over 80 mph and were stopped again. They were stopped for a third time at Petersburg. Turck gave a deposition while Burgess remonstrated high-handedly with the county police officer that he was a diplomat and therefore immune from arrest.[14]

The behavior of Burgess at the conference was even worse. He went on a bar crawl with the students and fell noisily asleep during the banquet. The ambassador was already displeased with the "unsatisfactory work" of his errant second secretary, and because of his "lack of thoroughness and balance on routine matters." The formal protest about Burgess's traffic violations, relaying the March 14 letter from Governor John Battle of Virginia, by the chief of protocol at the State Department proved the final straw. Sir Oliver Franks summoned Burgess and told him he was requesting Foreign Office approval for his recall. Burgess had a month in which to pack his bags and leave for England.[15]

That very weekend — March 19, 1951 — Burgess made another trip to New York. His mission undoubtedly was to report to his Soviet contact on the completion of the first stage of the operation. Meanwhile, the embassy booked passage for Burgess on the *Queen Mary* from New York sailing May 1. This allowed time for his mother, Mrs. Basset, to fulfill her plans to visit her son in America during April.

As soon as they had word of Burgess's sailing, it seems that the Soviets decided to provide a discreet alert to Maclean. His friends noted a dramatic change in his behavior around the beginning of April. Since taking on the job of head of the American desk the previous fall, Maclean had been a model Foreign Office commuter. Eschewing cocktail parties and London dinner invitations, he left the office with bowler hat and furled umbrella every evening to catch the 5:19 Kent train from Charing Cross to Sevenoaks. Now he began to stay overnight. He was seen at his old haunt, the Gargoyle Club, the late-night watering hole for London's intellectual literati throughout the forties and fifties.

Goronwy Rees ran into a "very drunk" Maclean at the Gargoyle on the night of April 2 — for the first time in fifteen years. "I know all about you," Maclean spat at Rees in a slurred voice. "You used to be one of us, but you ratted," Maclean ranted, then fell to his knees still pouring out a torrent of drunken abuse.[16]

At the end of another of those long evenings, Maclean surprised everyone by stating "I am the English Hiss." He made the remark for the benefit of the writer Cyril Connolly, whose friend's neighboring flat enabled Maclean to crash-land during his drinking sprees. The following morning, he challenged Connolly over breakfast: "What would you do if I told you I was a Communist agent? — Go on, report me." Connolly would later note in his own memoir how Maclean seemed burdened by some terrible strain.[17]

Connolly put down Maclean's strange outburst about being a Communist to alcoholic befuddlement. But he might have taken it more seriously had he known that Maclean was renting the darkroom above Ernest White's chemist shop, at Westerham near his Tatsfield home, to develop "very sensitive" films. Only after Maclean's defection did White tell the police how he had once found a crumpled portion of exposed film on which the pale-blue oval Foreign Office seal could just be made out.[18]

While Maclean was using the bottle to battle against the tightening noose, a chance encounter by Burgess with Michael Straight in Washington raised another threat to the Cambridge spy ring. Straight told me that he could not deny Burgess a ride downtown in his car when he met his fellow Trinityman one morning coming out of the British embassy. When Straight learned that despite their heated exchange five years earlier, Burgess was still on "special work" for the Foreign Office, he not only refused to lend his old friend his car, but delivered an ultimatum: Straight told Burgess that he had three months to resign from the Foreign service; otherwise he would "report him to the authorities." Reflecting on this last encounter with Burgess some twelve years later, Straight told the FBI that he did not know that Burgess intended to flee to Moscow before his three-month deadline was up.[19]

Although Burgess gave Straight no hint of his intentions, statements he made to others, which are found in the FBI files, suggest that his flight to Moscow was not some last-minute decision taken in London but a carefully planned operation that Burgess knew about long before he left Washington. "I'm v. depressed," he wrote to Mrs. Nicholas Roosevelt. These distant cousins of President Theodore Roosevelt were acquaintances of his stepfather, Major Basset, and they had put Burgess and his mother up at their South Carolina estate during the first week of April. They also lent him the money to pay his Fort Sumter Hotel bill on the way back to Washington.[20]

Burgess had much to be apprehensive about after he had seen his mother off on the plane to London. While he and Mrs. Basset had been sightseeing in Charleston, the sensational New York Rosenberg spy trial had concluded with Judge Kaufman pronouncing the death sentence "for a crime worse than murder" after the jury had convicted Ethel and Julius as the leaders in a Soviet atomic-espionage ring. Philby had also learned that the Foreign Office had narrowed the hunt for "Homer" down to two suspects — Paul Gore Booth and Donald Maclean. Both had been put under surveillance by MI5 and their phones were tapped as of April 17. Philby offered odds on the former because *Gomer*, a near anagram of Gore, was Russian for "Homer." But he knew that this could not long delay the exposure that he and Burgess understood was inevitable once Maclean's interrogations began.[21]

"Burgess did not look too happy, and I must have had an inkling of what was on his mind," Philby wrote disingenuously of his final briefing of Burgess the evening before he departed from Washington on April 28. Over a Chinese meal in the noisy Peking Restaurant, Philby braced Burgess on the need to adhere to the escape plan and not to arouse suspicion by rushing his fences. According to Philby, the instructions were for Burgess to call on Maclean when he reported to the Foreign Office. Burgess would hand him a piece of paper arranging a rendezvous where they could safely go over the details of the escape plan.[22]

"Don't you go, too," Philby says he reminded Burgess as he drove him to Union Station next morning. In the KGB-approved account calculated to camouflage the true extent of Soviet involvement in the defection, Philby suggests he gave this advice "half jocularly." But the FBI file makes it appear obvious that Burgess realized before he left for New York that London would be only a brief stopover on the road to permanent exile behind the Iron Curtain. This becomes clear from the FBI record of how he spent his last forty-eight hours in America in a state of semipermanent intoxication, while staying at the New York apartment of his old colleague from Broadcasting House, Norman Luker, who was with the BBC office in Rockefeller Center. In one of his brief moments of lucidity at his farewell party, Burgess prevailed upon Luker to let him use his BBC "sound mirror" machine to record his well-polished Winston Churchill story for posterity.[23]

President Truman had recalled General MacArthur from Korea three weeks earlier to prevent an escalation of the war, but Burgess left the United States issuing dire warnings that global war was "inevitable within the next ten days." Whether this was gallows humor, or his genuine belief, Burgess's depression was very apparent to Luker, who saw him aboard the *Queen Mary* on May 1, 1951. The American who shared cabin B-130 with Burgess during the five-day transatlantic crossing also recalled little about the British diplomat, except that he drank too much, and that he introduced him to a stocky New Yorker in his mid-twenties, named Bernard Miller, on the last day of the voyage.[24]

Six days later, when Burgess arrived in England, he reported to the Foreign Office. He was warned to expect a request for his resignation. But he made use of that visit to contact Maclean, who conveyed the need for extreme caution. Since April 17, Maclean said, he had received no top-secret papers. This led him to believe his phones were tapped, and he knew that Special Branch officers were tailing him to and from work. According to what Blunt told Robert Cecil, Burgess mistakenly assumed he, too, was under surveillance and appealed to Blunt to act as a "cutout" with the Soviet embassy.[25]

"We were longing for the end of three months of suspense," Sir Patrick Reilly wrote in 1986. As the undersecretary directly responsible for Foreign Office security, Reilly explained that the "long delay" before moving against Maclean was unavoidable. According to Reilly, the Foreign Office regarded itself as a "family," so the very idea that someone as senior as Maclean "should be a Soviet spy was something quite horrible and we had been living with this knowledge for months." But the problem was getting the evidence against Maclean, because there was "at that time no legally admissible evidence to support a prosecution under the Official Secrets Act." The Venona decrypts were too sensitive to be used in court, so MI5 had put Maclean under surveillance, hoping a slip would provide the evidence necessary to extract a confession. Reilly said that both Dick White, then the head of B (Counterintelligence Division), and Roger Hollis, the head of C Division, responsible for security, had stressed the need for getting a confession from Maclean. They had assigned their best interrogator, William Skardon, to the case.[26]

Reilly insists there was never any intention to "hush up his guilt" but rather they "wanted to get on with his confrontation. However, George Carey-Foster, then head of Foreign Office security, and Roger Makins (later Lord Sherfield), who was Maclean's immediate superior, have also gone on record as suggesting that the FBI was responsible for the "disastrous delay." They say that Sir William Strang, the Foreign Office undersecretary, coordinated "every detail of this joint Anglo-American exercise" with the FBI, "down to the actual date of Maclean's interrogation," and that for "various puzzling reasons, the FBI appeared to be in no desperate hurry." Reilly therefore finds it "impossible to understand" why Lamphere says that "the FO told MI5 not to keep the FBI informed."[27] FBI records state that Hoover "possessed no derogatory information re subjects [Burgess and Maclean] prior to their disappearance from England May 1951."

What this Foreign Office "insider's account" does not explain is *why* or *how* the FBI kept MI5 from applying to the home secretary for permission to interrogate Maclean until Friday, May 25, 1951. The British government did not speak on the matter until its 1955 White Paper, when it said that Maclean "was alerted and fled the country together with Burgess." Expanding on the White Paper version from his intimate inside knowledge of the sequence of events, Sir Patrick Reilly explained in 1986 that since all the messages from MI5 went through Philby in Washington, "he could have telephoned Burgess" or used the "safe channel of his Soviet contacts in Washington, who would have informed their colleagues in London, who must have told Burgess by the morning of the 25th since the latter spent the day preparing for the escape."[28]

It may be assumed that Philby, for reasons of KGB "disinformation" rather than "family" loyalty, concurred with the "insider's account" by explaining that he wrote a letter to Burgess telling him to "act at once or it would be too late" if he did not want his beloved Lincoln Continental, which he had abandoned in the embassy parking lot, sent to the scrap heap."[29]

Although Burgess's similarly suspect account does not mention this letter, he says that he and Maclean formulated their impromptu escape plans over a lunch in the RAC club. He told his biographer, Driberg, that he and a young American he had met on the *Queen Mary* "were thinking of going off to France for a jaunt, so I booked tickets for a weekend cruise to Saint-Malo and the Channel Islands." Burgess also arranged to have dinner at Maclean's home on Friday evening. "But until I got there I didn't know whether I was going to Moscow with Donald or to France with the American for a jolly jaunt. So I told the American to stay by the phone at his hotel until eight-thirty and packed two lots of things suitable for both purposes."[30]

According to the "insider's account" of the defection, MI5 was as vacillating as Burgess. Even after obtaining the foreign secretary's approval on the morning of Friday, May 25, to interrogate Maclean, there was some confusion in the Foreign Office over whether they intended to call in Maclean immediately or on the following Monday. Robert Cecil, who was then deputy head of the American desk Department, has also fueled the flames of controversy by saying that his boss, Roger Makins, need not have excused Maclean from his scheduled duty that Saturday morning because he (Cecil) was on vacation that week.[31]

After the defection, when Cecil went through Maclean's office papers, he was struck by how Maclean, an efficient bureaucrat to the last, had made meticulous notes of the Friday visit paid to him by the Argentine Counsellor to discuss an intricate trade issue. Cecil also discovered in Maclean's filing cabinet a numbered copy of the Cabinet paper reporting on Prime Minister Attlee's hurried visit to Washington in December 1950, when it appeared that MacArthur might get permission to use the atomic bomb against the Chinese forces who had joined the Korean War. So contrary to the assertion of some of his former colleagues, that Maclean had no access to very sensitive papers, Cecil says the Cabinet report he found was convincing proof that Maclean had continued to see secret information of great value to the Soviets.[32]

Roger Makins (now Lord Sherfield) disagrees. He insists that sensitive Anglo-American reports were deliberately kept from Maclean, but he does not specify the date when the reports began to be withheld. Lord Sherfield also believes Cecil was unfair in suggesting he could have refused Maclean's request to take Saturday morning off without arousing his suspicions. But Sherfield does concede that he failed to alert the head of security about this, saying that by the time he saw Maclean, Carey-Foster had gone home. Sherfield stated for the record that he then saw no reason to raise a "great hue and cry" because he knew Maclean was being trailed by MI5.[33]

What the Foreign Office officials did not know, however, was that the MI5 watchers who were trailing Maclean shadowed him no farther than the ticket barrier at Charing Cross station. Because his home in Tatsfield exceeded the fifty-mile travel limit imposed on Soviet diplomats, bureaucratic penny-pinching and the risk that Maclean would be "alerted by surveillance of his home in an isolated part of the country" had persuaded MI5 that it was unnecessary to follow him to Kent.[34]

The Special Branch "watcher" who waited until the 5:19 to Sevenoaks, with Maclean aboard, rumbled over Hungerford Bridge past the gleaming new exhibition buildings of the Festival of Britain site on the south bank of the Thames did not even guess that he was witnessing the start of a long journey to Moscow. Around the same time, a cream Austin A-40 saloon with Burgess at the wheel was weaving its way through the rush-hour traffic. It pulled up at the twelve-room house in Tatsfield only half an hour after Maclean arrived home. Maclean appears to have known that MI5 had bugged the house through the telephones, because he introduced Burgess to his wife as Roger Stiles, an old Foreign Office colleague.

Melinda later claimed not to have recognized Burgess. Although she was then entering the final month of her third pregnancy, Mrs. Maclean did not express dismay when, at the dinner table, her husband informed her he would be leaving the house — or so she would tell the police.

"Mr. Stiles and I have to keep a pressing engagement, but I don't expect to be back very late," Maclean told her. "I'll take an overnight bag just in case." They then climbed into the car and drove off. Burgess headed for Southampton, later claiming that Maclean "dillied and dallied" about leaving his wife, almost making them miss the 11:45 steamer SS *Falaise* for Saint-Malo. But their last-minute dash for the gangplank, abandoning their hired car on the dockside, with a reassuring shout of "Back Monday!," seems a deliberate ploy to rush through a sleepy immigration post that was about to shut down for the night.[35]

The next morning, when the *Falaise* docked at Saint-Malo around noon, a taxi driver recalled driving the pair to Rennes. There they picked up the Paris-bound express. From there the trail went cold, and there are almost as many theories as there are routes from France to Moscow. Some accounts have them traveling first to Austria, suggesting the fleeing diplomats included a stop in Switzerland, where they obtained Czech passports on the Monday before heading for Prague on Tuesday. But the authoritative account, provided by Kislitsyn, has it that their escape route "included an air passage over the border into Czechoslovakia." Kislitsyn then met Burgess and Maclean at the Moscow airport and, as the MVD officer detailed to take care of their "maintenance and welfare," drove them to a "comfortable house on the outskirts of Moscow."[36]

Whatever route Burgess and Maclean took to Moscow is of far less historical significance than the sequence of events that permitted them to escape from Britain. The "insider's account," which has been generally accepted up until now, is, as the FBI records reveal, nothing more than a travesty of the truth put out by the British government to cover up a chain of bureaucratic bungling and Soviet-inspired conspiracy at the highest levels of MI5.

The oddest aspect of the whole affair is that MI5's dcision to move against Maclean came on the Friday, *the day after the final element in the escape plan was in place.* By another uncanny coincidence, the defecting pair was given the entire weekend to effect an escape that new evidence suggests Moscow Center had planned down to the fine details. Furthermore, Blunt, it now emerges, had the primary responsibility for the smooth execution of the cover-up after he had been tipped off by the high-ranking Soviet mole in MI5.

The only justification offered by the "insider's account" to explain these two coincidences is that the MI5 decision triggering the defection was itself the result of a delay by the FBI. This buck passing by the British is categorically denied by the testimony of the head of the Soviet Espionage Section of the FBI and all the other American counterintelligence authorities I have consulted. Of greater significance is the fact that Hoover was told that the FBI "possessed no derogatory information" about Maclean or Burgess prior to their defection. The voluminous FBI case records that have been released to researchers under the Freedom of Information Act, from two separate archival sources, and the independent assessments of the affair in 1955 and 1957, confirm that the British *did not* alert the FBI.

The imputation that the memories of the ranking American officials are at fault, or that the extensive FBI record has been tampered with, continues to be made by surviving British officials. Yet these British officials cannot produce a single MI5 investigation report to support their argument, and they fall back on the 1955 White Paper that has been shown to be deliberately misleading and mendacious on no fewer than seventeen counts. The assertion of the "insider's account," that the FBI was kept fully informed, not only flies in the face of the statements by both British and American eyewitnesses (Robert Lamphere and Arthur Martin) but begs the question of why such an ardent pursuer of Communist agents as J. Edgar Hoover would have "sat" on damning information about Maclean.[37]

Nor does it explain why the FBI launched its own intensive investigation of Burgess and Maclean *on a scattershot basis* the moment it knew about the defection, or how it would have been possible to doctor the massive number of reports from scores of separate FBI interviews and leads. Lamphere, moreover, dismisses as ludicrous the notion that MI5 held up the interrogation of Maclean until Hoover gave his approval. As one of those FBI officers in almost daily contact with the MI5 and MI6 liaison officers in Washington, Lamphere notes that Patterson and Philby still behaved toward him as though *they* were the senior partners in the counterintelligence game.[38]

The British have found it necessary to attempt to denigrate the FBI Burgess and Maclean investigation because it conflicts so dramatically with the "insider's account" of the Foreign Office. One of the most important reassessments arises from the FBI interviews of Bernard Warren Miller, the young American Burgess met on the *Queen Mary*, who was unwittingly made to play — by both the Soviets and the British — a central role in the defection.

Miller was not the owner of an off-Broadway theater as Burgess claimed. This merely fit his convenient account that he was going away for a weekend jaunt with his newly acquired American pickup. Miller told the FBI, during the course of two long interrogations, that he had disembarked from the *Queen Mary* at Cherbourg on May 6. He then traveled to Switzerland, where he enrolled for a course at the University of Geneva Medical School. He explained that he returned to London on May 23, after spending a week in Paris, only because Burgess had promised to introduce him to a friend who was a doctor at London's Middlesex hospital. Miller insisted that he was not a homosexual, although he regarded "Burgess's sudden efforts in his behalf peculiar." He also told the FBI he was "aware of Burgess's general unhappiness and instability bordering on mental illness due to his recall to London."[39]

Contrary to every account published so far, the FBI records make it clear that Miller never discussed during the voyage, or planned to take, a weekend trip to France with Burgess. There is logic in his claim it was ridiculous to suggest that he would have gone back to Paris only two days after he had come to England from Paris on his way back to New York.

Miller's existence, it is now obvious, gave Burgess a plausible excuse for purchasing the boat tickets to Saint-Malo.

Anthony Blunt was in on the plot from the start. That is now clear from Jack Hewit's account. There must have been pressing reasons for Blunt to take the day off on Monday, May 7, to go down to Southampton to pick Burgess up at the Ocean Terminal. Nor did Burgess, his friend of fourteen years, come home to their flat in Lower Bond Street that evening. He spent the night at the director's flat at the Courtauld Institute. In the circumstances, it is believed that Blunt had already been in contact to discuss the details of the defection scheme with "Peters." He was Yuri Modin, the Soviet control officer, who operated under the cover of an attaché at the Russian embassy in Palace Garden Terrace.[40]

Moscow Center knew it could rely on Blunt to be a stickler for details. One of the problems that had yet to be taken care of was the possibility that Goronwy Rees would "rat" to the police when he learned that his old friend Burgess was safely in Moscow. This they decided was a job for Burgess to fix by appealing to old loyalties. So with his bags still unpacked, Burgess headed down to Sonning the next morning to see Rees at home. To reinforce his appeal, Burgess softened up Rees by stressing how McCarthyism was bringing the United States to the brink of war. He read out a long anti-American diatribe that he intended to be his official swan song to the Foreign Office. Rees had no doubt they would fire him. But Burgess told Rees that Michael Berry, an Etonian friend, had approached him in Washington with the suggestion that he might consider becoming a diplomatic correspondent on *The Daily Telegraph*, which the Berry family owned.

For all of Burgess's ebullience and scurrilous stories about Washington adventures, Rees noted he was "labouring under a tremendous sense of excitement, as if he were under intense external pressures." A letter in the FBI file from Burgess's stepfather to Mrs. Nicholas Roosevelt, written that Saturday, May 12, confirms that Burgess had been out of town for most of the first week of his return. By the second week Burgess was back with Hewit, but he too noted Burgess's violent mood swings. It was not simply alcohol, Hewit said, that made his old daredevil friend "maudlin one minute and up the next."[41]

On Saturday, May 19, Burgess visited the home of his wartime friend from MI5, Kemball Johnston, who lived at Henham not far from Cambridge. Timothy Johnston, who was then ten years old, remembers Burgess as a "fat, smelly, untidy man with a red face and slobbery lips who peed behind a bush in the garden instead of going to the lavatory like normal grown-ups." Burgess doodled cartoons for the Johnston boys, and the one of Stalin peering over a wall, captioned: "I wonder what *Kemball* is thinking?," seems to have a sinister purpose: Burgess was intent on reminding Johnston of the need to observe old loyalties. That it was a caution to a Marxist sympathizer is reinforced by FBI files that reveal how Burgess was already carefully laying the ground for his defection. He was dropping broad hints that weekend about an impending trip abroad. The FBI files record that Burgess and his old flame, Peter Pollock, were among the guests at a dinner party given by Douglas Collins, the U.K. president of the Goya cosmetics company. Collins later told the FBI that Burgess had announced he was "hoping to make a Mediterranean cruise."[42]

To preserve the cover story, Burgess did not buy the boat tickets for himself and Bernard Miller until after the American medical student had arrived in London on Wednesday, when he came to cocktails and dinner prepared by Hewit at the flat. Miller's FBI interrogation makes it clear that he never knew about the proposed trip, and Hewit recalls no discussion that evening about a weekend jaunt.

Next morning, Thursday, Burgess announced out of the blue that he was going on a weekend trip to France with Bernard Miller. This got Hewit's dander up. He told me he created quite a row about Burgess's going off with his "mousy" American "pickup." That morning Burgess made the two-block trip to Thomas Cook's travel bureau, where he booked two tickets for the Friday-night steamer to Saint-Malo, giving his own and Miller's name to the clerk. A twelve-hour crossing would seem an odd choice of escape route to the Continent. But the sleepy fishing port on the Brittany coast had obviously been carefully selected. If a hue and cry erupted in London, they hoped to rely on the British and French officials being less alert at Saint-Malo than at the busier, and more logical, Dover to Calais crossing.[43]

Philby goes out of the way in his account to suggest that Burgess decided to purchase the boat tickets as a result of his letter containing the coded message about Burgess's car being sent to the scrap heap. But even if the Soviets chose to rely on the vagaries of the transatlantic mails, the FBI records demolish the story because they show that Burgess never left his white Lincoln in the embassy parking lot. Blunt sought to add to the alibi by claiming that he too had seen the letter and that he had snatched it from under the very noses of Special Branch investigators during their search of Burgess's flat the following week.[44]

The Philby letter now seems to have been a red herring. It was planted at the instructions of the Soviets to draw suspicion away from whoever it was in MI5 who tipped off Burgess, or Blunt, about the meeting with the home secretary to give permission for Maclean's interrogation. Philby would not have been officially notified of the home secretary's action until *after* the approval was given on that Friday morning. With the five-hour time difference added to the enciphering and deciphering time required by such a secret message, Philby was in no position to tip off Burgess, even if he had been able to place a transatlantic telephone call, until late Friday afternoon.[45]

Miller's statement to the FBI makes it plain that Maclean was not on the Saint-Malo boat as a result of a hastily cobbled escape plan made by Burgess on May 25 after some last-minute tipoff by Philby. The sequence of events as they can now be reliably reconstructed precludes any involvement by Philby: First, he could not have known that MI5 surveillance did not extend to Maclean's home, making it safe for Burgess to drive there on the Friday evening to collect Maclean. Second, it is unlikely that Philby would have been cabled (if he was) of the foreign secretary's approval for MI5 to interrogate Maclean until *after* the decision had been taken on Friday morning. Moreover, several hours would have been taken up by the need to encipher, transmit, and decipher the top-secret cable, which (if it was communicated to Philby at all) could not have been in his hands until well into the afternoon, London time, when Burgess was already at the Reform Club with Miller.

All the evidence points to the tipoff about the imminent interrogation of Maclean coming from London, *the day before*, when the necessary reports for the foreign secretary were drawn up by his own staff and the senior MI5 officers involved. Whoever issued the crucial instruction *did so on Thursday at the latest* because of the time needed to draw up the report for Herbert Morrison to sign the following morning.

That Burgess picked Thursday to collect the boat tickets does not appear the result of mere fortuitous circumstances. In view of what the FBI files have revealed about Miller, even the most unenlightened analyst must conclude that the decision to submit the papers to the home secretary on a Friday has all the appearances of a carefully timed plan to prime the escape and was calculated to give the birds a two-day window of opportunity to fly the coop.

Once the final element of the plan was safely in place, Burgess celebrated with what appears suspiciously like a final pilgrimage to Eton. At the ancient educational cradle of the British Establishment, he took tea with the headmaster, Sir Robert Birley, who, as his former history teacher, had been one of the first to recognize and attempt to groom young Burgess's brilliance.

On Thursday afternoon when he returned from work, Hewit learned that Burgess was not going to France with Miller after all. Hewit thought for a moment he might go instead. But Burgess dashed his hopes by saying he would be taking a friend who was "in a spot of bother." Hewit went out to dinner without Burgess. When he came back to the flat after going out to dinner that Thursday night, he found the living-room door shut and sounds of a heated argument taking place in a foreign language. Fourteen years' experience had taught him better than to barge in on Burgess's private affairs, so he went into the bedroom. Burgess poked his head around the door to tell him he was trying to get rid of a drunk friend and not to worry. Hewit described the mysterious man as having a guttural accent, which even he recognized as not being French. But it is most unlikely he was a Russian agent, according to those familiar with Soviet operational practices. They would never have risked entering a house that might be under surveillance.[46]

When Hewit made a pot of tea for his friend the next morning, Burgess seemed in good spirits. When Burgess left the flat around nine, Hewit had no inkling that he might not be back. Burgess had told him about his invitation to dine with Michael Berry on May 29 to discuss the job offer at the *Telegraph*. Hewit says that because of this he expected to see Burgess the following Tuesday at the very latest.[47]

Burgess spent that Friday morning telephoning his old friends. One of those he tried to reach was W. H. Auden, who was staying with Stephen Spender. When Burgess telephoned, Auden was out. But Burgess told Spender how much he agreed with what Spender had said about his dalliance with communism in his recently published memoir *World Within World*. "It expresses the dilemma of a generation," Spender recalled Burgess congratulating him.[48]

Burgess then went to Welbeck Motors and hired a small saloon car for the weekend. He gave his address as "care of the Cavalry Club." When the garage retrieved the cream A-40 the following week from the Southampton dockside, a battered copy of a Jane Austen novel was in the glove compartment.[49]

While Donald Maclean went from the Foreign Office to Soho to join Cyril Connolly and his other friends for a lunchtime celebration of Maclean's thirty-eighth birthday, Burgess drove the car to the Reform Club, where the barman still served the tumblers full of port that were known as "Double Burgesses" in his honor.

At three o'clock, Miller arrived to meet Burgess at the Reform Club. He told the FBI that he was expecting to meet the influential medical friend. Instead, Burgess only gave him detailed instructions for his doctor friend who might be able to get him into a London medical school. Burgess told Miller that he should not try to get in touch with the contact at the Middlesex hospital before Monday, May 28. Miller found these instructions "strange," because his original understanding was that the introduction would be personal. But, he told the FBI, he did not ask for an explanation for the change.

Burgess told Miller that he was having dinner that evening with an unnamed friend who was "having marital difficulties," and that he was going away over the weekend "to help this friend help himself." After holding forth about the iniquities of General Douglas MacArthur and other unremembered matters, Miller said, Burgess left the Reform around five. They got into a car parked on Pall Mall outside the Reform Club. When Miller commented on the rental sticker on the windshield as they headed to the Green Park Hotel where Miller was staying, Burgess told him that it had been "rented by a friend who let him use it." There was no luggage on the backseat, so Burgess must have then returned to his Bond Street flat around 5:30 to pick up the suitcases that he later left behind on the boat to Saint-Malo.[50]

If Miller was telling the FBI the truth — and the declassified record gives no indication that Hoover's experienced interrogators had any reason to doubt his credibility — then Burgess could not have set off for Maclean's home in Kent much before six p.m. The FBI files also reveal that Melinda Maclean appears to have known more about her husband's abrupt disappearance than she admitted to the British detectives the following week.

The next morning, Saturday, May 26, when Mr. and Mrs. Robert Oetking, Melinda's American sister and her husband, arrived at Beaconshaw for a weekend visit, Melinda told them her husband would be "late coming from London." But when the Oetkings were interviewed by bureau investigators in 1954 — after Melinda had mysteriously vanished from a holiday trip to Geneva — they said it was "obvious that he was not expected as no place at the table had been set for him." On Sunday morning, when the two Maclean boys came into the Oetkings' bedroom, they glibly told their aunt and uncle that "their father would not be coming home."[51]

Melinda, however, told her sister, Nancy, later that same day that Maclean had "disappeared." She did not know where he was and appeared unconcerned. She said she was not going to advise the Foreign Office, but "would wait until they contacted her." Melinda Maclean did not get a telephone call from Whitehall until the middle of Monday morning.[52]

Melinda's account ties in suspiciously neatly to the 1955 White Paper, which has it that "Maclean's absence did not become known to the authorities until the morning of Monday 28th May," when he failed to report for work. But the official version, as Nigel West has pointed out, is "an extremely misleading account of what had taken place, not least because Maclean had been spotted leaving for France three days earlier."[53]

In 1986, sources formerly inside the British security service leaked to West the details of how an alert immigration official at Southampton had identified the name and number on Maclean's passport with a fresh entry on his "watch" list. (This standard MI5 practice calls for the circulation of the names of those under particular surveillance to all U.K. ports of entry and exit.) The Southampton immigration office, following procedure, immediately telephoned the news to the MI5 operational headquarters at Leconfield House. West has assured me he has been told that the secret office records show the phone call was logged in "soon after midnight" by the night-duty officer, who passed the word that Maclean had left the country to two of the officers working on the case, who "by chance, were still in the building conferring about the impending interrogation."[54]

The Southampton officer had also passed on the information that the *Falaise* would arrive at Saint-Malo just before noon the following day. This appeared to give ample time to arrange for the French police to pick up the two as they came ashore. But West contends on "reliable authority" that the French police did not receive an alert to look out for the two fugitive diplomats for more than forty-eight hours.[55]

The omission is astonishing and inexplicable. The more so because there are now *two* more corroborative reports that MI6 stations in Europe and North America received the alert within a matter of hours that Friday night. By Philby's own account, the signal came through at a "horribly early hour," when Geoffrey Patterson telephoned him at home to ask for Esther Whitfield's help in deciphering the Most Immediate telegram.

Philby fails to identify the day the momentous message arrived. But since Washington time was five hours behind London, if the first alarm about Maclean and Burgess had come in midmorning on Monday as the "insider's account" claimed, then there would have been no need to rouse Philby from his sleep. The cable would have come in during regular afternoon office hours. But 1 A.M. Saturday in London translated to 8 P.M. Friday in Washington. Since London's priorities would be to notify its agents in Europe first and its embassy in Washington second, the likelihood is that Washington was notified later during the night, which provides a more rational scenario for Philby's statement.[56]

"The bird has flown," Patterson told Philby when he came to the office, and he had to feign surprise when he heard that Maclean was missing. Within a matter of hours that Saturday Patterson and Philby had communicated the news to their opposite numbers at the FBI and the CIA. The impact of the message on the American intelligence community was "electric." This was the recollection of one American intelligence officer, who remembered how the news of the double defection shook everyone who heard about it that weekend.[57]

There was little that the FBI or CIA could do except to express amazement and pray that the British would take the necessary steps to apprehend the fleeing diplomats before they slipped behind the Iron Curtain. That was the mission given to MI6 agents all over Europe. One of them was Anthony Cavendish, who was then stationed in Berlin. Defying an injunction under the Official Secrets Act that forbade him to publish his memoirs, he included his recollections of that dramatic weekend in a privately printed "Christmas Card" that he sent out to all his friends in 1986.

"The weekend of May 25 to 27, 1951 proved to be a memorable one" for Cavendish and his MI6 colleagues at the Berlin station. They were all roused early from their billets by telephone and summoned to report to the British military headquarters at the Olympic Stadium, which also served as the main SIS office.

"I arrived and was surprised to find that all the officers of the station were assembling," wrote Cavendish. "But then our Station Commander began handing out photographs of two men." They were, he explained, two British diplomats, Donald Maclean and Guy Burgess, who intended to defect and might well pass through Berlin. Cavendish shared the "forty-eight hours sleepless weekend" with the fifty other officers then stationed as part of the "enormous" British MI6 presence in Germany. They fanned out to man the crossing points into the Soviet Sector until Monday, when the alert ended.[58]

FBI records also confirm that it was a very busy weekend for Anthony Blunt. His principal mission was damage control. This he did by setting up Bernard Miller to unwittingly lay down a false trail to cover up the real story behind the successful escape.

Many of the names of the leading participants involved in this masterful exercise of deception have been excised in the FBI records to meet the strict requirements of the Freedom of Information Act relating to living persons, or because of official British government requests. But in the thousands of pages that comprise the Burgess and Maclean file, there are scores of near-duplicate interviews and summaries, each of which yields clues to what lies under the censor's pen. When I had finished my own reconstruction, I compared the results with the research conducted independently on the same files by the writer Verne Newton.

The key passages of both our reconstructed files meshed to produce the same names. These were then discussed with Jack Hewit. He confirmed that his was almost certainly one of the names under the censor's ink, and that Tomas Harris was the likely candidate to have been brought in by Blunt to help "sell" a convincing cover story.

The reconstructed passages of the FBI Teletype report of the June 14 interview conducted by the New York field office reads: ON MAY TWENTY SIXTH MILLER SAID HE RECEIVED A TELEPHONE CALL FROM JACK HEWIT, THE ROOMMATE OF BURGESS, WHO TOLD HIM THAT BURGESS HAD NOT COME HOME THAT NIGHT. HEWIT WANTED TO KNOW IF MILLER HAD INFO REGARDING BURGESS WHEREABOUTS. MILLER TOLD HEWIT THAT HE HAD NO SUCH INFO BECAUSE HE HAD BEEN PREVIOUSLY INSTRUCTED BY BURGESS NOT TO TELL HEWIT OF HIS PLANS FOR THE WEEKEND.[59]

Miller said he had previously met several friends of Burgess at the Reform Club, Blunt and a diplomat friend who "recently returned from Moscow." But it was the summary of July 18, prepared for Hoover, that contains the evidence that implicates the art dealer Harris in Blunt's plot: "On May 27, 1951 MILLER said that he was contacted personally by PROFESSOR ANTHONY BLUNT and they drove to the home of TOM HARRIS who has been a friend of Burgess for many years. It was only then that MILLER told BLUNT of BURGESS' plan for the weekend. Both BLUNT and HARRIS were disturbed because BURGESS never went away without telling JACK and his mother (Mrs. Bassett [sic]). BLUNT and HARRIS seemed to think BURGESS was 'going down hill mentally' for a long time. HARRIS said that BURGESS used cocaine for relief from severe headaches, which were the result of a fall. He also said that BURGESS suffered from diabetes."[60]

Hewit says that the suggestion by Harris that Burgess was a cocaine addict and suffered from diabetes in 1951 was news to him. Hewit also denied that he had any communication with the American medical student after the defection, with the exception of the one telephone conversation.

Miller arrived back in New York on June 16, and he told the FBI he had received a letter from Blunt shortly afterward. Ten days later, the letter was followed by a cable: WORRIED. NO NEWS. DID YOU GET MY TWO LETTERS A. BLUNT. The FBI account that Miller had destroyed Blunt's letter corroborates that Miller was the innocent dupe. Had he been party to the plot he would have saved the letter as "evidence" for the FBI. But he did show Blunt's cable to the investigators and his reply advising Blunt that he was OK and telling Blunt his plans to go to the University of Geneva in late August.[61]

To all intents and purposes, the defection of Burgess and Maclean ended the operations of the Cambridge agents. There was still work to be done, however. It involved covering their tracks so that its achievements would be hard to discover, and protection of those who had helped them achieve its goals. This type of rearguard action could have been suicidal. But Anthony Blunt volunteered for the role because he had no intention of going to Moscow.

# CHAPTER 27

# *"I Let Him Go"*

"I'm certain where Guy's gone. He's gone to Moscow," Rees said when he came home and was told by his wife that Burgess had called that morning, Friday, May 25, and left the message: "Tell Goronwy that I'm about to do something almost incomprehensible, but I know he'll understand."[1]

Burgess could have called Rees at work in the bursar's office of Oxford's All Souls College. Instead of calming Rees, the message had the reverse effect from the one Burgess intended. Rees understood only too well what Burgess was doing. He wanted no part of it. He picked up the telephone and rang David Footman, told him his fears, and asked him to get Guy Liddell to call him. Footman was still with MI6, though under suspicion for his strong pro-Russian attitude. This could explain what Rees called "extraordinary slowness" in eliciting any response from MI5.[2]

On Sunday afternoon, Rees still had not heard from Liddell. So Rees telephoned Blunt to ask his advice. This was a mistake. Blunt read the signs of incipient panic in Rees's voice and rushed off to Rees's house to forestall a damaging confession from a former member of his network. Arriving in Sonning late that afternoon, he spent several hours talking Rees out of going to the authorities. He played down the idea that *anyone* in MI5 would believe Rees: "He told me I was a fool even to consider approaching MI5 with an unsubstantiated hunch — and why." Blunt tried to convince Rees that he would only bring himself under suspicion.[3]

'Blunt's cool reasoning did not deter me," Rees claimed. But it took another ten days — an astonishing loss of time in the circumstances — before he could get an appointment to see Liddell.

Blunt would admit — twenty-eight years later in his one and only press conference — that he had been in "direct contact" with the Soviets immediately after the Burgess and Maclean defection. He said: "It was at that point that I had *orders* to go to Russia and I refused." It was highly significant that he would use the term "orders," which contradicted his assertion that he had broken with Moscow six years earlier. He quickly tried to correct this slip by saying that the Soviets "probably assumed that I was still with them."[4]

"I was obviously going to be a prime suspect," Blunt conceded. He assumed that Burgess knew he "was not going to go" to Moscow. "I suppose he thought that if the thing got critical, they might simply take me out, not reckoning on the fact that . . ." Blunt checked himself again to say that he had not directly helped the two diplomats to escape.[5]

Blunt was proud of his successful defiance of Soviet orders. He cannot have been unaware of the risk that he might someday be "burned" to save a more productive agent, or that as ruthless a man as Beria might order a "wet affair" team to artfully arrange his suicide. But Blunt had no intention of giving up the director's flat at the Courtauld mansion, or his office at the Palace, for a utilitarian flat in one of the bleaker Moscow suburbs, as had Maclean and Burgess.

Blunt was counting on the fact that he could not be arrested on the circumstantial evidence of Rees. Blunt would have reminded his Russian controller that MI5 did not have the facilities of the Lubyanka prison, nor did the gentlemanly British police resort to extracting confessions under torture.

Blunt's friends in MI5, his "Royal" insurance policy, and his glacial cleverness evidently reassured the Soviets that, of all the Cambridge agents, he was the one least likely ever to find himself in a "critical" situation. They accepted his persuasive argument that he should remain as an immediate and practical one: his effectiveness as a damage-control agent. The defection of two of the prominent members of the Cambridge ring could have numbered his future usefulness in days, but he was able to move swiftly and effectively to seal off the other agents from suspicion.

The audaciousness with which Blunt discharged that damage-control mission enabled other members of the so-called Cambridge network — such as Alister Watson — to continue usefully serving Moscow for a dozen more years. But Blunt's greatest concern, after his preliminary pass at Rees, was to move swiftly to tidy up any paper trail that Burgess might have left in his flat.

Hewit remembers how Blunt called him and told him that Burgess probably was not coming back. Then Blunt asked for Hewit's keys and packed him off to stay with friends near Colchester. Hewit said he did not question this, because he was used to taking orders from Blunt. Blunt therefore had at least a day to scour through the closets, drawers, and guitar box of old love letters for any incriminating documents. Twenty-nine years later, Blunt would drop a hint to Rosamond Lehmann that she should not believe a word Rees had said about him, because Rees had helped him with that surreptitious "housecleaning."[6]

Whether Rees did participate, or whether it was Blunt's way of undermining Rees's credibility as a witness, cannot be established. But it was only when Blunt believed that no papers leading to the other members of his ring remained in the flat that he offered the keys to

MI5 to save them the inconvenience of having to apply for a search warrant. Blunt was present during the "official" examination of Burgess's belongings, and he later said he pocketed a compromising letter that Philby had sent from Washington.

Blunt's housecleaning was less thorough than he imagined because Special Branch found a twenty-five-page bundle of internal Treasury appreciations that dated back to 1940. An astute MI5 secretary identified them as having been written by John Cairncross, who was immediately put under surveillance by MI5. It was evident from Cairncross's wartime service at Bletchley Park that he should be a prime suspect, and this appeared confirmed when the tap on his telephone revealed a summons to a meet with a Soviet embassy official to discuss the Burgess and Maclean defection.[7]

MI5 watchers tailed Cairncross to a deserted wood in Surrey. But no Russian turned up. After several more abortive attempts to catch Cairncross red-handed, Arthur Martin eventually interviewed him. While Cairncross admitted giving nonclassified Treasury documents to his friend Burgess, he denied being a spy. The Treasury accepted Cairncross's resignation to go to Canada to take up a teaching post. He eventually went to Rome to work for the U.N. Food and Agriculture Organization.[8]

The failure to trap Cairncross was another indication that the Soviets had a direct line into MI5 in 1951. The tipoff could have come via Blunt, who was deeply involved in "assisting" Guy Liddell in the early stages of investigation into the Burgess and Maclean affair. It all struck Goronwy Rees as very odd when he arrived in London on June 7 for his long-awaited meeting with Liddell. Rees was "taken aback" to find that the deputy director of MI5 had not arranged a formal debriefing. Instead there was an informal chat over a lunch that included the intimidating presence of Anthony Blunt.

"The pair of them took up where Blunt had left off" was how Rees recalled his intense discomfort during the lunch that Thursday at Liddell's club. "They did their level best to convince me that I'd be wasting everyone's time if I went along and submitted the nebulous kind of evidence against Guy Burgess that I seemed determined to offer."[9]

That the deputy director of MI5 could be involved in Blunt's conspiracy was, on the face of it, ridiculous. But Rees could not forget the "peculiar circumstances" of that meeting. It convinced him there was "something sinister about the quiet protectiveness of Guy Liddell."

That very morning the story of the missing Burgess and Maclean had broken in the British press. The Foreign Office had managed to keep the lid on the incipient scandal for almost two weeks. But the day before, a member of the French Sûreté leaked the details to a journalist. *The Daily Express* and *Daily Herald* did not identify either Burgess or Maclean, but merely noted how "two British government employees" were "believed to have left London with the intention of getting to Moscow." The cat was now among the pigeons.[10]

Rees was not the only one outside the tight-lipped Foreign Office and intelligence communities who knew the identity of the missing officials. On June 7, Melinda Maclean received a telegram from France telling her that her husband had to leave "unexpectedly," and then Mrs. Basset got one from Rome saying her son had embarked on a "long Mediterranean cruise."[11]

"Even before their names were published, I was absolutely certain that Guy Burgess was one of the diplomats who had disappeared," Rosamond Lehmann told me. Sir Stewart Menzies was a friend of her cousin, so she called him from her home that Friday morning to report that she had known since 1937 that Burgess had been a Comintern agent.

"Yes, my dear girl, I would be delighted to talk with you, but it's Friday," Miss Lehmann recalled C saying. He then asked in his plummy voice: "Is it about A.B.?"

As a writer, Rosamond Lehmann possesses a remarkable eye for detail. But she was still trying to puzzle out who Menzies was referring to as he ran through a whole string of initials that ended with G.B. It finally dawned on her that the last one was Guy Burgess.

"Yes, it is," Miss Lehmann said. She asked if she could come up to London to see him on Monday. But Menzies astonished her by saying he would not be in town that day. "I could scarcely believe it when he told me he was accompanying his daughter to Ascot."[12]

It seemed odd to Miss Lehmann that the head of Britain's secret service elevated the demands of the social season over matters of national security. She saw her priorities otherwise. She called Harold Nicolson and arranged an appointment at the Curzon Street headquarters of MI5 early the following week. She was interviewed at length by William "Jim" Skardon, whose success with Fuchs had earned him the reputation of being the service's most skillful interrogator.

"I was very nervous and I told him all I knew about Burgess," Rosamond Lehmann told me. "He kept on asking: 'What can you tell us about G.R.?'" By then she had grasped that suspects were customarily referred to by their initials. But she stated that she genuinely believed that Goronwy Rees had refused to cooperate with Burgess.

When Skardon, whom Miss Lehmann recalled as a very patient man with a thin moustache, asked her about A.B., she realized that Menzies had been referring the previous Friday to Anthony Blunt. "I was absolutely astonished. He kept pressing me on what I knew about Anthony — they wanted to know anything and everything," she said. But she could tell them very little about Blunt. And when she left Leconfield House, Skardon asked her for an assurance she would not tell anyone about the meeting.[13]

The problem was that Rosamond Lehmann had already told her brother John, "in the strictest of confidence," about Burgess. He had "let the cat out of the bag" and written to Stephen Spender. The letter had ended up on the front page of *The Daily Express*. Lord Beaverbrook, the crusading newspaper's proprietor, had taken the lead initiating the hunt for the so-called "Third Man." It was to become a sensational Soviet spy story that preoccupied British journalists for the next three decades.[14]

Reports of a Communist connection in the case of the vanishing British diplomats also created a sensation in Washington. Busybodies and crackpots lined up at the British embassy. Among them, however, was one person who had the firsthand knowledge that could have solved the enigma. Michael Straight visited the embassy to tell the Information Service officer that he knew Burgess. But he says the officer on duty told him so dismissively that there were "so many witnesses" with the same story he decided not to take the matter any further. It would be another twelve years before Straight came forward again to provide the FBI with the testimony that incriminated Blunt.[15]

The significance of Rosamond Lehmann's account is that she makes it very clear that Blunt was under suspicion in 1951, within two weeks of the defection of Burgess and Maclean. Goronwy Rees also knew about Blunt's role in the conspiracy. He was familiar with the wartime coterie at Bentinck Street and with Blunt's highly placed friends linked with him. In contrast to Straight, Rees did not get cold feet after what he took to be a "warning" delivered by Blunt and Liddell at their "peculiar" luncheon. He insisted on telling what he knew to the MI5 investigators in two formal debriefing sessions conducted under the watchful authority of Dick White, the head of B Division and in charge of the investigation.

White is on record as having said that Rees "was as slippery as an eel and had a violent antipathy to Blunt." Rees may have been anxious to downplay his own guilt, but during the second, and more grueling session at MI5, he revealed how the "tortuous byways" of his friendship with Burgess had led to his discovery, in 1937, that Blunt was a Comintern conspirator. He also named half a dozen of his Oxbridge contemporaries whose secret faith in the Soviet Union, unlike his own, remained unshaken despite the traumatic impact on intellectual Marxist ideologies of the Nazi-Soviet pact and Stalin's bloody purges.[16]

"Goronwy knew the whole business," Andrew Boyle said. Boyle told me how Rees, even during his deathbed confession, made obscure jokes about the personalities involved. Rees named among his contemporaries Robin Zaehner, the former Tehran-based MI6 officer, and Stuart Hampshire, the philosophy don, as members of the informal Oxbridge network. However, he could offer no substantive proof. It was in the conclusions Rees drew from the apparent collusion between Liddell and Blunt, that he aroused the hostility of White, who made no secret of his intense distrust and dislike of the man who accused his friends and associates.[17]

"I thought he was a four-letter man," White is on the record as saying of Rees. "If he had really known all these things, why hadn't he come forward?"

White's attitude is somewhat understandable, given that the allegations made by Rees appeared inconceivable. The very suggestion that White's principal mentor in MI5 — the deputy head of the security service — could be a Soviet agent must have seemed "obscene." Such accusations played right into Blunt's hands. He salvaged his own credibility by branding Rees as a malicious liar, claiming Rees's accusations against him were as beneath contempt as the allegations against his friend Liddell.

Sir Dick White, moreover, asserts that Rees never actually said "Blunt was our man." Nor did Rees offer substantiation of Blunt's guilt beyond quoting Burgess's declaration that Blunt was a Comintern agent. Moreover, Rees was a grammar-school boy, an outsider to the old-boy network of the British intelligence services. The tight-knit community to which White belonged was already too shell-shocked by the Burgess and Maclean defection even to contemplate the possibility that a Soviet spy had made his way undetected into the senior ranks of their exclusive gentlemen's club.[18]

Meanwhile, the FBI had launched its own investigation of Burgess and Maclean. It included surveillance of Philby, and agents tailed him to what appeared to be an empty "dead drop" in a tree in the Virginia countryside. James Angleton at the CIA had also learned about Philby's experiences in the Communist underground from Teddy Kollek, the future mayor of Jerusalem, who was then a minister at the Israeli embassy in Washington. Kollek had known Philby in Vienna in 1934. But while the FBI and CIA now had good grounds for suspecting that Philby was implicated in the escape of the two British diplomats, they had no proof.[19]

The Americans were hesitant at first to communicate their suspicions to the British. But with Senator McCarthy's hearings making headlines in Washington, both Sillitoe and Menzies appreciated that they would have to move quickly to calm Washington's fears. What they needed was to reassure their transatlantic partners that the "Homer" investigation had not been bungled.

So when the FBI demanded to know the precise date on which B Division had targeted Maclean for surveillance, MI5 "lied" by putting the date back a fortnight. Liddell and White argued that they had to convince the Americans that their investigation had never produced any actionable suspicions against Maclean. This meant reconstructing the files to that effect. But to play the role of dissembler with Britain's most important ally offended Sir Percy Sillitoe. He protested that it was not his job to lie, no matter how important the purpose. But according to the recollections of one of those who attended the strategy meeting in the director's office, Sillitoe was eventually prevailed upon by senior MI5 officers to put a creative construction on the Burgess/Maclean case so that MI5 could salvage what little credibility it still had with the FBI.[20]

Sillitoe still insisted he could not carry off the artifice on his own. A decision was taken that an experienced officer would accompany him to help "sell" the doctored version of the case to the Americans. Significantly, Guy Liddell did *not* accompany Sillitoe on his June 11 trip to Washington. Instead, Arthur Martin was named his assistant. Their mission started off on the wrong foot with the failure of the scheme to get the pair aboard the BOAC flight unnoticed. Sir Percy Sillitoe, the "honest copper," and Arthur Martin, a former military policeman, had their photographs plastered all over the front pages next morning. *The Daily Express* might have had an even bigger field day if the reporters had known that Sillitoe's shoulder bag contained MI5 files on Burgess and Maclean that had been carefully doctored for Hoover's benefit.

The FBI files show that Hoover was told about this unfortunate publicity. That the press in London had correctly identified Sillitoe's mission did nothing to modify Hoover's opinion of British ineptness and general untrustworthiness. Hoover became even more concerned when he learned that Sillitoe had no real grasp of counterintelligence work. Sillitoe was visibly uneasy at having to lie to Hoover. But Sillitoe had no choice. The embarrassment was even greater for Martin, whose job it was to support him. But the FBI officials smelled a rat. They thought it odd that someone of the experience of Guy Liddell had not come to Washington. It was clear that the British were, once again, trying to pull the wool over American eyes.

When the FBI's domestic intelligence chief called the presentation of the British delegation "horseshit," he was expressing the bitter sentiments of many of his colleagues. It was left to Lamphere to discover in his one-on-one sessions with Arthur Martin why the MI5 delegation had been sent over to lie.[21]

"In our conversation Martin was so open with me, and so upset about having to admit MI5's bad faith, that I was almost sorry for him," Lamphere records. Martin said the blackout of information on Maclean was the result of instructions from the Foreign Office to MI5. Then Martin turned to the question of Philby, against whom he admitted the British now had "the gravest of suspicions." He handed Lamphere a seven-point case against Philby that began with his communism at Cambridge and concluded with the hypothesis that he had played a role in the disappearance of Burgess and Maclean. It was a telling indictment.[22]

"I'd never liked Philby, and now I began to hate him," Lamphere wrote. He realized that Philby's treachery had compromised the FBI's intelligence advantage with the Venona code-breaking operation, and Philby had probably wrecked a recent FBI request for MI5 to oversee a meet in London between one of the agency's double agents and a Soviet intelligence officer.[23]

At the CIA, Bill Harvey, the ex-FBI rough diamond who was then chief of staff "C" (Counterintelligence), had no doubt about Philby's guilt. In a cogent five-page memorandum submitted on June 13, 1951, he set out for the benefit of the director of the CIA why he believed Philby was a Soviet agent. Five days later, James Angleton delivered a second assessment to that effect. General Walter Bedell Smith, the head of the CIA, then enclosed both memoranda in a top secret, official communication to the head of the British Secret Intelligence Service. In polite words it amounted to an ultimatum: "Fire Philby or we break off the Special Relationship."[24]

The damage triggered by the defection of Burgess and Maclean is clear from declassified American documents. A report prepared for the Joint Chiefs of Staff in 1955 concluded that the Soviets had acquired, through Maclean, a vast amount of intelligence in "the field of US/UK/Canada planning on Atomic Energy, US/UK postwar planning and policy in Europe and all by-product information." According to the chairman of the U.S. Atomic Energy Commission, "practically everything was compromised up to the time of Mclean's [sic] dismissal. A *very* bad situation." Also compromised was any chance of Britain's sharing atomic energy secrets. Furthermore, as code-room supervisor and head of Chancellery at the British embassy, Maclean "had access to practically all high level plans and policy information" and "all UK and possibly some US diplomatic codes and ciphers in existence prior to 25 May 1951 are in possession of the Soviets and of no further use."[25]

The magnitude of the intelligence disaster was carefully concealed from the British public, but the secret record reveals that the timing of the defection was particularly embarrassing because a tripartite team that included British, American, and French representatives happened to be conducting an inspection of security facilities in the three countries. Originally set up to probe the leakages in France, their June 4 report focused instead on exposing the deficiencies of the security facilities in the United Kingdom. The full report is still a classified secret, but its contents are summarized in a 1955 report to the U.S. Joint Chiefs that indicated it came down hard on the British for their "system of personnel clearances for those handling high level information" and their "'old school tie' system in clearing their top people." The highest military authorities in Washington were told that "the suggestions made for improving their system were not particularly well received." Evidently the Americans had good reason to believe that the British had shelved the damaging report because the Joint Chiefs were told that although "some improvements have been made," "the current status of security conditions in the United Kingdom is lacking at this time and should be requested." Significantly, the chairman of the Joint Chiefs was told that both Burgess and Maclean had been able to function as Soviet agents "for many years prior to their defection" because they "were apparently protected from exposure and dismissal for a long time by other highly placed officials of the British Government, particularly the Foreign Office." The report concluded that it was "inconceivable that the pipeline dried up and operations stopped on 25 May 1951. It may be more appropriate to assume total compromise as of the defection date and continue inquiry into present and future security of Joint US/UK projects."[26]

The aftershock of the defections wore the "special relationship" very thin. Menzies had a keen diplomatic sense and moved swiftly to try to head off the storm building across the Atlantic. He had his deputy, Jack Easton, alert Philby to the possibility of recall in a personal letter of June 6 that was hand-carried to Washington. "It was an ugly picture," Philby said of his official order to report to London within a matter of days. During the thirteen-hour flight back to London by BOAC Stratocruiser, he had plenty of time to prepare his defense, confident in the knowledge that the "strong presumption of my guilt might be good enough for an intelligence officer," but it was "not good enough for a lawyer."[27]

Jack Easton arrived in Washington on July 13 to tell Hoover and Smith that Philby was "guilty of nothing worse than gross indiscretion, and that an inquiry was being mounted." He found himself confronting skeptics. When Easton returned home, however, he sat in on Dick White's interrogations and quickly concluded that Philby was "making no real effort to defend himself," and "looked and behaved like a rat in a trap."

"I let him go," Easton declared. Without a confession, and with nothing but circumstantial evidence, Easton had no choice. "But his attitude was such that everything being said against him was true and there was therefore a strong presumption of guilt against him," Easton observed thirty-five years later.[28]

Philby was then summoned to see Sir Stewart Menzies. White had already informed Philby that MI5 had received a strongly worded letter from the CIA that precluded his returning to Washington, so he knew what to expect. With under a year to go before his retirement, it was "with obvious distress" that C had to ask his onetime protégé for his resignation. The high-flyer who was once considered on his way to becoming the first house-raised director of MI6 was out of a job at the age of thirty-nine. Menzies offered him £4,000 in lieu of his pension, to be paid half down and the rest in six monthly installments to discourage him from defecting.[29]

Six months later, MI5 summoned Philby to Leconfield House for a "judicial inquiry." Helenus "Buster" Milmo was the examiner. A leading barrister with wartime service in the counterespionage section of MI5, Milmo made a formidable interrogator. But according to Philby's account, Milmo let only "two rabbits out of the bag" that he had not been expecting. One was the "spectacular rise" in radio traffic from the Soviet embassy in London at the time of the 1944 Volkov affair; the other was a similar increase after Philby's 1949 briefing about the "Homer" investigation. The chain of evidence assembled by MI5 surprised him. But he was relieved that it was all circumstantial. By meekly parrying Milmo's questions and permitting himself flashes of indignant anger when rebutting attacks on his character, Philby succeeded in what he set out to do: "to deny him the confession which he required as a lawyer."[30]

While Philby could not be brought to trial, Sir Jack Easton and Sir Patrick Reilly both agree that there was no doubt among senior MI6 officers of Philby's guilt. The same could not be said for MI5 when it came to putting its own house in order and investigating the charges leveled against Anthony Blunt by his close associates Goronwy Rees and Rosamond Lehmann.

When Rees's debriefing sessions with MI5 ended, he stepped out of

Leconfield House unburdened by his confession but worried that White did not believe the security service had been badly penetrated by Soviet agents. And, in fact, when Peter Wright in 1965 reexamined the file on those named by Rees fourteen years earlier, White — who had been moved over as head of MI6 — assured him that in 1951 he believed that Rees was making "malicious allegations."[31]

We can now see, with the advantage of hindsight, that despite White's skepticism about the reliability of Rees as a witness, Rees had dealt the security service all the cards it needed to play nothing but high trumps and roll up the so-called Cambridge network. That MI5 and MI6 were familiar with most of the cards in the pack is evident from Rosamond Lehmann's account.

MI5 was reluctant to play those cards and launch the same kind of systematic investigation in Britain that the FBI immediately conducted on the Cambridge agents and their connections in the United States. Sir Dick White has gone on record to insist that Rees's accusations lacked both substance and credibility. But Rees did implicate Blunt. It is also a matter of record that MI5 officers — including Dick White, Courtney Young, and Jim Skardon — conducted no fewer than fourteen separate interrogations of Blunt between 1951 and 1963. But MI5 insiders have told me that "cozy chats" would be a more appropriate way to describe these sessions.

Blunt considered both White and Young to be friendly, especially Courtney Young, who was his wartime partner in the diplomatic-bag operations, and who later became head of F Division. With such sympathetic "interrogators," Blunt had no problem explaining away his friendship with Burgess. White himself on occasion had accompanied the two Guys — Liddell and Burgess — to the Chelsea Palace of Varieties during the war. Nor, it seems, would Blunt have faced any serious questioning about Rees's allegations, since White not only distrusted Rees, but dismissed his charges as malicious fabrications.

Once again, connections and circumstances worked in Blunt's favor. There were very good political reasons why senior MI5 officers were reluctant in 1951 to entertain suspicions about their brother officers. An investigation would have smacked of "vulgar" American McCarthyism, and the consequences of even a limited internal investigation might have proved disastrous. The reputations of Britain's two intelligence services were already on the line with the FBI and CIA because of the successive debacles involving the atomic spies: Nunn, May, Fuchs, and Pontecorvo. Career officers such as Dick White had to weigh the damaging consequences to the special Anglo-American intelligence relationship if they acknowledged that there were further serious internal security problems.

Even more serious was the threat that these twin bastions of the privileged class would face in a "gloves off" confrontation with the current Labour Cabinet. It did not take much imagination to anticipate the outrage that would erupt from such a bluffly patriotic trade unionist as Herbert Morrison if the most senior officers of MI5 — an organization for which Morrison was responsible as home secretary — admitted that it was infiltrated by Soviet spies. The idea that British secrets had been systematically betrayed by this most hidebound of old-boy networks would have ignited in the Labour government a chain reaction of outrage and disgust of positively nuclear dimensions.

Meanwhile, there was the growing interest of both press and public in the Burgess/Maclean defection. This also promised to be disastrous for the reputations of MI5 and MI6. Despite the Official Secrets Act and the mechanism of the "D Notice" to muzzle inquisitive journalists, there was the risk of questions being asked in Parliament.

Most alarming was the prospect of a British Joe McCarthy, emerging not from the right but from the left. The essentially conservative White-hall Establishment would have found this the most alarming threat of all. In 1951, Attlee's administration was tottering toward a defeat in the general election that would restore Churchill and the Conservatives to power. Labour politicians were on the lookout for any issue that would rejuvenate the electorate's interest in their favor. If it leaked out that Soviet agents lurked in the privileged bastions of the secret services, the Labour party would have a powerful rallying cry against the fundamental faith of loyal Conservative supporters: the belief that the British upper class was mystically endowed with the right to rule England by virtue of privilege, public school, and an Oxbridge education.

The implications of the allegations Rees made against Blunt and Liddell were just too awful for any senior MI5 officer to contemplate. And so the Committee of Inquiry set up by the Home Office in July 1951 confined itself to the issue of the security clearance of Foreign Office employees. Its recommendation for "positive vetting" of all new applicants was quickly adopted. The question of what to do about those of questionable loyalty who were already in positions of influence in government was ignored.

James Robertson and Felix Johnston, the MI5 officers who investigated Burgess/Maclean, concluded that Blunt was a spy, but lacking concrete evidence, they were reluctant to start playing the cards dealt them in 1951. The declassified FBI "Blunt" file shows, however, that the Bureau wanted to interrogate Blunt in 1953 – but was evidently dissuaded from doing so by the British.[32]

It was ironic that the only casualty was Guy Liddell's career. There was unanimous agreement that while he could not possibly have been in any of Burgess's plots, his wartime friendships with Burgess and the Bentinck Street set appeared highly incautious. He was never a suspect and never interrogated. There was no official blemish on Liddell's reputation. But even he could not have failed to appreciate that he was compromised too badly to succeed to the top job in MI5. In the corridors of Leconfield House there were whispers that Liddell had "outlived his usefulness, since the Americans would no longer wish to work for him." By the time Dick White had leapfrogged into the director general's office in 1953 as Sir Percy Sillitoe's successor (with Roger Hollis as White's deputy), Liddell had already moved on to his consolation posting on retirement as security adviser to the Atomic Energy Authority.[33]

In Moscow, according to Kislitsyn, Burgess and Maclean underwent rigorous debriefing and became, for a time, advisers to the Ministry of Foreign Affairs. The Soviets forwarded money for Melinda Maclean through a Swiss bank. Kislitsyn told the defector Petrov about plans to get Mrs. Maclean to join her husband. But it was not until she left England to live with her mother in Geneva that Soviet intelligence agents considered it safe to get in touch with her. On September 11, 1953, she disappeared from her mother's house with her three children to go to Moscow.[34]

Despite what the KGB regarded as its generosity to the two defectors, it could not directly support Philby. For four years he had to keep his wife and five children going on the erratic earnings of a free-lance journalist. But he received financial support from Tomas Harris to repay a publisher's advance and take care of the private education of his children.

When Vladimir Petrov made headlines in 1954 with his defection in Australia, Philby had reason to be apprehensive. Petrov testified before a royal commission and might have provided some damning piece of evidence on which Philby could be arrested and tried. But the only light that Petrov shed on the Cambridge agents was what he had learned from Kislitsyn, who had made no mention of a "Third Man," as the popular press had dubbed the unnamed member of the network who tipped off Burgess and Maclean. The publicity created by Petrov nudged the British government into publishing its own White Paper on Burgess and Maclean. Drawn up as it was by MI5, the official version was ingeniously constructed to absolve everyone from blame and to answer as few leading questions as possible while attempting to counter any criticism of ministerial reticence.[35]

The year before the White Paper appeared in September 1955, Philby received a message from the Soviets via Blunt. At a Courtauld lecture, he recognized his "old" control, Yuri Modin, who handed him a postcard written by Burgess that fixed a rendezvous at 8:00 the following day in a North London pub. That Blunt responded to this direction shows that he was still under Soviet direction, if not control. When he arrived at the Angel in the Caledonia Road he was met by the Russian, who asked him to act as an intermediary in fixing a rendezvous with Philby. Moscow was attempting to bring Philby back under control just at the time he was getting the break that would rescue his career.[36]

This came on October 25, 1955, when Lieutenant Colonel Marcus Lipton, a Labour member of Parliament, rose to ask the prime minister whether he had "made up his mind to cover up at all costs the dubious Third Man activities of Mr. Harold Philby." Sir Anthony Eden said that he would get an answer from the foreign secretary in the following week's debate on the Burgess and Maclean affair. And Harold Macmillan then surprised the House of Commons with his unequivocal assurance: "I have no reason to conclude that Mr. Philby has at any time betrayed the interest of this country, or identify him with the so called 'Third Man,' if indeed there was one."[37]

"As far as I am concerned, the incident is closed," Philby told journalists at a hastily convened press conference at his mother's London home. Some of his former MI6 colleagues, including Nicholas Elliott and Count Frederick Vanden Heuvel, the former station chief in Switzerland, took Philby's public exoneration to mean that he could be reemployed. They arranged with sympathetic friends at *The Observer* and *The Economist* to share the cost of his services. By September 1956 Philby arrived in Beirut on the eve of the Franco-British military operation against Suez. For the next seven years he operated in the turbulent Middle East. Under his cover as a newspaper correspondent, he also operated as an intelligence agent for both London and Moscow.[38]

The year 1956 proved something of a watershed for the Cambridge network. Blunt was knighted by the queen and visited the United States for a lecture tour – prompting another FBI report. Burgess and Maclean reappeared in public at a Moscow press conference. Philby reestablished himself as an MI6 spy aided by his father's extensive Arab network.[39]

The worldwide headlines that greeted the Burgess and Maclean press conference in Moscow rekindled public interest in their case. As a result, Tom Driberg obtained the approval of Burgess – and the KGB – to publish a version of his story. This, in turn, prompted Goronwy Rees to write his own sensational version of events, which was serialized in *The People* that November. Neither Driberg, nor Rees, could name Blunt, who was protected by British libel law. But anticipation of the possible exposure of his role caused considerable apprehension and discomfort to the central figure in the drama. Sir Anthony Blunt was under such stress that he let his guard slip that memorable night in the taxi in Grosvenor Square when he broke down in tears before Rosamond Lehmann.

Driberg's memoir of Burgess was a careful pastiche of half-truths and misleading constructions. And Rees's second attempt to set the record straight backfired. The wrath of the Establishment cost him his college job and many of his remaining friends.

Now another botched operation by the secret service almost unseated Philby from his new respectability. The objective of the ill-planned exercise was to conduct an underwater survey of the hull of the new Soviet cruiser that had carried Marshal Bulganin and Nikita Khrushchev on their state visit to the United Kingdom in April 1956. While the Soviet leaders were in London for a reception at Buckingham Palace — which Blunt, to the surprise of his friends, declined to attend — Commander "Buster" Crabbe, an ex-navy diver, vanished in the murky waters of Portsmouth harbor. The press published the story while the Russian leaders were still in England, to the considerable embarrassment of the government. The head of MI6, General Sir John Sinclair, resigned. White, then head of MI5, replaced him. The unexpected move that put Sir Dick White in charge of both secret services led to his disturbing discovery that Philby was "back on the books."

White, whose conviction of Philby's guilt had been unshaken by his public exoneration a year earlier, could have ordered MI6 to sever its connection with him. But the new C decided to troll Philby as a bait to the Soviets in the hope that careful playing of the line would eventually produce the necessary evidence to bring Philby to trial. Philby continued to act in his dual capacity for both British and Soviet intelligence. But his usefulness to Moscow outweighed any contribution he made to MI6.

It was no coincidence that Philby met another member of the Cambridge spy ring that spring.

"I had a chat with [Norman] in Cairo not long before his death. What a shocking affair that was," Philby confided to Canadian journalist Eric Downton. Philby also said that he had known him "vaguely" as a brilliant Japanese scholar at Cambridge.[40]

Egerton Herbert Norman, the Canadian ambassador to Egypt, who had been named by witnesses as a Soviet agent to an investigating subcommittee of the Senate Judiciary Committee, had stepped off the topmost ledge of an eight-story apartment building in Cairo on the morning of April 4, 1957.

The bizarre circumstances of the suicide of the Canadian diplomat, who had played an instrumental role in General MacArthur's administration in Japan, became the subject of an international controversy. Norman's friends in Canada immediately charged the U.S. Congress with hounding an innocent man to his death. But others have claimed that Norman's suicide note suggests that he took his own life to protect his friend Lester B. Pearson — who was then Canada's external affairs minister and later became prime minister — from exposure as a fellow member of a Soviet network.[41]

Michael Straight, who knew Norman as another underground Trinity cell member, remains convinced that after Norman left Cambridge, he played a shadowy role as an important agent of influence for Moscow. Not only was Straight well informed but he was no Communist witch-hunter. He had kept the banner of liberalism flying as editor of *The New Republic* and had testified before congressional committees against what he termed the "spiritual corruption that characterized the McCarthy years."[42]

From his own experience, Straight was acutely aware of the insidious ways the Soviet intelligence service relentlessly exploited Communist ideologues. He suspected, too, that Blunt still had his lines to Moscow intact. So when he read in a newspaper that a "British scholar of Cambridge University might become chief of Intelligence" in Britain, his conscience once again moved him into action. Alarmed that this unnamed professor might be Blunt, Straight told the FBI in a 1975 re-interview that he had approached his cousin, C. Tracy Barnes, who was then a senior executive with the CIA, with his suspicions. The FBI could not prove or disprove this statement since Barnes was dead. But they questioned Straight extensively about Sergei Romanovich Striganov, a counselor at the Soviet embassy (later identified as a KGB officer) with whom he had regularly lunched in the early fifties. Straight insisted that the meetings were innocent journalistic exchanges. But Straight did tell the FBI that the contact had been made through Adam Watson, an old friend, whom Straight described as "a Soviet expert in the British embassy."[43]

The FBI took note of this further instance of the Cambridge connection leading to Moscow, but they concluded it was probably innocent since Straight's contacts with Striganov ceased in 1956 when he gave up the editor's chair at *The New Republic*.

The Straight case file shows, however, that the FBI was very keen to know why *The New Republic* had printed a series of articles on the Middle East from Kim Philby in 1957. But Straight pointed out that by then he no longer was editor of the magazine, even though his name was on the masthead. The FBI records also show that it had been told that Blunt made an effort to contact Straight the following year through Sir Philip Hendy, the director of the National Gallery, who was a friend of Straight's mother. Straight could not remember the approach. But he told his interviewer, "It doesn't mean it didn't happen." The FBI suggested that Hendy's approach represented an "attempt by Blunt, under SIS (Soviet Intelligence Service) direction, to reinstitute Straight's association with the SIS." Straight said this was impossible. He thought it likely that if Blunt was trying to contact him "it would have been to determine if Straight had informed [the] authorities about him."[44]

Blunt had every reason to worry about Straight. He shared, with Goronwy Rees, the dark secret that could bring Blunt down. He also may have realized that it would be more difficult to face down Straight's firsthand testimony of his role as the Cambridge recruiter than had been to dismiss the allegations made by Rees.

The higher Blunt's reputation soared as an art historian, the greater became his fear that his past might surface. There was also the possibility that Burgess would drop some indiscreet hint to the British foreign correspondents with whom he frequently drank in Moscow or, worse still, would carry out his threat to return to England. He confided in Harold Nicolson, who was then in correspondence with Burgess in Moscow, that MI5 had assured him that Burgess would be arrested if he set foot in England. The trial, at which he would be the chief witness, would cost him his job at the Palace and his directorship of the Courtauld. He told Nicolson "he had conveyed to Burgess that he must not return."[45]

Blunt, it appears, could still exercise his influence over Burgess *even in Moscow*. But he had no control over the information that other Soviet spies or defectors might provide. The latter threat became more real as the sixties began with a spate of high-level defectors.

In 1960, a colonel named Oleg Penkovsky volunteered himself as an MI6 mole. He was in the GRU, and for the next three years, his Minox camera provided the West with snapshots of the upper echelons of Soviet military intelligence. In 1961 came the defection of "Sniper," the code name given to Michal Goleniewski, a Polish intelligence officer with KGB affiliations, who helped uncover George Blake, the deep-cover Soviet spy in MI6 who had been captured in Korea and held during the war. Goleniewski's information also helped MI5 round up the "Portland Spy Ring," which was run by the KGB illegal Konon Molody. Under the alias of Gordon Lonsdale, Molody had run, via subagents Helen and Peter Kroger, an espionage network at Britain's main antisubmarine-warfare base. But it was another KGB defector, code-named "Kago" by the British and "Ae/Ladle" by the CIA, who provided the most damning evidence since Krivitsky of the KGB's extensive high-level penetration of Whitehall.[46]

Anatoli Golitsyn had been named earlier as a potential defector by Peter Deriabin, a KGB officer who defected in Vienna in 1954. Golitsyn spent six years at Moscow Center making mental notes of high-level files. This KGB major turned up at the home of the CIA station chief in Helsinki on the morning of December 15, 1961, asking asylum for himself and his family.

So detailed and extensive was Golitsyn's information on KGB penetration of Western governments that some on the CIA CI (Counter-intelligence) staff under James Angleton suspected he might be an *agent provocateur*. But Golitsyn established a remarkable track record, filling out the details of many cases that Goleniewski had been able only to hint at. His information was supplemented by the leads supplied by two other sources that the FBI and CIA had tapped in the Soviets' U.N. delegation. One was a GRU officer code-named "Fedora"; the other was a KGB source known as "Top Hat." Both later returned to the Soviet Union and were judged to be plants.[47]

This harvest of Soviet defections resulted in productive spy hunts in more than half a dozen Western countries. Among the agents success-fully uncovered were those in the "Sapphire" network in the French SDECE intelligence organization; Colonel Stig Wennestrom, of the Swedish air force; an American Foreign Service official in Warsaw; and Israel Beer, a KGB mole who had served as an aide to the chief of staff of the Israeli army.[48]

The most dramatic repercussions came in Britain. After the initial debriefing of Golitsyn in the United States, the CIA supplied the British with a list showing he knew of penetrations by at least *ten* Soviet agents. Golitsyn's information was tantalizingly incomplete in many of the cases. One referred to the MI6 spy Blake, who owed his conviction in 1961 and a record forty-two-year prison term to an investigation initiated by Goleniewski. A second serial led MI5 to John Vassal, a homosexual clerk in the Admiralty, who was arrested for passing on NATO secrets. A third serial pointed to a naval source who was identified as a senior commander who had already retired and against whom there was not enough evidence to proceed. A fourth serial relating to a KGB agent in an RAF missile base in Norfolk was also inconclusive.[49]

Golitsyn's other serials were the most alarming. They appeared to relate to a continuing history of Soviet penetration of MI5. About the Cambridge ring he was able to recall that it was a highly unusual KGB operation because its five members all knew one another and had all, at one time or another, been run by Yuri Modin. He provided positive identifications for Burgess, Maclean, and Philby, whose code-name he said was "Stanley." He was able to provide chapter and verse on the damage wrought by Burgess and Maclean. He also said that the Canadian ambassador, Herbert Norman, was "a long-term Communist and KGB agent." But when it came to identifying Blunt and Philby, Golitsyn's evidence could not have been used to obtain conviction.[50]

In March 1962 a British team led by Arthur Martin, who, in 1960, had become the head of MI5's D1 investigation division, and his opposite number from MI6, flew to Washington to make their own debriefing of Golitsyn. What gave them real cause for concern was Golitsyn's statement that the safe for British documents at KGB head-quarters in Moscow contained recent MI5 technical reports, that Commander Crabbe's mission had been betrayed, and that the Soviets were so confident of their sources in London that they had dispensed with the need for a *Soviet Kolony* (SK) agent to organize security at the embassy there. Golitsyn's statements pointed to ongoing high-level Soviet penetration of the British secret services.

The first target was to establish whether Philby really was a mole. Golitsyn had provided no new evidence that would be acceptable in a court of law. But even as Martin was sifting through the Golitsyn material for clues, Flora Solomon provided the breakthrough in the case. In August 1962 she was in Israel, where she ran into Lord Rothschild at the Weizmann Institute at Rehovot and pressed him to "do something" about Philby's anti-Israel articles in *The Observer*. On his return to London, Rothschild informed MI5. Martin's debriefing of Solomon provided the needed confirmation of Philby's Communist past.

Roger Hollis, now the director general of MI5, and his opposite number at MI6, Dick White, agreed that Philby should be confronted with the new evidence. They also agreed that Philby should be given assurances that he would not be prosecuted if he agreed to return to Britain and cooperate fully with MI5. The intelligence chiefs, and the Conservative government, were anxious to keep the embarrassing scandal covered up. But the offer of immunity in return for exposing the other Cambridge agents was to set a dangerous precedent.

It is difficult not to conclude that the old-boy network once again moved in to protect its own. Arthur Martin, who was originally detailed for the mission, was replaced at the last minute by Philby's friend, the former MI6 station chief Nicholas Elliott. The son of a former Eton master, Elliott, although now persuaded of his friend's treachery, was not the best man for the most difficult of counterintelligence missions: getting a spy to confess and then persuading him to return to face interrogation.

To the dismay of Arthur Martin, who had worked on the Philby case since 1951, Elliott blew it. He succeeded only in getting a general admission of guilt when Philby said he could not deny the long catalog of charges compiled against him. He even asked Elliott to break the news to his wife, Eleanor (an American whom he had married in Beirut in 1959), but he said he needed time to think about the immunity deal and returning to London. It was no surprise that Philby vanished from Beirut on January 23, 1963, a few days after Elliott returned with confirmation of what MI5 had suspected since 1951.

# CHAPTER 28

# *"The Final Sting"*

The news that Philby had been allowed to escape — or as he claimed in an interview twenty-five years later, his interrogation "was deliberately staged so as to push me into escaping" — exacerbated the relations between MI6 and the CIA. The British immediately released their official line on Philby. It sounded similar to what the British had said after the Burgess-Maclean defection in 1951. According to London, the Americans had been kept advised of the decision to interrogate Philby in Beirut.

"Advised? Hell no!" was the uncharacteristically explosive comment of James Angleton. The former chief of counterintelligence for the CIA believed he had been doubly betrayed, by Philby and by London, because, as he told an interviewer, Verne Newton, in 1986: "I had an agreement with them [MI6] that Philby would never be interrogated on foreign soil."[1]

The flight of the Third Man granted a reprieve to Blunt, who was out of England at the time. His British Council lecture tour of Europe may not have been a coincidence; it was the first extended trip he had made, except for a brief visit to New York the previous September. He had cut back his international travel schedule after suffering a severe bout of Bell's palsy in 1961, a neurological disorder that left him with a droop on the left side of his face.

MI5 had interviewed Blunt more than a dozen times by then. And the Philby defection prompted more of these polite interrogations. But Blunt knew that it was not only the security service who suspected him. In 1961 there came the first unnerving hint that someone outside the intelligence services had pieced together his complicity.

During an interview at the Reform Club, Blunt was asked: "Are you the Third Man?" The questioner was Douglas Sutherland, who was writing a book about the Burgess and Maclean affair. "If you print that I'll sue," Blunt told the former Foreign Office man turned investigative journalist. Sutherland noted: "His face was grim and his mouth untypically set."[2]

Sutherland might have pressed harder with the "circumstantial evidence" had he known that Blunt's old controller, Yuri Modin, had resurfaced in Beirut at the time of Philby's defection — and that Blunt had visited Lebanon shortly afterward. He stayed with his old friend Sir Moore Crosthwaite, the British ambassador in Beirut, in March while en route to a lecture at the Weizmann Institute. The possibility therefore exists that Modin met Blunt to tell him of the immunity deal offered to Philby.

Blunt would have returned to London fortified by the knowledge that with Philby in Moscow, if MI5 ever obtained hard evidence against him, it would offer him the same secret immunity deal. The thought would have reassured him. He would never need to flee to Moscow or spend the rest of his life in prison. Blunt had weathered another round of crises with his secret still intact and his future secure. His public reputation had soared to new heights the previous year when he stood next to the queen at the July opening of the Queen's Gallery in the Buckingham Palace mews. Blunt received — and deserved — much of the credit for persuading the royal family of the need for rotating exhibitions that would permit the public to see for the first time sections of the remarkable royal treasure house of more than 4,500 works of art that had been catalogued and restored under Blunt's supervision.

Art had lofted Blunt to great heights. It was ironic that six months after Philby's defection, it would be an artistic cause, and an American one at that, that would unleash his own Nemesis. At a White House luncheon on June 4, 1963, President Kennedy's special assistant, Arthur Schlesinger, told Michael Straight of his selection to succeed to the chairmanship of the newly created Advisory Council on the Arts. Straight's initial reaction was to accept the challenge of running what would become the National Endowment for the Arts. But when he heard he must undergo an FBI check before his candidacy could be submitted to Congress for approval, the specter of his Cambridge past "came flooding to the surface through the sinkhole of my memory.[3]

The next day, Straight told Schlesinger that he wanted his name withdrawn, and that he wanted to tell his story to the FBI. On June 7, 1963, Straight went to the Justice Department for the first of a series of interviews with Bill Sullivan, during which he made a clean breast of his Cambridge recruitment by Blunt, his association with Burgess, and his contacts with the Soviet intelligence service in Washington in the early part of World War II. It was, he admitted to the FBI, something "he realizes he should have done a long time ago." Straight said that until the presidential appointment came up he "lacked the resolution" to give his account to the authorities because he knew that it was not merely a matter of sharing his knowledge with a few officials.[4]

"My story would result in a trial in England," Straight declared, saying that he expected, "within a few months, I would be facing Anthony Blunt in an English courtroom." Since having to appear before a congressional committee was his primary concern, it would be surprising if he had not considered himself under an obligation to give Blunt the same sort of warning in 1963 that he had given Burgess twelve years earlier. Although Straight told the FBI that the June 4 offer from Schlesinger came as a surprise, in his autobiography he says that as early as May 1963, his friend Senator Paul Douglas of Illinois was proposing him for the chairmanship of the Fine Arts Commission.[5]

Straight had several weeks in which he could have alerted Blunt that an impending presidential appointment would require FBI clearance and would raise the possibility that the Cambridge connection would be uncovered. According to Stella Jeffries, an administrative secretary at the Courtauld, Straight appeared unannounced at the institute one day that summer. She says Blunt "was not keen to see him." Later, she heard Blunt telling someone "he — meaning Straight — was going to shop them." Jeffries claims the incident stuck in her mind because it occurred shortly before the director himself went off to America "at short notice."

Straight has admitted that he was in England that April, but he insists that he did not visit the Courtauld. The FBI files make no mention of his April trip, only that he took his family to their summer home on Martha's Vineyard at the end of June. If Straight had passed some warning to Blunt before his sessions with Sullivan, it could explain why Blunt suddenly changed his plans and decided to spend six weeks that summer in the United States.[6]

To the surprise of everyone at the Courtauld, the director suddenly decided on short notice to accept an invitation the institute had received to send a graduate student to lecture at a six-week summer course at Pennsylvania State University. Blunt's decision astonished — and delighted — the students and staff of the tiny art-history college in the heart of rural Pennsylvania.

"It was a bit like having a Harvard Law School professor come to teach a civics class to a country high school," recalls Desmond MacRae. He vividly recalls how amazed and delighted everyone was to have someone as grand as Blunt lecture them. They joked that it must have been the $5,000 fee or the Royal Art historian confused their small campus with the more famous University of Pennsylvania. MacRae, then a graduate student of art history, remembers how the lofty Blunt could never get used to the American custom of interrupting the lecturer with questions.[7]

Blunt's hauteur evaporated when his class took him on a tour of the local bars. "He let his hair down, singing off key some traditional British vaudeville ballads at the Millhein bar, which was decked out as an

English pub." MacRae was surprised to find that the surveyor of the queen's pictures was far to the left politically. "He held forth on the extraordinary egalitarian view that all men ought to be treated as equals in every way except intellectual ability," MacRae recalled. "He couldn't stand cant, and that is why we students found him very sympathetic." Although they had no idea that Blunt was a Communist, they found his socialist views oddly inconsistent with his intellectual fascination with the France of Louis XIV, in which every subject of the king had an assured place in society.

"Professor Blunt was obviously intrigued with the 'assured place' of subjects in an ordered society," MacRae says. He recalled that Blunt's own "assured place" as a royal courtier was deeply important to the English art professor. Blunt erupted once in barely controlled outrage when MacRae voiced novelist John Braine's scathing dismissal of the British monarchy as "a solitary gold filling in a mouth full of decay."[8]

It was part of Blunt's peculiarly schizophrenic character that while he did not disagree that British society was in a state of decay, he took any attack on the queen as a personal affront. Although MacRae and his fellow students did not appreciate the paradox, it must have been a bitter irony for their visiting professor that he was in the country that Burgess despised when the news came through that Burgess had died of liver disease on August 19, 1963. At the Moscow crematorium, it was left to Maclean to pay tribute to "a gifted and courageous man who devoted his life to the cause of making a better world."[9]

According to MacRae, Blunt was not noticeably moved by Burgess's death, about which several students commented. They knew Blunt's association with Burgess from his dedication to *Artistic Theory in Italy*, one of their standard texts. But Blunt was a past master at concealing his emotions, and if he was in contact with Straight, he would have known that his own denouement could not be long delayed.

In fact, it did not take place for another nine months. Although Straight agreed to the FBI's request that he meet with representatives of British intelligence that July, Sullivan did not recontact him until January 1964, when he arranged for him to meet Arthur Martin in the Mayflower Hotel. Straight told Martin about Blunt's activities in Cambridge, giving the names of other recruits including Leo Long.

"You may not believe this," Straight says Martin told him at the end of their talk, "but this is the first hard evidence that we've been able to obtain on Burgess and Blunt." Straight did not know that Martin had just finished interviewing John Cairncross at Northwestern University. Cairncross had made what Martin called only a "partial confession" to passing information to the Soviets. It was Straight's assurances that he would confront Blunt in court if necessary that provided the long-awaited breakthrough.[10]

Yet another three months elapsed before Blunt was confronted with Straight's confession. One explanation is that Roger Hollis, who had become director general, wanted to protect MI5's morale and reputation following a commission conducted by Lord Denning into the so-called Profumo Affair. The inquiry was ordered after the prime minister had been embarrassed that summer by having to admit that John Profumo, his defense minister, had lied to the House of Commons about his sexual liaisons with Christine Keeler and Mandy Rice-Davies. These two "showgirls," as they were euphemistically described by the press, had been introduced into Profumo's influential circle by Stephen Ward, an artist and "society osteopath." In turn, this led to liaisons with Captain Eugene Ivanov, a Soviet naval attaché, during wild weekend parties at Lord Astor's house at Cliveden.

What did not emerge in public, either at Ward's trial at the Old Bailey on charges of procuring, or in the Denning report, was MI5's role in the affair. Ward committed suicide the night the jury returned a guilty verdict. Some suggested that this was very convenient for his society friends, most of whom had deserted him. But it is now known that Ward believed he was assisting MI5 in the entrapment of Ivanov, who was known to be a Soviet intelligence officer. Nor was it known at the time that Blunt had done a service to the Palace by purchasing Ward's sketches of members of the royal family, which had been put on sale by Ward to raise money for his defense.[11]

It was not only Blunt's trivial role in this sex-spies-and-drugs scandal that convinced Roger Hollis to tread carefully in persuading the home secretary that to bring the royal art historian to trial would have public repercussions for the Establishment that would be too awful to contemplate. Professional counterintelligence officers, such as Arthur Martin, also argued against a trial. They, too, were in favor of an immunity deal that would enable them to extract fom Blunt the confession that Elliott had failed to get from Philby: a full list of those recruited and how they operated.

The immunity deal was finally approved by Humphrey Brooke — himself an old Marlburian contemporary — and it was conditional on Blunt's not having spied for the Soviets after 1945. Reliable sources confirm that Hollis obtained in advance approval for the deal from the queen's private secretary, because it required the continued presence of a traitor in the Palace. Sir Michael Adeane's concern was that at all costs the monarch should not be dragged into the affair, and this would best be served by a secret deal. Adeane knew, even if Hollis did not, that if Blunt ever came to trial, there was the risk of another, even more explosive, royal scandal.[12]

The immunity deal was a convenient but flawed solution for all concerned. It was predicated on the assumption by MI5 that Blunt would live up to his side of the bargain: That he would provide the full and detailed confession that they needed. Once Blunt had been given the guarantee against prosecution, it would be impossible to bring him or any of those he implicated to justice. The price of uncovering the Cambridge network was that none of its members could ever be called to account. Without Blunt's confession, however, there was no way of discovering how deeply the conspiracy had penetrated the British Establishment.

Considering what was at stake in Blunt's confession, it is astonishing that Arthur Martin was sent alone to confront Blunt on the morning of April 23, 1964. (American counterintelligence officers have assured me that the standard practice calls for at least two officers to be present.) Martin still believes that Blunt had been forewarned and held out for the immunity deal.

Martin says that he was met with a blank stare when he informed Blunt that Straight had told him all about his recruitment and dealings with the Russians. Blunt was too smart to be panicked into a confession. It was not until Martin told him that the attorney general had authorized formal immunity from prosecution that there was any reaction. With cool deliberation Blunt got up, walked to the window, and poured himself a drink. Only then did he turn round and say: "It is true."

While Martin was relieved to hear this confirmation, he made it clear to Blunt that immunity was conditional on his full cooperation. Blunt confirmed that Leo Long and John Cairncross were Soviet agents. Later, they were both interrogated by Martin, to whom they confessed on the understanding that they would not be prosecuted either. Straight was brought to London to confront Blunt in May 1964, again that September, and again in April 1965, in the hope of stimulating the flow of information. But as Martin affirms, Blunt's first twenty-five-minute confession was more productive than any other session in the more than six years of debriefings that followed.[13]

MI5 was provided with few really fresh leads by Blunt. Apart from Long and Cairncross, he volunteered only the name of the long-dead War Office clerk Tom Wylie as a prewar recruit of Burgess. The security service tried other tactics, which included confronting him with John Hilton, his Marlborough friend in MI6. This meeting ended sourly. So did a confrontation with Kemball Johnston. His son and daughter confirmed how their father had been summoned to the Courtauld to meet Blunt, in the summer of 1964. A very senior MI5 officer sat closely observing the pair while Blunt admitted he had been a Soviet spy. From what Johnston told his family after Blunt's public unmasking sixteen years later, Johnston evidently believed the meeting has been set up to find out whether he, too, had been a traitor. But his reaction was one of shock and astonishment — so much so that he went out and drank rather too much with Blunt over dinner after the session was over. MI5, however, appears not to have been totally convinced that Johnston's well-known anti-American pro-Marxist sympathies had left him quite so ignorant of Burgess and Blunt's activities. When MI5 knew that Johnston was away from home, an investigator calling himself Mr. Hendry questioned his wife about her Viennese brother-in-law, a left-wing banker. It was suggested that he had helped Melinda Maclean reach Russia in 1954 by using the Johnston family's passports. There was no truth to the story and Kemball Johnston was furious. Later the whole affair made a family joke. When they saw a French truck on the Dover ferry emblazoned with the name "Arthur Martin," Johnston told his children that MI5 was keeping them all under surveillance during their summer holiday on the Continent.

Arthur Martin, however, had already been taken off the Blunt case. Roger Hollis, the head of MI5, had replaced him with Peter Wright. To Wright fell the task of trying to wear Blunt down and persuade him to live up to his side of the bargain. It was proved a futile exercise because "although Blunt under pressure expanded his information, it always pointed at those who were either dead, long since retired, or else comfortably out of secret access and danger." According to American sources, Blunt's performance conformed exactly to the standard routine that the Soviets drilled their agents to adopt against interrogators.[14]

"I could never be a Whittaker Chambers," Wright says Blunt told him when he raised the question of Alister Watson. "It's so McCarthyite, naming names, informing witch-hunts." Wright says that he reminded Blunt that his acceptance of the immunity deal obligated him to play the role of Chambers. It was no good putting the hood on "if he would not point the finger." But Blunt did precious little finger pointing. He gave no evidence against Watson, who fitted Golitsyn's description of the fifth man in the Cambridge ring, and a face to face confrontation between Blunt, Watson, and two interrogators resulted only in bitter recriminations. Wright discovered that Lord Rothschild had written to Dick White in 1951 suggesting that Watson should be interrogated because of his Communist affiliations. But he never was. In 1965, Watson, who was still engaged in secret scientific work for the Admiralty, denied the allegations that he was ever a spy, even though he admitted he had met with Soviet agents on several occasions. This admission, and the discovery that he failed to declare his Communist sympathies, were grounds to remove his security clearance and transfer him to nonsecret work at the National Institute of Oceanography.[15]

Blunt was no more helpful when it came to investigating the allegations against Sir Dennis Proctor and Sir Stuart Hampshire. Wright interviewed them both and they vigorously denied that they had ever been involved in any espionage activities. In 1951 Rees had alleged that Hampshire was a part of Blunt's network, but Hampshire had denied this most emphatically in 1965. He did, however, recall a prewar dinner in Paris with Blunt, Burgess, and Klugmann, at which the trio might have targeted him for recruitment. But Hampshire insisted that he was never a part of their, or any other, espionage network. Klugmann died before he could be interrogated.

John Peter Astbury, one of the Communist Apostles "fathered" by Straight in 1937, was also a prime suspect of Wright's. According to his younger brother, Astbury had continued his political activities at London University before being called up to the Royal Corps of Signals. He later worked on radar development during the war and then at Manchester under Professor P.M.S. Blackett, another Marxist scientist, who made no secret of his sympathy for the Soviet Union. After prewar research at Imperial College, Astbury transferred to CERN in Geneva where he worked for many years on the European nuclear-accelerator project. He would, therefore, have been a valuable recruit for the Soviets. But his brother does not recall that he ever came under suspicion, and he says they were never close, recalling how in the fifties there was a "kerfuffle" with the press about his brother defecting during an extended holiday trip abroad. Straight told me that he had given Astbury's name to M15 in 1964 as one of his fellow Apostles who was recruited for the Soviets by Blunt or Burgess. Wright, moreover, confirmed to Chapman Pincher in 1981 that Astbury's scientific work made him an obvious candidate for investigation. But like a number of Cambridge suspects who declined to be interviewed, there was not enough evidence to proceed without their cooperation. Shortly before Astbury died in December 1987, Straight was told by surviving members of their old Cambridge circle, at their Trinity College reunion, that Astbury was studiously avoiding them. They suspected that M15 had renewed its investigations of him because of his connections to the CERN project.[16]

Blunt once said cryptically that any friend of Burgess's might be considered a potential recruit. Among the Cambridge contemporaries known to have made Wright's final list of suspects — all of whom denied the allegations — were the following: Ambassador Sir Anthony Rumbold, who was a close friend of Maclean; Sir George Clutton, the former British ambassador in Manila; Rosamond Lehmann's brother, John; Andrew King, a former MI6 officer; the publisher John McGibbon; and Sir Edward Playfair, a former permanent undersecretary, who had just retired as chairman of a major computer company. Permission to interview Rumbold, then ambassador to Austria, was declined although he had been identified through circumstantial evidence to tie him in as one of Krivitsky's Foreign Office sources. But Clutton was dead; Playfair denied he had been a spy, but he admitted he "had known a lot of Communists." McGibbon said he never made any secret he was once in the party but that "doesn't make me a spy." King's refutation was based on his declaration of Communist party membership when he joined MI6. Lehmann told MI5 that he had rejected an approach made to him in Vienna by a Soviet agent in the 1930s.[17]

One of the few valuable leads Blunt gave Wright was that his former Courtauld colleague Phoebe Pool, with whom he had written a book on Picasso, had acted as his courier in the thirties. MI5 arranged for Anita Brookner, another member of the Courtauld staff, to interview Pool, who confirmed Blunt's story and also said that she had acted as a go-between with Andrew Cohen and the Oxford graduate Jenifer Williams, plus two Oxford-educated brothers, Bernard and Peter Floud. This suggested that the Cambridge ring had spread its tentacles to Oxford, the alma mater of another suspect named Arthur Wynn, who was up for appointment as deputy secretary at the Board of Trade.[18]

Wright set out to see all those named. Williams, who had married Oxford professor Herbert Hart, a wartime MI5 officer, admitted being part of the Communist underground. But she declared that she had given up meeting her Soviet control officer when she joined the Home Office in 1938. Peter Floud, a former director of the Victoria and Albert Museum, was dead. Sir Andrew Cohen died from a heart attack before he could be interviewed. Bernard Floud, then a senior Labour M.P., committed suicide after his first inconclusive session with Wright. When shortly afterward Phoebe Pool threw herself under a subway train, the new director of MI5, Martin Furnival Jones, became so alarmed that the secret about Blunt would leak out that he summoned Wright to inform him that all the suicides would "ruin our image." He ordered

Wright to terminate the investigation — and there the matter rested, after some forty potential spies had been identified.[19]

Wright was confident he had exorcised the past and discovered "how far the conspiracy extended." But within a few years, another MI5 assessment cast doubt on this claim. Anne Orr-Ewing, another K branch officer, concluded that Blunt's assistance to Wright had been "entirely insincere." Nor had Wright discovered the damage that the transatlantic branch of the Cambridge network had caused the Americans — or the instrumental role that Philby had played in assisting the Soviet penetration of U.S. counterintelligence operations.[20]

The damage-control assessments within the CIA were initiated by James Angleton. They followed Golitsyn's defection in 1961. But it was not until after Philby's defection, the Straight confession, and the MI5 interrogations of Blunt that the CIA began to appreciate exactly how the sustained, high-level penetration of the British secret services might have affected the security of various American intelligence agencies. The discovery that George Blake was also a mole had serious implications for the CIA because he certainly told the KGB about Operation Gold. This was the successor to the tapping of Soviet telephone lines in Vienna by the British in 1951 — Operation Silver. Operation Gold was a 1,500-foot tunnel under the border into East Berlin. Gold cost $25 million, and it became operational in the spring of 1955. From then until its much publicized "discovery" eleven months later, in May 1956, the "Tunnel of Love," as it was dubbed by *The Washington Post*, provided a virtual Niagara of intercepted Soviet military and KGB traffic that kept a factory of translators working around the clock at CIA headquarters. But Blake's exposure five years later raised the question of how much of what had previously been regarded as reliable SIGINT was carefully manufactured Soviet disinformation.[21]

Golitsyn's confirmation that Philby was a spy proved American suspicions that he was responsible for the catastrophes that sabotaged the CIA's operations back in 1949. But since Philby was in the United States until 1951, he could not be held accountable for all the systematic failures that overtook other Anglo-American clandestine operations in Europe during that period.

For example, Anthony Cavendish, who was in R5 counterintelligence with MI6 in West Germany and Austria, had revealed that the operations he ran from Hamburg, to land émigré Latvian agents ashore, all turned sour. The MI6 men were rounded up. It was later discovered that the KGB then used the captured radio transmitters against the British. A similar fate plagued Project I, II, III, and IV, the code name given a series of operations in 1950 that parachuted two- or three-man teams of trained Ukrainian and Byelorussians back into their homelands inside the Soviet Union. Even Cavendish's personal efforts to cultivate contacts with Soviet officers, when he was in Vienna in 1951, seemed mysteriously doomed.[22]

Interestingly enough, Cavendish does not put the blame on the Communists and homosexuals whom he encountered in disproportionate numbers within MI6. He blames Philby. Philby was indeed responsible — but not in the way that Cavendish suggested. Philby was in Washington at the time. There is no reason to believe he would have been kept abreast of the details of purely British operations that were run from Europe. But from 1945 to 1947, Philby had been in charge of the MI6 anti-Soviet operations. One of his responsibilities was recruiting and vetting the Ukrainians, Byelorussians, and Poles who came from the Intermarium, Prometheus, and Abramtchik, factions of the ABN, the Anti-Bolshevik Bloc of Nations. These were the people MI6 trained and pressed into service as Cold War penetration agents.

The background checks on these agents had involved MI5's processing massive volumes of captured German Abwehr, Gestapo and SS files. Many members of these factions had become Hitler's puppet administrators or policemen and had helped enforce the ruthless German occupation in Eastern Europe. These people were thus regarded by the British as good anti-Communists. But as the Abwehr and SS had discovered, many of the émigré groups had been deeply infiltrated by underground agents of the Soviet intelligence service.[23]

Documentation in the formerly top-secret reports that are now in the process of being declassified in the U.S. National Archives, shows the extent to which the OSS and its successor organization(s) relied heavily on MI5 to weed out these Communists. Contributing to this vetting procedure, which involved checking the captured German counterintelligence files, were intelligence officers on the British Control Commission in Germany. It is significant that among them was Leo Long. And Blunt himself could have been involved because of his wartime operations against the Eastern Bloc governments in exile, and his extensive postwar travel in Germany. Also involved was MI5's F Division, where Roger Hollis and Graham Mitchell had spent the war logging the political connections of both Nazis and Communists.[24]

Agents of the "Cambridge network" were therefore remarkably well placed at the start of the Cold War to ensure that the MI5 and MI6 vetting slips carried the magic words "no traces against" when it came to the penetration of the ABN by Moscow. This ensured that a slew of

Soviet agents, including the White Russian general Anton Turkul, the Czech Intermarium chief Ferdinan Durcansky, the Ukrainian Stefan Bandera, and the Byelorussian leader Mikolai Abramtchik, were either directly involved or had staff members who ended up running and recruiting other agents for covert operations against the Soviet Union.

When Philby came to Washington in 1949, one of the missions he discharged simultaneously for both London and Moscow was to "sell" Frank Wisner, the assistant secretary of state for refugee affairs, the ABN networks. He claimed it was because the British government could no longer afford to support them. According to one former American intelligence officer, "the final sting" was that a number of these infiltrated networks were taken on by Wisner, and later passed into the CIA.[25]

After Philby came under suspicion in 1951, a reexamination of the bill of goods OPC had been sold caused it to drop its sponsorship of the Abramtchik faction. But it was not until after Philby defected to Moscow and the Blunt investigations revealed the true extent of the "Cambridge network" that James Angleton ordered a major reassessment of the CIA's European underground networks. This involved reviewing thousands of previous security checks for agents and sources who had earlier been cleared by MI5 and MI6.

Angleton knew from his own wartime experience in London the damage that double agents could cause. He suspected the British moles had laid the groundwork for a "Double-Cross" of the West's intelligence services that, if unchecked, would far exceed the disruption the Allies had caused the Germans in World War II. The new Soviet game would take them into what Angleton termed "a wilderness of mirrors." This telling and much misconstrued phrase he defined as that "myriad of stratagems, deceptions, artifices and all other devices of disinformation which the Soviet bloc and its coordinated intelligence services use to confuse and split the west."[26]

Angleton believed the CIA had the resources and experience to navigate in "the ever fluid landscape where fact and illusion merge" so as to confuse the KGB at its own game. This would be done by turning the infiltrators against the Soviets in a complex web of "Triple-Cross." But that involved taking risks. And some American counterintelligence officers lacked Angleton's precise logic. From the outset, they were skeptical of Golitsyn's obsession with the scope and deviousness of Soviet stratagems. But for Angleton it became something of a crusade when, in the wake of Philby's defection, Moscow stepped up its assault with a wave of false information and defectors in what Golitsyn warned was a carefully planned effort to protect its still undiscovered moles. The new assault by Moscow reinforced Golitsyn's most stunning allegaton: that the KGB already had an agent in the highest ranks of the U.S. intelligence service, and that Soviet defectors would be planted to build up his credibility.

The consequences of Philby's "final sting," and the appalling dimensions of the success of the "Cambridge moles," were seen as vindications of Golitsyn. "The Great Mole Hunt" resulted as the British and American intelligence services became preoccupied with the search for the other Soviet infiltrators. George Young, a former senior MI6 officer, suggested that Angleton was a gullible Machiavelli who "had been completely under Philby's influence and sought to whitewash himself by finding KGB agents in every British department and agency." But the record shows that the CIA counterintelligence chief had good reason for his concern. That was why the highest priority was given to the "Cambridge connection" in the housecleaning operations conducted by the American counterintelligence agencies in the mid-sixties.[27]

The FBI cooperated by recalling Michael Straight for a further interview in June 1966. He was given a list of eighty-five Americans who had attended Cambridge University between the years 1930 and 1934, from which he picked out one American, whom he knew casually at the Department of State. He then named two more Americans with whom he had studied at Cambridge between 1936 and 1937 and whom he knew to have been Trinity-cell members or Communist sympathizers. Although he did not name any at Oxford, he volunteered to look at any lists. The legal attaché who was the FBI representative in the U.S. embassy in London recommended a full review of all Americans who had studied at either Oxford or Cambridge before the war.[28]

Hoover initially balked at the resources needed for the job, and worried about the potential repercussions of an "investigation of over 500 American citizens with no basis for such inquiry in fact." But American intelligence officers confirm that he was persuaded by the CIA to change his mind. As a result, the records of nearly six hundred Americans who had attended either Oxford or Cambridge before World War II were carefully compiled, examined, and scrutinized.[29]

The British response to the damage they had suffered from the Cambridge moles and George Blake was to set up the so-called Fluency Committee. The need to reassure their American partners that MI5 and MI6 were at last taking steps to put their houses in order prompted the heads of the two organizations to agree to this joint committee, whose task was the evaluation of past infiltration and the possibilities of current penetration. An internal investigation code-named Peters was already under way in MI5 to examine the evidence that Arthur Martin had compiled indicating that Graham Mitchell, Roger Hollis's deputy, was a Soviet mole.

Hollis reluctantly agreed to the investigation of Mitchell, but used the word "Gestapo" to describe the inquiry, when Martin was transferred to MI6 in November 1964. Dick White insisted on nominating Martin as his representative on the Fluency Committee, whose principal contributor from MI5 was Peter Wright. The committee examined some 270 claims of Soviet penetration. After eliminating those that could be attributed to Blake, Philby, Burgess, or Maclean, they were left with some two hundred, which were later whittled down to twenty, plus three substantiated incidents that could not be accounted for. Two of the three final serials involved the twenty-year-old charges made by Volkov and Gouzenko that pointed to the high-level agent in MI5. The third defector, Goleniewski, had charged in 1960 that there was a middle-ranking agent in MI5 code-named "Harriet." After exhaustive investigation it was decided by the end of 1966 that the Polish defector had probably based his assertion on false information.[30]

The Fluency Committee was then left with the two historical cases. An intensive debriefing of the now-retired Mitchell led the committee to clear him of suspicion for lack of evidence. This wrapped up the "Peters" investigation, and led to the molehunt code-named Drat, which was led by Wright. Its target was Roger Hollis, the former director general, who was now retired. This investigation uncovered numerous incidents in which Hollis, as head of counterespionage and later director general, had delayed investigations or failed to act with the alacrity that might have been expected. Hollis also fit into two historical serials: As wartime head of F section he could fit Volkov's reference to "an acting head" of MI5; and he had traveled home from China in the thirties via the trans-Siberian railway, stopping off in Moscow, which gave him the "something Russian" in his background that fitted the code name "Elli."[31]

Wright was convinced from the evidence he dug up that Hollis was the "supermole." But the former director general denied the charges when he was finally brought in to be interviewed. Without a confession, the Drat case collapsed, and the ten volumes of Fluency Committee findings led to no certain conclusion.

In 1981, Wright, then in retirement in Australia, took his case to the public by telling the Hollis story to the journalist Chapman Pincher, who made it the focus of his best-selling book *Their Trade Is Treachery*. The prime minister denied in a House of Commons statement that any conclusive proof had ever been produced to show that Hollis was guilty. From the safety of his Australian retirement Wright successfully defied the Official Secrets Act and a lawsuit brought by the British government to publish his own indictment of MI5 in general and Hollis in particular in *Spycatcher*. The book made him an international sensation and a millionaire, but it did not "prove" Hollis guilty or shed any more light on the identity of the supermole in MI5.

The suggestion that the high-ranking Soviet spy was a figment of the feverish anti-Establishment imagination of molehunters such as Peter Wright and Arthur Martin is flatly rejected by Nigel West. In his book *Molehunt*, which summarizes the investigations and draws heavily on informed security-service sources, West concludes that "enquiries found overwhelming evidence to show that the original suspicions were amply justified." He tells us that "sixteen out of twenty-one molehunters, each an experienced counterintelligence expert, were convinced." On the basis of his sources, West concludes that either Roger Hollis or Graham Mitchell — or possibly both — was the traitor. He opts for Mitchell on the grounds that he authored the misleading 1955 White Paper.[32]

American intelligence sources, who have studied the cases and who have had links to the British, are not, however, nearly so certain that the answer is that simple. Some of them recall an observation made by Maurice Oldfield, former MI6 chief, that he would have put his money on the one candidate who escaped investigation altogether because he was believed to be above suspicion. His remark registered in Washington, and not just because of the candor of this unassuming Derbyshire farmer's son, during his tour as liaison officer in the capital in the early sixties at the time of Philby's defection, when he had earned the Americans' respect and helped heal the wounds in the MI6/CIA relationship. They also knew that when Oldfield took over as C in 1973, he reviewed the reports of the Fluency Committee and was struck by what he regarded as a curious and important omission. He duly passed his observations on to some of his American friends when the conversation turned to the old unsolved cases on a trip shortly before he retired in 1978.

"If I had been in charge of the investigation," Oldfield was recalled as saying, "I would have put Guy Liddell at the top of the list."[33]

Oldfield's comment cannot be dismissed as simply another shot in the partisan war with MI5. He was not known for dancing on dead men's graves, and as a staunch patriot, he considered it bad form to snipe at one's fellow countrymen in front of foreigners. That was why his remark stuck in the minds of those who heard him make it in the context of Liddell's suspiciously close association with "the Cambridges," as some CIA officers refer to Blunt, Burgess, Philby, Maclean, and their network of friends.

Within a month of the death of Goronwy Rees in December 1979, the charges of complicity he had made against Guy Liddell twenty-eight years earlier were published in *The Observer*. The reaction of two of Liddell's former protégés was immediate and indignant. TOP SPY MASTERS DENOUNCE NEW "PREPOSTEROUS SMEAR" was the headline on an unprecedented public statement by two of Britain's most senior MI5 figures, who had "top level clearance" to speak out in defense of their former boss.[34]

"It was a grotesque charge," said Sir Dick White, against "a devoted servant of this country." Guy Liddell was "a wonderful man," according to Jim Skardon, who told reporters that "any suggestion that he was a traitor was preposterous." He had merely shared "common artistic and cultural interests" with "a coterie" of people who included Burgess and Blunt.[35]

Despite their denunciation of Rees, neither White nor Skardon commented on why Liddell might have joined Blunt in trying to persuade Rees to remain silent about Burgess back in 1951. That issue was also sidestepped by Blunt, who wrote a letter to *The Times* about the credibility of Rees's various accounts. Andrew Boyle tartly reminded *Times* readers that Blunt, as a self-confessed liar and traitor, was not a reliable witness. "May I simply say that Rees had nothing to gain by telling me a pack of lies," he wrote. "His aim was to tell the truth and to do so more fully and openly than was legally possible when he published his book."[36]

"The accusation against Guy Liddell was palpably absurd," concluded Wright after reading Liddell's office diary, which was considered so secret that it was code-named Wallflowers. Wright, who listened to Liddell's taped historical memories of MI5, in which he made no mention of the Burgess and Maclean defection, thought him a "tragic figure" who had been "undone by unwise friendships."[37]

To Wright — and to Liddell's hand-picked recruits Dick White and Roger Hollis, who were then in charge of MI6 and MI5 — the former deputy director was a revered father figure. To many who served him, Liddell was the epitome of the fictional British spymaster: a thoughtful headmaster whose ruthless professional skills were tempered by artistic and musical sensibilities. The testimony to his universal popularity in the office was the large turnout at his funeral on December 6, 1958. He had died suddenly of a heart attack, but there were those who believed that his spirit had been broken when he was passed over for director general and then betrayed by the defection of his friend Guy Burgess.

Anthony Blunt was a conspicuous presence among the large crowd of mourners. For once he lost control of his emotions and he was observed weeping. But the tears he shed were more likely of remorse for having compromised Liddell than of regret that he had betrayed another friend.

The suggestion that the "officer and gentleman" who led Britain's secret war against the Soviets for forty years might have been a Soviet agent is still obscene to those who knew him. But in the context of the facts that are now available, Oldfield may have been correct to think the unthinkable. American intelligence experts who have reviewed the evidence do not find it impossible, or ludicrous, that Guy Liddell *could* have been the MI5 supermole.

The wilderness of mirrors corrodes gentlemanly constraint, and the discipline of counterintelligence theory demands rigorous examination of every potential suspect when penetration by a ruthless and hostile intelligence service is suspected. If possibilities translate to probabilities, then that probability has to be weighed against the facts. By these criteria it is now clear that MI5's lack of any independent research and analysis section contributed to the too-hasty dismissal by Liddell's protégés of the allegations Rees made against him as too absurd to be investigated. It is self-evident after Blunt, Philby, and Blake that what seemed an impossibility in 1951 should not have been so lightly rejected by Wright in 1965.

Not only is it *possible* to conceive that Liddell *could* have been recruited by the Soviets, but weighing the probabilities against the newly available evidence, a strong circumstantial case can be made that he was the most successful mole of all. Moreover, when it comes to the key Volkov and Gouzenko serials, Liddell is actually a better "fit" than either Hollis or Mitchell, the two candidates investigated by the Fluency Committee.

If by "*ispolnyayushchiy nachalnik*" Volkov really did mean "fulfilling the duties of" — as chief of the department rather than as "acting head of" — then Liddell, as director of B (Counterespionage) Division, was the obvious candidate for the Soviet source who in 1944 was "head of a section of the British Counterintelligence Directorate."[38]

In the case of "Elli," the GRU spy in "one of five of MI" in 1942, Gouzenko's recollection that communication was carried out only by *dubok* in a "split between two tombstones" once a month suggests that extraordinary precautions were taken to protect a very high-level source. Neither Hollis nor his deputy, Mitchell, was elevated enough in rank to warrant such precautions. But a full MI5 director of B Division, with twenty years' experience in anti-Soviet operations, *would* have insisted that this passive role offered him the maximum security because it avoided the risk of face-to-face communications with a Soviet controller or cutout.

A single train journey through the Soviet Union with a stopover in Moscow was considered enough evidence of "something Russian" in the background of Hollis to make him a good candidate for "Elli." Research shows a much more convincing Russian link for Liddell. In his days with Special Branch in the twenties, Liddell had strong contacts in the White Russian émigré community. One was the ubiquitous Anatoli Baykolov. This supposedly White Russian journalist was an associate of Sabline, the tsarist chargé d'affaires who had gone over to the Soviets in the twenties — and it is significant that they were *both* on friendly terms with Liddell. Baykolov continued as a contact until the fifties. In July 1944 he received a dubious communication from Liddell: "N. and F. have been returned to Paris, ostensibly for further duties, but Soldatenkov has been informed of this move and doubtless he will advise his people to pick them up in Paris."[39]

Why Baykolov, a supposed anti-Bolshevik, should have been involved with Soldatenkov, the Soviet embassy liaison officer at the War Office, is suspicious. What is more questionable is Liddell's involvement in what has every appearance of a plot to repatriate two unsuspecting Russians to the Soviets. It is difficult to conceive that the long-time head of MI5 counterespionage could have been unaware of Baykolov's Soviet connections. As late as February 1951, Liddell wrote to Lord Vansittart with information he obtained after he had "seen Baikolof," who was described as "very reputable."[40]

Analysis of Liddell's early performance in the MI5 case files discovered in the U.S. Archives reveals operational mishaps that must be added to the puzzling string of failures that occurred later, when he assumed full responsibility for MI5 counterespionage investigations in 1940. The anomalies are so numerous, and follow such a consistent pattern, that they suggest a prima facie case can be made that Liddell had been leaking information to the Soviets and systematically working to further their interests since the late twenties.

A partial list can now be compiled that raises serious questions about Liddell's competency, bad luck, or treachery. It includes such serials as:

- The allegations that the Arcos house was tipped off before the 1927 raid, and the failure to locate the planted RAF manual, forced the British government to reveal that it had broken the Soviet codes.

- The mishandling of the 1928 arrest of Ethel Chiles, which permitted the escape of Jacob Kirchstein, the Comintern's principal agent.

- MI5's failure to block the visas of Bukharin and the Soviet delegation, which enabled them to propagandize Britain's scientific community in 1931.

- The failure to sustain the wide-ranging surveillance of Cambridge Communists at the same levels as in the mid-twenties, after Liddell joined MI5 in 1931.

- MI5's failure to arrest either Maly (the master recruiter of the Cambridge ring) or his successor, Brandes, who were the Soviet agents running the Woolwich Arsenal spy ring in 1937.

- MI5's failure to keep track of the German Communist émigrés Kuczynski and Fuchs, despite MI6 notification that they were both Communist activists.

- The failure of the MI5 vetting procedure that permitted Fuchs and Nunn May to be given security clearances to work on the atomic-bomb project.

- MI5's failure to "bag" the Soviet agent running Captain King in 1940 when Krivitsky blew the Foreign Office code clerk.

- Liddell's personal recruitment of Blunt and approval of Burgess for secret-service appointments. Although C Division was technically responsible for security checks, and F Division under Hollis for monitoring subversive activities, Liddell's B Division had an authority that could override negative Registry traces.

- MI5's repeated failures to spot known Cambridge Communists such as Klugmann, Long, Cairncross, Watson, et al., who were all cleared for sensitive wartime military and intelligence positions.

- Liddell's failure to investigate the RSS reports on "Sonja's" radio transmissions or to put her under surveillance in 1947 when her record as a GRU agent runner was confirmed by a British defector from the Lucy Ring.

- Moscow's 1944 alert to Colonel Zabotkin, the GRU chief in Canada, to guard his network against the British "greens" prior to Liddell's visit to Canada and the United States.

- Liddell's approval of the decision to send F Division chief Roger Hollis to debrief Gouzenko instead of a senior counterespionage officer, and the failure to mount a proper investigation into "Elli."

- Liddell's repeated rejection of the reports by his Countersubversion Section chief, Maxwell Knight, that gave detailed warnings of Communist infiltration during World War II.

- The two years that it took MI5 to conduct the "Homer" investigation, or the Venona serial that exposed Maclean, and the decision to keep the FBI and CIA in the dark.

- The Liddell-Blunt relationship that was the probable source of the Thursday tipoff that the home secretary was to give approval on Friday for the interrogation of Maclean the following Monday.

- MI5's failure to maintain continuous surveillance of Maclean, and the lack of an alert to the French authorities to pick up Burgess and Maclean in Saint-Malo.

- Liddell's collusion with Blunt in the aftermath of the defection to dissuade Rees from making a confession to MI5.

- The repeated tipoffs to the Soviets that Cairncross was under MI5 surveillance after the defection.

- Liddell's sanctioning of the "creative" reconstruction of MI5's Fuchs and Burgess-Maclean files to mislead the FBI in 1951.

- The 1946 warning to Moscow of Skripkin's intended defection, and the significant absence of a single Soviet intelligence-service defector during Liddell's six-year tenure as deputy director of MI5.

There is, therefore, circumstantial evidence to suggest that Guy Liddell was either the "grandfather" Soviet mole, or was badly compromised by Blunt. Passive spies can be every bit as damaging as active ones. There can be no doubt that Liddell's passivity in the MI5 vetting process let in the Cambridge moles; passivity led to Krivitsky's warnings being ignored — and passivity slowed the "Homer" investigation into Maclean to a snail's pace. Yet when vital Soviet interests were threatened, as they were during the time of the Arcos raid, the Gousenko defection, and the escape of Maclean, Liddell appears to have played an activist role by discreetly raising the alarm for Moscow with such caution that he never came under suspicion. Yet his astonishing record of passivity, taken together with his compromising friendship with Blunt and Burgess, ought to have given MI5 investigators pause.

That it did not — and still does not — suggests that Liddell's former MI5 colleagues may have too hastily dismissed the probability because they could see no conceivable motive for his betrayal. But, as has been shown with Blunt, the mechanism of intellectual treachery is woven from subtle deceits and resentments. Nor should it be forgotten that the Liddells — like the Blunts — were a family with aristocratic connections dropping down the social scale. The backbiting cynicism of the homosexual milieu which he enjoyed may have fed a deep-seated resentment against the Establishment, exacerbated by his disastrous marriage. His passion for the cello and his connoisseurship grew in defiance of his stern military father and were nourished by a doting musician mother. Liddell's artistic temperament, like Blunt's, shaped by similar adolescent resentments against the underlying philistinism of British society, may well have sown the seeds of later treachery.[41]

Nor does the probability that the deputy director general of MI5 could have been a deep mole necessarily absolve the two other candidates: Roger Hollis or Graham Mitchell. As the Fluency Committee discovered, incidents such as the Crabbe affair and the botched confrontation with Philby indicate that there was an active mole in the upper reaches of MI5 *after* Liddell retired. But even if one — or both — were Soviet spies, their treachery does not explain the earlier series of prewar anomalies.

Espionage networks, like other living entities, have to proliferate to survive. So if Hollis and Mitchell were spies, whoever recruited them must be a prime suspect. Liddell was not only responsible for their admission into the elite ranks of the security service, he directly effected the entry of Blunt and Harris — and it was Harris who maneuvered Philby into MI6. Nor is it insignificant that Liddell's tenure as MI5 counterespionage director coincided with the high tide of Communist infiltration into the upper reaches of the British intelligence services. Only three explanations offer themselves: Either Liddell suffered from a run of bad luck that was so disastrous as to be incomprehensible; or he was incompetent to the point of criminal negligence; or he was the granddaddy Soviet mole in the British intelligence services.

Corroboration that Liddell may have been the primary deep-cover Soviet penetration agent is the fact that "Elli" worked for the GRU. Blunt and the Cambridge moles started out with the NKVD (later the

KGB). In fact, when Philby relayed the news about Gouzenko's defection to his controller in 1945, the telltale Venona decrypt revealed that the "Chiefs" of the Politburo had to give their permission for Moscow Center to consult its GRU "neighbors" about the spy whose existence Moscow Center was not aware of.

This indication that "Elli's" cover was jealously guarded in Moscow is another pointer to Liddell. By the late thirties, when Hollis and Mitchell would have been recruited, they would have worked for the NKVD (later the KGB). Since Elli was GRU, that would seem to rule them out. In the mid-twenties when Liddell was targeted because of his potential, Soviet military intelligence (GRU) was the dominant intelligence force in the UK. As an asset, the GRU would have kept Liddell from all their rivals because his unique position in British counterintelligence enabled him to sound the alarm when Soviet espionage rings were threatened. That could explain why the permission of the Politburo had to be obtained before his very existence could be revealed in 1945, as the result of the emergency caused by Gouzenko's defection.

In practice, unresolved counterintelligence cases are never closed. They still might contain the threat of systemic penetration. As Stalin used to say, "Espionage is a crime against the people." But the crime of espionage is difficult to prove in court unless the spy is caught red-handed, or can be persuaded to make a confession.

In the absence of incontrovertible proof of guilt, it is rare indeed for a counterintelligence service to develop a case that can be successfully prosecuted in a Western court of law. Occasionally evidence of a substantive nature is found in the reports of defectors and signals intelligence. But the prosecution is frequently inhibited from disclosing its sources and methods in a public trial. The putative cases against Hollis and Mitchell — like the one that can be made against Liddell — arise from careful analysis of their operational histories, their associates, their decisions (or the lack of them), and in the anomalies that come to light after their official service ends.

"Even the mere suggestion of a possible penetration has to be investigated thoroughly," a former top-ranked U.S. intelligence officer told me when I asked him to comment on the case against Guy Liddell. This intelligence officer pointed out, with considerable emphasis, that when allegations were made against James Angleton by a disgruntled junior officer, the FBI was immediately brought in to investigate the CIA's chief of counterintelligence. He also emphasized that it was an independent organization, the FBI and *not* the CIA, that handles internal-security matters.

"In terms of urgency, the report of a bomb aboard an aircraft ranks with information about a possible penetration of the security/ intelligence services," the intelligence officer said. "The bomb may take one hundred lives, but the latter could destroy a nation's capacity to defend itself."

Guy Liddell and James Angleton occupied similar positions in counterintelligence in MI5 and the CIA. But while the allegations against Angleton in Washington resulted in an immediate investigation, in London the allegations against Liddell were considered too grotesque to warrant any action at all. "Strange!" my intelligence source mused. "How very strange!"

Liddell was never caught red-handed. He made no confession. The case that he was "Elli" rests on the incomplete evidence of Soviet defectors. It is understandable that Liddell's former colleagues would rush to protect the reputation of a dead man who could not defend himself against the charges. But as the Blunt case shows, the cost that has been paid because of official rationalization, forgiveness, and indulgence has been too high.

A case officer's analysis of Anthony Blunt's life and times provides grim lessons that cannot be overlooked. Perhaps the most telling is the fact that Blunt's involvement in communism was probably known to MI5 as early as 1939, when Blunt was rejected for a post in army intelligence. Yet within twelve months, Guy Liddell personally recruited Blunt into MI5.

From an operational standpoint, American intelligence sources agree that it was unlikely that the Soviets would have told Blunt that his recruitment had been sponsored by one of their agents. If Liddell was indeed the "grandfather mole," Liddell would have been recruited and run by the GRU, which had good reason in the forties to keep such a deep operational secret concealed from the NKVD. And if Blunt ever suspected Liddell, it was one of the many secrets that died with him when he was struck by a heart attack at breakfast time on Saturday, March 26, 1983. His death came barely three weeks after Donald Maclean had died in Moscow.

Blunt's treachery left his obituary writers floundering. How could they weigh the contribution he might have made to British culture against the damage he had inflicted as a Soviet spy?

The paradox received official endorsement when the British government rejected as "inappropriate" the bequest of Blunt's Poussin painting in lieu of his estate taxes. Turned down by the National Gallery of Scotland, whose directors were mindful that the public regarded the painting as tainted by its owner's notoriety, the money to keep *Rebecca and Eliezer at the Well* in Britain was eventually put up by the Fitzwilliam Museum at Cambridge. Despite cleaning and restoration, this minor work by Poussin is a memento to Blunt's scholarly eye. There are no postcards of the painting at the gallery shop. But the alacrity with which the uniformed attendants spring forward to remind the souvenir-conscious that "Photography is *not* permitted" suggests that this particular Poussin has inherited an embarrassing curiosity value.

Curiosity drew a flock of reporters to the Putney Cemetery on March 29, 1983. But in contrast to Guy Liddell's interment there twenty-five years earlier, on this rainy morning there were no tearful crowds of former MI5 colleagues gathered for Blunt's last rites. The black cortege of cars drove past the press with indecent speed as they bore the spy's corpse and eleven anonymous wreaths through the acres of dripping tombstones.

The thirty mourners in dark coats were outnumbered by the line of police barring the television crews and newpaper photographers from entering the utilitarian crematorium chapel. One of the more diligent reporters noted how fitting it was that Blunt's funeral was taking place on the day of Holy Week traditionally known as "Spy Wednesday."[42]

In the brief service held at the crematorium chapel, the Reverend Thaddeus Birchard, incumbent of the parish once ministered to by Blunt's father, admonished the pews of stony faces: "All have sinned and fallen short of God." Later Wilfrid and Christopher Blunt would make a final pilgrimage to Martinsell Hill above Marlborough. There they cast their brother's ashes to the winds. Winds that Anthony once described as "more felt than seen," sweeping the "edge of the abyss," in a schoolboy poem that lovingly portrayed this ridge of Wiltshire downland as "fixed, immutable/Beyond the power of time."[43]

John Hilton, Blunt's close friend at Marlborough, suspects that Blunt would have approved of his own epitaph in preference to the Reverend Birchard's apologetic panegyric. Recalling how one of their masters at Marlborough had stressed loyalty to God, king, and parents "in that order," Hilton wryly observed: "If communism is counted as a religion, Anthony's later practice could be said to conform to this pattern, putting communism ahead of patriotism."[44]

In this context Blunt would have regarded himself not as a traitor but as a dedicated international Communist. To him this would have been proof of his emotional and intellectual detachment, qualities that he admired in his two great artistic heroes, Blake and Poussin. Their single-minded application of their individual and contrasting visions provided the creative dynamic that elevated them above contemporary moral and social constraints. So, too, did the intense personal revelations of the brooding seventeenth-century Roman architect Francesco Borromini — an icon of Blunt's baroque pantheon. In 1667, Borromini chose to perish in slow agony from a self-inflicted dagger wound rather than concede his subordinate position to his artistic rival Giovanni Lorenzo Bernini.

"To have been under a strain so violent that it drove him to this act of violence — if not madness — and yet immediately afterward to be able to dictate such a lucid account of the event," Blunt was to write approvingly of Borromini, "reveals a combination of intense emotional power and rational detachment which are among the qualities which go to make him such a great architect."[45]

This personal striving to combine "rational detachment" and "intense emotional power" was at the heart of Blunt's complex personality. It equipped him well for his role as a Soviet agent. His schizophrenic quest for artistic enlightenment, the intellectual authority that he derived from it, was paralleled by his personal goal of secret authority and power that was realized in his success as a Soviet agent. He was also a master of compartmentalization, in both his personality and his careers, and it made him the supreme Jekyll-and-Hyde character. Unlike the fictional doctor who had to wrestle with his twin identities, Blunt managed to resolve his different personae behind a mask of exquisite detachment that allowed him to live easily with his treachery.

Professor Steiner has pointed out that there is no modern parallel for Blunt's infamous achievement. He was an individual, Steiner says, who, "as a scholar and teacher, made veracity, scrupulous integrity, the touchstone of his work." He also managed "the co-existence within a single sensibility of the utmost truth and falsehood. . . ."[46]

Blunt may have succeeded in reconciling the irreconcilable while he lived. After he suffered the trauma of public exposure, he took comfort that the majority of his former students loyally defended his impeccable scholarship. Only a minority saw a link between his treachery and the self-assuredness of his own judgments — his preference for photographic analysis of a work of art at the expense of the painting itself.

This arrogance was attested to by Lord Annan. But as he pointed out: "Arrogance is well known in the academic world and is often inseparable from success in scholarship." Blunt's arrogance was so overweening it ensured that after his death, his haughty self-image would tarnish. As one of his former pupils told me: "Blunt wanted to carve his judgments in stone for all time and could never accommodate easily to criticism — least of all when it involved his beloved Poussin on whom he wanted to have the final word."[47]

No history, and certainly not that of such a diffuse discipline as art, can be cast as immutable. So after Blunt's death it was not surprising to find that his august reputation, while still acknowledged to be considerable, had lost some luster. Despite the argument that Blunt's academic achievements were separate from and outweighed his espionage, the tarnish has come with the recognition by some of his former colleagues that his inner moral degradation affected his professional judgment. To the dismay of Blunt's ardent admirers, cases have been documented where Blunt suppressed the scholarship of rivals and lent his considerable authority to ambiguous attributions for old master paintings and drawings. "Once you get away with lying on one subject, it spills over into the rest of your life — and that is what happened to Blunt" was how his fellow art historian Dennis Mahon chose to put it.[48]

"God dwells in the minutiae," Blunt was fond of drumming into his art students during lectures at the Courtauld. This dictum, on which he erected his professional reputation, was not his own. He had borrowed it from the pioneer German art historian Aby Warburg, in whose library Blunt honed the skills that launched his professional career. Warburg's recipe for an art historian demanded "a cool detached serenity which belongs to the categorizing and contemplations of things."

Blunt's philosophic detachment and his minute attention to detail may also account for his astonishing success as a Soviet agent. Ironically, it was the lack of these very qualities that was behind MI5's failure to counter Soviet penetration until too late. Blunt knew, so presumably Moscow did, too, that Britain's intelligence services did not have officers of collective intellectual caliber who could, by "cool and detached" research and analysis, root out the moles. The career MI5 and MI6 officers, recruited on the old-boy network, did not concern themselves with minutiae. They were too easily fooled by the outward appearances of Blunt, Philby, and their other wartime recruits from the Cambridge left-wing network.

The assumption that a public-school and Oxbridge education was an automatic guarantee of loyalty to the Crown proved as erroneous and myopically deadly as Senator McCarthy's belief that all American Communists posed a direct threat to national security. But the blind eyes of MI5 in general — and Guy Liddell in particular — were no less disastrous. It is an inescapable fact that Blunt's Marxist record ought to have barred him from MI5. That he gained admission to the inner sanctum of Britain's security service was a result of his cultivation of Liddell, without whom neither he nor Burgess could have engineered the admission of Philby to MI6.

Philby may have been the more dedicated and ruthless professional agent who has attracted the accolade of the "Spy of the Century." But his career cannot match the versatility or longevity of Blunt's service for the Soviets, which encompassed three distinct phases:

1. As the principal Cambridge recruiter of the original network of ideologically motivated Soviet moles
2. As an active double agent in World War II, who was instrumental in expanding the Soviet penetration of MI5 and MI6
3. As the unassailable "agent of influence" who helped thwart later investigations by laying false trails away from Philby and his fellow deep-cover spies who were still operational — and even after they had defected to Moscow.

Each facet of Blunt's treacherous career inflicted a particular harm to Crown and country, and the continuing damage to Anglo-American interests did not end with his death.

# The Legacy of the Cambridge Spies

On May 11, 1988, the Soviet news agency, Tass, announced the death of "the remarkable Soviet intelligence officer Kim Philby." Moscow's official news agency referred obliquely to his "exceptionally delicate work," describing his activities as "heroic" and his accomplishments as "multifaceted and vast in their geographic scope."[1]

The only survivor of the original founding fraternity of Cambridge spies died — probably of heart failure — just three months after he became a bizarre symbol of the new "openness" that Mikhail Gorbachev is bringing to the Soviet Union. But Philby's startling resurrection led many intelligence authorities to conclude that the KGB was still playing up to Lenin's decree that the key to successfully deceiving the West was to tell them what they want to hear.

Billed as "the most successful spy the KGB ever had," the seventy-six-year-old Philby understandably chose not to be photographed for the London *Sunday Times* in his Soviet general's uniform. Appropriately for the era of *glasnost*, he wore carpet slippers and a monogramed Cambridge-blue cashmere sweater. Beaming benignly, he mischievously held up a copy of *Spycatcher*. It was an appropriately cheeky gesture for the silver-haired spy — the book was still banned from publication in England by the British government.[2]

Philby's long silence had led to the conclusion that he had outlived his usefulness as a propaganda vehicle. But in the wake of the *Spycatcher* affair, the KGB evidently saw an opportunity to have its star spy play a final heroic role in his lifelong saga of deception. Suddenly, the old traitor was again making headlines outside of the Iron Curtain. He broke his silence of twenty-five years to tell the world that he was proud of being a spy, that he had no regrets, and that he "would do it all over again."

Rescued from the whiskey bottle, and rejuvenated by his fifth wife, a Russian twenty years his junior, Philby spoke of his unshakable faith in communism in six days of cozy tête-à-têtes involving Johnnie Walker Red Label, black and red caviar, smoked meats, and "fresh Egyptian oranges." Phillip Knightley of the *Sunday Times* was the first Western journalist to be invited to Philby's Moscow penthouse apartment, whose spacious twelve-thousand-volume library would put some Park Avenue residents to shame. There Knightley was shown the spy's trophies — a drawerful of Soviet, Hungarian, Cuban, and Bulgarian medals. Philby was especially proud of one. "It's the equivalent of a K, you know," Philby assured Knightley, singling out his Order of Lenin. "Of course there are different sorts of K's but the Order of Lenin is equivalent to one of the better ones."[3]

One of the reasons Philby gave for the unprecedented "interview" was his desire to dispel rumors that he was on his "uppers and abandoned by the KGB and anxious to return to Britain." Certainly one of the purposes behind the interview was to demonstrate to potential spies that the KGB "management" now offered its faithful agents something more rewarding on their retirement than the liquor-sodden exile that was the fate of Burgess and Maclean. Knightley obligingly reported that Philby was "slim, alert, bubbling with youthful good humor."[4]

"I was never a double agent," Philby told Knightley. "My loyalties were always to one side, the KGB." The England that Philby knew no longer existed and he was confident that he would be proved right by the verdict of history. The Soviet Union was now his country. He was proud to have served it for more than fifty years. "I want to be buried here," Philby declared, "I want my bones to rest where my work has been."[5]

The verdict that Philby delivered on himself at his final curtain call might have been written in Hollywood. Fate ensured that it was to become his epitaph. Three months later his bemedaled body was lying in state in the so-called Social Club of the KGB before his burial in a Moscow cemetery beneath a black granite headstone adorned by a single gold star.

Philby had delivered his final script and bowed out on cue. And Knightley justified his part in the final act with the statement that the "master of deception" had helped us to "understand the motives and compulsions of Philby and his ilk." The telling insights did not emerge from the interviews themselves but from Knightley's observations about the decor of Philby's apartment. The photographs of Che Guevara and St. John Philby in Arab burnous might have been set dressing, but the Roman engraving that Philby claimed to have received from a fellow Cambridge spy was significant. He said it arrived shortly after Blunt's exposure in 1979, the inference being that he too still held to the "faith." As Philby quipped conspiratorially, "So like Blunt to have done something like that." And the antique Spanish table was a gift from Tomas Harris. Since Harris now appears to have been deeply implicated in the conspiracy, it would have been interesting to know when and how this imposing piece of furniture reached Moscow.[6]

Philby's passion for Colman's mustard, Worcestershire sauce, and the *Times* crossword puzzle shed no more light on the central enigmas of his career than his refusal to discuss "KGB operational matters." His disparagement of "that bloody man Burgess" succeeded in persuading Knightley that Burgess had scuppered his career by defecting with Maclean in 1951. But this claim, like Philby's contention that his confrontation in 1963 in Beirut with Nick Elliot had been calculated by MI6 to precipitate his flight, was hardly "the fascinating new account" the *Sunday Times* promised its readers. Philby's "revelations" were subtly crafted to reopen the old feuds between the British and American intelligence services. As we have seen, there is no substance to Philby's claim that Maurice Dobb was the principal Soviet talent spotter at Cambridge, or in his denial that there was no organized Soviet spy ring at the university. Since we now have evidence that other Cambridge agents, particularly Cairncross and Klugmann, were also supplying Ultra direct to Moscow, there is also good reason to doubt Philby's claim that his most important contribution to Soviet wartime strategy was keeping Moscow apprised of the secret peace feelers put out by Admiral Canaris in 1943. Not surprisingly the verdict of one leading British newspaper on the Knightley articles was "Philby stirs up old suspicions."[7]

"In diplomatic circles it is accepted that the Knightley interviews — later to appear as part of a book — were sanctioned by the KGB at the highest level," observed the *Times* in a caveat that was published after the articles on Philby appeared. "But opinion is mixed whether the purpose was really to humor an old and much valued operative, or to try and muddy further the intelligence water in Britain."[8]

There is little doubt in the Western intelligence community that the KGB's intention was the latter. It emerged later that more than one Western journalist had been promised a "tell-all" interview with Philby. The Soviet press agency Novosti, itself known to be under close direction by the KGB, had also granted permission "from the highest level" in November 1987 for an Australian and an American writer in the intelligence field to have an exclusive interview.

Philby had gone so far as to agree to answer a detailed set of written questions based on documentation from the CIA and FBI that exposed just how extensively the British and Americans had recruited ex-Nazi intelligence agents — such as Klaus Barbie — for operations against the Soviet Union during the Cold War. The journalists had even received agreement from Novosti that the session could be taped. They accordingly sent an interviewer over to Moscow who sat out the month of

January at Soviet expense awaiting the promised invitation from Philby that never materialized.[9]

It is significant that the American writer insisted on videotaping Philby—albeit with the proviso that Novosti would have the right of censorship. In Philby's interview with Knightley, the old spy approvingly noted that the British reporter had "agreed to come without TV paraphernalia or tape recorders." Nor was Knightley apparently aware —as the American writer was—of the central role Philby had played in helping place Soviet penetration agents into anti-Bolshevik organizations, first in MI6 and then in American intelligence. The KGB's unwillingness to comment publicly on the devastating success of this particular exercise in deception may have been what finally killed the plans for the second interview. The Americans concluded that *glasnost* was circumscribed when it came to the operational secrets of the KGB. As Philby himself had reminded Knightley: "It's nonsense to say that intelligence knowledge is ever out of date."[10]

Prior to going to Moscow, Knightley had been publicly skeptical of the Hollis issue during the *Spycatcher* trials. He had written dismissively about Soviet defectors, especially Anatoli Golitsyn. It was his published view that intelligence agencies in both the East and the West were manifestly overpowerful parasitic organizations that fed on one another's paranoia.

"The CIA needs the KGB to justify its own existence; and how would the KGB fare without the threat of the CIA?" Knightley wrote in the introduction to his book *The Second Oldest Profession*. He promoted the theory that it was the British secret service that prompted Dzerzhinski to begin the search to "find an Englishman who would commit himself ideologically to Bolshevism and work for the Cheka." This search eventually produced "a young man so moved by social injustice or Marxist theory, or both, that he would be prepared to take the enormous step of committing himself to the Cheka for life, and to working against the country of his birth." According to Knightley: "In Britain, we so far know of only one—Kim Philby."[11]

Knightley's assertion that Philby must be viewed as an ideological spy is as astonishing as his claim that Ultra intelligence "did not win the war, and it is doubtful if it even shortened it." Knightley contends that "the failure to share it [Ultra] fully with the Russians so outraged several British officers working secretly for Soviet intelligence that they became absolutely convinced that their commitment was justified."[12]

A year after Knightley's book was published in the United States, Philby selected him to transmit his story that a deep Communist conviction motivated him to spy for the Soviet Union. "Come, come, only a fool would deny me my faith," he chided Knightley, who duly reported the "made-in-Moscow" myth. It became Philby's final legacy — and one of the KGB's finer deceptions.[13]

As this account has documented, adequate information has been released from the Western intelligence archives — not to mention the records of Cambridge University and the personal testimony of contemporaries — that exposes the Philby legend as a hoax.[14]

What really caused Philby to become a spy was not his deep political conviction — of which there is scant evidence in his anemic undergraduate socialism — but his calculating self-centered cynicism. That is why he later boasted that he felt no remorse for the victims caught in the web of lies: his first three wives, his children, his friends, his wartime colleagues, and his country — in fact, all who trusted him.

Philby and his Cambridge "soulmates" — Blunt, Maclean, and Burgess — were unashamed elitists. They looked down on their privileged contemporaries and, with the exception of the "rough trade" preyed upon by the homosexual Blunt and Burgess, they would have nothing to do with the lower classes. Blunt died a millionaire. Maclean once said: "There's nothing I enjoy so much as the comforts of my wealthy friends." The florid Burgess continued throughout his exile in Moscow to suck up to Harold Nicolson and his Establishment friends. And Philby's comfortable exile in the workers' paradise was one of splendor, far beyond the dreams of the average Russian.

Snobs as Communists? Elitists as ideologues? Hardly. The Cambridge spies were devoid of political convictions that they were willing to fight and die for. They shared a precocious adolescent rebelliousness and a rootless, elitist contempt for the institutions of democracy that isolated them from their Establishment surroundings.

Philby's admission, "I never felt I belonged," is far more revealing of his real motivations than his pretense of being an ardent Marxist. As General Orlov emphasized: The Soviet recruiters in the thirties wanted disaffected but essentially empty political vessels who could be molded into the perfect spies. Neither Philby nor Blunt could claim to be Communist, cast in the same heroic mold as John Cornford or Julian Bell. These were Cambridge's passionately motivated left-wing idealists. They spoke out and died for their beliefs; Blunt and Philby did neither. To contend otherwise would be another betrayal of their generation.

If Philby or Blunt had been true Marxist-Leninist converts, their consciences would never have permitted them to take orders from Moscow at a time when Stalin was bloodthirstily liquidating the true adherents of the Marxist faith. "I do not know what the position of Communist Party members is in . . . rabidly anti-communist countries," observed the Moscow correspondent of *The New York Times* in 1937, "but it is difficult to believe they face greater hazard than here, for here they are shooting them."[15]

The Cambridge spies were untroubled by Stalin's purges, which made a casualty of Theodore Maly, their venerated original controller. They ignored the Nazi-Soviet Pact of 1939. Of all the conspirators, only Maclean came close to being able to claim he was an ideological convert. That is why the Soviets moved so swiftly to evacuate him to the safety of Moscow in 1951. They had good reason to fear that he might make damaging admissions about his fellow conspirators and give an embarrassing recantation of Stalin's brand of communism in the witness box. Maclean's disillusionment with the Soviet Union in later years was made plain to visitors to his Moscow apartment with its wall plaque announcing "Anti-Semites not welcome here."[16]

How effectively the KGB succeeded in promoting the myth of the Cambridge spies as ideological believers was to be apparent when Philby's death brought the recognition — even in the Western press — that he was a hero of the Communist cause. "Philby was not blackmailed or bribed into betraying his country," *The Times* declared solemnly. "His service sprang from deeply held beliefs, a conviction so powerful that he was later able to say of his KGB work, 'I considered and still consider now, that by this work I also served my own English people.'" The Shakespearean construction of this analysis implied that Philby — like Caesar's assassin, Brutus — was "an honorable man." It was left to American newspapers to echo the sentiment that the treachery of Philby and his co-conspirators seems somehow less evil because they had been motivated by political conviction. Was not their spying motivated from high — if misguided — conviction rather than "cold" cash like the KGB's most recent recruits to be exposed in the United States: the Walker espionage ring?[17]

When writing of the magnitude of Philby's betrayal "of colleagues, class and country" *The New York Times* portrayed the Cambridge spies as "a kind of metaphor for the diffuse loyalties of the British that not only inspired a generation of spy fiction, most notably that of John le Carré, but also fed into the middle-class counterreaction in British Conservative politics exemplified by the current Prime Minister, Margaret Thatcher, who maintains a mistrust for both Foreign Office and career intelligence officers."[18]

It is still impossible to give a complete accounting of the damage and casualties inflicted by the Cambridge spies in that tumultuous decade of their operations that began with World War II. But there can be no doubt that one of their most enduring legacies was the shattering of the bonds of Anglo-American trust forged by the wartime "Special Relationship." Ever since the twenties it is clear now that all Western institutions (military, political, and intelligence) were targeted for penetration by the Soviets. This assault was accelerated dramatically during the war when Britain and the United States erroneously terminated or reduced their surveillance of Soviet operations within their borders after 1941 on the mistaken assumption that Russia was an ally in the struggle against Hitler.

On a strategic level the evidence of Soviet theft of wartime technology and ciphers and the spread of espionage was dismissed by Western political leaders while the illusion of cooperation was grimly maintained. On a tactical level, it has now been established that the Soviets penetrated the heart of the British Ultra operation at Bletchley Park and its American counterpart, the U.S. Army Security Agency. Both the American OSS and the British SOE included a number of active, Soviet-controlled agents. The Manhattan and Tube Alloys atomic bomb projects suffered significant losses to Soviet espionage. In the field of counterintelligence, we find that penetration agents like Blunt and Philby actively furthered Soviet military and political objectives. The British Foreign Office and the U.S. Department of State were penetrated and influenced by suborned Britons and Americans who were Soviet-controlled operatives.

The British and Americans took a long time to appreciate the Soviet dictum: "Peace is the continuation of war by other means." The postwar revelations of defecting Soviet agents, such as Gouzenko and Massing, together with the testimony of former Communist co-conspirators such as Chambers and Bentley, eventually convinced the FBI that penetrations of the U.S. government were plentiful and deep. But the vulnerability of British bureaucrats and ministers in the postwar Labour government, many of whom had themselves been Communists in the thirties, put the brake on the investigations of Soviet penetration in Britain. With the exceptions of the atomic spies Fuchs and Nunn May, prior to 1951 there were no such disclosures by the British government.

The American counterintelligence services, spurred by the growing problem, put mammoth resources into the investigation of leaks from the British embassy in Washington. The British government, to the amazement of concerned FBI and CIA officers, conveyed the assurance that it was proceeding with its own investigations — but only at glacial speed. These became accelerated after the defection of Burgess and

Maclean, followed by the forced recall of their Cambridge contemporary Philby because of American suspicion that he, too, was implicated.

Then with Blunt assisting — at the request of his friend Liddell, the deputy director of MI5 — witnesses were dismissed or ignored, trails obscured, and other Soviet agents in place were warned or protected.

When the dimensions of the Soviet plot could have been exposed by a thorough investigation of the Cambridge connections exposed by the Burgess and Maclean defection in 1951, MI5 continued its ostrichlike indifference. A comprehensive analysis by MI5 into the allegations made by Goronwy Rees, and the suspiciously compromised career of Guy Liddell, could have exposed not only Blunt but Philby, Watson, and the rest of the network. Instead, MI5 resorted to face-saving half measures that created a thirty-year saga of denial of the past. Peter Wright's account clearly indicates that neither he, nor any of the other MI5 investigating officers, ever came close to uncovering the extent, or sophistication, of how the Soviets recruited British penetration agents.

The Establishment and the Oxbridge intelligentsia closed ranks when the press assault began to expose the issue. This circling of the wagons was as much to conceal incompetence as from fear of the McCarthy-inspired anti-Communist hysteria erupting in Britain. The spinelessness of the Establishment enabled Philby to maneuver clear of exposure, and it permitted Blunt to put himself beyond reach of investigation until 1963. Golitsyn's revelations and Straight's accusations *after* Philby's defection forced the Establishment to give Blunt his double-edged immunity deal. The Establishment had insulated itself once again — but at the expense of allowing Blunt and his associates to escape being brought to account for their treachery.

Considering the wartime successes of MI5 — the XX Committee proved how the extensive penetration of a foreign intelligence service can lead to eventual control of an enemy's ability to conduct its own defense — it is inexplicable that this same institution did not grasp the implications of its own discoveries until too late.

Successive British governments, for domestic political reasons, kept the skeletons in the closet with the Official Secrets Act. Yet the KGB — from whom, as we have seen, few British secrets were concealed — continues to reap additional bonuses for its moles. This was a reward that could not have been foreseen when it launched its Trojan Horse strategy back in the early 1930s. As a result, Britain's intelligence services have been held up to ridicule and contempt. Counterintelligence officers face a difficult enough task as it is in Western societies. It could not be otherwise in governments that believe in individual freedom and

democratic rights. Soviet agents, whether native-born, or overseas re-
cruits, are, by contrast, well disciplined, carefully trained, and rewarded.
Compared to the controlled social order of Russia, where even in the
age of *glasnost*, freedom is still rationed and secrecy is an endemic trait,
Soviet and Eastern-bloc agents have a free rein in the countries of the
West.

Vigilance, as history shows us, is the price that has to be paid to guard
our democratic institutions from Soviet agents who have learned well
how to exploit and use our freedoms and laws against us to achieve their
totalitarian goals. Confronting the persistent Soviet penetration efforts,
counterintelligence organizations in Britain and the United States also
have to confront Moscow propaganda designed to reduce that vigilance.
This is implicit in the oft-heard argument that counterintelligence
destroys the rights of citizens by creating a government controlled by
a sinister "Big Brother" unaccountable to the electorate. Another KGB
expedient is encouragement of the belief that the democracies, by
practicing counterintelligence, encourage the Soviet Union to respond
in kind. A third and equally specious notion promotes the view that
all Soviet defectors, such as Anatoli Golitsyn, are either renegade
psychopaths, or planted agents under Moscow's control — and that spies
like Philby are the only true patriots.

This account has detailed the costly miscalculations made by Britain
and the United States about the dimensions and effectiveness of Soviet
penetration efforts.

If there is one lesson to be drawn from the career of Anthony Blunt
and his Cambridge co-conspirators, it is that the ethics of conspiracy
— and the motivations for betrayal — are not merely ideological, but
timeless and never-ending.

# Notes and Sources

CHAPTER 1: PAGES 23–42

1. Guy Rais interview, October 1986, and other details drawn from U.K. press coverage, principally *Daily Telegraph* and *Daily Mail* for February 13, 1980.

2. Interview with Mr. ————, New York City, February 1986.

3. Interview with Brian Sewell, October 1986. Whether Gaskin jumped or was pushed remains an enigma. The police treated the incident as a suicide attempt. But the mystery deepened on July 27, 1988, when Gaskin died under the wheels of a commuter train only a few yards from the Dundee home he had purchased just five months before.

4. Interview with Mr. ————, New York City, February 1986.

5. See J. R. Ackerly's frank personal memoir *My Father and Myself* (London: Bodley Head, 1968), p. 135. "His Majesty's brigade of Guards had a long history in homosexual prostitution. Perpetually short of cash, beer, and leisure occupation, they were easily to be found of an evening in their red tunics standing about in various pubs they frequented."

6. Interview with Mr. ————, New York City, February 1986.

7. Robert Cecil interview, July 1986.

8. Rosamond Lehmann interview, October 1986.

9. As quoted in Andrew Boyle, *The Climate of Treason*, rev. ed. (London: Coronet Books, 1979).

10. Elizabeth Bowen, *Death of the Heart* (London: Jonathan Cape, 1938).

11. Andrew Boyle, op. cit., preface to second edition.

12. Transcript of the press conference, *The Times* of London, November 29, 1979.

13. Official Secrets Act.

14. The term *mole* for an undercover agent has come into current use only recently, popularized by the spy novels of John Le Carré. Unlike much of his espionage argot, *mole* was never an operational term used by either British or American counterintelligence agencies according to Walter L. Pforzheimer, chairman of AFIO (Association of Former Intelligence Officers) and former legislative counsel of the CIA. His personal experience is extensive and his unique collection of espionage literature, books and documentation is probably the most comprehensive in private hands. I am most grateful to Mr. Pforzheimer for revealing how, during a trip to London in the early seventies, Sir Maurice Oldfield drew his attention to the first recorded use of "mole" to mean a spy. The then director of MI6 opened a leather-bound volume: *The Historie of the Raigne of King Henry VII*, published in 1622 by the Right Honorable Francis Lord Verulam, Viscount St. Albans. On page 240 the Elizabethan diplomat, poet, and statesman Francis Bacon noted: "As for Spialls, which hee did employ both at home and abroad by them to discover what practices and conspiracies were against him, surely his case required it: He had such Moles perpetually working and casting to undermine him."

15. See Hollis case "Drat" in Peter Wright with Paul Greengrass, *Spycatcher: The Candid Autobiography of a Senior Intelligence Officer* (New York: Viking, 1987).

16. Robert T. Crowley interviews, 1984–1988.

17. Peter Wright affidavit, and statement, *The Guardian*, December 9, 1986.


CHAPTER 2: PAGES 43–56

1. Wilfrid Blunt, *Slow on the Feather* (Salisbury, Eng.: Michael Russell, The Chantry Press, 1986), p. 243: "My Brother Anthony: A Postscript."

2. Ibid.

3. Blunt's press statement, *The Times*, November 29, 1979.

4. *Daily Telegraph*, November 29, 1979.

5. Blunt press statement, op. cit.

6. Ibid.

7. The 35,000-word handwritten manuscript was read by Wilfrid Blunt (according to his published comment) and was valued for probate at £125,000. As this was considered excessive, it was donated to the British Library on condition (probably insisted on by HMG) that it would not be released for 35 years.

8. Harry Chapman Pincher, *Their Trade Is Treachery* (London: Sidgwick & Jackson, 1981), p. 90; Nigel West, *MI5* (London: Bodley Head, 1981), p. 334; Nigel West, *The Circus* (New York: Stein & Day, 1983), p. 122.

9. Harry Chapman Pincher, *Their Trade Is Treachery* (New York: St. Martin's Press, 1984), p. 161.

10. Christopher Andrew, "R. H. Hinsley and the Cambridge Moles," in *Diplomacy and Intelligence in the Second World War* (Cambridge University Press, 1985), p. 25; Christopher Andrew, *Her Majesty's Secret Service* (London: Heinemann, 1985), p. 407.

11. Wilfrid Blunt, "Slow on the Feather," p. 243. "I still believe it was not until the following winter [1936] that he was ensnared by the machinations of Guy Burgess." His brother, who saw the draft, "begged me to remove the epithet"; Barry Penrose and Simon Freeman, *Conspiracy of Silence* (London: Grafton, 1986), p. 106.

12. "He [Blunt] talked of how he had joined the Soviet cause, recruited by the then youthful, brilliant Guy Burgess." Wright, *Spycatcher*, p. 226; Philby interviewed by Phillip Knightley, published in *The Sunday Times* March 27, 1988.

13. George Steiner, "The Cleric of Treason," *The New Yorker*, December 8, 1980; reprinted in full in *George Steiner: A Reader* (London: Penguin, 1984).

14. Wright affidavit, *The Guardian*, December 9, 1986; op. cit.

15. "It is the evidence of continued penetration of the service after Blunt retired in 1945 until at least the early 1960s which carried complete conviction among those working on the case," Martin wrote in an unprecedented public statement to protest how "the investigating team was disbanded" when the case against the form MI5 director general Sir Roger Hollis "failed to produce a conclusive answer." [*The Times* July 19, 1984.]; Peter Wright affidavit, *The Guardian*, December 9, 1986.

16. Rosamond Lehmann interview.

17. Wilfrid Blunt, "Slow on the Feather," p. 243.

18. Robert T. Crowley interviews.

19. Michael Straight, *After Long Silence* (New York: Norton, 1982), p. 104, and confirmed in interviews, 1985–1988.

20. Crowley interviews.

21. Wilfrid Blunt, *Married to a Single Life* (Salisbury, Eng.: Michael Russell, The Chantry Press, 1984), p. 1.

22. Ibid., pp. 8–15, pp. 80–89.

23. Anthony Blunt, "Bloomsbury to Marxism," *Studio International*, November 1922 (hereafter Blunt, "Bloomsbury").

24. "A History of the British Embassy Church Paris," published by the friends of St. Michael's Church, Paris.

25. Wilfrid Blunt, *Single Life*, p. 37.

26. Blunt, "Bloomsbury."

27. Wilfrid Blunt, *Single Life*, p. 37.

28. Ibid., p. 86.

29. Ibid.

30. Ibid., p. 93.

31. Blunt, "Bloomsbury."

32. Wilfrid Blunt, *Single Life*, p. 91.

## CHAPTER 3: PAGES 57–68

1. Robert Cecil interviews, July 1985–April 1988.

2. As quoted by Jonathan Gathorne Hardy, *The Public School Phenomenon* (London: Hodder & Stoughton, 1977), p. 80.

3. Wilfrid Blunt, *Single Life*, p. 58; T. C. Worsley, *Flannelled Fool* (London: The Hogarth Press, 1985), pp. 38–39.

4. Louis MacNeice, *The Strings Are False* (London: Faber & Faber, 1982), p. 80 (hereafter MacNeice, *Strings*).

5. Worsley, op. cit., p. 45.

6. MacNeice, *Strings*, p. 84.

7. Worsley, op. cit., p. 84; Wilfrid Blunt, *Single Life*.

8. Gathorne Hardy, op. cit., p. 101; See Alfred C. Kinsey et al., *The Sexual Behavior of the Human Male* (Philadelphia: Saunders, 1948). His ground-breaking research, although conducted exclusively in the United States, revealed that 95 percent of all boys in his sample of 12,000 were sexually active by the age of fifteen. He found no statistical evidence and "simply no cases which remain as clear-cut examples of sublimations."

9. Gathorne Hardy, op. cit., p. 234.

10. Lord Alfred Douglas as quoted in A. L. Rowse, *Homosexuals in History* (London: Weidenfeld & Nicolson, 1977), p. 167.

11. As quoted by Gathorne Hardy, op. cit., pp. 179–182. He concluded that on average, a quarter of the boys at any school were having sex with each other on a regular basis. Its extent ranged from "the crudest form of experiment and victimization" to establishments where "vice was sensational, with young boys being virtually raped"; Wilfrid Blunt, *Single Life*, p. 79.

12. Gathorne Hardy, op. cit., p. 193.

13. Wilfrid Blunt, *Single Life*, p. 79.

14. Worsley, op. cit., p. 47; MacNeice, op. cit., p. 100.

15. "Note on Anthony Blunt," kindly supplied by John Hilton (hereafter: Hilton, "Note"); MacNeice/Blunt letters, King's College (Cambridge) Modern Literary Archives (hereafter KCA).

16. Ibid.

17. Tom Driberg, *Ruling Passions* (London: Jonathan Cape, 1971), p. 15.

18. Anthony Blunt interviewed by the editors of *The Marlburian*, December 1967.

19. Cecil interviews, 1985–1988.

## CHAPTER 4: PAGES 69–86

1. John Bowle interview, September 1984.

2. MacNeice, *Strings*, p. 246.

3. Ibid., p. 95.

4. Worsley, *Flannelled Fool*, p. 40.

5. Anthony Blunt interview, *The Marlburian*, December 1967.

6. MacNeice letter to his mother, October 1925, MacNeice papers, Bodleian Library, Oxford (hereafter BO).

7. *The Marlburian*, December 1967.

8. Blunt, "Bloomsbury."

9. Bowle interview, 1984.

10. *The Marlburian*, December 1967.

11. Bowle interview, 1984.

12. *The Heretick*, June 1924; Hilton, "Note."

13. Bowle interview, 1984.

14. *The Marlburian*, December 1967.

15. Blunt, "Bloomsbury."

16. Dr. Cyril Norwood, *The English Tradition in Education*, as quoted by Gathorne Hardy, *The Public School Phenomenon*, p. 220.

17. The statistics are drawn from those compiled from official sources by J. M. Winter for his thorough study *World War I and the British People* (London: Macmillan, 1986). These put the military losses at:

Britain: 723,000; 63 per 1,000 males aged 15–49
Germany: 2,037,000; 125 per 1,000 males aged 15–49
France: 1,327,000; 133 per 1,000 males aged 15–49

British army casualty rates averaged out at 7.7 percent of the officer corps killed against 4.1 percent for other ranks over the four years of war. Winter's calculations from college records show that the Oxford and Cambridge death rates, particularly for the 20 to 24-year-olds, were above 26 percent and "well above the national figures" for other universities. This leads to his conclusion that "young Oxford and Cambridge men were more likely to be killed during the war than were their peers either within the population as a whole or members of other British universities" (pp. 97–98). Similarly with the public schools: The fifty-three studied "lost about one old boy of every five who served," leading to the Bishop of Malvern's statement at the dedication of Malvern College's war memorial that World War I "can only be described as the wiping out of a generation."

This popular myth of the so-called lost generation was reexamined by Robert Wohl in his groundbreaking study *The Generation of 1914* (Cambridge, Mass.: Harvard University Press, 1979), an analysis of the intellectual and cultural impact of World War I on European nations. His studies led Wohl to conclude that the term "missing generation" in England was distorted to mean "missing elite" and the subsequent "decimation, partial destruction, and psychological disorientation of the graduates of public schools and universities who had ruled England during the previous half century." He points out that the English generation of 1914 blamed the loss of their world on the war, but that in all the literature on the lost generation "one seldom has reason to remember that of the 700,000 British combatants who died in the war, only 37,452 were officers — and yet it is these 37,000 and not the troops they commanded who are enshrined in the myth" (pp. 120–121).

18. Harold Nicolson, *King George V* (London: Constable, 1951), p. 384.

19. As quoted in Stanley Hynes, *The Auden Generation* (Princeton, N.J.: Princeton University Press, 1982), p. 25.

20. Blunt, "Bloomsbury"; and *The Marlburian*, December 1967.

21. MacNeice, *Strings*, p. 95.

22. Ibid., p. 243.

23. Ibid., p. 100, p. 96.

24. I am grateful to Professor Jon Stallworthy, who is working on a MacNeice biography. He generously shared with me his impressions of his interview with Blunt and his own views on the curious intimacy of MacNeice's letters.

25. MacNeice, *Strings*, p. 249.

26. Hilton, "Note"; Blunt, "Bloomsbury."

27. MacNeice, *Strings*, p. 98; Blunt, "Bloomsbury."

28. Clive Bell, *Art* (London: Chatto & Windus, 1914).

29. MacNeice, *Strings*, p. 95.

30. Blunt, "Bloomsbury."

31. Ibid.

32. Henri Matisse had coined the name "Cubism" after being struck by the peculiarly

geometrical nature of a painting by Georges Braque at the 1908 Salon des Indepen-
dents. Picasso himself defined Cubism as "an art dealing primarily with forms." By
the twenties Picasso was already developing away from abstract Cubism.

33. MacNeice letter, September 1925, BO.

34. Blunt, "Bloomsbury."

35. MacNeice, *Strings*, p. 242, p. 247.

36. Blunt, "Bloomsbury."

37. MacNeice, *Strings*, p. 244.

38. Hilton letter of October 25, 1925; MacNeice, op. cit., Appendix B, p. 247.

39. Ibid., p. 244.

40. MacNeice letter, November 6, 1925, BO.

41. *The Marlburian*, December 1967.

42. MacNeice letter, January 1926, BO.

43. Ibid.

44. *The Marlburian*, July 1926.

45. MacNeice, *Strings*, p. 247; see also the Blunt poem in *The Marlburian*, March 29,
1926.

46. MacNeice, *Strings*, p. 247.

47. Ibid.

48. Report of Prize Day in *The Marlburian*, July 1926.

49. Ibid.

50. Ibid.

51. *The Marlburian*, July 1926.

52. Christopher Hughes article on art, *The Marlburian*, December 1927.

## CHAPTER 5: PAGES 87–116

1. The Comintern, as it came to be known, was the successor to the first International
Workingmen's Association called by Karl Marx in London in 1864 and the Social
Democratic Second International held in Paris in 1889.

2. W. Kendall, *The Revolutionary Movement in Britain, 1900–1921* (London: Weidenfeld & Nicolson, 1964).

3. David Morgan, *A Short History of the British People* (Leipzig: VEB, 1979), pp. 90–93.
This East German and Marxist view emphasizes the role played in the evolution
of the Labour party by the SDF and other British splinter groups.

4. Dr. L. J. Macfarlane, *The British Communist Party: Its Origins and Development*
(London: MacGibbon & Kee, 1966), pp. 24–25 and 68. See also W. Kendall, *The
Revolutionary Movement in Britain 1900–1921* (London: Weidenfeld & Nicolson,
1969).

5. WO (War Office) 32/10776, Public Record Office, Kew, England (hereafter PRO),

"Historical Sketch of the Directorate of Military Intelligence During the Great War," May 6, 1921.

6. U.S. Embassy London, Confidential Post Files, Decimal Filing System, Ref. 800 B(olshevik), Record Group 84, National Archives, Washington, D.C. (hereafter US Emb Lon 800 RG 84 NA), 9944-A-4/5 April 1918.

7. A dynamic if idiosyncratic "prefect" of the British Empire, Thompson was a product of Eton and Oxford who had been by turns prime minister of the Tonga Islands, tutor to the crown prince of Siam, and governor of Dartmoor Prison before heading the Criminal Investigation Division and Special Branch. [Cabinet Files (hereafter CAB) 24/52, August 18, 1918, PRO].

8. CAB 24/118 94308, January 6, 1921, PRO.

9. WO 32/3948, Report 14, February 2, 1920, PRO.

10. William R. Corson and Robert T. Crowley, *The New KGB* (New York: William Morrow, 1984), p. 80.

11. In 1920 the Cheka set up a special Counterespionage Department (Kontrarazvedy-vatelnyi Otdel), the KRO. Its agents operated overseas under the official cover of the Ministries of Foreign Affairs and Trade. Very soon the Cheka expanded its mission to provoke, entrap, and recruit foreigners as undercover agents. The Foreign Department (Inostrannyi Otdel, INO) was then established to direct the Cheka's foreign intelligence operations and to collaborate with the KRO in penetrating and destroying émigré organizations.

12. Robert Bruce Lockhart, the first Foreign Office diplomat in Russia after the Revolution, had invested a million rubles of the British government's money in a scheme that involved the legendary Sidney Reilly, to finance a revolt of Lettish troops in Moscow. The uprising was supposed to open the way for a southward march of the Allied expeditionary force, which had landed in Archangel. But the "Envoys' Plot" — as it was termed — was preempted by Fania Kaplan's ill-aimed bullet, which wounded Lenin on August 30.

   Reilly (or Sigmund Georgevich Rosenblum as he was known) became the principal target and victim of a sophisticated Cheka deception scheme known as "The Trust." He was the son of a Jewish landowner, whose enigmatic career has been surrounded in recent years by another layer of myths created by TV script-writers. The British did employ him as a secret agent because a Foreign Office report states: "We did at one time make considerable use of Reilly" because of his "violent hatred of the Bolsheviks, which coupled with a somewhat unscrupulous temperament, made him a rather double-edged tool." [As quoted in *Britain's Master Spy: The Adventures of Sidney Reilly* (a narrative written by Reilly and completed after his death by his wife) (New York: Harper Brothers, 1933).] Following the ill-fated Envoys' Plot, Lockhart was arrested but Reilly managed to slip back to England. This was seen as evidence of complicity with the Soviets by another of his associates, Xenophon Kalamatiano, an American engineer acting as a free-lance agent for the U.S. State Department, who ended up in prison. [Corson & Crowley, *The New KGB* pp. 61–63.] Was Reilly a victim of the Soviet plot — or was he the first in a long line of turncoats in the British intelligence services? Robert Bruce Lockhart's son, Robin, has suggested that he was "The First Man" in the Soviet penetration conspiracy [Robin Bruce Lockhart, *Reilly: The First Man* (New York: Penguin Books, 1987)]. But Natalie Grant Wraga, a former State Department official and widow of a ranking officer in the prewar Polish military-intelligence service, who is now the foremost authority on early Soviet undercover operations, argues convincingly that Reilly fell victim to The Trust. This brainchild of the

Cheka chief, Feliks Dzerzhinski, claimed to be the Monarchist Association for Central Russia, or "Tres." But The Trust, established in 1921, was an anti-Bolshevik front to lure into the clutches of the Soviet secret police the enemies of the Revolution. Wraga argues that The Trust agents in Finland were mobilized to organize the kidnapping of Reilly, who disappeared in 1925 after going to a villa near the Russian border belonging to Nicolai Bunakov, an employee of the British mission in Helsinki. Wraga's authoritative account suggests that Reilly fell victim to "internal party politics" rooted in the "Stalin-Trotsky Conflict." [Interview and telephone conversations with Natalie Grant Wraga, December 1987, and "Deception on a Grand Scale," *International Journal of Intelligence and Counter-intelligence*, Vol. 1, No. 4, 1986–1987.]

13. US Emb Lon, "Political Affairs" 1920, Vol. XLIII, 800 Britain, telegram, April 15 and letter from State Department to L. Lanier Wilson, April 16, 1920, RG 84 NA.

14. Captain Miller, Special Branch, to Winslow, June 4, 1920. US Emb Lon 800 1920, RG 84 NA.

15. Ibid.

16. Ibid., p. 6; that the "authorities" had permitted Rothenstein to operate from within a government department implies he was unwittingly acting as a double agent to monitor the activity of the extremist groups he was manipulating.

17. Ibid., p. 11; CAB 24/118, Annual Report of Directorate of Intelligence on "Revolutionary Movements in Britain" for 1920, p. 4 and p. 11, PRO.

18. Ibid.

19. R. H. Ullman, *Anglo-Soviet Relations 1917–1921* (Princeton, N.J.: Princeton University Press, 1961), Vol. III, pp. 44–52.

20. "Revolutionary Movements," CAB 24/118, PRO.

21. Ibid., p. 35.

22. Ibid.

23. CAB 24/118, Report No. 87, January 6, 1921, p. 5, PRO.

24. Memorandum by Commander Denniston dated 1944 (hereafter Den 1/4), Denniston Papers, Churchill College Archives, Cambridge (hereafter CCA).

25. The telegram was sent by Germany's foreign secretary, Arthur Zimmermann, to Count Johann von Bernstorf, the German ambassador to the United States, on January 16, 1917. It stated that in the event of war with the United States, Mexico was to be asked to enter the war as Germany's ally in return for the promise of the lost territory of Texas, New Mexico, and Arizona. Although control of GC&CS passed to the Foreign Office in 1922, the operation was originally established under the aegis of the director of naval intelligence. Admiral Sir Hugh Sinclair, who in 1923 became head of MI6, had prevailed upon the government to include in the 1919 revision of the Official Secrets Act a clause requiring commercial cable companies to hand over for scrutiny copies of all cable traffic passing over their systems.

26. Den 1/4, CCA.

27. Ullman, op. cit., Vol. III, p. 266.

28. Ibid.

29. "Memorandum on the proposal to expel Messrs. Kameneff & Krassin," September 2, 1920, Lloyd George MSS F/203/1/4, House of Lords Records Office.

30. "If this matter is raised through questions in Parliament, the answer will be that this work is done for the defense and security of the country against foreign agitators," the U.S. military attaché reported to Washington. "Officially the British MI5 is only concerned with civilian activities as they affect the army, but in reality and especially recently, they have concerned themselves in general with revolutionary and Bolshevik agents, using the Suspect List built up during the war and since added to, as a basis for operations." [U.S. Military Attaché Report 9944-A-166, November 15, 1920, RG 165 NA.]

31. CAB 24/118, PRO.

32. For an authoritatively detailed analysis of early Soviet operations, see John J. Dziak, *Chekisty: A History of the KGB* (Lexington, Mass.: Lexington Books, May 1988).

33. The young Armand Hammer is described in the report as a "close friend" of Dr. Zvye, a Columbia College lecturer who "is alleged to be an individual responsible for Technical Aid to Russia." US Emb Lon 800 B, Vol. 16, 1926, report dated November 9, 1926, RG 84 NA.

34. Joseph Finder, *Red Carpet* (New York: Holt, Rinehart & Winston, 1983), pp. 14–15.

35. US Emb Lon 800 B, October 21, 1926, RG 84 NA. Dr. Armand Hammer announced on June 13, 1922, the granting of a twenty-year concession to a vast asbestos deposit on the Asiatic side of the Urals. He claimed to have inspected the tract with Ludwig Martens, by now a Soviet official after his expulsion from New York the previous year. The Soviet State Bank required a $50,000 deposit in gold as surety for the concession. But Hammer declined to disclose the identity of those who financed the corporation. Dr. Julius Hammer, meanwhile, managed with the help of the Jewish Board of Guardians to get himself paroled after serving less than two years in the New York state penitentiary at Ossining, popularly known as Sing Sing. "Our turnover was considerably in excess of a million dollars," Julius wrote explaining why he needed to travel to his offices in Moscow, Berlin, Riga, Petrograd and Rostov. The burden of running his European interests had fallen on his son Armand, who "had no business training." Yet Dr. Julius Hammer's claims are strangely at odds with the State Department report that until 1924 Allied American Corporation "did little business and merely occupied desk space." (State Department report on Allied Chemical Corporation, March 5, 1924)

36. Ibid., p. 7; Department of Justice, Bureau of Investigation, J. Edgar Hoover letter of October 24, 1927, to Department of State; Military Intelligence Files, letter dated June 28, 1927, to War Department G-2 from G-2 Governors Island, New York, RG 165 NA.

37. U.S. Military Attaché Report No. 2655-H-260/19, RG 165 NA.

38. Cabinet Papers (CP) 273 (24) CAB (24) 166, PRO: Comintern Chief Zinoviev designated 1923 as the year in which the German working class was to be "saved" by the Revolution. By fall, Zinoviev realized he had overreached himself and the sporadic uprisings that erupted all over Germany were easily crushed. [Stephen Roskill, *Hankey: Man of Secrets* (London: Collins, 1972), Vol. II, pp. 72–74, CAB 24/166, PRO.]

39. Roskill, op. cit., pp. 72–74.

40. FO 371/1078, PRO. Keenly aware he was impaled on the horns of a dilemma, MacDonald decided to act by lodging a stern protest with the Russian chargé d'affaires. But on October 25 the conservative *Daily Mail* preempted his public statement by publishing the text of the so-called Zinoviev letter, which it had

obtained from Admiral "Blinker" Hall, the World War I code breaker who was now a Conservative M.P. The "Red Letter" campaign exploded on the eve of polling like a political bombshell. The Labour party, with some justification, believed it was the victim of a plot engineered by the Conservative Central Office, aided and abetted by right-wing intelligence officers. The Soviets disowned the letter as the product of a White Russian émigré "document factory." A British trade-union delegation that went to Moscow to examine the Comintern files was easily persuaded by the Soviets that the Zinoviev letter was a forgery. Natalie Wraga believes that recent assertions that Reilly forged the Zinoviev letter are "absurd." She believes that the notorious letter was a fabrication that was "received by the British intelligence service in the Baltic states from an agent of Moscow (possibly the Trust)." (Wraga, "Deception on a Grand Scale.") Wraga's authoritative view is consistent with the known efforts of Stalin's ally Dzerzhinski to discredit Trotsky and Zinoviev by bringing the Comintern into further disrepute. That the "Ace of Spies" fell into the trap engineered by The Trust a few months later seems to indicate that Dzerzhinski may have considered the elimination of Reilly essential to ensure that the origins of the Zinoviev letter remained an enigma.

41. Baldwin Papers, MS 113, JDG 10 Dec. 26, Cambridge University Library.

42. CAB 80 11/5/26, CP 236 (26), PRO.

43. Liddell asked for U.S. help on keeping track of a former Latvian, Jacob Kirchstein, a naturalized American, who "was one of the head centers of this whole movement." Since Liddell alluded to cryptic details in reports written by Kirchstein, it was obvious that the British had tapped into at least part of this extensive Comintern network. [Secret & Confidential Memo, March 29, 1926, US Emb Lon 800 B, and also, Secret Memorandum to Kirk, March 27, 1926, RG 84 NA.]

44. The Liddell family combined military and artistic traditions. The mother of Cecil, Guy, and David trained under the German violinist Joachim and was a founder member of an all-female string quartet. Their father's military career was in the tradition of his ancestor the Duke of Wellington, who defeated Napoleon. But he was also related to the Alice Liddell for whom the Reverend Lutwidge Dodgson wrote *Alice in Wonderland* and *Alice Through the Looking-Glass*. During World War I all three brothers served in the artillery, and each won the military cross for bravery. David, the oldest, pursued his artistic talents as a painter, but his two brothers continued in military-related careers that brought them together in World War II when Cecil Liddell served as an MI5 officer in Ireland. Guy's only son, Peter, told me that his father's career in intelligence very nearly came to an abrupt end after his marriage, when his uncle Rupert Baring, Lord Revelstoke, tried his best to persuade his brother-in-law to take a position in Baring's Bank in order to keep his sister Calypso in the style to which she was accustomed. But despite the lowly Special Branch pay, Guy Liddell declined a post that would have made him a rich man — he evidently relished the power that he exercised as one of Britain's leading counterintelligence specialists. [Interview with Peter J. Liddell, May 9, 1988; Liddell to Beal, May 25, 1926, US Emb Lon 800 B RG 84 NA.]

45. CP 236 (26), June 11, 1926, and CP 244 (26), June 15, "Russian Money," CAB 24/180, PRO. HMSO Command Paper 2682 (1926), "Communist Papers."

46. The foreign secretary considered the instructions received by the Communist party from Moscow too sensitive to circulate in writing. But from the cryptic references to the alarm in the Cabinet minutes of March 17, 1927, the attorney general endorsed Chamberlain's concern, noting that a "trustworthy" source (presumably a Special Branch infiltration of the CPGB) had confirmed renewed "interference

by Soviet Russia in affairs of this country." [CAB 14 (27)4, CAB 23/90B, PRO.] The London *Times* of May 3, 1927, carried a report of the trial and exposed the IWR. The scheme to persuade bourgeois sympathizers to "invest" in reconstructing Soviet industry was the brainchild of Willi Münzenberg, a German Comintern executive member who operated out of Arcos's German counterpart, Westwog, in Berlin. MI5 records show that American authorities also suspected Grüssfeld of espionage activity. [Confidential report and enclosure, "Moness & Chiles," January 1923, US Emb Lon 800 B 1926/27, RG 84 NA.]

47. The great degree of Anglo-American counterintelligence cooperation is indicated by the fact that to give the U.S. authorities time to move in, the British did not bring Grüssfeld to trial for two months. [Ibid., Confidential letter to State July 29, 1927, US Emb Lon 800, RG 84 NA.] But Moness had disappeared two months earlier, leaving a batch of unburned papers in a stove. When copies reached Britain, MI5 identified two of them as being in Grüssfeld's handwriting. [Ibid., Secret and Personal letter from Captain Miller of Special Branch to US Emb Lon 800 B, July 21, 1928, R6 84 NA.]

48. McCartney, an ex–World War I army intelligence officer, had gambled away the family fortune and served a nine-month prison term in 1926 for attempted shopbreaking of a jeweler's store. In jail he became a "sincere" convert to communism. He seems to have been acting as a free-lance agent for the Soviet embassy because he asked Monckland for any information he came across at Lloyd's on arms shipments to the Baltic neighbors of Russia. The approach left Monckland in no doubt that his gambling partner was a Soviet spy. And after receiving a questionnaire with the offer of £50 a month for information supplied, he contacted Admiral "Blinker" Hall, the wartime director of Naval Intelligence, now an outspokenly anti-Bolshevik member of Parliament. Hall turned Monckland over to Colonel Kell of MI5, who arranged for him to be run as a double agent. [For accounts of the McCartney case, *Times* of London, December 5, 6, 1927, January 17, 18, 19, 1928, and the accounts of *New York Times*, December 4, 1927, January 17, 18, 1928, which contain more details since they were not constrained by the Official Secrets Act. See also Wilfrid McCartney's own account, *ZigZag* (London: 1937), pp. 344–345.]

49. MI5 knew that a Soviet agent familiar with the RAF must have read the manual and Kell's trap was sprung. Confirmation that the Arcos raid was a carefully planned "sting" operation becomes clear from a Foreign Office cable sent out on May 24 ordering three critical amendments in the advance copies of the prime minister's statement on the raid, which had already been telegraphed to the Dominions.

   Comparing the changes with the prime minister's statement is most revealing. Baldwin's opening paragraphs referred to ongoing investigations of a group of Russian secret agents who were "engaged in endeavoring to obtain highly confidential documents relating to the armed forces of Great Britain." They were suspected of obtaining their instructions "from members of the Russian Trade Delegation, working at Soviet House, who arranged for the conveyance to Moscow of photographs or copies of the documents obtained."

   Suspicions about the illegal activities in Soviet House were, according to the prime minister's *original* draft, confirmed "*when a British subject in the Air Force was convicted under the Official Secrets Act of attempting to steal two such documents. The documents were recovered and the individual is now undergoing imprisonment. . . . A further document of an official and highly confidential nature, so marked, was recently found to be missing, and from information voluntarily furnished by a person lately in the employment of Arcos and supported by documentary evidence it became clear that this document has been conveyed to 49 Moorgate and there reproduced by means of photographic apparatus."*

The references to "Air Force" documents later "recovered" corroborate the Monckland/McCartney setup. But the government could not admit that MI5 had an informant *inside* Arcos, and this prompted the "Immediate Secret" cable of May 24 ordering revisions (underlined above) in the original draft of Baldwin's statement sent to the Dominions. Ordered omitted was "under Official Secrets Act"; and "attempting to steal" became "stealing." The cable ordered the reference to the information voluntarily provided by an Arcos employee deleted in its entirety. CAB 23/55, draft statement, "Search of Premises at 49 Moorgate on May 12, 1927," dated May 24 and FO 371/12591, copy of telegram from Secretary of State for Dominion Affairs to Governors-General of Canada, the Commonwealth of Australia, New Zealand, and the Union of South Africa, sent 4:20 P.M., May 24, 1927. PRO.

50. Details of the Arcos raid are from a confidential report of the U.S. military attaché in London, No. 19906, May 20, 1927, RG/65 NA, and reports in London *Times* and *New York Times* of May 12, 1927.

51. Papers found on Kolling showed that he was in communication with a man named Jilinsky in Moscow. Other documents revealed that until his return to Russia earlier that year, Jilinsky had combined his duties of Trade Delegation staff allotment officer with his function as a principal Soviet espionage and secret propaganda agent for Europe. [American military attaché G-2, Report No. 19964, June 8, 1927.]

52. Rosengolz's statement quoted in U.S. Military Attaché Report No. 19906, RG 165 NA.

53. Hansard – Parliamentary Debates (House of Commons), 5th Series, Vol. CCVI, May 17, 1927.

54. U.S. Military Attaché Report No. 19906, RG 165 NA.

55. Prime minister's statement dated May 24, 1927, CAB 23/55, PRO. Hansard – Parliamentary Debates (House of Commons), 5th Series, Vol. CCVI, May 26, 1927. For the intercepted Soviet cables made public in the prime minister's statement, see: "Russia No. 2: Documents Illustrating the Hostile Activities of the Soviet Government and Third International Against Great Britain," Commons Paper 2874, His Majesty's Stationery Office 1927. Note particularly the following cable:

Soviet Chargé d'Affaires to Commissariat for Foreign Affairs, Moscow
13 April 1927

I very much doubt the possibility of a raid on our Embassy. I would, however, consider it a very useful measure of precaution to suspend for a time the forwarding by post of documents of friends, "neighbors" and so forth from London to Moscow and vice versa. In the telegram sent in reply it is desirable to mention that the instructions emanate from the institutions concerned.

56. Ibid.

57. Ibid.

58. *New York Times*, May 24, 1927.

59. Report from US Emb Lon 800 B, November 15, 1927, RG 84 NA.

60. Unsigned fifteen-page report on Communist cell organizations, dated July 18, 1927, US Emb Lon 800 B, RG 84 NA.

61. The report confirmed the key role played by the London cell, which, "according to documents found during the raid," met at least twice a week. Members had a "definite obligation to carry out any orders that may be received from Moscow regarding subversive activities or espionage." Certain "specially trusted British Communists," by virtue of their position as "members of the Russian and the British Communist Parties," attended cell meetings "with the right to vote." The cell members responsible for maintaining contact with the British Communist party included Andrew Rothenstein, Edith Lunn, Leah Podolsky, and Alexander Squair. The secretary of the cell was "usually a Communist of very high rank, who with one or two others of equal importance form what is known as the Political Bureau" [Politburo], whose authority over the CPGB depended on "the status of its members in the Communist International." The London cell theoretically gave "direct instructions" to the British party only "in a time of crisis." But the records found at Soviet House revealed that the seniority of cell members was such that their suggestions "were invariably adopted."

Arcos staff members conducted their espionage "partly through the Technical Inspection Department and the Engineering Department of Arcos." Organizations outside Arcos operated "through certain trusted members of the revolutionary movement in this country," who obtained their information "from shop stewards working in factories where war material is being manufactured." Only the cell's Politburo discussed espionage, but orders to the espionage agents, who worked "very much in watertight compartments," came "direct from Moscow." Ensuring political reliability was the function of the Inspection Department, whose staff were "the most trusted agents" of the Soviet secret police," who "took instructions direct from Moscow." This MI5 had deduced "from a very much camouflaged account of its functions which was circulated in Arcos and the Trade Delegation." A senior member of the Inspection Department was on the cell Political Committee and often acted in a triple capacity "as agents of the GPU, as individuals engaged in espionage and as members of the Political Bureau." All employees of Arcos and its subsidiary companies were required to attend meetings of Mestkon, the Union of Soviet Employees. Members were "induced to bring their friends" to lectures that set out to "prove the superiority of the Soviet system and to make comparisons favorable to Russia."

The Society for Cultural Relations Between Britain and the Soviet Union was — according to MI5 — "completely in the hands of the Cell" by virtue of its control of the SCR executive committee. Founded in 1924, the SCR had particularly active branches in both Oxford and Cambridge universities. Margaret Llewelyn Davies, a Labour party activist, chaired the SCR's provisional committee, and as vice-president, she had assembled "*advanced* literary and artistic people." They included such distinguished British cultural figures as Maynard Keynes, Virginia Woolf, E. M. Forster, and H. G. Wells. But as the comprehensive MI5 report noted — and underlined for emphasis — five of the nine-member SCR executive "were employed in this country by the Russian Government, under the Anglo-Russian Trade Agreement, one of them being Andrew Rothenstein, perhaps the most dangerous agent of the Soviet Government in this country." [US Emb Lon 800 B, unsigned report dated July 18, 1927, RG 84 NA.]

62. Lawrence Badash, *Kapitza, Rutherford and the Kremlin* (New Haven: Yale University Press, 1985), pp. 5–6, and Albert Parry, ed., *Peter Kapitza on Life and Science* (New York: Macmillan, 1968), p. 4. The available evidence suggests that Kapitza must have been given his Cambridge assignment by Joffe, who maintained close contacts

with Bukharin, the most scientifically aware of the Bolshevik leaders. The available evidence suggests that Kapitza managed to gain admission to Britain as a scientist purchasing equipment under the auspices of Arcos and obtained his recommendation to the lofty Lord Rutherford from another Cambridge scientist (probably the Marxist physicist J. D. Bernal, who was one of the outspoken admirers of the Soviet Union's supposed dedication to science). On July 18, 1921, Kapitza wrote and assured Rutherford "how very grateful I am to you at having admitted me among your pupils" and that he was arriving in Cambridge that Thursday to "take up my work at once." [Letter from Kapitza to Rutherford, July 18, 1921, Churchill College Archives, Papers of Sir John Cockcroft, CKFT 20/15.] Kapitza's charm and immense practical ability made him one of the most popular scientists at the Cavendish and Rutherford's favorite pupil. [I. P. L. Kapitza, "Recollections of Lord Rutherford," *Proceedings of the Royal Society*, A294 (1966), p. 131.]

## CHAPTER 6: PAGES 117–132

1. T. E. B. Howarth, *Cambridge Between Two Wars* (London: William Collins, 1978), p. 148.

2. As quoted by Howarth, *Strings*, p. 52.

3. Ibid., p. 146.

4. Newton's *Philosophiae Naturalis Principia Mathematica*, which embraced his gravitation theories, was published in 1687.

5. The Cavendish took its title from the family name of William, Seventh Duke of Devonshire, who was chancellor of Cambridge University and who paid the entire expense of building and equipping the laboratory.

6. Quoted by Howarth, op. cit., p. 92; Kathleen Raine, an exact contemporary of Blunt, arrived in 1926 to read biology for the Natural Sciences Tripos. She found her creative aspirations stifled by "Russell's new logical positivism, Bloomsbury humanism (represented in King's College by Maynard Keynes and G. Lowes Dickinson) and the materialist science from the Cavendish Laboratory, that powerhouse that dominated all fields of Cambridge." [Kathleen Raine, *The Land Unknown* (London: Hamish Hamilton, 1975), p. 29.]

7. Richards's *Science and Poetry*, advocating an analytical approach to literary criticism, had just been published. He argued that Eliot's *The Waste Land* and its message of despair at the failure of the old values demanded the reorganization of cultural values to accord with a scientifically rationalist view of the world. Christopher Isherwood, who had attended Richards's lectures three years earlier, saw in "this pale, mild, muscular, curly headed young man" a prophet "who revealed to us in a succession of lightning strikes, the entire expanse of the Modern World." [Christopher Isherwood, *Lions and Shadows* (London: Methuen, 1985), p. 121.]

8. George E. Moore, *Principia Ethica* (1903) (Cambridge: Cambridge University Press, 1948), p. 34.

9. As quoted in Howarth, op. cit., p. 52. Bertrand Russell and Alfred North Whitehead's landmark work *Principia Mathematica*, was published in 1913. This mathematical approach to logic was later developed by Russell's protégé Ludwig Wittgenstein, a philosophy student of the Viennese positivist school who returned to Cambridge after World War I.

10. John Jacob Bronowski, *The Visionary Eye* (Cambridge, Mass.: MIT Press, 1978), p. 25.

11. Blunt, "Bloomsbury," p. 166.

12. Cecil Beaton, *The Wandering Years* (London: Weidenfeld & Nicolson, 1961), pp. 3–6.

13. Table of typical expenses in Cambridge University Student's Handbook 1926–1927; Prince Chula, *The Twain Hve Met, or An Eastern Prince Came West* (London: G. T. Foulis, 1956), p. 132.

14. MacNeice, op. cit., pp. 103–104.

15. "The University of Oxbridge" was the fictional alma mater of the hero of Victorian satirist William Makepeace Thackeray's 1850 autobiographical novel *Pendennis*. Oxbridge became a collective expression for the educational and social status of Britian's two senior universities.

16. Michael Robertson interview, April 1986.

17. Alastair MacDonald interviews, March 1987.

18. Isherwood, op. cit., pp. 20–38.

19. M. H. A. Newman essay on "Mathematics," in Cambridge University Studies (London: Nicholson & Watson, 1930), p. 33. As a scholar, Blunt would have been expected to submit six additional papers in his Part II final-year examination. These papers were the mathematical equivalent of a Jesuit tertianship and eventually became the separate Part III examination. Scholars were expected to devote their first-year time to preparing the easier Part II. [Andrew Hodges, *Alan Turing: An Enigma* (New York: Simon & Schuster, 1983), p. 60.]

20. These papers were also taken by candidates in the Natural Sciences Tripos.

21. MacDonald interviews, op. cit.

22. As quoted in Charles J. Hessian, *John Maynard Keynes* (New York: Macmillan, 1984), p. 38.

23. MacNeice letter, September 25, 1926, KCA; André Chastel, Blunt obituary, *The Burlington Magazine*, September 1983.

24. Ibid.; MacNeice refers to a reading list sent by Anthony, and to Marmeladov (*Crime and Punishment*) as "such a sympathetic charmer."

25. MacNeice, *Strings*, p. 104.

26. MacNeice letter, October 23, 1936, KCA.

27. MacNeice letter, October 3, 1926, KCA. Edward, according to MacDonald, was a boy in his house for whom he "had quite a passion." In an interhouse boxing match MacDonald had "clobbered" Edward and he remembered how "appalled" Blunt had been. Basil, according to MacDonald, was Basil Barr, another Marlborough boyfriend of Anthony's, who was a rather weak individual whom Blunt easily dominated. [Letter paraphrased and other names omitted at the request of the king's archivist because others referred to are still living.]

28. MacNeice letter, December 6, 1926, KCA.

29. Envelope, November 3, bearing message "Laurence Binyon's book on Blake is in the Union Library, but is not allowed to be taken out. M.R." KCA; MacNeice, op. cit., pp. 102, 105.

30. MacNeice letter, January 5, 1927, KCA.

31. MacNeice letter home, February 7, 1927, BO.

32. MacNeice letter, April 6, 1927, KCA.

33. MacNeice letter to Blunt, April 6, 1927, KCA; to mother, May 1927, BO.

34. MacNeice letter home, June 30, 1927, BO.

35. Hilton, "Note."

36. The hypothesis of language being "more relevant" is advanced by Penrose and Freeman, op. cit., p. 53.

37. MacNeice letter, June 14, 1927, KCA. This letter also contains an interesting insight into the homosexual milieu at Marlborough. Relaying the news that their hated housemaster, C. W. Guillebaud, had announced his engagement, MacNeice wrote: "I have decided he was in Love with me, which accounts for his assiduous attention to my personal appearance and his never getting married till I had left — and is also not compatible with his general tastes." MacNeice's aspersions appear confirmed when Guillebaud later broke off his engagement. [MacNeice, *Strings*, p. 264; MacNeice letter to "Dadie & Madre," June 1927, BO.] MacNeice, Blunt, and Hilton then spent several weeks together in London visiting the Russian ballet and the galleries, including the Royal Academy. They originally intended that Anthony would act as their guide for a July trip to Paris before heading for Italy. But it fell through. MacNeice and Hilton's visit to Paris was a disappointment. "The people looked so bourgeois," and instead of galleries overflowing with brightly colored Matisse paintings, they found only "muddy landscapes." [MacNeice, *Strings*, p. 110.]

38. Interviews with Jean and Peter Gimpel, October 1986.

## CHAPTER 7: PAGES 133–155

1. Blunt, "Bloomsbury."

2. MacNeice letters, November 7, 1927; December 31, 1927, KCA.

3. The covering letter asked, "Could you possibly get the Woolfs to read my novel and give me an opinion on it etc.?" MacNeice to Blunt, October 10, 1929, KCA; John Hilton diary entry quoted by MacNeice, *Strings*, p. 267.

4. MacNeice letter, June 8, 1929, KCA; MacNeice to mother, January 19, 1929, BO.

5. MacNeice letter, June 8, 1929, KCA; MacNeice to mother, March 7, 1928, BO; Cambridge University Student's Handbook for 1930–1931.

6. MacNeice letter, May 27, 1929, KCA.

7. As quoted by Wilfrid Blunt, *Single Life*, p. 207.

8. Michael Redgrave, *In My Mind's I: An Actor's Autobiography* (New York: Viking Press, 1983), pp. 60–61.

9. Ibid.

10. *Granta*, March 1, 1929.

11. MacNeice, *The Experiment*; Blunt, "Bloomsbury."

12. Michael Robertson interview; Hilton, "Note."

13. Anthony Blunt, ed., Introduction to *Baroque and Rococo* (New York: Harper & Row, 1978), p. 10.

14. *Rococo*, from French *rocaille*, "shell," strictly applies to decorative form rather than an architectural style. [Osbert Sitwell, *Southern Baroque Art* (London: Chatto & Windus, 1924), p. 56.]

15. Anthony Blunt, "Johann Michel Fischer and the Bavarian Rococo" *The Venture*, 1928, p. 132.

16. Anthony Blunt, ed. *Baroque*, p. 10.

17. Anthony Blunt, "Seurat," *Cambridge Review*, June 1929.

18. *Trinity Review* 1929; Anthony Blunt, "The Italian Exhibition," *Venture*, p. 315.

19. Anthony Blunt, "William Beckford," *Venture*, February 1929, p. 75.

20. John Lehmann, *In the Purely Pagan Sense* (London: GMP Publishers, 1985), p. 7. Although Lehmann asserted this was a "work of fiction," it illuminates many of the gaps in his more circumspect autobiography *The Whispering Gallery* (Philadelphia: West, 1954), p. 216.

21. Blunt, "Bloomsbury"; Professor Richard Braithwaite interview, October 1984.

22. Richard Deacon, author of *The Cambridge Apostles* (London: Robert Royce, 1985), kindly provided partially handwritten lists of members "from a source in Canada." But I am indebted to another senior Apostle with whose help it is now possible to publish, for the first time, an accurate and complete list of the Apostles for the interwar years.

23. Bertrand Russell (Lord Russell of Liverpool), as quoted in Deacon, p. 70, from *The Autobiography of Bertrand Russell*, 2 vols. (London: Allen & Unwin, 1967).

24. "The History of the Society," a paper read to the Apostles in 1985, kindly made available to the author.

25. As quoted in Deacon, p. 59, from Goldsworthy Lowes Dickinson, *The Autobiography of G. Lowes Dickinson and Other Unpublished Writings*, edited by Dennis Proctor, with a foreword by Noël Annan (London: Duckworth, 1973), p. 7. Dennis Proctor, Blunt's apostolic contemporary (and an MI5 suspect), was Dickinson's last undergraduate homosexual romance.

26. As quoted in Deacon, p. 49, from Michael Holroyd, *Lytton Strachey: A Critical Biography*, 2 vols. (London: Heinemann, 1977). Recent evidence of Rupert Brooke's active homosexual experience is in a revealing letter he wrote to James Strachey in July 1912 (in the Berg Collection, New York Public Library) discovered by Professor Paul Delaney and published in his controversial study *The Neo-Pagans* (London: Macmillan, 1987).

27. As quoted in Robert Skidelsky, *John Maynard Keynes* (London: Macmillan, 1986), p. 266.

28. Virginia Woolf, *Roger Fry* (London: Hogarth Press, 1940), p. 112.

29. T. E. B. Howarth, *Cambridge Between Two Wars*, p. 52.

30. As quoted in Deacon, op. cit., p. 98.

31. Russell, op. cit. Blunt's initial sponsor might well have been the former Apostle, or "angel," named Launcelot Charles Rolleston, the son of a Cambridge professor, who taught at Marlborough.

32. Julian Bell, *Essays, Poems and Letters*, edited by Quentin Bell (London: Hogarth Press, 1938), pp. 20–21.

33. Ibid., p. 21; Julian Bell letter to Vanessa Bell, March 14, 1939, Charleston Collection, KCA.

34. Roger Fry, *Exhibition of Flemish Art at Burlington House: A Critical Survey* (London: Chatto & Windus, 1927), p. 35; Anthony Blunt, "Breughel," *The Venture*, No. 5, November 1929, p. 163.

35. Blunt, "Bloomsbury"; "I should like to see your Breughel paper, if possible sometime. I am afraid my own paper will be very bad." MacNeice to Blunt, November 17, 1928, KCA.

36. Lord Annan interviews, April 1987–April 1988.

37. Westminster School Archives, researched by Jasper Wight of Busbys House.

38. Obituary of A. S. F. Gow, *The Times* of London, January 4, 1978.

39. Lord Annan; Gow letter of May 15, 1941; A. S. F. Gow, *Letters from Cambridge* (London: Jonathan Cape, 1945), p. 78.

40. Blunt on Gow, *The Times* of London, January 4, 1978.

41. Hilton, "Note."

42. Robertson interview, op. cit.

43. For a fuller exposition of the connotations of "homosocial," see Ben Pimlott's illuminating study of one of Gow's Cambridge contemporaries in *Hugh Dalton* (London: Macmillan, 1985), pp. 69–70.

44. Noël Annan, "The Cult of Homosexuality" (unpublished manuscript). I am most grateful to Lord Annan for providing a copy of the essay and for his advice on this sensitive subject.

45. Cited in "The Cult of Homosexuality."

46. Ibid.

47. Annan interviews.

48. Ibid.

49. Lehmann, *Pagan Sense*, p. 29. Lehmann's assertion that only one of his Cambridge undergraduate friends "liked older men" and "had yielded to importunities of a famous writer who used to visit Cambridge fairly frequently" appears to be a reference to E. M. Forster. [George Steiner, "The Cleric of Treason," in *The George Steiner Reader* (London: Penguin, 1985), p. 194, and interviews.]

50. Blunt, "Bloomsbury."

51. Julian Bell, op. cit., p. 20.

52. Letter from Julian to Vanessa Bell, March 14, 1929, KCA; Holroyd, op. cit., p. 929. Bell's letters prior to March 1929 expressed concern about his virginal state and afterward document his increasingly tangled heterosexual liaisons with a succession of Girton undergraduates. Lehmann's "gay" autobiography apparently hints at Bell's affair with Blunt: "A friend who had grown very close to me," Lehmann wrote, confessed that he "had agreed to go to bed with a young man who languished for him." The friend is identified only as a "non-Etonian" who was interested in "literary experiments." He "described the episode to me as if it had not been more than an interesting physical experiment and admitted that the physical side had slightly disgusted him." That Lehmann's literary friend "switched his attentions to the other sex and had a succession of mistresses" fits precisely with Julian Bell. [Lehmann, *Pagan Sense*, p. 9.]

53. MacNeice letter, March 18, 1929; inscribed MacNeice volume, KCA.

54. Bell letter, March 14, 1929.

55. John Hilton, Appendix to MacNeice, op. cit., p. 251.

56. Keynes letter to Vanessa Bell, May 24, 1929; Vanessa Bell's notebook on Julian's life, KCA.

57. Virginia Woolf, *The Diary*, Vol. II (New York: Harcourt, Brace Jovanovich, 1980), p. 255; letter, Julian Bell to Vanessa Bell, October 23, 1929, KCA; Lehmann, *Pagan Sense*, p. 29.

58. Peter Stansky and W. Abraham, *Journey to the Frontier: A Biography of Julian Bell and John Cornford* (London: Constable, 1970), pp. 45–47, p. 315.

59. Quentin Bell, Foreword to Julian Bell, *Essays*; Blunt, "Bloomsbury."

60. The senior Bloomsbury members including Fry and Strachey had been regular participants at the annual Pontigny "Decades" held in a former Cistercian abbey in Burgundy. Philosophers and writers from all over Europe gathered in the twenties and thirties for ten days of debate on a "crucial issue of the age" chosen by the organizer Paul Desjardins, a retired professor of classics at Paris University. Pontigny attracted the attention of the Comintern because it offered Marxist intellectuals a useful debating platform. [For accounts of the Pontigny Decades see: Bernard Wall, *Headlong into Change* (London: Harvill Press, 1969), pp. 56–59, and André Maurois, *I Remember, I Remember* (New York: Harper Brothers, 1942), pp. 140–143.] Another Pontigny regular was Prince Dimitrii Svjatopolk-Mirsky, a graduate of St. Petersburg University, who after service in the White Russian Army had been invited to England to become a lecturer in Russian literature and literary criticism at King's College, University of London. A frequenter of the Bloomsbury circles in London and Cambridge, Mirsky was a committee member of the Comintern-sponsored Society for Cultural Relations. He became a Marxist, joining the British Communist party in 1931. In 1932 Mirsky was attacked in the right-wing British press for exploiting his academic position to give militant Communist speeches at universities in support of the Friends of the Soviet Union. [Nina Lavroukine and Leonid Tchertkov, *D. S. Mirsky: Profile Critique et Bibliographique* (Paris: Institut d'Etudes Slaves, 1980).]

61. Ludwig Wittgenstein, *Tractatus Logico-Philosophicus*, quoted in Howarth, op. cit., p. 128.

62. Fanya (Feiga) Pascal, in *Recollections of Wittgenstein*, ed. Norman Malcolm (New York: Oxford University Press, 1984), p. 16; Paul Levy, *G. E. Moore and the Apostles* (London: Weidenfeld & Nicolson, 1979), p. 270; Keynes to Blunt, March 19, 1929, Keynes Papers, KCA.

63. Hilton, Appendix to MacNeice, op. cit., p. 259.

64. "An Epistle on the subject of ethical and aesthetic beliefs of Herr Ludwig Wittgenstein (Doctor of Philosophy) to Richard Braithwaite Esq. MA (Fellow of King's College)." The four pages of barbed couplets in the manner of Dryden's satiric verse in *The Venture* of February 1930, included:

In every company he shouts us down
And stops our sentence stuttering his own
Unceasing argues, harsh, irate and loud
Sure that he's right and of his rightness proud.

Three years later Bell noted that "this satire is not intended as a personal attack . . . but solely as a criticism of certain views on art and morals advocated by him three years ago." [Sherard Vines, ed., *Whips and Scorpions: Specimens of Modern Satiric Verse 1914–1931*, London: 1932.]

65. In the context of Blunt's relations with Julian Bell, it is interesting to note that Blunt kept not a single one of Julian's letters. This is curious. Blunt carefully preserved all MacNeice's correspondence. Perhaps Julian's letters — and those of MacNeice's that Blunt appears to have destroyed — contained the evidence that he was not as politically naïve as he later found it convenient to claim.

66. Lehmann, *The Whispering Gallery*, pp. 137–139. Significantly, it was Eddie Marsh who arranged with Churchill for Brooke's commission in the navy. He it was who wrote the eulogy that made his protégé the heroic sacrificial symbol of Britain's slaughtered youth. The bitter irony was that Brooke did not die in military action on the bloody beaches of the Dardanelles, but succumbed to septicemia caused by a mosquito bite

67. Steiner interviews.


## CHAPTER 8: PAGES 156–170

1. T.E.B. Howarth, *Cambridge Between Two Wars*, p. 146. Dennis Proctor was a member of the Apostles at the same time as Blunt and was also investigated by MI5 as a putative Soviet agent. Like Blunt, he sought to deemphasize the degree of politicization of Cambridge undergraduates of his generation. "Marx had crossed the Channel, but had not reached the Cam . . ." Proctor wrote; "the grim polarity of communism and fascism that haunted our successors had not yet forced its challenge to enroll under some 'student' banner on our attention." [Introduction, *The Autobiography of G. Lowes Dickinson*, edited by Dennis Proctor, p. 24.]

2. Alister Watson, "The Wisdom of Blake," in *The Venture*, Vol. I, p. 5.

3. Ibid., p. 6.

4. Report from Kapitza to chairman of the Committee of Magnetic Research, dated April 16, 1930, Cockcroft Papers (hereafter CKFT) 20/40, Churchill College Archives, Cambridge.

5. Letter from Kapitza to Cockcroft, August 30, 1930, CKFT 20/15. Biographical notes prepared in 1935 by Anna Kapitza as quoted from "Kapitza in Cambridge," *Kapitza, Rutherford and the Kremlin*, p. 17.

6. Arnost Kolman, *We Should Not Have Lived That Way* (New York: Chladize Publications, 1982), pp. 176–177. As quoted on page 18 of Lawrence Badash, *Kapitza*.

7. *The Times*, April 24, 1935.

8. A. M. Biew in *Kapitza: The Story of the British-Trained Scientist Who Invented the Russian Hydrogen Bomb* (London: Frederick Muller, 1956) was the first to claim, incorrectly, that Kapitza "fathered" the Soviet thermonuclear weapon. "Practically every detail which can be checked is wrong," Sir John Cockcroft wrote dismissively of this theory. "This book does not even qualify as science fiction." [Review in *Nature*, Vol. 175, February 23, 1957.] Twenty years later one of Kapitza's students, Professor David Shoenberg, criticized a similar claim made by Andrew Sinclair in *The Red and the Blue: Cambridge, Treason and Intelligence* (Boston: Little, Brown, 1986). "It is ludicrous to suggest the competence to build a Russian bomb was

brought from Cambridge to Moscow by Kapitza," Shoenberg wrote in a letter to *The Washington Post* published on April 29, 1987. In it Shoenberg pointed out that Kapitza's field was not nuclear physics but low-temperature physics. The nuclear-fission experiments that led to the atomic bomb were not performed by Cockcroft and Walton in Cambridge but by Hahn and Strassmann in Berlin more than four years *after* Kapitza's unplanned departure. Yet while Shoenberg and Kapitza's defenders are correct to point out that there is no *direct connection* between his low-temperature work and the bomb, they overlook the impetus his laboratory gave to Soviet scientific research and the crucial *indirect* contribution of technical expertise. Kapitza and Landau were awarded Nobel prizes. Many of those who worked for Kapitza at his Center for Physics Problems in Moscow certainly *did* go on to play a leading role in the nuclear research effort that eventually led to development — accelerated by wartime espionage of the Manhattan Project — of the Russian atomic and hydrogen bombs. Nor is it essential that Kapitza be a full-fledged GRU agent to contend that he could have been exploited by the Soviet scientific espionage operation. He was always fiercely proud of his Russian patriotism and during the war made strenuous efforts to persuade nuclear physicists exiled by the Nazis to seek refuge in the Soviet Union.

9. *Pravda*, June 14, 1935, quoted in report #248/5/75 from British embassy, Moscow, of same date, FO 371/19470 N 3170, PRO.

10. Harrison Salisbury, ed. *The Soviet Union: The Fifty Years* (New York: Harcourt Brace & World, 1967), p. 12; Jack L. Turck, "George Gamow: A Memorial Essay," in *Cosmology, Fusion and Other Matters* (Boulder, Colo.: Colorado Associated University Press, 1977), p. 192.

11. George Gamow, *My World Line* (New York: Viking, 1970).

12. Interviews with Dr. Arnold Kramish, 1986–88. The contribution that Cockcroft and Walton made in 1932 was to demonstrate that atoms of lithium could be split. Their experiment actually required the input of energy from the bombarding protons (stripped hydrogen atoms) produced by their accelerator. Not until seven years later did Otto Hahn and Fritz Strassmann in Berlin succeed in splitting uranium atoms with relatively slow-moving, low-energy neutrons. This demonstrated nuclear fission and opened up the theoretical possibility of the release of tremendous amounts of energy for war and peace.

13. Kapitza Club notebook, CKFT 7/2, CCA.

14. Kapitza Club records, ibid.; Howarth, op. cit., p. 191.

15. Neil Wood, *Communism and the British Intellectuals* (London: Gollancz, 1959), p. 120, "The Utopians of Science."

16. Charlotte Haldane, *The Truth Will Out* (London: Weidenfeld & Nicolson, 1949), pp. 25–60.

17. Wood, op. cit., p. 65.

18. Julian Huxley, *If I Were a Dictator* (London: Methuen, 1934), pp. 16–19; Wood, op. cit., p. 120; records of the Cambridge branch of the USW in the archives of Warwick University.

19. Bukharin's visa application reveals no such accreditation. He was designated as a "Fellow of the Academy of Sciences USSR and Head of the Research Department of the Supreme Council of National Economy." Bukharin File in HO 45/14449, PRO; N. Bukharin, Foreword to *Science at the Crossroads* (London: Kniga Ltd., 1929).

20. As quoted in thesis of Dr. Kay MacLeod, "Politics, Professionalization and the Organization of Scientists: The Association of Scientific Workers 1917–1942," University of Sussex thesis.

21. Metropolitan Police Special Branch letter, Miller to Scott, SB 320/Frs/2344, July 10, 1931, enclosing Intercept Great Northern Telegraph Co., July 5, 1931, to Press Tass Moscow, Bukharin File, HO 45/14449, PRO.

22. Lord Stanfordham to Balfour, report of September 1, 1925, Balfour Papers, as quoted in Kenneth Rose, *King George V* (London: Weidenfeld & Nicolson, 1983), p. 369. It is significant that three months before his death in May 1988, Kim Philby, in his first — and as it turned out last — "official" interview with a Western journalist assigned a key role in his recruitment to Maurice Dobb. The KGB obviously authorized the interview with Phillip Knightley, formerly of the London *Sunday Times*, who had been in correspondence with the exiled spy ever since he helped co-author the celebrated book on Philby in 1968. As might be expected of such a controlled encounter, no fresh insights emerged other than Philby's assertion that it was Maurice Dobb who steered him, not to the CPGB, but to a Communist group in Paris. This first step in his recruitment as a Soviet spy, Philby said, was taken after he sought out Dobb on his visit to Cambridge after his return from Vienna in the late spring of 1934. As the Soviet Union's most public and notorious spokesman at Cambridge, Dobb — who MI5 records show was under Special Branch surveillance — could *not* have been Moscow's sinister mastermind behind the Cambridge recruiting.

    What was headlined as Philby's final unraveling of the mystery appears more likely to have been nothing more nor less than a carefully orchestrated scheme by the KGB to use the old spy to lay yet another false trail away from the truth. [Interview with Philby by Phillip Knightley, *The Sunday Times*, March 23, 1988.]

23. Secret memorandum, "The Society for Cultural Relations," compiled by MI5 and Special Branch and passed to the U.S. embassy, London, in 1929, US Emb Lon 800 B, RG 84 NA.

24. Ibid.

25. Report, *The Times* of London, September 11, 1925.

26. Münzenberg to Montagu, October 21, 1927, HO 45/24871, PRO.

27. Letter written by Anatoli Lunarchevsky, first people's commissar for enlightenment, dated January 9, 1925, as quoted by Jay Leda, *Kino: A History of the Russian and Soviet Cinema* (London: 1960), p. 161.

28. "Notes for conversation with Mr. Brock Wilkinson," HO 45/24871, PRO.

29. Letter to Captain Miller (MI5) dated March 30, 1928; censorship list and memorandum dated July 19, 1929, HO 45/24871, PRO.

30. Ibid.

31. Ibid. Intercepted letter, Münzenberg to Burns, February 18, 1929, and Secret covering letter from MI5 dated February 22; SZ/5362, Personal and Confidential, dated November 22, 1929, HO 45/24871, PRO.

32. Ibid.

33. Intercepted letter, Dobb to Montagu, July 10, 1929, HO 45/24781/495308/57, PRO.

34. Intercepted letter, Dobb to Montagu, July 16, 1929; Miller to Scott, February 22, 1929; ibid.

35. Christopher Andrew, *Secret Service: The Making of the British Intelligence Community* (London: Heinemann, 1985), pp. 335–337.

36. Philip Spratt, *Blowing Up India* (Calcutta: 1955); and information from Felix Cowgill, who was in the Indian Police Service.

## CHAPTER 9: PAGES 171–184

1. MI5 and memorandum headed VOKS (All-Union Society for the Promotion of Cultural Relations with Countries Abroad) with a short note on the Friends of Soviet Russia organization, US Emb Lon 800 B, 1929, RG 84 NA.

2. Confidential State Department memorandum dated April 17, 1931, US Emb Lon 800 B, RG 84 NA. Liddell also spotted that Kreitz's address book contained a list of the ice-skating clubs in New York. This led him to believe Kreitz was a member of the same network as Albert Firebrand, a known Comintern agent employed as an instructor at the London Ice Club, who had made "a very rapid disappearance" from England in 1929. [Liddell to Atherton, May 10, 1931, ibid.]

3. Vernon Kell to Borum, April 8, 1932. US Emb Lon 800 B, RG 84 NA.

4. Krivitsky testimony, Vol. 9, "Hearings Before a Special Committee on Un-American Activities," House of Representatives, 76th Congress, September 1939, p. 5720 – "Investigation of Un-American Propaganda Activities in the United States."

5. See entry details and obituary notice on "Oldham, Ernest H.," in Foreign Officers List, HMSO, London, 1930. For a detailed examination of the Oldham case (dealt with under the pseudonym Scott because of official censorship), see Corson and Crowley, *The New KGB*, pp. 144–168. Declassified information from the reports of the U.S. military attaché in Paris reported on the unidentified British spy mentioned during debriefings of Grigoriy Bessedovsky. He was the chargé d'affaires of the Soviet embassy in Paris who defected in Paris in 1929. The British walk-in had initially been turned out of the embassy by the strong-armed Major Vladimir Voynovich, the embassy's senior OGPU officer. Voynovich had failed to keep the Englishman under surveillance. So when orders came from Moscow to cultivate such a valuable informant, the Paris OGPU agents discovered that their walk-in had only been visiting Paris with a British Foreign Office delegation. Weeks of patient detective work by a Soviet illegal sent to Britain from The Hague were required before this potentially valuable source was tracked down and brought under control. Oldham's controller has been identified on reliable authority as Hans Galleni, an OGPU illegal who traveled back and forth across the Channel posing as a Dutch art-materials supplier. He and his associate, Hans Pieck, proved skillful agent-runners because they also managed to involve Oldham's colleague, John Henry King, in the espionage network.

6. *The Times* obituary section, September 30, 1933.

7. See Arthur Koestler, *Darkness at Noon* (New York: Bantam, 1970), p. 68, for quote; see Corson, *KGB:* If Mrs. Oldham's death was indeed "arranged" by the Soviets to prevent her in 1945 from meeting Pieck and making the identification of Galleni, this could be attributed to the leak of Pieck's visit from the high-level MI5 mole.

8. Details of Pestrovsky's Byzantine CPGB maneuvers are given in L. J. MacFarlane, *The British Communist Party*, pp. 206–241.

9. For example, see the Secret and Personal correspondence of May 1929 regarding

Sir Edward Brotherton's donation of $100,000 to Ashridge (Conservative College) and subsequent recommendation for a peerage. [Davidson Papers, House of Lords Records Office.]

10. Robert Rhodes James, *Memoirs of a Conservative* (London: Macmillan, 1970), pp. 280–281. "Davidson's strategy had a brilliant simplicity. He introduced what was in effect a spy into the Gregory organization, whose task it was to obtain the list of Gregory's clients. Davidson then saw to it that no one on that list obtained any honor or award of any kind."

11. Ibid.

12. Information supplied by Natalie Wraga from her extensive files of contemporary White Russian records including the Paris émigré newspaper *Vozrozhdeniye*. The April and September 1930 editions and the Melgumov Archive 18/103, p. 2, state that Vladimir Petrovich Bogovout Kolomitzev "is a Soviet agent" of the OGPU and a partner in the "three B's" (Bogovout, Bessedovsky, Bogomelets). Although Bogovout Kolomitzev became one of the White Russians in Paris who openly espoused Soviet sympathy, he served as a Gestapo informer in World War II.

13. Richard Deacon in *The British Connection* (London: Hamish Hamilton, 1979), pp. 66–67, cites as his source "Roger," the former Soviet agent who operated in the Swiss network based in Geneva. Although "Roger" is now dead, Deacon considers it would be inadvisable to disclose his identity. But he did kindly provide coded entries (preceded by Pigou's signature, which appears genuine to those who know it) from the diaries. They do indeed confirm that they are based on a nine-cell key in which the letters of the alphabet are disposed in groups of three. Deacon has translated them to prove, to his satisfaction, that in August 1905 the rising young welfare economist and King's College fellow opened up a line to prominent Bolshevik revolutionaries in exile. Identified are Piatnitsky and "Josef Georgi," an alias used by Stalin when he was on the run from the Okhrana. Deacon, moreover, asserts from his decoding that after World War I, Pigou — then an economist of repute and part-time adviser to the British government on foreign exchanges — was also advising Theodore Rothenstein, the Comintern chief who was Moscow's ex-officio representative until he was expelled. Pigou was never openly involved with pro-Soviet groups, but his secret Russian connections were apparently suspected by the Special Branch Commissioner Basil Thompson. Information received from a confidential source confirms that Pigou was indeed "looked into" by the Fluency Committee, but according to a former very senior officer of MI6, nothing positive surfaced. The evidences of Pigou's involvement may be "circumstantial," as the source claimed, but it is intriguing that they were unknown to MI5 until the sixties. Deacon also told me that corroboration for his contention that Pigou — who sponsored Keynes at the beginning of his career — was a longtime secret supporter of the Soviet Union came from the noted economist Professor F. A. von Hayek.

14. Ibid.

15. Papers of J. C. C. Davidson, Beaverbrook Collection, House of Lords Records Office.

16. "Nobody knew to what extent Maundy Gregory would betray his past in desperation and financial stringency. We accordingly organized someone to go and see him, who told him that he couldn't avoid a term of imprisonment, but that if he kept silent we could bring pressure to bear on the authorities to let him live in France after his sentence had been served...." James, op. cit., p. 288. See also Gerald MacMillan, *Honours for Sale* (London: The Richards Press, 1954), p. 20. "When the summons under the Honours Act was issued he [Gregory] was offered a pension

of 1,000 pounds from the funds of one party, if he would plead guilty and then go abroad and stay there, and that Gregory held out for 3,000 pounds and got it."

17. Pestrovsky–Bennet's career ended when he was denounced on the streets of Moscow in 1930 by a Ukrainian worker who recognized, then exposed him as a former follower of the Ukrainian Menshevik leader of Petliuria who had been responsible in 1918 for the arrest of hundreds of Bolsheviks. ["Ypsilon," *Pattern of World Revolution* (New York: Ziff Davis, 1947), p. 233.]

18. "Internal Security of HM Forces During 1939," WO 32/3948 110/Gen/4399, PRO.

19. The amalgamation is reflected in the change of address on the intelligence com- munications supplied the U.S. embassy from "Metropolitan Police, Special Branch, Scotland House, London S.W.1," to "Oliver House, 35 Cromwell Road, South Kensington S.W.7" embossed with a half-inch-high SECRET. ["Security Intelli- gence in War" by Captain Eric Holt-Wilson, with attached note by Kell. Imperial War Museum, London.]

20. Report on Bessedovsky information sent to State Department by U.S. military attaché, Riga, Latvia, November 15, 1930, x-1 2037-1552, RG 165 NA.

21. Alexander Orlov, *Handbook of Intelligence and Guerrilla Warfar* (Ann Arbor: The University of Michigan Press, 1965). Orlov – or Leon Lazerevik Felbin – started his career as the brilliant Jewish law student Leon Felbin. He became a Bolshevik in 1917 under the name Lev Lazarevich Nikolsky. Joining the Red Army as an officer, he had come to the attention of Dzerzhinski in 1920 at the age of twenty-five for his counterintelligence work in Poland. After a brief spell as an assistant prosecutor of the Supreme Court, Felbin served in the economic directorate before becoming OGPU *resident* in France. After a spell as the intelligence chief in Berlin in 1928, attached to the Trade Delegation, Alexander Orlov, as he now called himself, returned to OGPU headquarters in Moscow in 1931 to head its economic- intelligence directorate. He served on the committee that evaluated the secret reports of the Foreign Department's spy rings in Europe, wrote a training manual for spies, and served as director of the counterintelligence section of the Central Military School until 1936. He was dispatched to head up Soviet undercover operations in Spain, whence he defected two years later after receiving a peremptory recall to Russia that he feared was a death warrant.

Orlov reached the United States by way of France and Canada. With his wife, he contrived to escape the notice of the U.S. authorities. He remained in seclusion for fifteen years in Cleveland, frequently changing names and residences, fearful that registering or taking a job would invite the long arm of Soviet retribution. On Stalin's death in 1953, Orlov surfaced and sold his story for $44,000 to *Life* magazine as a series of articles titled "The Ghastly Secrets of Stalin's Power."

The publicity brought Orlov to the attention of J. Edgar Hoover, and the FBI carried out an investigation of this top Soviet defector, followed by the CIA. He was rated one of the highest-ranking Soviet officers ever to defect and was debriefed extensively. Orlov provided valuable secret testimony about Soviet spy rings in the United States to the U.S. Senate Internal Security Subcommittee. Ten years before his death in 1973, Orlov authored a version of his personal experiences of Soviet intelligence methods and operations under the title *Handbook of Intelligence and Guerrilla Warfare*.

[For more background on Orlov/Felbin, see Corson, *The New KGB*, and also congressional record of the testimony of Alexander Orlov before the U.S. Senate Internal Security Subcommittee of the Judiciary Committee, September 1955 and February 1957.]

22. Ibid.

23. Ibid. Officially, Soviet agents abroad were subordinate to the senior diplomatic representative. But it was a measure of the Foreign Division's authority that by 1930 these agents overrode the diplomats because the OGPU was controlled by Stalin's subordinates on the Political Bureau of the Central Committee of the Communist party. The Secret Division worked against political parties opposed to the Soviet government, penetrated the White Russian organizations, and countered revisionists within the local Communist parties. Real or imagined reports of failure in the field fueled Stalin's paranoia about traitors. When he began his purges and show trials in the mid-thirties, the OGPU *rezidentury* were frequent targets of irrational suspicion because they were living abroad and subject to daily temptations to defect. Even minor failures to carry out Moscow Center's orders could lead to recall and a bullet in the back of the neck in the execution cells of the Lubianka prison. Fear became a powerful incentive to perform missions to the letter. But interdepartmental rivalries surfaced in 1929 when the OGPU initiated an industrial-intelligence operation that was intended to help accelerate the industrialization of the Soviet Union by stealing production secrets and new technological processes. This new function quickly led to friction with the Red Army whose Fourth Division of Military Intelligence had considered itself responsible for collecting its own information, especially on technical and military areas.

24. Orlov, op. cit., p. 10.

25. Ibid., pp. 108–110.

26. Ibid.

27. Ibid., p. 109.

28. Blunt's statement, November 29, 1979; H. A. R. Philby, *My Silent War* (New York: Grove Press, 1968), p. 14.

29. Orlov, op. cit., p. 119.

## CHAPTER 10: PAGES 185–199

1. Transcript of press conference published in *The Times* of London, November 21, 1979. The lack of specificity is very evident from his choice of words and quite deliberate since it was in response to the first question asked and one, moreover, which Blunt would have anticipated. His "1935–36" is therefore a significant fudge. So is the "let us say" which was not recorded in all the published accounts.

2. George Steiner, "The Cleric of Treason," p. 197.

3. George Steiner interview.

4. Lord Noël Annan's review of Andrew Boyle's *The Climate of Treason* in *The Times Literary Supplement*, December 7, 1979.

5. Lord Annan interviews, 1987–1988.

6. Ibid.

7. The full text of the relevant paragraph is: "We talk endlessly in the Society about Communism which is rather dull. Guy [Burgess] and Alister [Watson] and Richard [Llewelyn-]Davies speak with shining eyes and sweating foreheads about this all pervading topic, vehemently but somewhat illogically, it seems to me. (I believe I have discovered a fallacy in the whole racket; no doubt you could tell me a hundred.)

Hugh Sykes Davies prates endlessly about Sadism and Swinburne which I believe is due to the new Italian book; while Gray Walter and I content ourselves with obscure jokes about electric currents. The fact is an atmosphere of decadence is appearing and we need your presence . . . Yours ever, Victor R." [Rothschild to Keynes, undated, Keynes Papers, KCA.]

Although the letter is undated, it contains references to Rothschild's recent marriage to Barbara Hutchinson, placing it sometime in 1933, a year confirmed by the reference to the American biologist Apostle at King's, W. Gray Walter, who, Annan recalls, was preoccupied with the application of Marxism to science. Walter was elected in November 1933, suggesting that the letter can be dated in late 1933 or early 1934.

8. Roy Harrod, *John Maynard Keynes* (London: Macmillan, 1951), pp. 450–451.

9. Annan interviews.

10. Ibid.; Apostle's paper, "The History of the Society," 1985.

11. The King's College Register, December, 1988; information provided by Professor H. S. Ferns in a letter of July 30, 1987; L. P. Wilkinson, *A Century of Kingsmen* (Cambridge: King's College Provost & Fellows, 1980), pp. 193–194.

12. Obituary notice in King's College annual report, October 1983.

13. The King's College Register does not appear to have been consulted by MI5's self-appointed mole hunter Peter Wright — or his ghostwriter Paul Greengrass — who also happens to be a Cambridge graduate. *Spycatcher* on page 252 asserts that "Watson was a failure. He failed to gain a fellowship and took a job with the Admiralty." It is difficult to accept that MI5 Registry records would be incorrect about Watson, who was a King's fellow from 1933 to the outbreak of World War II in 1939.

14. The tipoff about Watson's communism came, as Wright reveals, in a 1951 (Chapman Pincher says Wright told him that it was 1956) letter that Lord Victor Rothschild sent to Sir Dick White, then head of B Division. Rothschild could attest to Watson's Marxist convictions because he had himself become an Apostle in 1932. When Wright found this reference in Watson's file in 1966, he was surprised not only that Rothschild's warning had been ignored, but that Watson had subsequently passed three high-level security vettings!

MI5 inquiries soon revealed by 1967 that Watson's wife and daughter were "current Communists" and in all probability so was Alister himself, although he had repeatedly concealed it during his security vettings. But because Watson was shortly due to leave for the United States to attend a briefing on the latest American antisubmarine-detection technology, the Admiralty pressured MI5 on the case. For six weeks, in 1967, Watson reported to the Ministry of Defense, where he was questioned by Patrick Stewart, the head of MI5's D1 Investigation Division. He would admit only that he knew Burgess and Blunt as Cambridge friends. But in the course of his questioning, he admitted several meetings with a mysterious Central European named "Otto," with slicked-down dark hair, because he "wanted to find out more about Russia." Nevertheless, Watson refused to confess he had spied for the Soviets even though he picked out from the MI5 photo file three KGB officers he had met on various occasions who were known by MI5 to be spy-runners. Through microphones MI5 surreptitiously secreted in the phones at his home, the suspect could be heard telling himself, "They've got something, but I don't know what it is. . . ." Six weeks later, punch-drunk and increasingly incoherent, Watson still would not change his story.

Wright and Patrick Stewart, the interrogating officer, remained convinced their subject was lying. Why should anyone in Watson's position at the head of a top-secret defense laboratory risk so many meetings with strange contacts who were obviously Soviet agents? Watson dismissed them as "too bourgeois" because one turned up in a blazer and walking a poodle. This information tallied with Soviet defector Anatoli Golitsin's revelation that a Sergei Kondrashev, who was running two top-level Admiralty spies, was recalled by Moscow because one of the British spies had taken strong exception to him.

When Watson disregarded an immunity deal in return for his confession, Stewart and Wright arranged for a session with Blunt at Brown's Hotel in the hope that this would persuade Watson to change his mind. After the old Apostles downed a bottle of Scotch and one of gin, Watson ignored the assurances about immunity and launched into a maudlin condemnation of Blunt, who continued to insist he had never recruited Watson.

In the absence of a confession from Watson, nothing could be done but take away his security clearance. He sustained a remarkable intellectual vitality to the end of his life, greeting an old friend at the 1981 King's College reunion dinner with a "proposition in four-dimensional geometry, a point about the structure of *Paradise Lost* and a surmise about the languages of Egypt." A year later Watson died from multiple strokes. [Wright, op. cit., pp. 252–257, and Watson's obituary in King's College Annual Register, October 1983.]

15. Llewelyn-Davies's obituary, *The Times*, October 28, 1981.

16. "Miss Margaret Llewelyn-Davies was elected Chairman of the Provisional Committee," Secret MI5 report on the SCR, dated January 23, 1926, HO 45/24861, PRO.

17. Watson obituary, op. cit.; reply to Professor Oakeshott in *Cambridge Review*, March 1934.

18. Wright, *Spycatcher*, p. 253.

19. Gide's search for an alternative to a Christian Utopia led him to make his declaration for Marxism at the 1935 Congress of Revolutionary Writers in Paris. For a detailed exposition of the philosophic impact of communism on the French intellectuals, see Raymond Aron, *The Opium of the Intellectuals* (New York: Doubleday, 1957), pp. 210–211.

20. Annan interviews.

21. Richard Deacon, *Apostles*, p. 127.

22. Sir Isaiah Berlin, on the authority of Sir Stuart Hampshire, announced in public that Llewelyn-Davies was a Communist. He was rebuffed by Lady Teresa Rothschild, who denied that her friend Richard Llewelyn-Davies was ever a member of the party. Information provided the author by confidential sources.

23. Confidential sources.

24. Ibid.

25. Sykes Davies, as quoted by Deacon, *Apostles*, p. 125.

26. The open-necked shirt worn by Alister Watson, and the fact that Llewelyn-Davies was elected at the end of April, indicate the picture was taken sometime in the 1932 summer term and certainly before the election of Burgess and Rothschild that November.

27. Letter from Earl Baldwin of Bewdley, dated August 1, 1962, to "Little" (Lady Davidson), Davidson Papers, House of Lords Records Office.

28. When MI5 spycatcher Peter Wright reopened the investigation on the Cambridge

Comintern after Blunt's confession, his suspicions were aroused by Proctor's sudden decision to leave the country in 1951 at the time of Burgess's and Maclean's defections. Proctor did not deny his friendship with Burgess, among whose abandoned papers had been found a Treasury report in Proctor's handwriting. He had "the classic Cambridge Comintern recruits' profile," and was identified to Wright as a "notable left-winger" by a dozen of his Oxbridge contemporaries. Proctor admitted he was "left-wing all my life," but denied he was ever a Communist or Soviet agent, when Wright journeyed to France in 1966 to interrogate him at his retirement home at Avignon. Proctor insisted that Burgess's defection had nothing to do with his equally abrupt decision to leave London for Copenhagen in 1951. Proctor explained — not very convincingly, according to Wright — that this had to do with the suicide of his first wife, Varda, which happened the same year. Wright remained convinced that Proctor had not told him the whole truth. He also discovered that Flora Solomon, the left-wing Russian émigré who befriended Kim Philby, played a more involved role than conceded in her autobiography. She advised Philby on potential recruits, although she protested that she herself did not join the Soviet conspiracy. Solomon conceded that after a dinner with Proctor, she had told Philby his left-wing Cambridge friend "had no backbone" and would not stand up under interrogation. Since Proctor did not confess to any illegal activity and gave no confession, no case could be made against him even though there was a strong circumstantial presumption of this model civil servant's underlying guilt. [Wright, op. cit., pp. 261–264; Flora Solomon and Barry Litvinoff, *A Woman's Way* (New York: Simon & Schuster, 1984), pp. 210–211, 215–216; supplemented by confidential informant.]

29. An indication of just how close Blunt and Pascal were was provided by Harry S. Ferns, emeritus professor of political science at Birmingham University. He said that Pascal shared an interest in art that he cultivated with Blunt's Marlborough friend Ellis Waterhouse, who became Barber Professor of Fine Arts in Birmingham from 1952 to 1970. Pascal also told Ferns that when Blunt was director of the Courtauld Institute, he had waived the academic admission rules in favor of the "completely unqualified" son of a close friend. [Harry S. Ferns interviews, 1986–1988.] Additional information via Ferns came from Professor R. F. Willerts (emeritus professor of Greek at Birmingham University), a protégé of Thompson's and himself a member of the CPGB. According to Willerts, Pascal "*did* convert George Thompson to Marxism and Communism *after* Thompson returned to Cambridge." This was also confirmed by Thompson's daughter, Dr. Margaret B. Alexion, professor of Greek at Harvard University. [Letter from Ferns, July 30, 1987.]

30. Annan interview.

31. Ferns interviews.

32. Norman Malcolm, ed., *Recollections of Wittgenstein*, essay by Fanya Pascal, p. 36.

33. Richard Deacon, *The British Connection*, p. 74.

34. T. E. B. Howarth, *Cambridge Between Two Wars*, p. 198.

35. Ferns interviews.

36. Ibid. Harry S. Ferns, *Reading from Left to Right: One Man's Political History* (Toronto: University of Toronto Press, 1983), p. 222.

37. Ibid.

## CHAPTER 11: PAGES 200–218

1. Secret report from First Secretary, U.S. Embassy, London, "Transmission of Biographical Letter re H. St. John Philby," prepared by the British Foreign Office, July 7, 1948, State Dept. Decimal File 111 20A/7-748 RG NA.

2. H. A. R. Philby, *My Silent War*; quoted in Andrew Boyle, *Climate of Treason*.

3. Harry St. John Philby had graduated from Trinity in 1907, Robertson in 1908; Goronwy Rees to Andrew Boyle.

4. Philby, op. cit.

5. Boyle, op. cit., p. 85, cited to a "confidential source."

6. David Armstrong Hedley, Burgess's Eton contemporary, went up to King's College, where Margot Heineman met him. She told Penrose and Freeman (*Conspiracy of Silence*, p. 100) that she fell in love with him, the relationship ending only when she met and began her affair with the charismatic Communist John Cornford. Hedley's family belonged to the King's intellectual aristocracy and he combined ardent communism with his academic studies. He demonstrated his brilliance by establishing his reputation as the top classicist of his year, taking a first in the tripos, the Browne Medal in 1932, and the Craven Scholarship in 1933. He then took a first in English in 1934 and was invited to become a Henry Fellow at Yale in 1934–1935. In New Haven — and later in San Francisco, where he became head of the California Labor School — Hedley played a leading part in the Communist International organization, rising to become secretary and head of its California chapter. Until 1948, according to the King's Register, Hedley "was still organizing communist cells in California when he died at the age of 37." While no evidence has come to light that Hedley was ever involved in Blunt's clandestine network, as an open campaigner for Moscow, Hedley must nonetheless be regarded as another of Stalin's Englishmen, who exported the Communist Revolution from Cambridge to the New World. [*A Century of Kingsmen*, p. 254.]

7. Goronwy Rees, *A Chaper of Accidents* (London: Chatto & Windus, 1972), p. 133.

8. The firsthand account Burgess gave to Tom Driberg in Moscow in 1956 discusses the relatively lengthy process of Burgess's own conversion. Driberg, then a prominent Labour M.P. and journalist (despite his Oxford communism and homosexuality), is now known to have been a Soviet agent. There seems no reason to doubt his detailed account of his friend Burgess's political enlightenment. The account was given firsthand by Burgess, six years before Blunt's secret confession. So there was at the time no need to serve Moscow's interest by developing a false cover story that was later to prove so much at odds with Blunt's account. Burgess told Driberg that "his interest in politics began to grow in his last year at Eton." He insisted, however, he "led the ordinary life of an Old Etonian undergraduate" during his first year at Cambridge. Jimmy Lees, a member of Dobb's and Pascal's Communist cell, a member of the Independent Labour party, and an "innocent and conscientious ex-miner from Nottingham," introduced Burgess to David Haden-Guest, an undergraduate Communist organizer, who persuaded Burgess to join the Anti-War Movement. Membership in this front organization led Burgess, after a discussion by Klugmann, to "his actual decision to join the Communist Party." He said he took this "intellectual and theoretical" decision after reading *The State and Revolution*, which confirmed his own elemental Marxist views. Helping organize a strike by Trinity waiters, a rent protest by council-house tenants,

the 1934 Hunger March and a trip that summer to Russia reinforced Burgess's Communist convictions. [Tom Driberg, *Guy Burgess: A Portrait with Background* (London: Weidenfeld & Nicolson, 1956), pp. 13–21.] In contrast to Blunt's later self-serving vagueness about precisely when his friend Burgess had persuaded him to make his "overnight" conversion to the Communist cause, Burgess makes no suggestion of a leap into communism. This process may not even have been completed until the end of 1931, or early 1932, when Burgess was in his third year. This timetable makes it yet more unlikely that Burgess could have become a full-fledged and trusted Soviet recruiter by 1934 on his return from Russia.

9. Ibid.; interviews with James Klugmann; Boyle, op. cit., p. 52.

10. Boyle, op. cit., p. 109; information supplied to Robert Cecil by Lord Thurlow, a Trinity contemporary. He recalled how Burgess hustled him out of his rooms to be alone with Maclean in circumstances that left Thurlow with no doubt that the seduction was consummated.

11. Ibid.

12. Boyle, op. cit.

13. Philby, op. cit., p. 15.

14. Driberg, *Portrait*, p. 20; Minute Book of Trinity Historical Society, Trinity College Archives.

15. Cyril Connolly, *The Missing Diplomats* (London: Queen Anne Press, 1952), p. 18; interviews with Jackie Hewit, friend and sometime homosexual lover of Guy Burgess, July 1985 and April 1988.

16. Blunt, "Bloomsbury."

17. Noël Annan, review of *The Climate of Treason*, *Times Literary Supplement*, December 7, 1979, and interviews.

18. Information supplied to Andrew Boyle by Charles Madge [Boyle, op. cit., p. 81]. The following May, after he had penned what was to become the celebrated invocational poem: "Lenin, would you were living at this hour/England has need of you . . . ," he abandoned Cambridge. But it was romance, not politics, that precipitated his elopement with poetess Kathleen Raine, the Marxist wife of Hugh Sykes Davies, the Communist Apostle. [Article by Charles Madge in "Viewpoint," *Times Literary Supplement*, September 14, 1979; Boyle, op. cit., p. 87, cited as information obtained from Robert Birley.]

19. Victor Rothschild letter to Keynes, 1933, Keynes Papers, op. cit., KCA.

20. Virginia Cowles, *The Rothschilds: A Family of Fortune* (London: Weidenfeld & Nicolson, 1979), p. 216; Victor Rothschild, *Meditations on a Broomstick* (London: Collins, 1977), p. 13.

21. Victor Rothschild, *Random Variables* (London: Collins, 1981), pp. 203–205; Rothschild, *Meditations*, p. 16.

22. Ibid., p. 17; ibid., p. 18.

23. Rothschild, *Variables*, p. 204.

24. Alastair MacDonald interviews; Rothschild, *Variables*, p. 205.

25. Boyle, op. cit., pp. 96–97.

26. Rothschild, *Variables*, p. 205.

27. Miriam Rothschild as quoted by Boyle, op. cit., p. 97.

28. Burgess, "Scamp into Scoundrel," *Times Literary Supplement*, 1972 (the review of Rees's *A Chapter of Accidents* was published anonymously in keeping with the then practice of the TLS). Lord Annan has confirmed he was the author; Driberg, *Portrait*, p. 15; information supplied to Andrew Boyle by Miriam Rothschild [see Boyle, op. cit., p. 120]. According to Driberg this was because of the appearance of a rival work by Professor Basil Wiley, *The Seventeenth Century Background*, which appeared in March 1934 and which Burgess reviewed for *The Spectator*. His attempt to switch to a Marxist interpretation for the Indian Mutiny was abandoned after his trip to Russia in the summer of 1934 [Driberg, *Portrait*, pp. 16–17].

29. Connolly, op. cit.

30. Interview with Lady Mary Dunn, September 1987.

31. Ibid.

32. Ibid.

33. Ibid.

34. MacNeice letter to Blunt, May 11, 1931, KCA.

35. Information was provided by three reliable sources but could not be confirmed because the two former female Cambridge undergraduates he named are still alive and, understandably, declined to comment.

36. Interviews with Robert T. Crowley and information supplied by other former CIA Soviet case officers.

37. Leonard Woolf, *Downhill All the Way* (London: Hogarth Press, 1967), p. 18.

38. Alexander Orlov, *Handbook of Intelligence*.

39. Hugh Thomas, *John Strachey* (London: Eyre Methuen, 1973), pp. 5–17; John Strachey, *The Coming Struggle for Power*, 1932.

40. Unlike so many others in the 1930 wave of Communist recruits, "Bugsy" Wolfe was neither at Trinity nor a liberal-arts scholar. He was a biologist and protégé of J. B. S. Haldane, the Marxist biochemistry professor. Haldane declined to openly join the Cambridge party itself, but he openly supported Dobb and Pascal. Wolfe was remembered as an "impassioned Communist" by Haldane's wife, who admitted seventeen years later that "it was he who first indoctrinated me with Marxist theory." [Charlotte Haldane, *The Truth Will Out*, p. 54]; Boyle: Information supplied by Professor Leonard Foster.

## CHAPTER 12: PAGES 219–229

1. Blunt, press conference, *The Times*, November 21, 1979.

2. Ibid.

3. Andrew Boyle as quoted in the *Daily Express*, November 21, 1979.

4. Interviews with Boyle, 1984–1988.

5. Goronwy Rees quoted by Boyle in *The Observer*, January 13, 1980.

6. Goronwy Rees, *A Chapter of Accidents*, p. 71.

7. Interviews with A. L. Rowse, 1984; A. L. Rowse, *A Cornishman at Oxford* (London: Jonathan Cape, 1965), p. 55.

8. A. J. P. Taylor, *A Personal History* (London: Hamish Hamilton, 1983), p. 78.

9. Rees, op. cit., p. 74.

10. Ibid., p. 116.

11. There is an important conflict of recollection and fact in Rees's testimony, which until now has not been recognized. Boyle confirms that in his discussions with Rees, he put this first meeting in 1932, as described so vividly in *A Chapter of Accidents*, p. 111. But Felix Frankfurter did not leave the United States during the 1932 election campaign of Franklin Roosevelt and, according to his own diary, crossed the Atlantic in June 1933 to take up his appointment as visiting law professor. He did not arrive in Oxford until late June 1933. [Felix Frankfurter, *From the Diaries of Felix Frankfurter*, notes by Joseph Plank (New York: Norton, 1965); and Liva Baker, *Felix Frankfurter* (New York: Coward-McCann, 1969).] This was not the first occasion when Rees was sloppy over dates (see below). That the Oxford meeting did take place there can be no doubt, but since Burgess did not become the dedicated Marxist encountered by Rees until sometime during his final year at Cambridge, the encounter was likely to have been in 1933 rather than 1932.

12. Rees, op. cit., p. 137.

13. Robert Crowley interviews. U.S. intelligence officers find it indicative of KGB disinformation ploys that Philby, in his January 1988 interviews, continues to give the impression that he was the "First Man," and that Burgess "maintained links with all of us" (*Sunday Times*, March 25, 1988).

14. Boyle interviews; Rosamond Lehmann interview.

15. Noël Annan, "Burgess," TLS 1972.

16. Boyle interviews.

17. *The Observer*, January 13, 1980.

18. Boyle interviews.

19. As quoted in *The Observer*, January 13, 1980.

20. *The Spectator*, May 5, 1933.

21. Ibid.

22. Peter Stansky and W. Abraham, *Journey to the Frontier*, p. 107.

23. Ibid., p. 109.

24. Cecil interviews.

25. Ibid.

26. Information supplied by Maclean's friend Christopher Gillie to Andrew Boyle [Boyle, *Climate of Treason*, pp. 116–117].

27. Information supplied to Andrew Boyle by Elizabeth Rea (Lady Clapham), Lady Grimond, Lady Felicity Rumbold, and others [Boyle, op. cit., p. 117].

28. Philby interview, *Sunday Times*, March 27, 1986; Lord Vansittart, *The Mist Procession* (London: Hutchinson, 1958), p. 490.

29. See E. H. Cookridge, *The Third Man* (New York: Putnam's, 1968); Patrick Seale and Maureen McConville, *Philby* (London: Hamish Hamilton, 1973), p. 67; Philby interviews, 1988.

30. Philby interview, *Sunday Times*, March 27, 1987.

31. H. A. R. Philby, *My Silent War*, p. 14.

32. Ibid.

## CHAPTER 13: PAGES 230–245

1. Philby, *My Silent War*, p. 14.

2. Blunt statement, *The Times*, November 12, 1979.

3. Confidential sources; Peter Wright, *Spycatcher*, p. 219.

4. Information supplied by a former senior MI5 officer, August 1987; Wright's own account in *Spycatcher* reveals that much of the damage could have been prevented if the British security services had properly applied the primary tools of counter-intelligence: research and analysis.

5. Blunt press conference, *The Times*, November 21, 1979; Blunt, "Bloomsbury"; Waterhouse, as quoted in Penrose and Freeman, *Conspiracy of Silence*, pp. 106–107.

6. "Thank you for your nice picture of the Casino, will look forward, as the view said, to hearing all your latest in's and out's," MacNeice wrote on September 29, adding "If you are still at home (which I doubt) do be a sweet child and bring your Rothschild friends to the enclosed Ball which we are meant to be running." [MacNeice to Blunt, September 29, KCA.]

7. 1933 *Spectators:* Renoir exhibition, September 22; Riviera style, September 29; Rhine and Danube styles, November 24; "Doctrinal Advertisement," Rome, January 5, 1934.

8. MacNeice letter addressed to Elizabethstrasse 23, München, Germany, KCA.

9. Blunt, "Bloomsbury."

10. West told me that his information had been provided by a reliable MI5 source at a dinner party. Interviews with Nigel West (Rupert Allason, M.P.), 1984–1988; Wright, op. cit., pp. 48, 336ff.

11. Quoted by Nigel West in *Molehunt* (London: Weidenfeld & Nicolson, 1988), p. 65. "Curiously, in 1971 K branch initiated a new assessment of Blunt which came to some depressing conclusions."

12. Nigel West told me that his interviews with Blunt led him to believe he was on "cozy" terms with the "office" since Wright had continued to consult him on matters of detail. When West contacted Wright in 1981, however, he recalls he did not get the impression that the former MI5 officer harbored anything like the doubt about Blunt's story that he conveys in *Spycatcher*.

13. *The People*, November 1956; Philby also says Burgess became a Communist in 1934 [*Sunday Times*, March 27, 1988].

14. Tom Driberg (*Portrait*, pp. 24–26) says Burgess claimed that the "principal organizer and initiator" of the trip and the one who obtained introductions was his friend David Astor, whose mother, Nancy, had visited the Soviet Union with George Bernard Shaw in 1931. Driberg, in an attempt to show that Rees was "not now a particularly credible witness," hinted that Rees himself was "very close to the Communist Party."

15. Andrew Boyle, *Climate of Treason*, p. 119.

16. After eleven letters in 1929, MacNeice's letter of April 22, 1930, refers to a previous telephone call and Anthony's Easter visit to Paris and talks of a forthcoming visit to Cambridge. That for July 13 refers to a visit that Blunt made to Oxford and discusses MacNeice's forthcoming marriage to Mary Ezra. *The only letter for 1931*, dated May 11, confirms that Blunt and MacNeice were still corresponding because it discusses a request from Blunt about a teaching post at the university for "your girlfriend." [This is probably a reference to Jean Stewart, who, like her father, Reverend R. H. Stewart of Trinity, was Cambridge lecturer in French.] The correspondence resumes with seven letters from 1932; the first, dated January 21, refers to a request from Blunt to see the typescript of MacNeice's new novel. [MacNeice/Blunt correspondence, KCA.]

17. MacNeice to Blunt, December 10, 1932; MacNeice, May 31, 1934; MacNeice, September 30, 1934, KCA.

18. Blunt, *The Spectator*, November 16, 1934.

19. MacNeice to Blunt, November 10, 1934, KCA.

20. *The Collected Poems of Louis MacNeice*, ed. E. R. Dodds (London: Faber & Faber, 1966), p. 22.

21. Michael Straight, *After Long Silence*, p. 104.

22. For details of the Hammer dealings and the $15 million worth of old masters sold between 1928 and 1933 by the Soviets to such notable Western collectors as Nubar Gulbenkian and A. W. Mellon, see Robert C. Williams, *Russian Art and American Money, 1900–1940* (Cambridge, Mass.: Harvard University Press, 1980), pp. 11–31.

23. Interviews with Christopher Wright, 1985–1988.

24. Christopher Wright interviews; Blunt, "Bloomsbury" and Gow obituary.

25. Anthony Blunt, *Artistic Theory in Italy, 1450–1660* (Oxford: The Clarendon Press, 1940), Foreword.

26. Blunt, "Bloomsbury."

27. Ibid.

28. Ibid.

29. *The Spectator*, March 2, 1934; *The Spectator*, August 4, 1933.

30. *The Spectator*, December 14, 1934.

31. *The Spectator*, August 20, 1937.

32. Ibid.

33. *The Spectator*, March 26, 1937.

34. *The Spectator*, July 12, 1935.

35. *The Spectator*, November 5, May 17, November 8, 1935.

36. *The Spectator*, August 16, 1935.

37. Steiner, "Cleric of Treason," p. 192.

38. Ibid.

39. Blunt, *The Spectator*, May 17, 1935; *The Times*, April 1971, as cited in *The Daily Telegraph*, November 16, 1979.

40. Maurice Dobb, *Soviet Russia and the World* (London: Wishart, 1932), p. 144.

41. Steiner, op. cit., p. 200.

42. Ibid., pp. 193–200.

43. Ibid.


## CHAPTER 14: PAGES 246–266

1. Interview with Leonard Miall, October 1986.

2. Ibid.

3. Interview with Leo Long, October 1986.

4. Ibid.

5. *Trinity Review*, May 1934; letter from Lord Thurlow, August 6, 1987.

6. Michael Straight interview, 1986–1988.

7. Profile of Straight, *Granta*, June 9, 1937; Michael Straight, *After Long Silence;* and interviews.

8. Ibid.

9. Ibid.

10. Ibid.

11. Ibid.

12. Victor Kiernan, "On Treason," *London Review of Books*, June 25, 1987.

13. Michael Straight, "A Red Mole of Martyr" *Toronto Globe and Mail*, October 9, 1986; James Barros, *No Sense of Evil: The Espionage Case of E. Herbert Norman* (New York: Ivy Books, 1987); for confirmation of Norman's Communist activities while at Cambridge, see H. S. Ferns, "Return to the Record: The Contribution of Herbert Norman," in *The Canadian Forum*, November 1986, p. 9: "Both of us studied in Trinity College, Cambridge; Norman from 1933 to 1935 and I from 1936 to 1939. Both of us were Marxists and Communists. Both of us did the same party work as students. Norman was in charge of "colonial work" at Cambridge; that is, the recruitment to the Communist Party and political education of students mainly from the British Empire in India and Ceylon. He was succeeded by an Englishman, Victor Kiernan, subsequently a fellow of Trinity College, Cambridge, and for most of his career a professor of history at the University of Edinburgh. I succeeded Kiernan from 1937 to 1939."

14. Straight interviews.

15. *The Spectator*, March 1, 1935.

16. *The Spectator*, June 7, 1935.

17. *The Spectator*, November 15, 1935.

18. Wilfrid Blunt, *Feather*, p. 295.

19. Interview with Sir Charles Fletcher-Cooke, September 1987.

20. Ibid.; Straight, op. cit., p. 63; Christopher Mayhew, *Time to Explain* (London: Hutchinson, 1987), p. 24.

21. Wilfrid Blunt, *Feather*, p. 295.

22. Straight interview.

23. Fletcher-Cooke interview; "Secret communication," Guy Liddell to Atherton, December 23, 1935, US Emb Lon 800 B RG 84 NA. In a letter to Atherton from General Kell of July 26, 1935, MI5 offered to extend the "present arrangement" of monitoring the names of U.S. citizens traveling to the U.S.S.R. on board Soviet ships to include "transmigrants travelling by other routes." This clearly indicates that MI5's monitoring of travel to and from Russia was indeed comprehensive and extensive throughout the thirties.

24. Blunt statement, November 21, 1979. Only *The Times*, fulfilling its obligation as Britain's newspaper of record, picked up the hesitation in answering this question.

25. *The Spectator*, September 20, 1935.

26. Ibid.

27. *The Spectator*, October 18, 1935.

28. *The Spectator*, October 11, 1935.

29. *The Spectator*, July 10, December 18, 1936.

30. Blunt review of *Modern Art* by Thomas Craven, *The Spectator*, October 18, 1934.

31. Interview with Professor G. M. Wickens, June 1987.

32. Ibid.

33. Straight, op. cit., p. 67.

34. Ibid.

35. Ibid., p. 71.

36. Straight interviews.

37. Ibid.

38. Ibid.; according to Straight, the themes that Burgess and Blunt stressed were very similar to those of Christopher Caudwell (the pseudonym of C. St. John Sprigg). A brilliant young Marxist journalist and poet who was killed in the Spanish Civil War, Caudwell's emphasis on science and art as the guides to human activity in *Further Studies in a Dying Culture* expanded further on a theme that inspired so many Communists in the middle thirties: namely, that revolutionary Marxism assigned them a role of action in the crusade to save the world.

39. Straight interviews.

40. Straight, op. cit., p. 91: Apostolic records show he was enrolled on March 8, 1935.

41. Straight interviews.

42. Straight interviews.

43. *The Spectator*, March 1935.

44. MacNeice to Blunt, March 12, 1936, KCA.

45. MacNeice, *Strings*, p. 161.

46. Ibid., p. 100.

47. MacNeice to Blunt, May 24, 1936, KCA; MacNeice, op. cit., p. 168; in this book

MacNeice puts his visit to Cambridge *before* the trip to Spain. The chronology of his letters, however, indicates that it was the other way about.

48. Ibid., p. 156; MacNeice to Blunt, May 7, 1936, KCA.

49. MacNeice, op. cit., p. 169.

50. Ibid., p. 156.

51. MacNeice to Blunt, May 7, 1936, KCA.

52. Undated Iceland card from Auden, MacNeice letters, KCA; "Auden and MacNeice: Their Last Will and Testament" in *Letters from Iceland* (London: Faber and Faber, 1985).

53. See MacNeice, op. cit., pp. 164–169. Professor Jon Stallworthy, MacNeice's biographer, was unable to establish precisely what caused the rupture with Blunt that the end of the correspondence indicated. He himself believes that it is more likely that some sexual pass by Blunt might have been responsible than that it was due to an attempted recruitment into the Soviet network. Significantly, the last surviving letter from MacNeice to his old friend, dating from August 3, 1936, was written in a fit of depression. He was clearing out his cottage near Birmingham prior to moving to London to begin his career as a full-time writer. He writes that he had "spent three days lately having a holocaust of letters and manuscripts. Most satisfactory." The bonfire presumably included Blunt's end of their correspondence and the novel that featured him. [MacNeice to Blunt, August 3, 1936, KCA.]

54. Stephen Spender, *The Thirties and After* (London: Fontana, 1978); MacNeice, op. cit., p. 168.

55. John Cornford, *Collected Writings*, ed. Jonathan.

56. Spender, op. cit., p. 29.

57. *The Spectator*, December 4, 1935; February 28, 1936; January 1, 1936.

58. *The Spectator*, December 20, 1935; April 9, 1937.

59. *The Spectator*, June 25, 1937.

60. *The Spectator*, August 6, 1937.

61. *The Spectator*, October 15, 1937.

62. Goronwy Rees, review of *Afterthoughts on the USSR* by André Gide, *The Spectator*, October 15, 1937.

63. *The Spectator*, January 8, 1937.

## CHAPTER 15: PAGES 267–275

1. *The Cambridge Review*, February 5, 1937; *Granta*, February 3, 1937; Straight, *After Long Silence*, p. 98.

2. Blunt, "Bloomsbury"; Straight interviews.

3. Straight, op. cit., pp. 101–102.

4. Ibid., p. 102.

5. Ibid.

6. Straight interviews.

7. Straight, op. cit., p. 104.

8. Straight interviews.

9. Straight, op. cit., p. 105.

10. Straight interviews.

11. Straight, op. cit., p. 120.

12. Ibid., p. 81.

13. Straight interviews.

14. Name provided in confidence.

15. Straight interviews.

16. As quoted by Roger Berthoud, "The Apostles with Different Creeds," *The Times*, November 22, 1979.

17. Straight's role in the election is confirmed by a letter from Keynes of February 3, 1937, asking him to contact Sheppard, the two Lucases, Rylands, Braithwaite, Watson, and Champernowne from Kings; Trevelyan, Moore, and Robertson from Trinity; Sykes Davies from John's; and "the younger people such as Blunt, Rothschild, and the others." [Reproduced in Straight, op. cit., p. 94.] This was an unusually full gathering and must have considered the membership issue, since the records show that three new members were elected two weeks later, followed by two more by June; information on Astbury from Straight; H. R. Astbury and the Record of Debates of the Cambridge Union 1937 in the University Library Manuscript Section at Cambridge; H. Chapman Pincher and H. S. Ferns.

18. Straight interviews.

19. Miall interview.

20. Ibid.

21. *The Spectator*, June 5, 1936; Frederick Muller, *The Mind in Chains*, Cecil Day Lewis, ed. (London: 1937). According to the editor, the leftist Oxford poet Cecil Day Lewis, all the contributors shared the "widespread belief of intellectual workers that the mind is really in chains today, that these chains have been forged by a dying system, that they can and must be broken — and in the Soviet Union have been broken" [p.17]; pp. 108, 114, 121, and 122. One of Lenin's few definitive cultural statements had been made to the German Communist leader Clara Zetkin.

22. Straight, op. cit., p. 121, and interviews.

23. Straight, op. cit., p. 122.


## CHAPTER 16: PAGES 276–287

1. *The Times*, Blunt press conference, November 29, 1979.

2. See article by Ernst Henri, "The Revolutionary Movement in Nazi Germany (I) The Groups of Five (Fünfergruppen) and (II) The Revolutionary Press and Agitation," printed in *The New Statesman and Nation*, August 1933. From his personal experience in Germany, Rostovsky, writing under his pseudonym, described the role to be played in the underground opposition to Hitler by the "revolutionary groups of five, a novel form of anti-Fascist organization." "Henri's" references were specifically to an underground *political* rather than espionage

movement. Dr. Andrew, among others, has argued that this article, later reprinted in book form in 1934 as *Hitler Over Europe*, influenced the romantic anti-fascist scheming of Guy Burgess and his Cambridge friends. But U.S. intelligence analysts dismiss the idea that the Soviet intelligence service would "openly" advertise for its recruits or publicly reveal its modus operandi.

3. The lack of information or alternative candidates left Andrew Boyle little choice in 1979 in *Climate of Treason*, pp. 98 and 120, but to settle on Cahan, aka Kahan or Kahann, as the recruiter. Penrose and Freeman in *Conspiracy of Silence*, p. 145; Christopher Andrew in his essay "F. H. Hinsley and the Cambridge Moles," in *Diplomacy and Intelligence in the Second World War*, pp. 24–25; and Robin Bruce Lockhart in *Reilly: The First Man*, pp. 42–52 opt for either Cahan or Ernst Henri as the Soviet *éminence grise*. It is significant that all these accounts were published *before* Wright, especially since Chapman Pincher, in *Their Trade Is Treachery* (published in 1981), adheres closely to Wright's account in *Spycatcher* of what he recalls Blunt *actually* telling MI5. Pincher appears to have been discounted by all other writers except Nigel West. In *MI5: British Security Service Operations 1909–1945*, pp. 332–333, and *The Circus: MI5 Operations 1945–1972*, pp. 122–123, West, who not only interviewed Blunt but also claims inside sources in the British security services, intriguingly avoids the issue by asserting that Blunt confessed he had been "recruited as a Russian spy by Guy Burgess in 1936." Anthony Cave Brown credits a Soviet spymaster, whom he identifies, from unsourced but very sparely quoted "files of the Central Intelligence Agency," as GRU agent Henri Robinson. Furthermore, he says Robinson "acquired" another "Red Army Military agent known as Harry II," who operated through an intermediary named Ernest Weiss, "who concentrated upon a small group of the sons of the higher bourgeoisie" and was probably a homosexual "for one of his earliest converts was Guy Francis de Moncy Burgess." [Anthony Cave Brown and Charles MacDonald in *On a Field of Red* (New York: Putnam's, 1981), pp. 459–460.] None of the former CIA officers consulted has been able to shed any light on the origins of Cave Brown's remarkably original theory, which flies in the face of the well-established fact that the Cambridge spies were run by the NKVD, not the GRU.

4. Wright, *Spycatcher*, p. 227; Pincher, *Their Trade Is Treachery*, p. 110, relying on the notes he made with Wright in 1980, draws attention to "Otto's" physical appearance, but *Spycatcher* describes how Philby alluded to an FBI file picture he had seen of "Otto," which had "fair curly hair." [Wright, op. cit., p. 227.]

5. Ibid.

6. Blunt as quoted by Wright, op. cit.

7. Philby, *Sunday Times*, March 1988; Elizabeth K. Poretsky in *Our Own People: A Memoir of Ignace Reiss and his Friends* (Ann Arbor: University of Michigan Press, 1963) recalls (p. 128) that Maly was then in Moscow and (p. 213) "Theodore Maly was also in Paris during that spring of 1937. He had finished his assignment in London and was waiting to be called back to the USSR." Poretsky was also a Pole who knew Maly and Krivitsky through her husband, Ignace Reiss, who was for twenty years an agent of the Fourth Department for the GRU. Her overall reliability is vouched for by former U.S. intelligence sources familiar with the assistance she was provided in writing her account. Poretsky details with the remarkable clarity of firsthand knowledge and insight the history of how the 1918 generation of foreign Comintern agents, including her husband, were suborned by Soviet intelligence and then eliminated by Stalin's purges of the late thirties. Orlov in his *Handbook*, p. 64, also makes reference to Mally [sic] as a "top flight NKVD intelligence officer" who traveled on a "genuine Austrian passport (obtained by fraud in Vienna)."

8. Brook-Shepherd, *The Storm Petrels* (London: Collins, 1977), pp. 175–178. Although no sources are cited for Gadar's role, Cookridge's disclosure that he had a relative named Shuster, who was second secretary at the Soviet Embassy, and Burgess's frequent trips to a favorite Chinese restaurant in the East End on mail-drop missions suggest an MI5 officer provided information. It is also perhaps significant that as early as November 1936 MacNeice records meeting Burgess "for a very good Chinese meal." Although he does not locate the restaurant, unlike today when Chinese food is ubiquitous, in the mid-thirties, aficionados trekked out to London's dockland for the "dim sum." [See MacNeice to Blunt, November 22, 1936, KCA.]

9. Poretsky, op. cit., pp. 128, 214.

10. Wright, op. cit., p. 227.

11. Noël Annan, "Et Tu, Anthony," *New York Review of Books*, October 22, 1987.

12. Essay by Arthur Koestler in *The God That Failed*, ed. R. H. S. Crossman (New York: Harper, 1950).

13. In 1981 Olga Gray, then in retirement in Canada, told author Anthony Masters the details of her role as Miss X, the celebrated undercover MI5 female agent. [Anthony Masters, *The Man Who Was M: The Life of Maxwell Knight* (New York: Blackwell, 1982), pp. 30–44, interview with Anthony Masters, July 1983.]

14. Ibid., p. 44. Corroboration is provided by the report on the "Woolwich Arsenal Spy Case" in *The Times* of London, February 4, 1938. In April Glading took to the flat a man introduced as "Mr. Peters." Miss X heard nothing discussed between these two, but in a casual conversation Peters was referred to as an "Austrian who had served during the War in the Russian cavalry."

15. Olga Gray's account in Masters, op. cit., p. 44; see also reference to Peters in confidential memorandum from US Emb Lon dated March 15, 1938, 800 B "Brandes." Liddell to US Emb Lon July 6, 1938; US Emb Lon 800 RG 89 NA. The newspaper reports of the Woolwich Arsenal spy trial have Stevens spelled "Stephens"; the contemporary MI5 reports contain both spellings but use "Stevens" as a heading.

16. Urgent and Confidential, Borum from Liddell, February 1, 1938. US Emb Lon 800 B "Brandes," RG 84 NA.

17. Ibid.; and Olga Gray's account in Masters, op. cit., p. 45.

18. *The Times*, February 4, 1938, and Masters, op. cit., p. 46.

19. *The Times*, February 4, 1938. Olga Gray's days as an agent were over; the only recognition she received was a lunch at the Ritz and a check for £500 as a termination fee. She later married a Canadian air force officer and lived the rest of her life in Toronto fearing Soviet retribution.

20. West, *MI5*, p. 82; Masters, op. cit., p. 46; West, *MI5*, p. 83.

21. The memo "Willy Brandes" (Mr. Stevens of the Miss X Case), which summarizes the investigation made by the Canadian authorities, showed that Brandes had obtained his false papers in 1936 with the assistance of Aaron Marcovitch. The same month Brandes married Mary Stern, and on the pretext he was a Hebrew teacher in Montreal anxious to leave on his honeymoon, Brandes quickly obtained a Canadian passport for himself and his wife. [Undated report supplied by MI5 to the US Emb Lon, 800 B "Brandes" 1938, RG 89 NA.]

22. MI5, it is clear from the later reports, *did* alert the French authorities to Brandes

because the Americans were told that the "French police have entirely failed to trace his arrival or departure from France. He may possibly of course have left this country on his British passport and landed in France on a French passport." [July 6, 1938 Emb Lon 800 B "Brandes," RG 84 NA.]

23. Poretsky, op. cit.

24. Crowley interviews.

25. Wright makes one reference that suggests Blunt removed Registry documents [*Spycatcher*, op. cit., p. 219]. Joan Miller, Knight's wartime assistant, also cites an instance in 1941 when the head of B(5)b Section took matters "into his own hands, of course, ignoring the rules when they got in his way; but I didn't expect to see him tamper with the office files which I had been taught to regard as inviolable. But there it was. He tore out a page which contained the Andrews/Darwell entry and replaced the file on the Registry shelf. The expression on my face as I watched this unlawful act simply made him smile." [Joan Miller's *One Woman's War: Personal Exploits in MI5's Most Secret Station* (Dublin: Brandon, 1986), p. 106.] After Joan Miller left Knight's department he told her "quite brutally" that "he had taken steps to ensure that the blame for destroying the Andrews/Darwell file would fall on me, should the matter ever be brought to light" [p. 154].

26. West interview, New York, September 23, 1987.

27. Ibid.

28. Ibid.

## CHAPTER 17: PAGES 288–313

1. At the request of the British government, the FBI has not made available any of the 1951 MI5 files under FOIA regarding suspicions about Maclean and Philby. [Information from a confidential source.]

2. Robert J. Lamphere interview, 1986–1988, and Robert J. Lamphere, *The FBI-KGB War* (New York: Random House, 1988), p. 242.

3. Burgess & Maclean [Espionage R], FBI Files 65-4648 (hereafter FBI B&M).

4. Lamphere interviews; Los Angeles FBI field agent's report of FBI interview with Isherwood, July 15, 1951, FBI B&M.

5. Lamphere interviews.

6. On July 18, 1951. Report to the director from SAC Los Angeles: Second Isherwood interview "able to identify the individual whom he had previously named as ----, a friend of Burgess, as ----------." Since the first part of the sentence uses the same construction as the cable referring to TONY the previous day, the ten spaces blanked out exactly coincide with Tony Blunt. The few pages of the FBI "Blunt" file on which all information has not been blacked out "in the interests of national defense or foreign policy" confirm that the Americans also had two other sources implicating Blunt by October 1951. See reports of July 15 and October 4. [FBI "Blunt" # 16294.]

7. Lamphere interviews.

8. In his book, Lamphere was requested to use STOTT, but I have been informed by another Washington source that SMOTH is the correct designation. (SMOTH is not an acronym, only a cryptic designation.)

9. Lamphere interviews.

10. FBI summary report, p. 37, FBI B&M.

11. While consul general in Tangier after World War I, in which he served as a private in the Scots Guards, Clark Kerr had been a regular visitor to the male brothels in the Casbah. [See Deacon, *British Connection*, p. 198.] Although a "confirmed bachelor," Kerr astonished his friends during his posting to Santiago de Chile by taking the attractive Maria-Teresa Díaz Salas as his wife before his appointment as ambassador to Baghdad. She was divorced on the grounds of desertion in 1945 — but two years later, on his return from Washington, Inverchapel caused another sensation by remarrying Lady Maria when he retired to his ancestral Argyllshire estates. Isherwood and Auden were evidently familiar with Inverchapel on the London homosexual circuit. They also stayed at the ambassador's residence in Shanghai's International Settlement during their trip to China in May 1938. Isherwood records how he and Auden spent the afternoons at a bathhouse where they were "erotically soaped and massaged" by the young Chinese attendants. "Of one thing they felt certain," Isherwood alluded knowingly in his autobiography: "If Archie did know about the bath-house, he wouldn't have been in the least shocked." [Isherwood, *Christopher and His Kind* (London: Eyre Methuen, 1977), p. 230.]

12. Robert Cecil interviews. Cecil became acquainted with Clark Kerr in the British mission in Iraq. He cited Frank Giles, who was Inverchapel's private secretary in Moscow, as joking that the ambassador's attitude to sex was "If it moves, go for it!" Giles also discussed Inverchapel's library of pornography at his ancestral Argyllshire home. Cecil confirms that his former boss was known to be bisexual when he was in Washington.

13. Ibid.

14. See Thomas Whiteside, *An Agent in Place: The Wennestrom Affair* (New York: Ballantine, 1983).

15. Stein entries in IRR and Shanghai Police Department files, NA. Chapman Pincher cites as the source for the Stein connection Gordon W. Creighton, who was Inverchapel's secretary [Pincher, *Their Trade Is Treachery*, p. 139]. See also Deacon, *British Connection*, pp. 198–199, quoting a former member (possibly also Creighton) of the British legation who said, "General Valery Chuikov, the Soviet military attaché in China, was a frequent visitor to the Ambassador. Sometimes they talked together alone for hours." Deacon also quotes a former missionary who "undertook intelligence work for the British in Chungking during World War II as having told him that there was a "safe house" used by the Russians a little way out of Chungking, where Clark Kerr used to meet with Stein, Chuikov, and an American journalist in Sorge's ring: Agnes Smedley.

16. Dame Rebecca West in *The Meaning of Treason*, revised 1965 (London: Penguin, 1965) says of Inverchapel: "Not least among his disadvantages was a steady passion for the Soviet Union. This he did not conceal from the Foreign Office, giving a pro-Soviet lecture to the experts employed during the war in the Far Eastern Section which none of them has ever forgotten." Anthony Glees in *The Secrets of the Service: British Intelligence and Communist Subversion 1939–51* (London: Cape, 1987), p. 271, insists that "there is absolutely no evidence" that Inverchapel was a "mole." He believes Inverchapel was "an eccentric pro-Bolshevik and because he was quite open about this, the chances that he was subverted are virtually nonexistent." American intelligence experts beg to disagree, pointing out the well-

documented Soviet ability to exploit homosexual "eccentricity" and his suspicious links to Wennestrom and Stein.

17. Stephen Spender, *Journals, 1939–1983* (New York: Random House, 1986), p. 264. Since Louis MacNeice was among the guests, it is possible that the literary gatherings were a cover for more sinister purposes: "Old MI5 records revealed during the debriefing of Blunt recalled that suspicion had been slightly aroused when Burgess had arranged a meeting between Lord Inverchapel (formerly Sir Archibald Clark Kerr) and Anatoli Gorski, the Soviet spymaster who was later found to have controlled Blunt." According to Pincher, the meeting had been arranged by an Austrian journalist, "who turned out to be a KGB agent," named Peter Smollett/Smolka. [Pincher, *Their Trade Is Treachery*, pp. 138–139.]

18. Cecil interviews.

19. Christopher Isherwood, *The Condor and the Crows* (New York: Random House, 1949), p. 192.

20. FBI report on interview with Rudolph Katz, July 31, 1931, FBI B&M 1955 Hoover.

21. "Summary Brief: Donald Duart Maclean; Guy de Moncy Burgess; Harold Adrian Russell Philby," prepared by J. Edgar Hoover for the Honorable Dillon Anderson, Special Assistant to President Dwight D. Eisenhower, dated November 8, 1955 (hereafter Hoover B&M 1955 report), page 17. FBI Series Box 10 Eisenhower Library. (In contrast to the FBI files, this report is much less heavily censored and many of the names removed from the Bureau material appear in context, including Lord Rothschild's. A simple cross-indexing with the key phrases enables many of the missing details to be reconstructed in the FBI investigation briefs of 1951.)

22. Ibid., p. 17.

23. FBI Isherwood interview, FBI B&M.

24. In his biography of Burgess, which must have been approved by the KGB, Driberg (*Portrait*, pp. 30–31) explains — presumably with Burgess's approval — that Mrs. Charles Rothschild was "much impressed by Guy's extemporaneous assessment of world affairs," especially his predictions about the nationalization of the railways in a Latin-American republic, which the Rothschilds' bank had not foreseen. Burgess had made a prediction by "academic political analysis" that armaments shares would rise and had specified Rolls-Royce — on which Lord Rothschild had made money and given Burgess a hundred pounds. Mrs. Charles Rothschild was most impressed. She gave him a list of all her personal investments and asked him to write her a monthly report, for which he was paid £100; Rees, *Accidents*, p. 117.

25. FBI Isherwood, op. cit.; FBI interview with Rolf Katz, report of July 21, 1951.

26. London *Daily Express*, June 14, 1951.

27. FBI Isherwood, op. cit.; Isherwood, *Condor*, p. 192. In 1948 he encountered Katz again in Buenos Aires, where he was editing an economic journal "which has a great reputation in government and stock-exchange circles" and had "lost a good deal of his political dogmatism. He no longer believes in the planned socialist state."

28. Katz is referred to in Rees's *Accidents*, p. 131, as a "grossly obese Central European whom I never knew by any other name than Ignatz." [Rees changed the names and Ignatz is obviously identical physically to Katz.]

29. Reference to earlier MI5 reports in Embassy files: Miller to Atherton, Secret, May 2, 1933, 800 B "Wagenknecht," US Emb Lon 800 RG 84 NA.

30. Liddell to Atherton, June 7, 1934, 800 B "General," US Emb Lon, RG 84 NA.

31. A dedicated founder member of the Communist International, Münzenberg was forced to flee from Berlin to France when Hitler came to power in 1933. But his strong loyalty to the International, rather than Moscow, aroused the suspicions of Stalin that his true loyalties remained with Trotsky's global revolution. In 1938 Münzenberg rashly protested the executions of the Communist leaders in the so-called Yezhov purges. He was summoned to Moscow. Anticipating his fate, he declined. In 1940, shortly after the fall of France, his decapitated body was found hanging from a tree in a village in the Massif Central. His widow and friends insisted that he had been liquidated by Stalin's agents. [See E. H. Cookridge, *The Third Man* (London: Arthur Barker, and New York: G. P. Putnam's Sons, 1968), p. 23 and footnote, and Arthur Koestler, *The Invisible Writing* (London: Hutchinson, 1969), pp. 197–199; Babette Gross (Münzenberg's widow), translated by Marian Jackson, *Willi Münzenberg: A Political Biography* (East Lansing: Michigan State University Press, 1974).]

32. Münzenberg had a "most persuasive way with the ladies," according to the British Communist Ivor Montagu, whose comments were cited by Betty D. Vernon, *Ellen Wilkinson, 1891–1947* (London: Croom Helm, 1979), p. 123; Lillian Hellman, *An Unfinished Woman* (Boston: Little Brown, 1967), p. 68.

33. Isherwood interrogation of July 14, 1951, FBI B&M.

34. Gross, *Münzenberg*, p. 312; Claude Cockburn, *Claude Cockburn Sums It Up* (London: Quartet Books, 1981); Cookridge, op. cit., p. 78.

35. N. D. Borum to Guy Liddell, June 14, 1939, 811.11 "Gibarti," US Emb Lon: files; for a more detailed discussion of the clandestine radio war see W. J. West, *Truth Betrayed* (London: Gerald Duckworth, 1987). The reference to "two stations operating in France on three wavelengths," which were "directed by Willi Münzenberg and are said to be in receipt of financial support from the French Government," is in a 1939 Foreign Office report [FO 371/23058; C20850/645/18, PRO]; French police records and interviews of survivors of the internment camp at Chambran near Lyons establish that Münzenberg probably struck out for Marseilles in the company of a mysterious twenty-five-year-old redheaded man who joined the Chambran camp shortly before it was dispersed. The French police regarded the case as a suicide, but Gross argues that her husband's consistent defiance of Stalin suggests that he was the victim of a classic NKVD assassination.

36. There are conflicting versions of Otto Katz's career after he left Münzenberg. The account most often cited is given in E. H. Cookridge, *The Third Man*. Cookridge was the pseudonym used by Edward Spiro, the son of the Austrian representative of a Manchester textile firm. He was by turns a socialist newspaper editor — when he met Philby in Vienna in 1934 — correspondent, prisoner of the Gestapo in Buchenwald, and free-lance MI6 agent. After World War II he made his name as a writer of spy books, including *Secrets of the British Service, Inside S.O.E., Shadow of a Spy, They Came from the Sky*, and *Traitor Betrayed*. Cookridge had encountered Otto Katz in 1939, and according to Andrew Boyle, who knew him, Cookridge based his account on information he had received from Guy Liddell and other friends formerly in the British intelligence service. Cookridge, however, created many composite characters and rounded out plots when he ran out of facts. Other accounts and MI5 records support Cookridge's assertions that Katz was a ranking NKVD agent in the prewar Comintern *but not* that he was a "drinking companion of Burgess." It is possible that both Burgess and Philby may have made Katz's acquaintance in London in 1934 during the Reichstag Hearings, or later in Paris

— presumably as Spiro did himself. But Otto Katz (as opposed to *Rudolph* Katz) was never in London for the length of time that Cookridge claimed. According to U.S. State Department records, Katz arrived in New York under his own name on a Czech passport on April 20, 1939, posing as a foreign correspondent for the French left-wing Communist paper *L'Ordre*. He returned on the *Queen Mary* and disembarked at Cherbourg, France, on August 28, 1939. Katz cannot have been in Britain after the war began because MI5 on March 8, 1940, asked the State Department for his whereabouts. The FBI confirmed that he had arrived in New York on the *President Adams* on January 21, 1940, on a temporary three-month visitor's visa and with a French visa issued in Paris valid until April 1, 1940. U.S. files show that Katz "was suspected of being a communist and also a Nazi agent, who has been a member of the OGPU" and his request for permanent residence was not granted. [US Emb Lon 800 B 1940 "Katz and Breda" RG 84 NA.] The American records therefore contradict Cookridge's assertion that Katz spent the war in Hollywood "establishing Communist front operations." Katz's visa ran out within six months and he appears to have left the United States for Mexico sometime in the summer or fall of 1940. [I am grateful for the assistance given in tracing the careers of Katz and Münzenberg by Stephen Koch of Columbia University, who is writing a detailed study of Communist intellectuals in the thirties.]

37. Koestler, *Invisible Writing*, p. 210; Cookridge, op. cit., p. 79; for a more factual record see Gross, op. cit., p. 313, and *Der Slanzsky-Prozess* (Prague: 1953), p. 253 et seq.

38. Since "Otto," like Katz/Simone/Breda, had a thick neck, darkish hair and was also claimed by Blunt to be a Czech, he obviously sensed the need for a plausible cover story.

39. Vernon, *Ellen*, op. cit., p. 163; references to Lord Listowel as a "communist sympathizer" who remained "closely associated" with Otto Katz are in State Department Decimal File 1955, 741.001/2-1353, RG 84 NA; statement made to Deacon by Lady Rhonda, a close friend of Ellen Wilkinson, cited in *The British Connection*, p. 173.

40. Secret Liddell to Atherton, December 6, 1934, US Emb Lon 800 B "Gottschalk," RG 84 NA, and Koestler, *Invisible Writing*, p. 209.

41. Memorandum from Home Secretary to Cabinet Committee on Aliens Restrictions, April 6, 1933, CAB 24/293, PRO.

42. See Liddell to US Emb Lon, RG 84 NA; Kuchinski, *Memorien* (East Berlin: Aufbau, 1983), pp. 270–271, and Fuchs's confession, Hoover to Souers, March 22, 1950, President's Secretary's Files, HST Library, as cited by Professor Robert Chadwell Williams in *Klaus Fuchs: Atom Spy* (Cambridge, Mass.: Harvard University Press, 1987). On p. 22 Professor Williams cites information (given to him from a former MI5 officer living in retirement in the United States) that in 1934 a British undercover agent in Kiel, code-named "Arthur," warned MI6 that Fuchs had been a KPD organizer at the local university.

43. Cookridge, op. cit., p. 40; as quoted from a letter to Andrew Boyle by the Honorable Mrs. Miriam Lee Boyle, in *Climate of Treason*, p. 122 and footnote.

44. Ibid.

45. Interrogation of Rudolph Katz, St. Regis Hotel, New York City, July 27, 1951, FBI B&M.

46. The principal promoter of Burgess in parliamentary and Foreign Office circles was

Harold Nicolson. His son, Nigel Nicolson, in his illuminating biography of his parents (*Portrait of a Marriage*, New York: Atheneum, 1980, pp. 135–137), provides a general insight into the homosexual relationships of his father, who was the husband of poet and novelist Victoria Sackville-West. "He had a series of relationships with men who were his intellectual equals, but the physical element in them was very secondary. He was never a passionate lover." Nicolson, a colorful M.P. and a one-time supporter of British fascist Oswald Mosley, was one of Burgess's most celebrated conquests. Although he is never mentioned as a "lover" in Nicolson's published diaries (*Diaries and Letters, 1930–1939*, London: Collins, 1966, pp. 252–361 passim), it is clear from the context of his references that Burgess was by March 1936 a part of Nicolson's Café Royal homosexual and literary entourage that included his Foreign Office friend Clark Kerr (Lord Inverchapel). In Driberg's autobiography, *Ruling Passions*, p. 233, he notes that Nicolson "remembered Guy with affection" and even continued to write to him in Moscow. Another influential friend of Burgess in the shadowy Establishment homosexual network was Sir Joseph Ball, a former assistant to MI6 chief Cumming in World War I, and then head of the Conservative Research Department. Their relation was rumored to have a homosexual basis: "This is possible since Sir Joseph was known to have such tendencies [Cookridge, op. cit., pp. 46–47]. Recommendations by both Ball and Nicolson nonetheless failed to persuade Baldwin's private secretary, Victor Cazalet, to give Burgess a job in the Research Department. Cazalet was evidently concerned that Burgess's dirty fingernails did not demonstrate a true recantation of his undergraduate Marxism. [Page, Leitch, and Knightley, *Philby: The Spy Who Betrayed a Generation* (London: André Deutsch, 1968), pp. 89–91. See also Boyle, op. cit., p. 95.]

47. Driberg, *Portrait*, p. 32.

48. Cookridge, op. cit., p. 43.

49. Richard Griffiths, *Fellow Travellers of the Right* (London: Constable, 1980), p. 52.

50. Sir Henry Channon, *Chips: The Diaries of Sir Henry Channon*, ed. Robert Rhodes James (London: Weidenfeld & Nicolson, 1967), p. 428.

51. Simon Haxey (pseudonym), *Tory MP* (London, 1939), p. 207. One of the leading propagandists for Germany in the later thirties. The Anglo-German Fellowship was founded on very substantial and respectable City support by Ernest Tennant, the merchant banker and assiduous cultivator of German business on behalf of Joachim von Ribbentrop, with whom he was personal friends. Like many of his well-heeled British supporters in the City, Tennant supported Hitler as a bulwark not just against a Communist takeover in Germany but as insurance against socialist revolution in Britain. Like many of his followers, Tennant paid lip service to the worldwide deprecation of Germany's treatment of the Jews, while declaring that the British press "should pay more attention to the constructive side of the Hitler movement." [Ernest Tennant, *True Account* (London, 1957), p. 156.] Ribbentrop appears to have been the inspiration for Tennant's decision to set up the Anglo-German Fellowship after the visit of the 1934 British Trade Delegation to Germany. Lord Mount-Temple was its chairman, and the council included the governor of the Bank of England, peers, merchant bankers, City businessmen and right-wing worthies. The Prince of Wales, through his liaison with Mrs. Wallis Simpson, had close connections with leading members of the pro-German faction. [Richard Griffiths, op. cit., especially pp. 183–187.]

52. Page et al., op. cit., p. 110; Cookridge, op. cit., p. 45.

53. Driberg, *Portrait*, p. 32.

54. Rees, op. cit., pp. 120–121.

55. Driberg, *Portrait*, p. 32.

56. Ibid., p. 30.

57. For a history of the Rothschilds' Palestine settlements, see Simon Schama, *Two Rothschilds and the House of Israel* (New York: Knopf, 1982), pp. 290–293.

58. John Reeves, *The House of Rothschild: The Financial Rulers of Nations* (New York: Gordon Press reprint, 1975), pp. 168–169; see also Richard Davis, *The English Rothschilds* (London: Collins, 1968). Davis who cites Lord Victor Rothschild's unpublished monograph "The Shadow of a Great Man" (1982) for his assertion that both the pigeon post and the size of the fortune that Nathan made have been exaggerated. It seems that Nathan nevertheless received early news of the battle of Waterloo through his highly effective courier service and that though he may have purchased government stock on the strength of it, his profit was less spectacular than popularly believed.

59. Rees, op. cit., p. 131.

60. Ibid., pp. 127, 131.

61. Ibid.

62. Philby, op. cit., pp. 189–190.

63. Ibid.

64. Rees, op. cit., p. 129.

65. Ibid.

66. Jackie Hewit interviews, July 1985.

67. Penrose and Freeman, op. cit., p. 203, misconstrue Jackie Hewit's account and quote him as having told them how he was "attacked by someone called *Otto* Katz, a great fat slob" [emphasis added]. A year before the publication of *Conspiracy of Silence*, Hewit confirmed to this author that the Katz he knew was Rolph – of this he was in no doubt. He never knew an Otto Katz. Moreover, Otto Katz, unlike his namesake Rolph or Rudolph, was neither a homosexual *nor* obese.

68. Ibid.

69. Wolfgang von und zu Putlitz, *The Putlitz Dossier* (London: Allan Wingate, 1957).

70. Vansittart – "Van" as he was known to his admirers – was the outspokenly anti-Communist and anti-Nazi permanent head of the Foreign Office from 1930–1938. He was a passionate devotee of intelligence, building up his own private network of German informants starting with Group Captain Malcolm Graham Christie, the former British air attaché in Washington, who had himself built up a network of German business contacts. Christie kept Van posted about Hitler's arms buildup in the thirties. Vansittart did not neglect MI6. He became one of the chief promoters of the Secret Intelligence Service, as it was officially known. He also encouraged Colonel Claude Dansey, senior MI6 officer in Switzerland, to develop a network of informants, which eventually became the so-called Z operation that conducted intelligence gathering in Germany and Italy semi-independently. [See Anthony Read and David Fisher, *Colonel Z: The Secret of a Master of Spies* (London: Hodder & Stoughton, 1984) for a useful, but undocumented account, Norman Rose, *Vansittart: Study of a Diplomat* (London: 1978), and Lord Vansittart's memoirs, *Lessons of My Life* (1944).] Vansittart unofficially supplied Churchill, whom he

greatly admired, with German intelligence. When he became disillusioned with Neville Chamberlain's appeasement policy, he was removed from the top Foreign Office post. After the Munich crisis in 1938, he was "kicked upstairs" as chief diplomatic adviser to the government. But this titular post enabled Vansittart, with his private information service, to keep abreast of Chamberlain's own intelligence about Hitler. On the outbreak of war, Vansittart urged the foreign secretary to form a committee of high-ranking German exiles, who, under British direction, would make propaganda broadcasts to Germany. Putlitz was one of the names put forward by Christie, along with Hitler's former opponents Otto Rauschning and Otto Strasser. [Vansittart memorandum accompanying the proposal by Christie to Eden, October 2, 1939, FO 371/23057; C18620/1645/18, PRO.]

71. Personal and Strictly Confidential telegram from Johnson (U.S. Embassy London) to Dunn (State Department), #1437, May 29, 1940, State Department Decimal File Index, "Putlitz," RG 84 NA.

72. FBI reports June 11–20, 1940, in 800.20211 "Putlitz," State Department Decimal Records for 1940–1945, RG 84 NA.

73. Biddle to Dunn from Netherlands Embassy, October 30, 1942, State Department Decimal Records, RG 84 NA.

74. Letter from Putlitz to Lord Vansittart, August 1, 1946. Vansittart Papers (VST) II 1/9, Churchill College Archives, Cambridge (hereafter CCA).

75. Putlitz, op. cit., p. 249; p. 247.

76. Putlitz, op. cit., Preface. Either Putlitz was unaware that Blunt had been knighted in 1956, or he mischievously insisted on using "Mr."

77. Anatoli Vasilievich Baykolov was one of those intriguers among the Russian émigrés who were suborned by the OGPU in the early thirties. As a former member of the prerevolutionary cooperative movement, in 1917 he arrived in England and was for many years employed as a translator and analyst, paid at the rate of "a guinea per thousand words." Through the Duchess of Atholl and Captain H. B. Kirby, M.P., Baykolov acted as a source of information on the Soviet Union to Winston Churchill, Vansittart, and Guy Liddell and MI5. In 1933 a Ukrainian named Korostorets warned émigré Russian leaders in Paris that Baykolov was really working for the Soviets and a warning to that effect appeared in the October 22 edition of *Zovrozhdeniye*. His activities interviewing recent Russian escapees, supposedly for a study of the Soviet judicial system, appear to have been tied up with his mission for the OGPU. He was an associate of Sabline, the former tsarist chargé d'affaires in London, who was later found to have been an undercover OGPU agent monitoring the White Russian exiles in Britain. He had links to Skoblin, the OGPU operative in Paris, who was involved in the 1932 kidnapping of General Miller, the Paris-based chairman of the Russian Military Union (ROVS). [Documents in the Vansittart file confirm that Baykolov was a longtime MI5 and Foreign Office source of Soviet intelligence; his contact was Guy Liddell. Information supplied from the files of Natalie Grant Wraga; interviews with Dr. Georg Knuppfer in 1981 and Richard Deacon; and Dziak, *Chekisty* (Lexington, Mass.: Lexington Books, 1987), pp. 48–50.]

78. Guy Liddell to Vansittart re Baykolov, February 15, 1950, VST, II 1/41 Churchill College. Deacon quotes, without attribution, that both Sabline and Baykolov "were on friendly terms with Guy Liddell of MI5." [Deacon, *The British Connection*, p. 204.]

79. Most Secret Memorandum dated February 14, 1936, Davidson Papers, House of

Lords Records Office. The source was Maurice Jenks, the former lord mayor of London, who had come to the prime minister "on a most secret and important matter." The Prince of Wales had used his influence to get Ernest Simpson admitted to the Masonic Lodge over which Jenks presided. After Wallis's husband had been turned down by the lodge, Jenks was sent for by the Prince of Wales, who demanded to know the reason. "Do you want the truth?" asked J. "Yes!" replied the P. of W. "It is because quite obviously we could not admit the husband of your mistress as it would produce a situation in which the fundamental law that no Mason may sleep with another Mason's wife would be broken." The Prince of Wales "denied that there was anything between himself and Mrs. S. and gave a pledge to that effect as a Mason." But later, when Simpson was "mari complaisant," he told Jenks "that the King wants to marry Mrs. S. (unbelievable) & that he — S — would like to leave England, only to do so would make divorce easier — what he wants is his wife back." Baldwin gave Jenks "a flat negative," saying he was the "King's chief minister not Mr. S's."

80. Although Hoesch was known to be lukewarm to Hitler, the British Secret Service could have reasoned that by eliminating Hoesch they would not only cut off Hitler's tie to Mrs. Simpson but bring in a hard-line Nazi. A Nazi ambassador in London would be less favorable to winning moderate support for the bridge-building aims of the Anglo-German Fellowship and this served the interests of the British government and the Soviets. Joachim von Ribbentrop, who the previous year had taken much of the credit for negotiating the naval treaty that permitted Hitler to rebuild the Kriegsmarine, was his replacement. See also the perhaps too-knowing speculation about Hoesch's death by Wolfgang von und zu Putlitz (p. 110). Since this "autobiography" was written after Putlitz "went home" to East Germany, its publication was calculated to provide the maximum discomfort to the British.

## CHAPTER 18: PAGES 314–334

1. Rees, *Accidents*, p. 126.

2. See "Pertinax" [André Géraud], *The Gravediggers of France* (New York: Doubleday, Doran, 1944), pp. 100, 49: "Ferdinand de Brion and Pfeiffer, the former secretary general of the Radical Socialist Party who later left this position to go into business — both 'appeasers' were close to Daladier." Most writers appear to have taken Burgess at his word: that Pfeiffer was chef du cabinet to Daladier in 1936. [See Page et al., *Philby*, p. 92; Boyle, *Climate of Treason*, p. 150.] But Daladier, the French premier from January to October 1933 and from January to February 1934, was not appointed prime minister of France again until September 1938. The confusion seems to have arisen from a misreading of Rees (op. cit., p. 131), who states that Pfeiffer "to my astonishment, suddenly emerged from what I had assumed to be an indecent obscurity as chef du cabinet to the Prime Minister of France, Edouard Daladier." But Marcel Clapier, not Pfeiffer, was Daladier's chef du cabinet in 1938.

3. Rees, op. cit., p. 132.

4. Rees, op. cit., p. 144; Page, op. cit., p. 93; Burgess as told to Driberg in Moscow is the citation given for this illuminating anecdote.

5. Rees, op. cit., p. 131.

6. Driberg, *Portrait*, p. 32.

7. Glees, *Secrets of the Service*, p. 391, who quotes Hollis's letter to his mother about

his unsuccessful interview at *The Times* with Peter Fleming (the brother of Ian Fleming, the creator of James Bond).

8. W. J. West's diligent researches in the BBC Written Archives Center at Caversham have uncovered the link between Burgess, Fulford, and Hollis to which he drew attention in his revealing study *Truth Betrayed* (London: Duckworth, 1987), pp. 46–53; ibid., p. 33: I am grateful for the assistance Mr. West provided from his extensive investigations of the BBC archives.

9. W. J. West (pp. 38–39) shows how the head of the Foreign Office News Department, Sir Reginald Leeper, exercised a powerful and direct control over the BBC political contents of BBC broadcasts before the war, amounting in many instances to government control and censorship.

10. Annan interviews; information conveyed to the author from two confidential sources of W. J. West.

11. W. J. West, op. cit., p. 47, based on private correspondence. I would like to express special thanks to Bill West for sharing the results of his groundbreaking research.

12. Microfilm records of John Hilton's programs and correspondence in the BBC Written Archives Center; Straight interviews; Hilton was a natural broadcaster who attracted a large following among the working classes, which some conservatives suspected was the result of his dangerously left-wing appeal. Burgess was one of his wartime producers. For a general biography see Edna Nixon, *John Hilton: The Story of His Life* (London: 1946).

13. See the correspondence in the Anthony Blunt Contributor File, BBC Written Archives Center, Caversham.

14. Ibid.; the Blunt script, "Spanish Painting" (January 1939, BBC Written Archives Center), reveals Blunt's political naïveté that derived from his blinkered belief in communism. By associating the Fascist forces with philistinism and iconoclasm, he failed to recognize that the Soviet Union was the "self-avowed home of iconoclasm" in the twentieth century.

15. According to Driberg, Burgess flew to Paris shortly after German troops marched into the demilitarized Rhineland on March 7, 1936. He met Pfeiffer, who passed on the information "decided by a majority of only one not to resist Hitler unilaterally." [Driberg, *Portrait*, p. 37.] But Daladier had resigned the premiership in 1934 and did not become prime minister again until April 1938, in the aftermath of the Austrian Anschluss nor did he rejoin the Cabinet as minister of war until June 1936. [Telford Taylor, *Munich: The Price of Peace* (New York: Doubleday, 1979), pp. 134–137 and p. 499.]

16. The journalist was André Géraud, who charges that "Pfeiffer and Marion (himself a former official of the Comintern) argued that I had been hostile to Russia until 1934 during the years when they had been a peace-loving society." [Pertinax, op. cit., p. 431.]

17. Driberg, *Portrait*, p. 37.

18. Footman's intense interest in the Soviet Union is evident in his books *Red Prelude* (1944), *The Primrose Path* (1946), *Civil War in Russia* (1961), and *The Russian Revolutions* (1962). He also edited a series of papers on Soviet affairs and communism for St. Anthony's College, Oxford. Robert Cecil, who knew Footman, has pointed out that he also wrote a biography of Ferdinand Lassalle, the pre-Marxist socialist who founded the German Social Democratic Party and was a friend and influence on both Marx and Engels. Cecil suggests it is a curious coincidence that Goronwy

Rees gave up an All Souls scholarship in 1933 to go to Germany to write a life of Lassalle.

19. Anthony Glees, *The Secrets of the Service*, p. 264. Quotes from a 1985 interview with Sir Patrick Reilly, who was from April 1942 until October 1943 the personal assistant to C, the head of MI6, Sir Stewart Menzies, and later chairman of the JIC.

20. Philby, *My Silent War*, p. 123.

21. Cecil interviews.

22. See W. J. West, op. cit., pp. 62–64, quoting the BBC correspondence with Footman's agents, from the David Footman Contributor File at the BBC Written Archives Center. "This form of approach was unusual for the BBC," West notes, "where speakers more often than not were drawn from a circle of acquaintances and accepted broadcasters; certainly Burgess never approached anyone else on this basis." Henlein quote cited in Taylor, op. cit., p. 654.

23. Hewit interviews; he is "Jimmy Younger" in Isherwood's *Christopher and His Kind*, p. 236.

24. Nicolson, *Diaries*, p. 340.

25. Driberg, *Portrait*, p. 40; Lord Halifax was still alive when Driberg's book was published so he could not refer to him directly.

26. See Taylor, op. cit., pp. 560–565.

27. Driberg, *Portrait*, p. 41.

28. Wright, *Spycatcher*, p. 228.

29. See West, *Molehunt*, p. 92. According to West, who is accurate on housekeeping details, MI5 had two "traces" against the name "Mrs. J. Hart." One referred to Dr. Tudor Hart's wife, and the other to Jennifer Hart, the wife of H. L. A. Hart, the former professor of jurisprudence at Oxford. He was an open member of the Communist party in the thirties and, as a civil servant in the Home Office, was, in 1938, working in the sensitive department that processed MI5's applications for telephone-tap warrants. Although Jennifer Hart denied passing any secrets to the Russians, she admitted she met clandestinely in Kew Gardens with a "Russian" who, Wright asserts, "from her description was definitely Otto" [Wright, op. cit., p. 265]. This appears to be only an assumption. It cannot be taken as reliable proof that this was the same agent as the one Blunt claimed recruited him. Only forty-eight pages earlier the mysterious "Otto" is characterized not as a Russian, but "a middle-class European, probably Czech" and no accurate physical description was given of him by Blunt.

30. Wright, op. cit., p. 265; also documents in State Department 800 B file showed that the United States was being notified of any American who applied for membership and give evidence that the King Street headquarters was under constant surveillance.

31. Wright, op. cit., p. 265.

32. See Blunt's letter of June 1937 to George Barnes over the Sistine Chapel program, in which Blunt gives his Paris address as the Hotel Récamier, Place St.-Sulpice, and says, "I may meet Guy there, in which case of course I will talk it over with him." [Blunt contributor files, BBC Written Archives Center.]

33. The DST (Direction de la Surveillance du Territoire) as well as a section under

the Paris Prefecture of Police that is a counterpart of the British Special Branch. The French were concerned primarily with espionage directed against France and, secondarily, political activities involving French nationals. Because they were numerous and efficient, it is unlikely that notice was not taken of all Soviet activities. The question, of course, is how much if any of the information collected was passed to the British through liaison. Two senior officers who served in responsible positions within the DST in the late thirties have independently informed me that a large volume of key DST files were trucked to the U.S. embassy in Paris in mid-May 1940. The files were said to have been shipped as diplomatic cargo to the United States for safekeeping. The French officers claimed that among the files that were destined "to Alexandria, Virginia," were records of French operations against the Soviets in New York City (there being no U.S. liaison counterpart in the twenties and thirties) which implicated several U.S. State Department officers in Soviet-controlled nets. Several major espionage attacks (e.g., Lydia Stahl, the Swiss couple, etc.) by the Soviets against the French had their origin in NYC [Confidential Information].

34. Philby, op. cit., p. 189. The date, it is clear, must have been sometime in the spring or early summer of 1937, before or shortly after he became *The Times* accredited correspondent in Spain; Rees, op. cit., pp. 147, 140.

35. Sir Dick White, as quoted by Penrose & Freeman, op. cit., p. 190, and confirmed by independent sources.

36. Information given confidentially from an MI5 officer to Boyle, op. cit., p. 183.

37. Rees, op. cit., p. 147.

38. See W. J. West, op. cit., pp. 138–139, quoting from the blow-by-blow record of the dispute with the Foreign Office censors that is in the Harold Nicolson Contributor File, BBC Written Archives Center; Nicolson, *Diaries*, p. 361.

39. Chamberlain broadcast, September 27, 1938, as reported in *The Times*, September 28, 1938.

40. Harold Nicolson Contributor File, BBC Written Archives Center.

41. Driberg, *Portrait*, p. 43; E. H. Carr Contributor File, BBC Written Archives Center.

42. Information supplied to Andrew Boyle by David Graham of Burgess's remarks at the BBC dinner to mark the retirement of Sir Richard Maconachie as head of Talks in 1945. [Boyle, op. cit., p. 181.]

43. W. S. Churchill Contributor File, 1938, BBC Written Archives Center.

44. Driberg, *Portrait*, p. 46. Stephen Spender, to whom Burgess showed the volume *Arms and the Covenant* in Moscow in 1960, says that it read: "To Guy Burgess, in agreement with his views, Winston S. Churchill." Underneath was penciled "And we *were* right." [Stephen Spender, *Journals 1939–1983*, ed. John Goldsmith (New York: Random House, 1986), p. 214.] Eden, who had been shown the book by Burgess during his 1951 trip to Washington, had declined to add his signature, but Burgess — according to Spender — was so carried away that he added it himself! Burgess was never tired of dining out on the story and, on the night before he left the United States, in May 1951 — as the FBI files show — made a soulful record during a farewell party thrown for him by Norman Luker, who was then head of the BBC office in New York. [Burgess File, FBI file.]

45. Driberg, *Portrait*, p. 44.

46. See W. J. West, op. cit., p. 58, which sheds the harsh light of documented fact on many of the myths about Burgess's time at the BBC that other popular accounts have promoted.

47. Information supplied to the author via W. J. West from a confidential source.

48. Cabinet Memorandum from Vansittart, February 1939, CAB 27/641, PRO; see Halifax Memorandum, FO 395/626; P:781/6/150, PRO; see correspondence on origins of the cover operation: General Manager Travel Association and the British Council, July 17, 1936, BW2/29, PRO.

49. Brigadier Bickham Sweet Escott, *Baker Street Irregular* (London: Methuen, 1965), pp. 20–21.

50. Hilda Matheson, JBC report, FO T 162/858/E39140/4, PRO.

51. The JBC also adopted, for bureaucratic and security convenience, the name of a genuine Committee on Broadcasting, which had been established in July 1936. It held meetings at the British Council on Chesham Place [See BW2/29, PRO]; see Driberg, *Portrait*, p. 56. It is interesting to note that Burgess, even in 1956, went out of his way when mentioning the JBC to claim misleadingly that its "main purpose was to get British propaganda on the American networks"; information supplied to W. J. West by a former member of the staff. [See West, op. cit., p. 116.]

52. Wilfrid Blunt, *Single Life*, pp. 198–231.

53. Minute by Rex Leeper to the Strategical Appreciation Subcommittee of the Committee of Imperial Defence, FO 395/647B; P1402/105/150, PRO.

54. W. J. West, op. cit., pp. 107–110; Driberg, *Portrait*, p. 55. Although Driberg's Burgess account makes it appear that his mission to Lichtenstein took place *after* the outbreak of the war, it is clear from the context of what is known about his work for the JBC that it must have been sometime early in 1939.

55. Hoover Personal and Confidential Report to Rear Adm. Sidney Souers, Special Consultant to the President, March 2, 1950, HST.

56. Boyle, op. cit., p. 184, and Page et al., op. cit., p. 123.

57. Page et al., op. cit., p. 99; Hewit interview.

58. Nigel West interview.

59. Ibid.

60. Rees, op. cit., p. 148.

## CHAPTER 19: PAGES 335–354

1. Hansard Parliamentary Reports, May 19, 1939.

2. Winston S. Churchill, *History of the Second World War: Vol. 1: The Gathering Storm* (London: Cassell, 1948) p. 391.

3. As quoted by William L. Shirer, *The Rise and Fall of the Third Reich* (New York: Simon & Schuster, 1959), p. 721.

4. Rees, *Accidents*, p. 149; Cecil interviews.

5. Cecil interviews; Blunt press conference.

6. Cecil interviews; Rees, op. cit., p. 149.

7. Ibid.

8. Cecil interviews.

9. Rees, op. cit., p. 149.

10. "Report on Fifth Column Activities," Report dated August 1, 1940, 800.02, US Emb Lon, RG 84 NR.

11. Statute of Edward III, 1351.

12. Correspondence and telephone interviews with A. A. Berends, December 1988. Berends was studying French at Downing and remembers encountering Blunt in 1935 after he had responded to the BBC appeal and reported to Mychett Barracks, Ash Vale near Aldershot, the CMP depot; Blunt press conference.

13. Penrose & Freeman, *Conspiracy of Silence*, p. 218; Malcolm Muggeridge, *Chronicles of Wasted Time: The Infernal Grove* (London: Collins, 1972); Interviews with Malcolm and Kitty Muggeridge, 1986–1987.

14. Interview with Brigadier John Shearer, *The Sunday Mirror*, November 27, 1979; Berends letter.

15. Blunt to Cecil; the suggestion has been made that MI5 was not the source of information that gave the army pause. Chapman Pincher, *Their Trade Is Treachery*, p. 92, says that he was "informed that there was no such information on Blunt's file in MI5." But this appears contradicted by both Blunt's admission to Cecil and standard operating procedure of the time. It therefore appears that Pincher's MI5 source (probably Wright) was referring to Blunt's file *after* Blunt weeded it.

16. Blunt on contemporary art, *The Spectator*, October 22, 1937; Blunt, "Standards II," *The Spectator*, May 16, 1938.

17. See "The Writings of Anthony Blunt," compiled by his former secretary Else Sheerer for the *Festschrift* published in honor of his sixty-fifth birthday in 1972.

18. Blunt to Cecil; Cecil interviews.

19. Berends interviews.

20. Ibid.

21. See Liddell covering letter of July 4, 1940, to Johnson, enclosing Lord Rothschild's MI5 report on "The Machine Tool Industry," 820 Britain (Machine Tools) Box 3, 1940, US Emb Lon RG 84 NA.

22. Organization Chart of "Security Service Organization" in US Emb Lon, Box 9, 820.02 1942, RG 84 NA.

23. Many of these communications are signed by Liddell *per pro* Colonel Sir Vernon Kell, then director of MI5. But by 1938 Liddell's signature began appearing on its own.

24. Hershel V. Johnson, Councillor, to J. Pierrepoint Moffat, March 15, 1938, US Emb Lon, RG 84 NA. The reference to Scotland Yard is a hangover from the late twenties when Liddell first began liaising with the U.S. embassy as a representative of Metropolitan Police Special Branch.

25. The full details of the "Rumrich Case" — including a copy of his letter to Mrs. Jordan — are contained in the eighteen-page report that Liddell prepared for MI5 on his return from the United States, a copy of which exists in the Vansittart Papers, VST I, 2/21 CCA.

26. Ibid.

27. Ibid. For a contemporary overblown account of this spy sensation, E. H. Cookridge, *Secrets of the Service* (London: Sampson Low, 1947), pp. 136–146, drawn from Leon G. Turrou, *The Nazi Spy Conspiracy in America* (New York: 1945).

28. Confidential, Johnson to Moffat, February 1, 1938, US Emb Lon, 800.00 "General" RG 84 NA.

29. Liddell report, VST I, op. cit., p. 11.

30. Ibid., p. 12.

31. Secret letter, Liddell to Johnson, February 8, 1939, 800 "China and Japan"; Dunn to Johnson, September 5, 1939. US Emb Lon, RG 84 NA.

32. James Dunn, a senior officer in the Department of State and former U.S. ambassador in Rome, was designated as the addressee of information passed by British "friends" to the designated contact in the U.S. embassy in London. For an extended period of time, Hershel V. Johnson, the first secretary, accepted and forwarded intelligence communications from the British. Although Dunn enjoyed the trust and full confidence of the president and the secretary of state, the military and FBI began to exert great pressure to eliminate the "knothole" in State through which all such material flowed.

   In 1940, General Clayton Bissell, G-2 of the army (and former military attaché in the London embassy), called a meeting with Assistant Secretary Adolf Berle and J. Edgar Hoover to demand that armed military couriers take over the handling of all diplomatic traffic, especially that which involved intelligence material. Bissell's argument was greatly reinforced by the fact that as many as eight U.S. embassies had suffered communications compromises and that even the department's recently installed "strip cipher" had been lost to the Soviets.

   Available department records do not disclose precisely what was done as a *direct* result of Bissell's demands, although the department was reorganized shortly after the meeting and communications security was much improved. Jimmy Dunn's monopoly was also a casualty of the expanded awareness in the U.S. government that the State Department's intelligence system, based on informal cottage-craft, was inadequate to the requirements of imminent war.

33. "General" Walter G. Krivitsky was the name Samuel Ginsburg adopted in the United States where he testified before the House Un-American Activities Committee in 1939. He was "promoted" to general by his New York publishers to enhance the sensational nature of his revelations, which were serialized in *The Saturday Evening Post* under the title of *In Stalin's Secret Service*. But during a long career (which began when he and Reiss were members of the Communist underground in Warsaw during the Russo-Polish War), Krivitsky used aliases that included Eduard Miller, Walter Poref, and Dr. Martin Lessner, his cover in Holland when he defected in 1937. He was a GRU officer, starting his career in the Third Section, Soviet Military Intelligence. [See Corson and Crowley, *The New KGB*, p. 412; Dziak, op. cit., p. 64.]

34. Committee on the Judiciary, U.S. House of Representatives, "Un-American Activities Committee Hearings," October 11, 1939, p. 5720, Records of 89th Congress; Waldman as quoted by Flora Lewis in "Who Killed Krivitsky?" *The Washington Post*, February 13, 1966.

35. HUAC, op. cit.

36. *Saturday Evening Post*, April 1939; see also Isaac Don Levine, *Stalin's Great Secret* (New York: Coward McCann, 1956), p. 140.

37. Unpublished handwritten originals of Cadogan Diaries, September 4, 1939, ACAD 1/8, Churchill College Archives, Cambridge.

38. Ibid., September 15: "Busy in the afternoon with Harper & Vyvian, who was putting OK & King through a Third degree examination." Brigadier A. A. A. (Jasper) Harker was the director of B Division — his deputy was Guy Liddell — whose responsibility was Counter Espionage. Colonel Valentine Vyvian was the head of Section V, the MI6 counterintelligence section; Cecil interviews.

39. Cadogan Diaries, September 25, 1939, ACAD 1/8, CCA.

40. Ibid., September 26, 1939.

41. Because of the British government's continuing efforts to conceal both the King and Oldham cases, there is nothing other than the brief 1956 official statement on which to draw conclusions. Nigel West in MI5, p. 90, provides a sketchy account of a confrontation in a Curzon Street pub with MI5's T. A. Robertson of B Division and William Codrington over "a series of large whiskies" when King supposedly became "intoxicated and mournfully admitted his involvement with the Russians." But this seems conveniently simplistic — especially as West precedes this colorful scene in the Bunch of Grapes with the assertion that MI5 had first "to be sure of his guilt." Since West provides no clue how that proof was obtained, other than by plying King with "large whiskies," it seems the more convincing account is given in Gordon Brook-Shepherd's The Storm Petrels (New York: Ballantine, 1982), pp. 177–179. Deacon in The British Connection, pp. 141–142, produces a composite version that relies on Brook-Shepherd (published two years earlier), which adds that King was arrested "on his way to a tea shop in Whitehall to meet his Russian contact." Deacon asks, with some justification, "Why did the authorities not follow him into the tea shop and arrest his contact as well?"

42. Cadogan to Treasury, December 2, 1939, T162 574/E40411, PRO. Cadogan, November 30 entry recording that Halifax broke the "most painful news" to the department.

43. Andrew, Secret Service, p. 432.

44. Interview with Lord Gladwyn; private informant quoted by Christopher Andrew, op. cit., p. 479.

45. West, MI5, p. 88.

46. Brook-Shepherd, op. cit., p. 182.

47. The Spectator, December 1937.

48. John Cairncross was transferred to the Treasury in 1939.

49. Wright, Spycatcher, p. 265.

50. Levine, Stalin's Great Secret, p. 102; Philby, My Silent War, p. 175.

51. Wright, op. cit., p. 325.

52. See Chapman Pincher, Too Secret Too Long (New York: St. Martin's Press, 1984), pp. 450–452, which details the Ellis investigation which Wright omits. Australian-born Charles Howard "Dick" Ellis had been posted to Berlin in 1924 — fresh from the Sorbonne — as MI6 station chief. His abilities as a linguist and his subsequent marriage to Lilia Zelensky had enabled him to tap into the White Russian networks in Europe. His father-in-law, Alexander Zelensky, who had become one of his subagents, was named by an Abwehr officer after the war as having been the source of valuable information about MI6 and its organization in Belgium. This "order of

battle" data could have been provided only by an insider and the Zelensky family connection not only made Dick Ellis the prime suspect in the leak that led to the Venlo incident, but also the MI6 source who disclosed that until 1940 the British had been able to tap into German Foreign Ministry telephone traffic. The Venona decrypts and our information provided by the FBI identified that the Soviets had sources inside William Stephenson's BSC operation in New York, where Ellis had been deputy chief from 1940 through 1944. Blunt also inferred during his 1964 confession that that was indeed a link between Philby and Ellis, who had inexplicably returned to Britain from a premature early retirement in Australia shortly before the Petrov defection in April 1953. Ellis was intensively questioned by MI5 interrogators Theodore Pantcheff and Christopher Phillpotts in 1967. Anticipating that he was about to be confronted by the Abwehr officer who had been Zelensky's contact, he finally provided a short, typed confession and conceded that he had turned information about MI6 over to Zelensky for the Germans because of shortage of money. Even when offered an immunity deal similar to Blunt's, Ellis vehemently denied passing information to the Soviets. But Ellis could not have been as unaware of the dangers posed by the deep NKVD penetrations of the White Russian émigré organizations in Paris. [Wright, op cit., p. 325 and Nigel West, *Friends*, pp. 153–155.]

53. Wright, op. cit., p. 325.

54. Boyle, *Climate of Treason*, p. 219.

55. Cadogan Diary MS, op. cit., January 26, 1940, CCA.

56. Report on Fifth Column Activities and Counter Measures in Great Britain, #5710, dated August 1, 1930, 820.02 Lon Emb Confidential Files 1940 RG 84 NA.

57. Ibid.

58. Secret British Memorandum, "The Security Executive," dated December 1941, US Emb Lon, Box 9, RG 84 NA.

59. Ibid.

60. Ibid.

61. Ibid., p. 21.

62. Ibid.


## CHAPTER 20: PAGES 367–397

1. Philby, now serving as a *Times* correspondent with BEF headquarters, also found himself caught up in the tidal wave of confusion that preceded the German onslaught. In the retreat from Amiens on May 19 he lost all his kit. Six days later he was among the group of British journalists evacuated through Boulogne as the scouts of the 2nd Panzer Division began probing the outskirts of the town in the morning. [Page et al., *Philby*, pp. 130–131.] Berends interviews.

2. George Curry, statement to *Daily Telegraph*, November 17, 1979.

3. Christopher Blunt, as quoted in Penrose and Freeman, *Conspiracy of Silence*, p. 222.

4. Anthony Blunt, Preface to *François Mansart and the Origin of French Classical Architecture* (London: The Warburg Institute, 1941).

5. Anthony Blunt, preface to *Artistic Theory in Italy*, dated June 28, 1940.

6. Chapman Pincher, *A Web of Deception: The Spycatcher Affair* (London: Sidgwick & Jackson, 1987), p. 143. Chapman Pincher assured me that the information given is correct because Lord Rothschild had sight of his manuscript before publication.

7. See Rothschild's own account of the operation about dismantling the booby-trap bomb in February 1944 in *Meditations on a Broomstick*, pp. 29–32. The decoration was a singular distinction for an MI5 officer since it had always been the custom *not* to award individual decorations to members of the security services because of the demands of secrecy.

8. Rothschild's report on the British Machine Tool Industry with a covering letter by Guy Liddell, dated July 4, 1940, US Emb Lon 820 Britain "Machine Tool," Box 5, RG 84 NA.

9. Blunt press conference, *The Times*, November 21, 1979.

10. West, *MI5*, p. 426: "Following a recommendation from an MI5 officer"; and Penrose and Freeman, op. cit., p. 237: "after appealing to a friend in MI5 who provided him with an excellent reference"; Cecil interview.

11. West, *Molehunt*, p. 85.

12. Pincher, *A Web of Deception*, p. 9, and footnote on p. 205.

13. West interviews.

14. West interviews, 1987, and confirmed November 1987.

15. Ibid.

16. Green, *Children of the Sun*, p. 315; Page et al., *Philby*, p. 126.

17. Pincher, *A Web of Deception*, p. 9.

18. MI5 organizational chart, US Emb Lon, Box 9, 1942, RG 84 NA.

19. West interviews confirmed by a confidential source.

20. Blunt press conference; West interviews.

21. The British Foreign Office Library diplomatic lists show that Anatoli arrived in London in the late spring of 1940. "Henry" aka Gorski/Gromov emerged from Wright's investigations as one of the most effective of the new breed of Soviet controllers who operated in the forties when the NKVD resumed running its agent under diplomatic cover. Unlike the non-Russian illegals of the thirties, these "legals" were diplomats and native Soviets, who were themselves tightly controlled by Moscow Center. "Henry" was the principal control officer for Blunt, Burgess, Philby, and Maclean as well as for Jürgen Kuczinski, after the German expatriate Communist was released from an alien internment camp in May 1940. [Pincher, *Treachery*, p. 48, citing Kuczinski's memoirs.] He moved on to Washington in 1944 and, using the cover name "Al," was for a time the controller of Elizabeth Bentley. [FBI "Gregory Case" file (Elizabeth Bentley).] According to Pincher, p. 416, Gromov ended up as a Professor Nikitin at the Moscow Institute of History.

22. Information provided by Christopher Harmer to Penrose and Freeman, op. cit., p. 249.

23. White as quoted by Penrose and Freeman, op. cit., p. 251, and confirmed.

24. Philby, op. cit., p. 80.

25. See Pincher, *Treachery*, pp. 112–113, for the details, which were subsequently confirmed by Wright, *Spycatcher*, p. 220.

26. Wright, op. cit., p. 20.

27. Cecil interviews.

28. Driberg, *Portrait*, p. 56; W. J. West, in *Truth Betrayed*, pp. 192–200, details the extent to which Burgess was involved with the clandestine radio war.

29. Rosamond Lehmann interview; Driberg, op. cit., p. 56. "In March 1940 he went to Paris with a distinguished woman novelist whose books were popular in France; it seemed desirable that she should do some broadcasts for the French Radio."

30. Ibid.; for a description of Grand's operations see M. R. D. Foote, *The S.O.E.* (London: 1984), p. 15; Bickham Sweet Escott, op. cit., p. 36.

31. Philby records that a Captain Leslie Sheridan of the War Office had telephoned Ralph Deakin, the editor of the *Times* foreign news desk "to ask whether I was available for war work." [*My Silent War*, pp. 22–23.] Burgess not only had friends in the homosexual network in the War Office, such as Tom Wylie, but he could also have dropped Philby's name to David Footman of the MI6 political section. That Philby was eventually assigned to Burgess as his assistant leaves little doubt that Burgess was the prime mover for his admission to the secret service.

32. Philby, op. cit., p. 27.

33. Ibid.

34. Philby, op. cit., p. 22. (See entries on Frank L. Birch in *Kingsmen of the Century*; he was the mutual friend and fellow broadcaster.)

35. It is curious that the reports Cookridge mentions were filed in 1934 by the *Daily Telegraph* correspondent in Vienna, who as an MI6 intelligence source would have reported that Philby was a member of the Communist underground. [Cookridge, *Third Man*.]

36. Driberg, op. cit., p. 58; Philby, op. cit., p. 31.

37. Straight, *Silence*, p. 141.

38. Confidential FBI report of interview conducted with Michael Straight on June 18, 1963, dated June 25, 1963, WFO 100-3644. Files obtained under FOIA by Michael Straight, who kindly provided them *in their entirety* to the author. Hereafter referred to as "FBI Straight."

39. In *After Long Silence*, Straight puts the first contact at April 1938. But his memoir was written *before* Straight had been able to "refresh" his memory from the 1963 FBI records, which state that he "related sometime between October, 1937, and March, 1938, and probably in December, 1937, he received a phone call at his home from an unknown man who identified himself as Michael Green." [FBI Straight, June 25, 1963, p. 5.]

40. Straight, op. cit., p. 129; FBI Straight, June 25, 1963, p. 5.

41. FBI Straight, p. 6.

42. FBI Straight report, July 31, 1975; June 25, 1963; Straight, op. cit., p. 129.

43. FBI Straight, June 25, 1963, p. 8.

44. Ibid., p. 11.

45. The FBI file shows that Straight identified Adler from FBI photographs as Solomon Aaron Linchinsky, who, he then recalled, had been linked to the revelations made by Elizabeth Bentley's Soviet espionage ring in the State Department.

46. Straight interviews.

47. Straight, op. cit., p. 134.

48. Ibid.

49. Philby, op. cit., p. 30.

50. T. A. Robertson, as quoted by Penrose and Freeman, op. cit., p. 253; Blunt's introduction to the Tomas Harris Memorial Exhibition; Muggeridge quoted by Boyle, op. cit., p. 185, and Philby, op. cit., p. 31.

51. See Deacon, *The British Connection*, p. 174. The former Soviet agent identified only by the pseudonym "Roger" was himself a member of the anti-Fascist INSA group in the early thirties in Switzerland and a member in a Soviet espionage network; Nigel West, *Friends* (London: Weidenfeld & Nicolson, 1988), p. 153.

52. Cited by Deacon in *The British Connection*, p. 175.

53. Report in Palma daily newspaper *Baleares*, January 28, 1964.

54. Solomon and Litvinoff, *A Woman's Way*.

55. Ibid., p. 163.

56. Philby interview, *Sunday Times*, March 1988; Solomon, op. cit., p. 169.

57. Ibid., p. 172.

58. Philby, op. cit., p. 211; Pincher, *Treachery*, p. 142.

59. Solomon, op. cit., p. 226.

60. Ibid.

61. Ibid.; Wright, *Spycatcher*, p. 172. Despite Lord Rothschild's reluctance, he permitted MI5 engineers to install a secret microphone in his telephone for the interview on the promise that they would remove it, because he was convinced that MI5 was clandestinely tapping him to find out details of his intimate connections with the Israelis.

62. Solomon, op. cit., p. 173. Solomon evidently told Martin more than she later admitted in her book. Wright says that she explained how Philby had taken her out to lunch to tell her he was working for the Comintern and that although she refused to accept Philby's invitation to join him, she told him he could always come back to her if he was desperate.

63. Wright then continues that Solomon said, "There is too much risk. You see what has happened to Tomas since I spoke to Victor," referring to the fact that one of Philby's friends, Tomas Harris, the art dealer, had recently died in a mysterious car accident in Spain. Wright's memory was playing him tricks because Harris was not killed until 1964, *two years after the Solomon interview!*

64. Information supplied by Nigel West in *MI6*, p. 226; Juan Pujol with Nigel West, *Garbo* (London: Weidenfeld & Nicolson, 1985), pp. 74–75; and Philby, op. cit., pp. 49–50.

65. Pujol with West, *Garbo*, p. 75; the interview with Peter Liddell confirmed his father's continuing close relationship with Harris and Blunt. He vividly remembers the El Grecos and flamenco dancers at the 1951 New Year's party at the Harris home, then in Logan Place.

66. Hilton and Macdonald interviews. (Macdonald recalled that the security vetting he

received came "3 or 4" months after he joined MI5, when he was sent to head-quarters in St. James's to see a former solicitor. The process consisted of taking a volume from the rows of leather-bound indexes of names and leafing through it cursorily. The extent of the MI5 files was such that he was surprised that "Macdonald" occupied a whole volume; Macdonald was impressed.) [Sir Dick White, as quoted by Penrose and Freeman, op. cit., p. 249.]

67. Sir Dick White, as quoted, Penrose and Freeman, op. cit., p. 249. White stood by his assertion about Liddell's refusal to have Burgess in the "office." In information conveyed to this author via an intermediary, he confirmed that MI5 continued to use information supplied by Burgess in connection with a diplomatic source in the Swiss Embassy.

68. Timothy Johnston interview, 1988; Christopher Harmer as quoted by Penrose and Freeman, op. cit., p. 259.

69. Information from Sir Dick White relayed to the author by a confidential inter-mediary.

70. Pincher, *A Web of Deception*, p. 8. Additional information on the Bentinck Street lease is from a confidential source.

71. Hewit interviews.

72. Blunt, *François Mansart*, Preface, in which he thanks "Miss Tess Mayor for taking down the first two lectures at my dictation"; Hewit interviews.

73. Ibid.

74. Ibid.

75. Rees, *Accidents*.

76. Goronwy Rees to Andrew Boyle, *Observer*, January 13, 1979, and Boyle, op. cit., p. 264.

77. Hewit interviews.

78. Malcolm Muggeridge, *Chronicles of Wasted Time: The Infernal Grove*, pp. 106– 107, and supplemental information supplied by Muggeridge in Boyle, op. cit., p. 233.

79. Hewit interviews.

80. Ibid; Geoffrey Wethered was one of the twelve RSLOs — regional security liaison officers — who managed B Division's liaison throughout Britain with the local army commanders and chief constables.

81. Hewit interviews.

82. Ibid.

83. Ibid.

84. Ibid.

85. Cecil interviews.

86. Ibid.

87. Ibid.

88. Ibid.

89. Cadogan Diaries, December 23, 1943, CCA.

## CHAPTER 21: PAGES 398–419

1. Hewit interviews.

2. Winston S. Churchill, *History of the Second World War, Vol. III, The Grand Alliance* (New York: Bantam Books, 1962), p. 39

3. Thümmel had originally been recruited by the Czech intelligence service in 1936. Code-named "A-54," he had provided accurate advance warning of every German move from the campaign against the Sudentenland and Czechoslovakia to the attack on Poland, Italy's entry into the war in 1940, and the attack on Greece. After Czech intelligence was evacuated to London, Thümmel's information was shared with MI6. It was from this most reliable source about the German Order of Battle that since October 1940 reports had filtered in indicating preparations under way for the campaign in the East. [Hinsley et al., *British Intelligence in the Second World War*, Vol. I (Cambridge University Press, 1979), pp. 58, 205, 368, 435–436, 472–473.]

4. As quoted in Hinsley, Vol. I, p. 452.

5. For a full discussion of the significance of the Enigma and Purple traffic in disclosing the attack on Russia, see Hinsley, Vol. I, pp. 463–465.

6. Joint Intelligence Committee (41) 252 (0) of June 12, 1941, quoted in Hinsley, Vol. I, p. 479.

7. Hinsley et al., *British Intelligence in the Second World War*, Vol. II (London: HMSO, 1981), p. 60.

8. Ronald Lewin, *Ultra Goes to War: The Secret Story* (New York: McGraw-Hill, 1978), p. 64.

9. Ibid; Hinsley, Vol. I, pp. 138–139.

10. Statement to Penrose and Freeman, *Conspiracy of Silence*, p. 273, confirmed by other MI5 sources.

11. Wright, *Spycatcher*, p. 265, citing Hart's admission to him that she had two other Oxford contacts including Bernard Floud, who she claimed recruited her. Wright was convinced that there was a "separate Ring based exclusively in Oxford University." But he said that investigating it "proved enormously difficult." [For other assessments of the Oxford Ring, see Christopher Andrew's interview with Mrs. Hart, quoted in *On Her Majesty's Secret Service*, p. 460.]; confidential source.

12. Harmer quoted in Penrose and Freeman, op. cit., pp. 273–274, and Pujol, *Garbo*, p. 74.

13. Hinsley, Vol. I., p. 668, where ISK is cited as Abwehr Enigma, and Hinsley, Vol. II, p. 20.

14. A nine-page draft report on "The Running of Double Agents." It was discovered among the private papers of Professor Norman Holmes Pearson, who was with the OSS counterintelligence team in London during the war. Undated and unsigned, the most likely author was Sir John Masterman, chairman of the Twenty Twenty Committee. (The report is hereafter referred to as "Double Agents.") [Norman Holmes Pearson Papers, YCAL Box 3, Beinecke Manuscript Library, Yale (hereafter "Pearson Yale").] See also Robin Winks, *Cloak and Gown* (New York: William Morrow, 1987), p. 284.

15. "Some of these were dropped by parachute (e.g. Tate) or were landed in this

country by the Germans (e.g. Mutt and Jeff); some were volunteers (Dragonfly and Garbo) who got in touch with the Germans themselves, were recruited by them and offered their services to us. Some, having been recruited by them in distant parts of Europe (e.g. Tricycle), informed our representative there, asked for our instructions and were able to carry on with the Germans and keep us informed." [Double Agents, Pearson Yale.]

16. The Twenty Twenty Committee exercised authority delegated from the Wireless Board that had been set up in June 1940 to monitor the "disinformation" passed back to Germany. Its members consisted of Guy Liddell from MI5; Stewart Menzies, the director of MI6; and the directors of military and naval intelligence. [Masterman, *Double Cross System*. For additional insights see Winks, op. cit., pp. 283–287, and Pujol, *Garbo*.]

17. Double Agents, Pearson Yale.

18. Ibid.

19. Ibid.

20. Ibid.

21. Ibid.

22. Dusko Popov, *Spy Counterspy* (New York: Grosset & Dunlap, 1974), which was supposedly substantiated by J. F. Bratzel and L. B. Rout, Jr., "Pearl Harbor, Microdots and J. Edgar Hoover," *The American Historical Review*, Vol. 87, No. 5, pp. 1342–1348. Former British military intelligence officer David Mure also tackled the "Tricycle" issue in *Master of Deception: Tangled Webs in London and the Middle East* (London: William Kimber, 1980), pp. 189–190. In the section of his manuscript that was cut before publication, Mure speculated that Guy Liddell or Kim Philby was responsible for routing Popov not to the U.S. military agencies but to the FBI, thereby wittingly playing a hand in the Pearl Harbor disaster. But this theory was predicated on the FBI blundering — and the documentary evidence shows that it did not. Moreover, Mure's extensive correspondence in 1979 with Tar Robertson and Felix Cowgill shows that they discounted Philby's involvement on the basis that he was not at that time senior enough in the Iberian section to have influenced the decisions made by Liddell over "Tricycle." [Excised typescript and letters are in the Mure Papers Manuscript Collection, The Imperial War Museum, London.]

23. Information from Natalie Grant Wraga; Krivitsky, *In Stalin's Secret Service*, p. 239; Sergueiev, who married an American army officer and became a U.S. citizen, does not touch on her Soviet connection in her account, *Secret Service Rendered*, published in America shortly before her death in 1966. But, significantly, her account attempts to blame the Germans for General Miller's abduction (p. 104) in defiance of the facts as they are now known: that Skoblin and his wife, Plentskaya (also referred to by Sergueiev), were the ones who engineered the assassination for the NKVD; Dziak, *Chekisty*, pp. 96–97.

24. Deacon, *The British Connection*, pp. 177–178, cited to a 1977 interview with Darling before his death. Darling had been responsible for managing the Iberian escape route for Lisbon until late 1943 under the guise of a British embassy official. According to the official S.O.E. history [M. R. D. Foote & J. M. Langley, *MI9 Escape and Evasion* (London: Bodley Head, 1979), p. 77], Darling "ran a one-man interrogation office which was invaluable for the work of MI9. . . . This enabled him to spot anybody who was trying to feed himself onto an MI9 line while in fact working for an Axis agency; a valuable safeguard."

25. Masterman, *Double Cross*, p. 168; Deacon, op. cit., p. 178, citing a letter to Deacon from Norman Holmes Pearson, October 3, 1977. Pearson was a "de facto" member of the XX Committee from 1943 as the ranking OSS counterintelligence officer in London; for a convincing exposé of the "Tramp"/"Treasure" Soviet link, see Deacon, *The British Connection*, pp. 177–179.

26. Leo Long interview, October 1987.

27. Ibid.

28. Ibid.

29. Martin Gilbert, *Winston S. Churchill*, Vol. V (Boston: Houghton Mifflin, 1981).

30. Long interviews.

31. Wright, op. cit., p. 221.

32. Long interview.

33. Long interview; Annan interviews.

34. These included signals from Russia's 17th Air Division, naval traffic, and the signaling system used by aircraft in the Leningrad area. [Information from still-secret GCHQ records not individually cited in Hinsley, Vol. II, p. 59; Dir/C Archive, 6883 of June 24, 1941, cited in Hinsley, Vol. II, p. 59.]

35. For an authoritative discussion of the abortive attempts at Anglo-Soviet intelligence cooperation, see Hinsley, Vol. II, pp. 59–66.

36. Wright, op. cit., pp. 221–223; Nigel West, *GCHQ: The Secret Wireless War 1900–1986* (London: Weidenfeld & Nicolson, 1986), pp. 150–155. For an authoritative insider's account, see Gordon Welchman, *The Hut Six Story* (New York: McGraw-Hill, 1986); Wilkinson, *Kingsmen of the Century*, p. 366.

37. The Enigma machine on which the Germans relied for the bulk of the secret communications was plaintext enciphered through a system of rotors, which advanced with each letter when the plaintext was entered through the typewriter keyboard. The internal wiring of the rotors, each position of which represented a letter of the alphabet, provided a primary encoding by routing the electrical current through a series of contacts on the wheels to illuminate a bulb indicating the encoded letter. The rotors advanced in relation to each other, and their initial position, along with the setting of a plug-board, determined the starting point for the cipher — the so-called *Enigma key*. Following the initial work on Enigma done by Polish and French intelligence before the outbreak of the war, Turing and Knox had played a leading role in devising the mathematical basis for cracking Enigma. But it was the primitive computing machine code-named Bombe, for which Turing is usually credited, that greatly accelerated the decrypting process. It automatically sifted through hundreds and thousands of combinations to establish which rotor setting constituted the key for that day and for that particular traffic. Once the settings of rotors and plug-board had been established, the messages could be read out by feeding them into a British-built analog of the German machines. [For an authoritative summary of Turing's contribution to Ultra, see Hinsley, Vol. I, Appendix 1, pp. 491–492.]

38. Andrew Hodges, *Alan Turing: The Enigma* (New York: Simon & Schuster, 1983), p. 409; Hodges doesn't quote in full an intriguing letter from Turing to his mother, May 26, 1933, KCA: "Am thinking of going to Russia some time in the vac, but have not quite made up my mind. I have joined an organization called the 'Anti-War Council.' Politically rather communist. Its program is principally to organize strikes

amongst munitions and chemical workers when the government intends to go to war." This suggests Turing might have been more vulnerable to Soviet pressure than has hitherto been believed.

39. Wright, op. cit., p. 222.

40. Information from Wright, quoted by Chapman Pincher, *Too Secret Too Long*, p. 396.

41. Ibid.; and see Vansittart confidential letter to Sir Frederick Morgan, dated March 9, 1950, detailing Klugmann's activities. [VST II 2/23 CCA.]

42. Wright, op. cit., p. 222.

43. Michael Straight, in *After Long Silence*, p. 143, records how Burgess, during his 1940 visit to Washington, had told him Blunt was "enraged" when another Apostle "tried unsuccessfully to seduce Leo during a drunken party that had followed the annual dinner of the society in 1938." Straight assumed that this suggested Long had been recruited by Blunt; Wright, op. cit., p. 250, says that Blunt told him "the situation was additionally complicated by the fact that Blunt was having an affair with the potential recruiter, although neither told the other about his designs on Long." Wright provided a further clue by saying that the Apostle worked on the deception (the Phantom Program) during the war and later left to pursue an academic career; Wright, op. cit., pp. 221–222.

44. Wright, op. cit., p. 251.

45. West, *MI5*, p. 427, first published the account originating from Arthur Martin, which has subsequently been repeated, with variations, by other writers.

46. Burgess later claimed to have provided the tipoff and led the raid. Neither claim is substantiated by declassified U.S. documentation. [Driberg, *Portrait*.]

47. Driberg, *Passions*, p. 150.

48. Joan Miller, *One Girl's War*, p. 65, and interview with Joan Miller, 1983.

49. Masters, *M*, p. 178.

50. Joan Miller, op. cit., p. 64; Chapman Pincher in *Too Secret Too Long*, p. 347. Pincher also quotes from his 1981 conversations with Wright, that Blunt also alerted the Soviets "within a week of the installations of the microphones" that the CPGB headquarters were being bugged.

51. West, *MI5*, p. 356. He also asserts that Springhall gave Anatoli Gorski as his contact at the Soviet embassy. But U.S. intelligence experts doubt whether "Henry," whose primary responsibility was running the Cambridge network, would have taken the risk of contacting anyone with such a high visibility to the MI5 "watchers" as the national organizer of the Communist party.

52. Wright, op. cit., p. 229.

53. Philby, op. cit., p. 48.

54. Hugh Trevor-Roper, *The Philby Affair* (London: William Kimber, 1968), p. 28.

55. Interview with Felix and Mrs. Cowgill, July 1986.

56. Philby, op. cit., p. 57; Cowgills' interview.

57. Philby, op. cit., p. 59; Hugh Trevor-Roper, op. cit., pp. 28–29.

58. Muggeridge, *The Infernal Grove*, p. 126.

59. Philby, op. cit., pp. 79–81.

60. In December 1938 Guy Liddell journeyed to the United States to conduct a successful custody battle in a Miami court for his four children whom his estranged wife had taken with her to Florida. For the father to be awarded custody was unprecedented at the time. He was greatly assisted by the evidence of his wife's incestuous relationship with her half brother, given by the butler and cook who were themselves then sued for defamation of character. The case made headlines on both sides of the Atlantic — but Liddell's triumph was short-lived. Although he took his children back to England, two years later Calypso Baring Liddell succeeded in having the court reverse the decision in order to have her children evacuated to safety from the Blitz. [Liddell interview.]

61. Hewit interviews.

62. Confidential but exceptionally well-informed source.

## CHAPTER 22: PAGES 420–442

1. Malcolm Muggeridge to Andrew Boyle, *Climate of Treason*, and interviews; Bickham Sweet-Escot as to Page, et al., *Philby*, p. 186.

2. Philby, *My Silent War*, p. 110; p. 81.

3. Ibid., p. 64.

4. Ibid., p. 85.

5. Undated memorandum, "British Recruitment and Handling of Agents," in Box 2, Pearson Yale.

6. Ibid.

7. Fourth report of the War Cabinet, "Panel on Security Arrangements in Government Departments," dated June 25, 1942, Copy #112 in Box 9, Confidential Files of U.S. Embassy London, RG 84 NA.

8. Winks, *Cloak and Gown*, p. 287; entry in appointments diary 1943; 1944 Box 1, Pearson Yale.

9. Undated letter draft, Box 2, Pearson Yale.

10. For a thorough and authoritative analysis of the role played by Norman Holmes Pearson, see Winks, op. cit., pp. 247–321.

11. Undated report, "Counter-Espionage — X2," Box 1, Pearson Yale; undated and untitled draft in Box 2, Pearson Yale.

12. Winks, op. cit., p. 341. For a reliable portrait of Angleton at war, see Winks's chapter on "The Theorist," pp. 322–469, a study based on many hours of close interviews with the often reticent and always enigmatic former CIA counterintelligence chief.

13. David Martin, *Wilderness of Mirrors;* and see Winks, op. cit., p. 537, for his interpretation of Angleton's phrase "the wilderness of mirrors."

14. Undated memorandum on "Theory of Counter Intelligence Operations," Box 2, Pearson Yale.

15. "Draft Suggestions for Talks on Russia," submitted by Guy Burgess on July 15, 1941, R51/520/1, BBC.

16. For a full analysis of the issues raised by the Christopher Hill employment, see Glees, op. cit., pp. 279–283.

17. Interview with Mrs. Kemball Johnston and Timothy Johnston; Dr. Christine Carpenter (née Johnston) and Peter Fairbairn, April 1988.

18. Cadogan Diaries, August 13, 1943, ACAD 1/111, CCA.

19. Anthony Cave Brown, *"C": The Secret Life of Sir Stewart Menzies, Spymaster to Winston Churchill* (New York: Macmillan, 1987), p. 474.

20. Air Vice Marshal Sir James Easton as quoted from interviews in 1986 by Cave Brown, op. cit., p. 474. But the Churchill cable, "I suppose you realize that we are weeding remorselessly every single known Communist from all the secret organizations," which Brown implies by juxtaposition was sent in August 1943 after the alarm was raised about "Communists in his organization," was not sent until April 6, 1944, *ten months after* "C" *met Cadogan!* [Cited by Martin Gilbert, *The Road to Victory: Winston Churchill, 1941–1945* (London: Heinemann, 1986), p. 729.]

21. Cowgill interviews; information from Robert Cecil.

22. Prime Minister's Personal Telegram, T 730/4, "Personal and Most Secret," No. 324 to Algiers, April 6, 1944: Churchill papers, 20/161, Churchill College Archives, Cambridge. [Not yet open to researchers, but cited in Gilbert, *Churchill*, Vol. VII, pp. 729–730.]

23. Application and note from Dick White dated December 31, 1944, 210.3, Assignment of Officers, SHAEF G-2 Intelligence, Target (T) Decimal File 1944–5, Box 156, SHAEF, RG 331 NA.

24. Patrick Howarth, *Intelligence Chief Extraordinary* (London: The Bodley Head, 1986), p. 163; Cecil interviews.

25. Draft information from Sir Dick White reconfirmed via an intermediary; Sir Dick White is quoted by Penrose and Freeman, op. cit., p. 286: "I was a member of Eisenhower's staff and head of counterintelligence. Blunt was not really at SHAEF."

26. Ibid.

27. SHAEF G-3 Administrative Section, Subject File "Fortitude," RG 331 NA.

28. Memorandum, "Planning and Organization," in Box 2, Pearson Yale.

29. Colonel R. F. Hesketh's Epilogue in Pujol, *Garbo*, p. 168.

30. Wing Commander Roman Garby-Czerniawiski had been imprisoned when the Germans occupied Paris and allowed to "escape" to England to provide his cover as an Abwehr agent. He was "turned" by Hugh Astor, who became his case officer. [Pujol, *Garbo*, pp. 134–136.]

31. Ibid., pp. 134–136; 145–149.

32. *Dictionary of National Biography, 1961–1970*, the Harris entry contributed by Blunt, p. 493.

33. Wright, *Spycatcher*, p. 228.

34. Pincher, *Too Secret Too Long*, p. 351; Wright, op. cit., p. 228.

35. Sir William Haley to Andrew Boyle, as quoted in *Climate of Treason*, p. 228.

36. Cowgill interview: The new Section IX is not to be confused with the prewar Section IX, headed by a Colonel Jeffreys, which dealt with codes and ciphers and

was amalgamated with GC&CS. [West, *MI6*, p. 386]; Cowgill's version of events contrasts somewhat with Philby's account. [*My Silent War*, pp. 113–114.] Philby suggests that Jane Archer, whom he acknowledges as "perhaps the ablest professional intelligence officer ever employed by MI5," was brought in *after* Philby had taken over Section IX in October 1944. Although he says that she was "a woman after my own heart," and professed admiration for her "tough-minded and rough-tongued" earthiness, Philby must have been uneasy lest she uncover his Communist past. He therefore always treated her with respect. He deflected her research into analysis of the Soviet support of the wartime national-liberation movements in Eastern Europe.

37. Cowgill interview.

38. Philby, op. cit., p. 101.

39. Ibid., p. 103.

40. Cowgill told me that apart from liaising with the FBI and OSS in Washington, his visit was made to try and arrange for the return of his son and daughters. But with D-Day near, there were very few civilian berths available, and Norman Holmes Pearson arranged for his wife in New Haven to take Cowgill's children in until transport to England became available.

41. Cowgill interviews.

42. Ibid.

43. Philby, op. cit., p. 108.

44. Cowgill interviews; drafts of an undated letter from Pearson to Cowgill. The final version he believes must have been sent sometime after they dined together for the last time on October 20, 1944. Letter from Cowgill to Pearson, January 19, 1945, notifying him officially that he had relinquished control of Section V and asking formally that the Americans extend "the same cooperation to Major T. I. Milne." [Pearson Yale.]

45. Philby, op. cit., p. 109; ibid.

46. See Cave Brown, op. cit., pp. 623–624, in which he discusses Donovan's December 1943 approach via U.S. Ambassador Averell Harriman in Moscow to exchange intelligence with the NKVD. Hoover's objection that there were already too many Soviet agents operating in the United States effectively killed this scheme. But C had also discovered that the OSS was "meddling" by pursuing an independent and "anticolonial" line against British interests in the Balkans; report by Lieutenant Commander W. M. Scott, USNR (Pearson's successor as chief of X-2 Mission in London), to Colonel William W. Quinn, OSS HQ Washington, dated April 30, 1946. [Pearson Yale.]

47. Muggeridge interviews, July 1986 and July 1987.

48. Muggeridge, *The Infernal Grove*, pp. 250–251.

49. Colonel Lord Rothschild was attached to 105 Special Counter Intelligence Unit. See letter to Lord Rothschild from Colonel Marshall, dated November 27, 1944 (letter of November 25 has been withdrawn at request of "GB/Intel"). [U.S. Seventh Army File #924, Box 71 Entry 13B, SHAEF G-3 Records, RG 331 NA.]

50. Muggeridge as quoted by Boyle, op. cit., p. 280, and confidential interviews.

51. Muggeridge interviews.

52. Muggeridge interviews.

## CHAPTER 23: PAGES 443–471

1. Sir Dick White as quoted and confirmed in Penrose and Freeman, *Climate of Treason*, p. 286.

2. A review of the SHAEF Headquarters Files for G-2 (Intelligence) and G-3 (Plans) disclosed the role played by Lieutenant-Colonel *Christopher* Blunt in the Censorship Section, but no direct evidence of any official position occupied by his brother Anthony. [RG 331 NA.]

3. Letter from Woolley to Colonel C. E. D. Bridge, dated April 17, 1944, 12 Army Group, RG 331 NA.

4. Letter to Kligender from Ellis Waterhouse, August 1, 1944, 12 Army Group, RG 331 NA.

5. Blunt's role with the Canadian divisions was apparently so minor that Colonel Roger Hesketh, who directed the "Special Means" section of Fortitude, cannot remember precisely what he was doing. [Letter dated July 27, 1983.]

6. Wright, *Spycatcher*, p. 223.

7. Ibid.

8. *Sunday Times*, November 25, 1979, added to by Penrose and Freeman, op. cit., p. 299.

9. *Sunday Times*, November 25, 1979.

10. Roper says that it was published shortly afterward in *The Times Literary Supplement*.

11. Philip Prinz von Hessen (1896–1960) was until 1943 one of the leading "royal" Nazis. A friend of Göring, Hesse had joined the National Socialist party in October 1930, joining the Stürmabteilung the same year and reaching the rank of Gruppenführer in the SA in 1933, the same year he became Oberpräsident of the Province of Hessen-Nassau. He studied art history in Rome, and his marriage to Princess Mafalda, the second daughter of King Victor Emmanuel II of Italy, made Prince Philip a useful ally when Hitler courted Mussolini. [Sources on Hesse family: Dieter Rebenstich, *Persönlichkeitsprofil und Karriereverlauf de nationalsozialistischen Aduhrungskader in Hessen 1928–1945* (Marburg: Sonderdruck aus Hessisches Jahrbuch für Landesgesichte, Vol. 33, 1983), pp. 303–305; Hans Philippi, *Das Haus Hessen: Ein europäisches Fürstengeschlecht* (Kassel: 1983), pp. 152–155.]

12. Roger Fulford, *Friedrichshof: The Home of the Empress Frederick* (Munich: Schness and Steiner Verlag, 1975).

13. Report on Nash and Durant arrests, *New York Times*, June 10, 1946.

14. Ibid.

15. Ibid.

16. Ibid.

17. See "Hesse" file in SHAEF G-2, entry 254-80, "Ashcan," entry 18A – Box 156, RG 331 NA.

18. *Sunday Times*, November 25, 1985.

19. Lady Diana Mosley, *The Duchess of Windsor* (London: Sidgwick & Jackson, 1980), p. 89.

20. Documents relating to German Foreign Policy, Volume I #5482/E382057 (US Government Printing Office, 1955).

21. Ibid.

22. Ralph G. Martin, *The Woman He Loved* (New York: Simon & Schuster 1974), as cited by Peter Allen in *The Crown and the Swastika* (London: Robert Hale, 1983, p. 87). Sir Dudley Forwood, a German-speaking attaché to the British ambassador in Vienna, was adjutant to the Duke of Windsor during the three years from the time of his abdication until the outbreak of the war. Forwood told me of the deep alienation between the Duke and the King following the denial of the HRH title to the Duchess on his marriage. "It broke his heart when I told him that it was not going to come from the Palace. He broke into tears on my shoulder," Forwood recalled. "'Well, Dudley, *you* think she's worth it.' I could only say, 'I will always have the greatest respect and honor for your Royal Highness's wife.'"

Forwood believes that from that moment on there was "intense bitterness" between the Duke — whom, despite his obvious regard for "HRH," Forwood characterized as a "middle-aged Romeo" — and his Juliet, the Duchess. "As much as I was honored to serve him," Sir Dudley said, "I'm afraid my late master was slightly unhinged. I have to say 'thank you' to Mrs. Simpson for taking from the throne a man who might have been an unstable king." [Interview with Sir Dudley Forwood, May 5, 1988.]

23. Forwood interview; *The New York Times*, October 23, 1937.

24. Ibid. For an exploration — but inadequately sourced discussion — of the Windsor/Bedaux connection, see Peter Allen, op. cit.

25. Frances Donaldson, *Edward VIII* (Philadelphia: Lippincott, 1973).

26. Report to Berth, January 27, 1940. [German Documents, 124/122667-8] None of the members of the *Fronde* were named by the ambassador in The Hague. But the principals in the "peace party" were identified in a cable from the German minister in Ireland dated July 22, 1940. They allegedly included Lord President of the Council Neville Chamberlain, Foreign Secretary Lord Halifax, Sir Samuel Hoare, the ambassador to Madrid, Sir Horace Wilson, who headed the Civil Service, Sir John Simon, and Lord Astor.

27. Ibid; for example, Zech-Burkesroda, February 19: "The D of Windsor, about whom I wrote you in my letter of 27th last month, has said that the Allied War Council devoted an exhaustive discussion at its last meeting to the situation that would arise if Germany invaded Belgium. Reference was made throughout to a German invasion plan said to have been found in an airplane that made a forced landing in Belgium."

28. Lord Halifax to Lord Lothian, cited in Donaldson, op. cit. p. 385; Stohrer to Berlin, June 23, 1940, and July 11, 1940. Cited in a proof copy of Top Secret Cabinet Memorandum C 53, "publication of Captured German Documents." [This was a copy to give to Lord Beaverbrook, September 4, 1953, by Churchill, Box 15, Beaverbrook Papers, House of Lords Records Office, CAB C 53, London.] Also reproduced in German Foreign Policy Documents, op. cit., B15/B002556 through B003633. For supporting SD documentation see R SS/1236 and E 035156, Bundesarchiv Freiberg.

29. Stohrer to Berlin, July 30, 1940, CAB C 53.

30. Stohrer to Berlin, August 3, 1940, CAB C 53.

31. Stohrer to Berlin, July 31, 1940, CAB C 53.

32. Stohrer to Berlin, August 3, 1940; Huene to Berlin, August 15, 1940, CAB C 53.

33. Cadogan Diary, October 25, 1945, ACAD/1/15, CCA.

34. Top Secret Report, "Discovery of Secret Archives of German Foreign Ministry," time-stamped May 25, 1945. [SHAEF G-2 "T" Force 655, Box 70, Entry 13 B, "Records of Allied Operational and Occupation Headquarters, World War II," RG 331 NA.]

35. Ibid.

36. Eisenhower to Churchill, Secret and Personal from the White House, dated July 2, 1953. Copy in "Secret Papers handed to Lord Beaverbrook by Mr. Churchill on 4 September 1953," Box 13, Beaverbrook Papers, HOL

37. Attlee to Churchill, August 25, 1945, Annex D, Top Secret Cabinet Memorandum C 53, dated August 1953, Box 13, Beaverbrook Papers, HOL.

38. Ibid.

39. Churchill to the President of the United States, "My Dear Friend," dated June 27, 1953; Churchill from "Ike," July 2, 1953, CAB C 53, Beaverbrook Papers, HOL.

40. Ibid.

41. Correspondence and interviews with John Loftus, 1987–1988.

42. State Department Decimal File Index 1940–45, "The Duchess of Windsor," RG 84 NA.

43. German Foreign Policy Documents #5482/E382057.

44. Letter from Morshead to Foreign Office dated November 18, 1948, FO 370/1698, PRO.

45. Memorandum from Morshead to Sir Alan Lascelles September 28, 1947, FO 370/1698 PRO; Pendant to Doorn Memorandum October 23, 1948.

46. Loftus interviews.

47. Telephone interview with Professor Donald Cameron Watt, January 1988.

48. There was also an OSS IAA Looting Investigation Unit established in late 1944; Norman Holmes Pearson, Pearson Yale.

49. The late Sir Ellis Waterhouse, as quoted by Penrose and Freeman, op. cit., p. 298.

50. The Washington Star, April 30, 1945.

51. Interviews with Robert Harbinson (Bryan), October 1986.

52. Anthony Blunt, The French Drawings in the Collection of HM The King at Windsor Castle (London: Phaidon Press, 1945).

53. Kenneth Clark, "Another Part of the Wood: A Self-Portrait" in Rose, Kings, Queens and Courtiers (London: Weidenfeld & Nicolson, 1986), p. 48.

54. Meryle Secrest, Kenneth Clark: A Biography (New York: Holt, Rinehart & Winston, 1985), p. 111.

55. The Spectator, September 20, 1986.

56. Blunt, The Queen's Lecture, delivered in Berlin on May 24, 1972.

57. Information supplied by Professor Peter Murray — see the Burlington Magazine 1946, LXXXVIII, p. 263, "Paintings by Sebastiano and Marco Ricci in the Royal Collection"; interviews with Jack Hewit.

58. Ellis Waterhouse as quoted by Penrose and Freeman, op. cit., p. 292; confidential information supplied by a former MI6 officer.

59. Philip Ziegler, *Mountbatten* (London: Collins, 1985), p. 52, supplemented by interview, October 1986.

60. There has always been speculation about the bisexuality of these two sons of King George V and their close friend and cousin, the late Earl Mountbatten of Burma. Philip Ziegler broke significant ground in 1985 by devoting nearly a page (pp. 52–53) of his illuminating biography of Lord Mountbatten to dismissing the rumors of "alleged homosexuality" that dogged his royal subject to the end of his long and distinguished career. He mentions Mountbatten's lifelong, left-wing Cambridge friend and alter ego, Peter Murphy, Mountbatten's homosexual naval servants, and his enjoyment of the company of "flamboyant homosexuals like Noël Coward." Although he quotes Mountbatten's admission that "Edwina and I spent all our married lives getting into other people's beds," Ziegler concludes that despite his spirited wife Edwina's well-publicized infidelities, Mountbatten "was never promiscuous." He claimed Mountbatten only ever had two protracted extra-marital affairs with women — although he "had an almost irresistible urge to use them as confidantes." As Ziegler puts it: "To suggest that such a man was actively homosexual seems to be flying not merely in the face of evidence but also of everything we understand about his character." Such a carefully constructed con-clusion avoids any possible bisexual element in Mountbatten arising from his preference for women as confidantes rather than sex partners; his exaggerated regard for himself as a "sexual athlete"; coupled with his fondness for homosexual company *and* his lifelong friendship with Murphy. A New York psychologist says he would think twice before categorizing such a complex personality as being straightforwardly heterosexual.

61. Harbinson interview, July 1985: There are many literary references to guards performing homosexual acts with upper-class Londoners (see J. R. Ackerly, *My Father and Myself*). Andrew Sinclair, noted author and Cambridge fellow, who was a guards officer in the late forties (and is not a homosexual), told me that it was common knowledge in the mess that their men hired themselves out. He named the three pubs as the Bag o'Nails, the Grenadier, and the Packenham.

62. Harbinson interviews.

63. Rose, *Kings, Queens and Courtiers*.

64. Ellis Waterhouse as quoted in Penrose and Freeman, op. cit., p. 292.

65. Blunt press conference.

66. Crowley interviews.

67. Cecil interviews.

68. Blunt press conference.

69. Crowley interviews.

70. Blunt press conference.

71. Long interview.

72. Ibid.

73. Wright, op. cit., pp. 221–222.

74. Annan interviews.

75. Nigel West, *Friends*, p. 23.

## CHAPTER 24: PAGES 472–500

1. Lord Moran, *Winston Churchill: The Struggle for Survival 1940–1945* (London: Constable), p. 231.

2. Hansard, February 7, 1945.

3. Annan interviews.

4. Winston Churchill, *History of World War II, Vol. VI: Triumph and Tragedy* (London: Cassell, 1959), p. 497.

5. Affidavit provided the U.S. embassy in Canberra, Australia, sworn by Petrov, in the PETROV file, Senate Internal Security Subcommittee records, RG 46 NA.

6. Ibid.

7. Ibid.

8. This Marxist study group met at the home of Moses Finkelstein, later Sir Moses Finley, professor of ancient history at Cambridge. Finkelstein denied knowing Wittfogel; he insists his Sunday evening meetings were a music circle. Recently released Senate Judiciary Committee records show that Wittfogel confirmed his testimony by letter to the Senate Judiciary Committee, August 22, 1951. [WITTFOGEL docket, Senate Judiciary Committee Internal Security Subcommittee (SSISC) records NA.] For an analysis of the conflicting loyalties and testimony concerning Herbert Norman, see Barros, *No Sense of Evil* (New York: Ivy Book, 1987), pp. 20–21.

9. JAFFE folder, SSISC, RG 46 NA.

10. Memorandum to File by Judge Robert Morris, April 30, 1957, in JAFFE folder, SSISC; according to the testimony of Louis Budenz at the hearing of the U.S. Senate Committee on the Judiciary: *The Institute of Pacific Relations*, Hearing Before the Subcommittee to Investigate the Administration of the Internal Security Act, 1951–52 (hereafter "IPR Hearings"), Part 2, p. 5.

11. U.S. Senate, Report on the Judiciary *Report on the Institute of Pacific Relations;* Report No. 2050, 83d Congress, 2nd Session (hereafter "IPR Report"), p. 97. See also IPR Hearings and IPR Report. Freda Utley, who had joined the party while a University of London student before marrying a Russian who later served the Comintern in China, recalled how Carter and Lattimore had come to Moscow in 1936 to meet the Soviet Council of the Institute of Pacific Relations. Lattimore was a remarkably unwavering adherent to Moscow's policy zigzags in relation to the Nazi-Soviet pact. He urged Americans to stay out of the conflict, which he described as "one between the established master races and the claimant master races." After Hitler's attack on Russia in 1941, he flipflopped to advocate intervention. [Budenz testimony at IPR Hearings, as quoted by Utley, p. 212.]

12. Interview with Andrew Roth, London, August 1986; Louis Budenz, the executive member of the CPUSA who had broken with the party in 1945, testified at the 1951 IPR Hearings that he knew from "official communications" that both Roth and Jaffe were Communist party members. *American Case*, House Report No. 2732, 79 Congress, 2nd Session, October 23, 1946.

13. Straight also told the FBI how he sponsored the entry into the USA of Duran's friend and comrade-in-arms, Gustave Regler, whom he described as "a Trotskyite." [FBI Straight WFO 100–3644.]

14. FBI Straight, December 1975; Benjamin Stolberg, "Muddled Millions, Capitalist Angels of Left-Wing Propaganda," *The Saturday Evening Post*, February 15, 1941; [FBI Memo, MICHAEL W. STRAIGHT and (another name deleted), dated January 7, 1942.]

15. FBI Investigation, Free World Association [File 100–43342, Internal Security (c) December 6, 1943, State Department Decimal Confidential File 800.0003, Free World Association, RG 84 NA.]

16. Dolivet, now a successful businessman and in his early eighties, continues to deny the accuracy of the extensive allegations made against him. Yet as early as 1943 sources told U.S. Military Intelligence that Dolivet had been a close associate of Willi Münzenberg. [War Department Intelligence Summary, "Subject Louis Dolivet," dated May 18, 1943, RG 165 NA.] The published record in France stated that Dolivet was born Ludwig Brecher of Romanian Jewish parents. He adopted the surname Udeanu when he was recruited into the Comintern in the late twenties to avoid anti-Semitism. Brecher, it was alleged, was by turn a member of the Communist parties of Switzerland and France, where in 1933 he became the Comintern's man on the *World*. This was the weekly founded by Henry Barbuse, the sage of French intellectual Marxists. On the outbreak of the war he was director of the International Peace Campaign whose co-chairmen were the peace activist Lord Robert Cecil and Pierre Cot, a French deputy and former minister in Daladier's prewar Cabinet. Intercepted messages from Soviet penetration agents in De Gaulle's Free French organization, later uncovered in the Venona traffic, confirm that Cot was an active Soviet spy. [Wright, *Spycatcher*, p. 239.] For a detailed analysis of Dolivet/Brecher's career see *La Revue Parlementaire 15 December 1949*, English translation in Department of State records with the note that "much of the material contained therein has been checked and verified by sources available to us" – the inference being that the U.S. embassy in Paris confirmed that the data in the article had been based on sources in the French DST.

17. Dolivet's magazine, which became *United Nations World* in 1943, began floundering when his marriage into the Straight family collapsed by the end of World War II. Allegations about his Communist past began surfacing in 1947, frustrating his search for wealthy backers. Two years later, when Beatrice was finally granted her divorce and custody of their son, Dolivet – still technically a French citizen – packed his bags and abandoned his bankrupt magazine. He sailed for France vowing to return with the *Légion d'Honneur*. [Straight op. cit., p. 256.] Republican congressmen moved to prevent his return by revealing Ludwig Brecher's Communist past on the floor of the House of Representatives on May 25, 1949. Their allegations about Dolivet/Brecher being a Communist prompted the State Department to cancel his visa despite Dolivet's protests that he was "thoroughly opposed to communism." [*Congressional Record*, May 25, 1949, p. 7764, and letter to Senator Pat McCarran from Louis Dolivet, editor of *United Nations World*, dated July 28, 1949.] Although Dolivet never took the witness stand to answer the charges, the record against him (which cannot be released to third parties until his death) was, however, sufficiently derogatory to persuade U.S. Attorney General James McGranery to reject Dolivet's request for a compassionate granting of an emergency visa in 1949 to attend the funeral of his son, Willard, drowned in a summer boating accident at Peekskill, N.Y. [Straight, *Silence*, p. 256.] Straight himself dismisses absolutely any suggestion that he and his brother-in-law Dolivet were ever "co-conspirators" in the secret machinations of Soviet intelligence. [Interviews with Straight and see Straight, *Silence*, p. 257.] These allegations resulted from the London *Sunday Times* investigation in 1981, but the story was killed when Dolivet,

by now a "wealthy entrepreneur" living with a young wife in Paris, "lost no time in flying to London and obtaining an injunction." Straight also confirmed that he did not withdraw his money from *United Nations World* in 1946 when other investors pulled out.

18. Reported in *The Washington Post*, March 10, 1942.

19. See FBI files 100–3476 on investigations that led to a report to the Criminal Division of the Justice Department on whether or not prosecution was warranted against Editorial Publications Limited, the *New Republic* holding company, for failure to register in compliance with the provisions of the Foreign Publications Act of 1938. The assistant attorney general evidently decided that "prosecution was not warranted." [Hoover to Special Agent in Charge, September 15, 1942, File 100-619296 – 26, FBI Straight June 24, 1963.]

20. Michael Straight, *Make This the Last War* (New York: Harcourt, Brace, Jovanovich, 1943).

21. FBI Straight #100-3644. The restaurant was dimly lit and the FBI records show that after a lapse of more than twenty years, Straight was unable to make a positive identification of the woman, only recalling that she was in early middle age, of "nice appearance," and that from her speech she must have been American. The FBI has blanked out its deductions about the likely identity of Mrs. Green. The remaining context suggests it suspected she was one of the known Soviet agents involved in running the Washington rings associated with Whittaker Chambers and Elizabeth Bentley.

    Straight dismisses the possibility that she was not really Mrs. Green at all, but Elizabeth Zubilin – "Comrade Lisa," who also went by the name "Helen" – and was one of the most experienced agent-runners that the NKVD had in the United States. From 1929 to 1930 she had worked under the cover of an official of Amtorg. She returned to the United States in 1934 with her husband Vassili Zubilin, also a high-ranking Soviet intelligence officer operating under diplomatic cover. "Helen" had flawless English, according to Hede Massing, who recalled her own encounters with Elizabeth Zubilin.

    Hede Massing, who defected to the FBI in 1947, was accompanied by "Bill," whom she had known since 1934 as "one of the most pedestrian of my Russian co-workers." Her description of "Bill" as "every inch the Soviet *apparatchik* or bureaucrat" fits exactly with Straight's recollection. His subsequent identification of Michael Green as William Grienke fits Massing's co-worker *Walter* Grienke. [Hede Massing, *This Deception* (New York: Ivy Books, 1987), pp. 191–192.] Elizabeth Zubilin and William Grienke were Soviet contacts of Elizabeth Bentley. If E. Zubilin was the "Helen" at the Longchamps meeting, it suggests that "Michael Green" was making a determined effort to bring Straight back into the Washington espionage network. This is supported by Straight's recollection of an earlier approach by Solomon Adler, whom Bentley had identified as a member of the Silvermaster network in the Treasury. The Czech with "stiff blond hair" who looked like "a ski instructor or storm trooper," with whom Straight refused to deal during Green's absence in 1941, matches Massing's description of "Anton," the philandering blond Czechoslovak who acted as the photographer of the Golos ring. [Massing, op. cit., pp. 154 and 167.] FBI Straight memorandum, dated July 31, 1975.

22. FBI Straight interviews of July 28, 1975.

23. Wallace Diary entry of March 9, 1944. Cited by Christopher Thorne, *Allies of a Kind* (New York: Oxford University Press, 1978), p. 438. Christopher Thorne, who

interviewed both Currie and Fairbank, states that they were "somewhat surprised when presented with the evidence that they had helped create the prevalent image of the Chinese as 'agrarian reformers.'" His thorough analysis [pp. 424–466] of the U.S. policy crisis in China in 1944 presents a convincingly objective picture of how Currie, Fairbank, and Service, with the aid of other members of the IPR group, helped create the terms of the debate in Washington that ultimately helped bring the Communists to power. He does not seek to enter the fray over whether this was a consciously directed conspiracy. [Owen Lattimore, *The Solution in Asia* (New York: 1945.]

24. *Foreign Relations of the United States, 1944* (Washington: 1965), Vol. VI, China, pp. 589–599, 97, 253.

25. Edgar Snow, "Must the East Go Red?" *Saturday Evening Post*, May 12, 1945.

26. IPR Hearings, Majority report, 1952.

27. As quoted in Utley, p. 163.

28. For a concise summary of the new evidence showing how Corcoran maneuvered to bury the affair, see Harvey Klehr and Ronald Radosh, "Anatomy of a Fix," *The New Republic*, April 26, 1986, and their book *Amerasia* (New York: Norton, 1988).

29. ROTH, Andrew, from a "Confidential Source" (probably FBI) in ROTH Folder, SSISC, RG 46 NA; interview with Andrew Roth, London, August 1986.

30. FBI memorandum dated November 25, 1945, reproduced in "Interlocking Subversion in Government Departments," Report of the Committee of the Judiciary, U.S. Senate, Subcommittee to Investigate the "Administration of the Internal Security Act and other Internal Security Laws," July 30, 1953 (hereafter ISH: "Interlocking Subversion Hearings 1953").

31. For a ghostwritten and carefully sanitized account see Elizabeth Bentley, *Out of Bondage* (with a documented Afterword by Hayden B. Peake) (New York: Ballantine, 1988). For details: see, for example, Bentley's testimony before the HUAC.

32. Memorandum dated August 24, 1948, for the director from Ladd, titled "NATHAN GREGORY SILVERMASTER et AL," ESPIONAGE 65-56402-3620XC2.

33. Bentley, "GREGORY CASE", FBI RECORDS

34. Whittaker Chambers, *Witness* (New York: Random House, 1952), p. 353.

35. Ibid., p. 26; Goldberger, before coming to the United States to act as a GRU agent and secret contact man between a succession of Soviet apparatuses and the Communist Party, had been an official of Bela Kun's Soviet government.

36. For an objective academic analysis of White's career and Communist connections, see David Rees, *Harry Dexter White: A Study in Paradox* (New York: Coward, McCann & Geoghegan, 1973). White's letter about his trip to Russia is reproduced on p. 39 and also in House Committee on Un-American Activities, Communist Espionage in the United States Government, Hearings, 80th Congress, 2nd Session (1948), p. 2570.

37. IPR Hearings, pp. 491–493; HUAC Hearings, 1948, p. 1180.

38. ISH, p. 4; IPR Hearings, p. 243.

39. IPR Hearings, p. 2; Lamphere, *FBI–KGB Wars*, p. 25.

40. ISH, p. 2.

41. HUAC Hearings, p. 540ff.

42. FBI file 65-56402 serial 220, Bentley (GREGORY CASE); ISH, p. 329.

43. Lamphere, op. cit., p. 34–35.

44. *The Report of the Royal Commission* (Ottawa: 1946), pp. 638–640.

45. See Boyle, op. cit., p. 169.

46. H. Montgomery Hyde, *The Atom Bomb Spies* (London: Hamish Hamilton, 1980).

47. Memorandum dated May 23, 1950, in Norman Papers in RCMP files obtained by James Barros and cited by him together with FBI File 100-346993-1 dated October 16, 1946, originated by Boston FBI in Barros, *No Sense of Evil*, p. 55. See also John Sawatsky, *Men in the Shadows* (Toronto: Doubleday, 1980), p. 145.

48. ISH, p. 71.

49. HUAC Hearings, pp. 113–114.

50. Notes of Harold D. Smith, Truman's budget director and confidante, May 11, July 6, 1945, as quoted in Robert J. Donovan, *Conflict and Crises: The Presidency of Harry S Truman, 1945–1948* (New York: Norton, 1977), p. 174.

51. Interviews with Robert J. Lamphere, 1986–88.

52. Ibid.

53. Ibid.

54. FBI Straight, July 18, 1975, File 100-61927-10.

55. Lamphere interviews.

56. Ibid.

57. Ibid.

58. As quoted by Professor David M. Oshinsky, *A Conspiracy So Immense: The World of Joe McCarthy* (New York: Macmillan, 1983), pp. 98–99. See also *The Specter: Original Essays on American Anti-Communism and the Origins of McCarthyism* (New York: Watts, 1974).

59. FBI Straight report, July 31, 1975; Straight, *Silence*, p. 231.

60. FBI Straight, 1963.

61. Straight, op. cit., p. 229. Over the conflict of dates, Straight told the FBI on June 10, 1963, that he *did* go to London after his release from the air force and repeated the claim at a second interview on June 18. It seems likely, therefore, that the confrontation in the RAC Club must have occurred *before* rather than *after* Straight took the halfhearted but nonetheless serious step of telling his wife to convey to her contact in the British embassy in 1948 that Burgess was a Communist. In *After Long Silence*, p. 229, Straight says that the argument was over the "Soviet occupation of Czechoslovakia." Since both American and Soviet troops occupied the country until 1945, this would not be inconsistent with Straight's declaration that his confrontation with Burgess and Blunt occurred in 1946. The actual takeover of Czechoslovakia by the Communists, who formed a Soviet-style regime that effectively eliminated democracy, was in 1948. It was not accompnied by an occupation by the Red Army.

62. Straight, op. cit., p. 230.

63. Straight explained how he met with CPGB chairman Harry Pollitt on the suggestion of Cornford's old girlfriend Margot Heinemann, and that he had been favorably

impressed by President Truman's proposals to internationalize atomic energy. (The Truman proposal for internationalizing the control of nuclear weapons was made in 1946, which also supports the accuracy of Straight's account to the FBI. [FBI Straight, June 24, 1963.]

64. In his famous essay originally published in the New York *Nation* in 1938 under the title "Two Cheers for Democracy," Forster had completed his oft-quoted pronouncement by explaining: "Love and loyalty to an individual can run counter to the claims of the State. When they do — down with the State, say I, which means the State would down me." But it is clear from context, not to mention the climate that gave birth to his individualistic philosophic credo — which at the time dismayed both orthodox patriots and orthodox Marxists — that the State he would betray was not so much the tolerant country for which he had just given "Two Cheers" but totalitarian regimes, Fascist, Nazi, and Communist. [E. M. Forster, *Two Cheers for Democracy* (New York: Harcourt Brace, 1951), p. 67; see also P. N. Furbank, *E. M. Forster: A Life* (Oxford University Press, 1979), pp. 224–251.]

65. FBI Straight; Straight, op. cit., p. 230. Straight told the FBI how he bumped into Burgess in 1947 in the Houses of Parliament while accompanying former Vice-President Henry Wallace on a "peace effort" sponsored by *The New Republic*. They had lunched together at the Savoy. Straight said he relayed the Truman administration's feelings of "complete frustration with the Soviets" who he believed were inviting "a terrible clash." Burgess inquired if he could impart this to his friends. Straight agreed he could. Significantly, he told the FBI that he did not take this to be a reference to the British foreign secretary, in whose outer office Burgess worked, but to his "Soviet principals." (FBI Straight, p. 14)

66. Editorial, *New Republic*, as quoted by Straight, op. cit., p. 231; FBI Straight.

67. 1986 correspondence between Dr. Welderhall and Verne Newton, to whom I am very grateful for permitting me access to this research. Newton also confirms that in conversation, the former Belinda Straight, now a practicing Washington psychiatrist, also confirms that only Burgess's name was mentioned; interview with the late James Angleton conducted by Verne Newton on February 23, 1984, to whom I am grateful for access to his notes of that meeting.

68. Information drawn from HUAC.

69. Hede Massing, *This Deception*, pp. 278–279. Alger Hiss stated at his trial and in his 1957 account *In the Court of Public Opinion* (New York: Knopf, p. 307) that he had known Noel Field, but insisted he "had never seen Mrs. Massing anywhere before the FBI in December 1948 arranged for me to see her and asked if I could identify her." The tenor of this book was that Massing and Chambers gave false testimony as part of an FBI plot to frame Hiss that included doctoring a Woodstock typewriter in order to forge the incriminating State Department digests on which his perjury conviction turned. In his 1988 memoir *Recollections of a Life* (New York: Seaver Books, Henry Holt and Company, pp. 202–211) Hiss amplifies his claim that he suffered a miscarriage of justice in a frameup "fabricated by an unholy trinity bound together by the theology of anti-Communism." Richard Nixon he charged with "falsifying the issues and the record" for "political opportunism." "Personal vindictiveness" allegedly motivated J. Edgar Hoover — "one of the most evil men in American public life" — who leaked "tales about me to Congress" and connived at the "suppression of evidence," particularly in regard to the serial numbers and date of manufacture of the typewriter. Whittaker Chambers, who Hiss sourly notes was posthumously awarded the Medal of Freedom by President Reagan in 1984, was not only a "closet homosexual" (according to a suppressed FBI report) but a

"possessed man and a psychopath," a "pawn in the hands of others." Hiss said Chambers was "without scruples or moral balance" and made use of an earlier kindness "to try to destroy me." But despite the sixty thousand pages of FBI and related trial documentation released under the Freedom of Information Act, the petition Hiss filed for writ of error *coram nobis* was rejected in 1982 and a writ of certiorari to set aside his conviction was denied by the U.S. Supreme Court a year later. Partisan debate will doubtless continue on the Hiss case.

70. As quoted by Harvey Klehr and Ronald Radosh, "Anatomy of a Fix."

71. Lamphere, op. cit., p. 142.

72. Professor Herbert Packer, *Ex-Communist Witnesses* (Stanford University Press, 1962), p. 107; Norman Redlich, *The Nation,* January 30, 1954, p. 86. I am grateful to Hayden Peake for drawing my attention to the *Nation* article, which quotes the liberal "sensible criteria of credibility" that are also used by counterintelligence officers and were "rather neatly put by Norman Redlich." For the first authoritative analysis of Elizabeth Bentley's credibility, based on the released FBI files and her testimony, see the Afterword by Hayden Peake to Elizabeth Bentley's *Out of Bondage.*

73. "Interlocking Hearings Report," p. 3–5.

74. Ibid., p. 15.

75. Ibid., p. 20.

76. Ibid., p. 21–22.

77. Lamphere interviews.

78. Scott report, April 6, 1946, Pearson Yale.


CHAPTER 25: PAGES 501–536

1. Quoted from separate interviews with Robertson by both Chapman Pincher (*Too Secret Too Long*, p. 351) and Penrose and Freeman (*Conspiracy of Silence*, p. 287). Pincher personally confirmed Robertson's statement to him.

2. MI5 sources quoted by Pincher, *Too Secret Too Long*, op. cit., p. 351.

3. Oliver Millar, *The Queen's Pictures* (London: Weidenfeld & Nicolson, 1977), p. 212.

4. Blunt's theory that the painting was a surviving section of the French master's *Adoration of the Golden Calf*, thought to have been destroyed in a 1647 Neapolitan revolt, was challenged on stylistic grounds. Blunt's theory was demolished when X-ray analysis revealed that the work had been overpainted on top of a landscape at right angles to the heads. For a full analysis of this "Poussin fragment" see Christopher Wright, *The Art of the Forger* (London: Gordon Fraser, 1984), pp. 142–144, and Christopher Wright, *Poussin Paintings: A Catalogue Raisonné* (New York: Hippocrene Books, 1985), p. 247; Professor Rees-Jones as quoted by Penrose and Freeman, op. cit., p. 295.

5. The late Lillian Gurry as quoted by Penrose and Freeman, op. cit., pp. 305–306.

6. Courtauld graduates accounted for most of the senior appointments at the National Gallery, the Tate, the Victoria and Albert Museum, the National Museum of Wales, the National Gallery of Scotland, and all the art departments of Britain's

universities. But Oxford and Cambridge tended to favor their own graduates — and the Courtauld influence is far less dominant in the great municipal galleries at Liverpool, Manchester, and Birmingham.

7. See the extensive listings in the Courtauld Institute Annual Reports: "Appointments of Former Students."

8. Cited by Pincher, *Too Secret Too Long*, pp. 204–205, who received a firsthand account from Reed.

9. Philby, *My Silent War*, pp. 126–127.

10. Pincher, *Too Secret Too Long*, p. 207. Information received from Wright.

11. Wright, *Spycatcher*, pp. 280–281, and Pincher, *Too Secret*, pp. 434–435 (his source was almost certainly his personal interviews with Wright).

12. Pincher, *Too Secret Too Long*, p. 434. Copy of original Russian and translation kindly supplied by Chapman Pincher.

13. Nigel West, *The Circus*, p. 19 and organization charts in Preface. West's information is usually regarded as reliable and confirms MI5 organization reports available in the U.S. archives; Glees, *The Secrets of the Service*, p. 309, quoting the note prepared by Sir Roger Fulford that states that Hollis was on sick leave from March to October 1942.

14. Philby, op. cit., pp. 125–134.

15. Wright, op. cit., pp. 244–245; West, *Molehunt*, p. 31; Glees, op. cit., p. 279.

16. Wright, op. cit., pp. 244–245. Hamburger was the first husband of Ruth Kuczynski, a GRU illegal who operated during the war as an undercover agent runner in the Oxford area for Klaus Fuchs and other scientists. But those familiar with Hamburger's career, such as Chapman Pincher, dispute this claim. See below.

17. Exhibit 23-J, Soviet Embassy Telegram, Report of the Royal Commission, GOU-ZENKO.

18. Ibid; Igor Gouzenko's memorandum to the RCMP made at the request of MI5 on May 6, 1962, reproduced in Pincher, *Too Secret Too Long*, pp. 623–625. Nigel West in *Molehunt* devotes no fewer than seven pages (pp. 54–61) to showing that Gouzenko's 1962 memorandum is unreliable and "an embroidered account." Yet West acknowledges that the Soviet defector's memory was "prodigious" when he was "the consummate expert witness" before the Royal Commission — and presumably, therefore, also to the British intelligence officers who debriefed him at the same time. His speculative contention that seven years' time had made Gouzenko an unreliable witness is an unconvincing circumstantial argument. Pincher confirms that his correspondence with Gouzenko (before his death nearly thirty years later) did not suggest any marked deterioration of his ability to fix details. Until the MI5 reports of the 1945 debriefing of Gouzenko are produced, it would therefore seem a logical assumption that Gouzenko *had* supplied the same details he gave the RCMP in 1952 — corroboration comes from the significant jump in Venona traffic when the Soviet embassy in London learned that Gouzenko had named the spy in MI5 (see also Wright, op. cit., pp. 284–285).

19. Ibid.

20. Ibid.

21. Ibid; Gouzenko said that this was: "In 1944 (the latter part, or maybe the beginning of 1945)" and Wright told Pincher in 1981 that reference to the records showed

that this could have tied in with one of Liddell's visits to Canada and Washington; Pincher confirmed to the author (telephone conversation, February 25, 1988) that Wright told him about Liddell's trip although he could not cite him as the source in *Too Secret Too Long*, p. 112.

22. Wright, op. cit., pp. 284–285.

23. Wright, op. cit., p. 285; Easton as quoted by Cave Brown in "*C*", p. 693.

24. Easton, ibid.; Philby named Milne, his former protégé, as a fellow conspirator in his two-page "confession" given to Nick Elliott in Beirut in 1963. Milne was investigated and found to be innocent, according to MI5 interrogators, but in deference to American objections, he was obliged to resign from MI6. [West, *Friends*, p. 145.]

25. Philby, op. cit., p. 115.

26. Confirmation from Sir William Stevenson, cited by Pincher, *Too Secret Too Long*, p. 107; William Stevenson, *Intrepid's Last Case* (New York: Villard Books, 1983), p. 74.

27. Cited by H. Montgomery Hyde, *The Atom Bomb Spies*, p. 42; confirmation of the Hollis tip provided by Robert Kaplan, then solicitor-general of Canada, at a press interview, March 26, 1981: see *Toronto Star*, March 27, 1981; information supplied by Gouzenko to Pincher as cited in *Too Secret Too Long*, p. 111.

28. Ibid.

29. During Skripkin's negotiations with British Naval Intelligence, he insisted on being flown to asylum in Australia because he said he knew that British intelligence was penetrated. His instructions were ignored and arrangements made to fly Rastvorov to Singapore to be handed over to SIFE (Security Intelligence Far East, a joint MI5–MI6 operation). When takeoff was delayed by a snowstorm at Tokyo airport, the would-be defector heard from crew chatter about his Singapore destination and promptly jumped from the plane and headed for the American embassy (Wright, op. cit., p. 286 — confirmed by U.S. intelligence sources); Wright, op. cit., pp. 188–189.

30. The Philby story that appears in Leonard Mosley, *Dulles* (New York: James Wade, Dial Press, 1978), p. 284, was denied to Verne Newton by Angleton himself; Winks, *Cloak and Gown*, p. 401.

31. Solomon, *A Woman's Way*, p. 210.

32. Easton quoted in Cave Brown, op. cit., p. 696. Akhmedov was later passed on to the CIA and settled in the United States.

33. Ismail Akhmedov, *In and Out of Stalin's KGB* (Frederick, Md.: University Publications, 1984), pp. 187–198.

34. Philby, op. cit., p. 151.

35. Ibid.

36. National Security Act, 80th Congress; for the most detailed and authoritative account of the early years of the CIA, see Thomas F. Troy, *Donovan and the CIA: A History of the Establishment of the Central Intelligence Agency* (Frederick, Md.: University Publications, 1981); John Ranelagh, *The Agency: The Rise and Decline of the CIA* (New York: Simon & Schuster, 1986), pp. 112–115.

37. Cave Brown, *Menzie*, p. 697.

38. Philby, op. cit., p. 152; Wright, op. cit., p. 193.

39. Nigel West, *GCHQ: The Secret Wireless War 1900–1986* (London: Weidenfeld & Nicolson, 1986), pp. 202–204; 222–224; confidential source.

40. Lamphere, op. cit., p. 81–83.

41. The reference to the captured Finnish MGB codebook appears to have been the message that Bentley told the FBI was relayed to her from Stettinius's assistant Alger Hiss; Lamphere interviews.

42. Article by Allen J. Mayer with David C. Martin, "Cracking a Soviet Cipher," *Newsweek*, May 19, 1980. (Lamphere assures me that the key information relating to the 1944 break-in was not supplied by him but by a CIA source. As part of his agreement with the FBI, he had not mentioned the duplicate Soviet one-time cipher pads being supplied to the MGB and the Purchasing mission.) Lamphere interviews, 1988; Lamphere, op. cit., p. 88.

43. Lamphere, op. cit., p. 87.

44. Ibid.

45. Top Secret memorandum prepared by J. Edgar Hoover for President Eisenhower, dated 1955, Dwight D. Eisenhower Presidential Library.

46. Lamphere, op. cit., p. 132.

47. Lamphere interviews.

48. Lamphere, op. cit., p. 135, used the word STOTT. Other members of the U.S. intelligence community have indicated that this was necessary to satisfy the restrictions under which he was writing. The correct term is SMOTH, an acronym that is entirely artificial.

49. Lamphere interviews.

50. West interviews.

51. See the FBI version of Fuchs's confession to Dr. Michael Perrin, a fellow nuclear physicist. [Hoover to Rear Admiral Sidney W. Souers, March 6, 1950, President's Secretary's Files, Harry S Truman Presidential Library, Independence, Missouri.

52. FBI summary report, Fuchs confession.

53. Fuchs worked as a graduate student at Bristol for Sir Neville Mott, who himself admitted he was "sympathetic to the Soviet cause." [Chadwell Williams, op. cit., p. 23.]

54. Rudolf Peierls, *Bird of Passage: Recollections of a Nuclear Physicist* (Princeton, N.J.: Princeton University Press, 1985), p. 148.

55. A revealing memorandum about Communist cells and extensive penetration of the faculty and student body of Birmingham is in Lord Vansittart's papers. (Professor Ferns confirms its general accuracy in regard to those of his colleagues who were named as active party members.) Dated 1951, the Vansittart memorandum appears based on detailed information provided him by his MI5 and Special Branch contacts. It and others were prepared as part of the campaign Vansittart hoped would alert the incoming British Conservative administration of his old friend Winston Churchill to how extensively communism had infiltrated the universities, civil service, BBC, and the trade unions. But he received little support from the House of Lords – or the Conservative Cabinet – who feared his campaign would result in witch-hunting that was then bringing notoriety to Senator McCarthy. [VST II 1/41 and associated files and reports, CCA.]

56. For a firsthand – though carefully sanitized – account, see Ruth Werner (aka Ruth Kuczynski, "Sonja"), *Sonja's Rapport* (Berlin: Verlag Neues Leben, 1977). Other elements derived from Alexander Foote, *Handbook for Spies* (Garden City, N.Y.: Doubleday, 1949). The first full evaluation of Sonja's role was presented by Chapman Pincher in *Too Secret Too Long*, derived in part from information supplied to him by Peter Wright.

57. Wright, op. cit., p. 186.

58. Ibid.

59. Information received from Chapman Pincher, who assures me he received it from a reliable and confidential source.

60. Williams, op. cit., p. 62; Klaus Fuchs, Case File I, U.S. Department of Justice, Washington, D.C.

61. Ibid.

62. Ibid, p. 100; for the secret British Cabinet decision to develop their own atomic bomb, see Kenneth Harris, *Attlee* (London: Weidenfeld & Nicolson, 1962), pp. 497–498.

63. John Saxon responded to an appeal in *The New York Times Review of Books* for anyone who knew about the Fuchs case. He said he was a former member of MI5, who was living in the United States. Williams, who is a distinguished historian and dean of Davidson College, North Carolina, was impressed with Saxon's depth of intimate knowledge of the case. Saxon, who had been a wartime recruit to MI6 before he transferred to MI5 shortly before Fuchs's return to England in 1946, told Williams that he knew from the files that an MI6 undercover agent code-named "Arthur," a worker on the Kiel Canal, had reported Fuchs as a KPD activist and Communist party organizer to London in 1934. [Williams, op. cit., p. 22.] In the course of several conversations in December 1985, Saxon also told Williams the British knew that Sonja not only met with Fuchs in 1946–47 but turned him over to her own case officer at the Soviet embassy. According to Saxon, MI5 knew of this because of the defection of a GRU agent in Ankara. [Williams, op. cit., p. 62.]

The publication of Williams's book in the fall of 1987 resulted in what appears to be an attempt to discredit both Saxon and the information he provided, an attempt that has been orchestrated in London. In April 1988 the attorney general, answering a written parliamentary question by Rupert Allason M.P. (Nigel West), told him enigmatically that the government contemplates taking no action against Saxon. In the aftermath of the "Spycatcher Affair," when the British government has made draconian attempts to prevent any other member of the security services from betraying his oath of confidentiality, this strikes West as tantamount to a signal that Saxon is not what he claims to be. West, moreover, has learned through his usually authoritative network of sources in the British intelligence community that none has heard of a former agent named Saxon – or of "Arthur," the Kiel Canal worker. He has written as much to Saxon.

When I was finally able to speak with John Saxon, he explained that he was reluctant to discuss the matter, especially since he had been hounded by British press correspondents ever since the publication of Williams's book. By disclosing some of my own knowledge, I was able to persuade him that the objective of my inquiries was to obtain corroboration for the facts already attributed to him regarding the Fuchs case. He did not express any great surprise about what appears to be an orchestrated attempt to discredit both him and his information. "They may have their reasons," Saxon said with the resigned air of an operative more used to carrying out orders than to giving them. "I've been out of the 'firm' for a long time now, I'm an old man. They know that the information is accurate, but they may very well have good reasons for denying it. I would have no objections to that, if it suits their current policy. I don't know what they are working at or what they are up to." When I suggested that "John Saxon" was not the name his former colleagues knew him by, he said, "You may draw your own conclusions."

In the course of our conversation it became clear that Saxon knew that it was Skardon who had been sent to see Sonja in 1947 and that the Fuchs files had been "reconstructed" for the FBI and CIA. Since neither of these telling facts has yet been published, this, together with his familiarity with other case details, his reticence, and the lack of bluster in someone whose bluff was being called, gave a convincing image of a knowledgeable former MI5 officer. Nor, on reflection, was "John Saxon" an inappropriate name for a seventy-year-old English intelligence officer in exile in the United States.

The situation is, therefore, rife with controversy. But behind the rumbles are sources who say "the real story is even worse." They say that in 1945 an MI5 officer added a note on the Fuchs file that his case warranted reexamination before he returned to atomic work in England. The recommendation was passed to higher authority – but no such investigation was ever made and Fuchs received routine clearance. When Fuchs confessed in 1949 to being a Soviet spy, Prime Minister Attlee demanded an explanation from Sir Percy Sillitoe, who, to protect the credibility of MI5 of which he had been made director general, was obliged to cover up for this glaring failure. Furious, Sillitoe returned to headquarters and summoned a meeting of senior staff in the canteen. He excoriated his counter-espionage officers, saying he had lied "for the good of the service." A senior member of B Division offered his resignation after the meeting. It was not accepted – and he went on to an even more distinguished career.

64. Cited as confidential information by Chapman Pincher, who confirmed that it was originally supplied during his interview with Wright, although *Spycatcher* makes no reference at all to Pontecorvo.

65. Ibid.

66. Information contained in a historical study, "The Trust," attributed to the Central Intelligence Agency and quoted by Cave Brown in "*C*," pp. 143–144. Further information supplied by Natalie Grant Wraga, and John Loftus, whose book, *The Belarus Secret* (New York: Alfred A. Knopf, 1982) tracks the Byelorussian underground network in detail. I am indebted to Mr. Loftus for sharing with me CIA and FBI documentation he has obtained under the Freedom of Information Act.

67. Information supplied by John Loftus. For documented details of the ABN recruiting, see Christopher Simpson, *Blowback* (New York: Weidenfeld & Nicolson, 1987), p. 269–273.

68. As quoted in Lord Nicholas Bethell, *The Great Betrayal: The Untold Story of Kim Philby's Biggest Coup* (London: Hodder & Stoughton, 1984), pp. 38–39.

69. Philby, op. cit., p. 161.

70. Bethell, op. cit.

71. Lamphere, op. cit., p. 240.

72. Letter from Sir Patrick Reilly to Dr. Anthony Glees, July 10, 1986, excerpted in Glees, op. cit., p. 359.

73. According to FBI reports, Maclean would later catch the train from Grand Central

to Hillsdale, New York, and take a taxi from there to Egremont, just across the Massachusetts state line; Lamphere interviews.

74. Reilly's letter in Glees, op. cit.

75. Lamphere letter to author, written after reading Sir Patrick Reilly's letter to Glees, July, 1987, with postscript: "You may use the above in any way you deem suitable."

76. George Carey-Foster interview, quoted in Penrose and Freeman, op. cit., p. 334.

77. See the minutes and records of the Joint Committee on Atomic Energy, 1956–77, RG 128, Box 316. See also FBI report 1955, B&M interview with "Carol Williams," head of AEA.

78. Brian Urquhart, *A Life in Peace and War* (New York: Harper & Row, 1987), p. 117.

79. See, for example, Burgess's memo on the JIC report of April 29, 1949, on "The Nature of Russian Air Assistance," cited in *The Times* of February 2, 1981.

80. Goronwy Rees, *Accidents*, p. 7; Carey-Foster as quoted in Penrose and Freeman, op. cit., p. 334.

81. Ibid., p. 189.

82. Philby, op. cit., p. 171.

83. Ibid.

## CHAPTER 26: PAGES 537–559

1. FBI B&M, Report to Director dated August 15, p. 71.

2. FBI, Blair Bolles interview. Burgess also sought to curry favor with Senator Claude Pepper, who regarded him as a "smart aleck" with "crackpot" ideas.

3. Rushmore, FBI summary interview, 1955 Report, p. 19.

4. FBI, Valentine Lawford interview, confirmed by personal interview, July 1987.

5. As quoted in Boyle, *Climate of Treason*, p. 379; Wilfrid Basil Mann, *Was There a Fifth Man?* (London: Pergamon, 1982), pp. 80–81, supplemented by interview with Dr. Mann, January 1988.

6. Blick's surveillance was both thorough and extensive, which is why he "could state with certainty that Burgess was known to be a homosexual." 1955 Summary Brief Prepared by J. Edgar Hoover, FBI B&M, p. 13; Whitfield summary, FBI B&M Hoover 1955.

7. See account given by Verne Newton in *The Washingtonian Magazine*, May 1984. Interviews with both Mann and Lamphere confirm Newton's account and that Burgess's drawing was not pornographic and that Harvey did not land a blow as other published accounts have suggested; Mann, op. cit., p. 81 and interviews.

8. Ibid.

9. Interview with Mann and information supplied by Verne Newton from his discussions with James Angleton.

10. Ibid.; FBI B&M, p. 100.

11. Ibid., FBI B&M.

12. Vladimir Petrov, "Statutory Declaration" prepared in Canberra on March 29, 1956, for the U.S. Embassy, SSISC, PETROV Folder, op. cit., RG 46 NA.

13. Philby, *My Silent War*, p. 176.

14. FBI B&M, deposition from TURCK.

15. *Report Concerning the Disappearance of Two Former Foreign Office Officials* (HMSO Command 9577, September 23, 1955 (Hereafter Cmmd 9577); On information from the embassy security officer Robert Mackenzie that Burgess emerged angry and remonstrative from the meeting with Franks, Cecil draws the conclusion that he was surprised to be sent home. But this could have been a deliberate act because the FBI files leave no doubt that his speeding offenses were no less deliberate.

16. Goronwy Rees, *Accidents*, pp. 191–192.

17. Cyril Connolly, *The Missing Diplomats*, p. 33; according to the FBI Dunbar interview, Maclean's homosexuality was known on "the family grapevine."

18. Boyle, op. cit., pp. 395–396.

19. Ibid., p. 15.

20. FBI B&M, Roosevelt interviews and undated letter received by Mrs. Roosevelt "at the end of April or beginning of May 1951."

21. Lamphere, op. cit., p. 237; Philby, op. cit., p. 176.

22. Other accounts (Penrose and Freeman, *Conspiracy of Silence*, p. 340) have commented on the "remarkable lack of urgency" surrounding Burgess's departure from the United States. But they do not take into account that to have canceled the prearranged visit of his mother or insisted on accelerating the bureaucratic process might have drawn unnecessary suspicion to his eagerness to return. Beside, it is clear from all the British accounts that the Foreign Office was proceeding very deliberately with the final stages of the "Homer" investigation — each step of which was being monitored by the MI5 mole. Burgess cannot therefore be said to have dawdled and he embarked on the *Queen Mary* within three days of his departure from Washington; Verne Newton, op. cit. I am grateful to Mr. Newton, who has been very generous with sharing some of the findings of his research into Burgess and Maclean, which are to be published shortly.

23. Philby, op. cit., p. 176–177.

24. FBI interview, Luker, B&M file.

25. Cecil interviews.

26. Reilly letter to Glees, quoted in *Secrets of the Service*, p. 361; White Paper on Burgess and Maclean defection, Cmmd 9577 1955. We now know that the contents of the Venona traffic had been used to interrogate Fuchs and get him to confess. It is another curious facet of the Maclean case that MI5 did not consider a similar move with Blunt. Glees, op. cit., p. 363.

27. As quoted in Glees, op. cit., p. 363; Boyle, op. cit., p. 394, cited to "information supplied to the author by Carey-Foster and Lord Sherfield." The FBI assessment of January 20, 1957, confirms that Hoover knew nothing of the investigation: "This was primarily a British case and of necessity [a] major portion of the investigation [was] conducted in England. We possessed no derogatory information re subjects [Burgess and Maclean] prior to their disappearance from England in May 1951. From what we know now of subjects' activities prior to their being assigned to this country, a routine investigation would have made them ineligible for government employment, according to our standards." [FBI to Director, January 20, 1957, B&M files.]

28. White Paper on Burgess & Maclean, Cmmd 9557 1955; letter from Reilly dated August 10, 1986, to Glees, reprinted in Glees, op. cit., p. 360.

29. Philby, op. cit., p. 177.

30. Driberg, *Portrait*, p. 89.

31. The White Paper, Cmmd 9557, states that "an additional reason for delaying the proposed interview until mid-June" was that the impending confinement of Mrs. Maclean would have given them a chance to search the house for evidence. Nigel West suggests that his MI5 sources insist the Foreign Office took this line in order to minimize its responsibility and that interrogations *were* scheduled to begin in the morning of Monday, May 28.

32. Cecil interviews.

33. Lord Sherfield interviewed in July 1985 and quoted by Glees, op. cit., p. 363.

34. White Paper on Burgess & Maclean, Cmmd 9557.

35. Melinda Maclean as quoted from confidential Foreign Office sources in Boyle, op. cit., p. 401.

36. Petrov affidavit.

37. For a detailed analysis of the White Paper's seventeen major factual misstatements, see West, *Molehunt*, pp. 185–194.

38. Interviews and written denial to author received from Robert Lamphere.

39. Although Burgess's American traveling companion did not appear to have pro-Russian attitudes, Miller told the FBI that he frequently raised the Korean War and several times mentioned his desire to live in Paris or settle down in Switzerland where he claimed to have a friend in Lugano. [FBI interviews with Bernard Miller, June 14, 1951]; I am indebted to Verne Newton of Washington, D.C., for permitting me to see the letter he received from the University of Geneva confirming that Miller did indeed enroll in the Medical School for the 1951–52 academic semester. Newton, a former doctoral student at Syracuse University and ex-officer at the Department of State, has been researching and interviewing over a number of years for a book about the American connections of Burgess, Maclean, and Philby. He has written on this subject for *The Washingtonian Magazine* and is a well-known writer, whose work has been published in *The New York Times*, New York *Herald Tribune*, and leading overseas newspapers.

40. Wright, op. cit.

41. Rees, op. cit., p. 236; Hewit interviews.

42. Letter from Timothy Johnston, April 1988; Dr. Christine Carpenter, in a July 1988 interview, said that she disagreed with my assessment of the significance of the Burgess drawing. She and her brother do not believe their father was ever knowingly part of Blunt's espionage conspiracy. They suggest that the cartoon of Stalin was more likely to have been an attempt by Burgess to try to discover how much Kemball Johnston knew about Burgess's Communist activities; FBI B&M; Hewit interview; FBI B&M, interview with Douglas Collins.

43. Hewit interviews.

44. Philby, op. cit., p. 177; FBI B&M, interview with Linwood Williams, the Mayflower Motors salesman who described Burgess as a "car nut." The Lincoln had never been at the embassy. It had been damaged when Philby's car rolled down the drive

into it, and after the insurance assessor's visit, it was delivered to the Alber Garage on Fourteenth Street and remained there until May 21, when Philby's secretary, Esther Whitfield, arranged for it to be taken to Mayflower Motors for a repair job; Blunt statement to Cecil.

45. The limited number of transatlantic lines then available meant that placing a Washington to London telephone call was an involved process, requiring bookings through an operator, a risky process since it would have left a trail of paper making both sender and receiver liable to being traced. The convenient "old-boy account" of the Foreign Office, endorsed by Sir Patrick Reilly in 1986 (see letter to Glees, op. cit.), that Philby provided the tipoff via the Soviet net, does not stand up to scrutiny unless it can be shown that he had news of the MI5 decision at an earlier date.

46. Hewit interviews; the identity of the mysterious foreigner is not clear. Because of Hewit's unfamiliarity with the language, it might have been Blunt speaking French in a final remonstration to Burgess to stick precisely to the escape plan.

47. Berry had in fact already changed his mind and decided that despite his offer to him in Washington, Burgess would be quite unsuited to the paper's staid conservative style.

48. Stephen Spender, *Journals 1939–1983*, ed. John Goldsmith (New York: Random House, 1986), p. 95. Nine years later, when Burgess contacted Spender during the writer's visit to Moscow in 1960, he told him that his purpose in making the call was to ask Auden if he could borrow his house in Ischia. He said that his plan had been to go there after dropping off Maclean in Prague "until the trouble blew over." But this appears to be either another piece of KGB misinformation or wishful thinking on Burgess's part, since Moscow Center never had any intention of leaving him to be interrogated.

49. FBI B&M, Miller interview, June 14, 1951.

50. Ibid.

51. FBI 1955 Summary Report on Burgess and Maclean, Oetking interview.

52. Ibid.

53. Nigel West, *Molehunt*, p. 135.

54. West interviews confirmed from a confidential source.

55. Ibid.; West's account of White's rush to the airport, only to find his passport had expired, according to information relayed from Sir Dick himself, related to an incident that occurred during an earlier trip to the United States.

56. Philby, op. cit., p. 177.

57. Information supplied from a confidential source and confirmed by two other Washington-based U.S. counterintelligence officers.

58. Anthony Cavendish, *Inside Intelligence* (privately published, 1987), p. 63.

59. FBI B&M, teletype to Washington from New York, DIRECTOR URGENT, in which line 14 mentions "JOHN OR JACK L[ast] N[ame] U[nknown], Burgess Roommate."

60. Miller interview of June 14, 1951; FBI Summary Report of July 16, 1951, pp. 22–23.

61. Teletype, Washington Field Office from New York to Director SAC, dated June 30, 1951; Verne Newton confirmed that Miller did attend Geneva University Medical School in 1951. Attempts to track down Miller have so far proved fruitless.

## CHAPTER 27: PAGES 560–579

1. Rees as quoted by Boyle, *Climate of Treason*, p. 410.

2. Ibid.

3. Boyle confirmed Rees's story with Footman.

4. Blunt press conference, *Times*, November 21, 1979.

5. Ibid.

6. Rosamond Lehmann as cited in Penrose and Freeman, *Conspiracy of Silence*.

7. Chapman Pincher, *Too Secret Too Long*, p. 394, and Nigel West, *MI5*, p. 50.

8. Pincher, *Too Secret Too Long*, pp. 394–395, and West *MI5*, pp. 50–51.

9. Ibid.

10. *Daily Express*, June 7, 1951.

11. FBI B&M.

12. Interview with Rosamond Lehmann, 1986.

13. Ibid.

14. Lehmann may have been hoping to send a warning by writing to Spender, who, wishing to demonstrate his "ignorance," as he put it thirty-five years later, allowed a *Daily Express* reporter to see the letter. [Spender, op. cit., pp. 95–96.]

15. FBI Straight.

16. Dick White as quoted by Penrose and Freeman, op. cit., p. 356.

17. Ibid. Also confirmed to the author by a confidential source.

18. Ibid.

19. Boyle, op. cit., p. 385, cited to confidential CIA sources, confirmed by this author.

20. West interviews, confirmed with Lamphere.

21. Ibid., confirmed with confidential source.

22. Lamphere, op. cit., p. 243.

23. Ibid. p. 249.

24. David Martin, *Wilderness of Mirrors*, p. 56; as quoted in Page et al., *Philby*, p. 271.

25. Top Secret memorandum for the chairman of the Joint Chiefs of Staff prepared by Colonel Robert Totten, acting DDI, dated October 18, 1955. [Chairman's file, COS Joint Chief of Staff, "Admiral Radford 1953–55," Box 46 RG 218 NA.] The news of the defection came at the very time when the Atomic Energy Commission and the CIA were on the brink of an agreement with Senator Brian McMahon, the chairman of the Joint Committee on Atomic Energy, permitting Britain access to secret information that had been denied it since 1945. Maclean's defection cost the British years in restoring the "special relationship" in the field of atomic energy because of the security-minded McMahon. [Walter Pforzheimer interviews — he was then assistant general counsel for the CIA and intimately involved in the negotiations on Capitol Hill.]

26. Memorandum for chairman of the Joint Chiefs of Staff, subject: "Safeguarding National Security," reference JCS 1712/5, dated November 25, 1955, prepared by Rear Admiral Edwin T. Layton, DDI. [Chairman's file, COS Joint Chiefs of Staff, "Admiral Radford 1953–55," Box 46 RG 218 NA.]

27. Philby, op. cit., p. 189.

28. Easton interview, as quoted by Cave Brown, "*C,*" p. 709.

29. Philby, op. cit., p. 189.

30. Ibid., p. 191.

31. Wright, *Spycatcher*, p. 244.

32. West, *Molehunt*, p. 28, identifies Robertson and Johnston as the investigating officers. MI5 wanted their names removed, but they slipped through by an oversight. MI5 appears to have sent a summary of the Rees testimony about Blunt to the FBI because although an "Espionage-R" file dealing with Blunt is almost totally blanked out, one sentence remains: "Burgess asked [Rees] to assist him in carrying out his work and stated that one of his other sources of information was ANTHONY BLUNT." [FBI "Blunt," 65-5648, dated October 4, 1951.] Similar censoring has obliterated a July 31 docket except for the final paragraph: "(2) After we learn from the State Department the reason given on Blunt's visa for his trip to the United States and after we have heard from our Legal Attaché [the FBI representative] we will give consideration to the advisability of interviewing Blunt if he actually arrives in this country." [FBI "Blunt," 100-374183-653, July 31, 1953.]

33. Boyle confirmed that his MI6 source was David Footman – whom Rees had telephoned on receiving Burgess's note of May 26. He also states that informed CIA sources confirmed that their suspicions after independent investigation of the circumstances of the defection of the two British diplomats in 1951 led to a firm refusal to deal with either Liddell or Philby.

34. Melinda Maclean later returned to the United States.

35. White Paper Cmmd 9577.

36. Pincher, *Too Secret Too Long*, p. 355, from information supplied by Wright.

37. Hansard, HOC, October 25, 1955.

38. *The Times*, October 26, 1955; Philby's assertion in January 1988 appears to confirm Nicholas Elliott's role in helping engineer his job at *The Observer* through the editor, David Astor. The files of the newspaper show that Philby – with an introduction from Malcolm Muggeridge – had first written for a job with his curriculum vitae in 1952. Astor had then told him there was no staff correspondent's job, although he had contributed two pieces on Spain for the *Observer*'s syndication service. In 1956 Philby had written to the news editor saying he was going to Saudi Arabia and reopening the possibility of writing for the newspaper, and as a result he was taken on as a stringer – nonstaff correspondent – for both *The Observer* and *The Economist*, with some help from the Foreign Office. [Michael Davie, *The Observer*, March 27, 1988.]

39. The report "ANTHONY BLUNT – Information Concerning" was originated by the Louisville FBI office. Intriguingly, the informant, it seems from wartime service, knew that Blunt was "connected with Military Intelligence." His attention had been caught by mention in a *U.S. News and World Report* story on Burgess and Maclean's press conference that Blunt had been the first to report their disappearance. Then syndicated columnist Drew Pearson had written about a coded

708 NOTES AND SOURCES

letter sent by a Communist agent, discovered in a library book at the British embassy in Cairo shortly after the defection in 1951: *It was postmarked Louisville, Kentucky*. Since Blunt was scheduled to stop over in Louisville to lecture after Cleveland, the informant suggested there might be some connection. What is significant about this FBI item is that the subsequent investigation reports are completely censored to the extent that even the subsequent identifying file numbers are "CLASSIFIED." [FBI "BLUNT" from SAC Louisville, March 16, 1963.]

40. Eric Downton, *War Without End* (Toronto: Stoddart, 1987), p. 297. Although Norman arrived to study at Trinity six months after Philby had graduated, it seems that they met when Philby had returned to Cambridge from Vienna in the following summer term when he addressed the Socialist Society.

41. Barros interviews and see Barros, *No Sense of Evil*, pp. 215–216.

42. Straight, *After Long Silence*, p. 290.

43. FBI Straight, 1975, p. 2.

44. FBI Straight, 1975, pp. 9–10.

45. Harold Nicolson, *Diaries and Letters 1930–1964* (London: Penguin, 1984).

46. For a synopsis of "Sniper's" contribution, see West, *MI5*, pp. 84–87. The most important information originating from defectors relates to knowledge of imminent hostile actions. The next most important data concerns possible penetrations of Western governments or services. The third phase involves extensive debriefing of the source to learn of current or planned operations of which the defector may have direct knowledge. A fourth stage consists of information about Soviet service personnel and organization. A never identified but most important collateral source is signals intelligence that bears on the interrogation. In the aggregate, these factors, when combined with technical collection data and other esoteric sources, help to establish the bona fides and corroborate data provided by the defector.

47. In attempting to divine the source, date, and precise content of counterintelligence information, a number of anomalies present themselves. Before any information is disseminated, the issue of source protection must be examined and the host service must also consider deception techniques that will provide advantages. As a consequence, versions of the processed information represent data released to the public, and because of the extended time lapse, attributions tend to be made to the most recent published source. Controversy still clouds the issue of whether "Fedora" and Top Hat" provided any reliable information, because they were later assessed to be Soviet agents provocateurs, who were deliberately planted on the CIA and FBI to discredit Golitsyn. "Fedora," who returned to the U.S.S.R. without defecting, was believed to have been Viktor M. Lessikovski, who became personal assistant to U.N. Secretary General U Thant from 1963 to 1966. Yuri Nosenko, "Foxtrot," did defect and spent three years in detention while the CIA tried unsuccessfully to prove that he was a Soviet agent provocateur.

48. Ibid. See also Martin, op. cit., Ranelagh, *The Agency*, pp. 564–565; Richard Deacon, *The Israeli Secret Service* (New York: Taplinger, 1985), pp. 164–165; Andrew, *On Her Majesty's Secret Service*, pp. 496–497. Information checked with confidential sources.

49. Wright, op. cit., pp. 170–171.

50. West, *MI5*, p. 97, and Barros, op. cit., pp. 120–121; West, *Friends*, p. 143.

## CHAPTER 28: PAGES 580–606

1. Interview on February 23, 1984, with the late James Angleton conducted by Verne Newton, to whom I am grateful for providing this information from his records of that meeting.

2. Douglas Sutherland, *The Fourth Man* (London: Secker & Warburg, 1980), p. 12.

3. Straight, *After Long Silence*, p. 318, and Memorandum to Mr. De Loach, subject: Michael Straight, Possible Presidential Appointee, June 7, 1963.

4. FBI Straight.

5. Straight, op. cit., p. 324.

6. Letters from Mrs. Stella Jeffries to Chapman Pincher dated May 4 and May 19, 1984, kindly given the author by Mr. Pincher. In her letters Mrs. Jeffries places the date as "July 1963," even though the handwritten letter she received from Blunt, who was teaching a summer course at Pennsylvania State University, is dated August 14, 1962. The Courtauld records and Desmond MacRae confirm that it was indeed 1963.

7. Interview with Desmond MacRae, New York, March 19, 1988.

8. Ibid.

9. *The Times*, August 20, 1963.

10. Straight, op. cit., p. 318; Wright, *Spycatcher*, p. 10. Despite Straight's willingness to testify, Arthur Martin and his superiors in MI5 knew there was no proof for his claims and an even adequate defense lawyer would be able to tear his assertions to shreds. Although Straight had provided a breakthrough, no British jury would bring in a conviction based on his uncorroborated testimony. A public trial was in any case out of the question because of Blunt's position in the Establishment. Martin knew that the only hope was a voluntary confession — but Blunt would have to be bluffed into it; Straight, op. cit., p. 324; Straight interviews.

11. An examination of the "Profumo Affair" is provided by Anthony Summers and Stephen Dorril, *Honeytrap: The Secret Worlds of Stephen Ward* (London: Weidenfeld & Nicolson, 1982); Harbinson interviews, corroborating Summers and Dorril.

12. Wright, op. cit., p. 253. The decision to grant Blunt an immunity deal is another gray area: It is claimed that the home secretary was not influenced by their common Marlborough background. But one of the principal Home Office solicitors advising him happened to be another Marlburian: G. B. T. Barr, who graduated in 1930 from Clare College as one of the star Cambridge academic lawyers of his generation. He appears to have been none other than "the Beautiful Basil" of the MacNeice letters — for whom Blunt had developed a romantic attachment while at school. According to Alastair MacDonald, Barr was a submissive character and "Anthony knew how to massage him." [MacDonald interviews.]

13. In *After Long Silence* Straight puts the first meeting with Martin in London as September, but confirmed from his passport that it was actually May 13–25, 1964. It was at this meeting that he first met Blunt, who requested fifteen minutes alone with Straight before Martin joined them. Since MI5 had bugged the Courtauld director's flat — and Blunt probably knew that — there were no sinister exchanges made in "the sort of scene that belongs in a movie," as Straight noted. There were

no recriminations. He was greeted by Blunt's thin-lipped smile and the cool assurance, "I just wanted to tell you: Thank God you did what you did ... I couldn't muster up the strength to go to the authorities myself." Blunt's apparent contrition and relief, as Straight was to find out, were more acted than heartfelt. The following year it appears he was already doing his level best to undermine Straight's account by pointing up inconsistencies. "The British authorities had come upon a minor discrepancy in my testimony, and Anthony, who had spent many days with them by then, was able to assist them in clearing it up," Straight wrote of his third visit to the MI5 safe house in South Audley Street, which took place sometime between April 6 and 20, 1965. Walking back up South Audley Street with Blunt after the meeting with MI5, "Blunt said the authorities had come to trust both of us; that was important to him, as it was to me." Straight's confidence in Blunt's good intentions toward him, however, were shaken when I showed him pages from his memoir *After Long Silence*, which I had obtained from a confidential source, in which Blunt had underlined passages where he claimed Straight was not telling the truth. They had been marked by Blunt before Straight was confronted in a hostile British television interview by Nigel West after the book was published in Britain in the fall of 1984. [Wright, op. cit., p. 253; Straight, *Silence*, p. 321, information supplied by Nigel West, and details supplied by Straight during interviews and in a letter of April 16, 1988, that confirmed dates from his passports.]

14. Wright, op. cit.; Crowley interviews.

15. Wright, op. cit., p. 257.

16. Straight interviews; interview and correspondence with the brother of John Astbury, May 2, 1988. Mr. H. R. Astbury doubts that "in any real sense" his elder brother was a spy. But confidential sources confirm that he was a suspect. No obituary of his elder brother was published and the rumor circulated among his Cambridge contemporaries that he took his own life because MI5 had revived its investigation in the summer of 1987.

17. Wright, op. cit., p. 242. [West, *Friends*, pp. 148–149.] Blunt also joked to Wright that it had given him great pleasure to blackball Playfair for the Apostles. [West, *Molehunt*, p. 157.] Sir Edward Playfair's denial was quoted in *The Sunday Times*, July 22, 1984.

18. Wright, op. cit., pp. 264–265; West, *Molehunt*, p. 65.

19. Wright, op. cit., p. 266–267.

20. West, *Molehunt*, p. 65.

21. Ranelagh, *The Agency*, p. 288–296.

22. Information given by Cavendish, *Intelligence Officer*, pp. 52–66

23. For a detailed documentary analysis of the postwar recruitment of the European factions but with respect to Nazi infiltrations, see Simpson, *Blowback*.

24. Samples drawn from the CIC name files in the IRR section that are still in the process of declassification reveal original, uncensored MI5 trace reports. For example No. KEL 3064, dated April 28, 1947, contains assessments requested by the OSS station in Austria for ten contacts of General Anton Turkul, a White Russian who had fought with the Germans, although it was thought that his intelligence chief Klat was a double agent for the Russians. Turkul was arrested in Salzburg, then released and employed as the White Russian representative in the American zone of Austria. On the strength of the 1947 MI5 report – "We have no

traces of any of the ten persons named" — the Americans concluded as late as 1956, "Investigation did not reveal any information that SUBJECT had been doubling as a Soviet agent."

25. Confidential source.

26. As quoted by Winks, *Cloak and Gown*, pp. 536–537.

27. George Young (former MI6 Officer), Foreword to Cavendish, op. cit.

28. FBI Straight; Director FBI to Legation London, PHILBY-ESPIONAGE RUSSIA April 28, 1966, FBI B&M; information supplied from two confidential sources.

29. West, *Molehunt*, p. 45; Wright, op. cit., pp. 302–304.

30. Wright, op. cit., pp. 302–344; West, *Molehunt*, p. 45; Gouzenko, RCMP Memorandum, May 6, 1952.

31. Wright, op. cit., pp. 278–286; West, *Molehunt*, p. 174.

32. West, *Molehunt*, pp. 177–183.

33. Information from a confidential source in the United States.

34. *Sunday Times*, January 20, 1980; *The Observer*, January 20, 1980.

35. Ibid.

36. *The Times*, February 23, 1980.

37. Wright, op. cit., p. 34.

38. I am grateful to a confidential source for supplying me with an original copy of the extracted Russian sentence and late-date GCHQ translation of the key sentence in Reed's report of his 1944 debriefing of Volkov.

39. Deacon, *The British Connection*, p. 204, sourced to "Baykolov Archives."

40. Letter to Lord Vansittart from Guy Liddell, February 15, 1950: "We have now seen Baikoloff [sic]. For your information, there are one or two gaps in his story; there is no real evidence to implicate Radulovic." [VST II 1/41 CCA.]

41. While it is of course impossible to do anything more than speculate on what personal frustrations and subtle external political forces *might* have led Guy Liddell to cast his lot in with the Soviets, certain obvious possibilities such as his artistic temperament, his long-term connections with Baykolov and the penetrated Russian émigré community in London — as well as the scars of his marriage — can be considered factors. In discussing his father with Peter Liddell, I was struck by his son's observation that in today's conservative Britain, his father would have considered himself a left-wing Tory. Peter also told me that doctors had repeatedly warned Liddell that his heart condition was aggravated by his hypertension and heavy smoking. This suggests that Liddell's famous ruminative demeanor concealed stress that he bottled up inside him and did not release in angry outbursts — or, like Blunt and the other Cambridge spies, in excessive liquor consumption. Then, too, other sources told me about Liddell's premarital love affair in the early twenties with a London University student (believed to still be alive), whose Marxism and links to the Communist party were well known to her contemporaries. This lead has so far proved impossible to corroborate, but if true, it could explain how one of the ranking officers in Special Branch might have become an early victim of a Soviet "honeytrap."

42. *The Daily Telegraph*, March 30, 1983.

43. *The Marlburian*, 1926.

44. Hilton, Note.

45. Anthony Blunt, *Borromini* (London: Allen Lane, 1979) as quoted by Steiner, *Cleric or Treason*, p. 191.

46. Steiner, pp. 191–192.

47. Annan interviews; Christopher Wright interviews.

48. Dennis Mahon, as quoted by Penrose and Freeman, op. cit., p. 295; examples include the supposed Poussin fragment he "discovered" for his MI5 friend Liddell. See also the investigations of the false authentications given to old-master drawings sold at Christie's later discovered to be fakes. *Daily Telegraph*, March 4, 1980.

## EPILOGUE: PAGES 607–615

1. Tass as quoted by *The New York Times*, May 12, 1988.

2. Philby interviews, *The Sunday Times*, March 20, 1988.

3. Ibid.

4. Ibid.

5. Ibid., March 27, 1988.

6. Ibid., March 20, 1988.

7. *The Observer*, March 27, 1988.

8. *The Times*, March 12, 1988.

9. Confidential information. The author was not involved in the events described.

10. *The Sunday Times*, March 20, 1988.

11. Phillip Knightley, *The Second Oldest Profession: The Spy as Bureaucrat, Patriot, Fantasist and Whore* (London: André Deutsch, 1986), p. 8; ibid., p. 77.

12. Ibid., p. 175; p. 172.

13. *The Sunday Times*, April 10, 1988.

14. *The Sunday Times*, March 20, 1988.

15. *The New York Times*, October 21, 1937.

16. Press accounts of March 1984 quoted by Corson and Crowley, *The New KGB*, p. 25.

17. *The Times*, May 12, 1988; *The Washington Post*, May 17, 1988.

18. *The New York Times*, May 12, 1988.

*Documents*

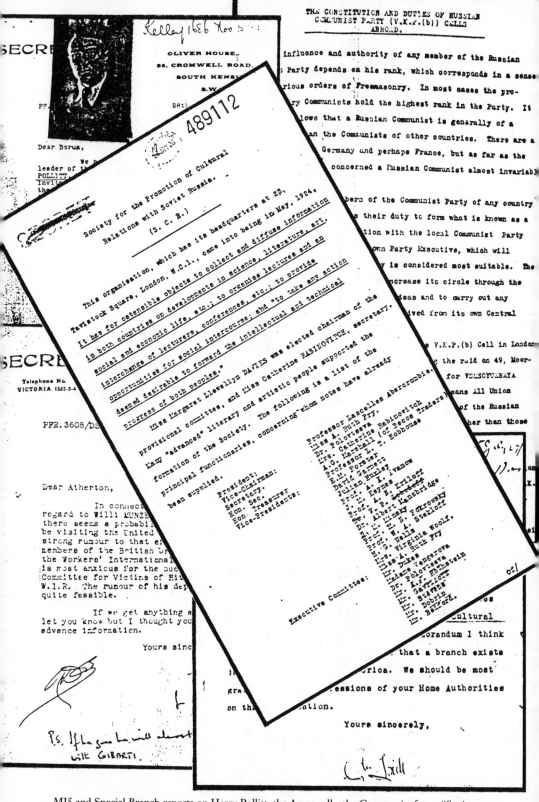

influence and authority of any member of the Russian

Party depends on his rank, which corresponds in a sense
rious orders of Freemasonry. In most cases the pro-
ry Communists hold the highest rank in the Party. It
lows that a Russian Communist is generally of a
an the Communists of other countries. There are a
Germany and perhaps France, but as far as the
concerned a Russian Communist almost invariab

bers of the Communist Party of any country
their duty to form what is known as a
tion with the local Communist Party
own Party Executive, which will
y is considered most suitable. The
ncrease its circle through the
deas and to carry out any
ived from its own Central

e V.K.P.(b) Cell in London
g the raid on 49, Moor-
for VSESOYUZNAYA
ans All Union
of the Russian
her than those

SECRE

OLIVER HOUSE,
33, CROMWELL ROAD,
SOUTH KENS
S.W.

Kelley 1686 No 5

PF

28t

489112

Dear Borum,

We
leader of th
POLLITT
Invite
th

SECRE

Telephone No.
VICTORIA 1532-3-4

PFR.3608/DS

## Society for the Promotion of Cultural
## Relations with Soviet Russia.
### (S. C. R.)

This organisation, which has its headquarters at 23,
Tavistock Square, London, W.C.1, came into being in May, 1924.
It has for ostensible objects to collect and diffuse information
in both countries on developments in science, literature, art,
social and economic life, etc.; to organise lectures and an
interchange of lecturers, conferences, etc.; to provide
opportunities for social intercourse; and "to take any action
deemed desirable to forward the intellectual and technical
progress of both peoples."

Miss Margaret Llewellyn DAVIES was elected chairman of the
provisional committee, and Miss Catherine RABINOVITCH, secretary.
Many "advanced" literary and artistic people supported the
formation of the Society. The following is a list of the
principal functionaries, concerning whom notes have already
been supplied.

President: Professor Lascelles Abercrombie
Vice-Chairman: Miss A. Ruth Fry.
Secretary: Dr. Polovtseva Rabinovitch
Hon. Sec.: Miss Catherine (of Becos Traders
Hon. Treasurer Mrs. Marshall L. T. Hobhouse
Vice-Presidents: A.G. Marshall
Professor L. T. Hobhouse
E.M. Forster
David Garnett
Julien Huxley
Prof. J. M. Keynes
J. M. Keynes
Prof. A. R. Kriloff
Prof. V. P. Volgin
Albert Mansbridge
Dr. A. Minsky
Prof. K. A. Fokromsky
Prof. W. A. Steklof.
G. Wells Woolf.
Mrs. Virginia Woolf.
Miss A. Ruth Fry
Mr. Dukes
Madame Yangerova
Mr. Polovtseva
Dr. A.F. Gavronstein
Mr. Gavrilov
Mr. Stefan
Mr. Dobrin
Mr. Belford.

Dear Atherton,

In connect
regard to Willi MUNZ
there seems a probabil
be visiting the United
strong rumour to that e
members of the British Un
the Workers' Internationa
is most anxious for the suc
Committee for Victims of Hi
W.I.R. The rumour of his dep
quite feasible.

If we get anything m
let you know but I thought you
advance information.

Yours sinc

ultural

orandum I think

that a branch exists

rica. We should be most

essions of your Home Authorities

on th ation.

Yours sincerely,

P.S. If the ga ... will almost
with GIBARTI.

MI5 and Special Branch reports on Harry Pollitt, the Arcos cells, the Communist front: "Society for the Promotion of Cultural Relations with the USSR," and Willi Münzenberg. (U.S. Embassy London, 800 B Confidential Files, RG 84 National Archives; Public Record Office [HO45/24861])

The Secret War 1915–69: Summary of the principal events, the rival chiefs of Soviet and British intelligence organizations, and the battles won and lost.

| | Bolshevik Revolution | | Sov. Trade Mission UK | Lenin's Death | | Rise of Stalin | | Trinity Cell | Hitler in power | | Nazi/Soviet Pact |
| | | | | | | Sov. Embassy Closed | | | | Poppy Day Demo | Munich |
| | Armistice | | | | UK Labor Govt | Arcos Raid Labor Govt | Sov. Emb. Reopened | | | Spanish Civil War | WWII |
| | | Comintern founded | | | | | | | | | |
| 1915 | 1917 | 1920 | | 1925 | | 1930 | | | 1935 | | 1940 |

Mil. Intel [Red Army 3rd Section     RU (Military and Industrial Espionage)

Security [– – – – Feliks Dzerzhinski – – – – – – – – – – – – – ][– – – – V. Menzhinsky – – – – – – – – – – – – – – – – G. Yagoda – – – – N. Yezhov– – – – – – L. Beria

Apparat   ===C H E K A=============O G P U===================N K V D ====

Diplomats          M. Litvinov              A. Rosengolz          I. Maisky          (S. Kahan)

Rezidentura   T. Rothenstein          Dip. Break          + + + + + + + + + + + + + + + + + + + + + + + + + + + + Theodore Maly + + + + + Brandes "Otto"?

Exporting          Comintern>>Fronts: Soc. Cultural Relation Int. Workers Relief; Anglo-Soviet Friendship Society

Revolution                    CPGB internal subversion>>>>>>>>>>>>>>>>>>>>>>>>>>>

[                    READING SOVIET CODES AND CIPHERS

[                    [– – – – – – – –Special Branch– – – – – – – – – – – – – – – – – – – –[Guy Liddell]– – – – – – – – – – – – – B Division MI5 (Counterintelligence)
                                                          McCartney Case                                                          Woolwich Case     Krivitsky

MI5 – – – – – – – – – – – – – – – – – Gen. Sir Vernon Kell DG – – – – – – – – – – – – – – – – – – – – – – – – – – – – – – – – – – – – – – – – – – – – ]
MI6 – – – Mansfield Cumming "C" – – – – – – – – – – ][– – – Adm Sinclair "C" – – – – – – – – – – – – – – – – – – – – – – – – – – – – – – – – – – – ]

SECRET US/UK EXCHANGES ON COMMUNIST SUBVERSION

Dunkirk  Hiroshima  Korean War  Stalin's death  USSR A Bomb  Suez Debacle  Cuban Crisis  Philby Defects
Russia attacked  Burgess & Maclean  Blunt Confesses

1940      1945      1950      1955      1960      1965      1969

2nd Chief Directorate                (Soviet Military Intelligence)

– – – – L. Beria – – – – – – – – – – – – – – – – I. Serov – – A. Shelepin – – V. Semichansty – – – – – Andropov

G R U

=====NKGB======MGB==============KGB===================

UK Control Officers
[– – – A. Gorski – – – ][– – – B. Krotov – – – ][– – – Y. Modin – – – – – – – – – – – – – – – –

Exposed Soviet Spies in UK

Capt. J. King    D. Springhall    A. Foote    K. Fuchs                        Portland Spy Ring
                 O. Uren          Nunn May    B. Pontecorvo                   Vassal Case
                                                                              George Blake

Principal Soviet    Volkov            The Petrovs              A. Golitsyn
Defectors           I. Gouzenko

MI5 – – – – – – – – – – – – – – – – Liddell deputy DG – – – – – – Harwell Security – – – – – – dies.

DG's – – – – – Sir David Petrie – – – – ][– – – – Sir P. Sillitoe – – – ][– – – Sir D.G. White – ][– – Sir R. Hollis – – – – – – ][– Sir F. Jones

MI6–"C" – – – – – Sir Stewart Menzies – – – – – – – – – – – – ][– – – Sir J. Sinclair – – ][– – – – – Sir D. G. White – – – – – – – – – – ]

Exposed Spies in US        Venona/Bride Sigint (Homer Fuchs & the Rosenbergs . . . . . . still yielding information . . . . .

                W. Chambers  H. Massing                                                                    M. Straight

        E. Bentley          The Rosenberg Ring

PRINCIPAL SOURCES: Corson & Crowley, *The New KGB*; John Dziak, *Chekisty*; Christopher Andrew, *Secret Service*; Nigel West's volumes on MI5 and MI6.

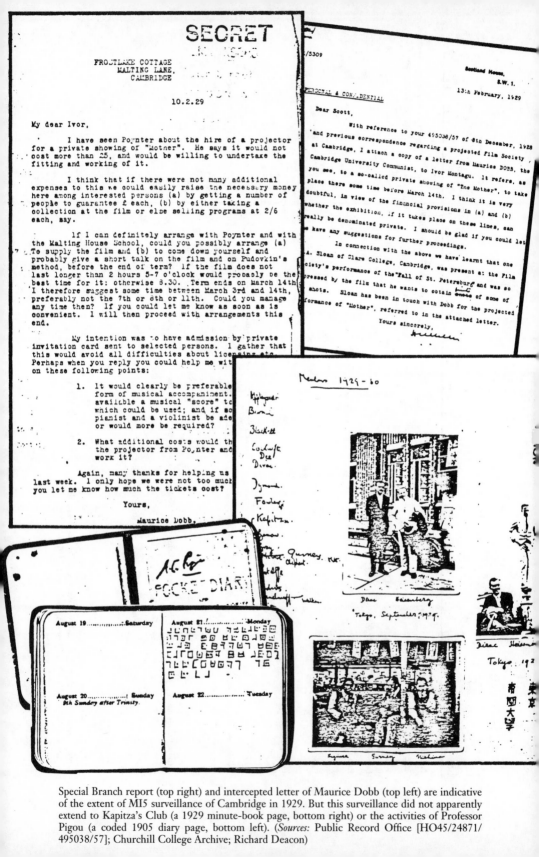

FROSTLAKE COTTAGE
MALTING LANE,
CAMBRIDGE

10.2.29

My dear Ivor,

I have seen Poynter about the hire of a projector for a private showing of "Mother". He says it would not cost more than £5, and would be willing to undertake the fitting and working of it.

I think that if there were not many additional expenses to this we could easily raise the necessary money here among interested persons (a) by getting a number of people to guarantee £ each, (b) by either taking a collection at the film or else selling programs at 2/6 each, say.

If I can definitely arrange with Poynter and with the Malting House School, could you possibly arrange (a) to supply the film and (b) to come down yourself and probably give a short talk on the film and on Pudovkin's method, before the end of term? If the film does not last longer than 2 hours 5-7 o'clock would probably be the best time for it: otherwise 8.30. Term ends on March 14th. I therefore suggest some time between March 3rd and 14th, preferably not the 7th or 8th or 11th. Could you manage any time then? If you could let me know as soon as is convenient. I will then proceed with arrangements this end.

My intention was to have admission by private invitation card sent to selected persons. I gather that this would avoid all difficulties about licensing etc. Perhaps when you reply you could help me with on these following points:

1.  It would clearly be preferable form of musical accompaniment. available a musical "score" to which could be used; and if so pianist and a violinist be ade or would more be required?

2.  What additional costs would th the projector from Poynter and work it?

Again, many thanks for helping us last week. I only hope we were not too much you let me know how much the tickets cost?

Yours,

Maurice Dobb.

---

/5309

PERSONAL & CONFIDENTIAL

Scotland House,
S.W.1.

13th February, 1929

Dear Scott,

With reference to your 495038/57 of 8th December, 1928 and previous correspondence regarding a projected Film Society at Cambridge, I attach a copy of a letter from Maurice DOBB, the Cambridge University Communist, to Ivor Montagu. It refers, as you see, to a so-called private showing of "The Mother", to take place there some time before March 14th. I think it is very doubtful, in view of the financial provisions in (a) and (b) whether the exhibition, if it takes place on these lines, can really be denominated private. I should be glad if you could let me have any suggestions for further proceedings.

In connection with the above we have learnt that one A. Sloan of Clare College, Cambridge, was present at the Film Society's performances of the "Fall of St. Petersburg" and was so impressed by the film that he wants to obtain some of shots. Sloan has been in touch with Dobb for the projected performance of "Mother", referred to in the attached letter.

Yours sincerely,

---

Special Branch report (top right) and intercepted letter of Maurice Dobb (top left) are indicative of the extent of MI5 surveillance of Cambridge in 1929. But this surveillance did not apparently extend to Kapitza's Club (a 1929 minute-book page, bottom right) or the activities of Professor Pigou (a coded 1905 diary page, bottom left). (*Sources:* Public Record Office [HO45/24871/495038/57]; Churchill College Archive; Richard Deacon)

BOX NO. 500
PARLIAMENT STREET, B.O.,
LONDON, S.W.1.

1st February, 1938.

URGENT & PERSONAL.

*for Sec. to Dept*

Dear Borum,

    As no doubt you have seen from the newspapers, we have at present four men under arrest here, charged with offences under the Official Secrets Act. These men are all members of a Soviet military espionage organisation operating here.

    We have definitely established that in October, 1937, an important document was photographed at the instigation, and with the assistance of two foreigners who hold Canadian passport No. 22247, issued 2nd October, 1936, to Willy BRANDES, native of Rumania, naturalised, aged 35, height 5" 8½', and his wife, Mary, height 5' 4", grey eyes, brown hair, aged 31.

    We have traces of BRANDES and his wife in this country from January 1937 until 6th November, 1937, when they left for Russia via Paris.

    Preliminary enquiries appear to show that [     ] t No. 22247 was unlawfully obtained, [     ] ther into this.

[     ] this country, BRANDES had [     ] and posed as an agent of the [     ] cs Company of New York, and had a [     ] les of Phantome Face Powder, the [     ] eared to be pushing here. He also [     ] e Charak Furniture Company, 444 [     ] York. The address of Phantome Red [     ] y also at 444 Madison Avenue, New

[     ] urgently necessary for us to obtain [     ] data which may enable us to [     ] entity of BRANDES, I should be most [     ] d cable an enquiry for us to New [     ] known both of these two companies

    Yours sincerely,

    Colonel Sir Vernon Kell.

---

BOX NO. 500
PARLIAMENT STREET, B.O.,
LONDON, S.W.1.

AMERICAN EMBASSY
24 SEP. 1935
DISBURSING OFFICE

RL.204/11/DS9.    23rd September 1935.

Dear Atherton,

    You may like to know that the following American citizens arrived in London from Leningrad on board the M.V. Smolny on 12.9.35:

      Michael STRAIGHT,
      Joseph LANDER.

    When the Smolny returned to Leningrad on 14.9.35, Ida Sonia SEGAL, an American citizen, was on board.

    Yours sincerely,

    Colonel Sir Vernon Kell.

Roy Atherton, Esq.,
United States Embassy.

Communications to the U.S. State department from MI5 regarding Michael Straight, who went to Russia with Blunt in 1935, and the Soviet illegal Willy Brandes, who was allowed to escape the rolling up of the Woolwich Arsenal spy ring in 1938. (*Source:* U.S. Embassy London, 800 B, R6 84 NA)

SECRET

The chairman has laid down that, to prevent confusion, but to preserve security, we should forthwith cease referring to A.J.B., but for his eyes only spell out the informant as either A.J. Bennett, or A.J. Bennet, taking great care that we get the spelling of the surname right according to which of the two it refers. The chairman feels this system would be less likely to arouse comment than the use of any code-name. This same method of reference is being used in communications with Balfour, Remnant and Bogovout-Kolomitzov in Paris.

28 / 11 / 28

Revealing documents discovered in the confidential papers of Tory party chairman J.C.C. Davidson: The SECRET note of November 28, 1928, indisputably refers to Comintern agent Pestrovsky using his alias of A. J. Bennet, which was confusingly close to A. J. Bennett, the Conservative party treasurer. Davidson's SECRET memorandum of February 4, 1936, raises suspicions communicated to the prime minister that Mrs. Wallis Simpson might not only be attempting to blackmail King Edward VII but also be relaying Cabinet secrets to the Germans. (*Source:* Davidson papers, House of Lords Record Office)

27 June, 1953.

My Dear Friend

     I have recently had my attention drawn to a series of telegrams about the attempt of German agents to bring pressure on the Duke of Windsor in Spain and Portugal during the summer of 1940. These documents were found in the German Archives at the end of the war. All these telegrams are from German sources and represent a Nazi-German intrigue to entangle and compromise a Royal Prince who had been driven out of France and had taken refuge in Portugal. If they were to be included in an official publication they might leave the impression that the Duke was in close touch with German Agents and was listening to suggestions that were disloyal. In fact it was because I foresaw that the Germans would try to entrap him verbally or even kidnap him especially if they got him into Spain, that I advised the late King to agree to his appointment as Governor of the Bahamas and made strenuous efforts to get him away from Europe beyond the

An exchange at the end of June 1953 between Churchill and Eisenhower that reveals the extent to which the prime minister was prepared to go to prevent the German Foreign Ministry Windsor files from ever being made public. (*Source:* Beaverbrook Collection, House of Lords Record Office)

THE WHITE HOUSE,
WASHINGTON.

July 2, 1953.

Dear Winston,

     Your letter of the twenty-seventh just this moment reached me. I am completely astonished to learn that a microfilm record was made of the documents to which you refer.

     At the time, in 1945, that the existence of these documents was called to my attention, I had them thoroughly examined by Ambassador Winant and by a member of my own Intelligence Staff. They completely agreed that there was no possible value to them, that they were obviously concocted with some idea of promoting German propaganda and weakening Western resistance, and that they were totally unfair to the Duke. As a consequence, they were turned over, upon capture, to the American Ambassador.

     At this moment I do not know exactly what it is possible for me to do because I do not even know in what classification these microfilms may be kept. I shall advise you further when I am able to do so.

     With my earnest prayers for your early return to full and vigorous health,

          as ever,

           IKE.

The Rt. Hon. Sir Winston Churchill,
    K.G., O.M., C.H., M.P.

Dear Colonel Bridge:

I am at length in a position to proceed collecting the British officers for M.F.A.&A. duty. Three such officers are likely to become available in the near future. They are, however, much better qualified both as to language and special knowledge to deal with French or Low Countries problems than German.

The officer I would prefer and could most strongly recommend as a capable man, a first rate German scholar and out of the top drawer as an art historian is Major Anthony Blunt, now serving with M.I.5. I have spoken to Major Blunt who promised to make strong representations to his C. O. but did not hold out much hope that he would be released. If there is anything you can do to help us to get the services of this officer I shall be more than gratified, as I am myself very anxious that the German end of this job should be in competent hands and that you should have a British officer in your section.

You will readily appreciate that the difficulties of finding officers among the British art historians is very considerable. At this stage of the war the qualified men are all either crocks [or] like Blunt, in responsible jobs in the [army] time and when they are really good [are] so useful that their C.O.'s are not [willing to] release them.

Yours sinc[erely]

Col. C. E. D. Bridge,
German Section.

6634

*From The Librarian, Windsor Castle, Berkshire.*

November 18,

My dear Passant,

Many thanks for your letter L 5824/2/402 of November 10 enclosi[ng] a copy of Wheeler-Bennett's memoran[dum] of 24 March 1947 concerning Haus Do[orn]. I do not know whether or not you ar[e] aware that in consequence thereof I [went] over to Holland in the following Au[tumn] with my colleague Anthony Blunt, to [see] the house and its contents on behal[f of] the King. In any case I send you h[erewith] my own aide-mémoire on the incident [in] order that, if necessary, you may b[ring] your file up to date. As this is my only copy may I ask for it back in due course?

Yours ever,

Owen Morshead

PENDANT TO THE DOORN MEMORANDUM.

23 Oct. 1948.

This morning the King came to the Castle and shewed me the Kaiser's two diamanté garter badges from the Cambridge sale, and also his other diamanté one: i.e. the three objects which I had seen at Doorn. The King was delighted with them, and took them away again to house with his others at Buckingham Palace.

His Majesty also brought, and handed to me, the miniature of the Duke of Clarence which I had spotted there. (It has no back, and I am to have a back fitted).

He also received from Doorn the Kaiser's complete Garter robes: not only the mantle and hat, but the full satin breeches etc.

He said nothing about the Field Marshal's baton, and I only remembered it afterwards: I do not know whether or not this has come over.

All these things have been quitely secured by Sir Neville Bland, our Ambassador at the Hague. The King expresaly told me that we only hold them on the same footing as we hold the things which I brought back from Frankfurt, i.e. if the German Family in the future want them back..... well, we have to title to them; we only hold them in security for them, over here in England where things are less unsettled.

O.F.M.

(Doorn itself is to be sold).

Documentation that confirms (top) that Blunt was *not* seconded to the SHAEF art operation in Europe as senior MI5 officers have claimed. The letter of November 18 from Royal Librarian Owen Morshead confirms that as late as 1948 they were still conducting secret missions for King George VII, retrieving documents and artifacts. The "pendant" of October 23, 1948 confirms that important "things" were collected from the Hesse archives in Frankfurt, to which the king had only tenuous title. (*Source:* Public Record Office, [FO370/1698, paper no. L6634/2/402])

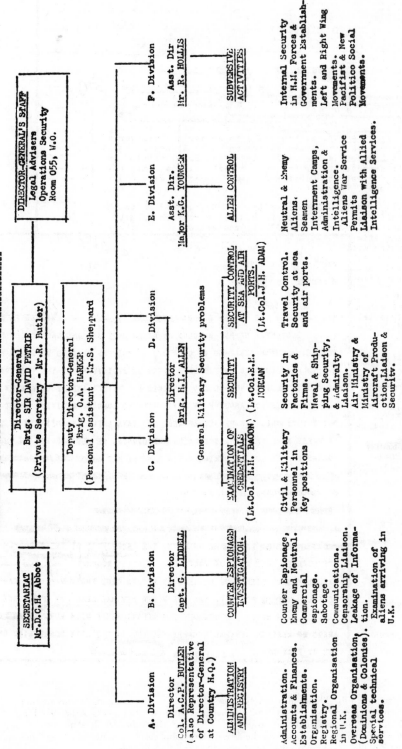

# SECURITY SERVICE ORGANISATION

**DIRECTOR-GENERAL**
Brig. SIR DAVID PETRIE
(Private Secretary – Mr.R.Butler)

**DIRECTOR-GENERAL'S STAFF**
Legal Advisers
Operations Security
Room 055, W.O.

**SECRETARIAT**
Mr.D.C.H. Abbot

**Deputy Director-General**
Brig. O.A. HARKER
(Personal Assistant – Mr.S. Sheppard)

**A. Division**

Director
Col. A.C.P. BUTLER
(also Representative of Director-General at Country H.Q.)

ADMINISTRATION AND REGISTRY

Administration.
Accounts & Finances.
Establishments.
Organisation.
Registry.
Regional Organisation in U.K.
Overseas Organisation. (Dominions & Colonies).
Special technical services.

**B. Division**

Director
Capt. G. LIDDELL

COUNTER ESPIONAGE INVESTIGATION.

Counter Espionage, Enemy and Neutral.
Commercial espionage.
Sabotage.
Communications.
Censorship Liaison.
Leakage of Information.
Examination of aliens arriving in U.K.

**C. Division**

**D. Division**

Director
Brig. H.I. ALLEN

General Military Security problems

EXAMINATION OF CREDENTIALS.
(Lt.Col. H.M. BACON)

Civil & Military Personnel in Key positions

SECURITY
(Lt.Col.E.F. MOLAN)

Security in Factories & Firms.
Naval & Shipping Security, & Admiralty Liaison.
Air Ministry & Ministry of Aircraft Production,Liaison & Security.

SECURITY CONTROL AT SEA AND AIR PORTS.
(Lt.Col.J.H. ADAM)

Travel Control.
Security at sea and air ports.

**E. Division**

Asst. Dir.
Major K.G. YOUNGER

ALIEN CONTROL

Neutral & Enemy Aliens.
Seamen
Internment Camps Administration & Intelligence.
Aliens War Service
Permits
Liaison with Allied Intelligence Services.

**F. Division**

Asst. Dir
Mr. R. HOLLIS

SUBVERSIVE ACTIVITIES

Internal Security in H.M. Forces & Government Establishments.
Left and Right Wing Movements.
Pacifist & New Political Social Movements.

The MI5 organization as communicated to the Americans in October 1942, noting the very extensive counterintelligence responsibility of B Division under Captain G. Liddell and that Roger Hollis's F Division was in charge of internal security in the armed forces in addition to left- and right-wing political movements in the civilian population. (*Source:* U.S. Embassy London, R6 84 NA)

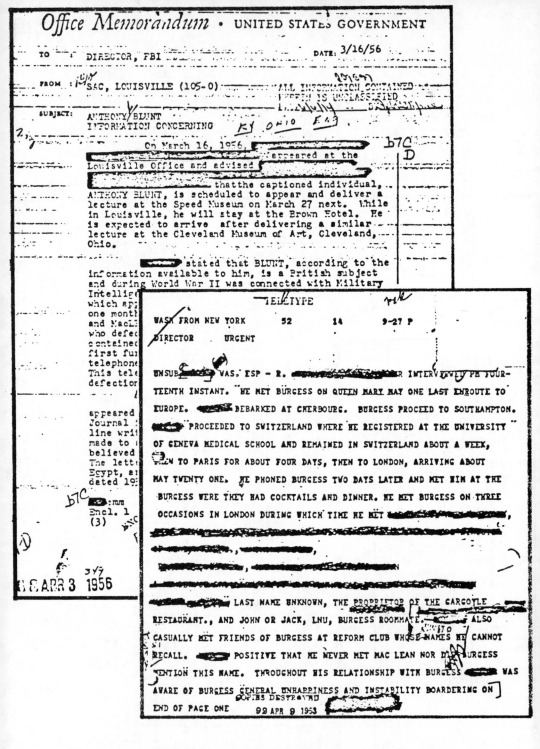

A page from the FBI "Blunt" file (top), revealing that the Bureau was paying serious attention to his movements as early as 1956. Its suspicions had been aroused within weeks of the 1951 Burgess and Maclean defection after the interrogations of Bernard Miller (below), the American medical student whom Burgess befriended on the *Queen Mary*. Only partially obliterated letters indicate Anthony Blunt is one of the blanked-out names. (*Source:* FOIA FBI files)

He explained that KATZ was a refugee
German Jew who left Germany in 1933 to escape punishment
by the Nazis because he is a writer and critical of the Nazi
regime. According to ISHERWOOD, KATZ first came to Paris
where he stayed for a few years and then on to London where
he stayed till the late 1930s, and then emigrated to South
America in 1939. According to ISHERWOOD, KATZ at the time
this interview was conducted, was publishing a news letter,
which was in the nature of a financial letter, in Buenos Aires.

With respect to the association between ROLF
KATZ and GUY BURGESS, ISHERWOOD believed that BURGESS worked
with KATZ "for a while", in 1936 and 1937 or 1937 and 1938,
in the publication of a magazine which devoted itself to a
survey of economic and political matters. ISHERWOOD stated
that he knew of no Communist Party activity or activities on
behalf of Soviet Russia on the part of ROLF KATZ, stating that
as far as he knew KATZ' field lay more in the line of economics
and finance, although he did indulge a bit in political analysis.

ISHERWOOD stated further that as far as he was
concerned KATZ was in no way identified with Communist Party
activity but was an independent thinker, whom he, ISHERWOOD,
very much admired.

On July 17, 1951 CHRISTOPHER ISHERWOOD was
interviewed a second time at Laguna Beach, California, by
Agents of the Los Angeles Office. At the time of this second
interview ISHERWOOD stated that upon reflection he believed
that he had met GUY BURGESS through ROLF KATZ in London in
the spring of 1936.

With further reference to RUDOLF KATZ, whom
he knew as ROLF KATZ, ISHERWOOD stated that in 1929 he went
to Germany to live and met ROLF KATZ in Berlin in 1931. With
respect to KATZ, ISHERWOOD stated at this time that he was
undoubtedly "Leftist" in some of his political thinking and that
he believed that at one time had probably adhered to the Communist
Party, but that it should be remembered that KATZ had quarreled
ints, and
KATZ as

8. CHRISTOPHER ISHERWOOD, 3000 Rustic Canyon Road,
Pacific Palisades, California, advised he met Burgess in
London in the late 1930's. He said he also met Burgess again
in 1947. Isherwood described Burgess as a drunkard, a
homosexual and an emotionally unstable person. He stated
he knew of no pro-Soviet acts on the part of Burgess other
than his support of the Loyalists during the Spanish Civil
War in 1937.

9. RUDOLPH KATZ advised that he met Burgess in
England in 1936, when he, Katz, was assisting Lord
Victor Rothschild. Burgess was a social acquaintance of the
Rothschild family. He stated he exchanged letters with
Burgess during 1937-38, while Katz was in South America, and
upon his return to England again had personal contact with
Burgess. He advised the last personal contact with Burgess
occurred between 1939 and 1940. Katz stated these contacts
were all of a social nature. It is noted that Katz was born
in Germany and joined the Communist Party in 1921. He fled
Germany to Paris and then to England, and in 1940 he was
ordered out of England due to homosexual contacts with
British naval personnel. In 1951 he was associated with
the Economic Commission for Latin American Affairs, which
is a regional body for the United Nations Economic and
Social Council, with headquarters at Santiago, Chile.

A page from the July 14, 1951, FBI interrogation report of Christopher Isherwood establishes the
connection of Rolf Katz (no relation to Otto Katz) to Burgess. The section of the 1955 Hoover
report to the White House reveals that the two met through Victor Rothschild. (*Source:* FBI FOIA
files, Harry S Truman Presidential Library)

d. The Federal Bureau of Investigation conducted an investigation at the time of the defection and promulgated a report, the contents of which were used to assist in preparing my memorandum of 18 October 1955. Under date of 19 June 1951, this report was addressed to the Assistant Chief of Staff, G-2, Army, with copies to Navy, State, Special Assistant to the President, Attorney General, Central Intelligence Agency, Atomic Energy Commission, and Office of Scientific Intelligence. Apparently no copy was furnished to the Chairman, Joint Chiefs of Staff, or any Joint Staff Agency. The Federal Bureau of Investigation has indicated interest in the current developments and have been briefed on the contemplated action of the Joint Chiefs of Staff and indicate concurrence therewith.

Very respectfully,

EDWIN T. LAYTON
Rear Admiral, USN
Deputy Director for Intelligence
The Joint Staff

---

THE JOINT CHIEFS OF STAFF
WASHINGTON 25. D. C.

25 November 1955

TOP SECRET

MEMORANDUM FOR: Chairman, Joint Chiefs of Staff

Subject: Safeguarding National Security

Reference: J.C.S. 1712/5

1. In response to your verbal query on 22 November 1955, as to whether any actions were taken by the military security agencies at the time of the Burgess-MacLean defection, or subsequently, the following is submitted:

a. Apparently no action that can be documented was taken by the Joint Chiefs of Staff subsequent to 25 May 1951 until the current study, which resulted in the report contained in the reference.

b. In April 1951, a tripartite group of inspectors from US/UK and France was conducting an inspection of security facilities in these three countries and were practically on the spot at the time of the defection. Their report of 4 June 1951, mentioned certain deficiencies in the security facilities in the United Kingdom, especially their system of personnel clearances for those handling classified high level information. Inasmuch as the British had in the past used the "old school tie" system in clearing their top level people, the suggestions made for improving this system were not particularly well received. There is evidence that since the defection incident, some improvements have been made, and are currently being made as a result of the recent publicity given the event in the British and world-wide press. However, definitive information on the current status of security conditions in United Kingdom is lacking at this time and should be requested.

c. All U. S. diplomatic codes and ciphers were changed immediately following the defection as a precautionary measure, following the same action instituted by the United Kingdom.

TOP SECRET

Rear Admiral Edwin T. Layton's damage-assessment report on the 1951 Burgess/Maclean defection for the U.S. Joint Chiefs of Staff in November 1955. (*Source:* JCS confidential files, National

*Index*